Achieving Secure and Transparent Supply Chains With Blockchain Technology

Mustafa Rehman Khan
UCSI University, Malaysia

Naveed Rehman Khan
UCSI University, Malaysia

Arsalan Mujahid Ghouri
London South Bank University, UK

IGI Global
PUBLISHER of TIMELY KNOWLEDGE

A volume in the Advances in Logistics, Operations, and Management Science (ALOMS) Book Series

Published in the United States of America by
IGI Global
Business Science Reference (an imprint of IGI Global)
701 E. Chocolate Avenue
Hershey PA, USA 17033
Tel: 717-533-8845
Fax: 717-533-8661
E-mail: cust@igi-global.com
Web site: http://www.igi-global.com

Library of Congress Cataloging-in-Publication Data

Names: Khan, Mustafa Rehman, 1990- editor. | Khan, Naveed R., 1982- editor. | Ghouri, Arsalan M., 1978- editor.
Title: Achieving secure and transparent supply chains with blockchain technology / edited by Mustafa Khan, Naveed R. Khan, Arsalan Ghouri.
Description: Hershey, PA : Business Science Reference, [2024] | Includes bibliographical references and index. | Summary: "This book gives an in-depth overview of the integration of supply chain and blockchain technology, and its potential applications while providing contemporary theoretical frameworks and the latest empirical findings"-- Provided by publisher.
Identifiers: LCCN 2023040225 (print) | LCCN 2023040226 (ebook) | ISBN 9798369304822 (hardcover) | ISBN 9798369304860 (paperback) | ISBN 9798369304839 (ebook)
Subjects: LCSH: Business logistics. | Blockchains (Databases)
Classification: LCC HD38.5 .A2964 2024 (print) | LCC HD38.5 (ebook) | DDC 658.7--dc23/eng/20230828
LC record available at https://lccn.loc.gov/2023040225
LC ebook record available at https://lccn.loc.gov/2023040226

This book is published in the IGI Global book series Advances in Logistics, Operations, and Management Science (ALOMS) (ISSN: 2327-350X; eISSN: 2327-3518)

British Cataloguing in Publication Data
A Cataloguing in Publication record for this book is available from the British Library.

For electronic access to this publication, please contact: eresources@igi-global.com.

Advances in Logistics, Operations, and Management Science (ALOMS) Book Series

John Wang
Montclair State University, USA

ISSN:2327-350X
EISSN:2327-3518

Mission

Operations research and management science continue to influence business processes, administration, and management information systems, particularly in covering the application methods for decision-making processes. New case studies and applications on management science, operations management, social sciences, and other behavioral sciences have been incorporated into business and organizations real-world objectives.

The **Advances in Logistics, Operations, and Management Science** (ALOMS) Book Series provides a collection of reference publications on the current trends, applications, theories, and practices in the management science field. Providing relevant and current research, this series and its individual publications would be useful for academics, researchers, scholars, and practitioners interested in improving decision making models and business functions.

Coverage

- Decision analysis and decision support
- Networks
- Marketing engineering
- Organizational Behavior
- Risk Management
- Computing and information technologies
- Production Management
- Services management
- Political Science
- Information Management

IGI Global is currently accepting manuscripts for publication within this series. To submit a proposal for a volume in this series, please contact our Acquisition Editors at Acquisitions@igi-global.com or visit: http://www.igi-global.com/publish/.

The Advances in Logistics, Operations, and Management Science (ALOMS) Book Series (ISSN 2327-350X) is published by IGI Global, 701 E. Chocolate Avenue, Hershey, PA 17033-1240, USA, www.igi-global.com. This series is composed of titles available for purchase individually; each title is edited to be contextually exclusive from any other title within the series. For pricing and ordering information please visit http://www.igi-global.com/book-series/advances-logistics-operations-management-science/37170. Postmaster: Send all address changes to above address.

Titles in this Series

For a list of additional titles in this series, please visit: www.igi-global.com/book-series

Strategies and Approaches of Corporate Social Responsibility Toward Multinational Enterprises
Erum Shaikh (Shaheed Benazir Bhutto University, Sanghar Campus, Pakistan)
Business Science Reference • copyright 2024 • 400pp • H/C (ISBN: 9798369303634) • US $275.00 (our price)

Cybersecurity Measures for Logistics Industry Framework
Noor Zaman Jhanjhi (Taylor's University, Malaysia) and Imdad Ali Shah (Taylor's University, Malaysia)
Information Science Reference • copyright 2024 • 310pp • H/C (ISBN: 9781668476253) • US $250.00 (our price)

Drivers of SME Growth and Sustainability in Emerging Markets
Sumesh Dadwal (Northumbrian University, UK) Pawan Kumar (Lovely Professional University, India) Rajesh Verma (Lovely Professional University, India) and Gursimranjit Singh (Dr.B.R Ambedkar National Institute of Technology, Jalandhar)
Business Science Reference • copyright 2024 • 330pp • H/C (ISBN: 9798369301111) • US $250.00 (our price)

Emerging Technologies in Digital Manufacturing and Smart Factories
Ahdi Hassan (Global Institute for Research Education and Scholarship, The Netherlands) Pushan Kumar Dutta (Amity University Kolkata, India) Subir Gupta (Swami Vivekanand University, India) Ebrahim Mattar (College of Engineering, University of Bahrain, Bahrain) and Satya Singh (Sharda University, Uzbekistan)
Business Science Reference • copyright 2024 • 291pp • H/C (ISBN: 9798369309209) • US $275.00 (our price)

Implementing Sustainable Development Goals in the Service Sector
Vipin Nadda (University of Sunderland, UK) Pankaj Kumar Tyagi (Chandigarh University, India) Rubina Moniz Vieira (St. Mary's University, London, UK) and Priyanka Tyagi (Chandigarh University, India)
Business Science Reference • copyright 2024 • 281pp • H/C (ISBN: 9798369320655) • US $275.00 (our price)

Effective Human Resources Management in the Multigenerational Workplace
Angela M. Even (Purdue University, USA) and Bryan Christiansen (Southern New Hampshire University, USA)
Business Science Reference • copyright 2024 • 304pp • H/C (ISBN: 9798369321737) • US $325.00 (our price)

Cases on Uncovering Corporate Governance Challenges in Asian Markets
Rashedul Hasan (Coventry University, UK)
Business Science Reference • copyright 2024 • 260pp • H/C (ISBN: 9781668498675) • US $235.00 (our price)

Innovation and Resource Management Strategies for Startups Development
Neeta Baporikar (Namibia University of Science and Technology, Namibia & SP Pune University, India)
Business Science Reference • copyright 2024 • 330pp • H/C (ISBN: 9798369320778) • US $275.00 (our price)

IGI Global
PUBLISHER of TIMELY KNOWLEDGE

701 East Chocolate Avenue, Hershey, PA 17033, USA
Tel: 717-533-8845 x100 • Fax: 717-533-8661
E-Mail: cust@igi-global.com • www.igi-global.com

Table of Contents

Detailed Table of Contents

with supply chain arrangement. Therefore, blockchain provides disseminated, irreversible, translucent records, which can also track possible communal and ecological prospects that can enact ecological, health, and well-being apprehensions.

This chapter focuses on the Chinese market and explores the use of blockchain technology in supply chain management. It explores actual Chinese case studies while explaining blockchain's basics and its promise for improving supply chain transparency, security, and efficiency. With a focus on enhanced traceability, robustness, and the function of smart contracts, this chapter examines Chinese supply chain models that make use of blockchain technology. Sustainable development goals in China are aligned with blockchain's environmental consequences, its use in carbon footprint tracking, and the promotion of circular supply chains. This chapter analyzes the obstacles to blockchain adoption in China from a legal and regulatory perspective, and suggests ways to overcome these roadblocks through policy reform. Finally, the chapter projects the future influence of blockchain technology on global supply chain management by analyzing the potential and constraints facing Chinese enterprises that deploy blockchain-based supply chain systems.

The aim of this chapter is to evaluate previous research, reports, and opinions of marketing specialists regarding the issue of transparency and trust in the existing supply chain of programmatic advertising. Literature shows that blockchain technology holds significant potential for improving transparency and trust in the programmatic advertising supply chain. Previous research highlights its advantages in enhancing advertising processes, securing transactions, and addressing industry challenges. The collaboration of industry organizations and the practical implementation of blockchain technology further demonstrate its efficacy. By embracing blockchain, the advertising industry can overcome the limitations of the current supply chain and create a more transparent, secure, and efficient ecosystem.

Blockchain technology has gained significant attention for its potential to enhance transparency, trust, and efficiency in supply chain operations. However, the adoption of blockchain in supply chains also introduces various security and privacy concerns that need to be addressed to ensure the integrity and confidentiality of sensitive information. This chapter examines these challenges, explores their implications, and discusses potential solutions to mitigate risks. The chapter begins by identifying the key security challenges associated with blockchain-based supply chain management. It delves into issues such as data tampering, malicious attacks on the blockchain network, vulnerabilities in smart contracts, and the risk of unauthorized access to sensitive supply chain data. Moreover, it highlights the privacy challenges, including the exposure of personally identifiable information (PII), the potential for data leakage, and the difficulty in achieving selective disclosure of information in a transparent blockchain environment.

The purpose of this chapter is to explore how blockchain technology can be used to transform supply chain management practices. Blockchain addresses longstanding supply chain challenges, such as transparency, traceability, and data integrity, through its decentralized, tamper-resistant nature. Through automated smart contracts, blockchain's secure and transparent ledger can enhance trust among stakeholders, mitigate fraud and counterfeiting risks, and streamline complex transactions. The chapter illustrates how blockchain integration can improve efficiency, reduce costs, and improve customer satisfaction through case studies across the pharmaceutical sector. In addition to addressing scalability, interoperability, and regulatory compliance, the chapter acknowledges existing obstacles in implementation of blockchain technology in supply chain management. Future advancements in blockchain technology promise to revolutionize supply chain management practices on a global scale.

Blockchain as a technology has potential for improving risk exposure through incorporation with risk management frameworks. There are aspects of the link between the two that facilitate a way of working outside that is possible by all but the very largest corporate entities. The use of enterprise risk management (ERM) frameworks, and in particular ISO31000, has become an increasingly accepted governance standard for companies, and any use of Blockchain technologies needs to integrate with those organisational processes. Doing so should result in practical benefits for most organisations engaging with their exposure to risk in a formalised manner. This chapter outlines risk management frameworks, the 'dimensions' in which integration with Blockchain may be realised, key benefits, challenges, and future development opportunities. The presently available implementation case studies are discussed throughout the chapter including potential usage in supply chain management, healthcare records, financial management, and corporate governance.

Data communication through Edge devices in a secured channel for real time applications is one of the biggest concerns. Software Defined Network is a suitable network opted for security. The Control Plane is more vulnerable to variety of attacks. Ensemble machine learning approach which composes of 3 times of Random Forest with one time of Linear Regression gives us the prediction of errors and loss of packets and hence the data will be transferred more securely. The Block Chain is integrated with the SDN controllers in the control plane to transfer the data from the edge devices in the form of a Block to the cloud layer. Federated Learning can be inculcated for security analysis prediction and then aggregating into a Global Model in the Central Cloud Layer. The majority of contemporary FL techniques do not explicitly address variances among client parameter estimates. An aggregation mechanism built on the Hessian matrix in order to close the gap. Moreover, we can use the Hessian as a scaling matrix using the second -order partial derivative information of the loss function

Blockchain technology has gained significant momentum in recent years, with many countries recognizing its potential for enhancing sustainability in supply chains. Countries around the world are increasingly exploring the potential of blockchain to enhance transparency, traceability, and accountability in their supply chains. Blockchain enables countries to establish a trusted and decentralized network where information can be securely stored and accessed by relevant stakeholders. This enables governments, businesses, and consumers to have a comprehensive view of the supply chain, from raw material sourcing to product delivery through transparency and traceability across which enabling better visibility into the origins and environmental impact of products by ensuring sustainability practices are adhered to at every stage of the supply chain. As more companies recognize the benefits of blockchain in ensuring sustainability, we can expect to see its widespread adoption in supply chains across various industries.

The digital transformation of industries, including the food delivery sector, has led to new challenges and opportunities. This comprehensive study explores into the complexities faced by Pakistan's food delivery industry, highlighting trust issues and customer loyalty. By integrating AI-driven blockchain technology, the purpose is to enhance credibility, transparency, and customer satisfaction within the sector. The research discloses a spectrum of challenges, ranging from food safety concerns to preservation of halal integrity. The amalgamation of AI-driven blockchain technology arises as a potential solution to such challenges, presenting real-time insights, boosted traceability, and enhanced accountability. However, ethical considerations associated with user consent, data privacy and fairness of algorithm must be addressed. The comprehensive analysis of the study led to conclusion that a balanced approach is crucial for unleashing the potential of it in revolutionizing Pakistan's food delivery sector, takes into account both technological benefits and ethical implications.

As we continue to navigate the 21st century, the interconnectedness of technological advancements and sustainable growth is becoming more evident. Among a plethora of technologies reshaping multiple sectors, blockchain emerges as a game-changer for supply chain management. Concurrently, the sustainable development goals (SDGs) established by the United Nations in 2015 offer a roadmap for sustainability worldwide. This chapter delves into the connection between these two significant constructs: blockchain technology and the SDGs, in relation to SCM.

Blockchain technology is revolutionizing countless areas of human life. It has gained significant attention because of its potential to transform supply chain management across various sectors, including education. This chapter explores possible benefits and obstacles associated with adopting a blockchain-enabled supply chain in the educational sector from a management perspective. With blockchain, universities will have more transparency, security, and efficiency in their system. However, implementing a new system includes several challenges in terms of technology, Infrastructure, Finance, Legal, and Human Resources. To overcome these challenges, a comprehensive understanding of the educational sector's unique supply chain requirements, stakeholders' participation, and careful planning are necessary. This chapter provides insights to decision-makers in formulating strategies to leverage blockchain technology effectively and maximize its potential in enhancing supply chain procedures in the educational sector.

The wide array of functions performed by a state referred to as public sector is increasingly applying the practices of supply chain management. The public sector has special emphasis on the aspects of transparency, efficiency, and resilience as increased awareness among the citizens is forcing the states to provide better value to the taxpayer money. Use of information and communication technologies has been attributed to improve the visibility and efficiency in public sector. Blockchain technology, being an emerging disruptive technology providing immutable distributed ledgers, has strong theoretical application in public sector. Following a systematic literature review the research establishes that Blockchain

Preface

In the era of Industrial Revolution 5.0, organizations grappled with unprecedented challenges in maintaining the effectiveness, transparency, and security of their operations, leading to disruptions in supply chain dynamics. Recognizing the transformative potential of blockchain technology, this edited reference book, *Achieving Secure and Transparent Supply Chains with Blockchain Technology*, emerges as a beacon of knowledge amid the complexities of contemporary supply chain management.

As editors of this comprehensive collection, we—Mustafa Khan, Naveed R. Khan, and Arsalan Ghouri—bring together diverse expertise from UCSI University, Malaysia, and London South Bank University, United Kingdom. Our collaborative effort aims to provide a thorough exploration of blockchain technology and its pivotal role in enhancing supply chain efficiency, security, and resilience. We delve into the challenges and opportunities inherent in integrating supply chain management with blockchain technology.

This book is a valuable resource offering contemporary theoretical frameworks and the latest empirical findings, catering to academics, practitioners, policymakers, researchers, professionals, and students. The scope is broad, and the content is meticulously curated to benefit individuals interested in supply chain and blockchain technology—whether engaged in fieldwork, research, teaching, or studying. Our intent is to provide a holistic understanding of the concepts, practices, and strategies shaping the intersection of supply chain and blockchain technology.

Key Features of the Book:

1. Introduction to Blockchain Technology and Its Applications in Supply Chain Management:
    a. A foundational exploration of blockchain and its relevance in modern supply chain frameworks.
2. Blockchain and Sustainability in Supply Chains:
    a. Examining the synergy between blockchain technology and sustainable supply chain practices.
3. Blockchain-Based Supply Chain Traceability:
    a. Unraveling the potential of blockchain for end-to-end traceability in supply chains.
4. Blockchain-Based Supply Chain Resilience, Transparency, and Efficiency:
    a. Analyzing how blockchain contributes to resilience, transparency, and efficiency in supply chain operations.
5. Blockchain for Supply Chain Security:
    a. Investigating the role of blockchain in fortifying the security of supply chain networks.

6. Smart Contracts for Supply Chain Management:
   a. Exploring the application of smart contracts as a catalyst for streamlined supply chain processes.
7. Blockchain-Based Supply Chain and Risk Management:
   a. Uncovering the transformative impact of blockchain on healthcare records, financial management, and corporate governance.
8. Sustainable Development Goals (SDGs) and Blockchain in Supply Chain Management:
   a. Aligning blockchain applications with Sustainable Development Goals in supply chain management.
9. Challenges and Opportunities for Blockchain-Based Supply Chain Management:
   a. Delving into the nuanced challenges and opportunities presented by blockchain in supply chain contexts.
10. Future Directions for Blockchain-Based Supply Chain Management:
    a. Anticipating and discussing the future trajectory of blockchain in shaping supply chain management.

This collection is a testament to the evolving landscape of supply chains and the transformative power of blockchain technology. We hope this compilation stimulates thought, sparks innovation, and serves as a valuable resource in navigating the intricate relationship between supply chain management and blockchain technology.

ORGANIZATION OF THE BOOK

Chapter 1: This chapter illuminates the intersection of supply chain digitalization, industry 4.0 technologies, and blockchain to achieve the United Nations Sustainable Development Goals (UNSDGs). The comprehensive discussion covers the 17 UNSDGs and 232 indicators established by the UN, emphasizing the successful integration of blockchain technology in supply chains for sustainable development. Practical implications for managers and policymakers are provided, offering insights into executing and encouraging blockchain adoption for achieving global sustainability.

Chapter 2: Examining blockchain as a key support for an invincible supply chain system, this chapter explores its implementation in various sectors. Focused on transparency and robust linkage, blockchain's role in ensuring sustainability in food, agriculture, healthcare, and pharmaceutical domains is emphasized. The chapter delves into the triple bottom line perspective, aligning ecological, social, and business stability. By providing distributed, irreversible, and translucent records, blockchain emerges as a transformative force for addressing ecological, health, and well-being concerns in supply chain arrangements.

Chapter 3: This chapter provides insights into the integration of blockchain technology in the Chinese supply chain, offering real-world case studies. Exploring the basics of blockchain and its potential for improving transparency, security, and efficiency, the discussion spans enhanced traceability, smart contracts, and alignment with Sustainable Development Goals (SDGs). The chapter addresses legal and regulatory obstacles in China and projects the future influence of blockchain on global supply chain management through the lens of Chinese enterprises.

Chapter 4: Evaluating research, reports, and opinions from marketing specialists, this chapter delves into the role of blockchain in enhancing transparency and trust in programmatic advertising supply chains. It highlights the advantages of blockchain in addressing industry challenges, securing transactions, and fostering collaboration among industry organizations. By embracing blockchain, the advertising sector can overcome limitations in the current supply chain, creating a more transparent, secure, and efficient ecosystem.

Chapter 5: While blockchain technology promises transparency and efficiency, this chapter addresses the security and privacy concerns associated with its adoption in supply chains. Identifying key challenges such as data tampering, malicious attacks, vulnerabilities in smart contracts, and privacy issues, the chapter explores potential solutions to mitigate risks. It emphasizes the need to balance the transformative potential of blockchain with safeguarding sensitive information and ensuring confidentiality in a transparent blockchain environment.

Chapter 6: Focused on transforming supply chain practices, this chapter explores the impact of blockchain technology. Highlighting its role in addressing challenges like transparency, traceability, and data integrity, the chapter presents case studies from the pharmaceutical sector. It discusses how blockchain's decentralized, tamper-resistant ledger and smart contracts enhance trust, mitigate fraud risks, and streamline transactions. The chapter also acknowledges existing obstacles and anticipates future advancements in global supply chain management.

Chapter 7: This chapter delves into the integration of blockchain technology with risk management frameworks, particularly Enterprise Risk Management (ERM) and ISO31000. By aligning blockchain with organizational processes, the chapter outlines key benefits, challenges, and future development opportunities. It explores implementation case studies in supply chain management, healthcare records, financial management, and corporate governance, emphasizing practical benefits for organizations engaging with risk in a formalized manner.

Chapter 8: Focusing on secure data communication through Edge devices, this chapter introduces the integration of blockchain with Software Defined Network (SDN). Emphasizing the vulnerability of the Control Plane and proposing an ensemble machine learning approach, the chapter explores the secure transfer of data from Edge devices to the cloud layer. It introduces Federated Learning for security analysis prediction and advocates the use of the Hessian matrix to address variances among client parameter estimates, ensuring a secure and scalable data transfer.

Chapter 9: This chapter explores the global momentum behind adopting blockchain technology to enhance sustainability in supply chains. It discusses how blockchain enables transparency, traceability, and accountability, offering stakeholders a comprehensive view of the supply chain. Governments, businesses, and consumers benefit from a decentralized network that ensures adherence to sustainability practices at every stage. The chapter anticipates widespread blockchain adoption in supply chains across various industries as more companies recognize its potential for ensuring sustainability.

Chapter 10: Examining the challenges faced by Pakistan's food delivery industry, this chapter proposes an integration of AI-driven blockchain technology to enhance credibility, transparency, and customer satisfaction. The research addresses concerns such as food safety, preservation of halal integrity, and the ethical considerations associated with user consent and data privacy. A balanced approach is advocated, considering both technological benefits and ethical implications for revolutionizing Pakistan's food delivery sector.

Chapter 11: Exploring the connection between blockchain technology and the United Nations Sustainable Development Goals (SDGs), this chapter navigates the intersection with supply chain management. It delves into the role of blockchain in reshaping supply chains and contributing to sustainability. Drawing parallels between technological advancements and sustainable growth, the chapter sheds light on the transformative potential of blockchain in achieving sustainable development goals within the context of supply chain management.

Chapter 13: Assessing the benefits and obstacles associated with adopting a blockchain-enabled supply chain in the educational sector, this chapter provides insights from a management perspective. Exploring transparency, security, and efficiency, the chapter acknowledges challenges related to technology, infrastructure, finance, legal aspects, and human resources. Decision-makers are offered strategies to leverage blockchain technology effectively, maximizing its potential in enhancing supply chain procedures in the educational sector.

Chapter 14: Highlighting the application of blockchain technology in the public sector's supply chain, this chapter explores its role in improving transparency, efficiency, and resilience. Drawing from a systematic literature review, the research establishes that blockchain enables key determinants of success in public sector supply chains. Existing research on the application of blockchain technology in the public sector is explored, providing insights into the current state of research, and proposing future directions.

Chapter 15: Concluding the edited reference book, this chapter explores the application of blockchain technology in achieving secure and transparent supply chains. Focused on addressing key challenges faced by modern supply chains, including counterfeiting and lack of traceability, the chapter emphasizes blockchain's features such as transparency, immutability, and decentralized consensus. It offers a promising solution to the critical challenge of ensuring the integrity and visibility of products throughout their lifecycle in an increasingly complex and globalized supply chain landscape.

CONCLUSION

In closing this edited reference book, *Achieving Secure and Transparent Supply Chains with Blockchain Technology*, we reflect on the collaborative effort that brought together diverse expertise from UCSI University, Malaysia; and London South Bank University, United Kingdom. As editors—Mustafa Khan, Naveed R. Khan, and Arsalan Ghouri—we embarked on a journey to illuminate the transformative potential of blockchain technology amid the challenges faced by organizations in the era of Industrial Revolution 5.0.

Our intention was to provide a comprehensive exploration of blockchain's pivotal role in enhancing supply chain efficiency, security, and resilience. From the foundational introduction to blockchain's applications in supply chain management to its potential in reshaping sustainability practices, each chapter in this collection contributes to a holistic understanding of the intersection between supply chains and blockchain technology.

The comprehensive organization of this book reflects the evolving landscape of supply chains and the undeniable impact of blockchain technology. We believe this compilation will stimulate thought, spark innovation, and serve as a valuable resource for individuals engaged in various capacities—be it academics, practitioners, policymakers, researchers, professionals, or students.

We extend our gratitude to the contributors for their valuable insights and dedication to advancing knowledge in this dynamic field. Our hope is that this book inspires further research, fosters collaboration, and contributes to the ongoing dialogue surrounding the intricate relationship between supply chain management and blockchain technology.

Mustafa Khan
UCSI University, Malaysia

Naveed R. Khan
UCSI University, Malaysia

Arsalan Ghouri
London South Bank University, UK

Chapter 1
Blockchain Technology and Supply Chain Sustainability: A View From UNSDG Perspective

Muhammad Rahies Khan
Bahria University, Karachi, Pakistan

Akhtiar Ali
University of Sufism and Modern Sciences, Bhitshah, Pakistan

Asad Ali Rind
University of South Champagne Business School, Y Schools, Troyes, France

ABSTRACT

Supply chain digitalization has revolutionized outcomes for firms in their business operations. Incorporating industry 4.0 technologies has witnessed a change in the supply chain process execution. Blockchain technology has been rigorously addressed in supply chain operations but achieving UNSDGs through blockchain technologies has rarely been witnessed. To fill this gap, this chapter discussed the United Nations sustainable development goals and revealed that the UN has established 17 goals with 232 indicators that will address sustainable development at the global level. Further, the chapter covered the integration of blockchain technology in the supply chain for achieving sustainability. The discussion revealed that the integration of blockchain has successfully helped firms in achieving sustainable development. The discussion resulted in the successful explanation of blockchain integration in addressing the UNSDGs sustainable development. This chapter has provided practical implications to managers and policymakers in executing and encouraging blockchain adoption.

INTRODUCTION

Rapid industrialization, globalization, and technological advancement brought exponential challenges to humanity, firms, and the environment (Jerath, 2021). To address these challenges, international regula-

DOI: 10.4018/979-8-3693-0482-2.ch001

tory bodies formulated suitable regulations at different times, however, they were incapable of providing adequate measures. Therefore, in 2015 United Nations formulated Sustainable Development Goals (UNSDGs). UNSDGs contain 232 indicators and 17 goals that are supposed to address issues in every sector. To address and implement these goals in developed and developing nations, trust, coordination and exchange of resources are an essential part. In this regard, developed countries have transferred a handsome amount of funds to these developing countries but unexpectedly, targeted goals have not been achieved due to a lack of several factors like a lack of trust, honesty, corruption, political instability, and weak governance (de Villiers et al., 2021). UNSDGs have been categorized into three categories first, UNSDGs with established methods and available data, second, UNSDGs with established methods but inadequate data availability and third UNSDGs with no established methods (Peltola et al., 2022). To enhance the quality of information and statistics, the UN's Global Partnership for Sustainable Development Data (GPSDD) has partnered with data revolution to promote sustainable development. The COVID-19 pandemic has affected the UNSDGs and promoted digitalization in every sector of life that accelerate automation and reduced human interference generating the philosophy of Industry 4.0 and Industry 5.0 (de Villiers et al., 2021).

Digitalization has brought challenges to sustainability, equity, and social inclusion at one end however acts as a strong enabler to address UNSDGs if implemented with true letter and spirit (Zheng & Walsham, 2008). In the field of the supply chain, blockchain technology was considered to be the primitive tool to address data sharing, information sharing and bring strong collaboration among trading partners. Blockchain technology is a decentralized and transactional database that provides resistant free transactions and facilitates a large number of trading partners through heterogeneous networks (nodes) (Beck et al., 2018). Kewell et al. (2017) suggested that due to the blockchain feature of being decentralized and resistant to free transactions, it can handle the challenges of trust, visibility, transparency, and decentralization among a large number of individuals, firms, institutions, and society at large. Due to its features, blockchain technology is discussed in a wider range named supply chain sustainability, certification, organizational competencies, smart contracts, and smart cities (Rossi et al., 2019). Additionally, the nexus of blockchain with sustainable development brought it to the core of research area in multidisciplinary areas (Lindman et al., 2017; Rossi et al., 2019).

The Majority of blockchain applications are directly associated with sustainable development initiatives. For example, blockchain technology can accelerate SC visibility, transparency, enhance information and data sharing, and provide sustenance to a circular economy (Khan et al., 2023; Mohamed et al., 2023). The implementation of blockchain technology is much evident during and after COVID-19 in supply chain management (Khan & Manzoor, 2021; Mohamed et al., 2023), public administration (Ølnes et al., 2017) and even in gender studies (Thylin & Duarte, 2019). Interestingly., the supply chain literature is abundant with blockchain applications however, little has been investigated to explore the role of blockchain technology in addressing sustainability (Chandan et al., 2023; Medaglia & Damsgaard, 2020) and how this technology can help achieve the UNSDG goals.

To address this potential gap, this chapter intends to discuss the core tenants of blockchain technology and also elaborate on the potential implications of blockchain technology in achieving SCM sustainability. Further, through the synthesis of previous literature on blockchain applications in SCM, we intend to examine and try to connect the research avenues with the UNSDGs. Predominantly, we are interested to answer the question that "how blockchain technology is helping firms in achieving supply chain sustainability and hence addressing the UNSDGs". Additionally, we also outline some of the potential challenges and barriers to the implementation of blockchain technology in achieving SCM sustainability and UNSDGs. In the next section, we investigate the intersection of some of the industry 4.0 technologies with blockchain technology and how this combination helps to address the sustainability and UNSDGs objectives. Lastly, we provide some of the future avenues for researchers to extend their thoughts on the blockchain technology application in addressing the UNSDGs.

BACKGROUND

Blockchain Technology and Supply Chain Sustainability

The triple bottom line concept was coined by Elkington (1998) encouraging firms to focus on economic, social, and environmental measures. Firms that implement these sustainability dimensions are successful to gain better competitive and economic performance (Carter & Rogers, 2008). Hence, it is worth mentioning that the three pillars of sustainability are equally important for firms' extensive competitiveness and sustainable outlook.

Economic Performance

The connectivity and demand and supply fulfillment between buyers and sellers was a crucial issue. Blockchain technology has provided disintermediation that serves to support and connect numerous buyers and sellers without any third-party intervention. This direct connection and support leads to the minimization of additional costs, complexity of transactions, and delayed product rejection by various customers. To eliminate these problems, blockchain serves as a direct connection between buyer and seller hence excluding the role of the third party by creating a network of trading partners. In this perspective, the combination of smart contracts and blockchain provides a workable, viable, transparent, trusted, and visible partnership between trading partners at global level supply chains. Additionally, the integration of blockchain also accelerates the firm's efficiency, agility, and responsiveness in addressing global supply chain challenges. Blockchain integration also enhances the digital traceability, verification, and authentication of food products from suppliers to store shelves.

Besides, real-time access to product information through blockchain technology enables the firms to identify the actual status of inventory and raw materials and hence make more holistic and integrated decisions at each stage of supply chains. Hence, blockchain provides time-saving competitiveness and makes the more complex stages and tasks by removing inefficient, procedures, paperwork, complex decision-making, and stringent organizational rules. Along with these benefits, real-time transactions and transfer of payments among trading partners can be made easy through blockchain integration. Therefore, it is evident that blockchain exponentially enhances operational performance, optimization of resource allocation, and provision of timely resources to address the demand and supply requirements in the market (Schmidt & Wagner, 2019).

Efficient integration of blockchain reduces several costs like product quality verification, transfer of ownership cost, and costs on inefficient business activities. Further, blockchain implementation enhances access to other markets by reducing the cost of physical networking among trading partners. Through the optimized allocation of resources, blockchain provides real-time information about underutilized inventories and logistics assets. Further, due to the digital capability of blockchain, sharing of information among trading partners enhance the availability and utilization of logistics resources and promotes the fair business economic model through sharing economy. This is because, the firms operating based on resource sharing remain under stringent monitoring, security, and supervision. According to Veuger (2018), blockchain can accelerate crowdfunding for small and medium businesses by simplification of procedures and by reducing the entry-level barriers and costs for lower capital firms. In a nutshell, blockchain promotes trust, enhances data security and integrity, is secure from fraud, and reduces cost.

Social Performance

According to Rahmanzadeh et al. (2020), blockchain promotes trust and offers widely accepted trusted platforms that serve as a common agreement on transparent, secure, and distributed ledgers. This nature of blockchain marginally reduces the risk and accelerates the fearless transactions among trading partners. The transparency of information and transactions on blockchain platforms helps in establishing a trustful mutual association between stakeholders (Veuger, 2018). Further, Lemieux (2016) indicated that to achieve the developmental objectives it is necessary to have more secure and trustful platforms for business trading partners which is made possible by integration on blockchain. The global supply chains are very difficult to manage as there involve numerous untrusted and unidentical trading partners however, this problem was solved by blockchain by providing (Wang et al., 2019). Hence, blockchain provides unique common values and platforms with well-defined goals and policies, stringent legislative and control mechanisms, and healthy connections that foster the firm's social capital namely trust.

Food security and safety are the chief concerns of customers in recent years as consumers are more and more interested to know the ingredients of food and their origin. Therefore, blockchain has solved this concern by providing the consumers' transparency and accountability of products and also serves the firms by providing them the real-time tracing of products. Further, consumers are more conscious of health issues and blockchain integration in food chains significantly reduces healthcare costs by strictly monitoring the quality of the product during the shipment hence improving the consumers' perception of the food industry. Similarly, Wang et al. (2019) revealed that blockchain-based product traceability enables retailers to quickly respond to the recalls of defective, rotten, and safety-compromising food products to reduce foodborne diseases.

Finally, during periods of crises and disruptions, blockchain served as humanitarian aid in the provision of timely medication and first aid. During the COVID-19 pandemic, humanitarian logistics was critically impacted at first glance but the incorporation of industry 4.0 technologies especially the blockchain provides the first way forward in the execution of the global supply chains. More importantly, blockchain transparency enhances the visibility to address human rights abuses, corruption, and child labor in a global context. Further, the blockchain helps to bring the general masses under the tax net and financial inclusion.

Environmental Performance

Blockchain played a crucial role in mitigating environmental issues by reducing the carbon footprint associated with logistic activities. Through blockchain integration, a monitoring setup in production processes like energy consumption, acquisition and processing of raw material, and gaseous emission helps in reducing environmental degradation. The digital nature of blockchain enables the stakeholders to launch low-carbon initiatives in daily activities, help them in integrating eco-friendly campaigns and promote the consumers' awareness and provide them access to clean and green energy and production (Ashley & Johnson, 2018). Blockchain also helps firms in the acquisition of eco-friendly raw material and also provide the way forward to invest in alternative, efficient, and sustainable energy resources that ultimately yield sustainable and durable products and services (Kouhizadeh et al., 2021). The transparent nature of blockchain monitors the chemical evaluation in the product eco-design phase and also enhances environmental sustainability by close environmental monitoring with trading partners.

Importantly, blockchain enhances the collaboration among trading partners and reduces the unnecessary steps in acquiring the raw material. The close nexus between suppliers and buyers promotes the transparent product eco-design process that helps in generating eco-friendly products. Blockchain technology empowers firms to trace the carbon emission of their products and provides them with the prospect of closely trading and monitoring carbon assets in markets (Saberi et al., 2019). In a nutshell, blockchain technology provides firms with real-time access and monitoring of carbon emissions and gives them analyses of greenhouse gases emission. Figure 1 below highlighted the transformation of the triple bottom-line approach to blockchain sustainable supply chain. Further, the integration of blockchain by Walmart and Unilever is explained in case 1 and 2 respectively.

Figure 1. Transformation of Traditional SCM to Blockchain driven SCM
Source: Munir et al. 2022

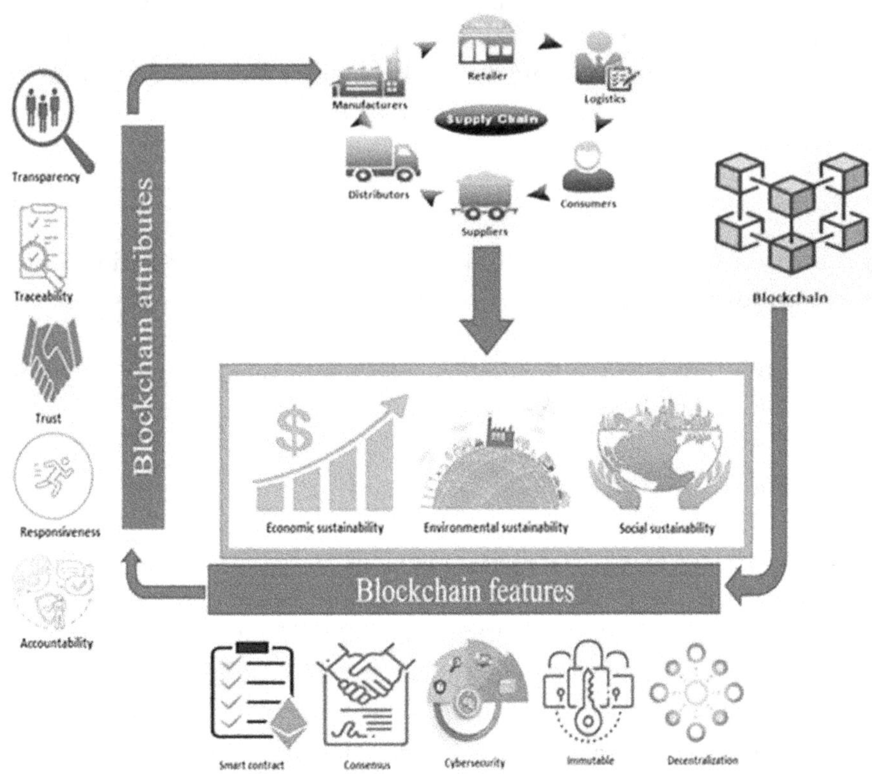

USE CASE One: BLOCKCHAIN AND FOOD RECALL MANAGEMENT

Case One: Blockchain and Food Recall Management

Food recalls happen when there's a risk that a product may cause a foodborne illness outbreak. The most common reasons for this are bacteria, parasites, and improper packaging. In this situation, food companies have to remove dangerous products from supermarket shelves as soon as possible to minimize public health risks and save their reputations. However, tracing affected products isn't so easy. On average, it takes about two months for food companies to do this, and even longer with global supply chains. Blockchain technology in supply chain networks helps businesses respond to recalls quickly. It logs all the events that food products go through on their way to the supermarket shelves. Companies can source defective products within seconds as a result. In addition to improving public safety, this also results in less waste and lower costs.

Real-Life Example

Since 2018, *Walmart* has been using blockchain to manage their suppliers of leafy greens. Their goal is to ensure the safety of the products they sell and to reduce the time it takes to provide evidence in the event of a claim. The solution gathers data about every step the greens go through, from when the seeds are planted. Once the greens are on the shelves, the company can continue to add data to the platform. For example, *Walmart* can specify how long the greens have been in the store and at what temperature they are being stored. With this information, *Walmart* can quickly determine the origin and location of compromised products. For example, sourcing the origin of sliced mangoes in their US stores takes two seconds with blockchain, while using traditional tracing methods would take a week.

Benefits

Reducing costs. Companies can manage recalls quickly, minimizing legal and investigative costs.

Minimizing waste. Businesses can localize contamination precisely to remove only the damaged products.

Saving reputation. With blockchain, food companies can respond to recalls before they become reputational disasters.

Case Two Blockchain for Sustainability

Today's businesses have to take care of the environment. Their environmental impact influences their reputation and investors' decisions. Sustainability credentials are also valued by consumers who tend to buy sustainable goods, even if they cost more. But, to label a product as sustainable, businesses have to be sure they're using 100% sustainable products coming from other suppliers. This isn't easy for companies that are toward the end of the supply chain. And the longer their supply chain is, the harder it is to find out. So, how can features of blockchain support sustainability efforts? The technology can create a supply chain model for any product. Each record along the blockchain will contain the necessary data on this product. It will also record every event and condition. For example, for a vegetable, it will record data from the vegetation period through to processing and transportation. This enables companies to see how sustainable the products they want to buy are.

Real-Time Example

Unilever aims to achieve a deforestation-free supply chain by the end of 2023, so they need to know how sustainable their supply chains are. Existing systems for sustainability certification are not enough to provide this information, so the company decided to use blockchain. They started a pilot project in Indonesia to trace the palm oil they bought. Their first-mile suppliers created digital tokens, which mirrored the flow of palm oil through the supply chain. As a result, *Unilever* could get information about the product, including the conditions in which it was grown and harvested.

Benefits

Verifying that the origin of raw materials is sustainable. Businesses can check how sustainable the raw materials they want to buy are.

Increasing consumer loyalty. Companies can prove the sustainability of their products to consumers for whom this is a priority.

Nexus Between Blockchain and UNSDGs

In 2015, United Nations formulated 17 UNSDGs with 232 indicators that almost cover every sector of life. The description of each UNSDG is provided briefly in Table 1 below. To address these UNSDGs, the UN has also formulated some ways forwards and mechanisms that could be beneficial and could better guide the governments and business communities globally. One of the supported mechanisms to accomplish these UNSDGs is the science, technology, and innovation initiative. Walsh et al (2020) developed a framework regarding the effective implementation of STIs by countries in achieving the UNSDGs 2030. Therefore, the effective implementation of blockchain technology could yield more fruitful results in this aspect. Several sectors have implemented blockchain and found significant positive outcomes in achieving the UNSDGs 2030. Some of the recent studies include the potential implications of blockchain in supply chain and smart contracts have evaluated their significance in addressing sustainability issues (Choi & Luo, 2019; Cole et al., 2019; Kamble et al., 2020; Kouhizadeh & Sarkis, 2018). Others like Saberi et al. (2019) evaluated the advantages of blockchain technology in enhancing the traceability, visibility, and security of supply chains. Similarly, Hasting and Sodhi (2020) also found transparent supply chains due to the application of blockchain in cobalt mining and pharmaceutical industries. Some of the studies also highlighted the economic-oriented benefits of blockchain integration in food supply chains (Astill et al., 2019; Duan et al., 2020; Howson, 2020).

Blockchain and Environmental SDGs

The implication of blockchain is widely accepted and has covered the areas of manufacturing, agro-food, and public administration besides the financial and insurance fields. Therefore, the influence of blockchain adoption on the sustainable aspects especially the environment is an essential element of research for the future world. Blockchain adoption has several effects on the SDGs and the environment as well and one of the prominent effects is on the SDG-7 Affordable and Clean Energy as blockchain played a significant role in the development of alternative energy especially renewable energy resources (Park et al., 2018). Further, Sharma et al. (2020) highlighted the role of blockchain in the electric battery recharge in vehicles and discussed their influence on the environment. Similarly, the integration of blockchain has a positive significant influence on the SDG-13 Climate Action providing an opportunity to frame the carbon emission exchange (Franke et al., 2020). Similarly, Thess et al. (2020) have indicated the implementation of cryptocurrency to initiate the incentive for appreciating low pollution behaviors. Some of the other scholars have also highlighted the tracking and traceability of supply chains that address the SDG-12 Responsible Consumption and Production (Saberi et al., 2019), to initiate the platforms for implementing and monitoring the energy utilization and waste management hence addressing the SDG-11 Sustainable Cities and Communities (Ahad et al., 2020) and lastly, the SDG-14 to promote the mechanism for sustainable and responsible behaviors for water conservation and reducing the water pollution and reducing the Biodiversity SDG-15 (França et al., 2020). On the contrary, some of the studies have highlighted the negative influence of blockchain technologies and indicated the massive utilization of these technologies in generating more carbon emission and energy consumption hence negatively influencing the SDG-13 Climate Action and some argue that the blockchain infrastructure requires a large landscape to construct buildings hence negatively affect the greener belt (Yadav & Singh, 2020).

In a nutshell, blockchain has some influential impacts on the economy shortly trying to achieve long-term transparency and economic growth with the consequences for a sustainable universe. Further, the above discussion has yielded a critical debate on the positive and negative effects of blockchain hence providing a potential avenue for developing a balancing mechanism.

Blockchain and Economic SDGs

Blockchain has also a strong nexus with economic growth such as the construction of new infrastructure to promote innovation and accelerate excellence in different sectors and achieve sustainable economic growth. This mechanism enables the nations to explore their demographic potentials, create and manage skilled and labor jobs and facilitate human resource practices. Blockchain implementation in different economic sectors like production, manufacturing, and distribution helps to accelerate the transparency, visibility, accuracy, and trust among all the trading partners and promotes real-time decision-making that helps firms in achieving sustainable growth. In the human resource sector, the execution and management of excellent and paperless recruitment processes provide the acquisition of efficient, skilled, and trained HR capital (Liu et al., 2020).

From the industrial growth perspective, blockchain accelerates innovation and automation in economic sectors like the automotive industry, banking sector, health care industry, media and entertainment, insurance, consumer goods, travel and tourism, transportation and logistics, etc. For example in the automotive industry, the automation of vehicles, the use of electricity as a substitute for fossil fuels and unmanned vehicles, in the health care sector, the automation of diagnostic machines and utilization of blockchain-based eWallet to execute the cashless payments accelerate the economic smoothness and sustainable performance in all these sectors (Miller, 2018). Similarly, the role of the agriculture and food sector in economic development is critical as it contributes 5.9% of global GDP and at least 35% to global employment. Therefore, the integration of digital technologies can enhance ecological and economic sustainability through traceability and visibility. The implementation of blockchain and other associated technologies are still in the infancy stage in agriculture however, yielded fruitful and excellent results in achieving the UNSDGs like reducing hunger, eradicating poverty, and sustainable agriculture. Besides, it provides the population with physical, social, and economic accessibility to safe, sufficient, and well-nourished food and meal at the global level to meet the dietary requirements of people. Alongside, achieving economic growth has an equal burden on the social and environment however, the adoption of digital technologies like IoT, blockchain and drones, and autonomous systems has made it possible.

IMPACT INVESTING CAN UNLOCK THE POTENTIAL OF BLOCKCHAIN IN AFRICA

The Global Impact Investing Network (GIIN) recently published research which revealed that global impact assets under management topped $502 billion in 2018. It is further proof if we needed any, of the exponential growth of impact investing in recent years, with new entrants both small and large coming to market.

However, despite this growth, there is still a plethora of untapped opportunities that impact investors have yet to take advantage of. Blockchain is one of the biggest and has the potential to transform millions of lives in some of the poorest regions of the world. In Africa, three converging trends will enable blockchain to have an exponential positive impact on the lives of low-income communities on the continent.

The Three Converging Trends

The first trend is that impact investing is becoming mainstream. This is, in part, driven by the intergenerational transfer of "wealth with purpose" from baby boomers to millennials, which Deloitte estimates could reach between $19 billion and $24 billion by 2020. Millennials are more likely to align their investments with a social purpose and according to Morgan Stanley, a significant majority of millennials (86%) are interested in sustainable investing. This has triggered the migration of large asset managers into impact investing, encouraged by this new generation of investors who are geared towards companies with positive impact at the very heart of their business model. The second trend is the rise of blended impact-first capital. Governments, supranational organizations, and non-governmental organizations (NGOs) are under pressure to receive less discretionary funding and show sustainable funding models. Therefore, grant and aid money is starting to interact with market-based models more. Blended finance structures allow not-for-profit and for-profit capital to sit alongside each other in the same investment vehicle.

A first loss layer is filled with grant or philanthropic capital, which has a catalytic effect to attract and protect senior layers of funding from the private sector at lower risk returns. Blended impact-first capital can scale small and medium-sized entrepreneurs (SMEs) and some investment vehicles serve the "missing middle" financing gap for SMEs in rural areas by providing them with small loans. The third and final trend is the exponential development of technology in Africa. In recent years, Africa has lived through the mobile phone revolution, which has triggered both the mobile money and distributed energy revolutions. The GSMA shows that unique mobile penetration in Sub-Saharan Africa was 44% and the regional subscriber base is set to grow at a CAGR of 4.8% for the period 2017-2022. These technological developments in Africa have provided people with increased connectivity to both the Internet and banking services, which has leapfrogged traditional infrastructure and formed the building blocks of a thriving digital economy on the continent at a price point that people can afford.

We have witnessed these three converging trends through our work at Bamboo Capital Partners. We have seen first-hand how African governments are willing to innovate to improve the lives of the poor. For example, BBOXX Togo, a portfolio company of our investment platform BEAM, in partnership with EDF and TogoCell, recently launched "Tomorrow's Connected Community". This smart village concept provides 300 houses and 4,000 people in the village of Sikpé Afidégnon in Togo via distributed solar energy, which helps power mobile-money financing, internet access, and domestic appliances – making it a next-generation concept.

The Case for Blockchain

The convergence of these three trends has made it possible for investors to seriously consider the potential of companies using blockchain in Africa. African governments are more willing to commit to innovation, there is a willing pool of investors wanting to invest in companies with a purpose, previous technological developments have provided a platform for companies using blockchain to grow and there is a financing structure that will develop and scale SMEs employing blockchain. However, there remain some barriers to growth. Blockchain arrives with a whole host of reputational challenges, mainly linked to cryptocurrencies. The Bitcoin rush in late 2017 left many retail investors out of pocket, while a series of fraudulent initial coin offerings (ICOs) in 2018 have caused serious reputational damage. However, the underlying technology is where the true value of blockchain lies, and some companies are already using it to generate a positive impact. One such company is Moeda Seeds Bank. It allows investors to invest in impact-led projects. The entire process uses blockchain, which provides security and transparency, from investors offering contributions to keeping track of the project's progress and accountability. Moeda invests in projects that align with the UN's Sustainable Development Goals (SDGs) and also supports rural women in frontier markets to scale their projects quicker, ultimately generating significant impact on the ground.

The Opportunity is There To Be Taken

At Bamboo, we have recognized the potential of blockchain. We launched the BLOC Fund, a first-of-its-kind global technology impact fund using blended finance. BLOC will leverage blockchain to provide investors with full traceability of their investments and invest in companies using new technologies, specifically blockchain, to benefit low-and middle-income populations in areas such as energy, education, FMCG, financial inclusion, and healthcare. Impact investors should wake up to the potential of blockchain. The positives of security and transparency via distributed ledgers outweigh the negative perceptions, such as the ICO bubble. It will have a significant impact on people's lives and investors should be helping SMEs using blockchain to scale their business.

Blockchain and Social SDGs

Blockchain integration is also accelerating social growth and addresses the SDGs related to social growth. In 2015, more than 736 million people were surviving on less than 1.90 USD per day, > 25% population of the world is living on 3.20 USD and approximately 50% were living on < 5.50 USD daily (World Bank, 2020). However, till the end of 2017, there were approximately 1.7 billion people globally have no banking accounts and 2/3 of them have no smartphones and do not have access to the internet as compared to their counterparts. To address the poverty issues (SDG-1) globally, the Asian Development Bank interacts with Everest, a centralized blockchain-based platform that enhances money transfer across the nations like Australia, New Zeeland, Samoa, etc. Similarly, M-Pesa, a renowned African mobile money system has claimed to alleviate > 194.000 households out of poverty which contributed approximately 2% of Kenya's population. Hence, it was possible due to the implication of blockchain that allow and interact with small brands like M-Pesa with digital wallets, remittances, and traditional banking systems.

Table 1 Description of SDGs

UNSDGs	Description
1 NO POVERTY	Eradication of poverty of all forms at all levels from the world till 2030 and to uplift the population for a prosperous universe.
2 ZERO HUNGER	The theme is to eradicate hunger of all forms at all levels and provide well-balanced nutrition to the undernourished population worldwide till 2030.
3 GOOD HEALTH AND WELL-BEING	This SDG aims to provide healthy life to a population that is free of diseases, declined infant and maternal mortality rates, and well-established mental health to all till 2030 to meet sustainable growth.
4 QUALITY EDUCATION	Making it feasible and possible for all to have a quality and discriminant free education to all across the world and especially to enhance the enrollment at primary level to reduce the number of children out of school till 2030.
5 GENDER EQUALITY	Provision of equal opportunities to women and girls in all sectors of life and empower them to gain sustainable economic and social growth.
6 CLEAN WATER AND SANITATION	The provision of clean water to all people globally which is free from all purities and sanitation of all societies and areas is the goal set under this SDG.
7 AFFORDABLE AND CLEAN ENERGY	Production of clean and green energy facilities to all populations which is affordable, accessible, and free from harm to society and the environment.
8 DECENT WORK AND ECONOMIC GROWTH	Provision of equal employment opportunities and decent and healthy working environment to all populations with equal growth opportunities free of discrimination till 2030.
9 INDUSTRY, INNOVATION AND INFRASTRUCTURE	Supporting infrastructure, innovation, and industrialization globally without harming the social and environmental elements is the key goal under this SDG as these factors act as catalysts for economic growth.

Table 1. continued

UNSDGs	Description
10 REDUCED INEQUALITIES	Balancing social prosperity through income equality and distribution of wealth among all populations to foster economic and social prosperity.
11 SUSTAINABLE CITIES AND COMMUNITIES	Maintaining a balance between urban and rural life through the construction of responsible and sustainable cities which include basic facilities equally.
12 RESPONSIBLE CONSUMPTION AND PRODUCTION	Balancing the economic growth by addressing the economic growth and environmental sustainability simultaneously through responsible production and consumption habits among all counties till 2030.
13 CLIMATE ACTION	Protecting the universe from natural disasters through sustainable utilization of natural resources and investing in low-carbon development.
14 LIFE BELOW WATER	Maintaining oceans' temperatures, chemistry, currents, and life below water through responsible behaviors at global, national, and international levels on Earth is required from countries till 2030.
15 LIFE ON LAND	The provision of healthy life to humans and species of the earth through a well-nourished diet, clean air, and water, and forestation is the goal under this SDG.
16 PEACE, JUSTICE AND STRONG INSTITUTIONS	Maintaining stability, human rights, and effective governance through effective implementation of the rule of law for peace, security, and prosperity.
17 PARTNERSHIPS FOR THE GOALS	Achieving SDGs through strong collaboration, partnership, and coordination at the global level for the exchange of all facilities and ties is the theme of this SDG that covers all 17 SDGs.

Similarly, another social issue hunger (SDG-2) is also on its rise with prominence from the African continent where > 820 million people are suffering from hunger and undernourishment till 2019 (ModusBox, 2017). Another aspect is the food loss which is about 14% globally between the harvest and retail supply chain operations and another food loss is during human consumption which represents about 1.6 gigatons in volume hence putting an economic cost of about USD 1 trillion yearly (Aysan et al., 2021). To address these inefficiencies in food supply chains, blockchain-based global food values can track and solve these issues by providing them with transparent supply chain operations that can reduce the wastage and loss of food. The execution of blockchain in the food supply chain simultaneously addresses multiple SDGs like SDG-13 by reducing carbon footprints in food supply chains, and conserving the biodiversity and ecosystems by minimizing water consumption and soil contamination through the feasible utilization of fertilizers and chemicals (SDGs 14,15) and lastly, control the food-borne diseases spread (SDG-3).

CONCLUSION

Among other Industry 4.0 technologies, blockchain was one of the primitive and remarkable innovations of the 21st century and its integration in different sectors yielded numerous economic, social, and environmental efficiencies. In a more fragile, dynamic, and competitive business environment, where technological innovation and sustainable dimensions go side by side, it is much evident that the association of blockchain integration and sustainable perspective should be examined. Therefore, our chapter has covered the integration of blockchain for sustainable performance in the domain of supply chain with a special look at achieving the UNSDGs. Literature indicated that the integration of blockchain is fruitful for achieving three sustainable performance dimensions namely economic, environmental, and social from the context of supply chain operations. In addition, blockchain integration is not only helpful in achieving sustainable and competitive performance measures but also equally helpful in addressing the UNSDGs. The application of blockchain in eradicating poverty and hunger (SDG-1,2) was addressed through the efforts of the Asian Development Bank from the transfer of freely and transparent funds from countries like Australia, New Zeeland, and Samoa to deserving nations and similarly, the M-Pesa to eradicate the hunger and poverty in African areas.

Further, discussion based on literature provide evidence of potential contribution of blockchain in achieving the SDGs associated with the economic and social dimensions. From an economic perspective application of blockchain in Sustainable Production and Consumption (SDG-12) was addressed in the industrial sector and enhances the resourceful utilization of renewable resources and energy (SDG-7) and clean and safe water consumption (SDG-11) and protecting the life of land and water (SDG-14,15). Similarly, the majority of the SDGs have been addressed through the application and adoption of the blockchain in various sectors of life. In short, we concluded that integration, adoption, and efficient execution of blockchain technology has numerous opportunities to create and manage a more competitive, efficient, and sustainable universe in accordance with the UNSDGs.

Our discussion also provides strong theoretical and practical implications as the chapter has covered almost all sectors by linking the sustainable orientation of supply chain operations and SDGs. Through the comprehensive discussion, we also portray the complex nature of the relationship between blockchain integration and supply chain sustainability from the context of the economic, environmental, and social perspectives.

Practical implications provide guidelines for managers and policymakers in applying the blockchain to achieve the potential benefits from economic, environmental, and social perspectives with specific reference to different indicators of SDGs. Discussion also provides implications to policymakers to accelerate the technological infrastructure that helps blockchain execution and facilitate the acquisition, implementation, and adoption of blockchain in private and public sectors to promote supply chain sustainability.

Future work on integration of blockchain and sustainability with specific refence to SDGs may include additional indicators of SDGs in order to provide comprehensive frame for maximum utilization of benefits of blockchain in SC and other fields to attend more efficient and transparent mechanism.

REFERENCES

Ahad, M. A., Paiva, S., Tripathi, G., & Feroz, N. (2020). Enabling technologies and sustainable smart cities. *Sustainable Cities and Society*, *61*, 102301. doi:10.1016/j.scs.2020.102301

Ashley, M. J., & Johnson, M. S. (2018). Establishing a secure, transparent, and autonomous blockchain of custody for renewable energy credits and carbon credits. *IEEE Engineering Management Review*, *46*(4), 100–102. doi:10.1109/EMR.2018.2874967

Astill, J., Dara, R. A., Campbell, M., Farber, J. M., Fraser, E. D., Sharif, S., & Yada, R. Y. (2019). Transparency in food supply chains: A review of enabling technology solutions. *Trends in Food Science & Technology*, *91*, 240–247. doi:10.1016/j.tifs.2019.07.024

Aysan, A. F., Bergigui, F., & Disli, M. (2021). Blockchain-based solutions in achieving SDGs after COVID-19. *Journal of Open Innovation*, *7*(2), 151. doi:10.3390/joitmc7020151

Beck, R., Müller-Bloch, C., & King, J. L. (2018). Governance in the blockchain economy: A framework and research agenda. *Journal of the Association for Information Systems*, *19*(10), 1. doi:10.17705/1jais.00518

Carter, C. R., & Rogers, D. S. (2008). A framework of sustainable supply chain management: Moving toward new theory. *International Journal of Physical Distribution & Logistics Management*, *38*(5), 360–387. doi:10.1108/09600030810882816

Chandan, A., John, M., & Potdar, V. (2023). Achieving UN SDGs in Food Supply Chain Using Blockchain Technology. *Sustainability (Basel)*, *15*(3), 2109. doi:10.3390u15032109

Choi, T.-M., & Luo, S. (2019). Data quality challenges for sustainable fashion supply chain operations in emerging markets: Roles of blockchain, government sponsors and environment taxes. *Transportation Research Part E, Logistics and Transportation Review*, *131*, 139–152. doi:10.1016/j.tre.2019.09.019

Cole, R., Stevenson, M., & Aitken, J. (2019). Blockchain technology: Implications for operations and supply chain management. *Supply Chain Management*, *24*(4), 469–483. doi:10.1108/SCM-09-2018-0309

de Villiers, C., Kuruppu, S., & Dissanayake, D. (2021). A (new) role for business – Promoting the United Nations' Sustainable Development Goals through the internet-of-things and blockchain technology. *Journal of Business Research*, *131*, 598–609. doi:10.1016/j.jbusres.2020.11.066

Duan, J., Zhang, C., Gong, Y., Brown, S., & Li, Z. (2020). A content-analysis based literature review in blockchain adoption within food supply chain. *International Journal of Environmental Research and Public Health*, *17*(5), 1784. doi:10.3390/ijerph17051784 PMID:32182951

Elkington, J. (1998). Partnerships from cannibals with forks: The triple bottom line of 21st-century business. *Environmental Quality Management*, *8*(1), 37–51. doi:10.1002/tqem.3310080106

França, A. S. L., Neto, J. A., Gonçalves, R. F., & Almeida, C. (2020). Proposing the use of blockchain to improve the solid waste management in small municipalities. *Journal of Cleaner Production*, *244*, 118529. doi:10.1016/j.jclepro.2019.118529

Franke, L., Schletz, M., & Salomo, S. (2020). Designing a blockchain model for the paris agreement's carbon market mechanism. *Sustainability (Basel)*, *12*(3), 1068. doi:10.3390u12031068

Hastig, G. M., & Sodhi, M. S. (2020). Blockchain for supply chain traceability: Business requirements and critical success factors. *Production and Operations Management*, *29*(4), 935–954. doi:10.1111/poms.13147

Howson, P. (2020). Building trust and equity in marine conservation and fisheries supply chain management with blockchain. *Marine Policy*, *115*, 103873. doi:10.1016/j.marpol.2020.103873

Jerath, K. S. (2021). Globalization and the Third and Fourth Industrial Revolution. *Science, Technology and Modernity: An Interdisciplinary Approach*, 119–130.

Kamble, S. S., Gunasekaran, A., & Gawankar, S. A. (2020). Achieving sustainable performance in a data-driven agriculture supply chain: A review for research and applications. *International Journal of Production Economics*, *219*, 179–194. doi:10.1016/j.ijpe.2019.05.022

Kewell, B., Adams, R., & Parry, G. (2017). Blockchain for good? *Strategic Change*, *26*(5), 429–437. doi:10.1002/jsc.2143

Khan, M. R., Khan, M. R., & Nallaluthan, K. (2023). Blockchain Supply Chain Management and Supply Chain Sustainability. In *Blockchain Driven Supply Chain Management: A Multi-dimensional Perspective* (pp. 155–180). Springer. doi:10.1007/978-981-99-0699-4_10

Khan, M. R., & Manzoor, A. (2021). Application and impact of new technologies in the supply chain management during COVID-19 pandemic: A systematic literature review. *International Journal of Economics and Business Administration*, *9*(2), 277–292.

Kouhizadeh, M., Saberi, S., & Sarkis, J. (2021). Blockchain technology and the sustainable supply chain: Theoretically exploring adoption barriers. *International Journal of Production Economics*, *231*, 107831. doi:10.1016/j.ijpe.2020.107831

Kouhizadeh, M., & Sarkis, J. (2018). Blockchain practices, potentials, and perspectives in greening supply chains. *Sustainability (Basel)*, *10*(10), 3652. doi:10.3390u10103652

Lemieux, V. L. (2016). Trusting records: Is Blockchain technology the answer? *Records Management Journal*, *26*(2), 110–139. doi:10.1108/RMJ-12-2015-0042

Lindman, J., Tuunainen, V. K., & Rossi, M. (2017). *Opportunities and risks of Blockchain Technologies–a research agenda.*

Liu, L., Han, M., Zhou, Y., Parizi, R. M., & Korayem, M. (2020). Blockchain-based certification for education, employment, and skill with incentive mechanism. *Blockchain Cybersecurity, Trust and Privacy*, 269–290.

Medaglia, R., & Damsgaard, J. (2020). Blockchain and the United Nations Sustainable Development Goals: Towards an Agenda for IS Research. *PACIS*, 36.

Miller, D. (2018). Blockchain and the internet of things in the industrial sector. *IT Professional*, *20*(3), 15–18. doi:10.1109/MITP.2018.032501742

ModusBox. (2017, October 24). Announcing Mojaloop.io – An Open-Source Software Platform for Financial Inclusion to Uplift the World's Poor. *Modusbox.Com.* https://modusboxcom1.wpengine.com/announcing-mojaloop-io-an-open-source-software-platform-for-financial-inclusion-to-uplift-the-worlds-poor/

Mohamed, S. K., Haddad, S., Barakat, M., & Rosi, B. (2023). Blockchain Technology Adoption for Improved Environmental Supply Chain Performance: The Mediation Effect of Supply Chain Resilience, Customer Integration, and Green Customer Information Sharing. *Sustainability (Basel), 15*(10), 7909. doi:10.3390u15107909

Ølnes, S., Ubacht, J., & Janssen, M. (2017). Blockchain in government: Benefits and implications of distributed ledger technology for information sharing. [). Elsevier.]. *Government Information Quarterly, 34*(3), 355–364. doi:10.1016/j.giq.2017.09.007

Park, L. W., Lee, S., & Chang, H. (2018). A sustainable home energy prosumer-chain methodology with energy tags over the blockchain. *Sustainability (Basel), 10*(3), 658. doi:10.3390u10030658

Peltola, A., Barnat, N., Chernova, E., Cristallo, D., Hoffmeister, O., & MacFeely, S. (2022). The role of international organizations in statistical standards setting and outreach: An overview of the UNCTAD contribution. *Statistical Journal of the IAOS, 38*(2), 501–509. doi:10.3233/SJI-210894

Rahmanzadeh, S., Pishvaee, M. S., & Rasouli, M. R. (2020). Integrated innovative product design and supply chain tactical planning within a blockchain platform. *International Journal of Production Research, 58*(7), 2242–2262. doi:10.1080/00207543.2019.1651947

Rossi, M., Mueller-Bloch, C., Thatcher, J. B., & Beck, R. (2019). Blockchain research in information systems: Current trends and an inclusive future research agenda. *Journal of the Association for Information Systems, 20*(9), 14. doi:10.17705/1jais.00571

Saberi, S., Kouhizadeh, M., Sarkis, J., & Shen, L. (2019). Blockchain technology and its relationships to sustainable supply chain management. *International Journal of Production Research, 57*(7), 2117–2135. doi:10.1080/00207543.2018.1533261

Schmidt, C. G., & Wagner, S. M. (2019). Blockchain and supply chain relations: A transaction cost theory perspective. *Journal of Purchasing and Supply Management, 25*(4), 100552. doi:10.1016/j.pursup.2019.100552

Sharma, P. K., Kumar, N., & Park, J. H. (2020). Blockchain technology toward green IoT: Opportunities and challenges. *IEEE Network, 34*(4), 263–269. doi:10.1109/MNET.001.1900526

Thess, A., Klein, M., Nienhaus, K., & Pregger, T. (2020). Global carbon surcharge for the reduction of anthropogenic emission of carbon dioxide. *Energy, Sustainability and Society, 10*(1), 1–9. doi:10.118613705-020-0242-z

Thylin, T., & Duarte, M. F. N. (2019). Leveraging blockchain technology in humanitarian settings–opportunities and risks for women and girls. *Gender and Development, 27*(2), 317–336. doi:10.1080/13552074.2019.1627778

Veuger, J. (2018). Trust in a viable real estate economy with disruption and blockchain. *Facilities, 36*(1/2), 103–120. doi:10.1108/F-11-2017-0106

Walsh, P. P., Murphy, E., & Horan, D. (2020). The role of science, technology and innovation in the UN 2030 agenda. *Technological Forecasting and Social Change, 154*, 119957. doi:10.1016/j.techfore.2020.119957

Wang, Y., Han, J. H., & Beynon-Davies, P. (2019). Understanding blockchain technology for future supply chains: A systematic literature review and research agenda. *Supply Chain Management*, *24*(1), 62–84. doi:10.1108/SCM-03-2018-0148

World Bank. (2020). Poverty and shared prosperity 2020: Reversals of fortune. The World Bank.

Yadav, S., & Singh, S. P. (2020). Blockchain critical success factors for sustainable supply chain. *Resources, Conservation and Recycling*, *152*, 104505. doi:10.1016/j.resconrec.2019.104505

Zheng, Y., & Walsham, G. (2008). Inequality of what? Social exclusion in the e-society as capability deprivation. *Information Technology & People*, *21*(3), 222–243. doi:10.1108/09593840810896000

Chapter 2
Towards Sustainable Supply Chains With Blockchain

Irum Gul
Balochistan University of Information Technology, Engineering, and Management Sciences, Pakistan

Abdul Raziq
Balochistan University of Information Technology, Engineering, and Management Sciences, Pakistan

Mustafa Rehman Khan
https://orcid.org/0000-0002-0250-9092
UCSI University, Malaysia

ABSTRACT

For constructing an irrepressible system for the supply chain, blockchain offers key support as a prominent implementation of the latest technological assistance by using a disseminated and dispersed system of records for mapping out the drive of merchandise and services within the supply chain. Prominently ensures transparency and vigorous linkage during the overall process. Blockchain contributes effectively towards diverse areas of the supply chain like foodstuff and agrarian domain, healthcare, and pharmacological domain for ensuring trustworthy supply chain arrangement. Besides other assistance, one of the crucial roles of blockchain is the perspective of supporting sustainability. This ensures the triple bottom line prospect which embraces the stability of ecological, communal, and governing business while dealing with supply chain arrangement. Therefore, blockchain provides disseminated, irreversible, translucent records, which can also track possible communal and ecological prospects that can enact ecological, health, and well-being apprehensions.

INTRODUCTION

The evolution of technological support is appraised from the perspective of innovation and improved performance of industries. Nevertheless, besides improving the performing capabilities of industries, the importance of these innovative technologies must also be assessed in terms of sustainable practices and

DOI: 10.4018/979-8-3693-0482-2.ch002

ensuring a sustainability agenda (Varriale et al., 2020). Supply chain management globally deals with encounters like immoral activities, deception, and damage to the environment (Chauduri et al., 2023). Changes around the world specifically due to the emergence of COVID imposed many concerns for business in terms of data exchanges and supply management systems and networks. While endeavoring to shape strong supply chain managing prospects, blockchain is becoming a noticeable instrument (Park & Li, 2021). This is one of the latest and most advanced technological supports designed to disperse and spread out a system to locate the movement of merchandise and services within supply chain prospects to ensure translucency and strong connection in the practice (Gul et al., 2023).

The Industrial Revolution and the emergence of industrial prospects of 4.0 are associated with the transfusion of societal apprehensions and the system of production and supply to customers by implying environmentally friendly and sustainable approaches (Parmentola et al., 2021). This transfusion is associated with the linkages of technological support with sustainability in organizational processes for ensuring a more sustainable society (Sharma et al., 2020). Therefore, industries are ever more changing by aligning profit maximization with the realization of environmental and societal welfare (Secinaro et al., 2020).

The supply chain system is changing with the changing demands of the industrial revolution and community, it becoming multifaceted due to the reasons, for example, inaccuracy chances, interrupted services, and environmental concerns. Literature asserted that 66% of inaccuracy is manmade. All the densities are the cause of a reduction in performance standards and monetary damage to industries (Punter, 2013). Businesses operating internationally, transport merchandise across borders. Which includes time and plenty of correspondence between parties. This process causes costs to the involved parties in the form of damage to merchandise, time, scams, and tariffs (Popper & Lohr, 2017).

While sustainability-focused supply chain arrangement consists of the coordination of participants/ shareholders, data, and assets included in the movement of merchandise and/ or services from traders to consumers, with the focus on avoiding the exhaustion of natural reserves while keeping environmental stability (Sunmola, 2021). Consequently, the goal of supply chain sustainability consists of the stakeholders who are linked with the sustainable agenda like commercial, communal, and ecological concerns. The basis of supply chain sustainability lies in the excellence of records, discernibility, and better judgment on choices (Barratt & Barratt, 2011). Within the supply chain system, discernibility represents the degree to which parties involved in the supply chain have entree to time-bound and accuracy of facts and records which are crucial and significant for overall supply chain systems and processes (Chen & Kitsis, 2017).

Old supply chain systems cannot be able to meet today's consumer mandate in terms of cost-effectiveness and excellence of quality, and at the same time, the latest and advanced system ensures sustainability as needed (Yadav & Singh, 2020). However, defies of this latest arrangement is not effective while excluding consumers and the incorporation of technological support. Thus, blockchain can be an advanced technological support for the supply chain system overall (Cole & Fernando, 2020). Who can moderate the cost associated with the arrangement, and assure quality while improving the sturdiness of the supply chain system (Catalini & Gans, 2020). Literature asserted the effectiveness of blockchain assimilation with the supply chain arrangement, as it affects the performance ability of businesses and relatively cheaper production with a focus on safeguarding the information and records (Perego et al., 2019). Supply chain systems are dependent on integrated and incongruent managing arrangements. This single-point fiasco is a crucial weakness of the central information arrangement, which puts the overall organism at risk of inaccuracy, hacking, fraud, or outbreak (Dong et al. 2017). Supply chain carries out and stratagems are also helpless to grow influences concerning sustainable approaches to supply chain (Swan, 2015).

Hence, one of the fundamental stratagem and competitiveness concerns within the supply chain arrangement is the validation and authentication that merchandise, practices, and methods in the supply chain meet the explicit sustainability criterion and accreditations (Benton et al., 2018). Therefore, sustainability concerns within the domain of the supply chain attaining substantial attention from literature and specialists (Fahimnia et al., 2015).

Therefore, establishing an organism while considering the sustainable approaches that hold cost-effective, communal, and ecological prospects is a critical concern in today's world (Hoekstra & Wiedmann, 2014). The modern world challenges need modern solutions. Blockchain technological support is achieving major attention as an innovative process that can achieve the goals of sustainable supply chains (Marsal-Llacuna, 2020). Blockchain is an uncluttered, disseminated record technological support that establishes the latest form of safeguarding and transferring records via peer-to-peer networking with the help of stable and confirmable proceedings of trades (Tillemann et al., 2019). From this point of view, blockchain technological prospect is considered a prospective sustainability-oriented innovation (SOI) (Friedman & Ormiston, 2022).

Blockchain as a disruptive technological arrangement offers certain benefits not only in terms of cost, tractability, and translucency but most importantly sustainable arrangement within the supply management system (Kouhizadeh et al., 2020). These features associated with smart contracts intensify and improve the environment with no requirements of arbitrators (Lacity, 2018). Amongst the various uses of blockchain, ensuring a supply chain sustainable system is a prime prospect (Saberi et al., 2019). The reason for focusing on the supply chain is the upsurge in complications due to the international grid system of the supply chain (Lambert & Enz, 2017). This involvedness makes the process challenging for effectual operations, tracing merchandise and records, and evaluating the facts available (Ivanov et al., 2019).

Today sustainable supply chain systems are gaining immense prominence and becoming a key driving factor concerning demand of the consumers and trustworthiness. This sustainable supply chain system ensures stability between three crucial dimensions including ecological prospects, communal concerns, and business targets. These societal, competitive, and governing motives advocate the need for a sustainability approach within the supply chain system (Saberi et al., 2018). Clients pursue to confirm sustainable products and need a reachable gateway related to the merchandizes and records (Nikolakis et al., 2018). Similarly, this condition puts stress on the vendors to ensure sustainability during transactions and trades worldwide or locally while being part of the supply chain system (Asif et al., 2019). However, the system works on volunteer databanks which put a question mark on the trustworthiness and legitimacy of the system. Blockchain technological support ensures sustainability accreditations that run deep in the system of the supply chain (Wang et al., 2019).

Case example: Airports are considered the hub of the supply chain to ensure supplies to the markets with multiple service providers. In such a supply chain hub, applying blockchain technological change can transform the performance in multiple ways. For example, this implication is airport supply chain can ensure sustainability, both from the perspective of ecologically sustainable prospects and economic perspectives, which confirms the reduction of disintegration, incompetence, and inept procedures (Hawlitscheck et al., 2018).

The implementation of digital incorporated arrangement impacts on regularity of flights which aid in reducing expenditures and adverse environmental concerns. Due to blockchain technology all the segments of flight, starting from the planning to flight operational stage and arrival, all stages are aligned as a solo procedure. Which helps in ensuring better air traffic control (Vaio & Varriale, 2020). At the same time, commercial and customer recompenses are associated with the blockchain technological invention. However, the responsiveness towards the societal and ecological prospects is limited (Kewell et al., 2017). Blockchain implications have been an important tool for ensuring sustainability goals (Giungato et al., 2017).

THE PROSPECTS OF BLOCKCHAIN

The technological prospects of blockchain have gained quite a popularity over a few decades (Polvora et al., 2020). The concept of blockchain was established in 2008 by Satoshi Nakamoto to avoid and control dual expenses associated with digital currencies (Nakamoto, 2008). The idea was to generate a platform for a peer-to-peer automated money system by using arithmetical signatures for every operation. The disseminated record and online system for trade are in focus while excluding arbitrators, for example, financial associations (Crosby et al., 2016). Blockchain is asserted as the "open, disseminated archive to record transactions amongst the parties competently while ensuring provable and enduring system. The tag "blockchain" explains the format of the technological regime; where info is put in storage on various blocks interconnected and establishes a series of certified data (Lansiti & Likhani, 2017). The technological prospect of blockchain is the amalgamation of three layers of functioning: 1) the storage facility for enduring, inflexible, and appraisable digitalized accounts that ensures data safety; 2) the interchange of digitalized possessions and ensuring transparent transactions; 3) the implementation of smart agreements and ensuring efficacy. These three layers of blockchain depict the decentralized prospect of the blockchain (Deloitte Insights, 2018). Hence, the major characteristics and elements of blockchain consist of a safe, transparent, efficacious, and decentralized system (Galen et al., 2018).

Ensuring Data Safety

The technological prospect of blockchain is associated with a much-secured method of data storage. As including each block based on the agreement of all parties included in the arrangement to validate the contract and transaction (Crosby et al., 2016). The peer-to-peer instrument ensures security against any kind of disruption (Wang et al., 2021). Where, at the same time without approval of all the prominences public records cannot be removed (Yli-Huumo et al., 2016). This characteristic of the blockchain system safeguards the data from alteration. All the approved participants collect their private key or encryption which allows the right of access to the records (Batwa & Norrman, 2020).

Ensuring a Transparent System

The systemization of secured entries of only approved and accredited parties and public visibility ensures the transparent system of the blockchain (Mukkamala et al., 2018). This makes the blockchain system only accessible to the ratified parties and only the affiliates can access the details of transactions. Members of the arrangement first validate the block with an agreement to ensure and confirm the authenticity of the records of transactions (Kim & Shin, 2019).

Ensuring Efficacy/ Competency of the System

Efficacy can be one of the crucial features of the blockchain system, as the arrangement is adapted digitalized and instantaneous system. This attribute of efficacy ensures the creation and implementation of smart agreements that are programmed and digitalized to decrease the psychological and computing/ data processing costs and at the same time guarantee security (Chang et al., 2019). Blockchain system provides a better evident way out of implementing contracts with the help of supporting immunity from damage and a clash-free system of substituting cost (Cong & He, 2019).

Providing a Decentralized System

The arrangement of the blockchain is designed to permit the authorized parties to establish a networking system within a P2P setting. Where every party has a copy of the record. Where information is distributed between the networking systems and therefore not kept in one consolidated databank (Wang et al., 2021). The prospect of decentralization makes certain that no sole party can regulate the system or databank, which ensures the transparency of the blockchain system (Batwa & Norrman, 2020).

Other than these primary characteristics of blockchain, the other aspects associated with the application of blockchain in businesses within supply management systems are also crucial (Kouhizadeh &Sarkis, 2018; Kshetri, 2020).

Lower Cost of Implementation

The literature asserted that there is not only a significant impact of blockchain on the supply chain management system but the lower cost associated with the implementation of blockchain in the industries also makes it easy for businesses on any level to adopt this technology (Kshetri, 2021). As no added investment is associated with the new expedients. Which can generate a coding system for even the smaller transactional prospects (Higgins, 2017).

Lower Cost (Internet of Things- Equipment)

the mechanisms associated with the IoT, for example, radars are cheaper and more manageable for businesses to implement the blockchain system (Hald & Kinra, 2019).

The above figure depicts the system of blockchain projections which safeguards protections and makes blocks to confirm disseminated unanimity, safety, traceability, verifiability, and transparency of data, all are considered crucial features.

Hence, disseminated unanimity, safety, traceability, verifiability, and transparency of data, all are considered crucial features (Dwivedi et al., 2019). Therefore, these prominent features of blockchain attracted numerous businesses and industries, for example, Walmart and Glencore who incorporated blockchain technological support within their supply chain networking system for refining the overall effectiveness, efficacy, and performing capacity (Mettler, 2016).

Figure 1. Blockchain system
Schinckus (2020)

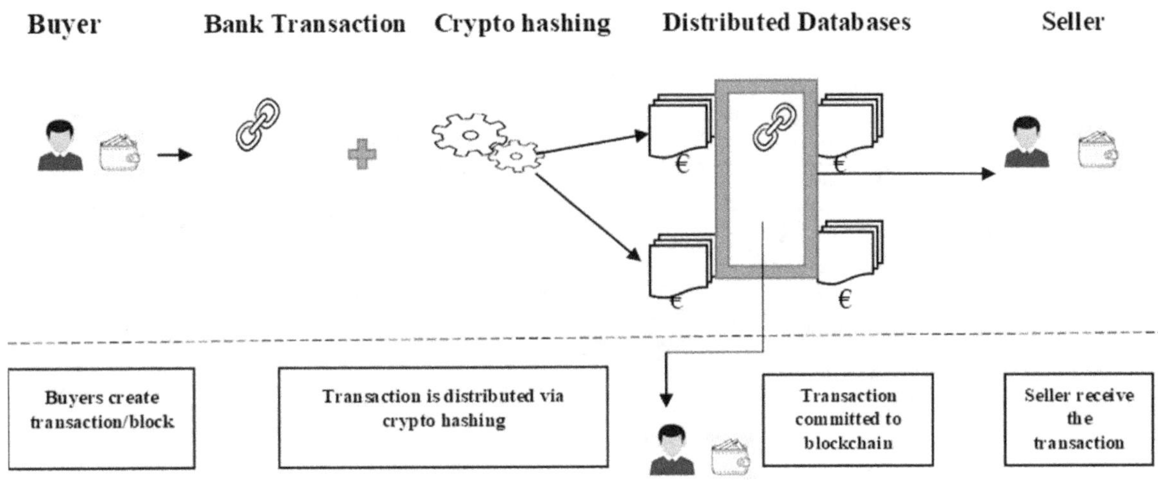

THE ROLE OF BLOCKCHAIN IN THE SUPPLY CHAIN AND PROSPECTS OF SUSTAINABILITY

Blockchain systems are designed to peer to peer-to-peer lucidity in which companies can interchange merchandise, services, and data while excluding the requisite of central arrangements for identification, validity of dealings, making enforced commitments, or eliminating the need for several arbitrators (Singh et al., 2019). In the initial phase, it supports the efficacy and also decreases the expenses for companies and other institutions involved by ensuring improved and quicker transactions that are dispersed and synced alphanumerically across various but limited parties (Polvora et al., 2020).

Blockchain is disrupting technological systems offering schemes, associations, set-ups, and the overall administration of supply chains. The blockchain serves as a guarantor of trustworthiness, and trackability of info and data, with the availability of smart contracts to control the risk and lack of trust involved within the supply chain system. Blockchain-centered supply chain system needs secure, and reserved, with the right to admission and approval with several but restricted parties (Tian, 2017). However, it also encourages a new public set of associations as well. Below is figure 2 demonstrates the revolution and alteration of the customary supply chain systems to blockchain-centered supply chain systems overall (Saberi et al., 2018).

The above figure depict the inclusion of blockchain within the supply chain management system, which includes important foundations like registrars, standard or quality-assuring entities, certifiers, and actors.

Important elements that constitute blockchain-centric supply chains are *registrars* (who are responsible for giving distinctive identities to the parties involved in the arrangement, quality maintenance entities, certifiers, and parties. *Standard or quality assuring entities* (states quality and the standard outlines, for example, ensuring trustworthiness within supply chain systems and blockchain guidelines and quality provisions. *Certifiers* (who are responsible for declaring the certificates or permits to the parties involved in the arrangement.

Figure 2. Implementation of blockchain to the supply chain management
Saberi et al (2018)

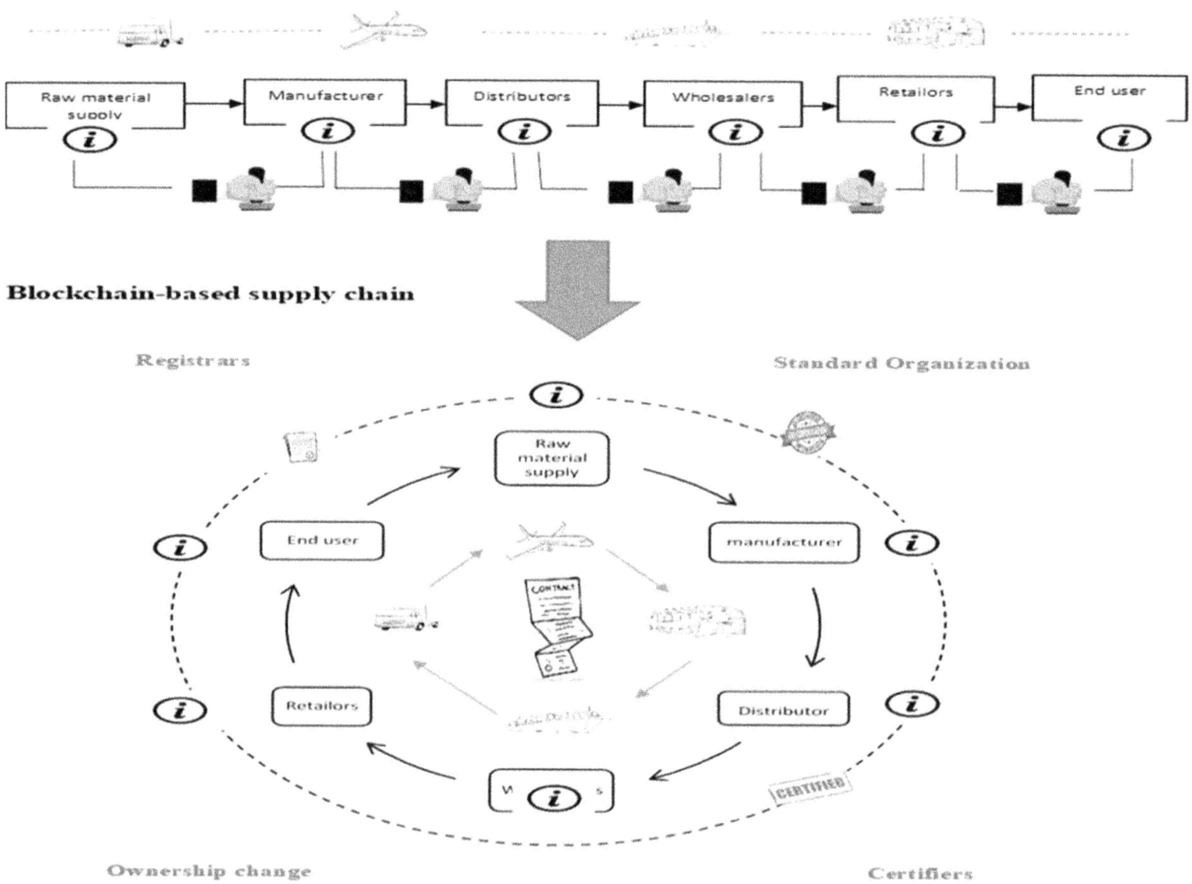

Actors/ parties (which can be companies, vendors, and customers should be licensed by the registrar or the certifiers to ensure the trustworthiness of the arrangement (Steiner & Baker, 2015). Experts approve of the significant impact of blockchain on helping businesses maintain the stresses of industry 4.0 agendas (Moll & Yigitbasioglu, 2019).

Integration of Blockchain With Supply Chain Sustainability

The demand for products in the market increased in the twentieth century which imposed pressure on the industries to submit to the risky but economical and cost-effective forms of producing goods and supplying those (Rajeev et al., 2017). Nevertheless, these actions most of the time ignore their effects on the community and environmental conditions on longer run (Bhatti et al., 2023). Since the early 2000s, the focus on ensuring sustainability in actions to combine the environmental concerns and communal prospects with the economic facets of the supply chain management system (Abas et al., 2022). This acquaintance was the reason for beginning the conception of "green supply chain management". Which prominently assesses and monitors the effect of the supply chain management system on the environment. However, the focus on the green supply chain management system excluded the communal concerns, which are included in the primary goals of "sustainability" (Ahi & Searcy, 2015). This development headed toward the occurrence of a sustainable supply chain system (Govindan et al., 2015).

The concept of industrial 4.0 or revolutionary agendas concerning industries was presented in 2011 (Lasi et al., 2014). Which demands improving the competencies of industries while strengthening the technology and its associated digital tools (Luthra et al., 2020). The vision of Industry 4.0 is associated with embracing smart processes by applying technological tools, and also focusing on also comprises alphanumeric and virtual technological tools for merchandizing and services prospects (de Sousa Jabbour et al., 2018). Which provides facilitation for records, data interchange, being up-to-date, intersected, value addition, automation of data, and communication (Lu, 2017). To achieve this combination, digitalized technological tools are the key dynamism for Industry 4.0 (Li et al., 2017). Blockchain ominously substitutes other applications for accounts and financial prospects, which offers entirely innovative industrial arrangements (Lee, 2019).

Blockchain intensively assures transparency in records sharing, improving practices of businesses, reducing operational expenditures, advancing cooperative efficacy, and improving the organism which does not include overt integration of the trust while controlling, for example, in supply chain management (Francisco & Swanson, 2018). Amongst the other benefits, blockchain is considerably addressing a series of sustainability concerns associated with the environment. This offers support for a sustainable environment with the help of three major tools associated with resource privileges, merchandise origins, and behavior-based inducements (Hughes et al., 2019).

Blockchain is currently applied in multiple areas and is widely used for improving environmentally concerned sustainable systems (Glavanits, 2020). Blockchain uncertainly facilitates the latest prospects from the perspective of green producing arrangements, the discerning and storing of data concerned with actions accountable for polluting and dreadful conditions of the environment, and real-time assortment and exploration of green and lesser carbon records for better decision-making mechanisms. Which makes the supply chain system as a whole more sustainable (Mora et al., 2021).

Currently, sustainability is one of the primary concerns of industrial experts to improve the consumer's experience and loyalty at the same time. Sustainability is the domain that forces environmental concerns, social or communal prospects, and business concerns (Queiroz & Wamba, 2019). Thus, sustainability is merged into three interconnected supporting pillars, which represent economic concerns, ecological concerns, and communal dynamics (Purvis et al., 2019). Those three supporting pillars are also entrenched in the United Nations' sustainability goals (United Nations, 2012), on the way to 2030, the emphasis is on economically concerned progression which is environmentally sensible, sustainable, and communally accountable (Beier et al., 2020).

The concept of 'sustainability' is one of the crucial concerns grabbing the attention of industries and ecological experts globally. The notion was first talked about by the World Commission on Environment and Development. However, the ideology of sustainability has been described several times over the last many years (Tanin et al., 2019). Economically the assertion of sustainability has been described as "to save the reserves for our upcoming generation". United Nations always stays focused on the vision of sustainability and asserted the conception into three primary dominions: ecological prospects, communal concerns, and economically sustainable societies, these are three fundamental pillars of sustainability (Park & Li, 2021). Defies of sustainability always demand combined attentiveness from the different sectors of society. This makes it crucial for businesses and industries to safeguard the alliance of the industrial or business concern activities consistent with the sustainability goals of the United Nations (Freiberg et al., 2020).

Globally the emphasis on climate conversion and other crucial concerns associated with environmental protection is increasing. The United Nations (UN) has been very thoughtful towards these climate rapid conversions. For this reason, the UN has given a list of seventeen goals concerning sustainability for the worldwide community (United Nations, 2018). The focus is that worldwide communal must be attentive and prioritize the concerns to ensure sustainability and a safe future. Environmental concerns and safety are categorized in goal 13 under the sustainable growth agenda of the UN. This goal stresses the activities and processes to battle climate conversion. To deal with such environmental and climate concerns role of technological transformation is very important (Lund et al., 2019). Similarly, the report by the UN "World Atlas of Illicit Trade" refers to the procurement of illegitimate merchandise and the transfer of them worldwide for illicit profit. According to the report, the major matter of concern is environmental criminality is considered the utmost money-making prospect associated with unlawful operations. Environment-concerned crimes comprise, for example, violation of forestry areas which are declared as safe zones, which also includes the concerns where trading merchandise is imported or exported (Nellemann et al., 2018).

Expressly, the three dominions of sustainability are revealed by the performance of the businesses from the perspective of environmental, communal, and governance perspectives. Where 'environment' concerned activities mainly depict the negative effect of businesses or industries externally, like on the environment overall (Venkatesh et al., 2020). The primary criterion of environmental sustainability comprises of deployment of reserves, energy efficacy, the concerns of the quantity of wastage, and the level of secretion from the business and industrial practices. 'Communal' prospects of the businesses are associated with important concerns like, workplace well-being and health of labor, diversity, impartiality in terms of opportunities, gender or ethnic discrimination in remunerations, and sweatshops (D'Eusanio et al., 2019). The 'governance/ administrative' perspective is associated with inside-the-company relationships and matters, communicating with the employees and other associated stakeholders (Son-Turan, 2019).

Overall, in the last decade, the attentiveness and importance of communal and environmental concerns about sustainable approaches have grown among the different stakeholders involved (Sanchez-Flores et al., 2020). At the same time, these features of sustainability are becoming a crucial driving factor of customer trustworthiness in businesses (Kouhizadeh et al., 2021). Now, customers need the right to the accessibility to information and records concerning merchandise and suppliers' sustainable approaches to operating the overall process (Mejias et al., 2019). This customer's attitude and interest growing immense stress on the businesses for monitoring the processes and operational setups of supplying through their comprehensive supply systems to ensure the implementation of accepted environmental concern processes and also protecting the harm to the labor laws and human rights to maintain the ethics of work (Najjar et al., 2020).

Now, supply systems and management are quite intricate and involve several allied (Sauer & Seuring, 2019) and geographically diverse groups which involve various industrial segments and social norms (Hannibal & Kauppi, 2019). Accordingly, have to offer economical and sustainability-focused merchandise and services to the clients (Sauer & Seuring, 2019). Literature supports the inclusion of blockchain systems within the supply chain networking to ensure sustainability concerns (Gold et al., 2017). For this reason, businesses adopt various managing systems, for example, accreditation methods, and ethical codes for monitoring and ensuring sustainability processes especially within the supply chain management system (Najjar et al., 2023). However, experts asserted several concerns about the usefulness of these arrangements (Govindan et al., 2020). As, in an overlong and multifarious supply system it is complex to be aware of the party 'who is liable for what practices' involved during the whole supply management arrangement (Choi et al., 2001).

The query arises; in all those prospects why concentrate on supply chains in this regard? The response to this query is clear. Due to the complications in the systemization of supply chain networking systems internationally (Azzi et al., 2019). These complications in the overall system of supply chains make it challenging to maintain and ensure transparency, track the production and data, and evaluate overall statistics (Inanov et al., 2019). Blockchain offers an advanced solution to the challenges of dealing with the complex system of global supply chain system (Dinh et al., 2018). The addition of cryptographies makes a system a chain that endures to the initiator, the initial block. Where, when each time the latest block is made known to the system, it's automatically allied with the precursor (Caro et al., 2018).

The sustainable supply chain networks are considered a crucial dominion with the inclusion of industry 4.0 agendas and are also considered the most important driving agent of improving demand and consumer trustworthiness (Chkanikova & Mont, 2015). Blockchain as a disruptive technological support can improve the sustainability concerns in supply chain networking systems. As, blockchain reinforces the assurance of a product's sustainable dominion and validity through a direct and precise tracking system for the supply chain streams (Adam et al., 2018).

Blockchain is considered the most compelling technological progression concerning this agenda, which is beneficial in facing the challenges of sustainable development (Upadhyay, 2020). Blockchain provides a crucial technological transformation as an instrument for dealing with the concerns of sustainable development. Blockchain supports local green energy production more extensively while also cultivating supply chain arrangements overall (Kshetri, 2018). After the 4th revolution emerged, the focus of social and communal systems prominently diverted and transmuted the whole system of producing goods and at the same time establishing a sustainable world community (Dubey et al., 2016). The attentiveness towards the need to transform the system to ensure sustainable social order. Therefore, the literature also asserts the need for the amalgamation of Industry 4.0 technological prospects with corporate sustainable transformation (Dubey et al., 2017). Focusing on aspects like Industry 4.0 will open the full probability of sustainability prospects of businesses with the use of philosophies and applications of Industry 4.0. Which safeguards and guarantees a more sustainable social structure and outstanding sustainability ensured business and manufacturing (Parmentola et al., 2021). The advancement of technological support can lead to a sustainable ecological system as a whole. Where environmental concerns technological progression can rouse ecological quality (Gouvea et al., 2018). At the same time, this novelty prospect of industry prototype can be of crucial importance towards the initial phase of sustainable industrialized value formation which is concerned with allocating resources, merchandise, supplies, and energy reserves more efficiently based on the latest sustainable models and business structures (Stock & Seliger, 2016). Similarly, industry 4.0 expedients and procedures also consider in prospective additional ecological sustainability concerned verdicts due to their improved strategical arrangement amongst the engaged I.T prospects and business objectives (de Sousa Jabbour et al., 2018). Therefore, literature and experts focus on investigating the impact of Industry 4.0 technological tools supporting a sustainable environment, especially from the perspective of sustainable industrial and supply chain systems (Kumar et al., 2018).

Blockchain technological support is considered a striking addition to the domain of the supply chain. The supply chain's new management purview aims to decrease waste and improve efficacy (Venkatesh et al., 2020). The support of blockchain in supply chain management can improve adeptness and efficacy and guarantee reducing the overheads and time (Xu et al., 2019). In this regard, improving the excellence of merchandise and producing them with sustainable approaches of "cleaner manufacturing" is focused on exceeding the boundaries locally and internationally (Lansiti & Lakhani, 2017). Blockchain is therefore, aligning supply chains with sustainable approaches via traceable and translucent systems (Ellen MacArthur Foundation, 2019) while decreasing the hard copy practices, and consumption of energy, boosting energy rejuvenation, and significantly reducing discarded leftovers in the supply chain management system. As blockchain is irretrievable, the accounts of assets apprise stakeholders can assist in producing cyclical practices of the supply chain. Moreover, the blockchain record system supports observing and the availability of the verifications for the parties involved, and at the same time ensures environmentally sustainable industrial tools. One of the prominent features of blockchain includes the protection of child labor laws and discouraging the violation of any laws concerning children and human rights in the overall process of manufacturing and supply chain systems (Dierksmeier & Seele, 2020). Consequently, with the help of alliance and data sharing within the blockchain support, the agenda of sustainable and socially reasonable approaches is achievable in supply chain management (Yigit, 2021).

LITERATURE AND MANAGERIAL IMPLICATIONS

In today's world, for industries being competitive and reasonable in the processes are the crucial concern. Industry 4.0 comes up with entirely new philosophies of business models and approaches that are consistent with the agenda of being profitable while not compromising the aim of transparency, and a sense of responsibility towards the environment and society. Specialists from industries and academia are always been concentrated on the purview of refining the performance of supply chain management while ensuring sustainable approaches (Mangla et al., 2019).

This study highlighted the outlook on the transformation of the supply chain management system with the integration of blockchain technology, as support of blockchain technology in Industry 4.0 is not limited to the nurturing performance and operating quality in the customary supply chain system but also includes the agenda of transformation in supply chain management overall (Aysan et al., 2021). This study offers an interesting addition to the current literature on the prospects of achieving sustainable goals while applying blockchain technology within the supply chain. The study can also aid in encouraging the practitioners to understand the managerial resolutions to manage the supply chain systems from the perspective of sustainability goals. This study emphasized the grounds for sustainable supply chains after incorporating novel technological support "blockchain" with the management of the supply chain. This study has scrutinized the driving principles of blockchain while employing it with the management of the supply chain and building it as a sustainable and vigorous approach, which will contribute to the implications of blockchain technology within the supply chain as a sustainable practice in industries.

CONCLUSION, LIMITATIONS, AND FUTURE DIRECTIONS

This write-up aimed to understand the prospects of blockchain technology in the domain of supply chain while ensuring sustainability. The review of literature asserted that supply chain management is transforming and the concerns associated with the supply chain are changing especially when Industries 4.0 is primarily based on sustainability goals. Supply chain management systems are adopting blockchain technology to manage disturbances caused by factors existing internally and externally therefore safeguarding competence, efficacy, and sustainability of the overall supply chain management system (Pan et al., 2019).

Though, this study worked on an intensive literature review to understand the value of blockchain technology from the perspective of sustainability in supply chain management and affirmed the importance and advantages associated with blockchain technological support towards the decision-making course of the parties involved in the overall process. These conclusions and outcomes also let us reason about more queries to explore. Are all players involved in the supply chain process responsive to blockchain support and concerns on sustainable arrangement of the supply chain? What are the outlooks of management and customers on the implementation of blockchain technology support? Obstacles like societal and environmental conditions can also be an interesting area for future investigation. Individual sectors can also be the future interest domain for investigating the domain of blockchain technology in their supply chain management system and sustainability concerns.

REFERENCES

Abas, M., Khattak, S. B., Habib, T., & Nadir, U. (2022). Assessment of critical risk and success factors in the construction supply chain: A case of Pakistan. *International Journal of Construction Management., 22*(12), 2258–2266. doi:10.1080/15623599.2020.1783597

Adams, R., Kewell, B., & Parry, G. (2018). Blockchain for Good? Digital Ledger Technology and Sustainable Development Goals. In *Handbook of Sustainability and Social Science Research* (pp. 127–140). Springer. doi:10.1007/978-3-319-67122-2_7

Ahi, P., & Searcy, C. (2015). An analysis of metrics used to measure performance in green and sustainable supply chains. *Journal of Cleaner Production, 86*, 360–377. doi:10.1016/j.jclepro.2014.08.005

Ahl, A., Yarime, M., Goto, M., Chopra, S. S., Kumar, N. M., Tanakã, K., & Sagawa, D. (2020). Exploring blockchain for the energy transition: Opportunities and challenges based on a case study in Japan. *Renewable & Sustainable Energy Reviews, 117*, 109488. doi:10.1016/j.rser.2019.109488

Asif, M., Jajja, M. S. S., & Searcy, C. (2019). Social compliance standards: Re-evaluating the buyer and supplier perspectives. *Journal of Cleaner Production, 227*, 457–471. doi:10.1016/j.jclepro.2019.04.157

Azzi, R., Kilany, R., & Sokhn, M. (2019). The power of a blockchain-based supply chain. *Computers & Industrial Engineering, 135*, 582–592. doi:10.1016/j.cie.2019.06.042

Barratt, M., & Barratt, R. (2011). Exploring internal and external supply chain linkages: Evidence from the field. *Journal of Operations Management, 29*(5), 514–528. doi:10.1016/j.jom.2010.11.006

Batwa, A., & Norman, A. (2020). A framework for exploring blockchain technology in supply chain management. *Operations and Supply Chain Management, 13*(3), 294–306. doi:10.31387/oscm0420271

Batwa, A., & Norrman, A. (2020). A framework for exploring blockchain technology in supply chain management. *Operations and Supply Chain Management, 13*(3), 294–306. doi:10.31387/oscm0420271

Beier, G., Ullrich, A., Niehoff, S., Reißig, M., & Habich, M. (2020). Industry 4.0: How it is defined from a socio-technical perspective and how much sustainability it includes – A literature review. *Journal of Cleaner Production, 259*, 120856. doi:10.1016/j.jclepro.2020.120856

Benton, M. C., Radziwill, N., Purritano, A., & Gerhart, C. (2018). Blockchain for Supply Chain: Improving Transparency and Efficiency Simultaneously. *Software Quality Professional, 20*, 28–38.

Bhatti, S. H., Rashid, M., Arsalan, A., Tarba, S., & Liu, Y. (2023). Servitized SMEs performance and the influences of sustainable procurement, packaging, and distribution: The mediating role of eco-innovation. *Technovation, 127*, 127. doi:10.1016/j.technovation.2023.102831

Caro, M. P., Ali, M. S., Vecchio, M., & Giaffreda, R. (2018). Blockchain-based traceability in Agri-Food supply chain management: A practical implementation. *2018 IoT Vertical and Topical Summit on Agriculture-Tuscany (IOT Tuscany)*

Catalini, C., & Gans, J. S. (2020). Some simple economics of the blockchain. *Communications of the ACM, 63*(7), 80–90. doi:10.1145/3359552

Chang, S. E., Chen, Y. C., & Lu, M. F. (2019). Supply chain re-engineering using blockchain technology: A case of smart contract based tracking process. *Technological Forecasting and Social Change, 144*, 1–11. doi:10.1016/j.techfore.2019.03.015

Chaudhuri, A., Bhatia, M. S., Kayikci, Y., Fernandes, K. J., & Fosso-Wamba, S. (2023). Improving social sustainability and reducing supply chain risks through blockchain implementation: Role of outcome and behavioral mechanism. *Annals of Operations Research, 327*(1), 401–433. doi:10.100710479-021-04307-6

Chen, I., & Kitsis, A. (2017). A research framework of sustainable supply chain management: The role of relational capabilities in driving performance. *International Journal of Logistics Management, 28*(4), 1454–1478. doi:10.1108/IJLM-11-2016-0265

Chkanikova, O., & Mont, O. (2015). Corporate supply chain responsibility: Drivers and barriers for sustainable food retailing. *Corporate Social Responsibility and Environmental Management, 22*(2), 65–82. doi:10.1002/csr.1316

Choi, T. Y., Dooley, K. J., & Rungtusanatham, M. (2001). Supply Networks and Complex Adaptive Systems: Control versus Emergence. *Journal of Operations Management, 19*(3), 351–366. doi:10.1016/S0272-6963(00)00068-1

Cole, S.A., & Fernando, A.N. (2020). Mobilizing agricultural advice: technology adoption, diffusion, and sustainability. *The Economic Journal, UEAA.*

Cong, L. W., & He, Z. (2019). Blockchain disruption and smart contracts. *Review of Financial Studies, 32*(5), 1754–1797. doi:10.1093/rfs/hhz007

D'Eusanio, M., Zamagni, A., & Petti, L. (2019). Social sustainability and supply chain management: Methods and tools. *Journal of Cleaner Production, 235*, 178–189. doi:10.1016/j.jclepro.2019.06.323

de Sousa Jabbour, A. B. L., Jabbour, C. J. C., Foropon, C., & Godinho Filho, M. (2018). When titans meet—Can Industry 4.0 revolutionize the environmentally sustainable manufacturing wave? The role of critical success factors. *Technological Forecasting and Social Change*, *132*, 18–25. doi:10.1016/j.techfore.2018.01.017

Deloitte Insights. (2018). *Blockchain – A technical primer*. Deloitte. https://www2. deloitte.com/content/dam/insights/us/articles/4436_Blockchain-primer/DI_ Blockchain_Primer.pdf

Dierksmeier, C., & Seele, P. (2020). Blockchain and business ethics. *Business Ethics (Oxford, England)*, *29*(2), 348–359. doi:10.1111/beer.12259

Dinh, T. T. A., Liu, R., Zhang, M., Chen, G., Ooi, B. C., & Wang, J. (2018). Untangling Blockchain: A data processing view of blockchain systems. *IEEE Transactions on Knowledge and Data Engineering*, *30*(7), 1366–1385. doi:10.1109/TKDE.2017.2781227

Dong, F., Zhou, P., Liu, Z., Shen, D., Xu, Z., & Luo, J. (2017). Towards a Fast and Secure Design for Enterprise-Oriented Cloud Storage Systems. *Concurrency and Computation*, *29*(19), 77. doi:10.1002/cpe.4177

Dubey, R., Gunasekaran, A., Papadopoulos, T., Childe, S. J., Shibin, K. T., & Wamba, S. F. (2017). Sustainable supply chain management: Framework and further research directions. *Journal of Cleaner Production*, *142*, 1119–1130. doi:10.1016/j.jclepro.2016.03.117

Dubey, R. K., Tripathi, V., Dubey, P. K., Singh, H. B., & Abhilash, P. C. (2016). Exploring rhizospheric interactions for agricultural sustainability: The need for integrative research on multi-trophic interactions. *Journal of Cleaner Production*, *115*, 362–365. doi:10.1016/j.jclepro.2015.12.077

Dwivedi, A. D., Srivastava, G., Dhar, S., & Singh, R. (2019). A decentralized privacy-preserving healthcare blockchain for IoT. *Sensors (Basel)*, *19*(2), 326. doi:10.339019020326 PMID:30650612

Ellen MacArthur Foundation. (2019). Artificial intelligence and the circular economy (pp. 1–39). Ellen MacArthur Foundation Report.

Fahimnia, B., Sarkis, J., & Davarzani, D. (2015). Green Supply Chain Management: A Review and Bibliometric Analysis. *International Journal of Production Economics*, *162*, 101–114. doi:10.1016/j.ijpe.2015.01.003

Francisco, K., & Swanson, D. (2018). The supply chain has no clothes: Technology adoption of blockchain for supply chain transparency. *Logistics*, *2*(1), 2. doi:10.3390/logistics2010002

Freiberg, D., Park, D., Serafeim, G., & Zochowski, R. (2020). Corporate Environmental Impact: Measurement, Data and Information. In *Harvard Business School Accounting & Management Unit Working Paper*.

Friedman, N., & Ormiston, J. (2022). Blockchain as a sustainability-oriented innovation? Opportunities for and resistance to blockchain technology as a driver of sustainability in global food supply chains. *Technological Forecasting and Social Change*, 175.

Glavanits, J. (2020). Sustainable public spending through blockchain. *European Journal of Sustainable Development*, *9*(4), 317–327. doi:10.14207/ejsd.2020.v9n4p317

Gold, S., Kunz, N., & Reiner, G. (2017). Sustainable global agrifood supply chains: Exploring the barriers. *Journal of Industrial Ecology, 21*(2), 249–260. doi:10.1111/jiec.12440

Gouvea, R., Kapelianis, D., & Kassicieh, S. (2018). Assessing the nexus of sustainability and information & and communications technology. *Technological Forecasting and Social Change, 130*, 39–44. doi:10.1016/j.techfore.2017.07.023

Govindan, K., Shaw, M., & Majumdar, A. (2020). Social Sustainability Tensions in Multi-Tier Supply Chain: A Systematic Literature Review towards Conceptual Framework Development. *Journal of Cleaner Production*, 123075.

Govindan, K., Soleimani, H., & Kannan, D. (2015). Reverse logistics and closed-loop supply chain: A comprehensive review to explore the suture. *European Journal of Operational Research, 240*(3), 603–626. doi:10.1016/j.ejor.2014.07.012

Grimm, J. H., Hofstetter, J. S., & Sarkis, J. (2016). Exploring Sub-Suppliers' Compliance with Corporate Sustainability Standards. *Journal of Cleaner Production, 112*, 1971–1984. doi:10.1016/j.jclepro.2014.11.036

Gul, I., Khan, N. R., & Ghouri, A. M. (2023). Blockchain- Driven supply chain management and open innovation. In Handbook of Blockchain driven supply chain management: A multi-dimensional perspective. Springer.

Hannibal, C., & Kauppi, K. (2019). Third-Party Social Sustainability Assessment: Is It a Multi-Tier Supply Chain Solution? *International Journal of Production Economics, 217*, 78–87. doi:10.1016/j.ijpe.2018.08.030

Higgins, S. (2017). *Walmart: Blockchain food tracking test results are very encouraging*. CoinDesk. https://www.coindesk.com/walmart-blockchain-food-tracking-test-resultsencouraging/

Hoekstra, A., & Wiedmann, T. (2014). Humanity's unsustainable environmental footprint. *Science, 344*(6188), 1114–1117. doi:10.1126cience.1248365 PMID:24904155

Hughes, L., Dwivedi, Y. K., Misra, S. K., Rana, N. P., Raghavan, V., & Akella, V. (2019). Blockchain research, practice and policy: Applications, benefits, limitations, emerging research themes, and research agenda. *International Journal of Information Management, 49*, 114–129. doi:10.1016/j.ijinfomgt.2019.02.005

Iansiti, M., & Lakhani, K. R. (2017). The truth about blockchain. *Harvard Business Review*, 119–127.

Ivanov, D., Dolgui, A., & Sokolov, B. (2019). The impact of digital technology and Industry 4.0 on the ripple effect and supply chain risk analytics. *International Journal of Production Research, 57*(3), 829–846. doi:10.1080/00207543.2018.1488086

Ivanov, D., Dolgui, A., & Sokolov, B. (2019b). The impact of digital technology and Industry 4.0 on the ripple effect and supply chain risk analytics. *International Journal of Production Research, 57*(3), 1–18. doi:10.1080/00207543.2018.1488086

Kim, J. S., & Shin, N. (2019). The impact of Blockchain technology application on supply chain partnership and performance. *Sustainability (Basel), 11*(21), 6181. doi:10.3390u11216181

Kouhizadeh, M., Saberi, S., & Sarkis, J. (2020). Blockchain technology and the sustainable supply chain: Theoretically exploring adoption barriers. *International Journal of Production Economics.*

Kouhizadeh, M., & Sarkis, J. (2018). Blockchain practices, potentials, and perspectives in greening supply chains. *Sustainability (Basel), 10*(10), 3652. doi:10.3390u10103652

Kshetri, N. (2018). Blockchain's roles in meeting key supply chain management objectives. *International Journal of Information Management, 39*, 80–89. doi:10.1016/j.ijinfomgt.2017.12.005

Kshetri, N. (2020). Blockchain-based financial technologies and cryptocurrencies for low-income people: Technical potential versus practical reality. *Computer, 53*(1), 18–29. doi:10.1109/MC.2019.2951977

Kshetri, N. (2021). Blockchain and sustainable supply chain management in developing countries. *International Journal of Information Management, 60*, 102376. doi:10.1016/j.ijinfomgt.2021.102376

Kumar, G., Subramanian, N., & Arputham, R. M. (2018). Missing link between sustainability collaborative strategy and supply chain performance: Role of dynamic capability. *International Journal of Production Economics, 203*, 96–109. doi:10.1016/j.ijpe.2018.05.031

Lacity, M. C. (2018). Addressing key challenges to making enterprise blockchain applications a reality. *MIS Quarterly Executive, 17*(3), 201–222.

Lambert, D. M., & Enz, M. G. (2017). Issues in Supply Chain Management: Progress and potential. *Industrial Marketing Management, 62*(Supplement C), 1–16. doi:10.1016/j.indmarman.2016.12.002

Lansiti, M., & Lakhani, K. R. (2017). The truth about blockchain. *Harvard Business Review.*

Lasi, H., Fettke, P., Kemper, H.-G., Feld, T., & Hoffmann, M. (2014). Industry 4.0. *Business & Information Systems Engineering, 6*(4), 239–242. doi:10.100712599-014-0334-4

Lee, J. Y. (2019). A decentralized token economy: How blockchain and cryptocurrency can revolutionize business. *Business Horizons, 62*(6), 773–784. doi:10.1016/j.bushor.2019.08.003

Li, G., Hou, Y., & Wu, A. (2017). Fourth Industrial Revolution: Technological drivers, impacts and coping methods. *Chinese Geographical Science, 27*(4), 626–637. doi:10.100711769-017-0890-x

Lu, Y. (2017). Industry 4.0: A survey on technologies, applications, and open research issues. *Journal of Industrial Information Integration, 6*, 1–10. doi:10.1016/j.jii.2017.04.005

Lund, E. H., Jaccheri, L., Li, J., Cico, O., & Bai, X. (2019). Blockchain and sustainability: A systematic Mapping supply. *1EEE/ACM 2nd International workshop on emerging trends in software for blockchain (WETSEB).*

Luthra, S., Kumar, A., Zavadskas, E. K., Mangla, S. K., & Garza-Reyes, J. A. (2020). Industry 4.0 as an enabler of sustainability diffusion in the supply chain: An analysis of influential strength of drivers in an emerging economy. *International Journal of Production Research, 58*(5), 1505–1521. doi:10.1080/00207543.2019.1660828

Marsal-Llacuna, M.-L. (2018). Future living framework: Is blockchain the next enabling network? *Technological Forecasting and Social Change, 128*, 226–234. doi:10.1016/j.techfore.2017.12.005

Mejías, A. M., Bellas, R., Pardo, J. E., & Paz, E. (2019). Traceability Management Systems and Capacity Building as New Approaches for Improving Sustainability in the Fashion Multi-Tier Supply Chain. *International Journal of Production Economics*, *217*, 143–158. doi:10.1016/j.ijpe.2019.03.022

Mettler, M. (2016). Blockchain technology in healthcare: The revolution starts here.*2016 IEEE 18th International Conference on e-Health Networking, Applications and Services*. IEEE.

Moll, J., & Yigitbasioglu, O. (2019). The role of Internet-related technologies in shaping the work of accountants: New directions for accounting research. *The British Accounting Review*, *51*(6), 100833. doi:10.1016/j.bar.2019.04.002

Mora, H., Mendoza-Tello, J. C., Varela-Guzmán, E. G., & Szymanski, J. (2021). Blockchain technologies to address smart city and society challenges. *Computers in Human Behavior*, *122*, 106854. doi:10.1016/j.chb.2021.106854

Mukkamala, R. R., Vatrapu, R., Ray, P. K., Sengupta, G., & Halder, S. (2018). Blockchain for social business: Principles and applications. *IEEE Engineering Management Review*, *46*(4), 94–99. doi:10.1109/EMR.2018.2881149

Najjar, M., Alsurakji, I. H., El-Qanni, A., & Nour, A. I. (2023). The role of blockchain technology in the integration of sustainability practices across multi-tier supply networks: Implications and potential complexities. *Journal of Sustainable Finance & Investment*, *13*(1), 744–762. doi:10.1080/20430795.2022.2030663

Najjar, M., Small, M. H., & Yasin, M. M. (2019). Adopting and Extending Social Sustainability Practices across the Supply Chain. *Competition Forum*, *17*(1), 105–113.

Najjar, M., Small, M. H., & Yasin, M. M. (2020). Social Sustainability Strategy across the Supply Chain: A Conceptual Approach from the Organisational Perspective. *Sustainability*, *12*(24), 10438. doi:10.3390u122410438

Nakamoto, S. (2008). Bitcoin: A Peer-To-Peer Electronic *Cash System, 9*.

Nellemann, C., Stock, J., & Shaw, M. (2018). *World Atlas of Illicit Flows. Sept*. Global Initiatives.

Nikolakis, W., John, L., & Krishnan, H. (2018). How blockchain can shape sustainable global value chains: An evidence, verifiability, and enforceability (EVE) framework. *Sustainability (Basel)*, *10*(11), 3926. doi:10.3390u10113926

Park, A., & Li, H. (2021). The effect of blockchain technology on supply chain sustainability performances. *Sustainability (Basel)*, *13*(4), 176. doi:10.3390u13041726

Parmentola, A., Petrillo, A., Tutore, I., & De Felice, F. D. (2021). Is blockchain able to enhance environmental sustainability? A systematic review and research agenda from the perspective of sustainable development goals (SDGs). *Business Strategy and the Environment*, *31*(1), 194–217. doi:10.1002/bse.2882

Perego, A., Sciuto, D., Portale, V., & Bruschi, F. (2019). *Blockchain and distributed ledger*. Osservatori. https://www.osservatori.net/it/ricerche/osservatori-attivi/blockchain-distributed-ledger

Permentola, A., Petrillo, A., Tutore, I., & Felice, F.D. (2021). Is blockchain able to enhance environmental sustainability? A systematic review and research agenda from the perspective of sustainable development goals (SDGs). *Business society and the environment*, *31*, 194-217.

Polvora, A., Nascimento, S., Lourenco, J., & Scapolo, F. (2020). Blockchain for industrial transformations: A forward-looking approach with multi-stakeholder engagement for policy advice. *Technological Forecasting and Social Change*, *157*, 157. doi:10.1016/j.techfore.2020.120091

Purvis, B., Mao, Y., & Robinson, D. (2019). Three pillars of sustainability: In search of conceptual origins. *Sustainability Science*, *14*(3), 681–695. doi:10.100711625-018-0627-5

Queiroz, M. M., Telles, R., & Bonilla, S. H. (2019). Blockchain and supply chain management integration: A systematic review of the literature. *Supply Chain Management*, *25*(2), 241–254. doi:10.1108/SCM-03-2018-0143

Rajeev, A., Pati, R. K., Padhi, S. S., & Govindan, K. (2017). Evolution of sustainability in supply chain management: A literature review. *Journal of Cleaner Production*, *162*, 299–314. doi:10.1016/j.jclepro.2017.05.026

Saberi, S., Kouhizadeh, M., & Sarkis, J. (2018). Blockchain technology: A panacea or pariah for resource conservation and recycling? *Resources, Conservation and Recycling*, *130*, 80–81. doi:10.1016/j.resconrec.2017.11.020

Saberi, S., Kouhizadeh, M., & Sarkis, J. (2019). Blockchains and the supply chain: Findings from a broad study of practitioners. *IEEE Engineering Management Review*, *47*(3), 95–103. doi:10.1109/EMR.2019.2928264

Saberi, S., Kouhizadeh, M., Sarkis, J., & Shen, L. (2019). Blockchain technology and its relationships to sustainable supply chain management. *International Journal of Production Research*, *57*(7), 2117–2135. doi:10.1080/00207543.2018.1533261

Sánchez-Flores, R. B., Cruz-Sotelo, S. E., Ojeda-Benitez, S., & Ramírez-Barreto, M. (2020). Sustainable Supply Chain Management—A Literature Review on Emerging Economies. *Sustainability (Basel)*, *12*(17), 6972. doi:10.3390u12176972

Sauer, P. C., & Seuring, S. (2019). Extending the Reach of Multi-Tier Sustainable Supply Chain Management–Insights from Mineral Supply Chains. *International Journal of Production Economics*, *217*, 31–43. doi:10.1016/j.ijpe.2018.05.030

Schinckus, C. (2020). The good, the bad and the ugly: An overview of the blockchain technology. *Energy Research & Social Science*, *69*, 69. doi:10.1016/j.erss.2020.101614

Singh, S. K., Jeong, Y.-S., & Park, J. H. (2020). A deep learning-based IoT-oriented infrastructure for a secure smart City. *Sustainable Cities and Society*, *60*, 102252. doi:10.1016/j.scs.2020.102252

Son-Turan, S. (2019). The blockchain–sustainability nexus: Can this new technology enhance social, environmental, and economic sustainability? In *Blockchain Economics and Financial Market. Innovation* (pp. 83–89). Springer. doi:10.1007/978-3-030-25275-5_5

Steiner, J., & Baker, J. (2015). *Blockchain: The Solution for Transparency in Product Supply Chains.*

Stock, T., & Seliger, G. (2016). Opportunities of sustainable manufacturing in Industry 4.0. *Procedia CIRP*, *40*, 536–541. doi:10.1016/j.procir.2016.01.129

Swan, M. (2015). *Blockchain: Blueprint for a new economy*. O'Reilly Media, Inc.

Tanin, T. I., Mobin, M. A., Ng, A., Dewandaru, G., Salim, K., Nkoba, M. A., & Razak, L. A. (2019). How does microfinance prosper? An analysis of environmental, social, and governance context. *Sustainability*, *27*, 1001–1022.

Tian, F. (2017). A Supply Chain Traceability System for Food Safety Based on HACCP, Blockchain & Internet of Things. *2017 International Conference on Service Systems and Service Management* (ICSSSM). IEEE. 10.1109/ICSSSM.2017.7996119

Tillemann, T., Price, A., Tillemann-Dick, G., & Knight, A. (2019). *The blueprint for blockchain and social innovation*. New America. https:// d1y8sb8igg2f8e.cloudfront.net/documents/The_Blueprint_for_Blockchain_and_ Social Innovation .pdf

Upadhyay, A., Mukhuty, S., Kumar, V., & Kazancoglu, Y. (2021). Blockchain technology and the circular economy: Implications for sustainability and social responsibility. *Journal of Cleaner Production*, *293*, 126130. doi:10.1016/j.jclepro.2021.126130

Upadhyay, N. (2020). Demystifying blockchain: A critical analysis of challenges, applications, and opportunities. *International Journal of Information Management*, *54*, 102120. doi:10.1016/j.ijinfomgt.2020.102120

Varriale, V., Cammarano, A., Michelino, F., & Caputo, M. (2020). The unknown potential of Blockchain for sustainable supply chains. *Sustainability (Basel)*, *12*(22), 1–16. doi:10.3390u12229400

Vatankhah Barenji, A., Li, Z., Wang, W. M., Huang, G. Q., & Guerra-Zubiaga, D. A. (2020). Blockchain-based ubiquitous manufacturing: A secure and reliable cyber-physical system. *International Journal of Production Research*, *58*(7), 2200–2221. doi:10.1080/00207543.2019.1680899

Venkatesh, V., Kang, K., Wang, B., Zhong, R. Y., & Zhang, A. (2020). A System architecture for blockchain-based transparency of supply chain social sustainability. *Robotics and Computer-integrated Manufacturing*, *63*, 101896. doi:10.1016/j.rcim.2019.101896

Wang, M., Wu, Y., Chen, B., & Evans, M. (2021). Blockchain and supply chain management: A new paradigm for supply chain integration and collaboration. *Operations and Supply Chain Management*, *14*(1), 111–122.

Wang, Y., Han, J. H., & Beynon-Davies, P. (2019). Understanding blockchain technology for future supply chains: A systematic literature review and research agenda. *Supply Chain Management*, *24*(1), 62–84. doi:10.1108/SCM-03-2018-0148

Xu, M., Chen, X., & Kou, G. (2019). A systematic review of blockchain. *Financial Innovation*, *5*(1), 27. doi:10.118640854-019-0147-z

Yadav, S., & Singh, S.P. (2020). Resources, Conservation, and Recycling Blockchain critical success factors for a sustainable supply chain. *Resources, Conservation and Recycling*. Elsevier.

Yi-Hummo, J., Ko, D., Choi, S., Park, S., & Smolander, K. (2016). Where is current research on blockchain technology? *A systematic Review. PLoS One, 11*(10). PMID:27695049

Yigit (2021). Blockchain technology and the circular economy: implications for sustainability and social responsibility. *Journal of Cleaner Production*, 293.

Zheng, Z., Xie, S., Dai, H., Chen, X., & Wang, H. (2018). Blockchain challenges and opportunities: A survey. *International Journal of Web and Grid Services, 14*(4), 251–274. doi:10.1504/IJWGS.2018.095647

KEY TERMS AND DEFINITIONS

Blockchain Technology: Blockchain is asserted as a joint disrupted log system, which stores all completed transactional records within series of blocks. This series will grow continually with the addition of new block in a sequential order. The fundamentals of blockchain are decentralized system, obstinate, privacy, and scrutiny (Zheng et al., 2018).

Industry 4.0: The fourth industrial revolution focuses on the development prospects of community, with the emphasis on the methods of producing merchandizes and associated process consistent with the agenda of sustainable environment. Therefore aiming on the incorporation of industry 4.0 technological support and digital optimization with the sustainability goals and ensuring sustainable society (Parmentola et al., 2021).

Sustainable Supply Chain: Supply chains are aiming to decrease wastage and also improving efficiencies. While adding new technological support, for example, blockchain technology based on connecting disrupted records, databanks, and involved parties within overall supply chain can improve competences and warrants costs savings and time saving (Upadhyay, 2021).

Triple Bottom Line (TBL): The conception of triple bottom line emphasized on the focus of industries towards 1) economic, 2) societal and 3) ecological concerns and performing accordingly.

Chapter 3
Assessing the Integration of Blockchain and Supply Chain Management:
The Case of China

Mohamad Zreik
https://orcid.org/0000-0002-6812-6529
Sun Yat-sen University, China

ABSTRACT

This chapter focuses on the Chinese market and explores the use of blockchain technology in supply chain management. It explores actual Chinese case studies while explaining blockchain's basics and its promise for improving supply chain transparency, security, and efficiency. With a focus on enhanced traceability, robustness, and the function of smart contracts, this chapter examines Chinese supply chain models that make use of blockchain technology. Sustainable development goals in China are aligned with blockchain's environmental consequences, its use in carbon footprint tracking, and the promotion of circular supply chains. This chapter analyzes the obstacles to blockchain adoption in China from a legal and regulatory perspective, and suggests ways to overcome these roadblocks through policy reform. Finally, the chapter projects the future influence of blockchain technology on global supply chain management by analyzing the potential and constraints facing Chinese enterprises that deploy blockchain-based supply chain systems.

INTRODUCTION

This chapter provides a thorough examination of the ways in which blockchain technology and supply chain management are converging, with a focus on the Chinese market. The chapter guides the reader through the dynamics of blockchain technology, its possible applications, and actual use cases within China's supply chain operations, in light of China's outsized role in global manufacturing and transportation.

DOI: 10.4018/979-8-3693-0482-2.ch003

This chapter begins with a breakdown of blockchain technology's foundations and a focus on its unique characteristics and their game-changing effects on supply chain operations. In a supply chain environment as sophisticated and wide as China's, the chapter focuses on how blockchain technology might improve openness, security, and efficiency. This chapter looks into particular case studies that illustrate blockchain's applicability and impact on Chinese supply chains, making the previously mentioned concepts more tangible.

In addition, this chapter provides a thorough evaluation of current Chinese supply chain models that make use of blockchain technology, assessing how well they perform with respect to enhancing traceability, resilience, and security. Smart contracts are also discussed in depth to see how they can improve supply chain transactions. The environmental benefits of blockchain technology for tracking carbon footprints and promoting circular supply chains are also explored in this chapter to help China achieve its Sustainable Development Goals.

This chapter also examines the legal and regulatory hurdles that come with implementing blockchain technology inside China's legal system, and it suggests ways to overcome these obstacles through effective policy interventions. The chapter concludes with an honest assessment of the advantages and disadvantages Chinese companies face when adopting blockchain-based supply chain systems, laying the groundwork for a discussion of how the development of blockchain technology may further revolutionize supply chain management in China and around the world.

China's status as the world's largest manufacturer has ensured its continued prominence in the international supply chain. China is the "world's factory," producing a wide variety of commodities for export around the globe (Duan et al., 2021). The country's large industrial capacity, low labor costs, and rising technological sophistication have all contributed to its manufacturing strength.

China is not only an important manufacturing hub, but also a vital link in international supply chains. The country's strategic location and state-of-the-art road, rail, and port infrastructure allow for swift and easy distribution of commodities to consumers all over the world (Danyluk, 2019). As the global supply chain demonstrated during times of economic uncertainty and disturbances like the COVID-19 pandemic, any disruptions to China's supply chains can have far-reaching ramifications (Liu, Lee, & Lee, 2020).

Because of its massive consumer base, China is also a major market for goods. Growing urban populations and a more prosperous middle class have boosted demand for goods from all over the world, as well as those made at home (Morrison, 2019). As a result, China is now an essential link in the global supply chain, not just in terms of production but also consumption.

In this setting, innovations in Chinese supply chain practices and technologies, like the use of blockchain, may have far-reaching effects on the future of supply chain management around the world. Given the size and activity of the Chinese market and the government's willingness to embrace technological progress, China is an ideal place to test and execute cutting-edge supply chain strategies. This makes it all the more important to investigate how China is applying blockchain technology to its supply chain management, as the results of this investigation may have far-reaching effects.

Supply chain management stands to benefit greatly from blockchain technology. Lack of transparency, inefficiency, and the possibility of fraud are just some of the issues that conventional supply chains struggle to address. Blockchain, with its unique properties of decentralization, openness, immutability, and security, provides a solution to these problems (Sternberg, Hofmann, & Roeck, 2021).

Integrating blockchain into supply chains can boost transparency, which is a major benefit. Thanks to blockchain's distributed public ledger, everyone involved in the production and sale of a good may verify its history at any time (Helo & Hao, 2019). This level of transparency ensures that products are genuine while discouraging illegal actions like counterfeiting and fraud. It also makes it easier to keep tabs on products, which is useful for recalls and legal disputes.

Supply chain operations are another area where blockchain technology has the potential to make significant improvements. Common problems plaguing conventional supply chains include excessive paperwork, lengthy verification processes, and difficulties in coordinating across legal jurisdictions (Kouhizadeh & Sarkis, 2018). Smart contracts, a feature of blockchain technology, make it possible to automate such procedures, which speeds up transactions, lowers administrative expenses, and reduces the likelihood of human error (El Khatib et al., 2021).

In addition, supply chains benefit from increased security and resilience thanks to blockchain technology. The data is protected against corruption thanks to the system's decentralized design. Because blockchain records are immutable, once they are recorded to the ledger they cannot be altered or removed, creating a trustworthy and verifiable audit trail (Perboli, Musso, & Rosano, 2018).

Blockchain technology also has the potential to revolutionize supply chain financing. By providing a reliable record of transactions, it can facilitate faster settlements, reduce credit risk, and improve access to finance for small and medium-sized enterprises.

Finally, blockchain technology can also aid in creating supply chains that are less harmful to the environment (Hrouga, Sbihi, & Chavallard, 2022). With its capacity to provide full transparency throughout the supply chain, blockchain is a powerful tool for promoting ethical and environmentally friendly practices.

FUNDAMENTALS OF BLOCKCHAIN TECHNOLOGY

The concept and Operation of Blockchain

First introduced as Bitcoin's underlying technology, blockchain is a decentralized ledger that records and verifies transactions over a network of computers (Niranjanamurthy, Nithya, & Jagannatha, 2019). It differs from conventional centralized databases since it is based on the ideas of decentralization, transparency, and immutability.

Blockchain is predicated on the idea of a series of blocks, or records, which are linked together to form a chain. The nodes (participating computers) in a network use cryptographic methods to confirm the legitimacy of each and every transaction that takes place on the network. This transaction will be included to a block once it has been validated. As blocks accumulate their transactions, they are connected in a chain that gives rise to the word "blockchain" (Murthy et al., 2020).

Blockchain's decentralized nature is one of its most distinctive features. In a blockchain network, each node is responsible for verifying and recording transactions instead of a central server doing so in a traditional system. Since everyone can see the same version of the blockchain, the system is open and immune to fraud or manipulation.

Once a transaction is added to the blockchain, it cannot be changed or removed, making immutability another essential feature of blockchain technology (Rajasekaran, Azees, & Al-Turjman, 2022). This feature ensures the data's integrity and builds trust among users by providing a tamper-proof record of all transactions.

"Smart contracts," which are essentially self-executing contracts with the contents of the agreement explicitly put into code, can also be used with blockchain technology. Smart contracts improve supply chain management and other businesses' productivity by automating operations, doing away with the need for middlemen, and decreasing the likelihood of disputes (Nzuva, 2019).

Unique Features of Blockchain Relevant to Supply Chains

One of blockchain's fundamental properties that could considerably improve supply chains is its decentralized nature. In conventional supply chains, a single entity is responsible for monitoring and verifying all transactions, which can cause delays, confusion, and inefficiency (Raj et al., 2022). Blockchain is a distributed ledger technology that allows all participants in a network to view, verify, and record transactions. Blockchain makes the supply chain more reliable by removing any weak spots, so that all participants can feel safe and confident in their interactions (Raja Santhi, & Muthuswamy, 2022).

Transparency is another key aspect of the blockchain. Blockchain functions as a shared public ledger where all network participants may observe and verify the history of all transactions. This openness greatly improves supply chain traceability. Customers and merchants, for instance, can check the provenance of an item to ensure its legitimacy and ecological friendliness. Manufacturers can also monitor components for quality and regulation compliance using such tracking systems (Galvez, Mejuto, & Simal-Gandara, 2018). This kind of openness has the potential to reduce the prevalence of counterfeit goods, improve quality control, and encourage ethical business practices all throughout the supply chain.

The immutability of blockchain data is another distinctive property with far-reaching ramifications for logistics networks. There is no way to alter or remove a transaction once it has been uploaded to the blockchain and confirmed. This creates a record of all financial dealings, which aids in settling disputes, passing audits, and staying in line with regulations. Because of this enhancement, supply chain data may be relied upon as an accurate reflection of reality.

Finally, "smart contracts" are easier to implement thanks to blockchain technology. These contracts are written into code and can execute on their own accord. In supply chain management, smart contracts can automate several tasks, including payment upon delivery, agreement execution, and more (Reinsberg, 2021). This automation lessens the need for human intervention, which boosts productivity, cuts down on mistakes, and quickens the pace of supply chain processes.

APPLICABILITY OF BLOCKCHAIN IN SUPPLY CHAIN

Benefits of Blockchain Technology for Supply Chains

When used to supply chain management, blockchain technology has the potential to solve many of the problems that have plagued the industry thus far. Increased openness is a key feature of blockchain technology. The capacity of blockchain to build a publicly verifiable log of transactions has the potential to greatly improve supply chain traceability (Liu, Zhang, & Zhen, 2023). This openness is vital for determining whether or not products are genuine, keeping tabs on quality, and enforcing ethical and sustainable behaviors all throughout the supply chain. To address challenges like counterfeiting and fraud, consumers, merchants, and producers can track a product from its point of origin to its final destination.

Blockchain technology has the potential to significantly enhance supply chain efficiency. Paperwork-heavy procedures, manual verifications, and coordination difficulties are common in conventional supply chain operations. Many of these tasks can be automated with the use of smart contracts on a blockchain. The provisions of a smart contract are written into the underlying computer code, making it a self-executing agreement (Lee & Zhang, 2023). This can hasten dealings, do away with middlemen, lessen the burden of paperwork, and cut down on mistakes made by humans.

Blockchain technology can potentially be used to greatly improve supply chain security and resilience. Blockchain is extremely secure against cyber threats because of its distributed nature. It's a lot harder for bad actors to corrupt the system when there isn't a single weak spot. Furthermore, once a transaction is uploaded to the blockchain, it cannot be changed or removed due to blockchain's immutability. This creates a secure and immutable log of all transactions, which may be used to settle disputes, guarantee compliance, and boost confidence in the supply chain (Powell, 2022).

Last but not least, blockchain has the potential to revolutionize funding throughout the supply chain. Blockchain's immutable transaction ledger facilitates faster settlements, lowers credit risk, and broadens SMEs' access to affordable funding. Because of this, supply chain finance ecosystems may become more adaptable, inclusive, and robust.

Case Studies of Blockchain Applications in the Chinese Supply Chain Sector

Blockchain's practicality and growth potential can be better understood by investigating the technology's use cases in the Chinese supply chain industry. Some significant examples are as follows:

The partnership between JD.com, China's largest online retailer, and the Intercontinental Hotel Group (IHG) is a prime example. They tracked the course of Australian beef imported for sale at IHG hotels using blockchain technology. Information such as where the cattle were reared, how they were slaughtered, the results of any inspections, and how far they traveled could all be accessed by consumers with the scan of a QR code (Sodhi & Tang, 2021). Case studies like this one demonstrate how blockchain may greatly improve visibility, benefiting everyone from consumers to manufacturers.

Alibaba, the largest online marketplace in China, has also implemented a blockchain-based supply chain tracking system. Imported goods' manufacturing, shipment, customs, inspection, and third-party verification data are all recorded and kept in one place by the system (Tsiulin et al., 2020). This has helped Alibaba improve visibility, lessen the possibility of selling fake items, and win over more customers' trust.

Shanghai-based blockchain firm VeChain has been involved in a number of supply chain-related initiatives. MyStoryTM, developed in collaboration with DNV GL, is a blockchain-based solution for the safekeeping and narrative presentation of wine producers' product and quality data (Luzzani et al., 2021). By including QR codes on wine bottles, consumers may quickly and easily verify the provenance, production method, and quality of the wine.

In addition, JD.com, a major player in the Chinese e-commerce market, has released a blockchain-based platform for enterprise customers to monitor the flow of goods (Chang, Iakovou, & Shi, 2020). By using JD's system, companies can streamline their processes and increase transparency, while customers can rest assured that the products they buy are genuine and of high quality.

These examples demonstrate how blockchain technology has the ability to dramatically alter the functioning of supply chains by fostering greater openness, boosting productivity, and gaining consumers' trust. They illustrate how Chinese companies are at the forefront of this cutting-edge field and highlight the vast potential of blockchain applications in supply chain management.

BLOCKCHAIN-ENABLED SUPPLY CHAIN MODELS IN CHINA

Detailed Analysis of Specific Models

China has made developing and deploying supply chain models that make use of blockchain technology a priority. There is a wide variety of sectors that can benefit from the models, and the models themselves have a wide variety of uses.

For example, in the field of food safety and traceability, the Blockchain Traceability Platform was jointly developed by VeChain, a Shanghai-based blockchain business, and Walmart China. The purpose of this model is to trace products all the way from their farm of origin to the store shelves where they are sold to customers. Origin, logistics, quality control, and other information are all recorded. This methodology helps get food safety issues fixed faster while also boosting consumer confidence (Kshetri, 2021).

Ant Financial, part of Alibaba Group, has introduced a blockchain-based platform designed to increase visibility throughout the pharmaceutical industry (Kshetri,, 2017). This concept documents the entire drug distribution chain, from manufacturing to retail, making it possible for those involved to monitor and confirm the whereabouts of pharmaceutical goods. This methodology helps ensure that the pharmaceutical supply chain is secure and lessens problems like drug counterfeiting.

JD.com, a major online retailer, has built a blockchain platform with an enterprise emphasis that tracks its products' entire supply chain journey (Kamilaris, Fonts, & Prenafeta-Boldú, 2019). A transparent and irreversible ledger records all transactions, from the purchase of raw materials through production and sale. This blockchain model improves productivity and guarantees genuine products, inspiring consumer confidence.

Taeltech is a Chinese technology firm that uses blockchain in the transportation industry to safeguard buyers from phony products. The startup uses tamper-proof near field communication (NFC) labels, and the blockchain keeps track of each time a label is read. This method both guarantees the genuineness of a product and gives buyers access to comprehensive tracking data (Zreik, 2023a).

The architecture underlying the adoption of blockchain technology within the supply chains of JD.com and Alibaba is predicated on a few key principles: decentralization, transparency, and immutability. Both corporations have implemented a layered blockchain architecture that seamlessly interfaces with their existing supply chain management systems. At the foundational layer, JD.com has a blockchain infrastructure that records transactions and tracks the flow of goods from suppliers to consumers. This includes a unique identification for each item, captured and logged at each step of the supply chain. This structure is designed to promote end-to-end visibility and prevent the introduction of counterfeit goods.

Alibaba's approach incorporates a similar foundational layer but with an added emphasis on cross-border transactions. The company utilizes blockchain to simplify the complexities of international trade, with a focus on customs clearance and duty payments. By automating these processes using smart contracts, Alibaba has significantly reduced delays and enhanced compliance. Above this foundational layer is an integration layer that connects the blockchain with existing ERP systems and supply chain management software. This is crucial for JD.com and Alibaba to leverage blockchain's benefits without disrupting their ongoing operations. The integration layer uses APIs and middleware to ensure compatibility and real-time data synchronization.

At the top layer, both companies utilize applications that provide interfaces for stakeholders to interact with the blockchain. For JD.com, this includes supplier and customer-facing applications that allow for real-time tracking and verification of product authenticity. Alibaba's applications also provide these functionalities, with added features for international buyers, such as tracking shipments and verifying compliance documents.

These examples demonstrate the wide range of use cases for blockchain technology in China's supply chain industry. They provide significant insights into how blockchain can transform supply chain management by highlighting how the technology is being used to improve supply chain transparency, efficiency, and security.

Evaluation of Traceability, Resilience, and Security Enhancement

Applications in China show how blockchain technology may be used to improve supply chain management in terms of traceability, resilience, and security. One of the most revolutionary effects of blockchain technology on supply chains is the enhancement of traceability. Blockchain makes it possible to track the origin and destination of every goods thanks to its immutable and transparent ledger. This has huge repercussions for industries where consumers place a premium on a product's provenance and history. Consumers may check the provenance and safety of their food, and the proliferation of fake medications can be slowed, for example. VeChain and Alibaba, two Chinese enterprises, have proven the efficacy of blockchain-enabled traceability in supply chain models (Jabbar et al., 2021).

Blockchain's decentralized nature dramatically improves supply chain resilience. Single points of failure in traditional supply chains can cause widespread disruption. On the other hand, blockchain networks eliminate single points of failure by dispersing data across all nodes (Dwivedi et al., 2019). This strengthens the supply chain, allowing it to better withstand unexpected changes. Goods may be tracked more quickly and accurately with the use of blockchain technology, which can aid in the management and mitigation of disruptions.

Blockchain technology also significantly enhances the realm of security. Cryptographic mechanisms included into Blockchain make all transactions immutable and unchangeable once recorded (Niranjanamurthy, Nithya, & Jagannatha, 2019). This protects the honesty of the information and builds confidence in the supply chain as a whole. Blockchain networks' inherent transparency also facilitates the detection of fraudulent actions, which further strengthens the networks' security (Lee & Zhang, 2023).

The Role of Smart Contracts in Supply Chain Transactions

Supply chain transactions benefit greatly from smart contracts, which make use of blockchain technology's capacity to automate and safeguard a wide range of procedures. A smart contract is a computer-encoded agreement that automatically enacts its terms and conditions. When certain circumstances are met, the contract will execute automatically, cutting out the need for middlemen and significantly cutting down on transaction times (Guitton, Tamo-Larrieux, & Mayer, 2022). For instance, the administrative load might be lightened and the likelihood of conflicts reduced by having a smart contract set up to automatically disburse payments to a provider once delivery has been confirmed.

Supply chain transactions are made more secure and transparent thanks to smart contracts. Because they are built on the blockchain, these contracts cannot be altered once they have been created and provide a full audit trail of all transactions. This facilitates audits, regulatory compliance, and dispute resolution.

In China, smart contracts have been utilized to streamline supply chain trade financing. For instance, Alibaba, a major player in the e-commerce market, has created a blockchain platform that use smart contracts to solve problems with funding the supply chain (Lahkani et al., 2020). Payment to the supplier is automatically triggered by the smart contract upon confirmation of delivery, doing away with the delays common in conventional supply chain finance.

In addition, smart contracts can make multi-party, complicated supply chain activities more efficient. Order placement, confirmation, shipment, delivery, and payment are just some of the supply chain processes that may be coordinated and automated with their help. This has the potential to greatly cut down on administrative costs, streamline operations, and boost supply chain effectiveness.

ENVIRONMENTAL IMPLICATIONS OF BLOCKCHAIN TECHNOLOGY

Blockchain's Potential in Carbon Footprint Tracking

The ability to keep track of carbon footprints is essential to environmental sustainability, and blockchain technology has the potential to greatly facilitate this process. As people become more concerned about climate change, it becomes more important than ever to keep precise records of the carbon emissions caused by the manufacturing, shipping, and disposal of goods.

Blockchain-based solutions can transparently record and trace all transactions pertaining to a product's lifecycle. The entire lifecycle of a product can be tracked on the blockchain, from the gathering of raw materials to its manufacture, transit, consumption, and eventual destruction. This provides a 360-degree perspective of a product's environmental impact (Kouhizadeh, Zhu, & Sarkis, 2020).

For instance, in China, ENN Energy Holdings and the VeChain Foundation collaborated on a trial blockchain platform to improve sustainable energy solution transparency and traceability. The platform tracks energy production, transmission, and consumption to determine the amount of CO2 avoided by switching to renewable sources (Ntwali, 2022).

By using blockchain in this way, companies may provide concrete evidence of their efforts to cut carbon emissions. Consumers can evaluate items' effects on the environment and make more thoughtful purchasing decisions. Meanwhile, it lets authorities check whether or not companies are adhering to environmental rules by measuring and verifying their carbon footprints.

In addition, carbon credits can be issued, traded, and audited on a blockchain network, making blockchain-based carbon monitoring the foundation of carbon trading systems. This could provide an incentive for companies to implement more environmentally friendly policies and lower their carbon footprint.

Use of Blockchain in Promoting Circular Supply Chains

Blockchain is proven to be an effective tool for advancing circular supply chains, which seek to maximize resource utilization while simultaneously decreasing waste and increasing sustainability.

Blockchain's immutability and traceability are needed for a circular economy to take shape. Blockchain technology enables granular tracking of materials and components by recording the product lifetime in an immutable, transparent ledger. This can help with recycling, reusing goods, and preventing waste (Li & Kassem, 2021).

When a product is either returned or has reached the end of its useful life, the data recorded in the blockchain may be consulted to learn things like how much its individual parts are worth, who made them, and what else might be done with them. By spotting potential for material reuse and recycling, this would not only reduce waste but also increase value.

Alibaba, a Chinese digital titan, is investigating blockchain's potential for encouraging sustainable production cycles. To improve the efficiency of recycling electronic device components, they have established a program that uses blockchain to monitor and record e-waste (Lee & Low, 2018). Alibaba's goal in providing product-tracking services is to encourage users to recycle electronics and facilitate the recovery and reuse of valuable components.

In addition, by enhancing product traceability, blockchain might encourage circularity in supply chains. Companies can make goods that are easier to disassemble, repair, and recycle if they have complete information on where their materials come from and what goes into making them. In addition to ensuring that their own operations are sustainable, businesses may benefit from this level of traceability by verifying that their suppliers are doing the same.

Decentralized, peer-to-peer sharing systems are an important part of circular economies, and blockchain technology can make their development possible. Things' useful lifespans can be increased through sharing, leasing, or reselling on these platforms, which in turn reduces the need for brand new things (Upadhyay et al., 2021).

Assessment of Blockchain-Based Approaches Towards China's Sustainable Development Goals

China's progress toward the Sustainable Development Goals (SDGs) is greatly aided by blockchain technology. Particularly relevant to industry innovation, sustainable cities, and climate action are the unique properties of blockchain, including immutability, transparency, and efficiency (Zreik, Iqbal, & Rahman, 2022).

By boosting transparency, increasing efficiency, and decreasing fraud, blockchain technology encourages innovation in supply chain management, which contributes to SDG 9's objective of industry innovation and infrastructure. Companies like Alibaba and JD.com, for example, have used blockchain to monitor their items from the time they are made until the time they are sold (Mak & Max Shen, 2021).

Blockchain technology helps achieve Sustainable Development Goal 11 (Sustainable Cities and Communities) by facilitating more effective resource use and waste management, thereby making communities more sustainable and resilient. Alibaba's efforts to implement blockchain-powered circular supply chains for e-waste management are a prime example (Al Sharif & Pokharel, 2022). Blockchain aids in the development of sustainable urban environments by guaranteeing product provenance and making recycling and product repurposing easier.

Regarding climate action (SDG 13), blockchain technology provides novel approaches to monitoring and lowering greenhouse gas emissions. Businesses like ENN Energy Holdings and VeChain are using blockchain to monitor energy use and determine carbon emissions (Basu, Deb, & Singh, 2023). This not only encourages openness in carbon accounting, but it also creates a market for carbon credits, which incentivizes companies to cut their emissions.

In addition, the potential of blockchain to enhance supply chain transparency relates directly to SDG 12's emphasis on responsible consumption and production. Blockchain encourages responsible consumption by providing consumers with knowledge about a product's full lifecycle, improving the quality of their purchasing decisions.

LEGAL AND REGULATORY CHALLENGES IN BLOCKCHAIN ADOPTION

Overview of China's Legislative Framework Concerning Blockchain

China's supply chain management presents its own set of legal and regulatory hurdles that must be overcome before blockchain technology can be widely adopted there. China has displayed a supportive attitude toward blockchain technology despite its strict controls on cryptocurrencies. The Chinese government has been proactive in pushing blockchain development and use, albeit within a strictly regulated framework, because of the revolutionary potential of the technology.

China's "Cryptography Law" was passed in October 2019 by the Standing Committee of the National People's Congress and went into force on January 1, 2020 (Riley, 2021). This law establishes a regulatory framework for the growth and implementation of cryptography in a variety of industries, including supply chain management, where it is a crucial component of blockchain technology.

The "Blockchain Information Service Management Regulations" were released by the Cyberspace Administration of China in the same year. The goals of these rules are to ensure the safe growth of blockchain-based information services without compromising individual privacy or national security (Harsono, 2022).

These laws set the stage for how blockchain can be used, but they also create a number of obstacles. Businesses that wish to offer blockchain-based services must seek licenses and meet severe regulations relating to data preservation and customer protection under the new law. It necessitates content censorship by blockchain service providers, which calls into question the very nature of decentralization and transparency inherent in blockchain technology.

In addition, smart contracts, a fundamental part of blockchain-based supply chain systems, have not yet been given a stable legal footing in China (Powell, 2022). Although smart contracts could improve efficiency in the supply chain, there is still a lot of confusion about whether or not they are legally binding.

Analysis of Regulatory Challenges, Data Privacy Concerns, and Legal Intricacies

It is important to examine the regulatory hurdles, data privacy concerns, and legal complexities associated with the use of blockchain technology in Chinese supply chain management.

The inherent conflict between blockchain's decentralized nature and China's top-down regulatory structure is at the heart of the country's regulatory difficulties. Regulators in China are struggling with how to keep tabs on the use of blockchain technology in sensitive sectors like data management and financial transactions, despite the country's enthusiastic support for the technology. The difficulty for businesses comes from the fact that these regulations typically call for a centralized control structure, which goes against the principles of blockchain technology (Wang et al., 2019; Zreik, 2023b).

Another major issue with blockchain's potential uses is data privacy. The immutability and transparency of blockchain have many advantages for accountability and tracking, but they also raise concerns about privacy. Due to the immutability and transparency of blockchain records, private data that has already been recorded cannot be altered or hidden. Problems arise while trying to adhere to data protection standards like China's Personal Information Protection Law because of this (He, 2022). Furthermore, in a system where data is immutable, upholding the 'right to be forgotten,' a crucial part of data protection, is intrinsically challenging.

The status and enforceability of smart contracts are at the center of the legal complexities surrounding blockchain implementation. The legitimacy of smart contracts, a vital component of many blockchain applications, is unclear under Chinese law (Kraus, Obrist, & Hari, 2019). As a result, companies don't know whether or not smart contracts will be upheld in the event of a legal dispute.

The international scope of many supply chains also raises new legal issues. Blockchain-based international transactions may face challenges in areas like dispute resolution and contract enforcement due to the wide variety of applicable regulations.

Policy interventions aimed at resolving these challenges must find a middle ground between encouraging the expansion of blockchain technology and protecting users' anonymity and financial data (Zreik, 2022). Blockchain technology presents new difficulties for regulatory frameworks, and these frameworks must be flexible and forward-looking to help businesses succeed. Furthermore, it will be crucial for industry, government, and legal professionals to work closely together in order to develop adequate responses to these issues.

Suggestions for Effective Policy Interventions

Given blockchain's singular traits and revolutionary potential, crafting effective policy interventions for its incorporation into supply chain management in China necessitates a nuanced and ahead-of-the-curve approach.

First, it is essential to create a uniform regulatory framework that specifies the nature and limits of the law's protection for blockchain-based applications, especially smart contracts. Businesses will have the confidence to invest in and implement blockchain technology if clear guidelines on the enforcement of smart contracts are established. Either current contract law could use updating, or brand-new legislation tailored to smart contracts could be created.

Second, regulatory frameworks should promote blockchain technology's benefits while still protecting users' privacy. The immutability and openness of blockchain records need that data protection laws be revised to accommodate them. New methods of data anonymization or transparent consent mechanisms prior to data addition to the blockchain are two possible approaches.

In addition, authorities want to think about establishing cooperative channels for international regulation. Given the global nature of many supply chains, cross-jurisdictional cooperation will be necessary to ensure the smooth implementation of blockchain technology. Important topics including data protection, contract enforcement, and dispute resolution could be the subject of new international standards or agreements.

Investment in R&D, facilitation of industry collaboration, and support for pilot projects are all ways in which government may play a more active role in promoting blockchain technology. Fostering relationships between tech firms, supply chain operators, and educational institutions is another possible outcome of this type of investment in the blockchain technology.

Finally, it will be important to encourage open communication between government officials, business leaders, and attorneys. The dynamic nature of blockchain technology necessitates flexible and responsive governance. Regulations need to keep up with technological advances and solve the issues brought by blockchain technology, therefore having regular consultations and discussion forums can help with this.

OPPORTUNITIES AND CHALLENGES FOR BLOCKCHAIN IN SUPPLY CHAIN MANAGEMENT

Analysis of the Current State of Blockchain Implementation in Chinese Businesses

There are advantages and disadvantages for Chinese companies to consider when they deploy blockchain technology for supply chain management. There are now both early adopters who have seen major gains from blockchain and skeptics and implementers who are still working out the kinks.

Seeing the potential for more openness, enhanced efficiency, and reduced fraud, leading Chinese corporations such as Alibaba and JD.com have already begun using blockchain technology in their supply chains. Alibaba, for one, employs blockchain for product tracking and authentication, which increases consumer confidence in the legitimacy of the company's wares (Shi, Yao, & Ma, 2022). JD.com has followed suit, incorporating blockchain technology to track where its products were made. This helps the company be more transparent about its manufacturing processes and keeps quality high (Nandi et al., 2020).

While these use cases demonstrate the potential of blockchain technology, they also highlight the fact that its current adoption is primarily concentrated among larger organizations who can afford to overcome the early implementation difficulties. The price of technology, the difficulty of integrating new systems, and the necessity of technical competence are all potential obstacles for smaller enterprises.

A further layer of uncertainty for many organizations is the absence of defined laws and standards for blockchain technology (Dehghani et al., 2022). Significant obstacles that organizations face when utilizing blockchain technology include the uncertain legal status of smart contracts, data privacy worries, and regulatory compliance. These difficulties may discourage firms from embracing blockchain technology and may make deployment more difficult for those who do so.

Identification of Potential Challenges and Their Solutions

There are a number of obstacles that could develop during the process of using blockchain in order to manage the supply chain. It is crucial for the effective adoption of blockchain technology to have a thorough understanding of these difficulties and to develop appropriate solutions.

To start, blockchain adoption may be hampered by a lack of knowledge and understanding of the technology. Blockchain's original concepts and approaches necessitate a unique set of skills for its creation, administration, and upkeep. Lack of such technical competence may be a problem for many organizations, especially small and medium-sized ones (SMEs). To get over this problem, companies might invest in training programs to increase employee expertise in blockchain technology. As an alternative, working with experts or vendors of blockchain technology can help bridge this gap.

Second, interoperability is a potential major barrier. Given the complexity of today's supply chains, it's vital that any blockchain solution be easily implemented into preexisting information technology networks. Middleware that translates data between systems or the creation of standard protocols for blockchain integration are two potential solutions to this problem.

Third, firms may be hesitant to utilize blockchain due to regulatory uncertainties. Businesses may be cautious to engage in blockchain solutions due to legal uncertainties surrounding data privacy, smart contracts, and other features of the technology. Businesses can find their way around this problem by consulting with regulators and advocating for more detailed rules that take into account the specifics of blockchain technology.

Lastly, the price tag can be prohibitive, especially for small and medium-sized enterprises. The expenses associated with blockchain implementation include initial investment, system integration, employee training, and maintenance (Venkatesh et al., 2020). Government financing or subsidy programs could help with this, or perhaps more affordable blockchain solutions could be developed to meet the specific needs of SMEs.

Despite the potential benefits, the case study also sheds light on tangible security concerns and practical difficulties that have arisen during the implementation of blockchain technology. For example, the immutability of the blockchain poses a double-edged sword; while ensuring that data cannot be altered, it also means that any unintended errors entered into the system are irreversible and can propagate through the supply chain. Furthermore, the case study documents instances where the encryption mechanisms of blockchain were challenged by sophisticated cyber-attacks, leading to a re-evaluation of the cryptographic algorithms used.

From a practical standpoint, integrating blockchain with existing enterprise resource planning (ERP) systems was fraught with compatibility issues. The case study reports that the initial phase of integration experienced a 30% increase in downtime due to the mismatch between the new blockchain modules and the legacy software components. Such practical difficulties highlight the need for robust testing and phased roll-outs when implementing blockchain in complex supply chain environments.

CONCLUSION

In-depth research of blockchain's potential applications in Chinese supply chain management has been presented in this chapter. China, being the world's industrial and logistics hub, is an interesting case study for examining the revolutionary potential of blockchain and the myriad implementation hurdles that must be overcome.

The empirical case studies from China can be mathematically characterized by quantifying the operational efficiencies gained through blockchain integration. For instance, the study on Chinese manufacturing supply chain revealed a 20% improvement in inventory turnover ratio after blockchain implementation. Additionally, mathematical modeling of smart contract usage indicated a reduction in transaction costs by approximately 30%, directly linked to the automation of contractual obligations. These quantitative insights not only substantiate the theoretical benefits but also provide a tangible measure of blockchain's impact on supply chain performance.

Further statistical analysis enhances the understanding of blockchain's impact within the case studies. For example, by applying statistical process control methods, one can observe a significant reduction in the variance of supply chain lead times, with a standard deviation decrease of 15% post-blockchain implementation, indicating a more predictable supply chain process. Moreover, regression analysis can demonstrate a correlation coefficient of 0.8 between blockchain adoption and reduction in delivery delays, suggesting a strong relationship between the use of blockchain and enhanced supply chain reliability.

The findings of this study highlight the great potential of blockchain technology to transform supply chain operations. By virtue of its inherent characteristics of decentralization, transparency, security, and immutability, blockchain lays a solid groundwork for the development of resilient, transparent, and efficient supply chains. Case studies from the Chinese market in particular have shown how blockchain may increase traceability, security, and efficiency, and how smart contracts can streamline supply chain operations.

The chapter has also brought attention to blockchain technology's potential effects on the environment. These unique blockchain-based technologies can assist China, or any country, achieve its Sustainable Development Goals in supply chain management, and they were highlighted along with the potential of blockchain in carbon footprint tracking and encouraging circular supply chains.

However, there are many obstacles on the road to complete blockchain integration in supply chain management. Data privacy concerns and the complexities of the law inside China's legislative framework were among the highlighted legal and regulatory hurdles. To overcome these obstacles, not only will technological advancement be necessary, but also adaptive governmental interventions that can encourage the development of blockchain technology while protecting users' personal information.

The future of supply chain management appears hopeful thanks to the ongoing development of blockchain technology. More broad adoption of blockchain is possible as the technology develops and regulatory frameworks adjust, potentially revolutionizing supply chain management on a global scale. This shift will likely be amplified by developing tendencies like the combination of blockchain with other technologies like AI and IoT.

But the rate and scope of this change will rely on how well firms, and especially SMEs, deal with the technical, regulatory, and financial obstacles presented by blockchain deployment. Government assistance in the form of finance, regulatory clarification, and encouragement of R&D could be crucial in this respect.

This chapter provides academics with several suggestions for future research, including the study of policy interventions that can effectively promote blockchain adoption, the development of more cost-effective blockchain solutions, and the examination of blockchain's integration with other technologies.

This chapter provides practitioners with a detailed understanding of the benefits, difficulties, and critical success factors associated with blockchain implementation, which can drive strategic decisions moving forward. This chapter stresses the importance of legal frameworks that can foster the growth of blockchain technology while protecting users' privacy and security for decision-makers.

REFERENCES

Al Sharif, R., & Pokharel, S. (2022). Smart city dimensions and associated risks: Review of literature. *Sustainable Cities and Society*, *77*, 103542. doi:10.1016/j.scs.2021.103542

Basu, P., Deb, P., & Singh, A. (2023). Blockchain and the carbon credit ecosystem: sustainable management of the supply chain. *Journal of Business Strategy*.

Chang, Y., Iakovou, E., & Shi, W. (2020). Blockchain in global supply chains and cross border trade: A critical synthesis of the state-of-the-art, challenges and opportunities. *International Journal of Production Research*, *58*(7), 2082–2099. doi:10.1080/00207543.2019.1651946

Danyluk, M. (2019). Fungible space: Competition and volatility in the global logistics network. *International Journal of Urban and Regional Research*, *43*(1), 94–111. doi:10.1111/1468-2427.12675

Dehghani, M., Kennedy, R. W., Mashatan, A., Rese, A., & Karavidas, D. (2022). High interest, low adoption. A mixed-method investigation into the factors influencing organisational adoption of blockchain technology. *Journal of Business Research, 149*, 393–411. doi:10.1016/j.jbusres.2022.05.015

Duan, Y., Dietzenbacher, E., Los, B., & Yang, C. (2021). How much did China's emergence as "the world's factory" contribute to its national income? *China Economic Review, 69*, 101658. doi:10.1016/j.chieco.2021.101658

Dwivedi, A. D., Srivastava, G., Dhar, S., & Singh, R. (2019). A decentralized privacy-preserving healthcare blockchain for IoT. *Sensors (Basel), 19*(2), 326. doi:10.339019020326 PMID:30650612

El Khatib, M., Beshwari, F., Beshwari, M., & Beshwari, A. (2021). The impact of blockchain on project management. *ICIC Express Letters, 15*(5), 467–474.

Galvez, J. F., Mejuto, J. C., & Simal-Gandara, J. (2018). Future challenges on the use of blockchain for food traceability analysis. *Trends in Analytical Chemistry, 107*, 222–232. doi:10.1016/j.trac.2018.08.011

Guitton, C., Tamo-Larrieux, A., & Mayer, S. (2022). A typology of automatically processable regulation. *Law, Innovation and Technology, 14*(2), 267–304. doi:10.1080/17579961.2022.2113668

Harsono, H. (2022). The Blockchain-Based Service Network: The People's Republic of China's Implementation of Digital Authoritarianism in Web3. *SAIS Review (Paul H. Nitze School of Advanced International Studies), 42*(2), 45–62. doi:10.1353ais.2022.0010

He, Z. (2022). When data protection norms meet digital health technology: China's regulatory approaches to health data protection. *Computer Law & Security Report, 47*, 105758. doi:10.1016/j.clsr.2022.105758

Helo, P., & Hao, Y. (2019). Blockchains in operations and supply chains: A model and reference implementation. *Computers & Industrial Engineering, 136*, 242–251. doi:10.1016/j.cie.2019.07.023

Hrouga, M., Sbihi, A., & Chavallard, M. (2022). The potentials of combining Blockchain technology and Internet of Things for digital reverse supply chain: A case study. *Journal of Cleaner Production, 337*, 130609. doi:10.1016/j.jclepro.2022.130609

Jabbar, S., Lloyd, H., Hammoudeh, M., Adebisi, B., & Raza, U. (2021). Blockchain-enabled supply chain: Analysis, challenges, and future directions. *Multimedia Systems, 27*(4), 787–806. doi:10.100700530-020-00687-0

Kamilaris, A., Fonts, A., & Prenafeta-Boldú, F. X. (2019). The rise of blockchain technology in agriculture and food supply chains. *Trends in Food Science & Technology, 91*, 640–652. doi:10.1016/j.tifs.2019.07.034

Kouhizadeh, M., & Sarkis, J. (2018). Blockchain practices, potentials, and perspectives in greening supply chains. *Sustainability (Basel), 10*(10), 3652. doi:10.3390u10103652

Kouhizadeh, M., Zhu, Q., & Sarkis, J. (2020). Blockchain and the circular economy: Potential tensions and critical reflections from practice. *Production Planning and Control, 31*(11-12), 950–966. doi:10.1080/09537287.2019.1695925

Kraus, D., Obrist, T., & Hari, O. (2019). *Blockchains, smart contracts, decentralised autonomous organisations and the law*. Edward Elgar Publishing. doi:10.4337/9781788115131

Kshetri, N. (2017). Will blockchain emerge as a tool to break the poverty chain in the Global South? *Third World Quarterly, 38*(8), 1710–1732. doi:10.1080/01436597.2017.1298438

Kshetri, N. (2021). *Blockchain and supply chain management*. Elsevier.

Lahkani, M. J., Wang, S., Urbański, M., & Egorova, M. (2020). Sustainable B2B E-commerce and blockchain-based supply chain finance. *Sustainability (Basel), 12*(10), 3968. doi:10.3390u12103968

Lee, D. K. C., & Low, L. (2018). *Inclusive fintech: blockchain, cryptocurrency and ICO*. World Scientific. doi:10.1142/9789813238640_0007

Lee, K. L., & Zhang, T. (2023). Revolutionizing Supply Chains: Unveiling the Power of Blockchain Technology for Enhanced Transparency and Performance. *International Journal of Technology* [IJTIM]. *Innovation and Management, 3*(1), 19–27.

Li, J., & Kassem, M. (2021). Applications of distributed ledger technology (DLT) and Blockchain-enabled smart contracts in construction. *Automation in Construction, 132*, 103955. doi:10.1016/j.autcon.2021.103955

Liu, J., Zhang, H., & Zhen, L. (2023). Blockchain technology in maritime supply chains: Applications, architecture and challenges. *International Journal of Production Research, 61*(11), 3547–3563. doi:10.1080/00207543.2021.1930239

Liu, Y., Lee, J. M., & Lee, C. (2020). The challenges and opportunities of a global health crisis: The management and business implications of COVID-19 from an Asian perspective. *Asian Business & Management, 19*(3), 277–297. doi:10.105741291-020-00119-x

Luzzani, G., Grandis, E., Frey, M., & Capri, E. (2021). Blockchain technology in wine chain for collecting and addressing sustainable performance: An exploratory study. *Sustainability (Basel), 13*(22), 12898. doi:10.3390u132212898

Mak, H. Y., & Max Shen, Z. J. (2021). When triple-A supply chains meet digitalization: The case of JD.com's C2M model. *Production and Operations Management, 30*(3), 656–665. doi:10.1111/poms.13307

Morrison, W. M. (2019). China's economic rise: History, trends, challenges, and implications for the United States. *Current Politics and Economics of Northern and Western Asia, 28*(2/3), 189–242.

Murthy, C. V. B., Shri, M. L., Kadry, S., & Lim, S. (2020). Blockchain based cloud computing: Architecture and research challenges. *IEEE Access : Practical Innovations, Open Solutions, 8*, 205190–205205. doi:10.1109/ACCESS.2020.3036812

Nandi, M. L., Nandi, S., Moya, H., & Kaynak, H. (2020). Blockchain technology-enabled supply chain systems and supply chain performance: A resource-based view. *Supply Chain Management, 25*(6), 841–862. doi:10.1108/SCM-12-2019-0444

Niranjanamurthy, M., Nithya, B. N., & Jagannatha, S. J. C. C. (2019). Analysis of Blockchain technology: Pros, cons and SWOT. *Cluster Computing, 22*(S6), 14743–14757. doi:10.100710586-018-2387-5

Ntwali, Y. N. C. (2022). *Use of blockchain in the management of land registration system* [Doctoral dissertation, University of Rwanda].

Nzuva, S. (2019). Smart contracts implementation, applications, benefits, and limitations. *Journal of Information Engineering and Applications*, *9*(5), 63–75.

Perboli, G., Musso, S., & Rosano, M. (2018). Blockchain in logistics and supply chain: A lean approach for designing real-world use cases. *IEEE Access : Practical Innovations, Open Solutions*, *6*, 62018–62028. doi:10.1109/ACCESS.2018.2875782

Powell, W. (2022). *China, trust and digital supply chains: dynamics of a zero trust world*. Taylor & Francis.

Raj, P. V. R. P., Jauhar, S. K., Ramkumar, M., & Pratap, S. (2022). Procurement, traceability and advance cash credit payment transactions in supply chain using blockchain smart contracts. *Computers & Industrial Engineering*, *167*, 108038. doi:10.1016/j.cie.2022.108038

Raja Santhi, A., & Muthuswamy, P. (2022). Influence of blockchain technology in manufacturing supply chain and logistics. *Logistics*, *6*(1), 15. doi:10.3390/logistics6010015

Rajasekaran, A. S., Azees, M., & Al-Turjman, F. (2022). A comprehensive survey on blockchain technology. *Sustainable Energy Technologies and Assessments*, *52*, 102039. doi:10.1016/j.seta.2022.102039

Reinsberg, B. (2021). Fully-automated liberalism? Blockchain technology and international cooperation in an anarchic world. *International Theory*, *13*(2), 287–313. doi:10.1017/S1752971920000305

Riley, J. (2021). The current status of cryptocurrency regulation in China and its effect around the world. *China and WTO Review*, *7*(1), 135–152. doi:10.14330/cwr.2021.7.1.06

Shi, X., Yao, S., & Ma, Y. (2022). When and how should cross-border platforms manage blockchain technology in the presence of purchasing agents? *Asia-Pacific Journal of Operational Research*, *39*(01), 2140020. doi:10.1142/S0217595921400200

Sodhi, M. S., & Tang, C. S. (2021). Supply chain management for extreme conditions: Research opportunities. *The Journal of Supply Chain Management*, *57*(1), 7–16. doi:10.1111/jscm.12255

Sternberg, H. S., Hofmann, E., & Roeck, D. (2021). The struggle is real: Insights from a supply chain blockchain case. *Journal of Business Logistics*, *42*(1), 71–87. doi:10.1111/jbl.12240

Tsiulin, S., Reinau, K. H., Hilmola, O. P., Goryaev, N., & Karam, A. (2020). Blockchain-based applications in shipping and port management: A literature review towards defining key conceptual frameworks. *Review of International Business and Strategy*, *30*(2), 201–224. doi:10.1108/RIBS-04-2019-0051

Upadhyay, A., Mukhuty, S., Kumar, V., & Kazancoglu, Y. (2021). Blockchain technology and the circular economy: Implications for sustainability and social responsibility. *Journal of Cleaner Production*, *293*, 126130. doi:10.1016/j.jclepro.2021.126130

Venkatesh, V. G., Kang, K., Wang, B., Zhong, R. Y., & Zhang, A. (2020). System architecture for blockchain based transparency of supply chain social sustainability. *Robotics and Computer-integrated Manufacturing*, *63*, 101896. doi:10.1016/j.rcim.2019.101896

Wang, S., Ding, W., Li, J., Yuan, Y., Ouyang, L., & Wang, F. Y. (2019). Decentralized autonomous organizations: Concept, model, and applications. *IEEE Transactions on Computational Social Systems*, *6*(5), 870–878. doi:10.1109/TCSS.2019.2938190

Zreik, M. (2022). The Regional Comprehensive Economic Partnership (RCEP) for the Asia–Pacific region and world. *Journal of Economic and Administrative Sciences*.

Zreik, M. (2023a). Analytical study on Foreign Direct Investment Divestment Inflows and Outflows in Developing Economies: Evidence of China. *Chinese Economy*, *56*(6), 415–430. doi:10.1080/10971475.2023.2193118

Zreik, M. (2023b). Sustainable and Smart Supply Chains in China: A Multidimensional Approach. In B. Bentalha, A. Hmioui, & L. Alla (Eds.), *Integrating Intelligence and Sustainability in Supply Chains* (pp. 179–197). IGI Global. doi:10.4018/979-8-3693-0225-5.ch010

Zreik, M., Iqbal, B. A., & Rahman, M. N. (2022). Outward FDI: determinants and flows in emerging economies: evidence from China. *China and WTO Review*, *8*(2), 385–402. doi:10.14330/cwr.2022.8.2.07

KEY TERMS AND DEFINITIONS

Blockchain Technology: A decentralized digital ledger system where transactions are recorded chronologically and publicly across a network of computers. It is known for its security, transparency, and immutability.

Cryptocurrency: A digital or virtual currency that uses cryptography for security and is typically based on blockchain technology. It is not controlled by any centralized authority, making it theoretically immune to government manipulation or interference.

Decentralization: The distribution of functions and powers away from a central location or authority. In the context of blockchain, it refers to the dispersal of data storage and decision-making across a network of computers.

Distributed Ledger Technology (DLT): A consensus of replicated, shared, and synchronized digital data geographically spread across multiple sites, countries, or institutions. Unlike traditional databases, DLT has no central data store or administration functionality.

Immutable Ledger: A ledger that is unchanging over time, one where records, once written, cannot be altered. This is a fundamental feature of blockchain technology, which ensures that transaction histories are permanently recorded.

Interoperability: The ability of different computer systems or software to exchange and make use of information. In blockchain, it refers to the capacity of different blockchain networks to communicate and transact with each other seamlessly.

Middleware: Software that acts as a bridge between an operating system or database and applications, especially on a network. For blockchain, middleware can facilitate the integration of blockchain technology with existing IT systems.

Regulatory Compliance: Adherence to laws, regulations, guidelines, and specifications relevant to an organization's business processes. In blockchain usage, it often refers to meeting legal standards in data management, financial transactions, and privacy.

Smart Contracts: Self-executing contracts with the terms of the agreement between buyer and seller directly written into lines of code. These contracts automatically enforce and execute the terms of an agreement based on predefined rules.

Supply Chain Management (SCM): The oversight of materials, information, and finances as they move from supplier to manufacturer to wholesaler to retailer to consumer. SCM involves coordinating and integrating these flows both within and among companies.

Chapter 4
Impact of Blockchain Technology on Transparency and Trust in Programmatic Advertising Supply Chain

Muhammad Ibrahim Khan
Iqra University, Karachi, Pakistan

ABSTRACT

The aim of this chapter is to evaluate previous research, reports, and opinions of marketing specialists regarding the issue of transparency and trust in the existing supply chain of programmatic advertising. Literature shows that blockchain technology holds significant potential for improving transparency and trust in the programmatic advertising supply chain. Previous research highlights its advantages in enhancing advertising processes, securing transactions, and addressing industry challenges. The collaboration of industry organizations and the practical implementation of blockchain technology further demonstrate its efficacy. By embracing blockchain, the advertising industry can overcome the limitations of the current supply chain and create a more transparent, secure, and efficient ecosystem.

INTRODUCTION

The advent of programmatic advertising has transformed the ad space buying and selling process, replacing manual interactions with automated systems. This shift has brought significant benefits to organizations, including cost and time savings, as well as a reduction in human error. However, the programmatic advertising industry continues to grapple with privacy and security challenges. Advertisers face the risk of fraudulent activities depleting their budgets, while publishers struggle with injected advertisements that generate no revenue and tarnish their reputation. Furthermore, consumers are increasingly concerned about security threats, such as malvertising, which exposes them to malware. Advertising fraud, commonly known as ad spam or ad fraud remains a prevalent issue in online advertising.

DOI: 10.4018/979-8-3693-0482-2.ch004

Nowadays, viewers may consume nearly any material produced and provided by the media at any time or place. The rapidly expanding use of mobile phones and the Internet has led to a rise in the adoption rate of virtual media (Truong, McColl, & Kitchen, 2010). Marketing executives now have more opportunities to leverage mobile phone-based interactions to establish consumer connections, advertise, and receive quick reactions from consumers (Andrews, Goehring, Hui, Pancras, & Thornswood e, 2016). For example, the advertising messages are delivered straight to customers' phones using mobile devices, negating the need for traditional delivery methods and enabling real-time consumer response.AI can assist in accurately targeting customers through programmatic advertising and the tailored content those results. According to the report, the majority of digital advertising operations are already being dominated by programmatic advertising. Advertisers benefit from this as they can target specific consumers (Klee, 2021).Programmatic advertising is now improving at a rate that cannot be understated. One of programmatic development's main goals is to employ technology to increase utility; in the era of full insight, this kind of advertising is worth expecting (Yan & Cao, 2021).

As today, advertising and marketing spending has involved in greater of applicable and reliable, automation technique of digital ads selling at the side of its powerful campaigning implementation has an essential function in helping to the web advertising this increase called "programmatic advertising." The programmatic advertising as converted the traditional technique of execution of ads, which might be worried in the advert inventory area, has normally used by the organization's publicity. Digital automation advertising has been a very critical tool, which creates green and powerful than manual systems. The sooner pattern of advertising and marketing observation process as seen progressively decline inside the marketing promotion technique and additionally has added less margin with extra fee for the ad companies within the field of commercial, which has forced the groups to undertake the innovative generation and structures for the competitive global. (Kiran & Arumugam, 2020).

Programmatic advertising has led to several advances. Among them are low-cost data storage, customization, marketing science, and quick data communication. The marketing industry now has more prospects because to these improvements. Using programmatic advertising strategies, all inventories may be optimized. The use of data-driven strategies boosts customer confidence in programmatic advertising strategies (cerezo, 2014).Innovations in technology has typically made firms and industries more competitive. The extent to which the benefits of technical breakthroughs are realized will depend on how often these technologies are employed (Mitropoulos & Tatum, 2000).

The programmatic advertising ecosystem is currently dealing with a number of significant issues, including the spread of fake news, data protection concerns, transparency and brand safety issues, advertising fraud, discriminatory practices, and the regulation of political advertising on platforms not covered by electoral law. These challenges impact publishers' revenue and the effectiveness of their advertising, and they could also have an impact on society as a whole (series, 2019).The programmatic advertising environment might be greatly enhanced by implementing smart contracts and tokenized assets (Spagnoletti & Terruli, 2021).

In light of the aforementioned challenges, there is a pressing need to explore the impact of blockchain technology on transparency and trust within the programmatic advertising supply chain. By leveraging the unique characteristics of blockchain, such as decentralization, immutability, and transparency, this research aims to uncover how blockchain can address the industry's challenges and revolutionize the programmatic advertising landscape. Specific research objectives are:

1. To assess the impact of blockchain technology on transparency and trust in the programmatic advertising supply chain.
2. To investigate how blockchain technology can address the challenges faced by the programmatic advertising industry, such as privacy, security, and ad fraud.
3. To explore the practical implications of implementing blockchain technology in programmatic advertising, including its potential to enhance contract transparency, prompt payment, and reduce bot activity and fraudulent traffic.

The programmatic advertising industry faces significant challenges related to ad fraud, transparency, trust, and data privacy. The integration of blockchain technology in this industry holds immense potential to address these challenges and revolutionize the way programmatic advertising operates. By exploring the impact of blockchain technology on transparency, trust-building, operational efficiency, and ad fraud mitigation, this study aims to provide valuable insights and practical implications for industry practitioners. Additionally, the study will identify the scope for future research, enabling stakeholders to take further steps towards maximizing the capabilities of blockchain in programmatic advertising.

METHODOLOGY

The primary goal of this extensive literature review is to analyze the body of research on how blockchain technology may enhance trust and transparency in the context of programmatic advertising. The review process followed PRISMA guidelines which provide a transparent and systematic approach to conduct literature review. Some major academic databases like Google Scholar, Pub Med, Semantic Scholar, IEEE Xplore, and Science Direct are searched with key words combinations like impact of blockchain technology on programmatic advertising, blockchain technology and marketing, and impact of blockchain technology on transparency and trust. To guarantee the quality and applicability of the chosen research, precise inclusion and exclusion standards are developed. Included are only peer-reviewed articles, conference papers, and pertinent grey literature that have been published within the last five to ten years. Excluded are studies that do not specifically address how blockchain affects transparency and trustworthiness. Total five databases were searched for collection of data. Five articles are found in duplicate out of 87 articles, reports and book chapters. 44 reports are excluded from record because of not matching with the objective of my study. 43 reports are sought for retrieval, out of which 22 are open access and downloaded and 21 were not retrieved because of we do not have access to these reports.

The results of the chosen research are analyzed and interpreted using a narrative synthesis approach. Some of the key findings from these studies are as follow

1. (Li et al., 2017) demonstrates how blockchain technology may increase marketing transparency through supply chain monitoring and verifiable advertising transactions using case studies and real-world examples. They also talks about the disadvantages of blockchain, such problems with scalability and user data protection, and stresses the need for standards and legal frameworks.
2. (Hammi et al., 2018) investigates the potential for blockchain technology's immutability, smart contracts, and decentralized consensus to foster trust among marketing stakeholders. They highlight the need of trust in marketing while also examining the possible benefits of blockchain in promoting trust.

3. (Demirkan, S. et al., 2020) draws attention to the potential applications and impacts of blockchain technology in marketing. The researchers highlight the potential benefits of blockchain technology for enhancing data security, transparency, and trust in marketing strategies. They also stress how crucial it is to conduct further research to see how blockchain technology may be used in various marketing domains.
4. (Yang, 2019) examines the benefits and challenges of using blockchain technology in marketing. He demonstrates how blockchain might enhance the transparency, reliability, and data security of marketing campaigns. Lu also highlights the information gaps and emphasizes the need for more study to thoroughly explore the application of blockchain in marketing.
5. (Viriyasitavat and Hoonsopon, 2019) investigates potential applications of blockchain technology in marketing. The researchers outline how blockchain technology might enhance data security, transparency, and trust in marketing strategies. They highlight the need for more study and advancement in this area while pointing out the challenges and limitations of blockchain technology in marketing.
6. (Khalid et al., 2023) recommended that marketing may benefit from the transparency, dependability, and data security that blockchain technology offers. Scalability, system integration, and the requirement for industry-wide standards should all be carefully considered. Establishing best practices and legal guidelines will enable the ethical and responsible use of blockchain technology in marketing. To fully exploit the benefits of blockchain technology in the marketing industry, cooperation between academic institutions, corporations, and the government is required.

   (Tan & Saraniemi, 2022) Gives some key findings from their study are as follow 1. Three distinct features of blockchain technology facilitate confidence in blockchain-enabled transactions: trust in exchange assets (digital escrows), trust in exchange actors (mathematics & encryption), and trust in exchange actions (information transparency). 2. By eliminating the requirement for a reliable third party, blockchain technology offers a new paradigm for economic coordination and governance in digital ecosystems. 3. Blockchain technology acts as a protector of institutionalized trust by symbolizing impersonal trust in transaction relationships. 4. A block chain's data is unchangeable and impenetrable, guaranteeing its integrity and thwarting illegal alterations. The consequences of these findings are significant for marketing researchers and practitioners, especially with regard to comprehending the increasing risks to customer trust, digital rights, privacy, and online advertising trust.

(Manzoor, Iqbal, & Baig, 2023)Blockchain has the ability to completely transform approaches to marketing by enabling more efficient marketing procedures, giving customers ownership over their data, and improving transaction security, transparency, and trust. Blockchain adoption and application in marketing is still in its infancy, thus a number of issues need to be resolved, including organizational preparedness, regulatory concerns, lack of understanding, and technological hurdles.

LITERATURE REVIEW

By tackling important issues with trust and transparency in the programmatic advertising supply chain, blockchain technology has the ability to completely transform the advertising sector. Prior research has emphasized how blockchain technology might enhance advertising procedures (Antoniadis & Kontsas,

2019). It provides improved transaction recording security and dependability along with an environment that is transparent and reliable (Ertemel, 2018). Moreover, blockchain reduces the need for middlemen like Amazon.com and AliExpress by facilitating true peer-to-peer exchange (Antoniadis & Kontsas, 2019). Transactions are streamlined and processing expenses are decreased by the tokenization of user reviews and the usage of designated currencies (Ghose, 2018).

There is a lack of transparency, compliance, and accurate measurement in the present media supply chain. PG's Chief Brand Officer, Marc Pritchard, brings attention to the supply chain's complexity, which reduces its efficacy and efficiency. But in order to solve these issues, IBM, MadHive, and TEGNA founded the non-profit Ad Ledger, which is tasked with creating standards and guidelines for the application of blockchain technology and cryptography in media and advertising (Ad Ledger, 2023). Ad Ledger focuses on raising industry transparency and accountability through research and partnerships with publishers, brands, agencies, and technology companies.

If we talk about the lean practices of adverting ecosystem so we will find ad fraud. Previous study sheds light on how well lean techniques work to enhance the operational performance of Pakistani manufacturing firms. Therefore, it is advised that businesses implement lean approaches in order to tackle the operational efficiency difficulty. By facilitating the implementation of these ideas in businesses, practitioners may be able to make better decisions by comprehending the connections between lean techniques and operational success (Haq, Khan, Parkash, & Jabeen, 2016). Technology always help human being to perform their job with efficiency and effectively. A study shows that in a highly dynamic company environment, RFID is thought to facilitate and encourage the development of a lean organization by having a substantial influence on operational operations. (Khan, Haq, Ghouri, Raziq, & Moiz, 2017).

Fake news, advertising fraud, and poor content creation are just a few of the major issues that the news business, digital advertising, and social media have to deal with. With its tamper-proofness, security, and decentralization, blockchain technology presents a fresh approach to solving these problems (Liu, Zhang, & Han, 2021). The advertising sector may overcome these obstacles and enhance overall operations by utilizing block chain's transparent and secure characteristics.

Blockchain technology has key components that solve important advertising problems. It guarantees security, trust, and transparency—all of which are essential for creating a stable advertising environment. According to Bezovski, Apasieva, and Temjanovski (2021) the application of blockchain technology can have an impact on a number of marketing domains, such as the creation of products and services, the assurance of trust and transparency, the elimination of middlemen, data privacy, customer retention programs, personalization, advertising, customer relationship management, click fraud prevention, income sharing models, and supply chain management. The decentralized and secure characteristics of blockchain technology will be advantageous to these fields.

Blockchain technology is already being used in advertising in a practical way. Blockchain company MetaX wants to use technology to address programmatic advertising's transparency and fraud problems. To identify dishonest affiliates and ad vendors along the programmatic supply chain, tools such as Ads.txt have been created (MetaX, n.d.). An over-the-top (OTT) advertising network called Premion and a technology firm called MadHive collaborated to create a blockchain-based OTT transaction platform. Using blockchain nodes, MadHive's decentralized MAD Network application aims to increase trust across all stakeholders in the advertising value chain (iab, 2018).

If we talk about the literature that what theories are supporting to adopt new technologies at organizational level we find supportive research work such as (Khan,N.R. et al., 2017) conducting a study which give empirical proof using technology, organizational structure, and environmental factors that affect technology adoption to support the Diffusion of Innovation (DOI) Theory and the TOE framework. Another research (Haq, M.A., et al., 2016) shows the support of programs theory. Programs theory is linked with the system, organization input and outputs.

In conclusion, blockchain technology holds significant potential for improving transparency and trust in the programmatic advertising supply chain. Previous research highlights its advantages in enhancing advertising processes, securing transactions, and addressing industry challenges. The collaboration of industry organizations and the practical implementation of blockchain technology further demonstrate its efficacy. By embracing blockchain, the advertising industry can overcome the limitations of the current supply chain and create a more transparent, secure, and efficient ecosystem.

Numerous research gaps in the area of blockchain technology in programmatic advertising are highlighted by this synthesis of the literature. A lack of understanding of industry adoption and challenges, a lack of empirical research on practical implementation and outcomes, a need to evaluate effectiveness and performance, a lack of exploration into user perception and acceptance, a lack of research on ethical and legal issues, and a lack of attention to long-term sustainability and scalability are some of the gaps. Filling in these research voids will yield insightful information and expand our understanding of how to use blockchain technology to increase trust and transparency in the supply chain for programmatic advertising.

Gap in Literature

The scholars of advertising field have been focusing on this arising trend, systematic research is still in its outset and there are numerous unexplored research domains (Helberger, Huh, Milne, Strycharz, & Sundaram, 2020).

Association of National Advertisers all over the world believes that the digital industry has arrived at an impasse where there is no transparency, an absence of quantifiability, unviewable promotion impressions and even ad fraud. Because of these variables and an absence of assurance to go digital advertisers are putting their clients off from following them into the advanced world(Sluis, 2015).However, clients would simply prefer not to see evidence of execution. Online advertising is additionally dependent upon the essential monetary standard by which steady effectiveness gains are expected to help efficiency and importance.

Digital marketing fraud prevention and loyalty programs are still relatively uncommon applications of blockchain technology (Stallone, Wetzels, & Klaas, 2021).

Programmatic Advertising History

Programmatic advertising is started with its debut as the Wired.com Banner in 1994.

The first ad servers were developed in 1996 to satisfy advertisers' excessive need for internet banner placement. The earliest ad server was probably DoubleClick, and it still provides advertising today. The said company was purchased by Google in 2007 for $ 1.3 billion.

Brands may now run advertisements across a wide range of websites and channels. Many more ad servers have been introduced afterwards, but notable ad networks that debuted before 2000 include 24/7 open Ad Stream, Advertising.com, Value Click, and Zedo.

Google launched its display advertising network, AdSense, in 2013. The Google Display Network (GDN) was restricted to Google/DoubleClick properties and accessible through Ad Words.

Demographic information, search terms, and fundamental behavioral targeting are used to construct targeted segments. The GDN software interprets the content on the webpage when Google crawls websites and when an impression is made. Relevant advertisements are then delivered once this is compared to the segment data. Programmatic is putting an increasing amount of emphasis on behavioral targeting and enhanced lead qualifying. Along with the development of AI, big data, and precise audience segmentation, I believe that the amount of data available to DSPs to bid for impressions will expand, making the ad experience nearly personal.(Schmid, 2017).

PROGRAMMATIC ADVERTISING

Data driven computational advertising is quickly extending and constraining key changes in the practices of advertising, advertising research and theory building. The advance advertising ecosystem is highly complex and involves multiple stakeholders(Helberger, Huh, Milne, Strycharz, & Sundaram, 2020).As today, advertising and marketing spending has involved in greater of applicable and reliable, automation technique of digital ads selling at the side of its powerful campaigning implementation has an essential function in helping to the web advertising this increase called "programmatic advertising." The programmatic advertising as converted the traditional technique of execution of ads, which might be worried in the advert inventory area, has normally used by organization's publicity. The digital automation advertising has been very critical tool, which creates green and powerful than manual system. The sooner pattern of advertising and marketing observation process as seen progressively decline inside the marketing promotion technique and additionally has added less margin with extra fee for the ad companies within the field of commercial which has forced the groups to undertake the innovative generation and structures for the competitive global. (Kiran & Arumugam, 2020).

The continuous increase of digital media technologies and smart phones, on-line marketing has ended up extra customized and engagement oriented. The trend in virtual advertising gadget has converted the advertising organizations to expand a system, which can assist in automation of commercials. Moreover, with the entry of exponential improvised and advance systems, this area is getting more innovative, aggressive and difficult (AdExchanger, 2015). This transformation may be seeing within the region of modern-day media after introduction the advertising automation. Virtual automation technology is one type supply for computerized system (programmed using machines and algorithms) for getting advert space in actual time.

One of the maximum essential advert networks was DoubleClick. Based in 1995, the company has been on the middle of the media attention numerous times, most substantially for having merged with Abacus Direct, an offline database of purchasers amidst fear of privateer's breach, for have been investigated by using The Federal change commission and for having been offered by means of Google in 2007. DoubleClick additionally implemented the first automatic model of advert serving generation with its DART (Dynamic advertising and marketing Reporting & focused on) a software which automated the advert buying technique for advertisers and minimized unsold stock for publishers. Ad serving technology is a vital building block of today's media buying and making plans. The fundamental functionalities of advert serving technology steadily evolved to reply to the need of publishers that wanted to sell the same advert slot to multiple marketers. At the start, advert serving changed into made of pieces of codes that rotated specific creative (the content material of an advert) into a single advert slot on a writer's web page. This accompanied by using the improvement of a hard and fast of metrics to optimize the ad shipping. A rating gadget called waterfall turned around the exclusive creative on the idea of a number of pre-set desires and performance metrics that related to person click on, publish-click on and post-affect activities and interactions. The statistics from these fundamental functionalities have been gradually incorporate into more state-of-the-art versions of serving era like the DART device that changed into able to help choice making in a more and more automatic way. The device ultimately integrated with Google DoubleClick ad exchange, the centralized marketplace of programmatic advertising surroundings (Alaimo & Kallinikos, 2018).

Programmatic Direct

Programmatic direct is a part of programmatic advertising that includes an immediate arrangement between advertisers and publishers, without including trade parties. In programmatic direct advertisers approach publishers directly to purchase ad space. The main advantage of programmatic direct is that advertiser can show ad on a publishers top pages, guaranteeing the best target audience reach, however do as such without physically designing the advertisements. With programmatic direct, advertisers and publishers can likewise negotiate on a decent CPM rate(Publift, 2023).

Programmatic direct deals can be classified into one of two kinds:

Preferred: This is balanced exchanging where the cost is indicated, and volume isn't fixed.
Programmatic Guaranteed: It comprises of balanced exchanging where the cost is indicated and the volumes are ensured.

Benefits/advantages of Programmatic Advertising

Numerous innovations have come from programmatic advertising. Fast data connectivity, marketing science, personalization, and low-cost data storage are a few of them. These changes have given the marketing sector new opportunities. The use of programmatic advertising techniques can optimize all inventories. Data-based techniques increase consumer trust in programmatic advertising practices (cerezo, 2014).

The competitive position of businesses and sectors has generally been improved by technological advancements. The amount to which these technologies are used will determine how much the advantages of technological advancements are realized (Mitropoulos & Tatum, 2000).

Disadvantages Challenges in Programmatic Advertising

Companies have been compelled to leave automation application in a number of instances as their advertisements were shown next to those of business competitors. This demonstrates the increased requirement for security and consideration for marketers that use programmatic advertising tools. Due to their lack of technical expertise of the program, which is beyond their comprehension, marketers may find this situation to be more challenging (Gertz & McGlashan, 2016).

Advertiser: advertisers are those who want to buy advertising space on internet.
Publisher: publishers are those want to sell adverting space on internet.

BLOCKCHAIN

Blockchain are alter obvious and alter safe computerized records carried out in a conveyed design (i.e., without a focal store) and generally without a focal power (i.e., a bank, organization, or government). At their fundamental level, they empower a local area of clients to keep exchanges in a common record inside that local area, to such an extent that under typical activity of the blockchain network no transaction can be changed once distributed. In 2008, the blockchain thought was joined with a few different advancements and processing ideas to make present day digital currencies: electronic money safeguarded through cryptographic systems rather than a focal authority. The first such blockchain based cryptographic money was Bit coin (Yaga, Roby, & Scarfone, 2018).

Smart Contracts

Smart contracts, a vital part of blockchain technology, are self-executing contracts with the details of the understanding straightforwardly composed into code. They work with, confirm, and uphold the discussion or execution of an agreement, eliminating the requirement for an outsider middle person. Quite possibly of the main way smart contracts are reforming advertising transactions is by improving transparency. With smart contracts, each transaction is recorded on a public ledger, furnishing advertisers with a reasonable perspective on where their cash is going. This degree of transparency is uncommon in the advertising business and is set to rethink trust among advertisers and publishers. Besides, smart contracts achieve expanded proficiency in advertising transactions. The mechanization of agreement execution decreases the time taken to handle transactions. Furthermore, the disposal of mediators prompts cost savings (Frackiewicz, 2023).

Projects and Software Already Used in Industry

The SaTT " Smart Advertisement Transition Token" solution wants to utilize the decentralized blockchain capabilities to unfathomably further develop the manner in which the digital advertising industry works today, and mechanizing transaction with smart contracts in a dispersed blockchain ledger could decrease costs, speedup exchange process, prevent fraud, and empower better and more precise observing of campaigns(Benshahar, 2021).

New opportunities for advertisers:

Blockchain has the potential to support programmatic media buying by enhancing programmatic technology. By making digital transactions more transparent, secure, reliable and effective all significant features for advertisers who need to run campaigns programmatically blockchain can offer exciting opportunities for those hoping to take on programmatic media buying(Butterworth, 2022).

CHALLENGES IN DIGITAL ADVERTING

Privacy Issue

According to Pixalate's evaluations show that 22% of App Store applications and 9% of Google Play Store applications that serve programmatic advertising don't have a privacy policy. This is huge on the grounds that generally archived instances of customer data are being abused as a component of ad fraud schemes (Pixalate, 2021). According to MINDK report there are multiple challenges for the current era of advertising like identity and privacy limitations, imminent, risk of ad fraud, measuring return on ad spend, ad creativity and lack of ad view ability (MINDK). Another report also tell almost the same challenges like ad fraud, lack of knowledge, inventory quality, ad creativity, brand safety(Bannerflow).

Ad Fraud

By definition, ad fraud is related with an activity where clicks, impressions, and actions are reported falsely for the purpose of earning and deception which is unethical. The purposes of ad fraud activities are not only to generate revenue but other non-revenue generating activities like noise creation are more common now days.

There are four kinds of ad fraud scheme

1. Impression fraud
2. Click fraud
3. Conversion fraud
4. Data fraud

In every one of these cases, detailing approves a visitor to be genuine, however it is really fake, these deceitful visitors can be totally mechanical, human or a blend of both(Kotila, Rumin, & Dhar, 2016).

Ad fraud is one of the major challenges in digital advertising now days. And everyone is familiar with it. However, few will take care of business. By 2026, according to the most recent estimates, global programmatic advertising spending will reach $726 billion. Over $490 billion was spent in 2022.Statista estimates that ad fraud will cost $81 billion in the United States alone in 2022, which is more than 30% of the total; spend on programmatic advertising that year(Tiago, 2023) It was assessed that the costs connected with digital advertising fraud all over the world increase dramatically within the four years between 2018 and 2023, from 35 billion to 100 billion U.S. dollars(statista, 2023).

REFERENCES

AdExchanger. (2015). *Defining Viewability: 'The Opportunity To Be Seen Can't Tell You If An Ad Worked Or Not'.* AdExchanger.

Alaimo, C., & Kallinikos, J. (2018). *Objects, Metrics and Practices: An Inquiry into the Programmatic Advertising Ecosystem.* Research Gate.

Andrews, M., Goehring, J., Hui, S., Pancras, J., & Thornswood, L. (2016). Mobile Promotions: A Framework and Research Priorities. *Journal of Interactive Marketing*, *34*, 15–24. doi:10.1016/j.intmar.2016.03.004

Antoniadis, I., & Kontsas, S. (2019). Blockchain Applications in Marketing. *7th International Conference on Contemporary Marketing*. Heraklion: ResearchGate.

Bannerflow. *The Challenges of Programmatic Advertising*.

Benshahar, A. (2021). *Bringing Smart Contracts To The Digital Advertising Industry- SaTT Review*. CryptoPotato.

Bezovski, Z., Apasieva, T. J., & Temjanovski, R. (2021). The Impact and the Potential Disruption of the Blockchain Technology on Marketing. *Journal of Economics*, *6*(1), 13–23. doi:10.46763/JOE216.10013b

Butterworth, P. (2022). *The Potential of Blockchain in Adtech and Programmatic – for advertisers*. Adwatch.

cerezo, p. (2014). *The media and the challenge of programmatic transformation*. IAB.

Chen, W., Shi, Z. X., & Zhao, Y. Z. (2018). A Survey of Blockchain Applications in Different Domains. Association for Computing Machinery, 17-21.

Chua, M. Y., Yee, G. O., Gu, Y. X., & Lung, C. H. (2020). Threats to Online Advertising and Countermeasures: A Technical Survey. *Digital Threats: Research and Practice*, 11.1-11.27.

Demirkan, S., Demirkan, I., & McKeec, A. (2020). Blockchain technology in the future of business cyber security and accounting. *Journal of Management Analytics*, 1-20.

Ertemel, A. V. (2018). Implications of Blockchain Technology on Marketing. *Journal of International Trade, Logistics and Law*, 35-44.

Frackiewicz, M. (2023). *The Role of Smart Contracts in Revolutionizing Advertising Transactions*. TS2.

Gertz, O., & McGlashan, D. (2016). Consumer-Centric Programmatic advertising. In Programmatic Advertising, Management for Professionals, (pp. 55-74). Springer. doi:10.1007/978-3-319-25023-6_5

Ghose, A. (2018). What Blockchain Could Mean for Marketing. *Harvard Business Review*.

Hammi, M. T., Hammi, B., Bellot, P., & Serhrouchni, A. (2018). Bubbles of Trust: A decentralized Blockchain-based authentication system for IoT. *Computers & Security*, *78*, 126–142. doi:10.1016/j.cose.2018.06.004

Haq, M. A., Khan, N. R., Parkash, R., & Jabeen, A. (2016). *Impact of JIT*. Waste Minimization, and Flow Management on Operational Performance of Manufacturing Companies in Pakistan.

Helberger, N., Huh, J., Milne, G., Strycharz, J., & Sundaram, H. (2020). Macro and Exogenous Factors in Computational Advertising: Key Issuesand New Research Directions. *Journal of Advertising*, 377-393.
iab. (2018). *Blockchain for Video Advertising:A Market Snapshot of Publisher and Buyer Use Cases*. Interactive Advertising Bureau.

Khalid, M. S., Upadhyay, A. K., Saxena, S., Yamang, C., & Bansa, S. (2023). BlockChain Technology in Marketing: A Systematic Review of its Potential for Transparency, Trust, and Data Security. *China Petroleum Processing and Petrochemical Technology*, 1882–1893.

Khan, N. R., Haq, M. A., Ghouri, A. M., Raziq, A., & Moiz, S. M. (2017). *Adaptation of RFID Technology in Business Supply Chain Success:Empirical Findings from a Developing Country Logistic Industry*. Calitatea.

Kiran, K. U., & Arumugam, T. (2020). Role of programmatic advertising on effective digital promotion strategy: A conceptual framework. *Journal of Physics: Conference Series*, 1–10.

Klee, C. (2021). AI in Marketing – Curse or Blessing? *Impacts of Programmatic Advertising and Personalized Content on Society.*

Kotila, M., Rumin, R. C., & Dhar, S. (2016). *Compendium of ad fraud knowledge for media investors.* World Federation of Advertisers.

Li, J., Liang, G., & Liu, T. (2017). A Novel Multi-link Integrated Factor Algorithm Considering Node Trust Degree for Blockchain-based Communication. *KSII Transactions on Internet and Information Systems*, 3766–3787.

Liu, L., Zhang, W., & Han, C. (2021). A survey for the application of blockchain technology in the media. *Peer-to-Peer Networking and Applications*, *14*(5), 3143–3165. doi:10.100712083-021-01168-5

Manzoor, U., Iqbal, M. S., & Baig, S. A. (2023). Blockchain Technology in Marketing: Potential Applications and Implications. *Perspective in Management and Society*, 12-23.

Mitropoulos, P., & Tatum, C. B. (2000). Forces Driving Adoption Of New Information Technologies. *journal of construction engineering and management*, 340-348.

Pixalate. (2021). *Navigating ad fraud and consumer privacy abuse in programmatic advertising.* TechCrunch.

Publift. (2023). *A Complete Guide to Programmatic Direct.* Publift.

Schmid, D. (2017). *The History of Programmatic Advertising: Everything You Need to Know.*

Sluis, S. (2015). *Procter & Gamble CMO Pritchard: Programmatic Delivers Business Lift.* ad Exchanger.

Spagnoletti, P., & Terruli, V. (2021). *The application of blockchain technology in the programmatic advertisement ecosystem.*

Stallone, V., Wetzels, M., & Klaas, M. (2021). *Applications of Blockchain Technology in marketing—A systematic review of marketing technology companies. Blockchain: Research and Applications, 1-9. statista. (2023). Estimated cost of digital ad fraud worldwide from 2018 to 2023.* Statista Research Department. doi:10.1016/j.bcra.2021.100023

Tan, T. M., & Saraniemi, S. (2022). Trust in blockchain-enabled exchanges: Future directions in blockchain marketing. *Journal of the Academy of Marketing Science.*

Terruli, V., & Spagnoletti, P. (2021). *The application of blockchain technology in the programmatic advertisement ecosystem.*

Tiago, J. (2023). *Why blockchain is the key to sustainable advertising and customer acquisition.* Open Mic.

Truong, Y., McColl, R., & Kitchen, P. (2010). Practitioners' perceptionsof advertising strategies for digital media. *International Journal of Advertising, 29*(5), 709–725. doi:10.2501/S0265048710201439

Viriyasitavat, W., & Hoonsopon, D. (2019). Blockchain characteristics and consensus in modern. *Journal of Industrial Information Integration, 13*, 32–39. doi:10.1016/j.jii.2018.07.004

Yaga, D., Roby, N., & Scarfone, K. (2018). *Blockchain Technology Overview*. National Institute of Standards and Technology. doi:10.6028/NIST.IR.8202

Yan, Y., & Cao, S. (2021). A Study on Data Monitoring and Effect Optimization of Programmed Advertising Platform: Taking "Ocean Engine" as an Example. *Journal of Physics: Conference Series, 1883*(1), 1–5. doi:10.1088/1742-6596/1883/1/012170

Yang, L. (2019). The blockchain: State-of-the-art and research challenges. *Journal of Industrial Information Integration*, 80–90.

Chapter 5
Security and Privacy Challenges in Blockchain-Based Supply Chain Management: A Comprehensive Analysis

Tarun Kumar Vashishth
https://orcid.org/0000-0001-9916-9575
IIMT University, India

Vikas Sharma
https://orcid.org/0000-0001-8173-4548
IIMT University, India

Kewal Krishan Sharma
https://orcid.org/0009-0001-2504-9607
IIMT University, India

Bhupendra Kumar
IIMT University, India

Sachin Chaudhary
https://orcid.org/0000-0002-8415-0043
IIMT University, India

Rajneesh Panwar
https://orcid.org/0009-0000-5974-191X
IIMT University, India

ABSTRACT

Blockchain technology has gained significant attention for its potential to enhance transparency, trust, and efficiency in supply chain operations. However, the adoption of blockchain in supply chains also introduces various security and privacy concerns that need to be addressed to ensure the integrity and confidentiality of sensitive information. This chapter examines these challenges, explores their implications, and discusses potential solutions to mitigate risks. The chapter begins by identifying the key security challenges associated with blockchain-based supply chain management. It delves into issues such as data tampering, malicious attacks on the blockchain network, vulnerabilities in smart contracts, and the risk of unauthorized access to sensitive supply chain data. Moreover, it highlights the privacy challenges, including the exposure of personally identifiable information (PII), the potential for data leakage, and the difficulty in achieving selective disclosure of information in a transparent blockchain environment.

DOI: 10.4018/979-8-3693-0482-2.ch005

INTRODUCTION

The global landscape of supply chain management is undergoing a profound transformation with the advent of blockchain technology. As organizations strive for enhanced transparency, traceability, and efficiency in their supply chain operations, blockchain presents itself as a promising solution. The inherent attributes of immutability, decentralization, and transparency make blockchain an ideal candidate for revolutionizing supply chain management. However, while blockchain holds immense potential, it also introduces a complex array of security and privacy challenges that demand comprehensive analysis and mitigation.

Background and Context of Blockchain Technology in Supply Chain Management

Supply chain management has long been a cornerstone of modern commerce, encompassing the complex networks of suppliers, manufacturers, distributors, retailers, and customers that collaborate to deliver goods and services to the market. However, this intricate web of interactions often faces challenges such as opacity, inefficiency, lack of transparency, and trust issues. In this context, blockchain technology has emerged as a transformative solution that holds the potential to reshape the landscape of supply chain management.

Blockchain technology, initially popularized by its association with cryptocurrencies like Bitcoin, introduces a novel approach to data management and transaction recording. At its core, blockchain is a distributed, decentralized, and immutable digital ledger that records transactions in a transparent and tamper-resistant manner. Each transaction, or "block," is linked to the previous one, creating a "chain" of information. This architecture ensures that once data is added to the blockchain, it cannot be altered or erased without the consensus of the network participants.

Blockchain offers several key advantages that align with the needs of modern supply chains:

Transparency and Traceability: Blockchain provides an immutable and transparent record of every transaction and movement within the supply chain. This enables real-time tracking of goods, ensuring transparency and traceability at each stage.

Reduced Intermediaries: By creating a decentralized and trusted network, blockchain reduces the need for intermediaries in supply chain processes. This streamlines processes, minimizes delays, and lowers costs.

Enhanced Security: Blockchain's cryptographic nature ensures data integrity and security. Once data is recorded, it is cryptographically linked to the previous block, making it virtually impossible to alter without consensus.

Smart Contracts: Smart contracts are self-executing contracts with the terms directly written into code. They automate and enforce contractual agreements, enabling automatic actions when predefined conditions are met.

Efficient Documentation: Traditional supply chains involve a plethora of documentation. Blockchain streamlines this process by digitizing and securely storing documents, reducing the risk of loss or manipulation.

Trust and Collaboration: Blockchain's consensus mechanism fosters trust among participants by ensuring that all parties agree on the accuracy of data. This collaborative environment encourages cooperation and reduces disputes.

Figure 1. Blockchain technology into supply chain management

Counterfeit Prevention: Blockchain can be employed to track the authenticity and provenance of products, preventing counterfeiting and ensuring the quality of goods.

The background and context of blockchain technology in supply chain management reflect a paradigm shift towards transparency, efficiency, and trust. As organizations across industries recognize the potential of blockchain to reshape traditional supply chain models, a deeper exploration of the benefits, challenges, and real-world applications becomes imperative. The subsequent sections of this chapter will delve into the security and privacy challenges that arise in this transformative landscape, offering insights into maintaining the integrity of blockchain-based supply chains.

Significance of Addressing Security and Privacy Challenges

The integration of blockchain technology into supply chain management holds the promise of revolutionizing traditional processes, enhancing transparency, and fostering trust among stakeholders. However, as this technology becomes more prevalent in supply chains, it brings with it a host of security and privacy challenges that must be diligently addressed. The significance of tackling these challenges cannot be overstated, as the successful implementation of blockchain-based supply chain management relies on maintaining the integrity of data, ensuring confidentiality, and safeguarding against malicious threats.

Data Integrity and Transparency: One of the key benefits of blockchain is its immutability, ensuring that once data is recorded, it cannot be altered without consensus. Any compromise to this integrity would erode the foundation of trust that blockchain aims to establish. Addressing security challenges ensures that the data recorded on the blockchain remains accurate and un tampered, upholding the promise of transparency throughout the supply chain.

Trust and Reliability: The adoption of blockchain is often driven by the need to enhance trust among supply chain participants. Security breaches or privacy breaches can shatter this trust, leading to scepticism about the reliability of the technology. Ensuring the security of blockchain-based supply chains bolsters confidence among stakeholders, encouraging wider adoption and collaboration.

Counteracting Malicious Activities: Blockchain networks are not immune to attacks, and supply chains are vulnerable to threats such as Distributed Denial of Service (DDoS) attacks, smart contract vulnerabilities, and consensus protocol breaches. Addressing these challenges is crucial to prevent malicious actors from exploiting vulnerabilities, which could lead to disruptions, financial losses, and reputational damage.

Figure 2. Security and privacy challenges in blockchain-based supply chain management

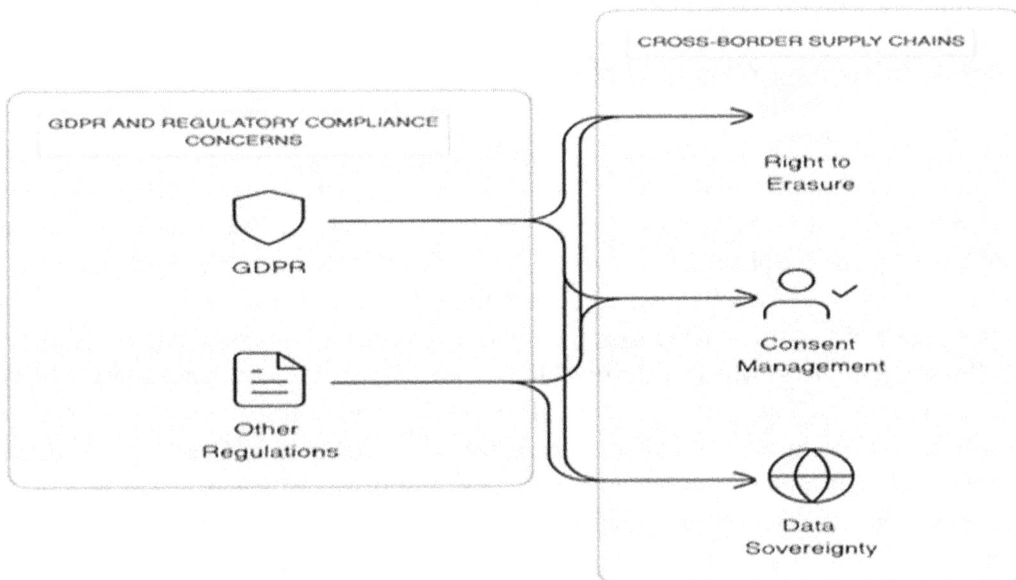

Data Privacy and Compliance: Privacy is a paramount concern in the digital age, and blockchain introduces unique challenges due to its transparent nature. Ensuring data privacy while maintaining the benefits of transparency is a delicate balancing act. Privacy breaches could lead to legal and regulatory repercussions, making it imperative to implement robust privacy measures.

Business Continuity and Resilience: Supply chains are critical to business continuity, and any disruption can have far-reaching consequences. Cybersecurity breaches could lead to disruptions in operations, financial losses, and delays. Addressing security challenges ensures the resilience of blockchain-based supply chains, mitigating the risk of disruptions.

Long-Term Viability and Adoption: The success of blockchain-based supply chain management relies on its long-term viability. Addressing security and privacy challenges early in the implementation phase contributes to building a sustainable and future-proof framework. Failure to address these challenges could result in the abandonment of blockchain solutions due to unforeseen complications.

Competitive Advantage: Organizations that proactively address security and privacy challenges position themselves as leaders in adopting innovative solutions. Demonstrating a commitment to protecting data and ensuring the security of supply chain operations can confer a competitive advantage and enhance brand reputation.

Stakeholder Confidence: Supply chains often involve multiple stakeholders, including suppliers, manufacturers, distributors, and customers. Demonstrating a robust approach to security and privacy instills confidence among these stakeholders, fostering better collaboration and partnership.

The significance of addressing security and privacy challenges in blockchain-based supply chain management is paramount to harnessing the transformative potential of the technology. By ensuring the integrity of data, protecting against malicious threats, and upholding privacy standards, organizations can unlock the full benefits of blockchain while establishing trust and reliability in their supply chain operations. The subsequent sections of this chapter will delve into a comprehensive analysis of the security and privacy challenges that emerge within the context of blockchain-based supply chain management.

Objectives and Scope of the Chapter

The primary objectives of this chapter are to comprehensively analyze the security and privacy challenges inherent in blockchain-based supply chain management and to provide insights into effective strategies for addressing these challenges. The chapter aims to offer a comprehensive understanding of the intricate landscape where blockchain intersects with supply chains, security, and privacy concerns. To achieve these objectives, the following scope is outlined:

In-depth Analysis of Security Challenges: The chapter will delve into a detailed examination of the security challenges that emerge when integrating blockchain into supply chain management. This analysis will encompass threats such as smart contract vulnerabilities, consensus protocol attacks, Distributed Denial of Service (DDoS) threats, and identity management challenges. Real-world examples and case studies will be used to illustrate the potential consequences of these challenges.

Discussion of Countermeasures and Solutions: A significant portion of the chapter will be dedicated to discussing viable countermeasures and solutions to address the security and privacy challenges identified earlier. The focus will be on both preventive and corrective measures, encompassing techniques such as smart contract auditing, consensus mechanism enhancements, encryption methodologies, and privacy-preserving techniques.

Real-world Case Studies: The chapter will present real-world case studies that illustrate instances of security breaches and privacy incidents in the context of blockchain-based supply chains. These case studies will provide practical insights into the potential ramifications of inadequate security measures and offer lessons learned for future implementations.

Regulatory and Compliance Considerations: The chapter will examine the regulatory and compliance landscape within which blockchain-based supply chain management operates. It will explore implications related to regulations such as GDPR, industry-specific compliance requirements and the ethical considerations tied to security and privacy.

Future Trends and Directions: The chapter will conclude by offering insights into the future trends and directions of blockchain-based supply chain security and privacy. This section will highlight advancements in consensus mechanisms, encryption techniques, and the integration of artificial intelligence for anomaly detection.

The scope of this chapter encompasses the comprehensive analysis of security and privacy challenges in the context of blockchain-based supply chain management. It aims to provide a holistic understanding of the multifaceted issues that arise and to equip readers with valuable insights into safeguarding the integrity of data and transactions while navigating the complexities of a rapidly evolving landscape. By addressing these challenges proactively, organizations can harness the transformative benefits of blockchain technology while ensuring the security and privacy of their supply chain operations.

LITERATURE REVIEW

Alzahrani & Bulusu (2018) introduce the concept of the block-supply chain, a decentralized supply chain paradigm leveraging blockchain and Near Field Communication (NFC) technologies to detect counterfeiting attacks. The proposed consensus protocol is unique in its full decentralization and effective balance between efficiency and security, redefining the conventional centralized supply chain design.

Biswas et al. (2017) present a novel blockchain-based solution for enhancing wine supply chain traceability, ensuring the immutability of recorded transactions within the chain while providing visibility to pertinent participants.

El Azzaoui et al. (2022) suggest enhancing security and privacy in critical systems like smart healthcare supply chain communication networks through the integration of Blockchain, smart contracts, and information hiding techniques.

Khan, Khan, and Nallaluthan's (2023) exploration of blockchain supply chain management and supply chain sustainability, while innovative, lacks a comprehensive exploration of the potential challenges and complexities in implementing blockchain technology in diverse supply chain environments.

Kishnani et al. (2023) conducted a classification of articles based on their alignment with different phases of the supply chain: upstream, midstream, downstream, and data management. Their analysis highlights the limited practical adoption of blockchain integration in oil and gas operations, despite its potential to enhance security and privacy within the supply chain.

Korpela et al. (2017) delve into the investigation of supply chain integration requisites and functionalities. They examine how cloud integration can present a cost-effective avenue for interoperable digital supply chains, further explaining how blockchain technology's integration can potentially bring about transformative changes in digital supply chains and networks.

Kumar et al. (2020) provide enterprises with a structured approach to comprehending the actual expenses and vulnerabilities associated with blockchain implementation. The insights garnered within the supply chain management context are applicable to diverse sectors like financial services and healthcare, where blockchain's potential can be fully harnessed.

Min (2010) investigates the suitability of diverse sub-fields of AI for addressing practical issues within supply chain management.

Mohanta et al. (2019) addresses challenges pertaining to the implementation of Blockchain technology and its interconnected security and privacy concerns.

Omar et al.'s (2020) study on enhancing vendor managed inventory supply chain operations using blockchain smart contracts, while technically sound, lacks a thorough discussion on the potential tradeoffs between the security benefits of blockchain and the complexity and cost of its implementation.

Tian et al. (2017) outline the creation of a real-time food tracing system within the food supply chain, integrating HACCP, blockchain, and the Internet of Things. This system aims to establish an information platform characterized by openness, transparency, neutrality, reliability, and security for all supply chain participants.

Toyoda et al. (2017) explore the concept of utilizing Bitcoin's blockchain principle of verifying balance ownership. Through their proposed Proof of Ownership Management System (POMS), customers can reject counterfeit purchases even if sellers possess authentic RFID tag information but lack ownership verification. Their work includes the implementation of a proof-of-concept experimental system on the Ethereum blockchain platform, with subsequent cost performance evaluation.

Tse et al. (2017) present the concept of Blockchain technology, discussing its application in enhancing information security within the food supply chain. The study contrasts this approach with the conventional supply chain system.

Uddin et al.'s (2023) case study on exploitation in the Bangladeshi ready-made garments supply chain, while revealing, lacks a comprehensive exploration of potential solutions and strategies for improving working conditions and promoting responsible capitalism in this industry.

Wen et al. (2023) offer an extensive overview and analysis of privacy protection, security supervision, and data exchange within blockchain-based applications. Their work provides a comprehensive analysis of the broad spectrum of blockchain's applications.

Wu et al. (2019) presents an exhaustive analysis encompassing the potential opportunities, emerging requisites, and fundamental design principles of Blockchain-integrated supply chain management (SCM) systems. The paper extensively outlines and deliberates upon four critical technical hurdles related to scalability, throughput, access control, and data retrieval, subsequently reviewing promising solutions in each aspect.

Yousuf and Svetinovic (2019) provide a conceptual overview of the intersections between blockchain and supply chain management, offering insights to guide future research and development endeavours.

Zyskind and Nathan (2015) present a decentralized personal data management system that empowers users with ownership and control over their data. They devise a protocol that transforms a blockchain into an automated access-control manager, eliminating the need for third-party trust. Unlike Bitcoin, their system's transactions encompass instructions beyond financial aspects, encompassing functions like data storage, querying, and sharing.

FUNDAMENTALS OF BLOCKCHAIN TECHNOLOGY IN SUPPLY CHAIN MANAGEMENT

Overview of Blockchain Technology and Its Features

Blockchain technology, originally introduced as the backbone of cryptocurrencies like Bitcoin, has evolved into a versatile tool with far-reaching applications across various industries, including supply chain management. At its core, blockchain is a decentralized and immutable digital ledger that records transactions in a secure, transparent, and tamper-resistant manner. This section provides an overview of the fundamental aspects of blockchain technology and its defining features.

Decentralization: Unlike traditional centralized databases, blockchain operates in a decentralized manner. Transactions are verified and recorded across a network of nodes, eliminating the need for a single controlling entity.

Immutability: Once data is recorded on the blockchain, it becomes nearly impossible to alter or delete without consensus from the network participants. This feature ensures the integrity and permanence of recorded information.

Transparency: Blockchain's transparent nature allows all participants in the network to view the same data in real-time. This transparency fosters trust among stakeholders and promotes accountability.

Security through Cryptography: Blockchain employs cryptographic techniques to secure transactions and data. Each transaction is encrypted and linked to the previous one, forming a chain of interconnected blocks.

Consensus Mechanisms: To validate transactions and maintain the integrity of the ledger, blockchain networks utilize consensus mechanisms. These mechanisms ensure that all network participants agree on the validity of transactions.

Figure 3. Block diagram of blockchain-based supply chain management

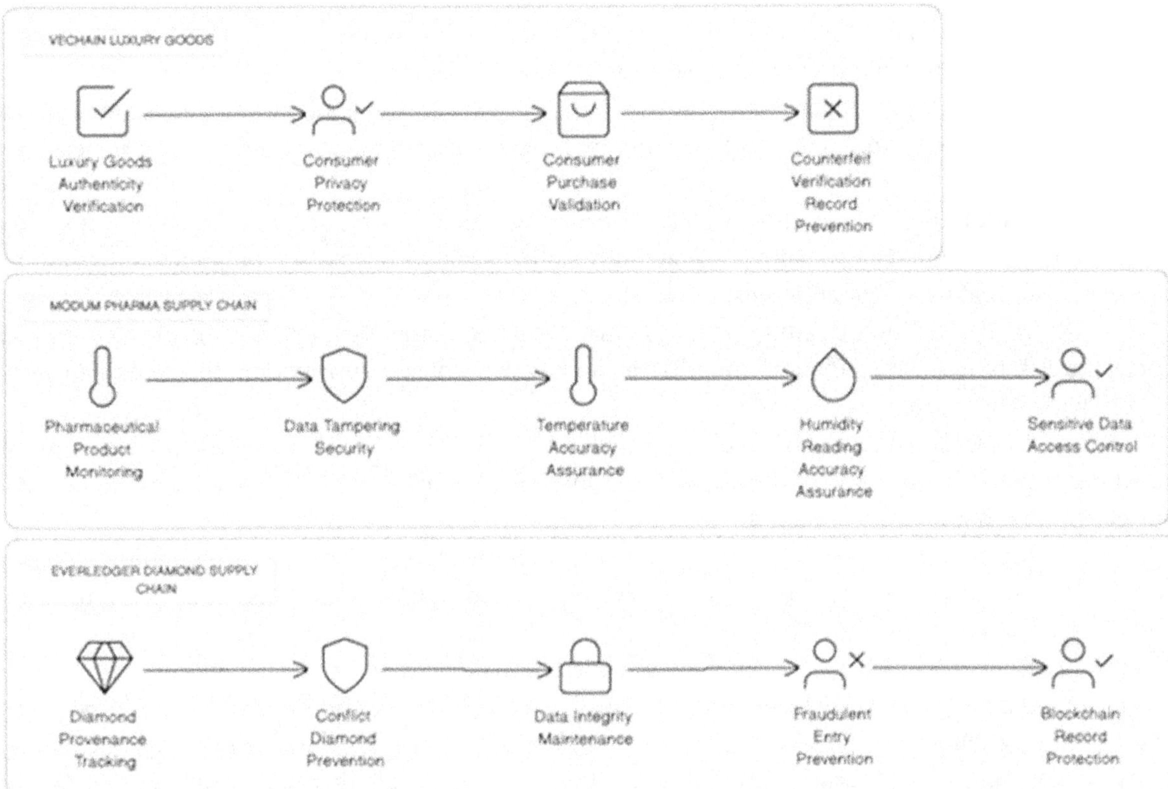

Applications of Blockchain in Supply Chain Management

Blockchain's attributes align seamlessly with the challenges faced by traditional supply chains, making it a promising technology for revolutionizing supply chain management. This section explores the diverse applications of blockchain technology in the context of supply chains.

Provenance and Traceability: Blockchain enables end-to-end traceability by recording every step of a product's journey. This is particularly beneficial in industries like food and luxury goods, where verifying authenticity and origin is crucial.

Supply Chain Visibility: Blockchain offers real-time visibility into supply chain processes by capturing data at every stage. This visibility enhances collaboration, enables informed decision-making, and reduces inefficiencies.

Smart Contracts: Smart contracts are self-executing agreements with terms directly written into code. These contracts automate processes, ensuring automatic execution of actions when predefined conditions are met. In supply chain management, smart contracts can automate payment release upon successful delivery, streamlining operations.

Quality Assurance and Compliance: Blockchain enables the recording of certifications, audits, and quality control measures at every stage of the supply chain. This facilitates compliance with industry standards and regulations.

Benefits of Using Blockchain for Supply Chain Transparency and Traceability

The adoption of blockchain technology in supply chain management offers a range of benefits that directly address the shortcomings of traditional supply chain models.

Enhanced Transparency: Blockchain's transparent nature ensures that all participants have access to the same, up-to-date information. This transparency reduces information asymmetry and fosters trust among stakeholders.

Immutable Audit Trails: The tamper-resistant nature of blockchain ensures that every transaction and interaction is recorded and cannot be altered retroactively. This creates an immutable audit trail that provides a historical record of activities.

Reduced Fraud and Counterfeiting: Blockchain's ability to authenticate and verify product origins reduces the risk of fraud and counterfeiting. By providing provenance information, blockchain technology deters malicious actors.

Real-time Tracking: Blockchain's real-time tracking capabilities allow for the monitoring of goods throughout their entire journey. This enhances supply chain visibility, making it easier to identify and address potential bottlenecks or delays.

Efficient Dispute Resolution: The transparent and auditable nature of blockchain simplifies dispute resolution by providing an accurate record of interactions and transactions. This reduces the time and resources required to resolve disputes.

The fundamentals of blockchain technology provide a solid foundation for understanding its application in supply chain management. By leveraging its features of decentralization, immutability, transparency, and security, blockchain introduces transformative possibilities for enhancing transparency, traceability, and efficiency within supply chains. The subsequent sections of this chapter will delve into the security and privacy challenges that arise when integrating blockchain into supply chain management, offering insights into strategies for mitigating these challenges and ensuring the success of blockchain implementations in this domain.

Figure 4. Benefits of blockchain in supply chain management

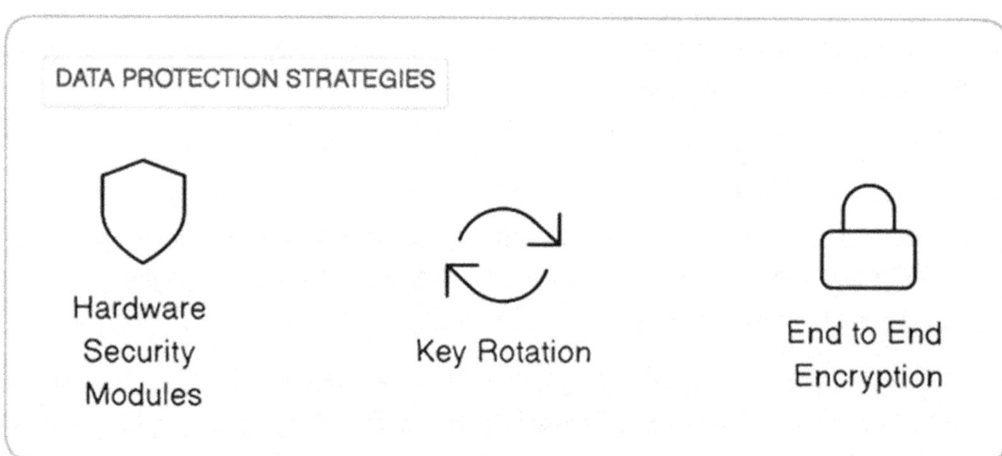

SECURITY CHALLENGES IN BLOCKCHAIN-BASED SUPPLY CHAIN MANAGEMENT

Security challenges in blockchain-based supply chain management are a critical concern that requires meticulous attention and comprehensive solutions. While blockchain offers transparency, immutability, and decentralization, it is not impervious to threats. One major challenge is ensuring the integrity of data entry and access control. Unauthorized or malicious actors can compromise the supply chain by tampering with data at the source, necessitating stringent identity verification and access controls. Moreover, ensuring the accuracy and reliability of data from IoT devices and sensors that feed information into the blockchain is essential, as any inaccurate data could have far-reaching consequences. Another security challenge is related to the vulnerabilities of smart contracts and interfaces connected to the blockchain. Smart contracts, which automate processes and transactions, must be thoroughly audited and tested to avoid vulnerabilities that can be exploited by attackers. The interfaces connecting the blockchain to the external world must also be secure to prevent unauthorized access and manipulation of data.

Privacy is a paramount concern, particularly in supply chain management involving sensitive business transactions and personally identifiable information. While blockchain offers pseudonymity, it is not inherently designed for anonymous data. Careful encryption and privacy-enhancing technologies must be employed to protect sensitive information while preserving the benefits of transparency and traceability.

Furthermore, regulatory compliance is a complex challenge, as the legal framework surrounding blockchain and supply chain management is still evolving. Companies need to navigate these legal uncertainties while ensuring that their blockchain-based solutions adhere to emerging regulations and standards. To address these security challenges effectively, a multi-pronged approach is necessary. This includes robust identity verification and access control mechanisms, comprehensive data integrity checks, careful smart contract development, continuous security audits and monitoring, and the implementation of encryption and privacy-enhancing technologies. Additionally, staying informed about evolving regulations and adapting blockchain-based supply chain management systems accordingly is crucial. As the technology continues to advance, finding innovative solutions to these security challenges is paramount to fully harnessing the potential of blockchain in revolutionizing supply chain management while maintaining the highest standards of security.

51% ATTACKS AND CONSENSUS MECHANISMS IN SUPPLY CHAIN NETWORKS

Consensus mechanisms are the backbone of blockchain security. This section explores the risks of 51% attacks, where a single entity gains control of the majority of a network's computational power.

51% Attacks: In proof-of-work (PoW) blockchains, an entity with over 51% of the network's computing power can manipulate transactions, compromise data integrity, and even double-spend.

Consensus Vulnerabilities: Centralization of mining power or inherent weaknesses in consensus protocols can render the network susceptible to various attacks.

In conclusion, security challenges in blockchain-based supply chain management highlight the need for robust measures to maintain data integrity, secure smart contracts, manage cryptographic keys, and ensure the resilience of consensus mechanisms. Addressing these challenges is pivotal to harnessing the transformative potential of blockchain while safeguarding the security of supply chain operations. The subsequent sections of this chapter will continue to explore the intricate landscape of security and privacy challenges in blockchain-based supply chain management, providing insights into effective strategies for mitigating these challenges and ensuring the success of blockchain implementations in this domain.

PRIVACY CHALLENGES IN BLOCKCHAIN-BASED SUPPLY CHAIN MANAGEMENT

Balancing Transparency and Privacy Requirements in a Public Ledger

Balancing transparency and privacy requirements in a public ledger, such as a blockchain, is a complex and delicate task. Public ledgers are designed to be transparent, immutable, and accessible to all participants, which can raise concerns when it comes to protecting sensitive or confidential information. To strike the right balance, various strategies can be employed, such as data anonymization and pseudonymization, which shield personal or sensitive data while maintaining transparency. Another approach is to implement permissioned blockchains, where access and participation are controlled, ensuring that only authorized parties have visibility into certain transactions or data. Smart contracts can be used to automate processes while preserving confidentiality by revealing only necessary information. It's a challenging but essential endeavor to meet both the demand for transparency and the need for data privacy, especially in industries where compliance with regulations like GDPR is mandatory. Finding the right equilibrium ensures that the benefits of public ledgers, such as trust and accountability, coexist with individual privacy and business confidentiality.

Pseudonymity and De-Anonymization Risks

Pseudonymity, the practice of using pseudonyms or aliases to conceal one's true identity in online interactions, offers a level of privacy and protection. However, it also comes with de-anonymization risks. De-anonymization refers to the process of revealing a person's real identity or sensitive information despite their use of pseudonyms. This risk arises when multiple pieces of seemingly innocuous data are correlated, analyzed, and pieced together to uncover an individual's actual identity. De-anonymization can be exploited by cybercriminals, marketers, or even government agencies. To mitigate these risks, individuals and organizations must be cautious about the data they share online, use secure and private communication tools, and stay informed about de-anonymization techniques. Additionally, employing strong encryption and adhering to best practices in online privacy can help safeguard against unwanted de-anonymization.

GDPR and Regulatory Compliance Concerns in Cross-Border Supply Chains

Global supply chains often span jurisdictions with varying data protection regulations, including the General Data Protection Regulation (GDPR). This section explores the challenges of ensuring compliance with GDPR and other regulations in cross-border supply chains.

Data Sovereignty: Data stored on a blockchain may be subject to regulations of multiple jurisdictions. Ensuring compliance with regulations related to data sovereignty and cross-border data transfers is complex.

Figure 5. General data protection regulation (GDPR) structure

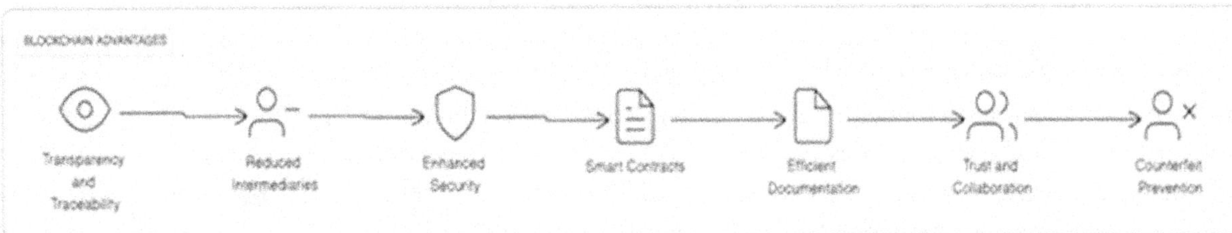

Right to Erasure: Blockchain's immutability poses challenges in adhering to GDPR's "right to erasure," as data cannot be easily deleted or modified once recorded.

Consent Management: Blockchain's transparency might conflict with GDPR's requirements for obtaining explicit consent from data subjects for data processing. Mechanisms for managing and revoking consent must be addressed.

Privacy-Enhancing Techniques in Blockchain, Such as Zero-Knowledge Proofs

To address privacy challenges in blockchain-based supply chain management, privacy-enhancing techniques like zero-knowledge proofs offer solutions. This section explores the concept of zero-knowledge proofs and their potential application.

Zero-Knowledge Proofs: Zero-knowledge proofs allow a party to prove the validity of a statement without revealing any specific details about the statement itself. This technique enhances privacy by providing proofs without exposing sensitive data.

Confidential Transactions: Confidential transactions use cryptographic techniques to encrypt transaction amounts, enhancing privacy by concealing financial information while ensuring transaction validity.

Selective Disclosure: Zero-knowledge proofs enable selective disclosure, where only specific information required for verification is revealed while keeping other details confidential.

The privacy challenges in blockchain-based supply chain management underscore the need for careful consideration of transparency, pseudonymity, regulatory compliance, and privacy-enhancing techniques. Striking a balance between transparency and data protection is vital to ensuring the successful implementation of blockchain solutions while safeguarding sensitive information. The subsequent sections of this chapter will continue to explore the complex landscape of security and privacy challenges in the context of blockchain-based supply chain management, offering insights into addressing these challenges to achieve a secure and privacy-conscious supply chain ecosystem.

DATA INTEROPERABILITY AND INTEGRATION CHALLENGES

Data interoperability and integration challenges within the context of blockchain-based supply chain management are intricately linked to the broader security and privacy challenges faced by this innovative approach. Interoperability issues arise when multiple stakeholders in a supply chain ecosystem employ different systems, data formats, and standards. Achieving seamless data integration is essential for harnessing the full potential of blockchain in enhancing transparency and traceability. One of the key security challenges in this context is the potential for unauthorized access and tampering of data as it moves between disparate systems and is integrated into the blockchain. Ensuring the integrity and authenticity of data during integration is crucial, and unauthorized changes can result in substantial supply chain disruptions and financial losses. Authentication mechanisms and secure APIs are essential for safeguarding the integration process. Additionally, the use of consensus mechanisms in blockchain networks helps ensure data integrity and prevents malicious actors from altering records without consensus.

Privacy challenges in data interoperability and integration primarily revolve around sensitive information sharing among supply chain participants. When data is integrated into a blockchain, it becomes accessible to all authorized participants, raising concerns about the exposure of proprietary or sensitive information. Achieving a balance between data transparency and privacy is essential. Techniques like data anonymization and pseudonymization can be employed to protect sensitive information while preserving transparency. Moreover, the implementation of permissioned blockchains, where access is controlled, allows organizations to restrict data visibility to only the relevant parties, enhancing data privacy.

In conclusion, addressing data interoperability and integration challenges in the context of blockchain-based supply chain management necessitates a comprehensive approach that considers both security and privacy implications. As blockchain technology continues to evolve, businesses and organizations must prioritize robust security measures, such as secure APIs, encryption, and consensus mechanisms, to protect data during integration. Simultaneously, they should leverage privacy-enhancing techniques and permissioned blockchains to strike a balance between transparency and data privacy. A well-executed strategy that addresses these challenges can unlock the potential for improved supply chain efficiency, accountability, and trust while maintaining the highest standards of security and data privacy.

SCALABILITY AND PERFORMANCE ISSUES

Scalability and performance issues are pivotal aspects that intersect with the overarching security and privacy challenges within blockchain-based supply chain management. While blockchain technology promises transparency and immutability, it grapples with inherent limitations in terms of scalability and transaction throughput. The decentralized nature of blockchain, where every participant in the network stores and validates all transactions, ensures security but hinders scalability. As more transactions are added to the ledger, the network's capacity to handle them can become a bottleneck, resulting in delays, higher costs, and decreased efficiency. These performance challenges can undermine the effectiveness of supply chain management, especially in scenarios where real-time visibility and responsiveness are critical.

To mitigate these scalability and performance challenges, various approaches are being explored. One approach involves optimizing consensus algorithms and network architecture. Transitioning from Proof of Work (PoW) to more efficient consensus mechanisms like Proof of Stake (PoS) or sharding can significantly increase transaction throughput. Moreover, layer-2 solutions, such as sidechains and state channels, can offload some of the transaction burden from the main blockchain, thereby improving overall performance. However, these scalability solutions must be implemented with careful consideration of the security and privacy challenges. Any changes to the blockchain's architecture must not compromise the integrity and transparency of supply chain data. Furthermore, enhancing performance should not come at the expense of data privacy or decentralization.

In conclusion, the scalability and performance issues faced by blockchain-based supply chain management are complex and interlinked with the broader security and privacy challenges. Achieving a balance between security, privacy, and scalability requires a multi-faceted approach that leverages innovative consensus algorithms and layer-2 solutions while safeguarding the core principles of blockchain technology. This ensures that the potential for enhanced transparency and traceability in supply chain management is realized without compromising data security and privacy.

CASE STUDIES: REAL-WORLD SECURITY AND PRIVACY CHALLENGES

Analysis of Notable Supply Chain Blockchain Projects and Their Challenges

This section presents an analysis of noteworthy supply chain blockchain projects, highlighting the security and privacy challenges they encountered during their implementations. By examining these cases, valuable insights can be gained into the real-world complexities of integrating blockchain technology into supply chain management.

IBM Food Trust: The IBM Food Trust platform focuses on enhancing transparency and traceability in the food supply chain. Analyze the challenges faced, such as ensuring data accuracy at each stage of the supply chain, addressing interoperability issues among diverse stakeholders, and managing privacy concerns when sharing sensitive information.

Everledger - Diamond Supply Chain: Everledger utilizes blockchain to track the provenance of diamonds and prevent the circulation of conflict diamonds. Explore the security challenges of maintaining the integrity of diamond data, preventing fraudulent entries, and safeguarding against malicious actors attempting to manipulate the blockchain records.

Modum - Pharma Supply Chain: Modum's blockchain-based solution aims to monitor pharmaceutical products' conditions during transit. Discuss challenges related to securing data from tampering, ensuring the accuracy of temperature and humidity readings, and managing access control to sensitive data.

VeChain - Luxury Goods: VeChain's platform focuses on verifying the authenticity of luxury goods. Analyze challenges such as protecting consumer privacy while ensuring that consumers can validate the legitimacy of their purchases, and preventing the creation of counterfeit verification records.

By delving into the challenges faced by these notable supply chain blockchain projects, organizations can gain a deeper understanding of the intricacies involved in implementing secure and privacy-aware solutions. The subsequent sections of this chapter will continue to explore the multifaceted landscape

Figure 6. Supply chain blockchain projects and their challenges

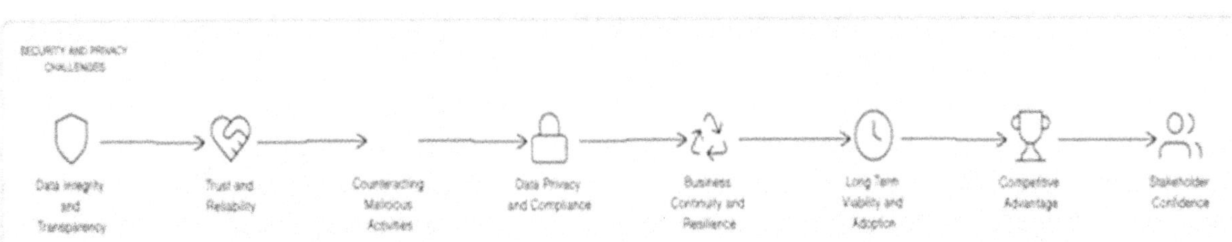

of security, privacy, data interoperability, scalability, and performance challenges in blockchain-based supply chain management. The insights gained from these case studies will contribute to developing effective strategies for addressing these challenges and fostering resilient, transparent, and efficient supply chain ecosystems.

Lessons Learned From Security Breaches or Privacy Lapses in Blockchain Supply Chain Implementations

This section delves into lessons learned from real-world incidents involving security breaches or privacy lapses in blockchain supply chain implementations. By examining these incidents, organizations can glean insights into potential vulnerabilities and best practices to prevent and mitigate such challenges.

Unintended Data Exposure: In the case of a pharmaceutical supply chain implementation, a misconfigured smart contract led to the exposure of sensitive patient data. The incident underscores the importance of thorough code reviews, testing, and proper access controls to prevent unintended data exposure.

Data Manipulation: An incident in a seafood supply chain project revealed that a participant maliciously altered blockchain records to reflect incorrect catch locations. This highlights the need for robust authentication mechanisms, consensus protocols, and auditing procedures to prevent data manipulation.

Privacy Breach: A clothing retailer's blockchain-based supply chain project suffered a privacy breach when consumer data was inadvertently exposed. The incident emphasizes the significance of data minimization, encryption, and clear consent mechanisms to protect sensitive information.

Smart Contract Vulnerability: An attack on a supply chain project's smart contract led to unauthorized fund transfers. This case underscores the necessity of rigorous smart contract auditing, continuous monitoring, and prompt response to vulnerabilities.

Interoperability Challenges: In a multi-partner supply chain project, interoperability issues between blockchain platforms hindered data exchange. The lesson learned is the importance of selecting compatible platforms, establishing data standards, and ensuring seamless integration.

By examining these real-world incidents and the lessons they offer, organizations can better prepare themselves to address security breaches, privacy lapses, and other challenges in blockchain-based supply chain implementations. The insights gained from these case studies contribute to fostering a secure, transparent, and resilient supply chain ecosystem. The subsequent sections of this chapter will continue to explore the complex landscape of security, privacy, data interoperability, scalability, and performance challenges in blockchain-based supply chain management, providing insights into effective strategies for mitigating these challenges and building robust supply chain solutions.

MITIGATION STRATEGIES AND BEST PRACTICES

Secure Smart Contract Development Practices

Secure smart contract development practices are paramount in addressing the security and privacy challenges within blockchain-based supply chain management. Smart contracts are self-executing programs that automate various processes and transactions on the blockchain. However, due to their immutable nature, any vulnerabilities or flaws in these contracts can have severe consequences, ranging from data breaches to financial losses. Secure smart contract development encompasses several essential practices,

Figure 7. Encryption and key management strategies

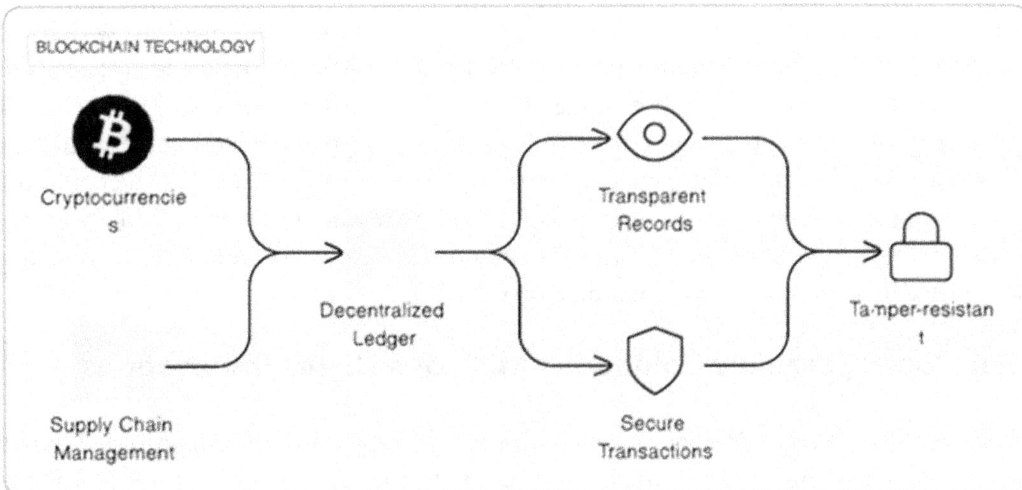

including code review and auditing to identify and rectify vulnerabilities, using formal verification tools to ensure the correctness of contract logic, and employing well-established security standards and best practices such as the OWASP Top Ten for Smart Contracts. Additionally, proper access control mechanisms must be implemented to safeguard sensitive supply chain data. Combining these practices with data anonymization and encryption can help strike a balance between transparency and data privacy, ensuring the integrity and security of the supply chain while preserving sensitive information.

Encryption and Key Management Strategies for Data Protection

Protecting data through encryption and robust key management is crucial for maintaining confidentiality. This section highlights key practices for safeguarding sensitive information.

End-to-End Encryption: Implement encryption mechanisms to ensure data confidentiality both in transit and at rest.

Key Rotation: Regularly update encryption keys to mitigate the impact of potential key compromise.

Hardware Security Modules (HSMs): Use HSMs to securely manage cryptographic keys and prevent unauthorized access.

FUTURE TRENDS AND RESEARCH DIRECTIONS

Emerging Technologies to Address Scalability and Privacy Challenges

In the realm of security and privacy challenges in blockchain-based supply chain management, future trends and research directions are expected to revolve around emerging technologies that specifically target scalability and privacy issues. As the demand for real-time visibility and efficiency in supply chain processes grows, addressing scalability challenges becomes paramount. Emerging consensus algorithms, such as Proof of Stake (PoS) and sharding, are poised to offer improved scalability without compromising security. On the privacy front, zero-knowledge proofs, such as zk-SNARKs and zk-STARKs, are gaining traction for their ability to validate data without revealing the data itself. Research will likely focus on the integration of these technologies into blockchain networks to enhance both scalability and data privacy, providing a holistic solution to the challenges faced in supply chain management. Additionally, exploring innovative approaches to smart contract development that combine security, privacy, and efficiency will be a key research avenue, as these self-executing contracts play a central role in the functioning of blockchain-based supply chains. Overall, future research endeavors will continue to adapt to the evolving landscape of blockchain technology and its applications in supply chain management to ensure the highest standards of security and data privacy.

Blockchain Interoperability Solutions and Cross-Chain Transactions

In the comprehensive analysis of security and privacy challenges in blockchain-based supply chain management, looking ahead to future trends and research directions is crucial. One prominent area of exploration is blockchain interoperability solutions and cross-chain transactions. As supply chains involve multiple stakeholders using different blockchain platforms, achieving seamless interoperability between these systems is vital. Research and development will likely focus on creating standardized protocols and bridges that enable the smooth exchange of data and assets between disparate blockchains while maintaining data security and privacy. This development can provide the foundation for a more interconnected and efficient supply chain ecosystem, allowing for real-time data sharing and decision-making while addressing the challenge of maintaining data confidentiality across multiple chains. As the blockchain landscape evolves, the pursuit of secure and private cross-chain transactions will be instrumental in overcoming the current challenges and unlocking the full potential of blockchain in supply chain management.

Evolving Regulatory Landscape and Its Impact on Blockchain-Based Supply Chain Management

In the comprehensive analysis of security and privacy challenges in blockchain-based supply chain management, the evolving regulatory landscape and its impact on this innovative approach are of utmost importance. As governments and international bodies increasingly recognize the potential of blockchain in enhancing transparency and traceability, they are also introducing new regulations and standards. Future research will likely delve into understanding and complying with these evolving regulatory requirements, ensuring that blockchain-based supply chain management solutions align with data privacy and security regulations, such as GDPR and HIPAA. Researchers and practitioners will need to navigate the intricate web of global, regional, and industry-specific compliance frameworks, which can impact how data is collected, stored, and shared on the blockchain. Addressing these regulatory challenges while preserving the fundamental principles of blockchain, such as decentralization and immutability, will be a critical aspect of future trends and research directions in supply chain management.

CONCLUSION

Recap of Security and Privacy Challenges in Blockchain-Based Supply Chain Management

This chapter has provided a comprehensive exploration of the security and privacy challenges inherent in blockchain-based supply chain management. By examining the multifaceted landscape of blockchain technology, supply chain dynamics, and evolving regulatory frameworks, we have gained insights into the complexities of ensuring secure, transparent, and efficient supply chain ecosystems. We began by delving into the fundamentals of blockchain technology and its applications in supply chain management. From there, we navigated through the intricate challenges of data security, privacy, interoperability, scalability, and performance that arise in the context of blockchain adoption.

The case studies illuminated real-world incidents, shedding light on the vulnerabilities and lessons learned from security breaches and privacy lapses. We explored mitigation strategies and best practices, highlighting the importance of secure smart contract development, encryption, privacy-preserving techniques, and collaboration to address these challenges effectively.

Furthermore, we projected into the future, identifying emerging technologies, blockchain interoperability solutions, and the evolving regulatory landscape as key trends that will shape the trajectory of blockchain-based supply chain management. These trends present opportunities to overcome existing challenges and create resilient, compliant, and innovative supply chain networks. By recapitulating the security and privacy challenges discussed in this chapter, we underscore the importance of acknowledging and addressing these issues in the pursuit of realizing the full potential of blockchain technology in supply chain management. As the blockchain landscape continues to evolve, collaboration, research, and innovation will be essential in building secure, transparent, and efficient supply chains that thrive in a dynamic and interconnected world.

This chapter has provided a foundation for understanding the intricacies of security and privacy challenges in blockchain-based supply chain management. As organizations continue to explore and implement blockchain solutions, the insights shared here will serve as a guiding compass, ensuring that security and privacy remain paramount in the pursuit of a transformed and empowered supply chain ecosystem.

Importance of Collaborative Efforts to Address These Challenges

This chapter has explored the multifaceted challenges that emerge when integrating blockchain technology into supply chain management. Throughout our examination of security, privacy, data interoperability, scalability, and regulatory considerations, one overarching theme has emerged—the critical importance of collaborative efforts in overcoming these challenges.

The complexities of blockchain-based supply chain management demand a collective approach that transcends organizational boundaries. The sheer diversity of stakeholders, ranging from manufacturers and suppliers to distributors and regulators, underscores the necessity of collaborative efforts to establish standardized practices, share insights, and develop innovative solutions. As we have witnessed, security and privacy challenges in blockchain-based supply chain management are not isolated incidents but rather shared concerns that affect the entire ecosystem. Mitigation strategies, the development of best practices, and the exploration of emerging technologies all require a collaborative approach that draws upon the expertise of multiple participants. Collaboration also extends to regulatory compliance. The evolving regulatory landscape underscores the need for open dialogue between blockchain innovators and regulatory authorities to ensure that technological advancements align with legal frameworks. The proactive establishment of regulatory sandboxes and partnerships can enable experimentation within controlled environments while adhering to compliance requirements.

Furthermore, the pursuit of blockchain interoperability and the realization of cross-chain transactions necessitate a collective effort to establish standards, protocols, and interfaces that allow different blockchain networks to seamlessly communicate. This collaborative endeavor will foster a cohesive blockchain ecosystem that thrives on cross-chain collaboration.

In conclusion, the successful integration of blockchain technology in supply chain management hinges upon the synergy of collaborative efforts. By working together, stakeholders can pool their knowledge, share their experiences, and collectively navigate the challenges that arise. As the supply chain landscape evolves, collaboration remains a cornerstone, ensuring that the transformative potential of blockchain is harnessed to its fullest extent.

This chapter has shed light on the importance of collaboration as a driving force behind the successful implementation of blockchain-based supply chain solutions. As organizations continue to embark on this transformative journey, the lessons learned from these collaborative endeavours will guide the way toward secure, transparent, and resilient supply chain ecosystems.

Call to Action for Organizations and Researchers to Ensure Secure and Privacy-Conscious Implementations of Blockchain in Supply Chains

In conclusion, the comprehensive analysis of security and privacy challenges in blockchain-based supply chain management underscores the pressing need for organizations and researchers to take proactive measures. Supply chains are the lifeblood of global commerce, and while blockchain offers transformative potential in enhancing transparency and traceability, it is essential to navigate the associated security and privacy hurdles. The call to action is clear: organizations must prioritize secure and privacy-conscious implementations of blockchain technology in their supply chain processes. This involves adopting best practices in smart contract development, data encryption, access control, and data anonymization to strike the delicate balance between transparency and data privacy. Researchers, on the other hand, have a crucial role in advancing the field by exploring innovative solutions that address scalability, data interoperability, and evolving regulatory requirements while maintaining the integrity of the blockchain. In this collaborative effort, both organizations and researchers can unlock the full potential of blockchain in supply chain management while upholding the highest standards of data security and privacy, fostering trust, and contributing to a more resilient and efficient global supply chain ecosystem.

REFERENCES

Al-Farsi, S., Rathore, M. M., & Bakiras, S. (2021). Security of blockchain-based supply chain management systems: Challenges and opportunities. *Applied Sciences (Basel, Switzerland)*, *11*(12), 5585. doi:10.3390/app11125585

Alzahrani, N., & Bulusu, N. (2018, June). Block-supply chain: A new anti-counterfeiting supply chain using NFC and blockchain. In *Proceedings of the 1st Workshop on Cryptocurrencies and Blockchains for Distributed Systems* (pp. 30-35). ACM. 10.1145/3211933.3211939

Biswas, K., Muthukkumarasamy, V., & Tan, W. L. (2017). Blockchain based wine supply chain traceability system. In *Future Technologies Conference (FTC) 2017* (pp. 56-62). The Science and Information Organization.

Chabani, Z., & Chabani, W. (2022). The role of blockchain technology in enhancing security management in the supply chain. In *Advances in Blockchain Technology for Cyber Physical Systems* (pp. 211–231). Springer International Publishing. doi:10.1007/978-3-030-93646-4_10

Chandra, N., Teotia, S., Chaudhary, A., Jain, V., Vashishtha, T., & Dwivedi, N. N. (2022). Noise Reduction Using Cellular Automata. *NeuroQuantology : An Interdisciplinary Journal of Neuroscience and Quantum Physics*, *20*(6), 4650–4672.

El Azzaoui, A., Chen, H., Kim, S. H., Pan, Y., & Park, J. H. (2022). Blockchain-based distributed information hiding framework for data privacy preserving in medical supply chain systems. *Sensors (Basel)*, *22*(4), 1371. doi:10.339022041371 PMID:35214273

Gao, N., Han, D., Weng, T. H., Xia, B., Li, D., Castiglione, A., & Li, K. C. (2022). Modeling and analysis of port supply chain system based on Fabric blockchain. *Computers & Industrial Engineering*, *172*, 108527. doi:10.1016/j.cie.2022.108527

Kant, R., Sharma, S., Vikas, V., Chaudhary, S., Jain, A. K., & Sharma, K. K. (2023). Blockchain – A Deployment Mechanism for IoT Based Security. *2023 International Conference on Computational Intelligence, Communication Technology and Networking (CICTN)*, Ghaziabad, India. 10.1109/CICTN57981.2023.10140715

Keresztes, É. R., Kovács, I., Horváth, A., & Zimányi, K. (2022). Exploratory analysis of blockchain platforms in supply chain management. *Economies*, *10*(9), 206. doi:10.3390/economies10090206

Khan, M. R., Khan, M. R., & Nallaluthan, K. (2023). Blockchain Supply Chain Management and Supply Chain Sustainability. In Blockchain Driven Supply Chain Management: A Multi-dimensional Perspective (pp. 155-180). Singapore: Springer Nature Singapore. doi:10.1007/978-981-99-0699-4_10

Kishnani, U., Madabhushi, S., & Das, S. (2023, July). Blockchain in Oil and Gas Supply Chain: A Literature Review from User Security and Privacy Perspective. In *International Symposium on Human Aspects of Information Security and Assurance* (pp. 296-309). Cham: Springer Nature Switzerland. 10.1007/978-3-031-38530-8_24

Korpela, K., Hallikas, J., & Dahlberg, T. (2017). *Digital supply chain transformation toward blockchain integration.*

Kumar, A., Liu, R., & Shan, Z. (2020). Is blockchain a silver bullet for supply chain management? Technical challenges and research opportunities. *Decision Sciences*, *51*(1), 8–37. doi:10.1111/deci.12396

Min, H. (2010). Artificial intelligence in supply chain management: Theory and applications. *International Journal of Logistics*, *13*(1), 13–39. doi:10.1080/13675560902736537

Mohanta, B. K., Jena, D., Panda, S. S., & Sobhanayak, S. (2019). Blockchain technology: A survey on applications and security privacy challenges. *Internet of Things : Engineering Cyber Physical Human Systems*, *8*, 100107. doi:10.1016/j.iot.2019.100107

Mohit, M., Kaur, S., & Singh, M. (2022). Design and implementation of transaction privacy by virtue of ownership and traceability in blockchain based supply chain. *Cluster Computing*, *25*(3), 1–18. doi:10.100710586-021-03425-x PMID:34744494

Omar, I. A., Jayaraman, R., Salah, K., Debe, M., & Omar, M. (2020). Enhancing vendor managed inventory supply chain operations using blockchain smart contracts. *IEEE Access : Practical Innovations, Open Solutions*, *8*, 182704–182719. doi:10.1109/ACCESS.2020.3028031

Patil, P., Sangeetha, M., & Bhaskar, V. (2021). Blockchain for IoT access control, security and privacy: A review. *Wireless Personal Communications*, *117*(3), 1815–1834. doi:10.100711277-020-07947-2

Tian, F. (2017, June). A supply chain traceability system for food safety based on HACCP, blockchain & Internet of things. In *2017 International conference on service systems and service management* (pp. 1-6). IEEE. DOI: 10.1109/ICSSSM.2017.7996119

Toyoda, K., Mathiopoulos, P. T., Sasase, I., & Ohtsuki, T. (2017). A novel blockchain-based product ownership management system (POMS) for anti-counterfeits in the post supply chain. *IEEE Access : Practical Innovations, Open Solutions*, *5*, 17465–17477. doi:10.1109/ACCESS.2017.2720760

Tse, D., Zhang, B., Yang, Y., Cheng, C., & Mu, H. (2017, December). Blockchain application in food supply information security. In *2017 IEEE international conference on industrial engineering and engineering management (IEEM)* (pp. 1357-1361). IEEE. DOI: doi:10.1109/IEEM.2017.8290114

Uddin, M. J., Azmat, F., Fujimoto, Y., & Hossain, F. (2023). Exploitation in Bangladeshi ready-made garments supply chain: A case of irresponsible capitalism? *International Journal of Logistics Management*, *34*(1), 164–188. doi:10.1108/IJLM-12-2021-0565

Vashishth, T. K., Chaudhary, S., Sharma, V., Sharma, S., & Gupat, V. K. (2023). Technological Implementation in Achieving Data Privacy Through Blockchain Technique. *International Journal of Research and Analytical Reviews*, *10*(2), 276–483.

Vashishth, T. K., Chaudhary, S., Sharma, V., Yadav, A., & Panwar, R. (2023). Next Generation Dynamic Distributed Honeypots System Based on Blockchain: A Real Time Network Defense Strategy. *International Journal of Research and Analytical Reviews*, *10*(2), 583–591.

Vashishth, T. K., Sharma, V., Chaudhary, S., Panwar, R., Sharma, S., & Kumar, P. (2023). Advanced Technologies and AI-Enabled IoT Applications in High-Tech Agriculture. In A. Khang (Ed.), *Handbook of Research on AI-Equipped IoT Applications in High-Tech Agriculture* (pp. 155–166). IGI Global., doi:10.4018/978-1-6684-9231-4.ch008

Verma, P. K., Sharma, V., Kumar, P., Sharma, S., Chaudhary, S., & Preety, P. (2023). IoT Enabled Real Time Appearance System using AI Camera and Deep Learning for Student Tracking. *International Journal on Recent and Innovation Trends in Computing and Communication*, *11*(6s), 249–254. doi:10.17762/ijritcc.v11i6s.6885

Wen, B., Wang, Y., Ding, Y., Zheng, H., Qin, B., & Yang, C. (2023). Security and privacy protection technologies in securing blockchain applications. *Information Sciences*, *119322*, 119322. Advance online publication. doi:10.1016/j.ins.2023.119322

Wu, H., Cao, J., Yang, Y., Tung, C. L., Jiang, S., Tang, B., & Deng, Y. (2019, July). Data management in supply chain using blockchain: Challenges and a case study. In *2019 28th international conference on computer communication and networks (ICCCN)* (pp. 1-8). IEEE.

Yousuf, S., & Svetinovic, D. (2019, October). Blockchain technology in supply chain management: Preliminary study. In *2019 sixth international conference on internet of things: systems, management and security (IOTSMS)* (pp. 537-538). IEEE. DOI: 10.1109/IOTSMS48152.2019.8939222

Zyskind, G., & Nathan, O. (2015, May). Decentralizing privacy: Using blockchain to protect personal data. In *2015 IEEE security and privacy workshops* (pp. 180-184). IEEE. DOI: doi:10.1109/SPW.2015.27

KEY TERMS AND DEFINITIONS

Blockchain: Blockchain is a decentralized and distributed digital ledger technology that records transactions across multiple computers in a secure and transparent manner. Each transaction is grouped into a "block" and linked to the previous one, forming a chronological chain of blocks. This ensures data integrity, immutability, and trust among participants without the need for a central authority.

Decentralized Autonomous Organizations (DAOs): Decentralized Autonomous Organizations (DAOs) are self-governing entities operating on blockchain technology. They use smart contracts to automate decision-making, governance, and resource allocation, enabling participants to collectively manage and control the organization's activities without a centralized authority. DAOs aim to create transparent, democratic, and trustless systems for various applications, including finance, governance, and community projects.

Decentralized Finance (DeFi): Decentralized Finance (DeFi) refers to a digital financial ecosystem built on blockchain technology, aiming to recreate traditional financial services, such as lending, trading, and borrowing, in a decentralized and permissionless manner. It eliminates intermediaries like banks and brokers, allowing users to interact directly with smart contracts and decentralized applications (DApps) to access financial services, often using cryptocurrencies as collateral or payment.

General Data Protection Regulation (GDPR): The General Data Protection Regulation (GDPR) is a comprehensive data protection regulation implemented by the European Union (EU) to safeguard individuals' personal data privacy and rights. It establishes rules for collecting, processing, and storing personal data by organizations, ensuring transparency, consent, and control over individuals' data, as well as imposing strict penalties for non-compliance.

Supply Chain Management: Supply chain management is the strategic coordination and oversight of the entire process involved in sourcing, producing, distributing, and delivering goods or services to customers. It encompasses the planning, execution, and monitoring of activities across various stages to optimize efficiency, minimize costs, and ensure the seamless flow of products from suppliers to end-users.

Chapter 6
Revolutionizing Pharmaceutical Supply Chains – Harnessing the Power of Blockchain Technology

Kasturi Laturkar
https://orcid.org/0000-0002-4985-909X
Validation Associates LLC, USA

Kaustubh Laturkar
https://orcid.org/0000-0002-2643-3942
Michigan State University, USA

ABSTRACT

The purpose of this chapter is to explore how blockchain technology can be used to transform supply chain management practices. Blockchain addresses longstanding supply chain challenges, such as transparency, traceability, and data integrity, through its decentralized, tamper-resistant nature. Through automated smart contracts, blockchain's secure and transparent ledger can enhance trust among stakeholders, mitigate fraud and counterfeiting risks, and streamline complex transactions. The chapter illustrates how blockchain integration can improve efficiency, reduce costs, and improve customer satisfaction through case studies across the pharmaceutical sector. In addition to addressing scalability, interoperability, and regulatory compliance, the chapter acknowledges existing obstacles in implementation of blockchain technology in supply chain management. Future advancements in blockchain technology promise to revolutionize supply chain management practices on a global scale.

INTRODUCTION

Blockchain technology has revolutionized industries, and its impact on supply chain management has been particularly profound. In essence, blockchain is a decentralized, distributed ledger technology that records transactions securely over a network of computers. With its inherent properties of transparency,

DOI: 10.4018/979-8-3693-0482-2.ch006

immutability, and traceability, this technology offers a paradigm shift in the way supply chains operate, overcoming long-standing challenges and inefficiencies.

It is common for information flow to be siloed in traditional supply chains, which creates opacity and hinders transparency. The lack of transparency can lead to counterfeit products, inaccurate records, delays, and difficulties in tracing the origin of goods. As a result of blockchain technology, all transactions are recorded transparently and immutably. Blocks in the chain contain timestamped records of transactions, cryptographically linked to previous blocks, ensuring the integrity and security of data (Amulya Gurtu, 2019).

As a decentralized network, blockchain eliminates the need for intermediaries and reduces the risk of data manipulation or fraud (Javed Aslama, 2021). With smart contracts, self-executing contracts with predefined rules encoded in the blockchain, processes are automated, terms and conditions are met, and actions are automatically triggered. Real-time tracking of goods, payments, and agreements across the supply chain is made possible through these contracts. The blockchain records every transaction immutably, providing a complete audit trail from the point of origin to the point of sale. As a result of this transparency, stakeholders are able to verify the authenticity and provenance of products, which reduces the risk of counterfeit goods and ensures compliance with quality standards.

As well as providing real-time visibility into the movement of goods, blockchain technology facilitates efficient inventory management. Optimizing inventory levels, reducing stockouts, and minimizing excess inventory can be achieved by tracking each stage of the supply chain, resulting in cost savings and improved operational efficiency. Additionally, blockchain facilitates collaboration and trust between participants in the supply chain ecosystem. Shared access to a common ledger allows stakeholders to exchange information securely and transparently, improving communication, dispute resolution, and coordination between suppliers, manufacturers, distributors, and consumers.

The blockchain has the potential to transform supply chain management by enhancing transparency, traceability, efficiency, and trust among stakeholders. A future where transparency and efficiency redefine global trade could be achieved through blockchain solutions.

SUPPLY CHAIN MANAGEMENT AT A GLANCE

In today's world, due to the globalization of industrial markets and the penetration of international borders, there is a greater sense of competition in the market. Further, organizations need to identify emerging digital technologies that can be used for the development of a new business model to survive and maintain a sustainable competitive advantage in this global economy. As a result, manufacturers have been forced to adopt advanced manufacturing technologies such as 3D printing, rapid prototyping, coupled with internet of things to collect and analyze data. The goal of every business in this competitive and turbulent environment is to provide their customers with the exact quality, quantity, and price of the product that they desire within a reasonable amount of time (Prakash Agrawal, 2018).

Supply chain is a logistics system that manages the flow of goods, services, finances, and information from a source to a customer by passing through three or more organizations. Consequently, supply chain management involves the proactive management of the movement of resources (such as raw materials, services, information, and funds) between the supply chain and end users (i.e., the various flows of resources) (John J. Coyle, 2021). The supply chain management system coordinates activities and flows across boundaries to improve operational efficiency. The management of supply chains is likely to be emphasized in organizations that have a focus on the supply chain. There is no doubt that supply chains consist of an interconnected set of internal and external activities, regardless of how they are defined or from what point of view they are seen. Most of these activities cross geographical boundaries and are complemented by individuals who come from a wide range of cultural backgrounds.

It is important to understand that supply chain management involves many activities, but an improved way of thinking about it is as a series of processes rather than discrete, often badly aligned tasks and activities. There are interrelated tasks or activities that are carried out in a process for the purpose of achieving a specific goal. The development of new products, the fulfillment of customer orders, the evaluation and selection of suppliers, the timely supply of the materials etc. are all important aspects of supply chain management, and many of these aspects are essential to its success. (Robert M. Monczka, 2020).

Due to the increasing importance of supply chain management, businesses must rethink how they are planning their purchasing and sourcing strategies so that they support broader business and supply chain objectives. It is important to understand that there are multiple organizations involved in supply chains, whether they are supplying raw materials or delivering products to the final customer.

ISSUES WITH SUPPLY CHAIN MANAGEMENT

For organizations to be able to develop and sustain efficient and effective supply chains, they must address a number of challenges (John J. Coyle, 2021). Some of these challenges are elucidated below. Figure 1 summarizes the current challenges for supply chain management.

An Overview of Supply Chain Networks

There are several facilities in supply chain that are important for the transportation of goods (plants, distribution centers, terminals, etc.). In the current dynamic, global environment, there is a need to have an effective network system as well. Changes can occur at such a rapid pace that it is a challenge to keep up with them. It is essential that organizations and companies have a network system that can respond to and change with the dynamics of the marketplace on a short-term and long-term basis so that they can remain competitive in the long run (Robert M. Monczka, 2020). In some situations, flexibility may be necessary for a short period of time, such as during port strikes, floods, hurricanes, political uprisings, terrorist attacks, and so on. There is no doubt that mitigating the risk of disruption in today's global networks is an essential part of managing this risk.

Grasping the Complexity

As a result of globalization and consolidation in the supply chain, SKUs (Stock Keeping Units), customer locations, supplier locations, transportation requirements, trade regulations, taxes, and so forth have become increasingly complex (John J. Coyle, 2021). For a company to simplify their supply chains as much as possible, they need to simplify a number of aspects of the process in order to achieve this goal. A number of organizations, for example, have recently expanded their number of SKUs, which increases the complexity of managing inventory and fulfilling orders for them. As a result of this, companies have rationalized their SKUs in order to eliminate items that are slow movers and are not profitable. Additionally, it is also necessary to analyze the locations so that duplication of services or high costs can be eliminated as well. It is essential to rationalize the alternatives for vendors and suppliers, as well as the level of customer service provided. To stay on top of the development of layers of complexity, organizations must continually evaluate the layers through process evaluations, personnel training and the use of new technology.

Deployment of Inventory Systems

Supply chains have two interesting characteristics: they are often characterized by duplicate inventory across the chain, and they are also characterized by a bullwhip effect along the chain (Amit Karamchandani, 2021). In most cases, inventory levels are reduced when supply chain management is implemented effectively in a company. Increasing the efficiency of the supply chain can be achieved through integration and co-ordination on both the horizontal (single firm) and vertical (multiple firms) levels to reduce inventory levels. There are also positive strategies, such as postponement and compression that can be implemented. Due to the associated costs and the potential for increasing efficiency of supply chain operations, inventory deployment is an important consideration for supply chains. There is no doubt that inventory is a necessary component of a successful supply chain, but it must be managed carefully in order to reduce working capital. The use of information technology is essential in order to manage inventory in an efficient manner.

Amount of Information

In the digital age, organizations can collect and store vast amounts of data using technology and communication systems. However, despite this, it is interesting to note that they may not be taking advantage of the wealth of data to develop the information systems they need to make better decisions. There is a great deal of value in accumulating and storing data during the supply chain, but it is largely useless unless it is shared horizontally, vertically, and used to improve inventory management, customer service, transportation, etc. (Gabriella M. Hastig, 2020). Information should be accurate, timely, easily manageable, and shareable for it to be useful. There are several factors that contribute to higher inventory levels, including safety stock accumulation. There is no doubt that sharing of information and ensuring the integrity of the collected data are the biggest challenges for supply chains, but they are also the most promising.

A Technology-Based Approach

In addition to being a driver of change, technology has the potential to also serve as a facilitator, which can increase efficiency and effectiveness (Arun Aryal, 2020). It is imperative that technology is evaluated and successfully implemented so that the desired improvements can be achieved. Technology is often thrown at a problem to solve it, which leads to frustration and failure as a result. To facilitate the implementation of the changes, processes need to be analyzed, then adapted or changed. People must be educated, and technology needs to be selected and implemented to make the changes possible. Skipping the first two steps of strategic planning is analogous to the notorious ready, fire, aim approach to planning that has been adopted for years. It is crucial to analyze and plan the available technologies to achieve the results that are expected from them. In order to solve or mitigate technology problems, it is important to perform an upfront analysis and planning process.

Supply Chain Security

The supply chain is expected to deliver products to customers in a safe and reliable manner. Previously, this was taken for granted, but now it is a source of concern and potential challenges might arise that must be addressed. Globalization has led to an increase in disruptions in supply chains because of the increased demand for products (Kim Sundtoft Hald, 2019). It is therefore essential that organizations are prepared to deal with disruptions as a result. The threat of disruption has changed some of the planning and preparation for supply chains, which now include some type of scenario analysis to consider potential threats, assess probability, and develop alternative solutions in order to deal with them. Thus, companies must be prepared for such a situation. In global supply chains, there is a high degree of vulnerability due to distance and complexity.

An Analysis of Cost and Value

There are challenges faced by supply chains when it comes to preventing suboptimization. There is a lot of competition between global supply chains today, so there is a great deal of focus on cost and value at the end of the supply chain (Md. Abdul Moktadir, 2018). Due to this reason, it can also be argued that supply chain collaboration is an important aspect of supply chain management. Throughout the supply chain, it is imperative that all members of the chain have an appreciation for and understanding of the challenges and issues involved. Supply chains can be suboptimized when individual segments or participants prioritize their own objectives without taking the broader objectives of the whole chain into consideration. As a result, supply chain operations can become inefficient, costly, and disrupted. While it's understandable to strive for cost-effectiveness at each step, it's also essential to realize that optimizing individual segments does not necessarily mean optimizing the whole process.

Figure 1. Current challenges for supply chain management

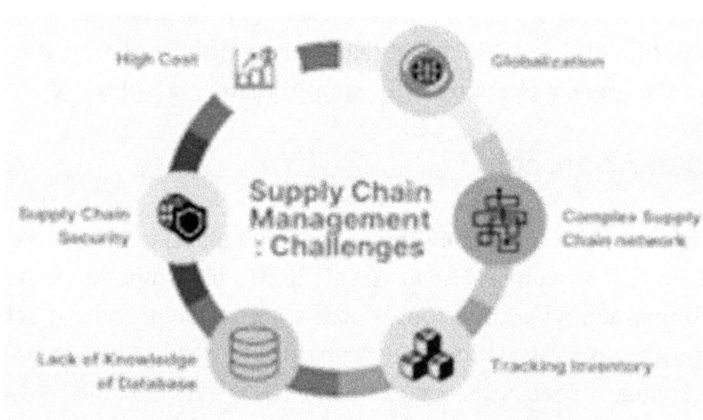

WHAT IS BLOCKCHAIN TECHNOLOGY?

Blockchain is a ledger technology where data is distributed between peer-to-peer networks in order to ensure that it is secure (Amulya Gurtu, 2019). With the help of a predefined protocol, network members can communicate and validate data without requiring a central authority to do so. A distributed ledger can be classified into two types: centralized ledgers, where specific users have special rights, and decentralized ledgers, where all users have the same rights (Gabriella M. Hastig, 2020). Considering that each node of a blockchain contains a copy of the ledger, blockchains are by nature distributed ledgers. Based on the type of the rights granted to the users in the ledger, decentralized ledgers or centralized ledgers can be designed. Decentralization is characterized by the fact that the decision-making is shared among multiple users whereas centralization is characterized by the fact that one central entity makes the primary decisions (Behzad Esmaeilian, 2020). Using blockchain technology will change the way administrative control and regulation are maintained and regulated on a digital level. Blockchains are used to convert data from paper to digital code, store it in shared databases, and have a higher level of transparency and immutability (Laturkar & Laturkar, 2022). A key advantage of the blockchain is its ability to digitally record every agreement, payment, and transaction in real time (Sobia Yaqoob, 2019). This information can be validated and shared by individuals, machines, algorithms, and organizations. Consequently, the need for intermediaries such as brokers, bankers, and lawyers has been reduced. A variety of industries rely on intermediaries to ensure the accuracy and veracity of their transactions. As a result of the blockchain technology, trust shifts from traditional agents and humans to computer codes when it comes to authenticating transactions. Figure 2 shows an example of how blockchain record can be implemented effectively at every step of supply chain.

Figure 2. Blockchain implementation in supply chain

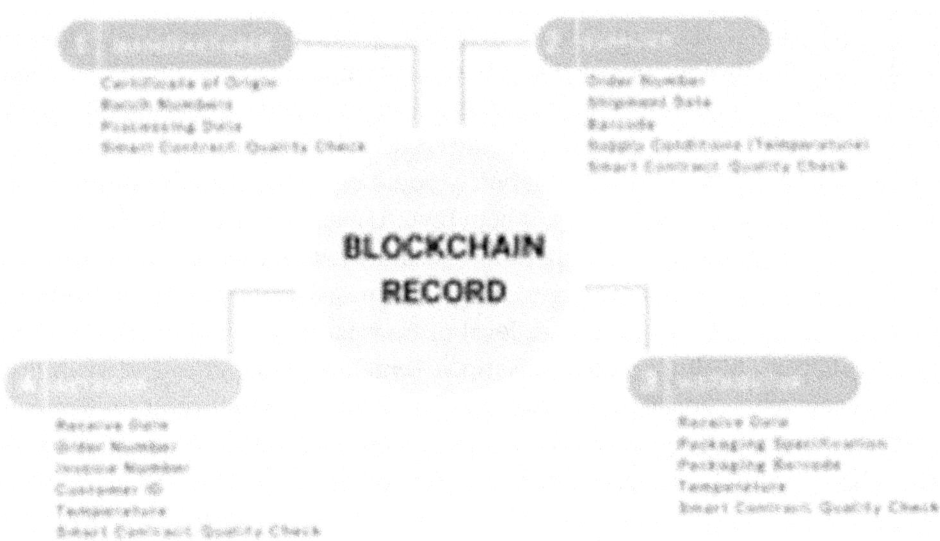

USE OF BLOCKCHAIN TECHNOLOGY FOR PHARMACEUTICAL SUPPLY CHAIN MANAGEMENT

It is the pharmaceutical supply chain (PSC) that is responsible for the provision of medicines to a wide range of stakeholders, including biotechnology companies, health regulatory agencies, pharmacies, hospitals, and patients. A shortage of medicines has become one of the top priorities for several governments due to the situation caused by Covid-19 and geopolitical circumstances. In accordance with the estimates of the World Health Organization (WHO), almost 10% of drugs in circulation are substandard, and almost 50% of medications sold over the internet are counterfeit. The pharmaceutical industry is producing more drugs containing toxic, dangerous ingredients (Seyyed-Mahdi Hosseini-Motlagh M. J., 2020), posing an increased health risk to the general public as a result (Shuchih E. Chang, 2020).

Specifically in the US, it is the responsibility of the Food and Drug Administration (FDA) to regulate pharmaceutical supply chains (PSCs) to ensure the safety, quality, and efficacy of drugs (Rita Azzia, 2019) . In accordance with the Drug Supply Chain Security Act, by 2023, all participants in the drug/medicine supply chain must develop an electronic and interoperable system that would trace prescribed drugs through their physical movement to their final destination. Despite the rigorous policies imposed by regulatory bodies and other collaborative initiatives by the pharmaceutical industry, there has been an increase in the number of drug breach incidents, putting millions of people at risk and costing the healthcare industry billions of dollars.

As a result of a lack of coordination between supply chain members and stakeholders, PSCs are not efficient (Md. Abdul Moktadir, 2018). In PSC, there is a fundamental reason why there is an increase in disease progression, drug resistance, and death as a result of a lack of transparency and visibility with regard to the supply of drugs. It is true that global sourcing and online markets make it easier to procure and supply medicines in different countries, but there is also an increased health risk because there is no way to determine where the medicines came from. Despite the application of stringent standards and the latest technologies like holograms, barcodes, and RFID tags, counterfeiting is still a major challenge for the global pharmaceutical supply chain.

Through blockchains, which are shared digital ledgers, peer-to-peer networks ensure immutable transactions by recording and executing them in a secure manner (Sara Saberi, 2019); (Mehrdokht Pournader, 2019); (Yingli Wang J. H.-D., 2019). In spite of increasing focus and successful attempts to implement Blockchain technology in other sectors such as finance, energy, food/agriculture, there seems to be a strong possibility for Blockchain's implementation in the pharmaceutical industry due to its distinct intrinsic attributes such as decentralization, immutability, and auditability (Amit Karamchandani, 2021). With the use of decentralization, healthcare hierarchy could be upended by creating new systems that will help patients manage their data in order to help them manage their health (Sobia Yaqoob, 2019). Using blockchain technology could provide the most accurate data for precision medicine, while at the same time maintaining the patients' sovereignty, control, and privacy over their personal information (Arvind Panwar, 2022). As a result of the high-level of transparency of the Blockchain, trust can also be improved in the delivery of drugs, conditions, documentation, and end-to-end visibility, especially in the case of cold chain management. Blockchain has been identified in several studies as having a big potential for pharmaceutical supply chains (e.g.: (H. M. Hussien, 2019); (Paula Fraga-Lamas, 2020); (Sandip Jangir, 2019); (Yanling Chang, 2020; Yingli Wang J. H.-D., 2019); (Seyed Mojtaba Hosseini Bamakan, 2021)).

It is the purpose of this chapter to conduct a comprehensive review of the adoption of blockchain technology in PSC and develop a conceptual framework for future research in this field. An in-depth review along with text mining methodology can be used to examine the advancements in Blockchain implementation in PSC through a systematic analysis (Francesco Galati, 2019). The thematic analysis can be used to generate an agenda for future research as well as develop a framework for the implementation of the research in a structured manner. This section lists out some of the advantages of blockchain implementation in the pharmaceutical supply chains. Figure 3 shows the various advantages of implementing blockchain technology in PSCs.

Improved Transparency and Visibility

To forecast demand for medicines/drugs, sensitive medical records of patients are scattered across hospitals, manufacturers and distributors, primarily for the purpose of demand planning. In spite of this, patients do not have access to the provenance information of the drugs they are using (Faisal Jamil, 2019); (Khizar Abbas, 2020); (Ahmad Musamih, 2021). As a result, achieving total transparency and visibility within PSCs is not as easy as it can be in other supply chains. However, blockchain implementation can help to increase collaboration, trust, and efficiency in the various PSC segments. The immutable, tamper-proof, and interoperable characteristics of blockchain are an important factor in overcoming the challenges discussed above (Hoek, 2019); (Gabriella M. Hastig, 2020); (Petri Helo, 2019); (Pedro M. Reyes, 2020).

The characteristics of blockchain make it highly attractive for managing personal health records in accordance with data protection laws while still adhering to regulatory requirements (Hao Sen Andrew Fang, 2021). PSC stakeholders will be able to access transactional information without having to expose that data to third parties (Aashima Sharma, 2021). Moreover, it contributes to the reduction of information delays which in turn helps to improve data accuracy. Recently through BlockRx, a pharma ecosystem, pharma manufacturers, retailers, and pharmacies have upgraded their existing information systems, broken down information silos, and provided enhanced transparency throughout the distribution chain (Ahmed Farouk, 2020).

Enhanced Data Security

There is no doubt that cloud storage of electronic medical records has proven to be a standard way of storing dispersed data, even though it is vulnerable and easy to be compromised by cyber-attacks (H. M. Hussien, 2019). As a result of the adoption of Blockchain technology, each transaction record will be grouped into time-stamped and immutable blocks which can be accessed via the decentralised distributed ledger, enabling it to be shared easily with authorized users (Thomas McGhin, 2019); (Nam Vu, 2021). It goes without saying that Blockchain is able to protect healthcare and medicine/drug data from being attacked by hackers or cybercriminals.

During the transportation of some pharmaceutical products, such as vaccines, it is necessary to maintain a delicate level of temperature and humidity monitoring (Laturkar & Laturkar, 2023). With the use of IoT devices (e.g. GPS, temperature sensors) during shipping, any unqualified environmental conditions for drugs can be captured quickly and an alert can be sent to the authorized parties in the blockchain platform so that they can act accordingly (Shanshan Zhao, 2019); (Fátima Leal, 2021).

Blockchain implementation can also ensure that the conditions of transportation of vaccines and other pharmaceutical products throughout the supply chain are safe (Rajani Singh, 2020). In this process, smart contracts can play a vital role in verifying the authenticity of products, requisitions as well as terminating the contracts and reimbursing clients as needed, contingent to pre-set protocols and rules (Hoek, 2019). Blockchain-based projects such as the SmartHub project can be used to track and trace pharmaceutical product characteristics - such as location, ingredients, temperature settings, etc. complete with product images (Petri Helo, 2019). In addition to this, a similar use case is the concept of LedgerDomain, which uses the Blockchain and bar-coding to trace and track drugs for patients (Md. Jahir Uddin Palas, 2021). There is, in essence, a need to ensure that drugs can be traced and secured in the PSC, which drives the implementation of Blockchain.

Improved Efficiency

The adoption of Blockchain technology improves the efficiency of the supply chain (Kim Sundtoft Hald, 2019); (Lai-Wan Wong, 2020). The pharmaceutical industry is expected to benefit from blockchain's ability to provide better analytics, speed up payment processes, and respond quickly to emergencies (Christoph G. Schmidt, 2019); (Pedro M. Reyes, 2020). The PSC's notification process and drug recall process were time-consuming due to the manual paperwork and fragmented, complex systems, leading to long response times and dissatisfied healthcare workers. As a result of the increased trust and transparency between the parties that are involved in the supply chain, Blockchain can substantially speed up the processing time and warn parties involved in the supply chain in a timely manner regarding any recalls of drugs (Seyyed-Mahdi Hosseini-Motlagh, 2021). Additionally, smart contracts can be used to eliminate other intermediates and reduce labor costs, since the validation process takes place within the Blockchain network, thereby reducing intermediary costs. As long as the pre-set conditions, rights, and obligations of each party of the self-executed agreement are met, the agreement will be valid and binding. Blockchain technology also increases the extent to which information is shared, which ultimately increases the efficiency of the pharmaceutical supply chain by identifying bottlenecks and eliminating overstocking.

Enforcement by Regulatory Bodies

The pharmaceutical industry is strictly regulated by government agencies such as the Food and Drug Administration (FDA), the Falsified Medication Directive (FMD), and other non-profit organizations such as the World Health Organization (WHO). Organizations are required to follow the regulations in order to prevent counterfeit products from being sold. In comparison to developing countries, developed countries are taking more practical measures in order to detect falsified drugs. Blockchain pilot projects, such as MediLedger and PharmaLedger are designed to collaborate with global pharmaceutical manufacturers, distributors, hospitals, and pharmacies to make transactions using the distributed ledger technology on a global scale. Similar to the FDA, the European Federation of Pharmaceutical Industries and Associations (EFPIA) is also focusing on detecting counterfeited products in the PSC and trying to eliminate unqualified drugs from the market. Blockchain projects are also being promoted by developing countries such as India and Brazil in order to improve the quality of healthcare services available in their countries (Devendra Dhagarra, 2019).

Figure 3. Advantages of implementing blockchain technology in pharmaceutical supply chains (PSC)

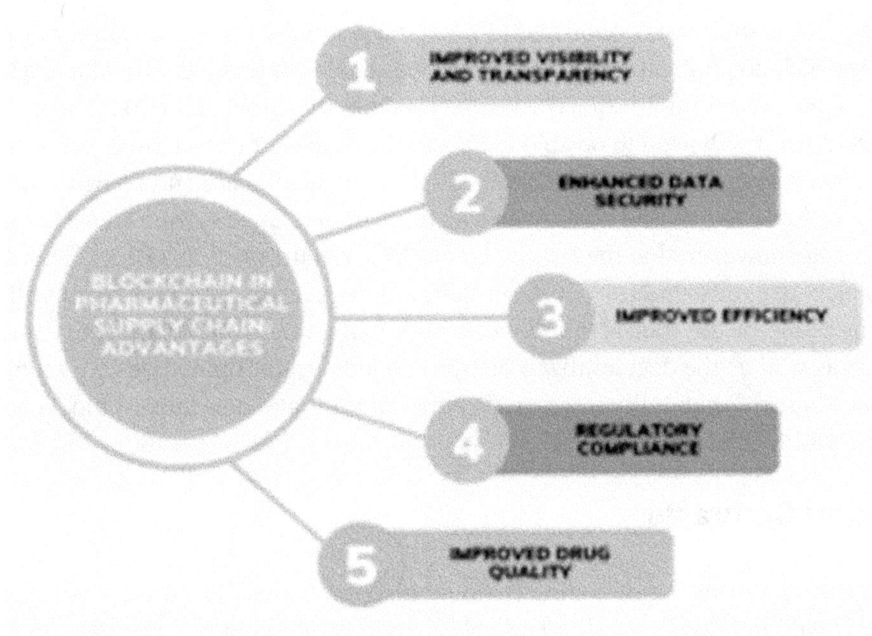

Improved Quality

Patients are increasingly interested in the provenance and ingredients of the medicines they use in order to make sure they are not going to have any side effects and comply with sustainability and quality certifications (Amit Karamchandani, 2021). The COVID-19 pandemic also restricted consumers' access to local pharmacies, which led to an increase in the number of people purchasing drugs online. It is for this reason that governments have demanded strict supervision of online pharmacies, especially their legitimacy and authenticity, in order to reduce chances of purchasing fake drugs from them. Through the implementation of blockchain in pharmaceutical manufacturing, distribution, and sale, emphasis is placed on bringing transparency to the supply chain. Medication authenticity and quality are verified through stringent documentation and traceability standards (Robert M. Monczka, 2020). Furthermore, governments are working with international organizations to create a unified approach to regulate online pharmacies. By adopting blockchain technology, certifications, licenses, and regulatory compliance could be checked in order to confirm that online pharmacies are legitimate.

LIMITATIONS OF BLOCKCHAIN IMPLEMENTATION IN SUPPLY CHAIN MANAGEMENT

There are several technical and operational issues that are experienced during blockchain implementation (Muhammad Haseeb, 2019); (Giuseppe Aceto, 2020). Scalability, smart contract design, and the high adoption costs of blockchain are ranked as the three most important barriers to the adoption of Blockchain in the multidisciplinary studies.

Scalability

There are hundreds of market tests conducted to prove the feasibility and plausibility of a new technology. Currently, blockchain applications in the pharmaceutical industry are still at an early stage, with a limited number of successful pilot projects to date. To scale the Blockchain to a supply chain network level, it is expected that it will need to be able to handle thousands of transactions per second and have a large amount of data capacity (Mohamad Kassab, 2019). The healthcare and pharmaceutical industries could produce 10 billion drugs based on Taiwan's healthcare insurance system (Jen-Hung Tseng, 2018). It is important to note, however, that the current Gcoin Blockchain system, a Blockchain-based solution for drug governance, can only process a million transactions per day, and thus there will be some time delay in verifying some of the transaction data. Additionally, due to the complexity, the large size of medical supplies, as well as the decentralized distributed ledger, multiple nodes are required to process every transaction. As such, scalability is a generic concern for wider adoption of blockchain technology and it stands true for PSCs as well.

Design of Smart Contracts

Apart from this, self-executing smart contracts would also make mistakes if there were several permissioned parties involved in both the design and verification of the contract. As an example, converting PSC operations and regulations to smart contracts can be a challenging process, because of the balance of conflicts and benefits that must be achieved between different stakeholders (Yingli Wang J. H.-D., 2019). As a result of the ambiguous clause generated in the interpretation, there is the possibility that the transaction will be unsuccessful or incorrect. Furthermore, the initial smart contracts are only capable of carrying out very simple processes, such as financial transactions, and laws and regulations are not included in the verification clauses of the contracts (Akhil Kumar, 2020). As transaction volumes and contractual agreements increase, smart contracts may become less effective at detecting counterfeit products because of an increase in transaction volumes. A crypto-anchor platform has been developed by IBM to overcome this problem by ensuring that the correct products are received through user authentication and certification (Miguel A. Prada-Delgado, 2021).

Costs Associated With Operations

Blockchain adoption is likely to be delayed as a result of the high costs associated with system adoption (mining) as well as the associated maintenance and consultant costs (Rosanna Cole, 2019). Pharmaceutical company practitioners are currently finding it difficult to see how the benefits of Blockchain in terms of improved efficiency and cost reduction could compensate for the high implementation costs associated with the new technology (Kshetri, 2018). In addition to this, the current 'immature' Blockchain technology market (Hoek, 2019) may lead to high system adoption costs as well as technical issues during the implementation process. It is predicted that large organizations will be 'early adopters' of this technology, whereas medium-sized and small enterprises may be hesitant to take the leap due to the financial risks associated with this technology. In addition, some scholars also recommend that Blockchain be used in combination with other technologies such as the cloud, IoT and RFID to achieve the best results (Arun Aryal, 2020) ; (Khizar Abbas, 2020); (Rajani Singh, 2020). This means that there would also be a high cost associated with integrating different systems. It would be expensive to implement Blockchain at the supply chain level due to the high cost of consultants and technical training for employees.

BLOCKCHAIN IMPLEMENTATION EXAMPLES IN PHARMACEUTICAL SUPPLY CHAIN

In the future, supply chains will be one of the most important segments of industries to use blockchain technology. There have been several research studies and publications that have shown the effectiveness of blockchain-based pharmaceutical and healthcare applications in recent years. In addition to improving workflow processes, they can also be used as data acquisition tools. Following are a few examples.

SmartHub Logistics

MVC Global, a Bahrain-based pharmaceutical track and trace company, partnered with Cox Logistics to open the SmartHub logistics blockchain warehouse solution for storing food and pharmaceuticals. For the distribution of food and medicines in Bahrain and the rest of the Gulf Cooperation Council (GCC) market, it is anticipated that the smart warehouse will use blockchain and other emerging technologies such as artificial intelligence (AI) (Ledger Insights, 2020).

A blockchain-based track and trace feature will be available in the 'SmartHub', while smart contracts will handle customs clearance and payments in the 'SmartPass'. It is this latter solution, known as 'SmartPass', that integrates supply chain finance and cross-border payments into one single method, allowing for government clearance and transactions across borders to take place simultaneously. In addition to its operational efficiency, SmartPass offers many other benefits which enhance supply chain reliability and speed. It is especially important in the context of pharmaceuticals, where timely and secure distribution can mean the difference between life and death. SmartHub contributes to supply chain resilience, ensuring that essential medications are delivered on time.

Furthermore, the SmartHub incorporates artificial intelligence (AI) to provide predictive and analytical capabilities. In addition to analyzing data from a variety of sources, AI algorithms can provide insights into demand patterns, inventory management, and potential disruptions. A data-driven approach to supply chain management allows for proactive decision-making, reducing stockouts and excess inventory, and optimizing overall supply chain efficiency.

MVC Global and Cox Logistics' collaboration demonstrates a commitment to leveraging technology to address the evolving challenges in logistics and supply chain. The SmartHub will likely set a precedent for similar initiatives across the globe, demonstrating how blockchain, AI, and smart contracts can transform traditional logistics practices into more secure, efficient, and transparent ones.

BlockRx Pharma Ecosystem

In the pharmaceutical industry, there is a market worth about $800bn that has a serious impact on patient safety as a result of serious diseases. According to the World Customs Organization, the counterfeit medicine business, currently estimated to have an annual value of $75-$200 billion, is a fast-growing, global epidemic with substantial human and financial costs (Securing Industry, 2017). The World Health Organization (WHO) estimates that ten to thirty percent of all medicines distributed around the world are counterfeit. There are more than 100,000 deaths each year and 90,000 direct and indirect job losses are predicted by the European Union. There is no doubt that there is an urgent need for an innovative solution to combat this epidemic now more than ever before, which is why BlockRx Pharma Ecosystem is crucial for the pharmaceutical industry. Using the BlockRx Token, the underlying platform will be able to optimize and secure a decentralized pharmaceutical supply chain, while at the same time providing patients with the ability to manage and share their health data as well.

BlockRx is partnering with Intel, one of the world's largest technology companies, and YourEncore, one of the industry's leading providers of proven expertise in the life sciences market. The BlockRx Pharma Ecosystem is a robust three-pronged solution incorporating Sawtooth by Intel, a high performance enterprise blockchain; the BlockRx Token for blockchain transactions and data exchange; as well as iSolve's Advanced Digital Ledger Technology (ADLT) to integrate legacy systems with the blockchain platform.

As a reward for using the blockchain as a vehicle for managing data entries pertaining to drug development and logistics, the BlockRx Token is the primary means to reward trade partners and consumers. Using the BlockRx Token, members of the BlockRx Pharma Ecosystem can exchange information with other trusted partners via the BlockRx Pharma Ecosystem, as well as use the token as a medium of exchange for the acquisition of intellectual property (IP), data, and services.

The Drug Supply Chain Security Act (DSCSA) Interoperability Pilot

Several studies have been conducted that investigate how blockchain technology can be used to track and trace certain prescription drugs throughout the supply chain in a more efficient and effective manner. With blockchain technology, pharmaceutical supply chain actors will be able to comply with DSCSA (a U.S. law that goes into effect in 2024), prevent the distribution of counterfeit drugs, ease the drug recall process, and many other things due to the transparency it offers.

The Drug Supply Chain Security Act (DSCSA) Interoperability Pilot was completed in December 2019 by KPMG, Merck, Walmart and IBM, as part of the U.S. Federal Drug Administration (FDA) pilot project program (IBM, 2019). It has been found that leveraging blockchain technology is able to significantly reduce the time it takes to trace a prescription drug - from up to 16 weeks to only two seconds - due to its high accuracy.

Having completed work for the FDA DSCSA Interoperability Pilot, IBM and its partners aim to formally launch and scale the blockchain-enabled solution to streamline and facilitate pharmaceutical supply chain stakeholders' compliance with the DSCSA as soon as possible. The DSCSA requires organizations to be able to digitally verify a drug product and its journey through the end-to-end supply chain in order to comply with the requirements of the act. As part of the pilot application, blockchain technology is used to digitally store pharmaceutical product profiles and track and trace pharmaceutical products at the unit level from the point of manufacture to the point of distribution.

As well as improving the visibility of the supply chain, the pilot also utilizes blockchain technology to enhance the safety of patients and the protection of their privacy. An illegitimate or suspect drug product can be identified, investigated, and communicated using the application quickly and effectively. The process of drug recall could be improved and expedited by eliminating data silos between supply chain actors.

PharmaLedger MediLedger

One of the most serious threats facing the pharmaceutical industry is the counterfeiting of drugs. According to the World Health Organization (WHO), nearly 10% of the drugs produced in the lesser developed countries, i.e., one out of ten medicines, are counterfeit and have serious side effects that can potentially lead to death (Uddin, 2021). There has been an increase in the number of online and internet-based pharmacies in recent years, which has led to a complexity and intricacy in the drug supply chain process in terms of its safety and security. An innovative track and trace blockchain-enabled Medledger system has been proposed that employs Hyperledger Fabric's blockchain platform with blockchain-enabled chaincodes (smart contracts). The proposed Medledger system is intended to help facilitate and secure the execution of drug supply chain transactions in a private permissioned distributed network of different stakeholders involved in the pharmaceutical industry. As a result, there will be no need for a centralized authority or intermediaries, which will result in an increase in efficiency and safety with high integrity, reliability, and security, thus reducing the possibility of meddling with the Medledger stored data. As part of the drug supply chain ecosystem, chaincodes are designed, coded, and implemented using sequence diagrams so they can govern and control the interaction amongst the stakeholders involved in the supply chain. With the proposed system, all activities, events, and transactions are perpetually stored and recorded on the immutable Medledger that is linked to peer-to-peer decentralized file systems such as IPFS, Swarm, filecoin, etc providing maximum transparency and traceability of data.

Anti-Counterfeit Management System

Pharmaceutical products are serialized and assigned security features so that they can be verified by consumers, allowing them to distinguish genuine products from counterfeits. The implementation of a blockchain system will enhance security through transparent and chaincode-based transactions. For the pharmaceutical industry to be successful, both trust and transparency are essential. This is because without trust, counterfeiting thrives, exposing the public to dangers resulting from the use of low-quality or substandard pharmaceutical products. Integrating blockchain technology into quality control and counterfeit drug detection can enhance safety and save lives (Nazik Zakari, 2022). In order to prevent counterfeiting, there are a number of approaches that can be used, including the Anti-Counterfeit Medicine System (ACMS). ACM uses the Interplanetary File System (IPFS) networks and the Ethereum blockchain to prevent cloning of medicines sold at retail and non-retail outlets, if the ownership criteria is established for both. It can also be used to build Ethereum based smart contracts to make it more functional.

As a result of the ACMS, fraud is effectively prevented. A chaincode is generated by the client as soon as the transaction is initiated. As soon as the signature is submitted, it is verified by endorsing peers, and once the endorsements have been collected, the endorsements are sent to the ordering services. The final step is to validate the transaction.

MeDShare for Data Sharing

The dissemination of patients' medical records results in various risks to patients' privacy as malicious activities conducted on these records have the potential to cause severe damage to the reputation, finances, and so on of all those involved directly or indirectly with those records. The current methods used to manage and protect medical records have proven to be insufficient to meet the current needs. The

MeDShare (Mingyue Wang, 2023) system is designed to address the issue of sharing medical data in a trust-less environment among the custodians of big medical data. It is a blockchain-based system that provides data provenance, auditing, and control of shared medical data in cloud repositories between big data entities (Laturkar & Laturkar, 2023). In the case of a data custodian system, MeDShare monitors entities that access data for the purpose of misusing it. A tamper-proof method has been developed for MeDShare, which ensures that all data transitions and sharing between entities, along with all actions performed on the MeDShare system, are recorded in a tamper-proof manner. Smart contracts and an access control mechanism are employed in the design to effectively track the behavior of the data and to revoke access to offending entities when it is detected that permissions have been violated. MeDShare will allow cloud service providers and other data guardians to achieve data provenance and auditing while sharing medical data with entities such as research and medical institutions with minimal privacy risks. There is no doubt that MeDShare performs better than current cutting edge solutions for data sharing among cloud service providers.

FUTURE DIRECTIONS

Enhance Sustainability and Circular Economy in the PSC Sector

There is a strong correlation between blockchain adoption in the PSC and environmental and social dimensions of sustainability (Yingjia Wang, 2020). With the implementation of Blockchain technology, it will be possible to ensure the confidentiality of personal information of patients and medical data, without compromising the accessibility of data for demand planning and other supply chain activities. The Shipchain on the other hand utilizes smart contracts to achieve a 100% digital transaction in order to reduce the amount of paper waste. The use of Blockchain in the pharmaceutical industry will allow researchers to investigate more sustainable and circular economy practices, including patient-centered drug supply and sustainable reuse and disposal of drugs (Ding, 2018).

Management of Drug Recalls in the Pharmaceutical Industry

Supply chain practitioners are still seeking proactive, efficient drug recall management systems, and with the help of Blockchain, it is possible to guarantee drug authenticity, ensure transparency and bring visibility across the supply chain networks (Seyyed-Mahdi Hosseini-Motlagh M. J., 2020); (Xuanping Wu, 2019). In addition to using Blockchain technology for reverse pharmaceutical logistics, a very exciting research direction that is being explored is the possibility of using Blockchain technology for expired or recalled drugs. As Blockchain is decentralized, information regarding expiration dates or recall status is securely recorded and easily accessible to authorized parties. By streamlining reverse logistics, it can be made more efficient and less error prone. As an added benefit, Blockchain's traceability features can help manage the disposal or destruction of expired or recalled drugs. Blockchain provides auditable proof of the proper handling and disposal of pharmaceutical products by maintaining an unalterable record of each transaction, minimizing the risk of illicit circulation.

Governing Standards and Regulations

The Blockchain ecosystem within the PSC is still in the early stages of development due to the lack of successfully implemented practices and clear regulations for this digital domain (Erikson Julio De Aguiar, 2020). It has been reported that pharmaceutical supply chain practitioners are concerned about the lack of regulations related to privacy policies related to sensitive data, which could stifle the adoption of Blockchain technology to a large extent. In addition, a Blockchain consortium is likely to update and change the governance model (Robbie Morrison, 2020) . Clearly, there is a lack of standardization of Blockchain practices and well-defined PSC regulations, which needs further research and analysis.

Enhancing the Interoperability and Compatibility

As a result of blockchain interoperability, it may be possible to collaborate between different Blockchain systems in the future. In spite of this, there are concerns that Blockchain interoperability in the healthcare/pharmaceutical system may be challenging due to the complex nature of the system. Additionally, integrating Blockchain with other support technologies such as IoT and RFID is beneficial to PSCs in improving supply chain traceability (Botcha & Chakravarthy, 2019); (Seyed Mojtaba Hosseini Bamakan, 2021); but this opportunity has not been fully exploited yet. There is an urgent need for ERP-integrated Blockchain systems to be created to better manage larger data sets. In the future, practitioners can explore further possibilities for enhancing Blockchain interoperability and compatibility with other disruptive technologies in order to make the technology more effective.

Establishing a Performance Measurement System

It is beneficial for organizations to evaluate the success and failures of the Blockchain performance optimization system in their industry and to decide whether or not this technology is really needed in that industry (Mengting Liu, 2019). With the growing number of Blockchain pilot projects in the PSC, there is a need to develop a performance measurement system in order to measure the effectiveness of the Blockchain system that has been implemented. As a result, organizations can follow benchmarking standards to evaluate their performance at each stage of the implementation process, and the whole supply chain activities can be improved. It is therefore necessary to carry out empirical/experimental studies in order to establish a link between Blockchain and PSC.

CONCLUSION

Ultimately, blockchain technology's integration into supply chain management has shown immense potential to revolutionize global trade and logistics. Blockchain addresses some of the most pressing challenges in the supply chain by providing secure, transparent, and decentralized solutions. In addition to ensuring accountability, it reduces risks of fraud, counterfeiting, and inefficiencies by providing a single source of truth for all stakeholders.

Supply chain management has already been impacted by blockchain in a variety of industries, including food and pharmaceuticals, luxury goods, and electronics. Processes are streamlined, collaboration is enhanced, and risk management is more effective when using the technology. In addition, smart contracts and real-time tracking facilitate trust among participants and simplify complex transactions, ultimately resulting in faster delivery times and better customer service.

There remain challenges, however, regarding scalability, interoperability with existing systems, and regulatory considerations. In order to address these challenges and ensure seamless integration of blockchain technology into existing supply chain infrastructures, stakeholders need to work collaboratively. Implementing blockchain in real-world supply chain management will require continued research and development in the coming years. Business, consumers, and the broader economy will benefit from the technology as it matures and becomes more widely adopted.

REFERENCES

Aashima Sharma, S. K. (2021). A comprehensive review on blockchain and Internet of Things in healthcare. *Transactions on Emerging Telecommunications Technologies.*

Ahmad Musamih, K. S.-H. (2021). A Blockchain-Based Approach for Drug Traceability in Healthcare Supply Chain. *IEEE Access : Practical Innovations, Open Solutions*, *9*, 9728–9743. doi:10.1109/ACCESS.2021.3049920

Ahmed Farouk, A. A. (2020). Blockchain Platform for Industrial Healthcare: Vision and Future opportunities. *Computer Communications*, *154*, 223–235. doi:10.1016/j.comcom.2020.02.058

Akhil Kumar, R. L. (2020). Is Blockchain a Silver Bullet for Supply Chain Management? Technical Challenges and Research Opportunities. *Decision Sciences*, *51*(1), 8–37. doi:10.1111/deci.12396

Amit Karamchandani, S. K. (2021). Analysing perceived role of blockchain technology in SCM context for the manufacturing industry. *International Journal of Production Research*, *59*(11), 3398–3429. doi:10.1080/00207543.2021.1883761

Amulya Gurtu, J. J. (2019). Potential of blockchain technology in supply chain management: A literature review. *International Journal of Physical Distribution & Logistics Management*, *49*(9), 881–900. doi:10.1108/IJPDLM-11-2018-0371

Arun Aryal, Y. L. (2020). The Emerging big Data Analytics and IoT in Supply Chain Management: A Systematic Review. *Supply Chain Management*, 141–156.

Arvind Panwar, V. B. (2022). A Blockchain Framework to Secure Personal Health Record (PHR) in IBM Cloud-Based Data Lake. *Computational Intelligence and Neuroscience*. PMID:35463293

Behzad Esmaeilian, J. S. (2020). Blockchain for the future of sustainable supply chain management in Industry 4.0. *Resources, Conservation and Recycling.*

Botcha, K. M., & Chakravarthy, V. V. (2019). Enhancing Traceability in Pharmaceutical Supply Chain Using Internet of Things (IoT) and Blockchain. *Proceedings - 2019 IEEE international conference on intelligent systems and green technology*, (pp. 45-48). IEEE.

Christoph, G., & Schmidt, S. M. (2019). Blockchain and Supply Chain Relations: A Transaction Cost Theory Perspective. *Journal of Purchasing and Supply Management.*

Devendra Dhagarra, M. G. (2019). Big Data and blockchain supported conceptual model for enhanced healthcare coverage: The Indian context. *Business Process Management Journal*, BPMJ-06-2018-0164. doi:10.1108/BPMJ-06-2018-0164

Ding, B. (2018). Pharma Industry 4.0: Literature Review and Research Opportunities in Sustainable Pharmaceutical Supply Chains. *Process Safety and Environmental Protection*, *119*, 115–130. doi:10.1016/j.psep.2018.06.031

Erikson Julio De Aguiar, B. S. (2020). A Survey of Blockchain-Based Strategies for Healthcare. ACM Computing Surveys. Association for Computing Machinery (ACM).

Faisal Jamil, L. H. (2019). A Novel Medical Blockchain Model for Drug Supply Chain Integrity Management in a Smart Hospital. *Electronics (Basel)*.

Fátima Leal, A. E.-V.-G.-G. (2021). *Smart Pharmaceutical Manufacturing: Ensuring end-to-end Traceability and Data Integrity in Medicine Production*. Big Data Research.

Francesco Galati, B. B. (2019). Industry 4.0: Emerging Themes and Future Research Avenues Using a Text Mining Approach. *Computers in Industry*, *109*, 100–113. doi:10.1016/j.compind.2019.04.018

Gabriella, M., & Hastig, M. S. (2020). Blockchain for Supply Chain Traceability: Business Requirements and Critical Success Factors. *Production and Operations Management*, 935–954.

Giuseppe Aceto, V. P. (2020). Industry 4.0 and Health: Internet of Things, Big Data, and Cloud Computing for Healthcare 4.0. *Journal of Industrial Information Integration*.

Hao Sen Andrew Fang, T. H. (2021). Blockchain Personal Health Records: Systematic Review. *Journal of Medical Internet Research*. PMID:33847591

Hoek, R. v. (2019). Developing a Framework for Considering Blockchain Pilots in the Supply Chain – Lessons from Early Industry adopters. *An International Journal, Emerald Group Publishing Ltd*, 115-121.

Hussien, H. M., Yasin, S. M., Udzir, S. N. I., Zaidan, A. A., & Zaidan, B. B. (2019). A Systematic Review for Enabling of Develop a Blockchain Technology in Healthcare Application: Taxonomy, Substantially Analysis, Motivations, Challenges, Recommendations, and Future Direction. *Journal of Medical Systems*, *43*(10), 320. doi:10.100710916-019-1445-8 PMID:31522262

IBM. (2019, December 16). *Protect Pharmaceutical Product Integrity with the Pharmaceutical Utility Network*. IBM. https://www.ibm.com/blog/protect-pharmaceutical-product-integrity-with-the-pharmaceutical-utility-network/

Insights, L. (2020, April 28). *Bahrain to Use Blockchain for Food, pharma traceability, customs amid COVID-19*. Ledger Insights. https://www.ledgerinsights.com/bahrain-to-use-blockchain-for-food-pharma-traceability-customs-amid-covid-19/

Javed Aslama, A. S. (2021). Factors influencing blockchain adoption in supply chain management practices: A study based on the oil industry. *Journal of Innovation and Knowledge*, 124-134.

Jen-Hung Tseng, Y.-C. L.-w. (2018). Governance on the Drug Supply Chain via Gcoin Blockchain. *International Journal of Environmental Research and Public Health*. PMID:29882861

John J. Coyle, C. J. (2021). *Supply Chain Management: A Logistics Perspective.* Singapore: Cengage Learning.

Khizar Abbas, M. A.-C. (2020). A Blockchain and Machine Learning-Based Drug Supply Chain Management and Recommendation System for Smart Pharmaceutical Industry. *Electronics (Basel).*

Kim Sundtoft Hald, A. K. (2019). How the Blockchain Enables and Constrains Supply Chain Performance. *International Journal of Physical Distribution & Logistics Management, 49*(4), 376–397. doi:10.1108/IJPDLM-02-2019-0063

Kshetri, N. (2018). 1 Blockchain's Roles in Meeting key Supply Chain Management objectives. *International Journal of Information Management, 39*, 80–89. doi:10.1016/j.ijinfomgt.2017.12.005

Lai-Wan Wong, G. W.-H.-H.-B. (2020). Unearthing the Determinants of Blockchain Adoption in Supply Chain Management. *International Journal of Production Research, 58*(7), 2100–2123. doi:10.1080/00207543.2020.1730463

Laturkar, K., & Laturkar, K. (2022, April). Blockchain and the downstream segment: Increasing efficiency through technology. *Hydrocarbon Processing.*

Laturkar, K., & Laturkar, K. (2023). A Blockchain-Based Approach to Revolutionizing Healthcare. Springer. doi:10.4018/978-1-6684-6509-7.ch003

Laturkar, K., & Laturkar, K. (2023). *Internet of Things: Architectures.* Applications, and Challenges. doi:10.4018/978-1-6684-8145-5.ch023

Liu, M. F. R. (2019). Performance Optimization for Blockchain-Enabled Industrial Internet of Things (IIoT) Systems: A Deep Reinforcement Learning Approach. IEEE Transactions on Industrial Informatics. IEEE Computer Society, 3559-3570. IEEE.

Md. Abdul Moktadir, S. M.-R. (2018). Decision modeling of risks in pharmaceutical supply chains. *Industrial Management & Data Systems.*

Md. Jahir Uddin Palas, R. B. (2021). Exploring Interpretations of Blockchain's Value in Healthcare: A Multi-Stakeholder Approach. *Information Technology & People*, 453–495.

Mehrdokht Pournader, Y. S. (2019). Blockchain Applications in Supply Chains, Transport and logistics: A systematic review of the literature. *International Journal of Production Research.*

Miguel A. Prada-Delgado, G. D. (2021). A Blockchain-Based Crypto-Anchor Platform for Interoperable Product Authentication. *IEEE international symposium on circuits and systems (ISCAS)*, (pp. 1-5). IEEE.

Mingyue Wang, Y. G. (2023). MedShare: A Privacy-Preserving Medical Data Sharing System by Using Blockchain. *IEEE Transactions on Services Computing.*

Mohamad Kassab, J. D. (2019). Exploring Research in Blockchain for Healthcare and a Roadmap for the Future. *IEEE Transactions on Emerging Topics in Computing*, 1835–1852.

Muhammad Haseeb, H. I. (2019). Industry 4.0: A Solution Towards Technology Challenges of Sustainable Business Performance. *Social Sciences.*

Nam Vu, A. G. (2021). Blockchain Adoption in Food Supply Chains: A Review and Implementation Framework. *Production Planning and Control*, 1–18.

Nazik Zakari, M. A.-R. (2022). Blockchain technology in the pharmaceutical industry: A systematic review. *PeerJ. Computer Science*. PMID:35634106

Paula Fraga-Lamas, T. M.-C. (2020). Fake News, Disinformation, and Deepfakes: Leveraging Distributed Ledger Technologies and Blockchain to Combat Digital Deception and Counterfeit Reality. IT Professional. IEEE.

Pedro, M., & Reyes, J. K. (2020). Managing the Dynamics of New Technologies in the Global Supply Chain. *IEEE Engineering Management Review*, 156–162.

Petri Helo, Y. H. (2019). Blockchains in Operations and Supply Chains: A Model and Reference Implementation. *Computers & Industrial Engineering*, *136*, 242–251. doi:10.1016/j.cie.2019.07.023

Prakash Agrawal, R. N. (2018). Digital supply chain management: An Overview. *IOP Conference Series. Materials Science and Engineering*.

Rajani Singh, A. D. (2020). Internet of Things Based Blockchain for Temperature Monitoring and Counterfeit Pharmaceutical Prevention. *Sensors (Basel)*. PMID:32708588

Rita Azzia, R. K. (2019). The power of a blockchain-based supply chain. *Computers & Industrial Engineering*, *135*, 582–592. doi:10.1016/j.cie.2019.06.042

Robbie Morrison, N. C. (2020). The DAO Controversy: The Case for a New Species of Corporate Governance? *Frontiers in Blockchain*.

Robert M. Monczka, R. B. (2020). *Purchasing and Supply Chain Management.* Cengage Learning.

Rosanna Cole, M. S. (2019). Blockchain Technology: Implications for Operations and Supply Chain Management. *Supply Chain Management*, *24*(4), 469–483. doi:10.1108/SCM-09-2018-0309

Sandip Jangir, A. M. (2019). A Novel Framework for Pharmaceutical Supply Chain Management using Distributed Ledger and Smart Contracts. *International Conference on Computing, Communication and Networking Technologies (ICCCNT)*. IEEE.

Sara Saberi, M. K. (2019). Blockchain technology and its relationships to sustainable supply chain management. *International Journal of Production Research*, *57*(7), 2117–2135. doi:10.1080/00207543.2018.1533261

Securing Industry. (2017, August 24). *BlockRx announces powerhouse partners before the first pharmaceutical ICO offering hits the market*. Securing Industry. https://www.securingindustry.com/press-releases/blockrx-announces-powerhouse-partners-before-the-first-pharmaceutical-ico-offering-hits-the-market/s135/a5484/

Seyed Mojtaba Hosseini Bamakan, S. G. (2021). Blockchain-enabled Pharmaceutical Cold Chain: Applications, key Challenges, and Future Trends. *Journal of Cleaner Production.*

Seyednima Khezr, M. M. (2019). *Blockchain Technology in Healthcare: A Comprehensive Review and Directions for Future Research.* Applied Sciences.

Seyyed-Mahdi Hosseini-Motlagh, M. J. (2020). Recall management in pharmaceutical industry through supply chain coordination. *Annals of Operations Research.*

Seyyed-Mahdi Hosseini-Motlagh, M. J. (2020). Recall Management in Pharmaceutical Industry through Supply Chain Coordination. *Annals of Operations Research*, 1–39.

Seyyed-Mahdi Hosseini-Motlagh, M. N. (2021). Drug Recall Management and Channel Coordination Under Stochastic Product Defect Severity: A Game-Theoretic Analytical Study. *International Journal of Production Research*, *59*(6), 1649–1675. doi:10.1080/00207543.2020.1723813

Shanshan Zhao, S. L. (2019). Blockchain Enabled Industrial Internet of Things Technology. *IEEE Transactions on Computational Social Systems*, *6*(6), 1442–1453. doi:10.1109/TCSS.2019.2924054

Shuchih E. Chang, Y. C. (2020). When Blockchain Meets Supply Chain: A Systematic Literature Review on Current Development and Potential Applications. *IEEE Access, Institute of Electrical and Electronics Engineers Inc*. IEEE.

Sobia Yaqoob, M. M. (2019). Use of Blockchain in Healthcare: A Systematic Literature Review. *International Journal of Advanced Computer Science and Applications*, 644–653.

Thomas McGhin, K.-K. R. (2019). Blockchain in Healthcare Applications: Research Challenges and opportunities. *Journal of Network and Computer Applications*, *135*, 62–75. doi:10.1016/j.jnca.2019.02.027

Uddin, M. (2021). Blockchain Medledger: Hyperledger fabric enabled drug traceability system for counterfeit drugs in pharmaceutical industry. *International Journal of Pharmaceutics*, *597*, 120235. doi:10.1016/j.ijpharm.2021.120235 PMID:33549813

Xuanping Wu, Y. L. (2019). Blockchain Recall Management in Pharmaceutical Industry. *Procedia CIRP*, 590–595.

Yanling Chang, E. I. (2020). Blockchain in global supply chains and cross border trade: A critical synthesis of the state-of the-art, challenges and opportunities. *International Journal of Production Research*, 1–18.

Yingjia Wang, J. L.-M. (2020). Gray Market and Counterfeiting in Supply Chains: A Review of the Operations Literature and Implications to Luxury industries. *Transportation Research Part E, Logistics and Transportation Review*.

Yingli Wang, J. H.-D. (2019). *Supply Chain Management*, 62–84. doi:10.1108/SCM-03-2018-0148

Yingli Wang, J. H.-D. (2019). Understanding Blockchain Technology for Future Supply Chains: A Systematic Literature Review and Research Agenda. *Supply Chain Management*, *24*(1), 62–84. doi:10.1108/SCM-03-2018-0148

Chapter 7
Risk Management Frameworks and the Implementation of Blockchain Technology

Gregory Barnes
Leeds Beckett University, UK

ABSTRACT

Blockchain as a technology has potential for improving risk exposure through incorporation with risk management frameworks. There are aspects of the link between the two that facilitate a way of working outside that is possible by all but the very largest corporate entities. The use of enterprise risk management (ERM) frameworks, and in particular ISO31000, has become an increasingly accepted governance standard for companies, and any use of Blockchain technologies needs to integrate with those organisational processes. Doing so should result in practical benefits for most organisations engaging with their exposure to risk in a formalised manner. This chapter outlines risk management frameworks, the 'dimensions' in which integration with Blockchain may be realised, key benefits, challenges, and future development opportunities. The presently available implementation case studies are discussed throughout the chapter including potential usage in supply chain management, healthcare records, financial management, and corporate governance.

INTRODUCTION

There has been an increasing adoption of Enterprise Risk Management (ERM) standard ISO31000 in corporate contexts following the publication of the first version of the standard in 2009. A revision in 2018 updated the standard to include more modern approaches and areas of interfacing with the organisation (Hamir & Sum 2021). Missing thus far in scholarly literature has been an explicit attempt to integrate new organisational approaches offered by Blockchain (BC) technology with the ISO31000 ERM framework conceptually. This chapter views the issue as one of 'dimensions of integration' in the implementation of BC. This offers a conceptual viewpoint for practitioners to judge the use of BC and ISO31000 / ERM adoption. In an environment where managers are seeking to leverage the advantages

DOI: 10.4018/979-8-3693-0482-2.ch007

of disruptive digital technology, consideration of the dimensions should ensure coherency within an organisation. The definitions of 'disruptive technology' or digitalisation are very broad and move between the practical 'user' end (for example Augmented Reality) to the basic underpinning of information and communication management (Artificial intelligence) (Rodriguez-Espindola etal 2020).

As with any discussion of BC technology, we are in a period of rapid development and thus run the risk of obsolescence of any discussion on the topic. I hope to transcend some of the pitfalls associated with this by focusing on the principles behind how BC may be used in this context. Risk Management is a discipline that is founded not only on formal governance processes, but also perspectives and conceptual foundations that underpin approaches to the topic. Every context within which risk is debated has complex inter-relationships and as a result, the principles discussed matter more than the formalised processes (which would be subject to change at the point of implementation).

Risk Management as a discipline concerns the full range of corporate and organisational processes. It is built into the foundation of governance within companies in a manner that seeks to protect stakeholder value and maximise the return on uncertain circumstances. However, some aspects of Risk Management processes are exposed to issues relating to data integrity, and the transparency of relationships between parties and layers of organisational structures. Blockchain offers a technology solution to some of these challenges, but the nature of the technology exposes organisations in new ways. We will explore some of these principles in this chapter.

What is Risk?

Risk is commonly conceptualised as having negative connotations. It is worth our while to move beyond that narrow view and towards seeing it as any area of uncertainty. As a result, we could view risk as both positive (upside) and negative (downside). Once this step has been taken, we can begin to view any management processes as being not about reducing exposure, but about providing certainty.

ISO Guide 73:2009 embraces this principle by defining risk as being the "effect of uncertainty on objectives" which is contextualised but outcome neutral in emphasis (ISO 2009). This means that while risk is commonly discussed in business senses as being potentially focused on the 'downside' outcomes, we may equally need to manage the 'upside' outcomes and their maximisation.

In most management arenas, certainty is the key aspiration: Customers are not concerned at lead times, only that a lead time that has been agreed is kept, management processes need to be realised in an efficient and consistent manner and so on. As a result, any Framework for management should seek to ensure that consistency is achieved. This involves not only hitting agreed deadlines but doing so in a consistent manner on which operational efficiency can then be constructed. The use of BC within a risk environment then should be to increase the relative certainty around processes by offering a 'governed' approach to data handling and information.

RISK MANAGEMENT FRAMEWORKS: AN OVERVIEW

Large corporations use systems often described as being Enterprise Risk Management (ERM) systems. These are corporate systems that provide a framework for the governance of risk for an organisation. In general, they are supported by, rather than being focused on, IT systems and are overall management systems and overlapping processes that support the understanding of risk for the company. Risk Management (RM) is, at heart, built upon a four-step process associated with the awareness, then treatment of uncertainties. Risk frameworks then build upon these core principles to provide managerial structures in their support. The four steps are: Identification, Assessment, Mitigation, and then monitoring.

While I have laid these steps out in a linear manner, it should be recognised that they are not necessarily realised in that sense. The Corporate Governance Institute (CGI) for example suggests that Monitoring of risk is undertaken before any Mitigation to support the validity of the assessment (Ashby 2019). Similarly, most definitions suggest that a circular process of continual incrementalism is applied to these steps with potential loop backs at each step.

Risk Identification

There are many potential processes involved in the identification of risks. Commonly this involves the systematic review of empirical information regarding operation and performance of the organisation. Modelling of the operations can then lead to an understanding of areas of deficiency or exposure in the organisation.

Qualitative and normative reviews of organisational situation can also be conducted. Identification tools include the use of checklists to gauge situations against existing knowledge, process mapping of systems of operation, use of Risk Breakdown Structure (RBS) diagrams, and Root Cause Analysis techniques.

BC presents an opportunity to create a single unified ledger of the operational transactions and processes. This would enable a deeper level of empirical information collection and resulting analysis than may otherwise be available. When looking at the whole system involved with the organisation (including supply chain) there is the potential to span several organisations and therefore gain a broader AND deeper insight into the operational efficacy.

There is a normative benefit as well from the use of BC. The requirement for greater levels of integration would itself lead to a potential deeper cultural integration between partners. This is of course a causality dilemma: greater cultural integration is required to realise the use of BC across a system (as will be discussed later) but equally BC would assist in facilitating this integration. We will see that ISO31000 requires this additional level of integration to be successfully realised.

Risk Assessment

The fundamental relationship between risks is a function of the two main factors: likelihood and impact. These two factors are then multiplied to provide an estimation of the 'risk exposure' for the activity being assessed.

Likelihood is variably expressed as a qualitative or numerical value but fundamentally relates to probabilities of activities occurring. The use of empirical information improves the basic understanding of the likelihood of an occurrence, and it is here that more data based approaches have yielded benefits for risk management. Financial institutions obviously lead the way in understanding the probabilities of market activities, and there is a lot to be learned for supply chain and operational organisations. Governance officers also have a great deal to learn

Impact is an estimation or calculated function of the resulting consequences of an uncertainty. The level of impact is, without empirical information relating to the specific losses or implications of a risk, an area of uncertainty that has a largely qualitative judgement associated. For many organisations, this impact level can be judged as the financial implications, but it is the opportunity cost that has a larger impact, and in many instances the organisational effort exerted is difficult to assess. In both likelihood and impact, BC can be seen to offer benefits from the increased level of information available to the analysis. Most importantly it can, if enacted as a systemic level, integrate data perspectives from across the partners to generate a more accurate picture than traditional approaches.

Risk Mitigation

Mitigations are the actions taken to either ameliorate against negative connotations from risks, or the maximise potential outcomes and returns from opportunities. They are typically described as falling under transference, treatment, or termination actions that lead to an improvement to the level of exposure the organisation is exposed to.

Risk Monitoring

Monitoring the exposure to risk over time is important in terms of evaluation of the level of exposure calculated, and the efficacy of any mitigation actions undertaken. ISO3100 places an emphasis on this aspect as being a wraparound of the four-stage process; one that is continually enacted rather than taken as a snapshot measurement of exposure. This is a change in the view of risk management from being an organisational 'cross sectional' viewpoint, and one that encompasses data longitudinally. This periodic view results in a potential delay in the response to risks.

BC has the potential to facilitate real-time risk monitoring through the continual measurement and update of the ledger. Data would be generated inherently as part of the use of BC rather than a 'certification' route for actions. Data can continually be collected, aggregated into a pool, and then analysed. Emerging risks would be highlighted much more rapidly. Additionally, the use of Smart Contracts could result in actions being highlighted across the system / supply chain in order to initiate activity by multiple partners.

ISO31000 as a Risk Management Framework.

The International Standards Organisation ISO has a number of published standards relating to risk. The primary one in terms of enterprise and corporate governance is ISO31000. The initial formulation of ISO31000 was published in 2009 to encompass the remit of Enterprise Risk Management (ERM) operations that encompass organisational level risk. This moves 'risk' from a practice of management associated with projects, or specific activities, and into one that tackles overall governance and organisational systems and practices.

Unlike some of the other ISO systems, 31000 is not organised to provide accreditation of a company's systems and processes. It is instead intended to provide an organisational framework for both internal and external auditors. As a result, it has a 'best in class' approach to the management of risk that matches the primary requirements of global stock markets and liberal democratic country legal frameworks.

ISO31000 takes the basic 4 step process outlined above and expands upon that framework in several ways. Figure 1 outlines the basic elements of this expanded framework. The key addition is the overall emphasis that ISO31000 places on risk management. It presumes heterogeneity in applications to allow for a diverse approach to the development of organisational structures to support the *ethos* of robust risk

Figure 1. ISO31000:2018 risk management framework elements
Adapted from ISO (2018)

Area	Framework	Principles	Process
Emphasis	Leadership and Commitment	Value Creation and Protection	Identification and Treatment
Components	Integration	Integrated	Scope, Context
	Design	Structured	Risk Assessment
	Implementation	Customized	Risk Treatment
	Evaluation	Inclusive	(Recording and Reporting)
	Improvement	Dynamic	(Monitoring and Review)
		Best Information Available	(Communication and Consultation)
		Human and Cultural Factors	
		Continual Improvement	

management. This is done by breaking down 'Risk Management' into three components: Principles, Framework, and Process.

Process we have covered in section 2.1 to 2.4. It is the formalised workflow of identification to monitoring of uncertainty for the organisation. This is however expanded further through the inclusion of a feedback loop based on reporting and recording elements of the RM process.

Principles are the underlying cognitive and aspirational aspects. They are the socio-cultural elements of the framework that support behaviours of the organisation and offer a guiding light as to the direction of travel for the subsequently established elements.

Framework refers to the 'hard' managerial structures associated with the framework. They are the aspects of management that need to be put into place at a structural level in order to realise success.

Other ERM Frameworks

Other standards exist in specific industry spaces. Two notable examples include COSO and COBIT5. Both are more specific in their emphasis, but are important in the context of discussions around using BC in the management of Risk:

The Committee of Sponsoring Organisations (COSO) standard approaches the risk as a major area of weakness for organisational success. Their framework is a paid standard that integrates five aspects into a unified framework. The inclusion of BC within this framework has been discussed previously by Vincent and Barkhi (2021) with the conclusion that the use of the framework for the operation of 'smart contracts' allows for effective and transparent operation. COSO overall emphasises a financial management rather than the broader aspects potentially touched upon by ISO31000.

The Control Objectives for Information and Related Technologies (COBIT) framework for IT governance is presently at the fifth revision, and the scope of such a framework lends itself readily for discussion in this context. The principal emphasis of the system is the application of a singular network approach. Management and governance is separated to ensure that one is critically positioned to review and improve the other. In terms of the scope of COBIT, we are in the realm of a singular approach to the implementation of BC rather than the overall governance of the organisation that is offered by ISO3100. There may however be benefits to this approach within the case study applications discussed later in this chapter (Setadi, Soetomo, Mahawan 2018 p76).

IMENSIONS OF BLOCKCHAIN INTEGRATION

Blockchain integration in this chapter relates to the degree to which BC is integrated into the processes and working of the system within which it is employed. ISO31000 encourages the customisation of processes and practices in order to best fit the organisational aspirations. As a result, the level of integration that may be considered needs to be judged on a per case basis. To facilitate such discussions, I offer here a framework for analysis based on 'dimensions' of integration of the elements of the 'system'.

For ease, the terminology used herein adopts 'organisation' as the key 'target' or 'case' company, 'supply chain' is the longitudinal up / downstream of the organisation, and 'systemic structure' is the overarching construct that the 'organisation' and 'supply chain' inhabits.

The systemic structure, and the constituent components are outlined in Figure 2. The dimensions within the systemic structure are arranged along an Internal / External dichotomy. These is not however a binary position, but a porous boundary between the two extremes to do with the proximity, or efficacy offered to the stakeholders / actors in each area.

For the sake of this analysis, the 'Business Environment' is viewed as an entirely external factor outside of the systemic structure. The intention behind this exclusion is to allow us to view within the 'black box' of the system without the business environment being allowed to cloud our view of the interactions within. The 'Business Environment' in Risk Frameworks is most commonly dealt with in terms of the 'PESTLE' or 'STEEPLED' factors of analysis. Indeed, ISO31000 specifically encourages the categorisations of risks, and the definitions of their sources, to be under the auspices of the Organisation rather than externally validated. This customisation again allows for effective alignment of the practices with the organisation's aspirations. The following sections describe the various elements of the systemic construction:

Transaction Tracking and 'Workflow'

The first category relates to transactions within the system. This is the area of the system where goods and services are transacted with supply chain partners and remittances for the same are resolved. For obvious reasons, any interface with materiel or contracts between parties would benefit from verification processes such as those facilitated by BC. With regards to SCM utilisations, the framework offered by Rauniyar etal (2021) would be applicable as a way to judge appropriateness for inclusion. Their conclusion was that monitoring of goods, fraud, cyber risk, and 'tamper proofing' (to name a few) would all benefit from BC technology (p262).

There are socio-cultural elements that would benefit from this area of integration specifically around the increased transparency. Such a move would be a major shift towards 'partnering' and away from 'transacting' relationships (which may prompt a revision in this dimensional framework at a later date).

Figure 2. Dimensions of Blockchain integration within the Risk Management Environment

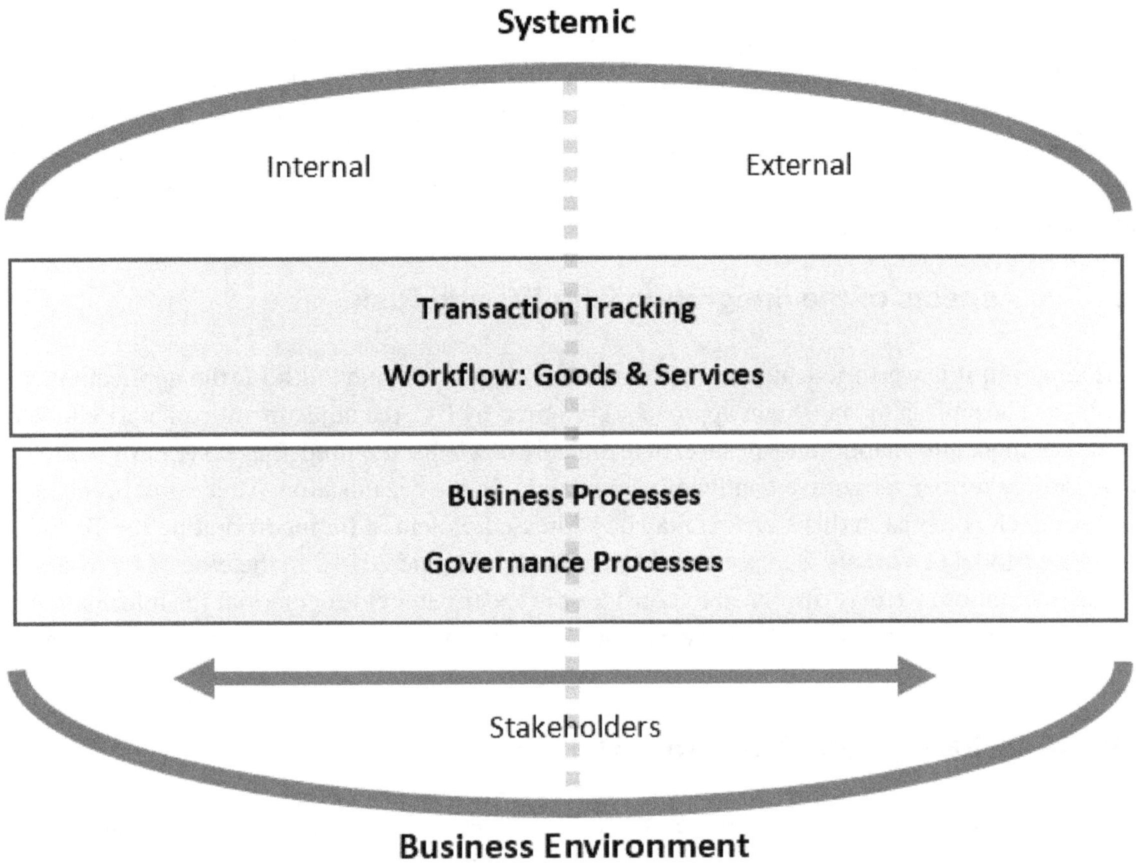

Business Processes and Governance Processes

The practices and processes of an organisation at a higher level of integration systemically require a view across all participating organisations. Using BC would facilitate an immutable system of information storage. Business processes include operational elements such as the internal ordering, allocation of resources, and project management. Governance processes usually relate to the allocation of approvals, audit, and oversight across the organisation.

In this newly integrated system, some of these practices and processes would require systemic integration in order to be effectively utilised. BC in this context therefore becomes a motivator for increasing partnership between parties across the supply chain.

External interfacing with not only regular partners but also outside agents and agencies would be more effectively managed. For example, the use of BC for tracking carbon emissions or tier 3/4 emissions across a supply chain effectively would suit the use of BC. In each instance, the principles of ERM are supported through the effective level of transparency offered by the technology integration. The increasing transparency offered would allow for greater efficiency identification and exposure.

Stakeholder Engagement

ERM systems foreground the inclusion of stakeholders; according to the 'Five Lines of Assurance' (Leech 2016) within the organisation, this should include all levels of the operational and management structures. Our perspective of a systemic level of consideration using BC would extend this consideration outwards into including all organisational and systemic actors internally and externally where possible. BC would facilitate a transparent access to data through the distributed ledger that should allow for this broader vision of the system for the relevant parties.

Cognitive Aspects of the Integration with BC and Risk

As a final point, it is worth touching upon the issue of cognitive bandwidth for the application of this technology. The shift in management approaches required by BC, the adjustment from periodic to real-time management information, and the level of technical knowledge required, may potentially lead to what may be loosely termed 'cognitive bandwidth constraints' in the organisation. There is certainly a great deal of research potential in this area that may be addressed. Potential for incorporating the Technology Acceptance Model (TAM) are also present (Marangunić & Granić 2014). In the case of ERM adoption and implementation, we may also need to consider the sheer bandwidth potential for information consideration and decision making offered by traditional board and organisational governance structures.

APPLICATIONS IN EXISTING CASE STUDIES

There have been several studies on the use of Blockchain technology already completed and these are highly instructive in demonstrating the benefits and challenges to the implementation of the technology in a risk context. These examples studies are an introduction to the practical implementations of BC in high-risk enterprise environments. In each case there will be a variable implementation as the markets and industries are at differing levels of sophistication. Importantly, the implementation of any BC technology in these contexts will have to be defined by the intended outcomes: relating back to our model of BC 'Dimensions' one may look to understand the extent to which 'workflow' or broader aspects may be included.

Supply Chain Management

There are several aspects of BC that facilitate the effective operation of Supply Chains through process and relationship optimisation. The major impetus in the use of BC in this context is around the complexity of actors and processes within the supply chain. The earlier sections of this chapter have addressed this context specifically at several points and particularly in reference to the 'systemic construction' and the integration of BC within risk management dimensions.

SCM was particularly important in the context of the pandemic. This is due to the direct implications of the disruption caused by the virus on the workers within the companies in the supply chain, and the indirect implications of country and regional spikes in infection leading to localised lockdowns and restrictions of movement. The period when the globe was recovering from the pandemic was also marked by an increase in demand for goods following pent up demand from consumers for goods (with a deficit in services being available), and a backlog in supply chain movement leading to increases in costs. EL Baz and Ruel (2021) suggest that the pressures on the market because of recovery from such a shock require additional tools such as the use of BC to optimise processes.

Calls for such a paradigm shift in informational capacity are in line with discussions around 'Industry 4.0' but outside the common practices in many mid-sized companies. Particularly apposite in this context would be the capacity for Blockchain 2.0 to allow for 'Smart Contracts' within their structure. The important element here therefore is that these SCs allow for rapid and accurate generation of contracting relationships between parties. The result has been a focus on the potential for Supply Chain Management (SCM) to utilise this aspect of BC for interorganisational relationships. The research by Etemadi etal (2021) suggests that many of the key areas of organisational risk resolvable through the use of BC revolve around transparent contracting and verification between parties. This should assist in the improvement of confidence between agents and therefore reduction in transaction costs.

Healthcare Management Using Blockchain

Patient record keeping digitisation has been a consistent aim across developed economies for decades. There have been some notable successes in the field, including the UK system which now has a single integrated database for patient care information across the National Health Service (NHS). Of critical importance is the need for immutability within the realm of healthcare information. Patient records must be seen to be singular and linked to only a single individual. Security issues are also abound in the area of patient records as there are examples of where lack of information security may lead to significant harm or embarrassment.

Workflow systems need to be interrogated by other systems in order to provide interoperability without the opportunity to compromise the other systems. Advancements in the practice of 'digital first' interaction with patients may include several systems, practices, and levels of interrogation of a ledger (Rodgers etal 2019). Furthermore, government regulation requires consideration of the principles of data protection in many countries with blocs such as the EU imposing significant fines on those actors and organisations that breach the GDPR.

Healthcare therefore is emblematic of sensitive information storage and manipulation services run by centralised providers. The issues applying to such organisations is similar to that of banking services with similar levels of harm potentially liable where there is a breach in the integrity of the service.

CHALLENGES AND LIMITATIONS

While there are a number of areas where the application of Blockchain is a positive contribution, there are also a number of areas where use is more challenging. This is particularly acute when looking at the context of risk management frameworks and the areas of operation and governance that concern them.

Scalability and Performance

Risk management has evolved into a discipline that is founded on empirical information wherever possible. Where this is not possible, there is an expectation that a rigorous, transparent and timely evaluation of risks will be established.

As BC ledgers grow, there is a consequent implication for the performance of the system. We have seen the increasing hash 'cost' of applied BC solutions resulting in ever higher performance tolls on computing power in order to be operationalised. The same would result over time in a complex system.

The number of transactions and movements of goods associated with an FMCG group could overtime result in an increased level of demand on the system that would outweigh the benefits from the operation of it. One of the questions around the implications of this burden is the level of 'proof of stake' that is needed to verify ownership of the BC ledger item. Where this is set at a higher level in order to ensure transaction probity, then the calculative burden will be exponentially higher.

Finally, the most common risk monitoring tool in use is a 'risk register' of some sort which includes information on principal and emerging risks, exposure, and owner of the mitigation actions. Any implementation of BC in this context would require a significant revision of such a register format to allow for the increasing informational bandwidth, or to make such a simple tool irrelevant. Scaling and effectively managing and communicating risk would become an issue in an integrated system.

Alignment with Internal Governance Processes

Audit controls to an extent rely on the accurate and transparent operation of processes. These processes are then auditable by both internal officers and external auditors. The application of BC in any context results in a higher technology threshold for the operation of SCM. The consequence is therefore twofold: firstly, that the audit function is technically incapable of adequately evaluating the risks associated with the operation of a BC enabled supply chain. This type of situation has been seen in other contexts such as banking where the financial crash was in part facilitated by esoteric risk modelling that obfuscated and obscured the relationships between parties and areas of exposure.

As a result, the verification of the application of such processes in this context is constrained without appropriate oversight. The principles of the three lines of defence and the five lines of assurance are undermined through the inability to engage with the technology. A potential implication is that the technology understanding required to evaluate such activities requires an 'insider' mindset OR the explicit explanation of processes in such a way that allows a 'layman' to evaluate the processes.

Five lines of assurance is particularly important in this context as it is aligned with the aspirations of ISO31000. The principle is that every key (internal) organisational stakeholder should be involved in the management of risks across the organisation, from board to operative. The level of technical awareness therefore needs to be improved to allow for board education on technology solutions such as we are discussing herein.

Further, the utilisation of BC with partners would also require a coherency and application of similar governance across the networks to ensure the system was applied in a robust manner. This may require additional reform of governance across partners in the supply chain as well (Vincent, Barkhi 2021). Governance and consensus around standard setting would lead to a level of integration (see dimensions above) that may be beyond many relationships.

Exposure of Transparent Data to Supply Chain Partners

One of the principal benefits espoused by BC advocates in the area of SCM are transparent and open logging of transactions with partners. Operating in this manner would allow all partners to be able to view the ledger and therefore interact with the supply chain equally. In terms of ISO31000, this principle fits exceptionally well with the

This opens transactions logs with partners however and runs the risk of undermining a beneficial asymmetry of information for one of key organisations. To be clear, aspirations for supply chains are that they will be run openly in a spirit of partnership with all other parties. This is not always the case however, and there exist asymmetries where market failure allows for excessive concentration of power with one party. External regulation is therefore required to resolve such situations. It is uncertain as to whether transparency would lead to a reduction in the requirement for independent state regulation that laissez faire economists might assume to be possible.

COMPARATIVE ANALYSIS: BLOCKCHAIN VS TRADITIONAL RISK MANAGEMENT

The following areas for consideration are some of the principle issues that differentiate 'traditional' management approaches of risk to those that may utilise BC technology. The key here is that the areas highlighted are conceptual or 'higher level' areas of consideration rather than more prosaic or operational functions.

Flexibility and Rigidity

RM frameworks are deterministic in nature. They are based on externally designed and (potentially) validated application of principles and processes which can be audited against a standard benchmark. ISO31000 however seeks to allow for customisation of the system at a fundamental level. This is achieved by allowing the organisation to define categorisations of risk that align with their own perception / operational matrices. As a result, there is a high level of flexibility for an organisation to adapt the principles underpinning ERM to the needs of the strategic direction of the organisation, and the stakeholders involved.

Blockchain however is determined by the technology that underpins it. There is a rigidity inherent that benefits the system at a fundamental level. While implementations may be adaptable, there is no such fluidity or ambiguity possible in the ledger, in the data stored, or in the validity without undermining the entire BC. As a result, when viewing the differences between BC and traditional ERM one must view the context as critically important and understand that there are certain 'fixed points' in the use of BC that may not be amended ad hoc. This is a useful principle for 'governance' of a system, but less useful when one needs to be adaptable.

Approaches to Data

Use of cryptography enhances data security, particularly around financial data. Not only in terms of security of access, but also security of salience (Nordgren, A; Weckström, E W 2019).

There are of course routes into the data systems offered by BC due to the improvement in technology such as Quantum Computing. Attack opportunities need to be considered within the ERM as a result of the system being potentially crackable by quantum brute forcing of a password-based system (Campbell 2020).

Cost Benefits of Using BC with Risk Management Frameworks

Considering the benefits of any system implementation is a process that needs to encompass all the principle stakeholders of an organisation. In the case of BC however, the added complexity and external implications for the organisation means that there is an overall systemic implication. As a result, the porous nature of the implementation will require a Whole Life Costing (WLC) to be attempted that involves contracting or systemic partners.

Systemic Maturity

The maturity of the systemic structures, and the included partners is of critical importance. In 2023 at the time of writing this article, we are not in a position where many industries will be positioned to allow for fully systemic engagement with BC. While reports and papers abound regarding the number and types of industries that may implement the disruptive technologies, there are fewer examples of full systems where such integration may be enacted.

In terms of maturity then, we may view this through the veil of supply chain integration, global value chains, or process improvements (such as the adoption of Six Sigma). BC implementation then would require a review of the likely potential for adoption not only of system wide ERM, but also the spine of the dimensions across the whole system. The following case studies in section 7 touch upon this issue by highlighting two areas where maturity preconditions may have been reached.

FUTURE DEVELOPMENTS AND RESEARCH

There are a number of areas of Risk and BC integration that would benefit from further research. The effective testing of the conceptual dimensions of integration for Risk Management offered in this chapter would be a good starting point for a future research agenda. Further areas include, Interoperability, Scalability, Systemic Maturity, and the use of Hybrid systems.

Interoperability and Standardisation

The improvement of SC information systems has a positive impact on the resilience of the parties using those systems and the SC overall (Gu, Yang, Huo 2021). There is a difference between exploitation and exploration that is interesting in this context. Exploration involves the investigation of dimensions of performance outside of the exploitation of existing data to enhance the robustness of systems. Therefore, we are looking beyond the use of data to reinforce processes, and instead looking to it for provision of fresh insights and presentation of foreknowledge.

All parties need to be involved in the processes and have commensurate IT and technical capabilities. Where this is not available, asymmetries exist between parties and the resulting misalignment can lead to further SC instability. We therefore return to the risk of engaging once again with asymmetrical data provision and technical capabilities.

Scalability and Performance of BC and RM Systems

We discussed the potential challenges from the scaling of BC within organisations, and the level of scaling within RM could lead to consequent new challenges and areas of risk to be considered. There is certainly a research thread opportunity in this area as optimisation of the elements that are required to be included in the ledger would be of interest.

This would be therefore an exercise in establishing the optimum efficient level of information and data to be captured by the BC system alongside the conceptualisations of the dimensions of BC integration. Doing so would assist us in realising the most effective data to be captured for the purposes that are required to give managers *information* rather than just a pool of unregulated data.

Systemic Maturity

There is an opportunity to look at the systemic maturity, factors associated with the implementation potentially with reference to a framework such as the Technology Acceptance Model (TAM) or derivative perspectives that offer an enhanced model of system integration. Of key importance here is the need to balance the overall systemic maturity with the level of organisational maturity of the participant agents to avoid asymmetry of power relations.

Hybrid Approaches to RM

There is the potential for incorporation of other technology and conceptual options within the realm of the BC and ERM integration. If one is implementing BC then this may require a higher level of monitoring than might otherwise be the case under traditional management processes. BC will lead to a resulting increase in data and potential for ML and data mining opportunities. This is particularly pertinent in the context of AI developments in the early 2020s. The automation of aspects of the 4 steps of risk management frameworks (for example Risk Identification) would be highly advantageous. In particular, model building involving risk identification, trend analysis, and probability calculations could be far more accurate.

Integrating additional technologies using IOT in the tracking of goods and services provisions (the workflow aspects of our dimensions of integration) would additionally lead to benefits for the application of Smart Contracts. Contracts could be initiated between parties at a much more accurate point in time, meeting the timeliness of contract initiation and reducing ambiguity in the risk allocation. This would be particularly important when transactions include insurance risk transference to other parties.

Finally, rather than looking at technology solutions, there exist additional hybridisation options relating to the conceptual nature of BC and distributed ledger structures. This would lead us into the realms of discussing the nature of Market Instruments and the role of BC in the implementation of markets as a transaction medium (Callon etal 2007, Fligstein 2001). The nature of markets changes as the information and tools relating to them frames the debate around their operation. When this is combined with the additional governance and risk management concepts presented by BC integration with ERM, we can see that an alternative view of ownership, and market participation may be fostered.

CONCLUSION

This chapter has drawn together several points around the conceptualisation and implementation of BC and RM frameworks. There are several conclusions that would be beneficial to reiterate here.

Firstly, that the holistic implications of Risk Management means that consideration of many more facets of the systemic structure of the organisation and context need to be taken account of before implementation is considered. There are a number of dimensions outlined in section 3 but they themselves are not exhaustive, and more research on each of the elements discussed would be beneficial to enhance our empirical understanding.

Secondly, there is a conceptual tension at the heart of the debate around BC and RM Frameworks. RM Frameworks are adaptable according to certain principles but require expansion across the entire system. This inherently imposes a standardised approach from a third party on a system as opposed to allowing the system to generate its own approach to RM. While this may seem arbitrary in practice, conceptually we are coming up against a tension between deterministic approaches of standardisation organisations, and the adaptability and agility required by contemporary business structures.

Thirdly, there are several benefits of the application of Blockchain in a risk management framework. Section 4 of this chapter runs through these main benefits and the principal ways in which ISO31000 may be adapted to use BC applications. These benefits however need to be viewed in the light of the critical perspectives offered in section 5. The conclusion of this chapter is that the context matters. While there are applications which will benefit all parties, it is the maturity of the system that will determine the overall applicability of either the RM Framework or the application of BC.

REFERENCES

Agarwal, U., Rishiwal, V., Tanwar, S., Chaudhary, R., Sharma, G., Bokoro, P. N., & Sharma, R. (2022). Blockchain Technology for Secure Supply Chain Management: A Comprehensive Review. *IEEE Access : Practical Innovations, Open Solutions*, *10*, 2022. doi:10.1109/ACCESS.2022.3194319

Callon, M., Yuval, M., & Muniesa, F. (Eds.). (2007). *Market Devices*. Blackwell Publishing.

Chang, S. E., & Chen, Y. (2020). When Blockchain Meets Supply Chain: A systematic literature review on current developments and potential applications. *IEEE Access : Practical Innovations, Open Solutions*, *8*, 2020. doi:10.1109/ACCESS.2020.2983601

Choo, B., & Goh, J. C.-L. (2014) Adapting the ISO31000:2009 Enterprise Risk Management Framework Using the Six-Sigma Approach. *Proceedings of the 2014 IEEE IEEM January 2015* (pp. 39-43). IEEE. 10.1109/IEEM.2014.7058596

Choo Campbell, R. (2020). The Need for Cyber Resilient Enterprise Distributed Ledger Risk Management Framework. *The Journal of the British Blockchain Association*, *3*(1), 1–9. doi:10.31585/jbba-3-1-(5)2020

El Baz, J., & Ruel, S. (2021). Can supply chain risk management practices mitigate the disruption impacts on supply chains' resilience and robustness? Evidence from an empirical survey in a COVID19 outbreak era. *International Journal of Production Economics*, *233*, 107972. doi:10.1016/j.ijpe.2020.107972 PMID:36567758

Etemadi, N., Borbon-Galvez, Y., Strozzi, F., & Etemade, T. (2021). Supply Chain Disruption Risk Management with Blockchain: A Dynamic Literature Review. *Information (Basel)*, *12*(2), 70. doi:10.3390/info12020070

Fligstein, N. (2001) The Architecture of Markets: An Economic Sociology of Twenty First Century Capitalist Societies). Princeton, Oxford.

Gu, M., Yang, L., & Huo, B. (2021). The Impact of information technology usage on supply chain resilience and performance: An Ambidextrous View. *International Journal of Production Economics*, *232*, 107956. Advance online publication. doi:10.1016/j.ijpe.2020.107956 PMID:33071462

Hamir, H; Sum, R M (2021) An Analysis of Risk Management Processes and Comparison with ISO31000:2018. *Asian Journal of Research in Business and Management, 3*, 16-30.

ISO. (2009). *ISO Guide 73:2009 Risk Management Vocabulary*. ISO.

ISO. (2018). *ISO31000 Risk Management*. International Organisation for Standardization.

Iyer, S. S. (2022) Application of Digital Technologies: Integrated Blockchain with Emerging Technologies. Handbook of Research on Supply Chain Resiliency, Efficiency and Visibility in the Post-Pandemic Era. IGI Global. doi:10.4018/978-1-7998-9506-0.ch014

Leech, T., & Hanlon, L. (2016). Three Lines of Defense versus Five Lines of Assurance: Elevating the Role of the Board and CEO in Risk Governance. The Handbook of Board Governance: A Comprehensive Guide to Public, Private and Not for Profit Board Members. Wiley, London.

Nordgren, A., & Weckström, E. W. (2019). Blockchain in the Fields of Finance and Accounting: A Distruptive Technology or an Overhyped Phenomenon? *ACRN Journal of Finance and Risk Perspectives*, *8*, 47–58.

Rauniyar, K., Wu, X., Gupta, S., Modgil, S., & Jabbour, A. B. (2021). *Risk Management of Supply Chains in the Digital Transformation Era: Contribution and Challenges of Blockchain Technology*. Industrial Management and Data System. doi:10.1108/IMDS-04-2021-0235

Rodgers, M., Raine, G., Thomas, S., Harden, M., & Eastwood, A. (2019). Informing NHS policy in 'digital-first primary care': A rapid evidence synthesis. *Health Services and Delivery Research*, *7*(41), 1–124. doi:10.3310/hsdr07410 PMID:31869020

Rodriguez-Espindola, O., Chowdhury, S., Beltagui, A., & Albores, A. (2020). The potential of emergent disruptive technologies for humanitarian supply chains: The integration of blockchain, artificial intelligence and 3D Printing. *International Journal of Production Research*, *58*(15), 15. doi:10.1080/00207543.2020.1761565

Setiadi, R., Soetomo, M. A., & Mahawan, B. (2018). Blockchain Governance: An Evaluation from COBIT5 Perspective. *Proceedings of Annual Conference on Management and Information Technology (ACMIT) 2018*. ACM.

Vincent, N. E., & Barkhi, R. (2021). Evaluating Blockchain Using COSO. *Current Issues in Auditing*, *15*(1), 57–71. doi:10.2308/CIIA-2019-509

Chapter 8
Blockchain-Enabled Federated Learning for Secured Edge Data Communication Through a Decentralized Software-Defined Network

S. Selvi
https://orcid.org/0000-0002-0884-908X
Builders Engineering College, India

G. Revathy
https://orcid.org/0000-0002-0691-1687
SASTRA University, India

P. Brindha
Builders Engineering College, India

ABSTRACT

Data communication through Edge devices in a secured channel for real time applications is one of the biggest concerns. Software Defined Network is a suitable network opted for security. The Control Plane is more vulnerable to variety of attacks. Ensemble machine learning approach which composes of 3 times of Random Forest with one time of Linear Regression gives us the prediction of errors and loss of packets and hence the data will be transferred more securely. The Block Chain is integrated with the SDN controllers in the control plane to transfer the data from the edge devices in the form of a Block to the cloud layer. Federated Learning can be inculcated for security analysis prediction and then aggregating into a Global Model in the Central Cloud Layer. The majority of contemporary FL techniques do not explicitly address variances among client parameter estimates. An aggregation mechanism built on the Hessian matrix in order to close the gap. Moreover, we can use the Hessian as a scaling matrix using the second -order partial derivative information of the loss function

DOI: 10.4018/979-8-3693-0482-2.ch008

1. INTRODUCTION

A Software Defined Network (SDN) is a virtual, programmable networking architecture which is primarily meant for detecting the behaviour of the entire network. SDN is a dynamic architecture and hence it has its unique attention towards industry and research environment. Due to its scalability, adaptability and less structural complexity, the SDN has its wide usage in various real time applications recently. Apart from these, it has a higher privilege of building a securable environment for communication of data packets when compared to traditional TCP/IT network. SDN is broadly classified into three planes: Application plane, Control plane and Data plane. Though SDN overcomes several security limitations of traditional networks, it still faces some security breaches and has a vulnerable projection in Control plane. Due to security threats in the Control plane, there are still few packet losses. As a result, some data are left unnoticeable, could not be taken into account and it has a serious effect on final project conclusions.

This chapter concentrates on overcoming the security concerns in the Control plane and the techniques proposed to eradicate the unseen challenges. SDN builds a novel security mechanism by encompassing Blockchain based data packet transmission. The presence of SDN Controller in the Control plane manages the network traffic and aims at regulating the packets based on the application request from the Application plane.

Blockchain building a secured architecture by integrating with SDN, can be able to strike a good balance between scalability, irrespective of the size of the query from the Application plane and at the performance level, throughput and latency metrics are perfectly achieved. Every node in the network separately assembles the BC. Each block includes information on some or all of the most recent transactions that were not included in the block before it. Each block is made up of two parts: (i) a block header with the current and previous cryptographic block hash values, a timestamp, and a nonce; and (ii) the main body with the transaction hash value, sender and receiver identities, and signatures for each transaction. Block chain is the primary aspect of providing security against threats, where it could be accomplished by Miners. Miners are users who pool their computing resources to check the validity of the transactions contained in blocks in exchange for rewards. To confirm the most recent transactions and record them all in the global ledger, they must solve a statistical problem based on the computation of a cryptographic hash function. A block is typically extracted every five to ten minutes.

Federated Learning (FL) approach is the most preferable ensemble based prediction learning model since the training data remains distributed locally (Nguyen et al., 2021) and demands strict privacy over the data. Federated learning (FL) is a distributed AI strategy that works by coordinating several devices to do AI training without sharing raw data in order to protect privacy and conserve network resources (such bandwidth).This would prominently reduce the probability of data transmission for longer distances which in turn security threats are minimized. The local training model collects the data from the nearby Edge devices; convert into a block, thus supporting the decentralization, immutability and traceability. Decentralised data ledgers can be used to achieve federated learning without the need for a central server, which reduces the risk of single-point failures. The unexpected update of events and dynamic network behaviours are all being tracked by the network entities. This would probably mitigate the Distributed Denial of Attacks (DDoA). The integration of FL and Blockchain enhances trust among the devices and improves the scalability of intelligent Edge networks.

FL is an iterative improvement model, where the local model is trained over the data in a continuous iteration process until the model is completely trained and the prediction performance is highly achieved.

At each and every iteration, all the local updates are sent back to the cloud and the aggregation followed by final prediction is accomplished in Cloud.

In the Cloud Layer, the global model is obtained and the prediction is measured. In order to improve the prediction performance and minimize the errors, the conventional gradient descent optimization and its versions are less suitable, since it follows the first order derivative of the features. Also the average gradients for the model weight updates are based on the quantity of training data for each client. The convergence to local minima and the curvature of the loss function can be effectively handled by Hessian Matrix Optimization (HMO), as it comprises of the second-order partial derivatives of the loss function. Hessian Matrix leverages down the effect of variations in client parameters and avoids a sensitive global model aggregation in Cloud. In spite of lower convergence, the different levels of data quality in client models can be well captured by Hessian Matrix. The convergence could be accelerated by inculcating Hessian scaling matrix with Quasi-Newton approaches.

The conventional Hessian matrix is computationally expensive, since the matrix has to be computed at each epoch due to the explicit calculation of second-order derivative. The proposed Quasi Newton approach lessens the computation as Hessian need not to be computed at each epoch.

This chapter presents the following novel contributions towards addressing multiple security breaches in the control plane of SDN and enhances the prediction performance of the data provided to the application plane of SDN as and when required.

- Blockchain based secured data transmission to overcome dynamic security threats and effectively handling applications encompassing Big data.
- Applications of different data sizes can be effectively handled and network behaviours could be recorded in Blockchain, thereby providing a reliable environment.
- SDN can be able to withstand any type of security challenges irrespective of the size of Big data.
- Introducing Federated Learning prediction mechanism in Cloud layer, aggregating the local prediction results and developing a global model.
- Quasi-Newton approach is incorporated to eradicate the client parameter variations among the edge devices in the Cloud layer and lessening the computational cost.

The above mentioned aspects are highly important because of faster storing of big data, easy access and secure computing.

2. LITERATURE SURVEY

Researchers had made their contribution in their works earlier and some pitfalls had been identified on security challenges during survey.

Maimoona Bint et. al. (2022) suggested a secure routing architecture for the Internet of Sensor Things (IoST) based on Blockchain. For detecting malicious types of nodes, Genetic Algorithm based Support Vector Machines (GA-SVM) and Genetic Algorithm based Decision Tree (GA-DT) were introduced in their work. A Hybrid combination of Machine Learning algorithms and Block Chain were proposed by the authors to provide a secure transmission of data in the network. Rana Faisal Hayat et. al. (2022) developed a Hyperledger Caliper to eliminate the malicious devices in IoT environments. But the work has to be extended to concentrate on Cyberattacks in a dynamic and flexible nature of the network.

Various security challenges were highlighted by Dinh et. al. (2021) and Chaoyang Zhu et. al. (2022) when providing Federated Learning based Blockchain solutions to Edge devices and UAV Edge Computing Network. Enhancement of security by maintaining integrity of the data throughout the network was a novel approach introduced by Abhiroop (2022) et. al. and the work attempted to equip Machine Learning algorithms at Edge devices. The work has introduced heterogeneity classes of Machine Learning in the Edge devices for predicting and sensing the malignant nodes. However, the work did not concentrate on providing a formal security framework for a continuous type of data. An intelligent Medical Analytics based Unmanned Aerial Vehicle (UAV) had been proposed by Chaoyang Zhu et. al. (2022). The authors had tried to manipulate Blockchain with distributed and immutable features and Federated Learning approach among multiple untrusted parties. The essential research challenges and its proposed solutions due to the integration of Blockchain and Federated Learning are discussed in this paper. The possible issues in terms of communication cost, resource allocation mechanisms, security and privacy protection schemes in Block chain enabled Federated Learning architecture in UAV are being highlighted.

Various challenges faced due to smart contracts and its certain technical advances had been enlisted with few case study applications by ZibinZheng et. al (2019). A survey of incorporating various smart contracts in Block chain for security reasons was studied in the work by the authors. A new dimensionality of enhancing security against Distributed Denial of Attacks (DDoS) to the data flow through Software Defined Network (SDN) was introduced by Seungwon et. al. (2016). The authors facilitated with a flexible deployment of security functions in SDN, however SDN could also be leveraged to advance security functions. In Jiasi et al. (2019), the security concerns over the transmission of nodes in SDN were procured and deduced a Blockchain based solution to overcome the threats. The probability of vulnerability between the control plane and data plane was prioritized and the proposed model guarantees authenticity, traceability, and accountability of the application data flows in SDN. Due to this, the problem of single-point failure and network scalability were rectified, but failed to effectively handle the dynamic security threats over the network through predictive algorithms.

An OpenFlow–based SDN architecture (Li et al., 2016) was unveiled against scanning, spoofing attacks, Denial-of-service (DoS), etc. by means of CIA triad model. The authors designated this novel architecture to setup a trust mechanism between the nodes through strong encryption mechanism. This proposed model ensures security against threats to controllers and switches so that network behaviours are sealed against DoS attacks. Sultan Algarnier et. al. (2022) developed a token-based authentication model to manipulate SDN controller resources and offered an North Bound Interface design. Here the Blockchain's computational overhead was limited by proposing a light-weight Blockchain architecture and attempted to prevent malicious activities. The application behaviour was monitored by enforcing an access control policy and devised an application trust model. The framework proved to provide an effective protection against CIA threats, but it failed to address data consistency issues.

The management of large scale networks in SDN environment against threats like false data injection, topology inconsistency among controllers were taken into account by Derhabet. al(2021) and put forward a Blockchain-based Multicontroller architecture with adaptive fading reputation strategies. Also the paper aimed at ensuring a secure and trustworthy intercontroller communication in SDN. However the paper did not provide any security implementation for the southbound interfaces.

Though BC and SDN offered a significant secured solution to larger networks, some emerging technological trends could be introduced for securing real time applications (Rahman et al., 2022). Synchronization in SDN was still compromised and there was a lack of standardization to achieve. Further Federated Learning (FL) techniques could be promoted for threats prediction and the problem of slow convergence in building a Global model could be avoided by employing Quasi-Newton (QN) methodologies (Ahmad et al., 2023). Also to deal with the loss function, QN could be supported with Hessian scaling matrix representation. B.B. Sezer et. al. (2023) has developed PPF chain for a secured privacy-preserving framework using BC and FL technologies, aiming at interoperability, low-cost and a higher performance. The framework encompasses off-chain fog based computation, however the latency is yet to be improvised. Similarly Baucas et al. (2023) addressed and provided solutions for security challenges of wearable IOT devices in Health Care Analytics. An adaptive and dynamic network is created by utilizing the Fog-IoT network distributive structure. The authors have still yet to address propagation delay between the Fog and the Cloud. A decentralized protocol has been designed in Riahi et al. (2023) to enhance mutual trust among local models during information exchange and to improve the data skewness. The proposed technique has implemented Reinforcement Learning mechanism for faster convergence and saves 70% of the cost for homogeneous type of data. The privacy data leakage is still a promising challenge and it negatively affects the convergence (Wael, 2023) with an increased probability of inference attacks. An asynchronous mechanism of global model is suggested for heterogeneous devices in IoT networks. Prediction of malicious attacks and unlawful transactions are still under research in Block chain networks. An AI-enabled smart contract is a new direction of solution to be concentrated for avoiding such types of attacks.

In Singh et al. (2022) and Abou El Houda et al. (2023), the authors outlined how the fusion of FL and BC has applied for implementing privacy preserving mechanism in the network. In addition, Abou El Houda et al. (2023) had also developed a distributed secured architecture for maintaining the collaboration of multiple SDN domains. But still they are still lacking in the concentration of large scale attacks in the industrial environments. The fusion of FL and BC has a significant impact in real time scenarios like traffic management system (Sharma & Seetharaman, 2023) and they are intelligent in defending the network against Sybil attacks and Byzantine attacks. Many researchers focussed on achieving trust worthiness for various objectives like leveraging a secure enclave (Kalapaaking, Khalil, & Atiquzzaman, 2022), energy trade within edge devices (Otoum et al., 2023) and Internet of things .The authors aimed at improving the accuracy of threats prediction using FL and BC. Other than SDN, the solutions are provided for fixing the malicious nodes in Wireless Sensor Networks (Gebremariam, 2023) (WSN).

Federated Learning has its wide range of applications in skin care systems (Sharma & Bhadula, 2023) and the need for data privacy is met out. Though it is highly recommended by Sachin Sharma et. al, data heterogeneity is not effectively targeted. A multi signature technique is focussed by Adithya et. al. (2022) in Block Chain for tamper proof storage policy and their experimental; results achieved a reduction inaccuracy when training the secure conclave. To improve the accuracy a light weight authentication mechanism (Ji et al., 2023) was introduced in Block Chain technology, but failed to prove the efficiency for many real world scenarios with unknown attacks.

The proposed model discussed in Chapter 3 has more advancements in means of fast storage and secure when compared with state of art models.

Figure 1. Layered architecture model

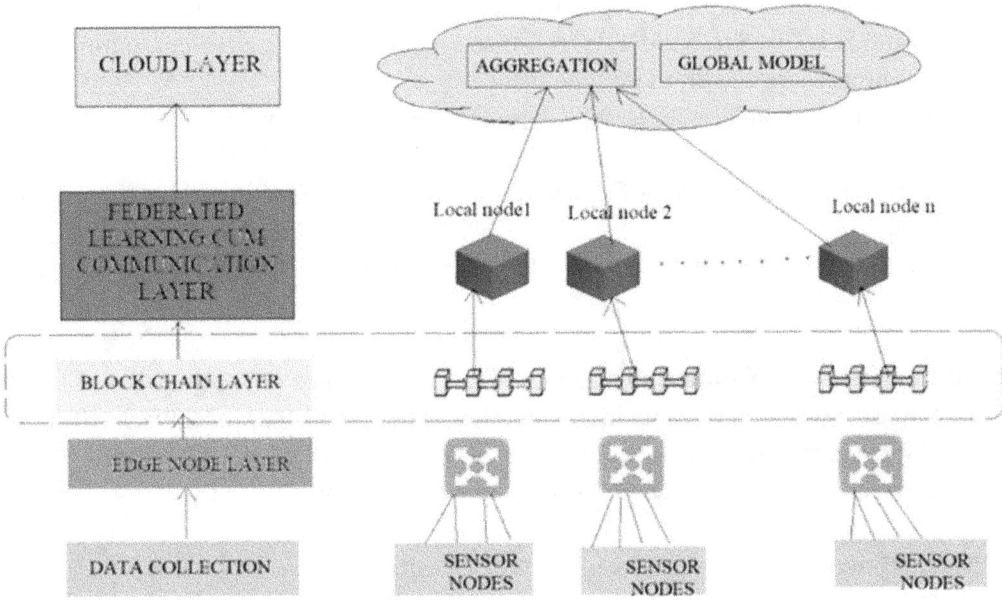

3. PROPOSED MODEL

3.1 Layered Architecture Model

The proposed secured intelligent layer is composed of Data Collection Layer, Edge Node Layer, Block Chain Layer, Federated Learning cum Communication Layer and Cloud Layer. The main objective of the intelligent model is to transmit the data in a secured and a robust communication channel violating the dynamic threat barriers throughout the network, and the recipient could obtain a continuous, integrated data. The Figure 1 depicts the layered architecture of a tenable and a strong model.

Data Collection Layer: This layer replicates the sources of data from various types of devices. The data may be collected through sensors incubated from mobile gadgets, vehicles, satellites, living organisms, etc. The data is continuous in nature and should provide an uninterrupted supply to its connected Edge nodes.

Edge Node Layer: This layer is a distributed paradigm that brings computation and data close to the data sources. The unique feature of edge computing is that it is a topological platform with location sensitive technology that receives data from nearby sources and directs it to the Edge server. The uncomplicated and simple computations are carried out within the Edge nodes, and only the complex part of the computation is submitted to the central Cloud server for further computation. The easier tasks like normalising the real-time data, visualisation of the normalised data, caching and buffering, data filtering, etc. are taken care of by the Edge nodes. The risks of higher latency, higher communication costs, and handling of lower internet bandwidth are eliminated by this layer.

Block Chain Layer: One of the most significant layers is the Block Chain layer, which provides a common data base that could be shared by multiple parties enabling transactions among different individuals, organisations, etc. Edge computing nodes infuse Block Chain and assist in alleviating the energy consumption and time lagging issues of Block Chain. Without a single point of control, Block chain technology might be used to build a decentralised marketplace for edge computing that connects providers of edge infrastructure with those who need it.

Also, the Edge nodes integrate with Block Chain for the following two reasons:

a. The resource-constrained nature of Edge nodes and their security limitations are overcome using Block Chain.
b. Block Chain limits the amount of sensitive data that is sent to the cloud, thereby resolving privacy concerns.

Federated Learning cum Communication Layer: This layer lies above the Block Chain layer and trains the Block of data received from its immediate lower layer. This approach varies from traditional centralised machine learning techniques, which call for the submission of all local datasets to a single server. Federated layer is being introduced for the following reasons:

a. To add an additional layer of security to the created Block.
b. Lessening the real-time predictable and unpredictable threats in the Cloud Layer.
c. Avoids the sensitive data being transmitted across the network, instead it facilitates in sharing the updates of locally trained models (Local Privacy).
d. Accomplishment of anonymization and encryption techniques ensures the data to be protected against untrusted parties except the central server (Global Privacy).

Horizontal Federated Learning (HFL) and Vertical Federated Learning(VFL) are the types of mechanisms (Liu et al., 2022) and exploited based on different use cases. HFL is best suited for training local models, since it encompasses less number of repetition samples and more overlapping feature attributes. However, VFL is applicable for uses case scenarios where it requires same sample data set and less overlapping feature attributes.

FL model would shield the training data against Data Poisoning attacks, Collusion attacks and data theft of malicious local nodes (Liu et al., 2022), thereby diminishing the risk probability of data and behaviour auditing phase of the FL model. To ensure the creditability of FL, data quality assessment is worked out and the historical behaviour of the local worker nodes are evaluated frequently.

Apart from the threats arising in local worker nodes, the central server and communication channels are also viable to different attacks. White Box attacks are predictable during the transmission of gradient information to the central Cloud server. Also, the eavesdropping attacks are predictable to occur, leading to the meaningful data tampering by the opponents. Gradient compression techniques and cryptology gradients (Liu et al., 2022) are few of the techniques adapted to prevail over the above said attacks.

Cloud Layer: A Generalization is induced at the Cloud layer by aggregating the local models from the edge devices and converged to a new generic model (Sannara, 2021). The generic model is sent back to all the local nodes at the edge layer and the machine starts learning again. This process is repeated till a satisfied précised model is obtained.

The Cloud layer poses the following challenges:

a. In the midst of transmission paradigm, the data are to be protected against DDoS attacks, Man in the Middle attack, etc.
b. There is more probability to influence the global model disproportionately by multiple fake devices using Sybil attacks, Byzantine attacks (Khordadpour, 2023), etc. The global model may get compromised and the learning process may get disrupted with incorrect updates from the local devices.

A robust aggregation technique is hence required to strengthen the global model at the Cloud layer. Hessian scaling matrix is proposed to close the above said gap.

3.2 The Proposed SDN Secured Framework

The control plane is more vulnerable to unseen attacks and the risk of unauthorized access or exploitation is highly probable. The control plane in an SDN is responsible for managing and controlling the network's behaviour, including routing decisions, traffic management, and network configuration. If unauthorized individuals gain access to the control plane, they can potentially manipulate network traffic, disrupt network operations, or launch attacks on other network components.

The hypothesis for this vulnerability could be that if an attacker gains unauthorized access to the control plane of an SDN, they can exploit it to disrupt network operations, manipulate traffic, or compromise network security.

An Overview Analysis on Potential Exploits in Control Plane of SDN:

- **Control plane spoofing:** Attackers may attempt to impersonate a legitimate controller or manipulate control plane messages to gain unauthorized control over the network. This can lead to unauthorized changes in network behaviour or configuration.
- **Control plane flooding:** Attackers can flood the control plane with a high volume of malicious or bogus requests, overwhelming the network's processing capabilities and causing a denial-of-service situation. This can disrupt network operations and impact the availability of network services.
- **Control plane injection:** Attackers may attempt to inject malicious commands or configuration changes into the control plane messages. This can lead to unauthorized modifications in routing decisions, traffic redirection, or other network behaviour.
- **Control plane information leakage:** Vulnerabilities in the control plane implementation may allow attackers to gather sensitive information about the network, such as network topology, configuration details, or security policies. This information can be exploited to plan further attacks or gain unauthorized access to other network components.

To mitigate the vulnerability in the control plane of an SDN, several strategies are being implemented by the researchers earlier. The proposed technologies of integration of Block Chain with Federated Learning attempt to upgrade the mitigation strategies, so that Business organizations can take steps to reduce the risk associated with vulnerabilities in the control plane of an SDN and enhance the security and resilience of their software-defined networks.

Figure 2. The proposed secured SDN with Blockchain enabled

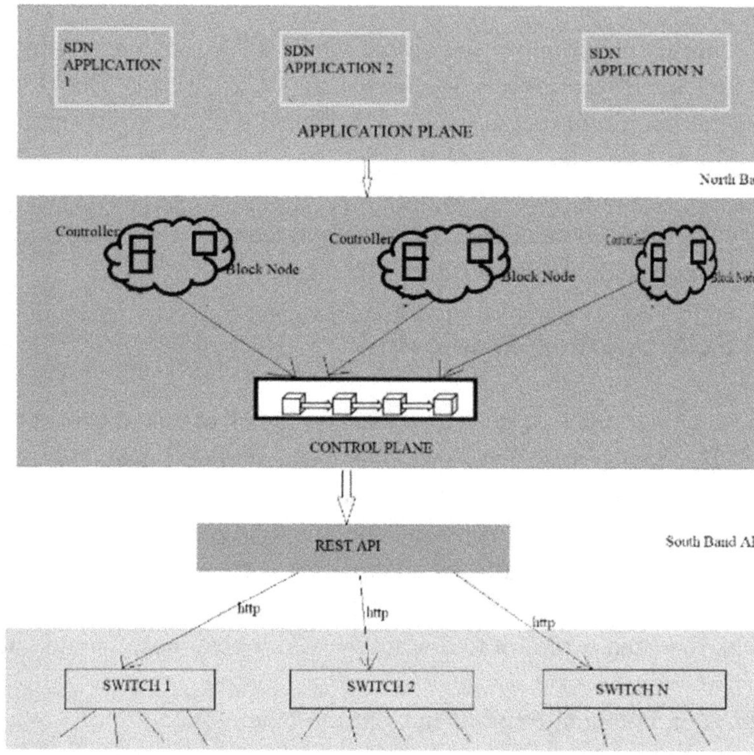

3.3 Impact of Hessian Scaling Matrix in Global Model Aggregation

Quasi Newton approach and Hessian Scaling matrix are both optimization algorithms. Both the approaches converge faster than first order methods like Gradient Descent. Quasi Newton is applicable for various types of optimizations including unconstrained optimization, constrained optimization and machine learning algorithms.

However, Hessian Scaling Matrix is more preferable to Federated Learning, since the matrix balances the heterogeneous contributions of different clients at their local Edge devices. The influence of each client's update is adjusted by the matrix and the loss gets minimized.

The Hessian scaling matrix is a square matrix that provides information about the second-order partial derivatives of a function. It plays a crucial role in optimization algorithms, such as Newton's method and Quasi-Newton methods, for finding the minimum or maximum of a function.

The Hessian matrix is derived by taking the second-order partial derivatives of a multivariable function with respect to its variables. For a function f(x1, x2, ..., xn), the Hessian matrix is constructed by computing the second-order partial derivatives:

$$\text{Hessian matrix } (H) = [[\partial^2 f/\partial x1^2, \partial^2 f/(\partial x1 \partial x2), ..., \partial^2 f/(\partial x1 \partial xn)],$$

$$[\partial^2 f/(\partial x2 \partial x1), \partial^2 f/\partial x2^2, ..., \partial^2 f/(\partial x2 \partial xn)],$$

[∂^2f/(∂xn∂x1), ∂^2f/(∂xn∂x2), ..., ∂^2f/∂xn^2]]

The elements of the Hessian matrix provide valuable information about the curvature and shape of the function at a particular point. Positive values in the diagonal elements indicate concavity, while negative values indicate convexity. The off-diagonal elements represent the interaction between variables.

The Hessian scaling matrix is used to adjust the Hessian matrix during optimization processes. Scaling can help balance the influence of different variables and improve the convergence and stability of optimization algorithms. Various techniques, such as diagonal scaling, can be applied to modify the Hessian matrix and enhance optimization performance.

By utilizing the Hessian scaling matrix in optimization algorithms, the convergence speed and accuracy of finding the optimal solution for a function can be improved. The Hessian matrix provides valuable information about the curvature and shape of the function, enabling efficient optimization techniques and algorithms to navigate the function's landscape.

By incorporating the Hessian scaling matrix, federated learning can account for variations in local data distributions and ensure that the global model reflects the contributions of different clients appropriately. This helps to mitigate the impact of data heterogeneity and improve the overall performance and generalization of the global model in federated learning scenarios.

Following is the step by step procedure describing how Hessian scaling matrix is typically used in the global model aggregation process of federated learning.

Step 1: Local Model Training by the participating Edge Devices using its local data set. The Central server will then aggregate the local models. The local models are being personalized at the Edge devices and it provides a better experience. Each and every Edge devices have their individual learning models.

Step 2: Before evaluating the local model, the client partitions its local dataset into two parts: training data and validation data. The training data is used to train the local model, while the validation data is used for model evaluation. Local Models are evaluated for its model's performance using validation data set. The outcome of the evaluation will provide the loss and gradient calculation. The loss function measures the discrepancy between the predicted outputs of the model and the actual labels/targets from the validation data. This evaluation process helps determine the contribution of each client's local model to the global model and ensures that only well-performing models are included in the aggregation process. The model parameters are then updated using optimization algorithms using Gradient Descent.

Step 3: Along with the loss function, the client computes various evaluation metrics to assess the performance of the local model. These metrics depend on the specific task or problem being solved. For example, in image classification tasks, metrics like accuracy, precision, recall, or F1 score can be used.

Step 4: By using the Hessian approximation based on gradients, federated learning incorporates information about the curvature of the loss function around the current model parameters. This helps to improve the optimization process, enhance convergence, and ensure accurate updates to the global model.

Step 5: In Hessian approximation, assume the off-diagonal elements of the Hessian matrix are negligible compared to the diagonal elements. This simplification reduces the computational complexity while still capturing important information about the curvature. The diagonal elements represent the second-order partial derivatives. Each diagonal element is estimated using the corresponding gradient component.

Step 6: To improve the Hessian approximation, a scaling factor can be applied to each diagonal element. Normalizing the Scaling Matrix based on Local Data distribution and the characteristics of Loss Function. The scaling factor accounts for the learning rate or step size used in the optimization algorithm. It helps balance the influence of the gradients and ensures that the Hessian approximation captures the curvature accurately.

Step 7: The diagonal Hessian approximation, along with the scaling factors, is organized into a matrix called the Hessian scaling matrix. The Hessian scaling matrix is then used in the global model aggregation process to adjust the influence of each client's update based on the estimated curvature information.

Step 8: In Cloud Layer, central server receives and aggregates the local models with approximate weighting on the Hessian Scaling Matrix. At the cloud central server, federated learning can leverage the collective knowledge from multiple devices or clients while preserving data privacy.

Step 9: The Global Model Aggregation process is performed iteratively with multiple rounds of model updates and aggregation

3.4 Implications of Hessian Scaling Matrix for Enhancing SDN Security

There are also supplementary reasons the Hessian Matrix is used in SDN security. Hessian Matrix plays a vital role in accurately predicting against threats and attacks.

3.4.1 Intrusion Detection

Anomalies in the patterns of network traffic can be identified by examining the curvature of the loss function. By contrasting the Hessian matrices of the regular traffic and the current traffic, anomalous or malicious activity can be detected. By doing so, network threats can be detected and unapproved access to the SDN can be stopped.

3.4.2 Anomaly Detection

Observing the curvature of the loss function allows one to spot deviations from the norm. Any anomalies or security breaches within the SDN can be detected by any sudden changes in the Hessian matrix. This can aid in real-time detection and mitigation of potential security issues.

3.4.3 Traffic Classification

Within an SDN, the Hessian matrix can help with traffic classification and application identification. Different network applications-specific patterns can be found by examining the loss function's curvature. This can be used to distinguish between genuine communication and traffic that can be malicious, improving the SDN's security.

3.4.4 Defence Against Evasion Attacks

Attacks that alter network traffic aim to get around security protections. In SDNs, such assaults can be recognised and defended against using the Hessian matrix. Changes in the traffic pattern brought on by evasion strategies can be located by examining the loss function's curvature. This gives the SDN the ability to modify its security controls and thwart effective evasion assaults.

3.4.5 Optimization of Security Measures

The positioning and setting up of security mechanisms within an SDN can be optimised using the Hessian matrix. Potential vulnerabilities and weak areas in the network can be found by examining the loss function's curvature. In order to increase the overall security of the SDN, this information can be utilised to deploy security equipment, such as firewalls or intrusion prevention systems, in the best possible locations.

4. CONCLUSION

This Chapter encompasses Block Chain for secured data communication in the control plane of Software Defined Network. Hashed Data security is provided to the local data of the edge devices and Federated Learning approach is proposed for two reasons: to efficiently handle the data of different calibrations and to further strengthen the data against threats and attacks like Evasion attacks, DDoS attacks, Man in the middle attack, etc. Block Chain cum Federated Learning explores the security features at each and every stage of the data in the network. Block Chain shields the data near the Edge devices, and Federated Learning approach guards the data by managing the heterogeneous data and defending against the future possible attacks by predicting the malicious, unwanted threats accurately. The accuracy of the prediction can be enhanced by incorporating Hessian Scaling Matrix at the central server in Cloud layer during Global aggregation process. Hessian Scaling plays a dual role of optimizing the global aggregation and threat prediction. This would lessen the loss of curvature and holds accountability for increasing the learning rate of the model.

REFERENCES

Abdelouahid, D., Guerroumi, G., Belaoued, M., & Cheikhrouhou, O. (2021). BMC-SDN: Blockchain-Based Multicontroller Architecture for Secure Software-Defined Networks. *Journal of Wireless Communications and Mobile Computing*. . doi:10.1155/2021/9984666

Abhiroop, T. (2022). A Machine Learning Consensus Based Light-WeightBlockchain Architecture for Internet of Things. *14th International Conference on Communication Systems & Networks*. IEEE. 10.1109/COMSNETS53615.2022.9668487

Abou El Houda, Z., Hafid, A. S., & Khoukhi, L. (2023). MiTFed: A Privacy Preserving Collaborative Network Attack Mitigation Framework Based on Federated Learning Using SDN and Blockchain. *IEEE Transactions on Network Science and Engineering*, *10*(4), 1985–2001. doi:10.1109/TNSE.2023.3237367

Ahmad, A., Luo W., & Robles-Kelly, A. (2023). Robust federated learning under statistical heterogeneity via hessian-weighted aggregation. *Journal of Pattern Recognitio n*10.1016/j.patcog.2023.109635

Al Asqah M., & Moulahi, T. (2023). Federated Learning and Blockchain Integration for Privacy Protection in the Internet of Things: Challenges and Solutions. *Journal of Future Internet.*. doi:10.3390/fi15060203

Algarni, S. (2022) BCNBI: A Blockchain-Based Security Framework forNorthbound Interface in Software-Defined Networking. *Journal of Electronics (China).* doi:10.3390/electronics11070996

Baucas, M. J. Petros, S. & Plataniotis, K. (2023). Federated Learning and Blockchain-Enabled Fog-IoT Platform for Wearables in Predictive Healthcare. *IEEE Transactions on Computational Social Systems.* IEEE.

Bugra, B., Turkmen, H., & Nuriyev, U. (2023),"PPFchain: A novel framework privacy-preserving blockchain-based federated learning method for senor networks", Elseveir: Internet of Things, ISSN: 2542-6605.

Gebremariam, G., Panda, J., & Indu, S. (2023). Blockchain-Based Secure Localization against Malicious Nodes in IoT-Based Wireless Sensor Networks Using Federated Learning. *Hindawi Journal of Wireless Communications and Mobile Computing.*. doi:10.1155/2023/8068038

Hayat, R. F., Aurangzeb, S., & Aleem, M. (2022). ML-DDoS: A Blockchain-Based Multilevel DDoSMitigation Mechanism for IoT Environments. *IEEE Transactions on Engineering Management.* doi:10.1109/TEM.2022.3170519

Ijaz, A. Namaly, S., Ylianttilaz M., & Gurtov, S. (2015). Security in Software Defined Networks: A Survey. *IEEE Communications Surveys & Tutorials, 17*(4).

Ji, S., Zhang, J., Zhang, Y., Han, Z., & Ma, C. (2023). *LAFED: A lightweight authentication mechanism for blockchain-enabled federated learning system.* Elseveir Journal of Future Generation Computer Systems. doi:10.1016/j.future.2023.03.014

Jiasi, W. J., Liu, J., & Zhang, Y. (2019). Secure Software-Defined Networking Based on Blockchain. *Journal of Cryptography and Security.* doi:/arXiv.1906.04342 doi:10.48550

Kalapaaking, A. P., Khalil, I., & Atiquzzaman, M. (2022). *Blockchain-Enabled and Multisignature-Powered Verifiable Model for Securing Federated Learning Systems.* IEEE Transactions on Internets of Things.

KhordadpourP. (2023). Proposed Smart 5G Framework: Incorporating Federated Learning and Transfer Learning. *Tech.* doi:10.36227/techrxiv.22814831.v1

Li, W., Meng, W., & Kwok, L. F. (2016, June). A Survey on OpenFlow-based Software Defined Networks:Security Challenges and Countermeasures. *Journal of Network and Computer Applications, 68*, 126–139. doi:10.1016/j.jnca.2016.04.011

Liu, P., Xu, X., & Wang, W. (2022). *Threats, attacks and defenses to federated learning: issues, taxonomy and perspectives.* Cyber Security, Springer Open Access.. doi:10.1186/s42400-021-00105-6

Maimoona Bint, E. (2022). Exploiting Machine Learning to Detect Malicious Nodes in Intelligent Sensor-Based Systems Using Blockchain. *Hindawi Journal of Wireless Communications and Mobile Computing.* doi:10.1155/2022/7386049

Nguyen, D., Ding, M., Pham, Q., Pathirana, P., & Long, B. (2021). Federated Learning Meets Blockchain in Edge Computing: Opportunities and Challenges. *IEEE Journal of Internet of Things.*

Otoum, S., Al Ridhawi, I., & Mouftah, H. (2023). A Federated Learning and Blockchain-Enabled Sustainable Energy Trade at the Edge:A Framework for Industry 4.0. *IEEE Internet of Things Journal, 10*(4), 3018–3026. doi:10.1109/JIOT.2022.3140430

Qammar, A., Karim, A., Ning H., & Ding, J. (2022). Securing federated learning with blockchain: a systematic literature review. *Journal of Artificial Intelligence Review.* . doi:10.1007/s10462-022-10271-9

Qi, X., Ye, W., Tao, Z., Wu, J., & Li, Q. (2021). A survey of federated learning for edge computing: Research problems and solutions. *Journal of High-Confidence Computing.* . doi:10.1016/j.hcc.2021.100008

Rahman, AMontieri, AKundu, DKarim, MIslam, JUmme, SNascita, APescapé, A. (2022). On the Integration ofBlockchain and SDN: Overview, Applications, and Future Perspectives. *Journal of Network and Systems Management.* doi:10.100710922-022-09682-4

Riahi, A., Mohamed, A., & Erbad, A. (2023). RL-Based Federated Learning Framework Over Blockchain (RL-FL-BC). *IEEE Transactions on Network and Service Management, 20*(2), 1587–1599. doi:10.1109/TNSM.2023.3241437

Sannara, E. K. (2021). A Federated Learning Aggregation Algorithm for Pervasive Computing: Evaluation and Comparison. *IEEE International Conference on Pervasive Computing and Communications.* IEEE. 10.1109/PERCOM50583.2021.9439129

Sharma, S., & Bhadula, S. (2023). Secure Federated Learning for Intelligent Industry 4.0 IoT Enabled Self Skin Care Application System. *IEEE Xplore proceedings of the Second International Conference on Applied Artificial Intelligence and Computing (ICAAIC 2023).* IEEE. 10.1109/ICAAIC56838.2023.10141028

Sharma, V., & Seetharaman, T. (2023). Blockchain and Federated Learning Enabled Smart Traffic Management System for Smart Cities. *4th International Conference on Intelligent Engineering and Management (ICIEM 2023).* IEEE. http://Doi: 10.1109/ICIEM59379.2023.10167236

Shin, S., Xu, L., & Hong, S. & Gu, G. (2016). Enhancing Network Security through Software Defined Networking (SDN)",IEEE Explore. *25th International Conference on Computer Communication and Networks (ICCCN).* IEEE. 10.1109/ICCCN.2016.7568520

Singh, S. K., Yang, L. T., & Park, J. H. (2022). FusionFedBlock: Fusion of blockchain and federated learning to preserve privacy in industry 5.0. *Information Fusion, 90,* 233–240. doi:10.1016/j.inffus.2022.09.027

Wael, I. (2023), Blockchain-Based Federated Learning for Securing Internet of Things: A Comprehensive Survey. ACM Computing Surveys, 55(9) . doi:10.1145/3560816

Zhu, C., Zhu, X., Ren, J., & Qin, T. (2022). Blockchain-Enabled Federated Learning for UAV Edge Computing Network: Issues and Solutions. *IEEE Access : Practical Innovations, Open Solutions, 10,* 56591–56610. Advance online publication. doi:10.1109/ACCESS.2022.3174865

Zibin, Z., Chen, W., Chen, X., Weng, J., & Imran, M. (2019). An Overview on Smart Contracts: Challenges, Advances and Platforms. *Journal of Future Generation of Computer System.* . doi:10.1016/j.future.2019.12.019

Chapter 9
Blockchain and Sustainability in Supply Chains

Syed Danish Bukhari
https://orcid.org/0000-0002-2478-0297
Sir Syed CASE Institute of Technology, Islamabad, Pakistan

ABSTRACT

Blockchain technology has gained significant momentum in recent years, with many countries recognizing its potential for enhancing sustainability in supply chains. Countries around the world are increasingly exploring the potential of blockchain to enhance transparency, traceability, and accountability in their supply chains. Blockchain enables countries to establish a trusted and decentralized network where information can be securely stored and accessed by relevant stakeholders. This enables governments, businesses, and consumers to have a comprehensive view of the supply chain, from raw material sourcing to product delivery through transparency and traceability across which enabling better visibility into the origins and environmental impact of products by ensuring sustainability practices are adhered to at every stage of the supply chain. As more companies recognize the benefits of blockchain in ensuring sustainability, we can expect to see its widespread adoption in supply chains across various industries.

INTRODUCTION

In the business world, before the pandemic, the Supply Chain (SC) consisted of three subcategories: handling, storage, and transportation of products. These categories have been strengthened by ensuring the right product, in the right condition, is delivered at the right time, to the right place, for the right client, at the right cost, and in the right quantity. To achieve these, it is crucial to carefully manage the transactions involved in the SC process, from the delivery of goods through the flow of materials from production to the final client. The SC expanded into the global market, which increased complexity and required digitalization to improve the flow of information between SC partners. Digitalization has significantly improved income with the help of real-time information flow, which increases customer satisfaction (Muduli et al., 2022). However, the flow of information through digitization has increased the risk of cyberattacks and hackers can manipulate, steal, or delete information, posing a serious threat.

DOI: 10.4018/979-8-3693-0482-2.ch009

In this regard, blockchain is a more advanced and sophisticated technology that can combat these risks by enhancing both the security and efficiency of the SC through transforming the entire process of product creation, marketing, and transportation for expediting purchase order execution, streamlined invoice processing and accelerated payment reconciliation (Mazumder & Bhaumik, 2022). The SC experts applied a range of transaction-related data to create distinctive and easily verifiable identities for purchase orders, inventory units, and bills of lading, which create loyalty and trust among end users towards brands and corporate leaders with the help of mitigating risks of documentation, errors, delays, and fraud, by improving supply chain performance (Ashcroft, 2022), (Mazumder & Bhaumik, 2022). Resultantly, the global market share of block chain in SC has approximately $253 million in 2020, out of which the global market share of blockchain in the food SC has up to $128.87 million in 2020 (Markets and Markets, 2023), (Science Soft, 2023). The COVID-19 pandemic has a detrimental impact, but the blockchain has the potential to mitigate its effects by presenting businesses with the opportunity to improve their processes and address inefficiencies (Sinistra, 2020), (Xiong et al., 2021). This situation highlights the importance of adapting and seizing change-related possibilities, and the significance of this function may vary for different companies based on how the pandemic has disrupted their supply networks. For example, Sonoco, the leading provider of temperature assurance packaging for pharmaceutical distribution, enhances supply chain transparency by utilizing blockchain technology. This involves tracking data throughout the entire journey of a package, integrating it with information from other commercial sources, and sharing it with SC partners. Notably, online retailers such as Alibaba and JD.com also rely on blockchain to ensure real-time product tracking in their operations (Xiong et al., 2021). Hence, the global coronavirus pandemic has brought about significant changes in the landscape of blockchain technology and its application to SC management (Mazumder & Bhaumik, 2022).

BACKGROUND AND LITERATURE REVIEW

Background

Origin and Function of Block Chain

The fundamental concepts of blockchain technology were developed by Leslie Lamport in the late 1980s and early 1990s. After that, in 2008, Satoshi Nakamoto created a digital ledger system that served as the foundation for the creation of the virtual currency known as Bitcoin. The blockchain is built on cryptocurrencies like Bitcoin, Litecoin, and Ethereum. In a distributed ledger, they function to keep track of transactions. Blockchains are available in two types: public and private. Peer-to-peer transactions are made possible by public blockchain, which includes cryptocurrencies like Bitcoin. Using a private cloud infrastructure, private blockchain uses blockchain-based platforms like Ethereum or Blockchain-as-a-Service. A public blockchain is the internet, whereas a private blockchain is an intranet. Although blockchain technology was designed to be completely open and distributed, private blockchains have also been created. One or more entities have control over private blockchains. Otherwise, there are no differences between private and public blockchains (Alharthi et al., 2020). Blockchain is a distributed database system with a consensus mechanism that stores information about transactions and other types of data. Asymmetric encryption methods, distributed data storage, consensus algorithms, and smart contracts are the four main components of blockchain technology. The symmetric encryption methods use many coding schemes, they are more secure. Blockchain offers a distributed consensus system that makes sure all participating entities are aware of every transaction by recording it incontrovertibly in the public ledger. Distributed data storage and encryption techniques secure the data in the system. To execute the peer-to-peer transfer, smart contracts are created collaboratively with network users. The blocks that make up a blockchain are interconnected, and it is simple to follow the history of transactions through earlier blocks. Blocks function as a container with batch information. A new block is added to the list of current blocks whenever a new record or transaction is initiated on the blockchain. The difficulty target value, nonce, previous hash, timestamp, Merkle root hash, and block version number are all included in the block header. The timestamp contains the block's creation time and is 4 bytes in size. Merkle uses root logic to establish an immutable, secure distributed ledger. The difficulty goal specifies the degree of difficulty of the proof of work. Miners are supposed to test all potential values for the nonce to obtain the unique hash value, which is the hash of the whole block. Nonce is the sequence of integers that fulfills the proof of work and is used to construct this hash value. In the blockchain system, exchanges between network participants take place, and records of these exchanges are gathered in the form of blocks. These blocks are added to a running list that is stored on all network members' computers after being validated by other network users. All transactions are timestamped, grouped in chronological order, linked to the preceding block, and made irreversible once they are uploaded to the network. They are all validated and recorded by users on that network. Blockchain is a trustworthy technology because of its extensive structure. For managing interactions between several parties in a safe, effective, and decentralized way, blockchain is recognized as a reliable and affordable technology (Yontar, 2023).

Origin and Function of Sustainable Supply Chain

The phrase sustainable development was originally used in 1980 by the International Union for Conservation of Nature to describe a scenario in which development is both beneficial and damaging to the environment. The International Union for Conservation of Nature, in conjunction with the United Nations Environment Programme, the World-Wide Fund for Nature, UNESCO, and the Food and Agriculture Organisation of the United Nations, presented a strategic plan for sustainable living in 1991. According to this approach, sustainable development means that as the capacity of supporting ecosystems grows, so does the quality of human existence. Elkington originally proposed Systainable Supply Chain (SSC) in 1998 with the intention of encouraging business owners to analyze their performance in addition to the traditional goal of boosting profitability. Compared to the conventional supply chain, the sustainable supply chain necessitates a broader perspective and greater collaboration between the participating businesses. Cooperation and integration are necessary at all points along the supply chain, from the acquisition of raw materials to the point of consumer consumption, in order to convert it into a sustainable supply chain (SSC). SSCs are not just for ethical and sustainable supply chains. The operational procedures that must be carried out in the social, environmental, and economic dimensions determine the quality of what is produced. SSCM stands for transparent social, environmental, and economic goal integration and attainment through efficient internal organisational process coordination. The Supply Chain Management Professional Council amended the definition of sustainability as an enterprise endeavour to adhere to the principles of sustainable development in 2013, taking into consideration stakeholder and CSR needs. Organisations must rebuild their present supply chains in order to integrate sustainability goals into all aspects of their operations, from procurement through distribution, in order to achieve sustainability.In addition to completing the economic dimension, a real SSC also takes care of the environment and society (noneconomic dimensions). Some of the similar characteristics in the definitions of SSCM presented in the literature include organisational collaboration, enhancing chain performance overall, and paying respect to stakeholder concerns (Amirian et al., 2022).

Literature Review

BlockChain in Sustainable Supply Chain

The sustainability of supply networks includes social and environmental considerations in addition to economic ones. Social, economic, and environmental sustainability are the three key goals that blockchain technology may influence. Blockchain technology's attributes, such as data immutability, decentralization, neutrality, security, and transparency, may be used to gather, manage, store, and support product information in SC data. The blockchain has significant drawbacks, but it also has the potential to reduce some sustainability-related problems and promote the realization of the circular economy. The pressure of sustainable SC is present in many modern industries. Global consumers are growing more conscientious and cautious about the goods they buy, particularly those in the food and beverage sector. The combination of IoT with blockchain, including the usage of Radio Frequency Identification (RFID) tags, can be utilized to provide real-time food tracing. RFID tags in the agriculture industry may also be used to record events in the SC. Since only authorized parties may access the information, unethical providers who really hurt society are discovered, and along with that, fake products can be avoided. Any organisation and its SC benefit from the implementation of blockchain technology from a commercial perspective, which boosts their economic performance. Blockchains can lead to the disintermediation of production networks, wherein fewer layers result in decreased time and exchange costs, reducing corporate waste in SC. The ability of blockchain to quickly communicate changes to any data reduces human error and transaction delays. By making data more trustworthy and preventing unwanted data change, blockchain technology can secure the data's validity and safety while also lowering corporate costs. Transparency on the blockchain will increase trust, which will encourage customers to purchase more goods and benefit businesses financially. Blockchain, a revolutionary technology, has the potential to improve SC social sustainability. Because information in blockchain-based SC cannot be changed without the agreement of the parties, it can stop unscrupulous activities. Governments can quickly recognize these malevolent actors and take appropriate action against them thanks to their ability to hold corrupt individuals responsible. Human rights abuses in the SC may be found thanks to blockchain traceability and transparency, and a safe workplace can be set up with ease. Governmental authorities may also seize illegitimate assets. Blockchain technology can also help with environmental sustainability. There are several uses for blockchain technology in environmental sustainability. The use of blockchain technology can help accomplish significant environmental goals. For instance, blockchain technology's tracking capabilities can assist minimize product recalls. The reduction of carbon footprint is another use case for blockchain technology. It can assist in determining the true carbon footprint of any product, which can help decide the exact tax that needs to be collected from the producer. Giving rewards in the form of bitcoin to those who take part in deposit-based programs helps with product recycling as well. Blockchain also improves the efficacy of outflow exchange schemes by reducing deception and enhancing the stability of the system (Kumar & Dagar, 2021).

Application of Blockchain for Sustainability Supply Chain

The blockchain has been actively used by businesses all over the world to build a more sustainable supply chain system.However, some of example are: Coca-Cola declared in 2019 that it will use blockchain technology to increase supply chain transparency and sustainability. To establish a secure registration of employees in its bottling facilities in the Philippines, the corporation has teamed up with three blockchain startups. The system's goals are to avoid violations of human rights and advance moral workplace behavior. Ford said in 2020 that it will collaborate with IBM to utilize blockchain technology to trace the cobalt used in its electric vehicle batteries. Ford can use the technology to track the cobalt down to the mine that produced it, guaranteeing that it was supplied ethically and sustainably (Freeman FRSA,2023).A blockchain-based technology named TradeLens was introduced in 2018 by the world's largest shipping company Maersk to increase efficiency and transparency in the global supply chain. The technology, created in collaboration with IBM, enables shippers, freight forwarders, and customs officers to securely share transportation data and documents. TradeLens lowers paperwork and delays while simultaneously encouraging transparency and sustainability by digitising and simplifying the SC (Freeman FRSA,2023). The French retail behemoth Carrefour has used blockchain technology to increase the openness and traceability of its food supply chain. The business tracks the food products' path from the farm to the shop using blockchain, enabling customers to confirm the legitimacy and calibre of the goods they buy. The approach also promotes ethical sourcing methods and lessens food waste (Freeman FRSA,2023). Global consumer products firm Unilever and IBM have joined together to implement blockchain technology to enhance the traceability and sustainability of their supply chain. To ensure that tea, palm oil, and other raw materials are produced responsibly and without causing harm to the environment or local populations, the firm employs blockchain to trace their origin. Small-scale farmers' lives are also improved by the system by giving them better access to markets and information. These instances show how blockchain technology has the power to revolutionize SCM and advance sustainability in a variety of sectors. Blockchain may assist businesses in reducing waste, promoting ethical practices, and improving efficiency while also allowing customers to make knowledgeable decisions about the items they purchase. This is done by enabling more precise monitoring of resources and products. In the years to come, we may witness even more cutting-edge applications for sustainable supply chain management as blockchain technology develops (Freeman Frsa,2023).

Countries adopted Blockchain for Sustainable Supply Chain

Today's online payment industries and merchants continue to show interest in the global market for blockchain technology and cryptocurrencies. The majority of established and developing countries are dominating the cryptocurrency and blockchain technology markets, according to surveys, and the global digital industry is steadily gaining speed. There are various countries that has adopted blockchain for SC: A supportive environment for blockchain and cryptocurrency firms has been actively built in Portugal. The country has aggressively implemented blockchain technology in SCM, healthcare, and public services. In 2019, the Portuguese government unveiled the Blockchain Panorama platform, which aims to promote communication and collaboration among those involved in the blockchain industry. Since then, a pro-crypto atmosphere enabling the option to utilise BTC in real life, including paying bills and taxes with the cryptocurrency, has drawn a large population of Bitcoiners and crypto fans to the area. With a Spanish business called BitBase striving to expand the number of Bitcoin ATMs and storefronts in key cities, merchant usage has also surged. To encourage tech-based innovation, the Portuguese government adopted a decree in 2021 that laid out the fundamental requirements for the development of technical free zones. Through testing and experimentation, it involves assisting with the adoption of blockchain technology. Since then, the nation has been implementing stricter controls on cryptocurrency taxation in order to comply with the laws of other European nations. The government announced the repeal of a long-standing tax provision that excluded earnings from cryptocurrencies on the grounds that they are not considered legal cash until 2022 (Lacapra, 2023).Malta began to encourage blockchain use in 2017 after establishing several industry laws to hasten the development of blockchain technology. At the time, Malta was known as blockchain. Three laws establishing a legal framework for blockchain technology and virtual currencies, including ICOs, digital assets, virtual currencies, and associated services, were approved by the Maltese parliament in 2018. Regarding the taxation of cryptocurrency assets, Malta said that utility tokens and electronic money are not classified as capital assets under the Income Tax Act, making them exempt from capital gains tax. Securities and virtual financial assets, however, are regarded as capital assets and are taxed. The Maltese government committed to supporting the technology by including blockchain and artificial intelligence (AI) in its commercial guide outlook and framework at the end of 2021. The purpose is to encourage foreign businesses to establish themselves in Malta in order to test and use blockchain technology. Malta has not yet become a blockchain island. The island's government adopted less liberal policies towards the sector as a result of ongoing and heightened foreign monitoring of domestic political and economic developments on the island. But a lot of blockchain and cryptocurrency-focused firms are doing well. For example, companies utilizing blockchain in the supply chain of products, like wine and olive oil, are a tangible reality on the island (Lacapra, 2023). In India, the National Institution for Transforming India (NITI) Aayog, the country's policy think tank, and ConsenSys Ventures, a blockchain software company, collaborated on the implementation of blockchain in a land titling initiative. Additionally, ConsenSys Ventures inked a contract with the state of Andhra Pradesh for several applications of its technology, including land titling, supply chains, and health records (Reiff, 2023). To provide microloans to vendors in Kenya, IBM collaborated with Twiga Foods, an African business-to-business logistics network for kiosks and food stalls. These loans were designed to assist merchants in acquiring and controlling additional inventory. Building a blockchain-enabled loan infrastructure that could assess the creditworthiness of the food providers was IBM's contribution. In Nigeria, where efforts are being made to clean up the river belt, blockchain technology has being utilised to track toxic levels. These statistics are necessary for the reporting needs of the international organisations supporting these initiatives (Reiff, 2023).Haiti, which has suffered from hurricane and earthquake destruction over the past ten years, has much to gain from blockchain. The Haitian government has proposed using blockchain technology to track and register votes, intellectual property, property transfers, and other parts of the bureaucracy. The Haitian Gourde will soon be available digitally thanks to a trial program that the La Banque de la Rēpublique d'Hati said it was investigating in 2019. The project's objectives are to enhance Haiti's domestic payment system and advance financial inclusion. The Business Development and Investment program (BDI) in Haiti has aided hundreds of manufacturers during the past few years. Due to natural catastrophes, the COVID-19 epidemic, the killing of its president, lockdown because of sociopolitical upheaval, and gang-fueled insecurity, the BDI project—which was created to help the reconstruction efforts following Haiti's 2010 earthquake—had to step up its operations. The initiative originally planned to facilitate the export of current high-quality agricultural goods but eventually changed its focus to attracting private sector investment through the construction of special industrial zones. The initiative assisted in building the ability of third-party service providers by giving them access to quality transport and logistics services, standard operating procedures, and working capital to help farmers receive higher prices. The success of the entire operation depended on a blockchain system for payments and traceability that allowed for direct payments to farmers (Reiff, 2023).China announced restrictions on cryptocurrencies and mining, but it hasn't stopped experimenting with the development of blockchain-based services. The Chinese government officially supports blockchain technology and seems to be the technology's greatest and most impressive global advocate. With the advent of a developed blockchain industrial framework, the government is expanding distributed network usage to integrate the technology into its financial and growth goals. To support blockchain-based firms, the nation plans to develop industrial standards, licensed property insurance, and tariff incentives. From its educational system to its judicial system, China has included blockchain. The nation has also made several notable attempts to enhance blockchain-based advancements. Effectively, it supports TRON, NEO, VeChain, and Qtum as well as its own smart contract software. The Chinese authorities are open to the idea that blockchain may be the most purposefully important early global invention. The crackdown issues in China are typically linked to instances of blockchain technology use that violate specific governmental regulations and guidelines, such as fake behaviour, token sales, particularly to retail customers, and other crimes like illegal tax laundering and capital controls evasion (Kumar Sharma, 2002). United States is not lagging behind any other nation in adopting blockchain technology. The nation has taken every step imaginable to adopt and implement blockchain technology, from establishing research organizations to installing ATMs that only accept Bitcoin. It will become a part of the government's normal operating procedure. New blockchain-based enterprises are reportedly most welcome in states like Texas and Montana. Only in the US can you find over 40% of the whole blockchain startup market. The nation has a huge impact on the bitcoin and blockchain environment. The United States Federal Government anticipates increasing investment in blockchain development 10 times over, according to the most recent study. Before the end of 2021, it is anticipated that the amount spent on blockchain development would increase to 123.5 million dollars from its first measurement of 10.7 million dollars in 2017. (Kumar Sharma, 2002).

MAIN FOCUS OF CHAPTER

Sustainability Supply Chain Governance

In attempts to mobilize blockchain as sub technology, three crucial aspects of global supply chains and their governance are repeated, aggravated, and eventually depoliticized. The dominance of hierarchical and exploitative corporate power structures over global supply networks comes first. The second topic is audit culture, which is strongly tied to managerialist models of governance. Thirdly, outside consulting firms reinforce these dual dynamics. These topics were gathered from current supply chain governance research in order to situate the larger stakes involved in our politicization of the shift to blockchain as supply chain sub technology. First, corporate influence in the regulation of the global supply chain. The preservation of the most profitable parts of production processes by top companies in the supply chain serves as the clearest illustration of this. Supply chains are progressively being divided into their component portions across sectors and areas, with the most expensive and dangerous tasks being leased out to auxiliary personnel and locations. It is claimed that integrating geographically scattered locations and processes into global supply chains is a crucial path to development and the eradication of poverty. These assertions, however, acknowledge the enduring power disparities that underlie the corporate-centered globalization of production. Numerous studies from numerous academic fields relate the structure of global supply networks to the hyper exploitation of various types of forced labor. Due to ingrained inclinations towards the hyper exploitation of peripheral workers, global supply networks are better understood as global poverty chains. The logistics and transport activities related to the operation of global supply chains have also been blamed for a significant increase in carbon emissions, in addition to supply chains propensity to externalize ecological deterioration. The complex, ostensibly universal mechanisms of coordination across time and location have since materialized and sustained the hierarchical and exploitative structures of the global supply chain. The second is the need of management coordinating strategies. This refers to the methodically unequal use of standardization, measurement, and competition-fostering practices in international supply chains that serves as the foundation for abusive corporate dominance. Continuous expansion and capture of value are described as methods for managerial types of coordination. As a form of government that espouses the ambition of a logically ordered world while depending on professional knowledge of calculation and predictability, managerialism has several challenges that are universal in nature. Managerialism has, in fact, increased the social and ecological costs and repercussions that are disproportionately being paid for by workers and communities in the Global South. In this regard, managerialism discussions are quite similar to anthropological studies of audit cultures. These latter have highlighted in particular how the calculative rationalities of contemporary financial accounting systems designed for measuring and auditing cast governance issues as merely technical and administrative tasks, carried out by remote technocrats in ways that diminish the role of local knowledge and professional expertise. The integration of financial bookkeeping and human management, sometimes known as human accounting, emphasises accomplishment and efficiency through measuring and rating as the fundamental set of principles guiding audit culture. Through the use of top-down, external, predetermined criteria, such methods frequently serve to make grassroots communities knowable and answerable to market-based development authorities. Local, bottom-up solutions to sustainability problems are frequently replaced by these processes and depoliticized as a result. The increased understanding of such costs has frequently extended increasingly complicated forms of private, corporate-led governance rather than signaling a move away from managerial inclinations. Most notably, since the early 2000s, major companies involved in global supply chains have worked to ease worries about socio-environmental costs by releasing a wide range of codes of conduct and sourcing policies specific to respective sectors. Multi-stakeholder initiatives involving numerous public and private actors as well as professional services companies like the Big Four Deloitte & Touche (D&T), Ernst and Young (EY), KPMG, and Price Waterhouse Cooper (PwC) have increasingly supplemented early Corporate Social Responsibility (CSR) schemes and corporate codes of conduct for suppliers. The solutions employed by efforts headed by the business sector to solve these issues are last but certainly not least. These tend to strengthen the identical circumstances that initially gave rise to worker and environmental exploitation. There are two ways that this process has happened. First, as industry actors have had more freedom to pick and choose which voluntary norms to follow, encouraging a race to the bottom, corporate dominance has increased. Despite offering protection from pressure to at least take some action to address the sustainability problem, the proliferation of private sustainability standards has served to further strengthen the influence of foreign stakeholders over local populations throughout the Global South. The latter generally employ local expertise in an effort to tackle sustainability issues at a scale that is less global but perhaps more successful. Private codes of conduct, principles, and other similar forms of governance are mainly prevented from truly addressing the issues they are positioned as answering by the ease with which they can be evaded and the difficulty with which they can be enforced under international voluntary norms. Multiple evolving environmental and labor norms have been found to, at best, replace environmental and labor infractions rather than reduce them. In the worst-case scenario, the flurry of private codes of conduct has increased the costs of monitoring and compliance on smaller local suppliers and subcontractors without reducing the pressure from leading firms to deliver raw materials quickly and affordably while minimizing labor and environmental abuses. Notably, studies have generally concluded that where changes have been made, these successes were often the result of political pressure from civil society organizations or the inclusion of worker participation and voice. The private standards and codes have a propensity to rely on pre-existing repertoires of supply chain management and coordination, which ultimately strengthens the control of transnational corporations over the organisation of production and exacerbates the unequal capture of value within supply chains. Instead of addressing the more complicated socio-political, ecological, and socioeconomic problems that exploitation by these powerful actors has made possible, the rise of such governing at a distance produces numerical forms of technical transparency that serve the interests of distant corporate actors in quantitative data. In the paragraphs that follow, it is argue that the shift to blockchain in reaction to these persistent failures creates a veil of transparency over the socio-political consequences of efforts to make sustainable supply chains, doing so in ways that may eventually reinforce current failures and depoliticize them (Bernards et al., 2022).

Blockchain Repurposed as Sub Technology

It has been demonstrated that the development of platform capitalism and information communication technologies (ICTs) has extended and intensified managerialism practices by giving managers more precise tools to manage the labor process, such as algorithms and digital tracking technologies. In order to ostensibly improve the openness, visibility, and readability of actors and resource flows in global sustainability governance, a variety of developing digital technologies have been put to use. Blockchain is one of them that businesses, governments, and international organizations have given a lot of attention to. Blockchain applications codify both the salient features of the types of private government mentioned above as well as their pathologies, despite their anti-financial system beginnings. In a nutshell, blockchains materialize audit culture. They encourage data and information responsibility along economic lines, and they calibrate messy human trade and interaction using calculable and auditable reasoning. As a result, this collection of tools turns the human into a type of unadulterated economic, calculable, and auditable rationality. In order to further the technical viewpoint that all issues are engineering challenges, blockchains are frequently touted as offering universalist answers. Additionally, blockchains are frequently explicitly considered as transcend geopolitical conflicts between people. In other words, technology is frequently used to flatten diverse activity zones towards a single competitive market conduct as an unquestionable universal global good. Blockchain technology, when envisioned as a value accounting infrastructure, has the potential to enable more cooperative governance of shared resources. For instance, technology has the ability to foster new forms of organization and governance and give rise to ecosystems of creative cooperation by adopting a commons-centric value logic and assisting a worldwide transition towards a more egalitarian communitarian future. However, far more deliberate plans are required to shift sovereignty from elites to the people in financial, service, and national infrastructures in order to really realize these possibilities. In other words, a lot depends on politicking the particular social ties that are used to create and implement blockchain technologies. By contrast, as we will demonstrate in the following sections, managerial controlling logic and top-down power relations of the sorts outlined in the preceding section are used to expand and guide blockchain systems for supply chain governance in practice. Technology is being used to strengthen management logic and increase corporate control. Through a veneer of openness, this depoliticizes unsustainable practices. In particular, the so-called distributed ledger technology (PLT) or permission version of blockchain that has gained popularity in corporate alliances and PPPs is frequently presented as a natural solution for resolving the two main issues impeding private-led initiatives to improve the sustainability of the global supply. First, it is claimed that blockchains can aid in overcoming the proliferation of norms and standards in international supply chain governance. According to the World Economic Forum's lead for blockchain, the supply chain sector is fragmented, with stakeholders taking a siloed approach. Technology like blockchain and distributed ledgers may promote standardization and transparency. There is a lot of paperwork involved in the coordination between supply chain actors including manufacturers, transportation firms, and banking institutions. Initiatives to create permissioned blockchain-based networks to store and enable data on international trade flows are part of the expanding digitalization of global logistics. One of these is the 2021-launched Global Shipping Business Network. However, there are still issues with complying with antitrust and competition rules as well as other restrictions in cross-border settings. Second, it is claimed that blockchain applications encourage data transparency by producing shared, permanent records of transactions that, in principle, can be accessed by all and changed only by network members who have reached consensus. The sustainability of global supply chain governance depends on these activities. Blockchain is thought to offer reasonably priced solutions for enhancing visibility and traceability as supply chains become more complicated. The technology is believed to reduce the costs of data collection and exchange, but more crucially, for the sustainability of the global supply chain, it is said to display and validate the identity of commodities effectively, including their condition and provenance. But even while blockchain may increase the visibility of some supply chain elements, real management choices along the (block) chain harden well-established top-down paths outlined by managerialism and audit culture. Contrarily, the greater legibility of some aspects of products and their movements made possible by blockchain also makes new invisibilities possible, making sociopolitical, ecological, and economic problems less visible rather than more transparent (Bernards et al., 2022).

Practical Example of Blockchain and Sustainable Supply Chains

Blockchains can have an impact on networks of sustainable supply chains because they are distributed, immutable, transparent, and reliable databases that are shared by a community. A significant application area for the blockchain is tracking possible social and environmental factors that might pose risks to the environment, human health, and safety. There are real-world instances. According to China's Carbon Emission Reduction for the Paris Agreement, businesses may generate carbon assets more effectively thanks to blockchains created in China for carbon asset markets. Human rights and ethical workplace practices are better guaranteed by a supply chain built on the blockchain. For instance, a clear history of the product guarantees consumers that the things they are buying are supplied and produced from sources that have been shown to be morally upright. Smart contracts may be particularly capable of enforcing or managing regulations that autonomously track and regulate sustainable terms and regulatory policy. Academics and professionals alike are becoming increasingly interested in sustainable supply chains. In addition to the importance of the commercial aspects of the supply chain for sustainable supply chains, including the environmental and social aspects has given the supply chain a more all-encompassing and universal viewpoint. Given the intricacy of the triple-bottom-line of sustainability—economic, social, and environmental—blockchain technology's promise attributes may be the answer. Thus, recording and locating examples of sustainable supply chains may demonstrate the range of uses for blockchain technology. Data collection, storage, and administration may be supported by blockchain technology, supporting important product and supply chain information. Openness, transparency, impartiality, dependability, and security for all supply chain participants are possible in this technology environment. There are strains on the food and beverage industry's supply chain sustainability. In this perspective, combining RFID and blockchain technology to equip the food supply chain with a traceability system for real-time food tracking based on Hazard Analysis and Critical Control Points (HACCP) guidelines is an intriguing application. It can capture events in the agricultural supply chain. Since all information can only be recorded by authorised participants, blockchain can help supply chains identify unethical suppliers and counterfeit goods, which can cause considerable social harm.Adopting blockchain technology may help a company and its supply chain economically by improving many business metrics that have an impact on their financial performance. Here are a few of the numerous instances that may be used to support the business and economic case for blockchain technology in the supply chain. Blockchain technology has the potential to disintermediate the supply chain, resulting in lower transaction costs and transaction times and less corporate waste overall. By instantaneously sharing any change to the data, blockchain technology might possibly speed up the rollout of goods and procedures while reducing human error and transaction delays. With the use of blockchain technology, it will be cheaper to protect data from willful and arbitrary change, which will increase supply chain risks and decrease business dependability. Additionally, the government and consumers increasingly demand supply chain transparency. Pioneering businesses recognised the competitive advantage of openness, which increases consumers' confidence and encourages them to spend more money with them. Blockchain technology has the potential to improve the sustainability of social supply chains. One strategy to increase the social sustainability of the supply chain is to make information durable and irreversible. Blockchains can stop dishonest persons, governments, or organisations from wrongfully stealing people's assets since information cannot be changed without the permission of permitted participants. Blockchain technology may also stop malicious actors and make the corrupt responsible for both societal and personal wrongdoing. Sustainability is aided by blockchain traceability through improved assurance of human rights and just, safe work practises. For instance, having access to a product's history gives buyers more assurance that the items they are buying are from moral producers. Sustainability of the supply chain for the environment is also aided by blockchain technology. It is capable of doing so from a wide range of applications. First, eliminating rework and recall can minimise resource consumption and greenhouse gas emissions by properly monitoring defective items and detecting subsequent transactions of the products. A peer-to-peer network based on blockchain technology for energy systems can eliminate the need to transport power over long distances and, as a result, save a significant amount of energy that would otherwise be squandered during long distance transmission. Traditional energy systems are centralised. Additionally, it would decrease the demand for energy storage, saving resources. Echchain, Electric Chain, and Sun Contract are a few power systems built on blockchain technology that aim to cut down on supply chain waste. Second, blockchains might be used to verify the environmental friendliness of allegedly green items. Green product processing data is frequently elusive and challenging to validate. Customers that care about the environment can be more inclined to buy green items if the production method of a product is confirmed to be green in terms of greenhouse gas emissions level. For instance, Ikea sells a desk constructed from wood harvested from an Indonesian forest that is managed sustainably. In order to ensure that the desks are indeed manufactured from this particular wood, Ikea must track the wood from the time it is cut through production to the finished product. Although this procedure is complicated, blockchain technology may be used to manage it. One such instance is the Endorsement of the Forestry Certification project, which uses blockchain technology to trace the origin of about 740 million acres of certified forests worldwide. A another illustration of environmental supply chain sustainability relates to the carbon price. The carbon footprint of any product is challenging to quantify using conventional technologies. Blockchain technology makes it simpler to track the product footprint of a certain firm. It can assist in calculating how much carbon tax a corporation should pay. Customers may choose to purchase a product with a low carbon footprint if it is more expensive but has a larger carbon impact. To fulfil customer demand, businesses may need to rethink and reorganise their supply chains in light of this new knowledge and pressure from the market or consumers. By offering the building blocks for supply chain mapping and implementing low-carbon product design, production, and transportation methods, blockchain technology can cut carbon emissions along the product's journey. A methodology for evaluating the carbon emissions of each entity participating in supply chains and the life cycle of products is proposed by the Supply Chain Environmental Analysis Tool (SCEnAT). A brand-new tool called SCEnAT 4.0 combines cutting-edge technologies like blockchain, the Internet of Things (IoT), artificial intelligence, and machine learning to better manage big data and connect organizations in the supply chain in support of Industry 4.0 regulations, carbon reduction efforts, and environmental assessments. Trading of carbon assets may change as a result of blockchain technology. For instance, IBM and Energy Blockchain Labs Inc. China is creating a blockchain-based platform for green assets that enables businesses to manage and quantify their carbon footprint, fulfill CER regulations, and promote the creation and trade of carbon assets. Organizations may collaborate and exchange their carbon assets more effectively in the green asset markets thanks to the blockchain's real-time, transparent, secure information. Thirdly, recycling might be enhanced via blockchain. It's possible that businesses and individuals lack the motivation to engage in recycling activities. In Northern Europe, blockchain technology has been utilised to compensate individuals for depositing recyclables like plastic bottles, cans, and containers with money in the form of cryptographic tokens. While this is going on, comparing and tracking the effects of various recycling initiatives is challenging. Blockchain enables data tracking for assessing the effectiveness of various projects. For instance, Social Plastic is a blockchain-based startup that promises to minimise plastic waste by converting it into currency. Another blockchain application that enables consumers to return plastic containers is Recycle to Coin. Blockchain is suitable for new ideas like the circular economy because of the opportunities for this kind of work for closed-loop supply chains. Fourth, the effectiveness of emission trading schemes (ETS) is increased thanks to blockchain. Due to blockchain's trustworthiness and openness, fraud may be avoided with its implementation. As a result, a reputation-based system is developed to address the shortcomings of the ETS and to motivate all participants who are motivated by the financial rewards of good reputation to devise long-term emission reduction strategies. It will be difficult to employ blockchain technology as a method for supply chain governance and information management, especially in a sustainable network. Long- or short-term, disruptive innovations often confront difficulties. As a result, supply chain players need to be ready for it to be an opportunity rather than a danger because it might put the relationships inside the supply chain at risk. These instances demonstrate the potential for managing environmental, social, and economic (sustainability) factors in a supply chain that uses blockchain technology (Saberi et al., 2018).

Benefits of Blockchain for Sustainable Supply Chain

Due to its potential to revolutionise supply chain operations, blockchain technology has attracted a lot of interest recently. It has attributes like decentralisation, immutability, transparency, and better security that can help with issues with supply chain data management, provenance, and traceability. Blockchain technology has been shown to improve supply chain transparency, lower fraud and counterfeiting, improve traceability, and enable more effective and sustainable supply chain operations, according to research. Additionally, a number of earlier studies looked at the application of blockchain technology in other industries. the potential advantages of blockchain technology in lowering mistakes, data redundancy, order delays, and damage to items within various businesses. the use of blockchain technology in the maritime sector, with a focus on how it might help with problems with digital trust and data synchronisation. The adoption of blockchain technology in the field of accounting, highlighting its importance in ensuring accurate and trustworthy database transactions. These studies, along with others, help us understand the benefits, drawbacks, and prospective uses of blockchain technology across a range of industries. However, the idea of the supply chain as a web of businesses engaged in creating value for the client. the emergence of Industry 4.0 and its potential to enhance supply chain processes. The all-encompassing character of Industry 4.0 and its effects on sustainability, productivity, speed, and flexibility. They emphasised Logistics 4.0's significance in integrating processes across company borders and opening the door for new monitoring techniques utilising intelligent pallets, containers, and vehicles. the significance of big data for Industry 4.0 and Logistics 4.0 since it facilitates improved decision-making. They also noted that the growth of blockchain technology is built on the use of big data.The advantages of using blockchain in supply chain and logistics management, such as better asset monitoring, order management, and information exchange between suppliers and vendors. It showed how blockchain technology may help reduce problems including delays, inaccuracies, and unidentified product origins. Review of blockchain's applicability in industrial supply networks and its potential for establishing supply chain transparency. The use of blockchain in guaranteeing participant privacy while assuring the validity and traceability of items throughout the supply chain. Last but not least, even with straightforward uses, blockchain technology may significantly enhance the supply chain. They affirm that better supply chain management results from recording product transfers on a digital ledger. Customs port procedures, however, are of utmost significance in global trade. They strengthen international trade ties, enable trade facilitation, create income, protect product safety, and maintain regulatory compliance. Governments and companies may promote smooth international commerce, improve supply chain effectiveness, and support economic growth and development by establishing efficient and transparent customs operations (Ababneh et al., 2023).

BARRIES AND FUTURE RESEARCH

Barriers for Blockchain and Sustainable Supply Chain

The first barrier is Information techonology barrier. Although BT offers the potential for SCM, there are many obstacles to its implementation. Implementation is hampered by technical constraints including scalability, usability, and interoperability problems. Slower transaction times and fewer transactions are caused by latency issues. Blockchain splitting can be caused by issues with security, including vulnerability to hacking and system assaults, and disagreements amongst blockchain organizations. Another difficulty is the constrained availability of blockchain data and information. Although data immutability is an important property, it can be troublesome if mistakes from the past continue to exist. Adoption may be hampered by the dark web's bad connotation with illicit activity, but as more people use it, perceptions may gradually alter. Due to their pseudonymous nature, cryptocurrencies, blockchain technology, and illicit activities on the dark web are likely related since these technologies have been used in certain illegal transactions. The immutability of blockchain has been used by criminals to conceal their activities. Despite the fact that the technology is neutral, it's critical to note that how it is applied can have either positive or negative impacts. The second barrier is strategy barriers The adoption of BT in SCM is impacted by a number of internal organisational difficulties and circumstances. Financial difficulties arise from the installation of BT since it necessitates significant expenditures in infrastructure maintenance, software, hardware, and infrastructure. To guarantee that BT is integrated with environmental management, public relations, and corporate responsibility for sustainability, cross-disciplinary collaboration is also required. The perceived value of blockchain applications in SCM, however, might be severely impacted by a lack of commitment from middle or senior management. Additionally, if management does not prioritise sustainability, the value of blockchain technology can go unnoticed. Adoption is hampered by organisations' lack of expertise and understanding of blockchain and sustainability. Furthermore, the lack of standardisation in BT makes it more difficult to use it in SCM, forcing organisational changes for new blockchain and sustainability requirements. However, if management does not view sustainability as a core value, it is possible that the potential benefits of blockchain technology in attaining sustainability goals would be overlooked or underappreciated. The management's goals, vision, decisions about resource allocation, and impact on organisational culture all have a substantial impact on the adoption of blockchain technology as a tool for sustainability inside a firm. The third barrier is supply chain barriers external impediments that are unrelated to enterprises or technology are impeding the implementation of BT in SCM. A fundamental obstacle in SC concerns is the lack of consumer comprehension of the relationship between blockchain and sustainability as a result of inadequate communication and cooperation among partners. Businesses frequently lack sustainability knowledge and don't apply sustainable practises throughout the SC, which makes integrating BT more difficult. While BT can provide an encrypted blockchain and data security safeguards, companies are only ready to exchange information if it helps their customers and preserves the protection and privacy of their private information. These constraints are further exacerbated by the sensitivity of sustainability information owing to ethical and legal concerns. The integration of SC with sustainability and blockchain presents obstacles that must be solved via reengineering corporate procedures, however this may cause advances in sustainable performance to be delayed. It might be difficult to apply consistent blockchain solutions due to differing concepts of sustainability, especially social sustainability, among SC partners who are diverse in terms of geography and culture. The forth barrier is Legislation Barriers, legal barrier in blockchain technology is a difficulty or issue that inhibits the usage, acceptance, or operation of blockchain systems due of laws, regulations, or a lack thereof. These barriers, which have an impact on many aspects of blockchain technology, may be caused by the legal and regulatory systems of a particular country or region. Government regulations are still not entirely in favour of BT, which makes its adoption in the SC more challenging. The absence of legislative sustainability frameworks and rules is a significant issue that impedes the creation of integrated systems and blockchain standards. The fifth barrier is External parties from a variety of sectors, including governments, companies, institutions, communities, and non-governmental organisations, are impeding the adoption of sustainability and blockchain in SCM. These obstacles could prevent blockchain and sustainability from working together, which would ultimately thwart attempts to expand the economy in a way that is both a profitable and sustainable. Lack of market awareness and unpredictability are other obstacles that may cause businesses to be afraid about the introduction of new sustainable products (Al Amin et al., 2023).

Future Research on Blockchain and Sustainable Supply Chain

With the help of closed-loop digitalization on the blockchain, social and environmental issues may be integrated into commercial operations. The development of an evolving business ecosystem as a result of this transformation ensures compliance monitoring, quality assurance, and active incentivization. This encourages future research in three areas, namely the circular economy, the digital economy, and the sharing economy, to address problems related to the evolving complexity of a closed-loop SC, such as disagreements regarding the adoption of new practises by SC members at various levels. The 6R model, which involves rethinking methods, lowering material consumption and waste, reusing products, recycling materials, and repairing and repurposing goods, can be used to express the idea of a circular economy. Effective application of the 6R model involves behavioural consensus among stakeholders (e.g., authorities, customers, business rivals, non-governmental organisations), not only technological consensus via the blockchain platform, in order to speed up sustainable development projects. Conflict and behavioural inconsistencies among SC participants significantly hinder the unmatched scalability of blockchain technology. In order to strengthen the interorganizational relationship in the circular economy model using blockchain technology, future research should concentrate on developing social mechanisms centred on policy formulation, sensitization campaigns, a mutually collaborative working forum, an incentive-for-performance structure, as well as a penalty structure for non-compliant activities.The suggested solutions for the circular economy model also present a window of research opportunities for the digital economy model. However, a number of studies indicate that the SC's limited technological infrastructure prevents the broad implementation of blockchain technology. This suggests that businesses in these economies who want to use blockchain in their operations have little influence over their SC partners. Researchers now have the chance to investigate and evaluate the usefulness of blockchain technology for SC in developing nations, as well as to show that pilot programmes are successful in order to promote widespread implementation. Data security and safety may seem as significant issues in these situations. In order to uncover various enablers for a successful system deployment utilising blockchain for SSCM in the context of a developing economy, future research should also adopt a qualitative approach. Researchers can suggest and create a variety of maturity model frameworks, based on an inclusive investigative scope of varied industries, to assess a firm's preparedness to adopt blockchain technology in their SC operations. Additionally, it has been suggested that prospects for research into how information systems in organisations may use blockchain technology to optimise resources to achieve sustainability in SC operations. To ascertain how much adoption of blockchain technology influences the execution of sustainability operations inside SCs, longitudinal studies are required. Finally, because the sharing economy model is linked to sustainability in SC operations, more study might be done to develop new organisational governance frameworks for resource sharing among SC members to realise mutually beneficial sustainable aims. Researchers have suggested examining how businesses are enhancing their two-way communication with customers and the sharing of information with stakeholders by using social media channels like Facebook, LinkedIn, and Twitter. This is because customers have begun to demand greater visibility into the SCs of the products they buy. Further study is required to determine the full degree of this strategy's effects, which are anticipated to improve brand reputation and customer happiness. Future research should concentrate on topics like financing strategies for eco-startups, managing sustainability in omni-channel retailing, and auditing of sustainable operations given that blockchain technology has the potential to be used as a source of automated audit verification procedures. This is because blockchain technology has its roots in the financial sector. That is to say, auditors may examine transactions on openly available blockchain ledgers rather of requesting bank statements or sending confirmation requests to the appropriate parties. In this context, researchers might investigate the accelerators that might help automated audit verification approaches work more effectively in a variety of industries. Further investigation is needed to determine how publishing financial data of businesses using blockchain impacts their overall performance because the idea of the sharing economy for creating transparent SCs is still in its infancy. (Sahoo et al., 2022).

CONCLUSION

Blockchain enables countries to establish a trusted and decentralized network, allowing governments, businesses, and consumers to have a comprehensive view of the SC, from raw material sourcing to product delivery. This provides transparency and traceability, enabling better visibility into the origins and environmental impact of products. This transparency and fair system help companies set and achieve sustainability goals while improving operational efficiency. By integrating smart contracts into SC processes, businesses can incentivize suppliers to adopt eco-friendly practices, such as reducing carbon emissions or using renewable energy sources. This eliminates the need for intermediaries, reducing costs and friction in SC transactions and increased transparency not only helps identify potential bottlenecks but also ensures that ethical and sustainable practices are followed throughout the SC. With end-to-end visibility and real-time tracking capabilities, blockchain ensures the continuity of essential goods and services, fostering collaboration and trust among SC partners. The adoption of blockchain for sustainability in SC is gaining momentum across industries, with businesses of all sizes exploring blockchain solutions to create a more sustainable and ethical SC. As more companies recognize the benefits of blockchain in ensuring sustainability, it is expected to see widespread adoption in supply chains across various industries.

Definitions

i. Blockchain is decentralized, distributed, and open digital ledger called a blockchain is used to log transactions across a number of computers in a way that makes it impossible to modify the record in the past without also changing all subsequent blocks and getting network consensus.
ii. Supply Chain Management is from the acquisition of raw materials until the delivery of the product at its intended location, management of the flow of commodities, data, and money associated to a good or service.
iii. Supply Chain Process is management of the flow of goods, information, and money related to a good or service from the procurement of raw materials to the delivery of the product at its intended destination.

iv. Substantiality in Supply Chain is incorporating environmental, social, or corporate governance concerns into the sourcing of raw materials, the creation of goods, and the delivery of those items to market.

REFERENCES

Ababneh, A. M., Almarashdah, M. A., Jebril, I., Al-Zaqeba, M. A. A., & Assaf, N. (2023). Driving sustainable supply chains: Blockchain-enabled eco-efficiency for resilient customs ports. *Uncertain Supply Chain Management, 11*(4), 1719–1734. doi:10.5267/j.uscm.2023.6.018

Al Amin, M., Nabil, D. H., Baldacci, R., & Rahman, M. H. (2023, September 19). Exploring Blockchain Implementation Challenges for Sustainable Supply Chains: An Integrated Fuzzy TOPSIS–ISM Approach. *Sustainability (Basel), 15*(18), 13891. doi:10.3390u151813891

Alharthi, S., Cerotti, P. R. C., & Maleki Far, S. (2020, October 6). An Exploration of The Role of Blockchain in The Sustainability and Effectiveness of The Pharmaceutical Supply Chain. *Journal of Supply Chain and Customer Relationship Management*, 1–29. doi:10.5171/2020.562376

Amirian, S., Amiri, M., & Taghavifard, M. T. (2022, September 27). The Emergence of a Sustainable and Reliable Supply Chain Paradigm in Supply Chain Network Design. *Complexity, 2022*, 1–29. doi:10.1155/2022/9415465

Ashcroft. (2022, October 14). Timeline: Evolution of blockchain tech in supply chain. *Supply Chain Magazine*. https://supplychaindigital.com/digital-supply-chain/timeline-evolution-of-blockchain-tech-in-supply-chain

Bernards, N., Campbell-Verduyn, M., & Rodima-Taylor, D. (2022, November 25). The veil of transparency: Blockchain and sustainability governance in global supply chains. *Environment and Planning C. Politics and Space, 239965442211427*. doi:10.1177/23996544221142763

Freeman, F. R. S. A. O. J. (2023, March 22). 10 Companies Using Blockchain Technology for Sustainable Supply Chain. *Medium*. https://medium.com/@OjFRSA/10-companies-using-blockchain-technology-for-sustainable-supply-chain-6d17ca8cca25

Kumar & Dagar. (2021, December 12). Sustainability in Supply Chain with Blockchain: Understanding the Adoption Barriers and Scalability Solution. *International Research Journal of Engineering and Technology, 8*(12), 1135–1144.

Kumar, S. (2002, December 16). *Top 10 Countries Leading Blockchain Technology In The World*. Blockchain Council. https://www.blockchain-council.org/blockchain/top-10-countries-leading-blockchain-technology-in-the-world/

Lacapra, C. (2023, March 9). *5 countries leading blockchain adoption*. Cointelegraph. https://cointelegraph.com/news/5-countries-leading-the-blockchain-adoption

Mazumder, S., & Bhaumik, A. (2022, June 30). Blockchain: Transforming Supply Chain Management Amidst Covid-19. *International Journal of Engineering Trends and Technology*, *70*(6), 100–105. doi:10.14445/22315381/IJETT-V70I6P212

Muduli, K., Raut, R., Narkhede, B. E., & Shee, H. (2022, March 11). Blockchain Technology for Enhancing Supply Chain Performance and Reducing the Threats Arising from the COVID-19 Pandemic. *Sustainability (Basel)*, *14*(6), 3290. doi:10.3390u14063290

Reiff. (2023, June 5). *How Blockchain Can Help Emerging Economies*. Investopedia. https://www.investopedia.com/tech/how-blockchain-can-help-failing-economies/

Saberi, S., Kouhizadeh, M., Sarkis, J., & Shen, L. (2018, October 17). Blockchain technology and its relationships to sustainable supply chain management. *International Journal of Production Research*, *57*(7), 2117–2135. doi:10.1080/00207543.2018.1533261

Sahoo, S., Kumar, S., Sivarajah, U., Lim, W. M., Westland, J. C., & Kumar, A. (2022, May 27). Blockchain for sustainable supply chain management: Trends and ways forward. *Electronic Commerce Research*. doi:10.100710660-022-09569-1

Sinistra, P. (2020, November 3). *Future of Blockchain Technology in Supply Chain Management*. Vault Security Systems AG – Blockchain for Supply Chain. https://vaultsecurity.io/blockchain-technology-supply-chain-management

Xiong, Y., Lam, H. K., Kumar, A., Ngai, E. W., Xiu, C., & Wang, X. (2021, July 13). The mitigating role of blockchain-enabled supply chains during the COVID-19 pandemic. *International Journal of Operations & Production Management*, *41*(9), 1495–1521. doi:10.1108/IJOPM-12-2020-0901

Yontar, E. (2023, September). The role of blockchain technology in the sustainability of supply chain management: Grey based dematel implementation. *Cleaner Logistics and Supply Chain*, *8*, 100113. doi:10.1016/j.clscn.2023.100113

Chapter 10
Enhancing Customer Trust and Loyalty in the Pakistani Food Delivery Sector Through AI-Driven Blockchain Supply Chain

Muhammad Inshal
https://orcid.org/0009-0001-0467-5860
Iqra University, Pakistan

Mirza A. Haq
Iqra University, Pakistan

Pervaiz Akhtar
University of Aberdeen, UK

ABSTRACT

The digital transformation of industries, including the food delivery sector, has led to new challenges and opportunities. This comprehensive study explores into the complexities faced by Pakistan's food delivery industry, highlighting trust issues and customer loyalty. By integrating AI-driven blockchain technology, the purpose is to enhance credibility, transparency, and customer satisfaction within the sector. The research discloses a spectrum of challenges, ranging from food safety concerns to preservation of halal integrity. The amalgamation of AI-driven blockchain technology arises as a potential solution to such challenges, presenting real-time insights, boosted traceability, and enhanced accountability. However, ethical considerations associated with user consent, data privacy and fairness of algorithm must be addressed. The comprehensive analysis of the study led to conclusion that a balanced approach is crucial for unleashing the potential of it in revolutionizing Pakistan's food delivery sector, takes into account both technological benefits and ethical implications.

DOI: 10.4018/979-8-3693-0482-2.ch010

INTRODUCTION

Traditional supply chains face persistent challenges, often plagued by lack of trust and transparency (Ghouri et al., 2023; Calvera Isabal et al., 2023; Flores-Vivar & García-Peñalvo, 2023; Shaoliu & Tongbai, 2023). This opacity hinders efficiency and leaves room for fraud (Khan et al., 2017). Addressing these issues is crucial for long-term viability, and this is where the transformative power of Supply Chain Management (SCM) shines (Khan et al., 2017; Haq, Khan, Parkash & Jabeen, 2016). By incorporating digital technologies, businesses can achieve unprecedented levels of visibility and accountability, fostering trust and paving the way for a more efficient and resilient future.

An inspiring example of such transformation is the global online food delivery sector. This industry connects consumers to diverse food providers through platforms, acting as a matchmaker between desire and delivery (Yuen et al., 2019; Galati et al., 2020). Its success relies on collaboration among restaurants, customers, and intermediaries, facilitated by technology that improves precision and consistency (Kulkarni, 2021).

The global food service market, driven by online delivery, has seen significant growth, reaching $2.52 trillion in 2021 and projected to reach $4.43 trillion by 2028 (Statista, 2023). Notable platforms like Uber Eats, Grubhub, and Doordash are driving this growth (Meemken et al., 2022). In Pakistan, the food delivery sector has also experienced a surge, with online food consumption increasing by 300% in just three years (CISPL, 2020). Local players like Foodpanda, EatMubarak, and Cheetay play a significant role in this expansion, demonstrating the potential of this transformative approach in diverse markets (Raza et al., 2023; Sjahroeddin, 2018).

However, in Muslim-majority countries like Pakistan, globalization has introduced complexities in ensuring halal food standards since the food products which are consumed, are not necessarily produced in the same country (Dağ & Erbasi-Gonc, 2013), which has increased the chances of cross-contamination (Yusoff et al. 2015). Therefore, now-a-days, Muslims are concerned about their product's halal status or questioning about products' integrity or authenticity (Dağ & Erbasi-Gonc, 2013). In a nutshell, challenges in food delivery sector of Pakistan include maintaining the integrity of halal food throughout the supply chain, transparency, traceability (Ellahi, 2023), and adherence to varying international and national standards (Sabreen, 2021). To tackle these challenges, the implication of a blockchain-based system can create transparency in supply chains, allowing stakeholders to trace food origin, confirm authenticity, track custody, and ensure product integrity (Montecchi et al., 2019). Also, with artificial intelligence food fraud (Jiménez-Carvelo, 2022) and fake reviews can be tackled (Mohawesh et al., 2021).

The primary focus of this study is to thoroughly investigate and determine the main challenges within the food delivery sector of Pakistan, specifically related to food safety, trust, and customer retention. Despite significant industry growth, there is a scarcity of comprehensive scholarly literature addressing these complexities, especially in the Pakistani context. Driven by specific objectives, the research also seeks to explore innovative solutions using cutting-edge technology, particularly AI-driven blockchain supply chain systems, its impact on customer feedback and reputation management, and to examine its enhancements in food traceability and transparency.

BACKGROUND

The food delivery sector in Pakistan has witnessed astonishing growth driven by the digital age and a 300% surge in online food consumption over the last three years (CISPL, 2020; Raza et al., 2023). The key platforms of this market like Foodpanda, EatMubarak, and Cheetay (Sjahroeddin, 2018) have played important roles in reshaping how consumers access and enjoy their meals.

Despite significant growth, the food delivery sector in Pakistan faces challenges that impact its trajectory. Globalization has made it difficult to guarantee the halal status of food products due to the complexities of sourcing raw materials and ensuring halal practices throughout the supply chain (Dağ & Erbasi-Gonc, 2013). In addition, the lack of uniform halal standards in Pakistan, compounded by varying standards from different organizations, further complicates matters (Sabreen, 2021). Also, the struggles of the traditional food supply chain with issues like transparency, traceability, food safety, food fraud (Ellahi, 2023), and halal integrity have been exposed in the wake of globalization and technological advancements.

In the digital era, online reputation management has become crucial for businesses, and online reviews significantly influence consumer choices, with 93% of consumers considering online reviews when making purchasing decisions (Vimaladevi & Dhanabhakaym, 2012). However, the challenge of fake reviews (Shi et al., 2023) and false or misleading label claims persists (van Ruth et al., 2017), affecting customer trust and damaging the credibility of online businesses (Karode & Werapun, 2022).

To address these challenges and strengthen trust and loyalty of customer in the Pakistani food delivery sector, the integration of blockchain and artificial intelligence presents a potential solution. Blockchain, which is a secure and distributed database, having prominent features like decentralization, immutable records, transparency, peer-to-peer communication (Rajasekaran et al., 2022), time stamping, traceability and secured even it can not be virtually hacked (Malik et al., 2019). In addition, with blockchain technology, companies can grant selective access to not only customers but also halal authorities, enhancing transparency about sourcing, processes, and distribution, which maintain customer trust in Halal products and provides authorities an alternative means to verify compliance (Hendayani & Fernando, 2022), and has potential to deliver a reliable and transparent system for customer reviews (Puri et al., 2023). However, there is a drawback of using blockchain, that is its ability to store accurate and truthful data depends on the reliability of the provided information, or in other words, it is not immune to the storing of inaccurate or already manipulated data, and challenges like data confidentiality and the verification of external data sources remain unresolved in this sector (Giannoni et al., 2023). At the end of the day, the accountability for data inaccuracy rests with the data provider, as they are the ones who have the control of the data. However, by developing automated systems using AI's machine learning algorithms, such as text mining, the challenge of identifying fake reviews within data can be resolved. Given the possible harm fake reviews pose to businesses, it is vital to employ accurate detection tools. Differentiating fake reviews from real ones in large datasets is challenging for individuals or companies, however machine learning algorithms, known for uncovering hidden patterns, are suitable for this particular task (Mohawesh et al., 2021).

In conclusion, the integration of AI and blockchain in supply chain systems appears as a promising solution to enhance trust and loyalty of customers in Pakistan's food delivery sector. These technologies address critical issues related to transparency, traceability, and data integrity, particularly concerning with food fraud, provenance, authenticity, fake reviews, and halal integrity.

Figure 1. Research protocol

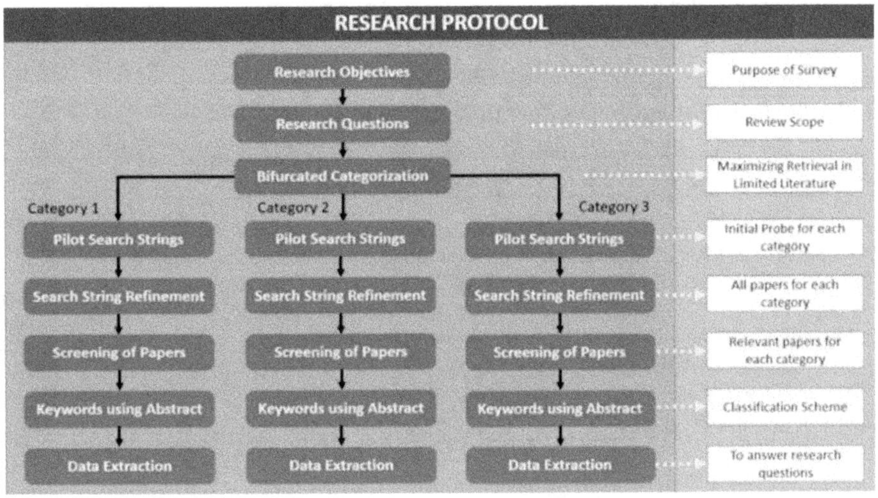

RESEARCH METHODOLOGY

This research establishes a review protocol to conduct a systematic literature review that outlines the methods for minimizing any potential biases in the study, and the diagram depicted in Figure 1 illustrates the research protocol that is adhered to throughout this study.

Research Questions

1. What are the primary challenges faced by the food delivery sector in Pakistan concerning food safety, trust, and customer retention?
2. How does the implementation of an AI-driven blockchain supply chain impact customer feedback and reputation management in the food delivery sector?
3. How does the adoption of an AI-driven blockchain supply chain improve food traceability and transparency, and how does it address issues related to food fraud, fraudulent labelling, provenance, halal supply chain, and fake reviews in the food delivery sector?

Search Strings

For the relevance of studies in the systematic literature review (SLR), the selection criteria must align with the SLR objectives. Balancing high recall and precision is essential (Avci et al., 2020). Pilot search strings, primarily created with operators like "AND" and "OR" and combining wildcard characters, help refine the search (Avci et al., 2020). The plan of search strings with the right keywords is vital for optimal results (Avci et al., 2020). Testing search strings on Google Scholar helps identify the most effective string for each category, maximizing relevant keywords.

Key Challenges Faced by Food Delivery Sector in Pakistan Related to Food Safety, Trust, and Customer Retention

Table 1. Search string (Key challenges in Pakistan's food delivery sector)

Source	Search String	Context
Google Scholar	"Pakistan" AND ("Food Delivery" OR "halal food" OR Food*) AND ("Food Safety" OR "food authenticity") AND "Halal Supply chain" AND "blockchain" AND ("AI" OR "artificial intelligence") AND ("reputation" OR "trust" OR "customer retention")	Key challenges faced by Pakistan's food delivery sector in context of Halal supply chain, food safety, trust and customer retention

AI-Driven Blockchain in the Food Delivery Sector With Main Focus on Fake Reviews

Table 2. Search string (Main focus on fake reviews or customer feedback)

Source	Search String	Context
Google Scholar	("fake reviews" OR "customer feedback" OR "online reviews") AND ("food delivery" OR food*) AND ("AI" OR "artificial intelligence") AND ("hybrid blockchain" OR "blockchain") AND "food fraud" AND ("reputation" OR "reputation management") AND "trust"	AI-driven Blockchain in food delivery sector with main focus on fake reviews or customer feedback

AI-Driven Blockchain in the Food Delivery Sector With Main Focus on Halal Supply Chain and Labeling

Table 3. Search string (Main focus on Halal supply chain and labeling)

Source	Search String	Context
Google Scholar	("food delivery" OR food*) AND "hybrid blockchain" AND ("AI" OR "artificial intelligence") AND ("provenance" OR "halal supply chain") AND ("mislabel" OR label* OR "label fraud") AND ("Certification" OR certif*)	AI-driven Blockchain with main focus on Halal Supply Chain and labeling

Screening of Relevant Papers

For precision in aligning papers with research questions, we utilized Dybå and Dingsøyr's (2008) search process for screening. The first phase required selecting papers based on titles, excluding those unrelated to the research area. For instance, the keyword protocol retrieved articles on blockchain and AI in different contexts, leading to their exclusion as they were irrelevant to the study. In the second phase, the abstracts of selected papers were assessed, applying inclusion and exclusion criteria.

The following types of papers were excluded:

Table 4. Quality criteria. JCR: Journal citation reports

Sources	Ranking	Score
Journal	Q1	2
	Q2	1.5
	Q3 or Q4	1
	If article is not in a JCR ranking	0
Conference	CORE A	1.5
	CORE B	1
	CORE C	0.5
	If article is not in a CORE ranking	0

Each study gets a score for each question, and the cumulative score is presented as an integer ranging from -1 to 5.

- Articles not available in English language.
- Articles with no relevancy to the search string used.
- Articles with non-availability of full text.
- Articles released outside of journals, conferences, technical reports, and patent.

Selected papers advanced to the next screening stage after these criteria were applied.

Quality Assessment

For SLRs, quality assessment (QA) is crucial (Farooq et al., 2020). In this study, we established a questionnaire aligned with the QA approach used in a previous mapping study (Fernandez et al., 2011).

The assessment encompassed the following dimensions:

(a) The study's contribution to the AI and blockchain in the food domain was evaluated with responses as "Yes (+1)" or "No (0)."
(b) The study's effectiveness in providing a coherent solution in the food domain through blockchain and/or AI was assessed with responses as "Yes (+1)," "partially (0.5)," or "No (0)."
(c) The number of citations received by the article was assessed, ranging from "No (−1)" for zero citations, "partially (0)" for 1 to 5 citations, to "Yes (+1)" for more than five citations.
(d) The study's source credibility was determined by examining its origin from reputable and established publication sources, referencing Journal Citation Reports (JCR) lists, and the CORE ranking of computer science conferences, detailed in Table 4.

Study Selection Process

In this systematic literature review, we defined three categories: challenges in the food delivery sector, an AI-driven blockchain supply chain focusing on fake reviews, and one focusing on the halal supply chain and labeling. While search string characteristics for "fake reviews" and "halal supply chain and labeling" are similar, the distinction lies in their specific focal points. The study selection process has two

Figure 2. PRISMA flowchart for key challenges faced by Food delivery sector in Pakistan

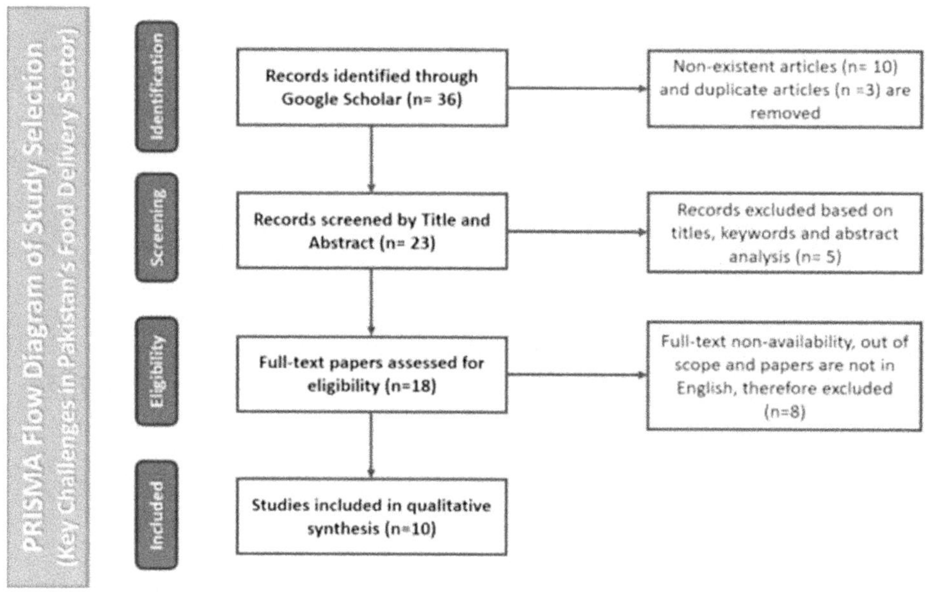

sections: the first addressing key challenges and the second consolidating "Fake Reviews" and "Halal Supply Chain and Labeling." PRISMA flowcharts guide our study selection process.

Selection of Eligible Studies Addressing Key Challenges in the Food Delivery Sector in Pakistan

In the initial search, 36 articles were identified. After eliminating non-existent articles (n=10) and duplicates (n=3), 23 studies remained. Following screening, 5 records were excluded for irrelevance, and 8 studies were removed due to full-text unavailability or being out of scope. The final qualitative synthesis included 10 studies. See Figure 2 for the selection and search outcomes.

Selection of Eligible Studies Addressing AI-driven blockchain Supply Chain for Food Delivery sector

This subsection has the following additional three sections:

a. **For Food Delivery Sector through AI-Driven Blockchain Supply Chain with Main Focus on Fake Reviews**. In the initial search, 24 articles were identified. After eliminating non-existent articles (n=10), 14 studies remained for screening. Following screening, 2 records were omitted for irrelevance. The final qualitative synthesis included 12 studies. Refer to Figure 3 for the selection and search outcomes.

b. **For Food Delivery Sector through AI-Driven Blockchain Supply Chain with Main Focus on Halal Supply Chain and Labeling**. In the initial search, 42 articles were identified. After removing non-existent articles (n=11) and duplicates (n=1), 31 studies remained for screening. Following screening, 15 records were excluded for irrelevance. The final qualitative synthesis included 16 studies. See Figure 4 for the selection and search outcomes.

Figure 3. PRIMSA flowchart for food delivery sector through AI-driven blockchain supply chain with main focus on fake reviews

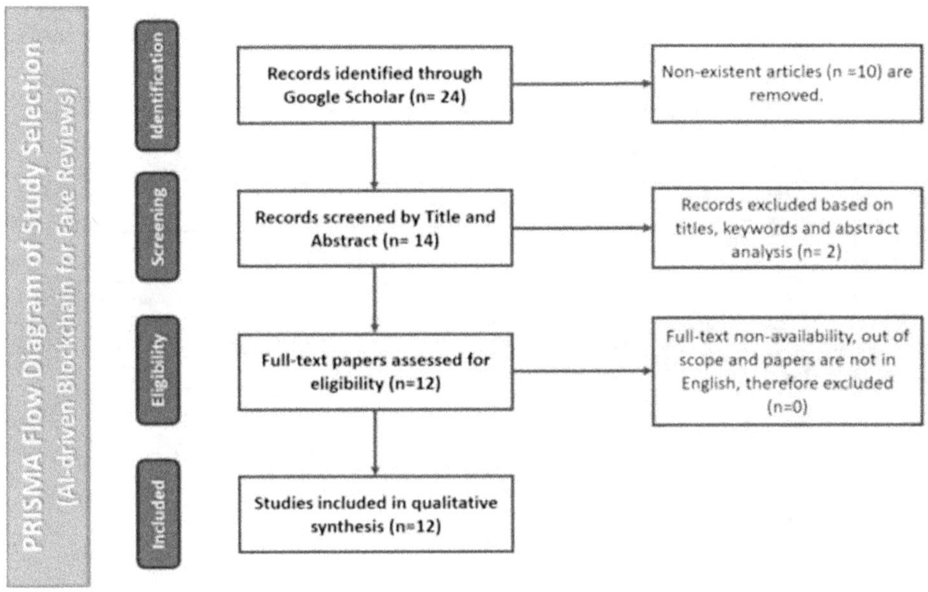

Figure 4. PRISMA flowchart for food delivery sector through AI-Driven blockchain supply chain with main focus on halal supply chain and labelling

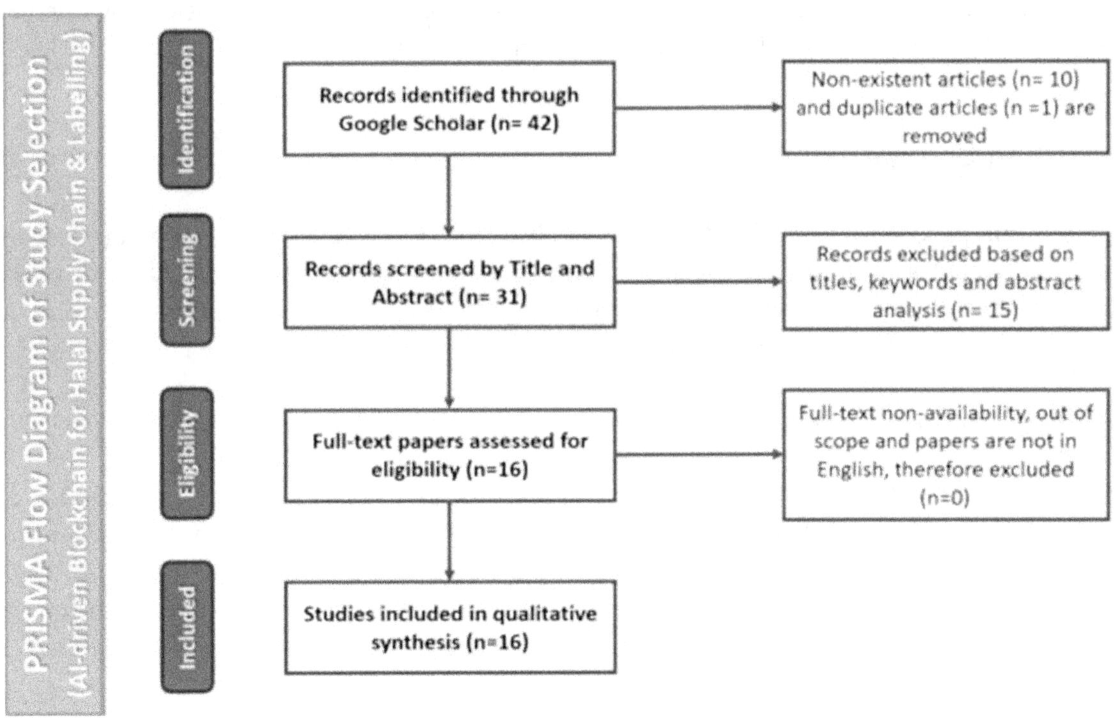

Figure 5. Consolidated PRISMA flow for the development of classification scheme

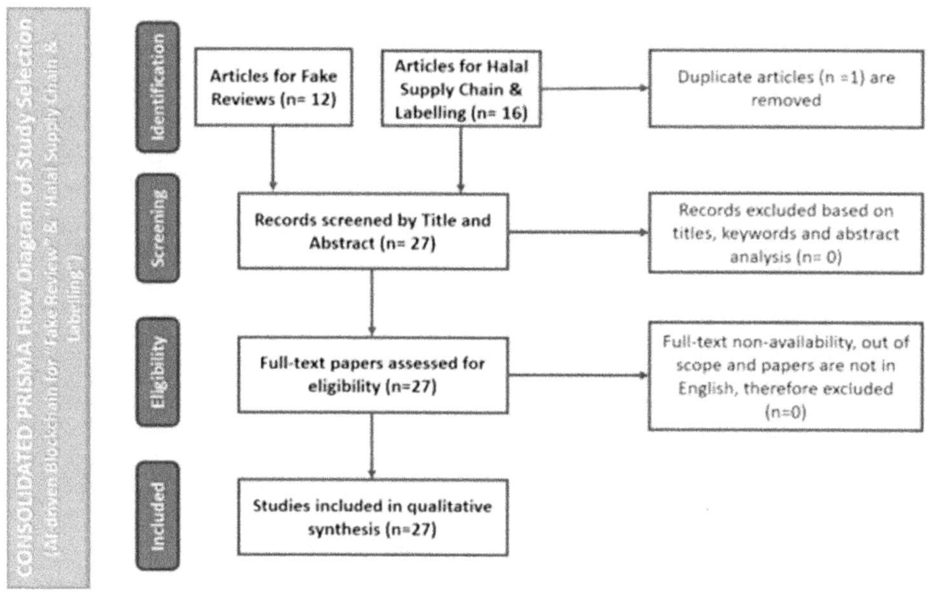

c. **Consolidation for Food Delivery Sector through AI-Driven Blockchain Supply Chain with Main Focus on "Fake Review" and "Halal Supply Chain and Labeling"**. A total of 28 articles were included, with 12 focusing on fake reviews and 16 on the halal supply chain and labeling. After removing one duplicated article, 27 studies were included for the classification scheme development. See Figure 5 for the selection and search outcomes.

Keywording Using Abstract

To find relevant papers using specific keywords in abstracts, the Petersen et al. (2008) approach was applied. This includes observing abstracts to extract main ideas and keywords related to the research questions. Keywords were then used to organize and classify the reviews. In cases of poor abstract quality, reviewers had the choice to explore introduction or conclusion sections.

Classification Schemes

Applying the classification scheme methodology outlined by Petersen et al. (2008), two distinct classification schemes are formulated in table 5 and table 6. Below is Table 5, which presents the primary challenges faced within the food delivery sector:

Table 6 underscores AI-driven blockchain supply chain benefits in the food delivery sector, covering feedback and transparency. The established categories of 'fake reviews' and 'Halal supply chain and labeling' were consolidated for a unified classification scheme.

Table 5. Classification scheme: Key challenges faced by food delivery sector

Research Question	Classification	Themes
RQ1	Food Safety and Quality	Food Safety Concerns, Contamination Risks and Handling
		Halal Integrity and Authentication Challenges
	Trust and Transparency	Trust Erosion and Importance of Accountability
		Maintaining Halal Integrity and Consumer Trust
	Customer Experience and Retention	Customer Satisfaction, Loyalty, and Expectations
		Impact of Negative Experiences on Customer Retention
	Supply Chain Challenges	Risks, Coordination, and Integrity in the Supply Chain
	Regulatory Compliance and Technology	Regulatory Framework, Standards, and Compliance
		Role of Technology in Enhancing Safety and Transparency
	Ethical Considerations and Sustainability	Ethical and Environmental Factors in Food Choices
		Importance of Sustainable Practices in Food Delivery

ANALYSIS

In the analysis section, results related to the SLR questions are discussed. After selecting studies through screening, answers to each research question are provided. This section has three sub-sections: the first on key challenges in the food delivery sector in Pakistan (RQ1), the second covering customer feedback, reputation management, food traceability, transparency, and related challenges through AI-Driven Blockchain Supply Chain (RQ2, RQ3), and the third addressing overall quality assessment scores.

Key Challenges Faced by the Food Delivery Sector in Pakistan

This subsection addresses key challenges in the food delivery sector in Pakistan. The classification scheme by Petersen et al. (2008) is applied to ten articles using the PRISMA method, as shown in Table 7. Moreover, Table 8 is constructed for quality assessment

Assessment of RQ1: What Are the Primary Challenges Faced by the Food Delivery Sector in Pakistan Concerning Food Safety, Trust, and Customer Retention?

As per table 7, the identified key challenges faced by Muslim countries like Pakistan include:

a. ***Food Safety and Quality.*** Various researchers have highlighted food safety concerns and contamination risks. Such concerns are widespread due to potential mishandling and contamination during the process of food delivery. Moreover, challenges associated with preserving halal integrity and authentication are a recurring issue, which is important for Muslim consumers.
b. **Trust and Transparency.** The next identified and significant challenges encompass trust erosion and the significance of accountability. Ensuring transparency throughout the process, whether in food sourcing, preparation or delivery, is crucial for maintaining consumer trust.

Table 6. AI-driven blockchain supply chain enhancements and consolidated classification scheme for the food delivery sector

Research Question	Classification	Themes
RQ2	AI-Driven Blockchain Supply Chain Implementation	Integration of AI and blockchain technology.
		Real-time data collection and analysis.
		Automation of processes.
		Enhanced monitoring and tracking.
	Customer Feedback Enhancement	Real-time feedback collection.
		Data-driven insights.
		Personalized customer interactions.
		Improved feedback accuracy.
	Reputation Management Enhancement	Building trust and transparency.
		Immutable and transparent record-keeping.
		Trustworthy reputation tracking.
		Addressing negative feedback.
	Operational Efficiency and Decision Making	Automated feedback analysis.
		Data-driven improvements.
		Continuous service enhancement.
RQ3	Enhanced Traceability and Transparency	Real-time tracking of products.
		Immutable record-keeping.
		Supply chain visibility.
	Addressing Food Industry Challenges	Food fraud prevention.
		Provenance verification.
		Labeling accuracy.
		Halal supply chain assurance.
		Mitigation of fake reviews.
	Authenticity and Integrity	Verification of product authenticity.
		Detection of counterfeit products.
		Halal certification validation.
	Review Authenticity and Reliability	Blockchain-based review verification.
		Trustworthy and verified customer feedback.
		Prevention of fake reviews.

c. **Customer Experience and Retention.** Customer satisfaction, loyalty, and meeting expectations are central concerns for any organization. Unfortunately, negative experiences can have a direct impact on customer retention.

d. **Supply Chain Challenges.** Risks, coordination, and integrity within the supply chain are considered as a commonly identified challenges. Therefore, ensuring the quality and integrity of the supply chain is essential.

Table 7. Classification of key challenges faced by the food delivery sector in Pakistan

Classification						
RQ1						
Reference	Food Safety and Quality	Trust and Transparency	Customer Experience and Retention	Supply Chain Challenges	Regulatory Compliance and Technology	Ethical Considerations and Sustainability
Bux et al. (2022)	-Food Safety Concerns -Halal Integrity and Authentication Challenges	-Trust Erosion and Importance of Accountability -Maintaining Halal Integrity and Consumer Trust	-Customer Satisfaction, Loyalty, and Expectations -Impact of Negative Experiences on Customer Retention	-Risks, Coordination, and Integrity in the Supply Chain	-Regulatory Framework, Standards, and Compliance -Role of Technology in Enhancing Safety and Transparency	-Ethical and Environmental Factors in Food Choices -Importance of Sustainable Practices in Food Delivery
Sarwar et al. (2021)				-Risks, Coordination, and Integrity in the Supply Chain	-Regulatory Framework, Standards, and Compliance -Role of Technology in Enhancing Safety and Transparency	-Ethical and Environmental Factors in Food Choices -Importance of Sustainable Practices in Food Delivery
Xu et al. (2022)	-Food Safety Concerns, Contamination Risks, and Handling -Halal Integrity and Authentication Challenges	-Trust Erosion and Importance of Accountability -Maintaining Halal Integrity and Consumer Trust		-Risks, Coordination, and Integrity in the Supply Chain	-Regulatory Framework, Standards, and Compliance -Role of Technology in Enhancing Safety and Transparency	-Ethical and Environmental Factors in Food Choices -Importance of Sustainable Practices in Food Delivery
Masood & Rahim (2021)		-Trust Erosion and Importance of Accountability -Maintaining Halal Integrity and Consumer Trust	-Customer Satisfaction, Loyalty, and Expectations -Impact of Negative Experiences on Customer Retention		-Regulatory Framework, Standards, and Compliance -Role of Technology in Enhancing Safety and Transparency	-Ethical and Environmental Factors in Food Choices -Importance of Sustainable Practices in Food Delivery
Zhao et al. (2022)	-Food Safety Concerns, Contamination Risks, and Handling -Halal Integrity and Authentication Challenges	-Trust Erosion and Importance of Accountability -Maintaining Halal Integrity and Consumer Trust	-Customer Satisfaction, Loyalty, and Expectations -Impact of Negative Experiences on Customer Retention	-Risks, Coordination, and Integrity in the Supply Chain	-Regulatory Framework, Standards, and Compliance -Role of Technology in Enhancing Safety and Transparency	-Ethical and Environmental Factors in Food Choices -Importance of Sustainable Practices in Food Delivery
Nafik Hadi Ryandono et al. (2023)	-Food Safety Concerns -Contamination Risks and Handling			-Risks and Coordination in the Supply Chain	Regulatory Framework and Standards	

continued on following page

Table 7. Continued

Classification						
RQ1						
Reference	**Food Safety and Quality**	**Trust and Transparency**	**Customer Experience and Retention**	**Supply Chain Challenges**	**Regulatory Compliance and Technology**	**Ethical Considerations and Sustainability**
Hashim et al. (2022)	-Food Safety Concerns -Contamination Risks and Handling -Halal Integrity and Authentication Challenges	-Trust Erosion and Consumer Confidence -Maintaining Halal Integrity and Consumer Trust	-Customer Satisfaction and Expectations -Impact of Negative Experiences on Customer Retention	-Risks in the Supply Chain -Coordination and Integrity in the Supply Chain	-Regulatory Compliance and Standards -Role of Technology in Enhancing Safety and Transparency	-Ethical Factors in Food Choices -Importance of Sustainable Practices in Food Delivery
Priantina & Sapian (2021)	-Food Safety Concerns -Contamination Risks and Handling	-Trust Erosion and Importance of Accountability -Maintaining Halal Integrity and Consumer Trust		-Risks in the Supply Chain -Coordination Challenges -Ensuring Integrity in the Supply Chain	-Regulatory Framework and Standards -Role of Technology in Enhancing Safety and Transparency	-Ethical Factors in Food Choices -Environmental Impact of Food Choices -Importance of Sustainable Practices in Food Delivery
Kagan et al. (2020)	-Food Safety Concerns and Contamination Risks -Challenges in Halal Integrity and Authentication	-Erosion of Trust and the Importance of Accountability -Maintaining Halal Integrity to Build and Sustain Consumer Trust	-Ensuring Customer Satisfaction, Loyalty, and Meeting Expectations -Understanding the Impact of Negative Experiences on Customer Retention	-Identifying Risks, Coordination Challenges, and Maintaining Integrity in the Supply Chain	-Navigating Regulatory Frameworks, Standards, and Ensuring Compliance -Utilizing Technology to Enhance Safety, Transparency, and Accountability	-Recognizing Ethical and Environmental Factors in Food Choices -Emphasizing the Importance of Sustainable Practices in Food Delivery
Marotta (2023)	-Food Safety Concerns -Contamination Risks and Handling -Halal Integrity and Authentication Challenges	-Trust Erosion and Importance of Accountability -Maintaining Halal Integrity and Consumer Trust	-Customer Satisfaction, Loyalty, and Expectations -Impact of Negative Experiences on Customer Retention	-Risks -Coordination -Integrity in the Supply Chain	-Regulatory Framework, Standards, and Compliance -Role of Technology in Enhancing Safety and Transparency	-Ethical and Environmental Factors in Food Choices -Importance of Sustainable Practices in Food Delivery

Table 8. Quality assessment score (Key challenges faced by the food delivery sector in Pakistan)

Classification					Quality Assessment				
Reference	**Year**	**Publication Channel**	**Journal/ Conference ranking**	**Cited by**	**a**	**b**	**c**	**d**	**Scores**
Bux et al. (2022)	2022	Journal	Q1	32	1	1	1	2	5
Sarwar et al. (2021)	2021	Symposium	0	4	1	0	0	0	1
Xu et al. (2022)	2022	Journal	Q1	56	1	0.5	1	2	4.5
Masood & Rahim (2021)	2021	Conference	0	0	1	1	-1	0	1
Zhao et al. (2022)	2022	Journal	Q1	2	1	0.5	0	2	3.5
Nafik Hadi Ryandono et al. (2023)	2023	Journal	Q1	7	0	0	1	2	3
Hashim et al. (2022)	2022	Journal	0	3	1	0	0	0	1
Priantina & Sapian (2021)	2021	Journal	0	2	1	0	0	0	1
Kagan et al. (2020)	2020	Journal	0	2	1	0.5	0	0	1.5
Marotta (2023)	2023	Symposium	0	0	1	0.5	-1	0	0.5

e. **Regulatory Compliance and Technology.** Regulatory frameworks, standards, and compliance have potential to pose challenges. Therefore, a balancing act is needed to meet regulatory requirements while leveraging technology to enhance safety and transparency.
f. **Ethical Considerations and Sustainability.** Ethical and environmental factors in food choices are highlighted as important considerations, and sustainable practices in food delivery are increasingly important in addressing consumer concerns.

To conclude, the food delivery sector in Muslim countries experiences diverse challenges, covering safety, trust, customer satisfaction, supply chain complexities, regulatory compliance, technology adoption, and ethical and sustainability concerns.

Enhancing Food Delivery Sector through AI-Driven Blockchain Supply Chain: Feedback and Transparency

This subsection divided into two further sections: one on research question 2 regarding AI-driven blockchain for customer feedback and reputation management, and the second on its impact on food traceability and transparency. The classification scheme by Petersen et al. (2008) is applied using the PRISMA method. Tables 9 and 11 emphasis on the food delivery sector through AI-driven blockchain with a focus on fake reviews and halal supply chain, respectively. Tables 10 and 12 cover quality assessment for each focus area.

Table 9. Classification: Food delivery sector through ai-driven blockchain supply chain (With main focus on fake reviews)

Classification								
	RQ2				RQ3			
Reference	**AI-Driven Blockchain Supply Chain Implementation**	**Customer Feedback Enhancement**	**Reputation Management Enhancement**	**Operational Efficiency and Decision Making**	**Enhanced Traceability and Transparency**	**Addressing Food Industry Challenges**	**Authenticity and Integrity**	**Review Authenticity and Reliability**
Treiblmaier & Garaus (2023)	Integration of AI and blockchain technology. Real-time data collection and analysis. Automation of processes. Enhanced monitoring and tracking. Automated feedback analysis. Data-driven improvements. Continuous service enhancement.	Real-time feedback collection. Data-driven insights. Personalized customer interactions. Improved feedback accuracy.	Building trust and transparency. Immutable and transparent record-keeping. Trustworthy reputation tracking. Addressing negative feedback.		Real-time tracking of products. Immutable record-keeping. Supply chain visibility.	Food fraud prevention. Provenance verification. Labeling accuracy. Halal supply chain assurance. Mitigation of fake reviews.	Verification of product authenticity. Detection of counterfeit products. Halal certification validation.	Blockchain-based review verification. Trustworthy and verified customer feedback. Prevention of fake reviews.
Wünsche & Fernqvist (2022)	Integration of AI and blockchain technology. Real-time data collection and analysis. Automation of processes. Enhanced monitoring and tracking.				Real-time tracking of products. Immutable record-keeping. Supply chain visibility.		Verification of product authenticity. Detection of counterfeit products.	
Chen et al. (2021)	Integration of AI and blockchain technology. Real-time data collection and analysis. Automation of processes. Enhanced monitoring and tracking.	Real-time feedback collection. Data-driven insights. Personalized customer interactions. Improved feedback accuracy.	Building trust and transparency. Immutable and transparent record-keeping. Trustworthy reputation tracking. Addressing negative feedback.	Automated feedback analysis. Data-driven improvements. Continuous service enhancement.	Real-time tracking of products. Immutable record-keeping. Supply chain visibility.	Food fraud prevention. Provenance verification. Labeling accuracy. Halal supply chain assurance. Mitigation of fake reviews.	Verification of product authenticity. Detection of counterfeit products. Halal certification validation.	Blockchain-based review verification. Trustworthy and verified customer feedback. Prevention of fake reviews.
Hassoun et al. (2022)					Real-time tracking of products. Immutable record-keeping. Supply chain visibility. Provenance verification. Labeling accuracy. Halal supply chain assurance.			Blockchain-based review verification. Trustworthy and verified customer feedback. Prevention of fake reviews.

continued on following page

Table 9. Continued

Classification								
	RQ2				RQ3			
Reference	**AI-Driven Blockchain Supply Chain Implementation**	**Customer Feedback Enhancement**	**Reputation Management Enhancement**	**Operational Efficiency and Decision Making**	**Enhanced Traceability and Transparency**	**Addressing Food Industry Challenges**	**Authenticity and Integrity**	**Review Authenticity and Reliability**
Agarwal (2018)	Integration of AI and blockchain technology. Real-time data collection and analysis. Automation of processes. Enhanced monitoring and tracking.	Real-time feedback collection. Data-driven insights. Personalized customer interactions. Improved feedback accuracy.	Building trust and transparency. Immutable and transparent record-keeping. Trustworthy reputation tracking. Addressing negative feedback.	Automated feedback analysis. Data-driven improvements. Continuous service enhancement.		Food fraud prevention. Provenance verification. Labeling accuracy. Mitigation of fake reviews.		Blockchain-based review verification. Trustworthy and verified customer feedback. Prevention of fake reviews.
Rejeb & Karim (2019)		Real-time feedback collection. Data-driven insights. Personalized customer interactions. Improved feedback accuracy.	Building trust and transparency. Immutable and transparent record-keeping. Trustworthy reputation tracking. Addressing negative feedback.	Automated processes and data-driven improvements. Continuous service enhancement. Real-time data collection and analysis. Enhanced monitoring and tracking.	Real-time tracking of products. Immutable record-keeping. Supply chain visibility. Verification of product authenticity.	Food fraud prevention. Provenance verification. Labeling accuracy. Halal supply chain assurance. Mitigation of fake reviews.		Blockchain-based review verification. Trustworthy and verified customer feedback. Prevention of fake reviews.
Majer (2018)	Integration of AI and blockchain technology. Real-time data collection and analysis. Automation of processes. Enhanced monitoring and tracking.		Building trust and transparency. Immutable and transparent record-keeping. Addressing negative feedback.		Real-time tracking of products. Immutable record-keeping. Supply chain visibility.			Blockchain-based review verification. Trustworthy and verified customer feedback.
Qian et al. (2022)	Integration of AI and blockchain technology. Real-time data collection and analysis. Automation of processes.	Personalized customer interactions.	Building trust and transparency. Addressing negative feedback.					
Oates (2022)	Integration of AI and blockchain technology. Real-time data collection and analysis. Automation of processes. Enhanced monitoring, tracking, and visibility.	Real-time feedback collection and analysis. Data-driven insights. Personalized customer interactions.	Building trust, transparency, and accountability. Immutable and transparent record-keeping. Addressing negative feedback and challenges.	Automated feedback analysis and improvements. Data-driven enhancements. Continuous service improvement.	Real-time tracking and monitoring of products. Immutable and transparent record-keeping. Supply chain visibility and provenance verification.		Verification of product authenticity and quality. Detection of counterfeit products and fraud prevention. Certification validation and assurance.	

continued on following page

Table 9. Continued

	Classification							
	RQ2				RQ3			
Reference	AI-Driven Blockchain Supply Chain Implementation	Customer Feedback Enhancement	Reputation Management Enhancement	Operational Efficiency and Decision Making	Enhanced Traceability and Transparency	Addressing Food Industry Challenges	Authenticity and Integrity	Review Authenticity and Reliability
Latino et al. (2022)	Integration of AI and blockchain technology. Real-time data collection and analysis. Automation of processes. Enhanced monitoring and tracking.	Real-time feedback collection. Data-driven insights. Personalized customer interactions. Improved feedback accuracy.	Building trust and transparency. Immutable and transparent record-keeping. Trustworthy reputation tracking. Addressing negative feedback.	Automated feedback analysis. Data-driven improvements. Continuous service enhancement.	Real-time tracking of products. Immutable record-keeping. Supply chain visibility.	Food fraud prevention. Provenance verification. Labeling accuracy. Halal supply chain assurance. Mitigation of fake reviews.	Verification of product authenticity. Detection of counterfeit products. Halal certification validation.	Blockchain-based review verification. Trustworthy and verified customer feedback. Prevention of fake reviews.
McKinna & Wall (2020)	Integration of AI and blockchain technology. Real-time data collection and analysis. Automation of processes. Enhanced monitoring and tracking.	Real-time feedback collection. Data-driven insights. Personalized customer interactions. Improved feedback accuracy.	Building trust and transparency. Immutable and transparent record-keeping. Trustworthy reputation tracking. Addressing negative feedback.	Automated feedback analysis. Data-driven improvements. Continuous service enhancement.	Real-time tracking of products. Immutable record-keeping. Supply chain visibility.	Food fraud prevention. Provenance verification. Labeling accuracy. Halal supply chain assurance.	Verification of product authenticity. Detection of counterfeit products. Halal certification validation.	Blockchain-based review verification. Trustworthy and verified customer feedback. Prevention of fake reviews.
Javeed et al. (2022)	Integration of AI and blockchain technology. Real-time data collection and analysis. Automation of processes. Enhanced monitoring and tracking.				Real-time tracking of products. Immutable record-keeping. Supply chain visibility.	Food fraud prevention. Provenance verification. Labeling accuracy. Halal supply chain assurance.		Blockchain-based review verification. Trustworthy and verified customer feedback. Prevention of fake reviews.

Assessment of RQ2: How Does the Implementation of an AI-Driven Blockchain Supply Chain Impact Customer Feedback and Reputation Management in the Food Delivery Sector?

The aim of this research question is to explore how the implementation of an AI-driven blockchain supply chain can improve customer feedback and reputation management in the food delivery sector. Notably, the references in Tables 9 and 11 consistently highlight the following aspects:

a. **AI-Driven Blockchain Supply Chain Implementation.** Essential components consist of integrating AI and blockchain, real-time data analysis, process automation, and improved monitoring, offering operational efficiencies and decision-making enhancements.
b. **Customer Feedback Enhancement.** Significant elements involve real-time feedback collection, data-driven insights, personalized interactions, and improved accuracy, contributing to data-driven service quality improvements.

Table 10. Quality assessment score (Food delivery sector through AI-driven blockchain supply chain-with main focus on fake reviews)

Classification					Quality Assessment				
Reference	**Year**	**Publication Channel**	**Journal/ Conference ranking**	**Cited by**	**a**	**b**	**c**	**d**	**Scores**
Treiblmaier & Garaus (2023)	2023	Journal	Q1	41	1	1	1	2	5
Wünsche & Fernqvist (2022)	2022	Journal	Q2	15	1	0.5	1	1.5	4
Chen et al. (2021)	2021	Journal	Q2	113	1	1	1	1.5	4.5
Hassoun et al. (2022)	2022	Journal	Q1	76	1	0.5	1	2	4.5
Agarwal (2018)	2018	Dissertation	0	12	1	1	1	0	3
Rejeb & Karim (2019)	2019	Journal	0	49	1	1	1	0	3
Majer (2018)	2018	Other	0	0	1	1	-1	0	1
Qian et al. (2022)	2022	Journal	Q1	1	1	1	0	2	4
Oates (2022)	2022	Thesis	0	0	1	0.5	-1	0	0.5
Latino et al. (2022)	2022	Journal	Q2	7	1	0.5	1	1.5	4
McKinna & Wall (2020)	2020	Report	0	1	1	0.5	0	0	1.5
Javeed et al. (2022)	2022	Journal	Q2	1	1	1	0	1.5	3.5

c. **Reputation Management Enhancement.** Highlighted themes include building trust and transparency, transparent record-keeping, trustworthy reputation tracking, and addressing negative feedback, reinforcing reputation management through AI-driven blockchain solutions.

d. **Operational Efficiency and Decision Making.** Linked to AI-driven blockchain components, operational efficiency and decision-making improve with real-time data collection, process automation, and enhanced monitoring.

The consistent findings suggest that AI-driven blockchain supply chain integration has the potential to boost customer feedback, reputation management, and operational efficiency in the food delivery sector, emphasizing the importance of integrating AI and blockchain for these improvements.

Assessment of RQ3: How Does the Adoption of an AI-Driven Blockchain Supply Chain Improve Food Traceability And transparency, and How Does it Address Issues Related to Food Fraud, Fraudulent Labelling, Provenance, Halal Supply Chain, and Fake Reviews in the Food Delivery Sector?

This research question explores how adopting an AI-driven blockchain supply chain in the food delivery sector improves traceability, transparency, and addresses challenges like food fraud, labeling accuracy,

Table 11. Classification: Food delivery sector through AI-driven blockchain supply chain (With main focus on Halal supply chain)

Classification								
	RQ2				RQ3			
Reference	**AI-Driven Blockchain Supply Chain Implementation**	**Customer Feedback Enhancement**	**Reputation Management Enhancement**	**Operational Efficiency and Decision Making**	**Enhanced Traceability and Transparency**	**Addressing Food Industry Challenges**	**Authenticity and Integrity**	**Review Authenticity and Reliability**
Thanujan et al. (2021)	Integration of AI and blockchain technology, Real-time data collection and analysis, Automation of processes, Enhanced monitoring and tracking.	Real-time feedback collection, Data-driven insights, Personalized customer interactions, Improved feedback accuracy.	Building trust and transparency, Immutable and transparent record-keeping, Trustworthy reputation tracking, Addressing negative feedback		Real-time tracking of products, Immutable record-keeping, Supply chain visibility.	Food fraud prevention, Provenance verification, Labeling accuracy.	Verification of product authenticity, Detection of counterfeit products, Halal certification validation.	Blockchain-based review verification, Trustworthy and verified customer feedback, Prevention of fake reviews.
Domínguez & Roseiro (2020)		Real-time feedback collection Personalized customer interactions Improved feedback accuracy	Building trust and transparency Trustworthy reputation tracking Addressing negative feedback			Food fraud prevention Provenance verification Labeling accuracy Halal supply chain assurance Mitigation of fake reviews		Blockchain-based review verification Trustworthy and verified customer feedback Prevention of fake reviews
Raja Santhi & Muthuswamy (2022)	Integration of AI and blockchain technology. Real-time data collection and analysis. Automation of processes. Enhanced monitoring and tracking.	Real-time feedback collection. Data-driven insights. Personalized customer interactions. Improved feedback accuracy.	Building trust and transparency. Immutable and transparent record-keeping. Trustworthy reputation tracking. Addressing negative feedback.		Real-time tracking of products. Immutable record-keeping. Supply chain visibility. Verification of product authenticity. Detection of counterfeit products.	Food fraud prevention. Provenance verification. Labeling accuracy. Mitigation of fake reviews.	Verification of product authenticity. Detection of counterfeit products.	Blockchain-based review verification. Trustworthy and verified customer feedback.
Tsoukas et al. (2022)	Integration of AI and blockchain technology. Real-time data collection and analysis. Automation of processes. Enhanced monitoring and tracking.				Real-time tracking of products. Immutable record-keeping. Supply chain visibility.	Food fraud prevention. Provenance verification. Labeling accuracy. Mitigation of fake reviews.		Blockchain-based review verification. Trustworthy and verified customer feedback. Prevention of fake reviews.
Tanwar et al. (2022)	Integration of AI and blockchain technology. Implementation Real-time data collection and analysis. Automation of processes. Enhanced monitoring and tracking.	Real-time feedback collection. Data-driven insights. Personalized customer interactions. Improved feedback accuracy.	Building trust and transparency. Immutable and transparent record-keeping. Trustworthy reputation tracking. Addressing negative feedback.		Real-time tracking of products. Immutable record-keeping. Supply chain visibility.	Food fraud prevention. Provenance verification. Labeling accuracy. Mitigation of fake reviews.	Verification of product authenticity. Detection of counterfeit products. Halal certification validation.	Blockchain-based review verification. Trustworthy and verified customer feedback. Prevention of fake reviews.

continued on following page

Table 11. Continued

Classification								
	RQ2				RQ3			
Reference	AI-Driven Blockchain Supply Chain Implementation	Customer Feedback Enhancement	Reputation Management Enhancement	Operational Efficiency and Decision Making	Enhanced Traceability and Transparency	Addressing Food Industry Challenges	Authenticity and Integrity	Review Authenticity and Reliability
Tharatipyakul & Pongnumkul (2021)	Integration of AI and blockchain technology. Real-time data collection and analysis. Automation of processes. Enhanced monitoring and tracking.	Real-time feedback collection. Data-driven insights. Personalized customer interactions. Improved feedback accuracy.	Building trust and transparency. Immutable and transparent record-keeping. Trustworthy reputation tracking. Addressing negative feedback.		Real-time tracking of products. Immutable record-keeping. Supply chain visibility.	Food fraud prevention. Provenance verification. Labeling accuracy. Halal supply chain assurance. Mitigation of fake reviews.	Verification of product authenticity. Detection of counterfeit products. Halal certification validation.	Blockchain-based review verification. Trustworthy and verified customer feedback. Prevention of fake reviews.
Agarwal (2018)	Integration of AI and blockchain technology. Real-time data collection and analysis. Automation of processes. Enhanced monitoring and tracking.	Real-time feedback collection. Data-driven insights. Personalized customer interactions. Improved feedback accuracy.	Building trust and transparency. Immutable and transparent record-keeping. Trustworthy reputation tracking. Addressing negative feedback.	Automated feedback analysis. Data-driven improvements. Continuous service enhancement.		Food fraud prevention. Provenance verification. Labeling accuracy. Mitigation of fake reviews.		Blockchain-based review verification. Trustworthy and verified customer feedback. Prevention of fake reviews.
Gómez González (2021)	Integration of AI and blockchain technology. Real-time data collection and analysis. Automation of processes. Enhanced monitoring and tracking.	Real-time feedback collection. Data-driven insights. Personalized customer interactions. Improved feedback accuracy.	Building trust and transparency. Immutable and transparent record-keeping. Trustworthy reputation tracking. Addressing negative feedback.			Food fraud prevention. Provenance verification. Labeling accuracy. Halal supply chain assurance.		Blockchain-based review verification. Trustworthy and verified customer feedback. Prevention of fake reviews.
Hellani et al. (2021)	Integration of AI and blockchain technology. Real-time data collection and analysis. Automation of processes. Enhanced monitoring and tracking.	Real-time feedback collection. Data-driven insights. Improved feedback accuracy.	Building trust and transparency. Immutable and transparent record-keeping. Trustworthy reputation tracking. Addressing negative feedback.		Real-time tracking of products. Immutable record-keeping. Supply chain visibility.	Food fraud prevention. Provenance verification. Labeling accuracy. Halal supply chain assurance. Mitigation of fake reviews.	Verification of product authenticity. Detection of counterfeit products. Halal certification validation.	Blockchain-based review verification. Trustworthy and verified customer feedback. Prevention of fake reviews.
Engbers & Kloppenburg (2020)	Integration of AI and blockchain technology. Real-time data collection and analysis. Automation of processes. Enhanced monitoring and tracking.	Real-time feedback collection. Data-driven insights. Personalized customer interactions. Improved feedback accuracy.	Building trust and transparency. Immutable and transparent record-keeping. Trustworthy reputation tracking.		Real-time tracking of products. Immutable record-keeping. Supply chain visibility.	Food fraud prevention. Provenance verification. Labeling accuracy.	Verification of product authenticity. Detection of counterfeit products.	Blockchain-based review verification. Trustworthy and verified customer feedback.

continued on following page

Table 11. Continued

	Classification							
	RQ2				RQ3			
Reference	**AI-Driven Blockchain Supply Chain Implementation**	**Customer Feedback Enhancement**	**Reputation Management Enhancement**	**Operational Efficiency and Decision Making**	**Enhanced Traceability and Transparency**	**Addressing Food Industry Challenges**	**Authenticity and Integrity**	**Review Authenticity and Reliability**
Facchini Amondarain (2019)	Integration of AI and blockchain technology. Real-time data collection and analysis. Automation of processes. Enhanced monitoring and tracking.	Real-time feedback collection. Data-driven insights. Improved feedback accuracy.	Building trust and transparency. Immutable and transparent record-keeping. Addressing negative feedback.	Automated feedback analysis. Data-driven improvements. Continuous service enhancement.	Real-time tracking of products. Immutable record-keeping. Supply chain visibility.	Food fraud prevention. Provenance verification. Labeling accuracy. Mitigation of fake reviews.	Verification of product authenticity. Detection of counterfeit products. Halal certification validation.	Blockchain-based review verification. Trustworthy and verified customer feedback. Prevention of fake reviews.
Crittenden (2020)	Integration of AI and blockchain technology. Real-time data collection and analysis. Automation of processes. Enhanced monitoring and tracking.	Real-time feedback collection. Data-driven insights. Personalized customer interactions. Improved feedback accuracy.	Building trust and transparency. Immutable and transparent record-keeping. Trustworthy reputation tracking. Addressing negative feedback.	Automated feedback analysis. Data-driven improvements. Continuous service enhancement.	Real-time tracking of products. Immutable record-keeping. Supply chain visibility.	Food fraud prevention. Provenance verification. Labeling accuracy.	Verification of product authenticity. Detection of counterfeit products.	Blockchain-based review verification. Trustworthy and verified customer feedback.
Paggi (2022)	Integration of AI and blockchain technology. Real-time data collection and analysis. Automation of processes. Enhanced monitoring and tracking.	Real-time feedback collection. Data-driven insights. Personalized customer interactions. Improved feedback accuracy.	Building trust and transparency. Immutable and transparent record-keeping. Trustworthy reputation tracking. Addressing negative feedback.		Real-time tracking of products. Immutable record-keeping. Supply chain visibility.	Food fraud prevention. Provenance verification. Labeling accuracy. Halal supply chain assurance. Mitigation of fake reviews.	Verification of product authenticity. Detection of counterfeit products. Halal certification validation.	Blockchain-based review verification. Trustworthy and verified customer feedback. Prevention of fake reviews.
Beserra (2021)	Integration of AI and blockchain technology. Real-time data collection and analysis. Automation of processes.	Real-time feedback collection. Data-driven insights.	Building trust and transparency. Immutable and transparent record-keeping. Addressing negative feedback.	Automated feedback analysis. Data-driven improvements.	Real-time tracking of products. Immutable record-keeping.	Food fraud prevention. Provenance verification. Labeling accuracy.	Verification of product authenticity. Detection of counterfeit products. Halal certification validation.	Blockchain-based review verification. Trustworthy and verified customer feedback.
Cording & Lückander (2023)	Integration of AI and blockchain technology. Real-time data collection and analysis. Automation of processes.			Automated feedback analysis. Data-driven improvements.	Real-time tracking of products. Immutable record-keeping. Supply chain visibility.			
Sadri, S. (2021)	Integration of AI and blockchain technology. Real-time data collection and analysis. Automation of processes. Enhanced monitoring and tracking.	Real-time feedback collection. Data-driven insights. Personalized customer interactions. Improved feedback accuracy.	Building trust and transparency. Addressing negative feedback.	Automated feedback analysis. Data-driven improvements. Continuous service enhancement.	Real-time tracking of products. Immutable record-keeping.	Food fraud prevention. Provenance verification. Labeling accuracy. Halal supply chain assurance.		Blockchain-based review verification. Trustworthy and verified customer feedback. Prevention of fake reviews.

Table 12. Quality assessment score (Food delivery sector through AI-driven blockchain supply chain-with main focus on Halal supply chain)

Classification					Quality Assessment				
Reference	**Year**	**Publication Channel**	**Journal/ Conference ranking**	**Cited by**	**a**	**b**	**C**	**d**	**Scores**
Thanujan et al. (2021)	2021	Conference	0	3	1	0.5	0	0	1.5
Domínguez & Roseiro (2020)	2020	Journal	0	17	1	0.5	1	0	2.5
Raja Santhi & Muthuswamy (2022)	2022	Journal	Q1	66	1	0.5	1	2	4.5
Tsoukas et al. (2022)	2022	Journal	Q2	23	1	1	1	1.5	4.5
Tanwar et al. (2022)	2022	Journal	Q2	6	1	0.5	1	1.5	4
Tharatipyakul & Pongnumkul (2021)	2021	Journal	Q1	33	1	1	1	2	5
Agarwal (2018)	2018	Dissertation	0	12	1	1	1	0	3
Gómez González (2021)	2021	Bachelor's thesis	0	0	1	1	-1	0	1
Hellani et al. (2021)	2021	Journal	Q1	31	1	1	1	2	5
Engbers & Kloppenburg (2020)	2020	Master's thesis	0	0	1	0.5	-1	0	0.5
Facchini Amondarain (2019)	2019	Report	0	0	1	0.5	-1	0	0.5
Crittenden (2020)	2020	Report	0	2	1	1	0	0	2
Paggi (2022)	2022	Information not available	0	2	1	0.5	0	0	1.5
Beserra (2021)	2021	Dissertation	0	0	1	0.5	-1	0	0.5
Cording & Lückander (2023)	2023	Degree Project	0	0	1	1	-1	0	1
Sadri. (2021)	2021	Master's thesis	0	0	1	1	-1	0	1

and halal supply chain authenticity. Findings from Tables 9 and 11 reveal the impacts of this adoption on key themes:

a. **Enhanced Traceability and Transparency.** Common themes include real-time tracking, immutable record-keeping, and supply chain visibility, enhancing transparency and allowing stakeholders to trace food product journeys.
b. **Addressing Food Industry Challenges.** Multiple references have mentioned the usage of AI-driven blockchain to address challenges like food fraud prevention, provenance verification, labeling accuracy, and assurance of halal supply chain. This reflects that the adoption of such systems can assist in tackling various issues affecting the food industry.

Table 13. Overall quality assessment score

References	Score	Total	Percentage	
Bux et al. (2022); Treiblmaier & Garaus (2023); Tharatipyakul & Pongnumkul (2021); Hellani et al. (2021)	5	4	10.81%	
Xu et al. (2022); Chen et al. (2021); Hassoun et al. (2022); Raja Santhi & Muthuswamy (2022); Tsoukas et al. (2022)	4.5	5	13.51%	
Wünsche & Fernqvist (2022); Qian et al. (2022); Latino et al. (2022); Tanwar et al. (2022)	4	4	10.81%	**51.35%**
Zhao et al. (2022); Javeed et al. (2022)	3.5	2	5.41%	
Nafik Hadi Ryandono et al. (2023); Agarwal (2018); Rejeb & Karim (2019)	3	3	8.11%	
Domínguez & Roseiro (2020)	2.5	1	2.70%	
Crittenden (2020)	2	1	2.70%	**2.70%**
Kagan et al. (2020); McKinna & Wall (2020); Thanujan et al. (2021); Paggi (2022)	1.5	4	10.81%	
Sarwar et al. (2021); Masood & Rahim (2021); Hashim et al. (2022); Priantina & Sapian (2021); Majer (2018); Gómez González (2021); Cording & Lückander (2023); Sadri (2021)	1	8	21.62%	**45.95%**
Marotta (2023); Oates (2022); Engbers & Kloppenburg (2020); Facchini Amondarain (2019); Beserra (2021)	0.5	5	13.51%	

c. **Authenticity and Integrity.** Across the references, verification of product authenticity, detection of counterfeit products, and the blockchain's immutability and cryptographic features ensure product information integrity.

d. **Review Authenticity and Reliability.** Blockchain-based review verification, trustworthy feedback, and preventing fake reviews contribute to sustaining customer review credibility in the food delivery sector.

To conclude, the data from table 9 and table 11 recommends that the adoption of an AI-driven blockchain supply chain can certainly have a positive impact on various aspects of the food delivery sector.

Overall Quality Assessment Score

According to Farooq et al. (2020), the quality assessment scores range from -1 to 5. The average score calculated is 2. The table 13 indicates that 2.7% of papers have an average score, the majority (51.35%) have an above-average score, and 45.95% have a below-average score.

DISCUSSION

The discussion section of this research paper explores findings related to the research questions, addressing challenges faced by the food delivery sector in Muslim countries like Pakistan, and benefits of implementing AI-driven blockchain.

The analysis of existing literature revealed a set of key challenges that the food delivery sector in Muslim countries like Pakistan encounters. These challenges cover a wide range of issues including food safety, trust erosion, customer satisfaction, supply chain complexities, regulatory compliance, and ethical and sustainability concerns. Moreover, the preservation of halal integrity emerged as a noteworthy challenge, especially in Muslim-majority countries like Pakistan.

The findings suggest that the integration of an AI-driven blockchain supply chain has the potential to address many of the identified challenges. By leveraging real-time data collection, process automation, and enhanced monitoring, this integration offers opportunities to improve customer feedback and reputation management.

In addition, the transparency and accountability inherent in blockchain technology powered by AI can bolster trust and address issues related to food fraud, provenance, labeling accuracy, fake reviews, and halal supply chains. Lastly, the potential for enhanced operational efficiency and data-driven decision-making adds another layer of benefits to the implementation.

The discussion concludes that AI-driven blockchain integration in the food delivery sector holds significant potential to not only overcome the challenges, but also to reshape operations, improve traceability, transparency, and accountability.

CONCLUSION

This research investigates into challenges faced by the food delivery sector in Muslim countries, particularly Pakistan, covering issues like food safety, trust erosion, customer retention, supply chain complexities, regulatory compliance, and ethical concerns, particularly preserving halal integrity. The conclusion highlights the potential of AI-driven blockchain to revolutionize Pakistan's food delivery sector by improving traceability, transparency, and accountability, while emphasizing the importance of balancing technological benefits with societal considerations in a dynamic landscape.

Despite the contributions of this research paper, it has notable limitations. It lacks a comprehensive investigation of technical challenges, scalability issues, ethical considerations and industry-specific hurdles related to blockchain and AI in the context of the food delivery sector in Pakistan. The selected studies fall short in exploring the barriers and potential advantages thoroughly. Although the importance of accurate AI analysis is recognized, the retrieved articles do not adequately research into the technical and cost-effectiveness challenges of integrating blockchain and AI solutions, nor do they appropriately address the potential impacts on traditional supply chain systems. Methodological limitations, such as overseeing complicated customer feedback patterns and nuanced ethical considerations in diverse cultural contexts, bound the depth of analysis. Biases stemming from reliance on obsolete news articles and limited sources also reduce the research's overall comprehensiveness. Furthermore, the research fails to capture recent industry dynamics and shifts, limiting the applicability of its insights to the progressing landscape of food delivery.

To deal with limitations and advance research in this field, the following recommendations are proposed: Starting with broaden the research scope beyond Halal food to cover a wider array of challenges in the food delivery sector within Muslim countries like Pakistan, including socio-economic factors and changing industry dynamics. Secondly, an in-depth analysis of the barriers and costs tied to implementing blockchain technology in food delivery is needed in order to further explore potential benefits and transparency effects. Next, the integration of AI solutions is needed to explore deeper, considering technical hurdles and implications for traditional supply chains, for a more holistic understanding of role of AI. Moreover, to counter biases, diverse methodologies need to be adopted, uniting diverse data sources and analyzing complex customer feedback patterns. Above all, in order to ensure comprehensive analysis, depend on current, diverse literature and even consult experts both within and outside the industry. Lastly, stay familiar to industry shifts to sustain relevance and accuracy. By following these recommendations, future research can successfully address limitations and provide insights into the opportunities and challenges, including ethical considerations, in the food delivery sector throughout all Muslim countries.

REFERENCES

Agarwal, S. (2018). *Blockchain technology in supply chain and logistics* [Doctoral dissertation, Massachusetts Institute of Technology].

Avci, C., Tekinerdogan, B., & Athanasiadis, I. N. (2020). Software architectures for big data: A systematic literature review. *Big Data Analytics*, *5*(1), 1–53. doi:10.118641044-020-00045-1

Beserra, P. B. (2021). *Blockchain Technology to Improve Supply Chain Management-A Systematic Literature Review* [Doctoral dissertation, Universidade do Algarve (Portugal)].

Bux, C., Varese, E., Amicarelli, V., & Lombardi, M. (2022). Halal Food Sustainability between Certification and Blockchain: A Review. *Sustainability (Basel)*, *14*(4), 2152. doi:10.3390u14042152

Calvera Isabal, M., Santos, P., Hoppe, H., & Schulten, C. (2023). Cómo automatizar la extracción y análisis de información sobre ciencia ciudadana con propósitos educativos. *Comunicar.*, *31*(74), 13.

Chen, S., Liu, X., Yan, J., Hu, G., & Shi, Y. (2021). Processes, benefits, and challenges for adoption of blockchain technologies in food supply chains: A thematic analysis. *Information Systems and e-Business Management*, *19*(3), 909–935. doi:10.100710257-020-00467-3

CISPL. (2020). *Pros & cons of online food delivery services*. SISPL. https://cispl.com/pros-cons-online-food-delivery-services/

Cording, R., & Lückander, J. (2023). *Blockchain for supply chain transparency and traceability-A contingency framework to implementation challenges*.

Crittenden, C. (2020). Blockchain in California: A Roadmap. *UC Berkeley: Center for Information Technology Research in the Interest of Society (CITRIS)*. https://escholarship.org/uc/item/2j9596dp

Dağ, H., & Erbasi-Gonc, E. (2013). SMIIC and halal food standards. *Journal of Chemical Metrology*, *7*(1).

Domínguez, J., & Roseiro, P. (2020). *Blockchain: a brief review of agri-food supply chain solutions and opportunities*.

Dybå, T., & Dingsøyr, T. (2008). Empirical studies of agile software development: A systematic review. *Information and Software Technology*, *50*(9-10), 833–859. doi:10.1016/j.infsof.2008.01.006

Ellahi, R. M., Wood, L. C., & Bekhit, A. E. D. A. (2023). Blockchain-Based Frameworks for Food Traceability: A Systematic Review. *Foods*, *12*(16), 3026. doi:10.3390/foods12163026 PMID:37628025

Engbers, N., & Kloppenburg, S. (2020). Bananas Blockchained.

Facchini Amondarain, F. (2019). *Study of the functional and economic feasibility of the application of Blockchain in a food sector company's supply chain* [Bachelor's thesis, Universitat Politècnica de Catalunya].

Farooq, M. S., Riaz, S., Abid, A., Umer, T., & Zikria, Y. B. (2020). Role of IoT technology in agriculture: A systematic literature review. *Electronics (Basel)*, *9*(2), 319. doi:10.3390/electronics9020319

Fernandez, A., Insfran, E., & Abrahão, S. (2011). Usability evaluation methods for the web: A systematic mapping study. *Information and Software Technology*, *53*(8), 789–817. doi:10.1016/j.infsof.2011.02.007

Flores-Vivar, J. M., & García-Peñalvo, F. J. (2023). Reflexiones sobre la ética, potencialidades y retos de la Inteligencia Artificial en el marco de la Educación de Calidad (ODS4). *Comunicar*, *31*(74). Advance online publication. doi:10.3916/C74-2023-03

Galati, A., Crescimanno, M., Vrontis, D., & Siggia, D. (2020). Contribution to the sustainability challenges of the food-delivery sector: Finding from the deliveroo italy case study. *Sustainability (Basel)*, *12*(17), 7045. doi:10.3390u12177045

Ghouri, A., Akhtar, P., Venkatesh, V. G., Ashraf, A., Arsenyan, G., Tarba, S. Y., & Khan, Z. (2023). Enhancing supply chain innovation and operational agility through knowledge acquisition from the social media: A microfoundational approach. *IEEE Transactions on Engineering Management*, 1–15. doi:10.1109/TEM.2023.3316119

GiannoniC.MeddaF.BartolucciS. (2023). Blockchain Technologies and Art: Opportunities and Open Challenges. *Available at* SSRN 4439318. doi:10.2139/ssrn.4439318

Gómez González, C. (2021). *Blockchain applications in food marketing*.

Haq, M. A., Khan, N. R., Parkash, R., & Jabeen, A. (2016). Impact of JIT, waste minimization, and flow management on operational performance of manufacturing companies. *Quality - Access to Success*, *17*(153), 48.

Hashim, Y. Z. H. Y., Ahmad, A. N., Samsudin, N., Abd Lateef, M. H., & Majlan, N. S. (2022). The Evolution Of Halal Research: A Bibliometric For 1996–2020. *Journal of Fatwa Management and Research*, *27*(3), 1–38. doi:10.33102/jfatwa.vol27no3.443

Hassoun, A., Aït-Kaddour, A., Abu-Mahfouz, A. M., Rathod, N. B., Bader, F., Barba, F. J., & Regenstein, J. (2022). The fourth industrial revolution in the food industry—Part I: Industry 4.0 technologies. *Critical Reviews in Food Science and Nutrition*, 1–17. PMID:35114860

Hellani, H., Sliman, L., Samhat, A. E., & Exposito, E. (2021). On blockchain integration with supply chain: Overview on data transparency. *Logistics*, *5*(3), 46. doi:10.3390/logistics5030046

Hendayani, R., & Fernando, Y. (2022). Adoption of blockchain technology to improve Halal supply chain performance and competitiveness. *Journal of Islamic Marketing*.

Javeed, A., Aljuaid, M., Khan, Z., Mahmood, Z., & Shahid, D. (2022). Role of extrinsic Cues in the formation of quality perceptions. *Frontiers in Psychology*, *13*, 913836. doi:10.3389/fpsyg.2022.913836 PMID:35959058

Jiménez-Carvelo, A. M., Li, P., Erasmus, S. W., Wang, H., & van Ruth, S. M. (2022). Spatial-Temporal Event Analysis as a Prospective Approach for Signalling Emerging Food Fraud-Related Anomalies in Supply Chains. *Foods*, *12*(1), 61. doi:10.3390/foods12010061 PMID:36613277

Kagan, A., Draeger, K., & Olive, R. (2020). *Halal and Kosher Minnesota Meat Market Assessment: Analysis*. Implications and Recommendations.

Karode, T., & Werapun, W. (2022). Robustness against fraudulent activities of a blockchain-based online review system. *Peer-to-Peer Networking and Applications*, *15*(1), 92–106. doi:10.100712083-021-01225-z

Khan, N. R., Haq, M. A., Ghouri, A. M., Raziq, A., & Moiz, S. M. (2017). Adaptation of RFID technology in business supply chain success: Empirical findings from a developing country logistic industry. *Quality - Access to Success*, *18*(160), 93.

Kulkarni, A. (2021). Review of Online Food Delivery Industry of India. *International Journal of Engineering and Advanced Technology*, *11*(2), 75–77. doi:10.35940/ijeat.B3317.1211221

Latino, M. E., Corallo, A., Menegoli, M., & Nuzzo, B. (2022). An integrative conceptual framework of food certifications: Systematic review, research agenda, and macromarketing implications. *Journal of Macromarketing*, *42*(1), 71–99. doi:10.1177/02761467211049071

Majer, A. (2018). *How Blockchain Could Help Regulators*.

Malik, A., Gautam, S., Abidin, S., & Bhushan, B. (2019, July). Blockchain technology-future of IoT: including structure, limitations and various possible attacks. In *2019 2nd international conference on intelligent computing, instrumentation and control technologies (ICICICT)* (Vol. 1, pp. 1100-1104). IEEE. 10.1109/ICICICT46008.2019.8993144

Marotta, A. (2023). Halal as more than a market benchmark: from certification issues to 'Eco-Islam'up to Vegan Muslims. *Amministrativ@ mente-Rivista di ateneo dell'Università degli Studi di Roma "Foro Italico,"* (4).

Masood, A., & Rahim, A. A. (2021). Addressing Halal Industry Sustainability Through Halal Certification Bodies and IR. 4.0 Techonology.

McKinna, D., & Wall, C. (2020). *Commercial application of supply chain integrity and shelf life systems*. Technical Report. Meat and Livestock Australia Limited.

Meemken, E. M., Bellemare, M. F., Reardon, T., & Vargas, C. M. (2022). Research and policy for the food-delivery revolution. *Science*, *377*(6608), 810–813. doi:10.1126cience.abo2182 PMID:35981021

Mohawesh, R., Xu, S., Tran, S. N., Ollington, R., Springer, M., Jararweh, Y., & Maqsood, S. (2021). Fake reviews detection: A survey. *IEEE Access : Practical Innovations, Open Solutions*, *9*, 65771–65802. doi:10.1109/ACCESS.2021.3075573

Montecchi, M., Plangger, K., & Etter, M. (2019). It's real, trust me! Establishing supply chain provenance using blockchain. *Business Horizons*, *62*(3), 283–293. doi:10.1016/j.bushor.2019.01.008

Nafik Hadi Ryandono, M., Mawardi, I., Nugraha Rani, L., Widiastuti, T., Tri Ratnasari, R., & Kusuma Wardhana, A. (2023). Trends of research topics related to Halal meat as a commodity between Scopus and Web of Science: A systematic review. *F1000 Research*, *11*, 1562. doi:10.12688/f1000research.123005.2

Oates, N. L. (2022). *Blockchain from farm to fork-a new business model for tracing local South African market food supply chains using blockchain technology* [Master's thesis, Faculty of Commerce].

Paggi, E. (2022). Blockchain in finance: focus on securitization.

Petersen, K., Feldt, R., Mujtaba, S., & Mattsson, M. (2008, June). Systematic mapping studies in software engineering. In *12th International Conference on Evaluation and Assessment in Software Engineering (EASE) 12* (pp. 1-10). IEEE.

Priantina, A., & Sapian, S. M. (2021). Halal Food and Compliance: A Bibliometric Analysis.

Puri, V., Mondal, S., Das, S., & Vrana, V. G. (2023, January). Blockchain propels tourism industry—An attempt to explore topics and information in smart tourism management through text mining and machine learning. [). MDPI.]. *Informatics (MDPI), 10*(1), 9. doi:10.3390/informatics10010009

Qian, C., Liu, Y., Barnett-Neefs, C., Salgia, S., Serbetci, O., Adalja, A., & Wiedmann, M. (2022). A perspective on data sharing in digital food safety systems. *Critical Reviews in Food Science and Nutrition*, 1–17. PMID:35880485

Raja Santhi, A., & Muthuswamy, P. (2022). Influence of blockchain technology in manufacturing supply chain and logistics. *Logistics*, *6*(1), 15. doi:10.3390/logistics6010015

Rajasekaran, A. S., Azees, M., & Al-Turjman, F. (2022). A comprehensive survey on blockchain technology. *Sustainable Energy Technologies and Assessments*, *52*, 102039. doi:10.1016/j.seta.2022.102039

Raza, A., Asif, M., & Akram, M. (2023). Give your hunger a new option: Understanding consumers' continuous intention to use online food delivery apps using trust transfer theory. *International Journal of Consumer Studies*, *47*(2), 474–495. doi:10.1111/ijcs.12845

Rejeb, A., & Karim, R. (2019). Blockchain technology in tourism: Applications and possibilities. *World Scientific News*, *137*, 119–144.

Sabreen, M. (2021). Legislation on Halal Food in Pakistan: An Analytical Study. *Journal of Islamic and Religious Studies*, *6*(1), 27–40. doi:10.36476/JIRS.6:1.06.2021.14

Sadri, S. (2021). *Enhancing healthcare using blockchain technology: blood donation supply chain* [Doctoral dissertation, École de technologie supérieure].

Sarwar, A., Zafar, A., & Qadir, A. (2021). Analysis and prioritization of risk factors in the management of Halal supply chain management. *Discover Sustainability*, *2*(1), 1–10. doi:10.100743621-021-00039-6

Shaoliu, D., & Tongbai, L. (2023). Ideological and Physical Education Integration in Higher Education: Strategies for Mental Health Education. *Journal of Sport Psychology*, *32*(4), 203–212.

Shi, X., Yao, S., & Luo, S. (2023). Innovative platform operations with the use of technologies in the blockchain era. *International Journal of Production Research*, *61*(11), 3651–3669. doi:10.1080/00207543.2021.1953182

Sjahroeddin, F. (2018, October). The role of ES-Qual and food quality on customer satisfaction in online food delivery service. In *Prosiding Industrial Research Workshop and National Seminar* (Vol. 9, pp. 551-558).

Statista. (2023, April 27). *Food service industry: global market size 2021-2028.* https://www.statista.com/statistics/1095667/global-food-service-market-size/#statisticContainer

Tanwar, S., Parmar, A., Kumari, A., Jadav, N. K., Hong, W. C., & Sharma, R. (2022). Blockchain adoption to secure the food industry: Opportunities and challenges. *Sustainability (Basel), 14*(12), 7036. doi:10.3390u14127036

Thanujan, T., Rajapakse, C., & Wickramaarachchi, D. (2021, September). A community-based hybrid blockchain architecture for the organic food supply chain. In *2021 International Research Conference on Smart Computing and Systems Engineering (SCSE)* (Vol. 4, pp. 77-83). IEEE. 10.1109/SCSE53661.2021.9568325

Tharatipyakul, A., & Pongnumkul, S. (2021). User interface of blockchain-based agri-food traceability applications: A review. *IEEE Access : Practical Innovations, Open Solutions, 9*, 82909–82929. doi:10.1109/ACCESS.2021.3085982

Treiblmaier, H., & Garaus, M. (2023). Using blockchain to signal quality in the food supply chain: The impact on consumer purchase intentions and the moderating effect of brand familiarity. *International Journal of Information Management, 68*, 102514. doi:10.1016/j.ijinfomgt.2022.102514

Tsoukas, V., Gkogkidis, A., Kampa, A., Spathoulas, G., & Kakarountas, A. (2022). Enhancing food supply chain security through the use of blockchain and TinyML. *Information (Basel), 13*(5), 213. doi:10.3390/info13050213

van Ruth, S. M., Huisman, W., & Luning, P. A. (2017). Food fraud vulnerability and its key factors. *Trends in Food Science & Technology, 67*, 70–75. doi:10.1016/j.tifs.2017.06.017

Vimaladevi, K., & Dhanabhakaym, M. (2012). A study on the effects of online consumer reviews on purchasing decision. *Prestige In. J. Manag., 7*(1), 51–99. doi:10.37922/PIJMIT.2012.V01i01.005

Wünsche, J. F., & Fernqvist, F. (2022). The potential of blockchain technology in the transition towards sustainable food systems. *Sustainability (Basel), 14*(13), 7739. doi:10.3390u14137739

Xu, Y., Li, X., Zeng, X., Cao, J., & Jiang, W. (2022). Application of blockchain technology in food safety control: Current trends and future prospects. *Critical Reviews in Food Science and Nutrition, 62*(10), 2800–2819. doi:10.1080/10408398.2020.1858752 PMID:33307729

Yuen, K. F., Wang, X., Ma, F., & Wong, Y. D. (2019). The determinants of customers' intention to use smart lockers for last-mile deliveries. *Journal of Retailing and Consumer Services, 49*, 316–326. doi:10.1016/j.jretconser.2019.03.022

Yusoff, F. A. M., Yusof, R. N. R., & Hussin, S. R. (2015). Halal Food Supply Chain Knowledge and Purchase Intention. *International Journal of Economics & Management, 9.*

Zhao, G., Olan, F., Liu, S., Hormazabal, J. H., Lopez, C., Zubairu, N., Zhang, J., & Chen, X. (2022). Links between risk source identification and resilience capability building in agri-food supply chains: A comprehensive analysis. *IEEE Transactions on Engineering Management*, 1–18. doi:10.1109/TEM.2022.3221361

Chapter 11
Blockchain in Supply Chain Management and Sustainable Development Goals (SDGs)

Muhammad Rafiq
https://orcid.org/0000-0001-5037-6485
UCSI Graduate Business School, UCSI University, Kuala Lumpur, Malaysia

Omkar Dastane
https://orcid.org/0000-0002-9921-859X
UCSI Graduate Business School, UCSI University, Kuala Lumpur, Malaysia

Duan Xiuqing
UCSI Graduate Business School, UCSI University, Kuala Lumpur, Malaysia

ABSTRACT

As we continue to navigate the 21st century, the interconnectedness of technological advancements and sustainable growth is becoming more evident. Among a plethora of technologies reshaping multiple sectors, blockchain emerges as a game-changer for supply chain management. Concurrently, the sustainable development goals (SDGs) established by the United Nations in 2015 offer a roadmap for sustainability worldwide. This chapter delves into the connection between these two significant constructs: blockchain technology and the SDGs, in relation to SCM.

BACKGROUND AND INTRODUCTION

As we continue to navigate the 21st century, the interconnectedness of technological advancements and sustainable growth is becoming more evident (Smits, 2002). Among a plethora of technologies reshaping multiple sectors, blockchain emerges as a game-changer for supply chain management (SCM; Kopyto, Lechler, von der Gracht, & Hartmann, 2020). Concurrently, the Sustainable Development Goals (SDGs) established by the United Nations in 2015 offer a roadmap for sustainability worldwide (Tsalis, Mal-

DOI: 10.4018/979-8-3693-0482-2.ch011

amateniou, Koulouriotis, & Nikolaou, 2020). This chapter delves into the connection between these two significant constructs: blockchain technology and the SDGs, in relation to SCM.

In today's world, supply chains have become intricate and globally dispersed, posing challenges for businesses to oversee and control each stage effectively. This obscurity can lead to inefficiencies, unethical actions, and environmental harm. For example, the creation of a simple T-shirt involves multiple continents, several stakeholders, and can have a considerable impact on the environment. Thus, fostering sustainability in such complex supply chains calls for groundbreaking solutions - a potential that blockchain technology aspires to realize.

Blockchain, initially invented as a public ledger for Bitcoin transactions, has far-reaching implications (Block, 2023). It's a decentralized, unchangeable, and transparent system capable of securely and efficiently tracking transactions (Hemdan, El-Shafai, & Sayed, 2023). Within the framework of supply chains, blockchain can enhance visibility, confirm product genuineness, and promote trust among participants (Agrawal, Angelis, Khilji, Kalaiarasan, & Wiktorsson, 2023). By recording and tracing every transaction, it enables consumers, businesses, and regulators to authenticate product origins and supply chain reliability. Consequently, blockchain can help tackle numerous sustainability-related issues prevalent in contemporary supply chains.

Meanwhile, the SDGs offer a worldwide schema for sustainability, including 17 goals that cover areas from eradicating poverty and eliminating hunger to encouraging responsible consumption and production. Supply chains play a crucial role in attaining these goals, given their importance to global trade, job generation, and resource distribution (Dou, Xu, Zhu, & Keenan, 2023). For instance, SDG 12, advocating for responsible consumption and production, directly involves supply chain functions. Other SDGs like SDG 8 (decent work and economic growth) and SDG 9 (industry, innovation, and infrastructure) also entail significant supply chain implications.

Considering blockchain technology's capability to alleviate numerous challenges related to achieving the SDGs in SCM, a study of this link is both opportune and pertinent. This chapter is designed to offer a comprehensive view of this intersection, highlighting how blockchain can support sustainable SCM and how supply chains can assist in accomplishing the SDGs. It will share real-world instances of this symbiosis, discuss the associated challenges and possibilities, and deliver insights for supply chain experts, sustainability proponents, and policymakers.

This chapter seeks to contribute to both the scholarly dialogue on sustainability and blockchain and provide practical guidance for SCM practitioners. The primary aim is to enhance comprehension of how cutting-edge technologies can be employed to develop more sustainable and equitable supply chains, hence contributing to the global mission of achieving the SDGs. The upcoming section discusses the relevance of SDGs in the context of SCM.

The SDGs are a collection of 17 interconnected global objectives established by the United Nations General Assembly, aimed at fostering a more sustainable future. These goals cover various areas including responsible consumption and production, decent work, and economic growth, all of which have implications for SCM. This section explores the specific relevance of SDGs to supply chain operations and sustainability.

BLOCKCHAIN IS A GROUNDBREAKING TECHNOLOGY FOR SUPPLY CHAINS

Blockchain technology, in the beginning recognised for its knots with cryptocurrencies (Meland, Bayoumy, & Sindre, 2020), has since extended its pressure, proving itself as a groundbreaking technology in numerous areas, including SCM. SCM, which are complicated nets of numerous businesses team up to deliver products or services from origin to terminal point, can momentously advantage from blockchain's exclusive structures in tackling persistent glitches such as absence of transparency, deception, incompetence, and the need for mutual trust among varied members.

What is Blockchain? If we focus on its core, it is a variant of shared ledger technology that records an ever-mounting list of 'blocks' coupled through cryptographic approaches. Each block contains a cryptographic hash of the preceding block, a timestamp, and operation data. The dispersed, transparent, and immutable characteristics of blockchain make it an effective tool for challenging several supply chain obstacles.

The most significant vantage of blockchain is its probable to boost SCM clarity. Conventional supply chains commonly undergo from limited prospect due to the involvement of a array of events around the globe. Yet, blockchain nets offer a solution to this obstacle with their permanent, shared transaction logbooks. This level of transparency allows different patrons, including end clients, to trace a product's path from its source to its final delivery point. For example, retailers can leverage blockchain to verify a product's ethical sourcing by tracing its origins. This heightened visibility can contribute to the eradication of unethical practices and promote sustainability by enabling stakeholders to make well-informed decisions in buying and selling.

A further benefit is blockchain's ability to eliminate supply chain fraud and counterfeiting. Its inherent security features like immutability and cryptographic validation make data manipulation or introduction of fraudulent products into the supply chain extremely challenging. As per an estimate by the Organization for Economic Co-operation and Development (OECD), counterfeit trade might have reached a staggering USD 509 billion in 2016. Blockchain's capacity to guarantee product authenticity could be a game-changer in combating this global issue.

Blockchain improves SCM efficiency (Gurtu & Johny, 2019). Bills of lading, invoices, and customs forms are common in traditional supply chains (Natanelov, Cao, Foth, & Dulleck, 2022). Processing these documents can be prone to errors and delays, resulting in inefficiencies. Blockchain can digitize and automate these processes with smart contracts (contracts that automatically execute when certain conditions are met), streamlining supply chain operations and reducing administrative costs.

Blockchain also serves a critical role in supply chain dispute resolution (Kumar, Liu, & Shan, 2020). Traditional supply chain systems often suffer from discrepancies and errors leading to disputes, which can be time and resource-intensive to resolve. The use of blockchain, providing a single, shared, and unalterable record of transactions, can simplify this process (Helo & Hao, 2019). Moreover, smart contracts can minimize disputes by ensuring that contractual obligations are met as soon as the specified conditions are fulfilled.

An exemplar of blockchain application in supply chains can be seen in the food industry. Utilizing blockchain to trace food items from their source to the consumer allows stakeholders to promptly identify and isolate food safety concerns. A compelling example of this was when Walmart traced a package of sliced mangoes back to its origin within seconds using blockchain technology, a process that previously took almost a week. In scenarios involving food safety crises like disease outbreaks, this feature could prove to be lifesaving.

Despite the promising benefits of blockchain in supply chains, its implementation is not without hurdles (Sternberg, Hofmann, & Roeck, 2021). The nascent stage of this technology and the lack of technical expertise among businesses can pose challenges. Additionally, concerns surrounding data privacy and the legal status of blockchain transactions present further obstacles. Not all supply chain stakeholders may have the capacity or willingness to participate in a blockchain network. Finally, the environmental implications of blockchain, especially those using proof-of-work algorithms, must be considered within the context of sustainable SCM.

While blockchain has the potential to revolutionize SCM by enhancing transparency, curtailing fraud, boosting efficiency, and simplifying dispute resolution, there are considerable technical, regulatory, and adoption hurdles to overcome (Jahid, Alsharif, & Hall, 2023). As the technology matures and these challenges are addressed, it's likely that blockchain will assume a crucial role in fostering more efficient, transparent, and sustainable supply chains, thereby contributing to the attainment of the SDGs (Palomares et al., 2021).

RELATIONSHIP BETWEEN SDGS AND BLOCKCHAIN IN SCM

To completely comprehend this interaction, it's fundamental to recognize the central hurdles that endure in participating supply chain operations with SDGs (Liou & Rao-Nicholson, 2021). The set of 17 SDGs are committed to solving the best decisive social, financial, and green issues by 2030. They cover a wide array of troubles like poverty, discrimination, climate change, ecological degradation, peace, and integrity. A number of these goals are clearly linked to supply chain operations, such as SDG 8 (Decent Work and Economic Growth), SDG 9 (Industry, Innovation, and Infrastructure), and SDG 12 (Responsible Consumption and Production).

Even so, the apprehension of these goals within supply chains often faces hurdles like lack of clarity, wastefulness, and uncertainty among stakeholders. This is the juncture where blockchain can deliver possible resolutions. With a permanent, apparent, and secure log of transactions, blockchain can amplify transparency, cut inefficiencies, and build trust among supply chain stakeholders (Liou & Rao-Nicholson, 2021).

The transparency enabled by blockchain can significantly influence to SDG 12, which advocates responsible consumption and production (Tham & Sigala, 2020). The traceability offered by blockchain enables consumers, companies, and regulators to authenticate the origins of products, thereby fostering responsible consumption and production. For instance, the legitimacy of claims about products being organic, ethically sourced, or carbon-neutral can be validated through blockchain, promoting responsible consumer behavior and corporate practices.

Blockchain can also support SDG 8 by encouraging decent work and economic growth. The secure and transparent attributes of blockchain can discourage unethical labor practices that are often concealed in complicated, global supply chains. For example, blockchain can confirm fair payment and acceptable working conditions for workers at every stage of the supply chain, supporting the goal of decent work for all.

Likewise, the efficiency gains and cost reductions brought about by blockchain can stimulate economic growth, making supply chains more profitable and resilient. This is particularly beneficial for small and medium-sized enterprises (SMEs), which often find it hard to compete with larger entities in the supply chain. This aligns with SDG 9, which highlights the importance of industry, innovation, and infrastructure.

Some case studies illustrate the interaction of blockchain and SDGs in SCM. For instance, De Beers' adoption of blockchain to trace diamonds from the mine to the customer ensures the diamonds are conflict-free, thereby promoting SDG 16 (Peace, Justice, and Strong Institutions). Another example is the Food and Agriculture Organization's (FAO) application of blockchain to trace the supply chains of fish products, contributing to SDG 14 (Life Below Water).

Yet, it's crucial to understand that the incorporation of blockchain technology into supply chains isn't a straightforward solution. Numerous challenges, including technical complexity, privacy issues, and regulatory uncertainties, need to be tackled. Moreover, the successful application of blockchain is reliant on the willingness and capability of all supply chain stakeholders to engage in the blockchain network.

Notwithstanding the challenges, the possible interaction between SDGs and blockchain in SCM presents exciting opportunities. Blockchain can help surmount significant obstacles in achieving SDGs in supply chains by enhancing transparency, efficiency, and trust. It is anticipated that the discourse in this chapter will stimulate further investigation and innovation in this domain, contributing to a more sustainable and inclusive future.

OPPORTUNITIES AND CHALLENGES

The blend of SDGs and blockchain technology in SCM brings with it both hypothetical payback and barriers (Moro-Visconti, 2022). As we persist our quest for more reorganized, environmentally friendly, and equitable supply chains, it becomes crucial to delve deeply into these elements. This research discusses the opportunities that emerge from the intersection of SDGs and blockchain and the hurdles we need to overcome for this groundbreaking fusion to thrive.

Opportunities

The union of SDGs and blockchain technology yields numerous prospects in supply chain management. These are some of the most significant ones:

Lucidity and Trackability

Blockchain technology profoundly lifts the level of lucidity and trackability within supply chains, representing a significant opportunity (Peres, Schreier, Schweidel, & Sorescu, 2023). The definitive nature of blockchain records each transaction, facilitating comprehensive oversight throughout the entire supply chain. This feature proves vital in concentrating numerous SDGs, exceptionally SDG 12, which focuses on Responsible Consumption and Production. For illustration, blockchain allows the ability to authenticate a product's organic or ethically sourced assertions by meticulously tracing its route from origin to retail. This degree of transparency, unlike anything before, encourages companies to incorporate more eco-friendly practices, while empowering consumers to make more sustainable purchasing decisions (Khan, Badghish, Kaur, Sharma, & Dhir, 2023).

Annihilation of Unethical Practices

The underlying transparency of blockchain technology can deter unethical behaviour, thereby facilitating the achievement of SDG 8, which promotes Decent Work and Economic Growth. As an illustration, in the realm of the apparel industry, the usage of blockchain can ascertain that clothes are not manufactured in exploitative environments, as it can monitor and authenticate each phase of the production process (Mandolla, Petruzzelli, Percoco, & Urbinati, 2019). In a similar vein, within the food sector, blockchain can certify the adherence to equitable trade principles by supplying incontrovertible evidence of a commodity's trajectory from its agricultural origins to the end consumer.

Cost Reduction and Efficiency

Blockchain has the potential to optimise supply chain processes through the digitization and automation of processes such as products monitoring and contract execution (Wang, Singgih, Wang, & Rit, 2019). It increases supply chain productivity while decreasing costs by reducing documentation and administrative costs. This enhancement goes hand in hand with SDG 9 (Industry, Innovation, and Infrastructure), as it promotes technological advancements and economic progress.

Enhanced Stakeholder Trust

The immutability of blockchain records inspires confidence among key stakeholders, including providers, producers, traders, and end users (Wang, Han, & Beynon-Davies, 2019). This garnered trust is decisive in creating and preserving robust, effective, and reasonable supply chains, necessary elements in the attainment of numerous SDGs.

Challenges

The combination of blockchain technology and the SDGs in supply chain management presents both intriguing opportunities and substantial challenges.

Technical intricacy

The complexity of blockchain technology and the specialised knowledge required for its deployment can impede its incorporation (Steenwinckel et al., 2021). This is especially challenging for small and medium-sized enterprises (SMEs), as they might lack the essential capabilities and resources to establish and sustain a blockchain infrastructure.

Anonymity or Privacy

Even with the innate security mechanisms that blockchain offers, data privacy continues to be a concern (Farahani, Firouzi, & Luecking, 2021). For example, the transparency that is often hailed as a significant benefit of blockchain could inadvertently reveal sensitive corporate information to rival companies. Moreover, despite the robust security of the blockchain infrastructure itself, access points such as web applications might still be susceptible to cybersecurity threats.

Ambiguous Regulations

The rules and legislation surrounding blockchain are still in development, resulting in ambiguity regarding aspects such as the legality of blockchain-based transactions. This lack of clarity might discourage companies from integrating blockchain into their supply chains (Hastig & Sodhi, 2020). The array of opportunities and challenges underscores the intricacy of fusing SDGs and blockchain within SCM. Evidently, blockchain holds substantial potential to advance SDGs in supply chains, but realising this potential requires overcoming substantial obstacles.

FUTURE AGENDA

An area that is rapidly developing in the field of SCM is the interaction between blockchain and the SDGs. The in-depth discussion in this chapter sheds light on the immense possibilities and obstacles linked with this fusion. As we gaze into what lies ahead, it is of vital importance to ponder possible pathways and initiatives that can expedite the actualization of these possibilities. The statements that follow consider these possible directions for the future.

Developing Skills and Education

Blockchain technology's complexity is a major barrier to its mainstream adoption. A comprehensive educational and skill enhancement program is required to provide businesses, especially SMEs, with the technical know-how needed to effectively operate within the realm of blockchain. Higher education institutions, vocational training centers, and industry bodies hold substantial potential in creating and executing such instructional programs. Collaboration between these academic institutions and commercial organisations may offer priceless, practical learning opportunities, developing a workforce skilled in blockchain technology in the supply chain industry.

Measures to Enhance Security and Privacy

Despite the built-in security features of blockchain, challenges with data security and privacy persist. The emphasis for future initiatives should be to devise and deploy superior security strategies that safeguard confidential business data, while not compromising the transparency that blockchain technology brings to the table. Promising solutions may lie in methods such as zero-knowledge proofs and homomorphic encryption, both of which allow data validation without the necessity to expose the underlying data. In order to safeguard against potential cyber risks, it is essential to establish reliable and secure access points to blockchain systems.

Advancement of Regulatory Frameworks

The regulatory environment surrounding blockchain technology is constantly evolving and is in a state of flux, which can breed confusion and perhaps prevent its widespread adoption. It becomes crucial, therefore, for legislators, commercial entities, and those proficient in blockchain technology to collaborate and devise regulatory structures that are both supportive and unambiguous. Such structures need to not only tackle current hurdles but also exhibit the elasticity to accommodate forthcoming advancements. Cross-border cooperation can significantly contribute to aligning regulatory strategies among various nations, thus smoothing the path for the global integration of blockchain in supply chain systems.

Collaboration between Multi-stakeholders

Implementing the integration of blockchain technology and SDGs inside SCM calls for a collaborative strategy including several parties. This collaboration should encompass corporations, blockchain innovators, experts in SDGs, legislators, and end-users who work jointly to establish sector norms, promote exemplary procedures, and expedite blockchain's uptake. Such synergies can encourage the exchange of knowledge, build mutual trust, and define group goals for sustainable supply chains.

Achieving Inclusive Blockchain Solutions

The benefits of blockchain should not only be available to big businesses. Future research must put a strong emphasis on creating blockchain solutions that Small and Medium-sized Enterprises (SMEs) can use and afford. These could take the shape of open-source blockchain platforms or a blockchain-as-a-service model that demands fewer resources and less expertise for deployment and maintenance.

By concentrating on these areas, we can leverage blockchain technology's disruptive powers to advance the SDGs inside the supply chain ecosystem. Nonetheless, it is vital to acknowledge that blockchain isn't a one-size-fits-all solution. Despite its manifold benefits, the inclusion of blockchain in supply chains should be supplemented with additional sustainability measures and initiatives. A thorough and multifaceted approach must be adopted if supply networks are to be really sustainable.

CONCLUSION

SDGs and blockchain technology might at the outset seem irrelevant. Though, further examination exposes a possibly impactful junction between these two realms in the field of SCM. This chapter delves into the potential of blockchain in furthering SDGs within supply chain operations and how supply chains aligned with SDGs can leverage the benefits of blockchain solutions. The extraordinary potential of blockchain to further the attainment of SDGs within the sphere of supply chain management cannot be understated. Our exploration revealed that blockchain's incorporation into supply chains can magnify transparency, escalate efficiency, and enhance trust amongst all involved parties - all key factors in actualizing numerous SDGs such as responsible consumption and production, decent work and economic growth, and industry, innovation, and infrastructure. Blockchain's capacity to produce an immutable and clear record of transactions could be harnessed to promote responsible consumption and production. Through facilitating comprehensive traceability, blockchain can assist in verifying product authenticity, securing ethical sourcing of materials, and preventing deceptive practices. This amplified supply chain visibility can also promote decent work and economic growth by ensuring equitable labor practices and ethical business operations at all stages of the supply chain. Besides, the efficiency gains and cost reductions facilitated by blockchain can stimulate innovation and economic expansion in the supply chain industry. Through digitizing and automating several processes, blockchain technology can make supply chains more robust, profitable, and sustainable. The trust that blockchain instills can also boost collaboration and partnership amongst stakeholders, vital for achieving a more sustainable and inclusive supply chain sector. Yet, we should not disregard the obstacles that exist in the path of integrating blockchain into supply chains. The intricacies of the technology, concerns about privacy and security, and regulatory uncertainties are substantial challenges that need to be surmounted. Particularly for small and medium-sized enterprises (SMEs), the elevated costs and specialized expertise required to implement and manage a blockchain system could be prohibitive. Likewise, while blockchain improves transparency, it could potentially reveal sensitive business data, raising apprehensions about data privacy and security. The evolving regulatory environment for blockchain also adds uncertainties that can dissuade businesses from adopting this technology. Despite these hurdles, the inclusion of blockchain technology into supply chains is an achievable reality. Numerous innovative businesses and organizations have already begun utilizing blockchain to further their sustainability goals. Noteworthy examples include De Beers' application of blockchain to certify their diamonds as conflict-free, and the Food and Agriculture Organization's use of blockchain to trace fish product supply chains. These initiatives provide invaluable insights and lessons for other businesses and industries aiming to incorporate blockchain into their supply chains. As we progress, nurturing an environment that supports the adoption of blockchain in supply chains is paramount. This involves investing in capacity building to provide businesses with the required skills and knowledge to implement blockchain, fostering collaborations amongst multiple stakeholders to develop and implement industry standards for blockchain in supply chains, and sculpting a supportive regulatory framework that addresses the unique challenges and opportunities offered by blockchain technology. While the journey ahead may be filled with obstacles, the prospect of a more sustainable, efficient, and inclusive supply chain sector, which can greatly contribute to the attainment of SDGs, is an opportunity worth pursuing. As we persist in our exploration and innovation at the juncture of blockchain and supply chains, we uncover fresh avenues for progressing sustainable development in our increasingly interconnected world.

REFERENCES

Agrawal, T. K., Angelis, J., Khilji, W. A., Kalaiarasan, R., & Wiktorsson, M. (2023). Demonstration of a blockchain-based framework using smart contracts for supply chain collaboration. *International Journal of Production Research*, *61*(5), 1497–1516. doi:10.1080/00207543.2022.2039413

Block, S. (2023). Legal Requirements in the Field of Virtual Currencies. In M. Užík, C. Schmitz, & S. Block (Eds.), *Financial Innovation and Value Creation: The Impact of Disruptive Technologies on the Digital World* (pp. 75–86). Springer International Publishing. doi:10.1007/978-3-031-22426-3_5

Dou, S., Xu, D., Zhu, Y., & Keenan, R. (2023). Critical mineral sustainable supply: Challenges and governance. *Futures*, *146*, 103101. doi:10.1016/j.futures.2023.103101

Farahani, B., Firouzi, F., & Luecking, M. (2021). The convergence of IoT and distributed ledger technologies (DLT): Opportunities, challenges, and solutions. *Journal of Network and Computer Applications*, *177*, 102936. doi:10.1016/j.jnca.2020.102936

Gurtu, A., & Johny, J. (2019). Potential of blockchain technology in supply chain management: A literature review. *International Journal of Physical Distribution & Logistics Management*, *49*(9), 881–900. doi:10.1108/IJPDLM-11-2018-0371

Hastig, G. M., & Sodhi, M. S. (2020). Blockchain for Supply Chain Traceability: Business Requirements and Critical Success Factors. *Production and Operations Management*, *29*(4), 935–954. doi:10.1111/poms.13147

Helo, P., & Hao, Y. (2019). Blockchains in operations and supply chains: A model and reference implementation. *Computers & Industrial Engineering*, *136*, 242–251. doi:10.1016/j.cie.2019.07.023

Hemdan, E. E.-D., El-Shafai, W., & Sayed, A. (2023). Integrating Digital Twins with IoT-Based Blockchain: Concept, Architecture, Challenges, and Future Scope. *Wireless Personal Communications*, *131*(3), 2193–2216. doi:10.100711277-023-10538-6 PMID:37360142

Jahid, A., Alsharif, M. H., & Hall, T. J. (2023). The convergence of blockchain, IoT and 6G: Potential, opportunities, challenges and research roadmap. *Journal of Network and Computer Applications*, *217*, 103677. doi:10.1016/j.jnca.2023.103677

Khan, S. J., Badghish, S., Kaur, P., Sharma, R., & Dhir, A. (2023). What motivates the purchasing of green apparel products? A systematic review and future research agenda. *Business Strategy and the Environment*. doi:10.1002/bse.3360

Kopyto, M., Lechler, S., von der Gracht, H. A., & Hartmann, E. (2020). Potentials of blockchain technology in supply chain management: Long-term judgments of an international expert panel. *Technological Forecasting and Social Change*, *161*, 120330. doi:10.1016/j.techfore.2020.120330

Kumar, A., Liu, R., & Shan, Z. (2020). Is Blockchain a Silver Bullet for Supply Chain Management? Technical Challenges and Research Opportunities. *Decision Sciences*, *51*(1), 8–37. doi:10.1111/deci.12396

Liou, R.-S., & Rao-Nicholson, R. (2021). Multinational enterprises and Sustainable Development Goals: A foreign subsidiary perspective on tackling wicked problems. *Journal of International Business Policy*, *4*(1), 136–151. doi:10.105742214-020-00080-8

Mandolla, C., Petruzzelli, A. M., Percoco, G., & Urbinati, A. (2019). Building a digital twin for additive manufacturing through the exploitation of blockchain: A case analysis of the aircraft industry. *Computers in Industry*, *109*, 134–152. doi:10.1016/j.compind.2019.04.011

Meland, P. H., Bayoumy, Y. F. F., & Sindre, G. (2020). The Ransomware-as-a-Service economy within the darknet. *Computers & Security*, *92*, 101762. doi:10.1016/j.cose.2020.101762

Moro-Visconti, R. (2022). ESG-Driven Valuation: From Father Profit to Mother Nature. In R. Moro-Visconti (Ed.), *Augmented Corporate Valuation: From Digital Networking to ESG Compliance* (pp. 235–314). Springer International Publishing. doi:10.1007/978-3-030-97117-5_8

Natanelov, V., Cao, S., Foth, M., & Dulleck, U. (2022). Blockchain smart contracts for supply chain finance: Mapping the innovation potential in Australia-China beef supply chains. *Journal of Industrial Information Integration*, *30*, 100389. doi:10.1016/j.jii.2022.100389

Palomares, I., Martínez-Cámara, E., Montes, R., García-Moral, P., Chiachio, M., Chiachio, J., Alonso, S., Melero, F. J., Molina, D., Fernández, B., Moral, C., Marchena, R., de Vargas, J. P., & Herrera, F. (2021). A panoramic view and swot analysis of artificial intelligence for achieving the sustainable development goals by 2030: Progress and prospects. *Applied Intelligence*, *51*(9), 6497–6527. doi:10.100710489-021-02264-y PMID:34764606

Peres, R., Schreier, M., Schweidel, D. A., & Sorescu, A. (2023). Blockchain meets marketing: Opportunities, threats, and avenues for future research. *International Journal of Research in Marketing*, *40*(1), 1–11. doi:10.1016/j.ijresmar.2022.08.001

Smits, R. (2002). Innovation studies in the 21st century; Questions from a user's perspective. *Technological Forecasting and Social Change*, *69*(9), 861–883. doi:10.1016/S0040-1625(01)00181-0

Steenwinckel, B., De Paepe, D., Vanden Hautte, S., Heyvaert, P., Bentefrit, M., Moens, P., Dimou, A., Van Den Bossche, B., De Turck, F., Van Hoecke, S., & Ongenae, F. (2021). FLAGS: A methodology for adaptive anomaly detection and root cause analysis on sensor data streams by fusing expert knowledge with machine learning. *Future Generation Computer Systems*, *116*, 30–48. doi:10.1016/j.future.2020.10.015

Sternberg, H. S., Hofmann, E., & Roeck, D. (2021). The Struggle is Real: Insights from a Supply Chain Blockchain Case. *Journal of Business Logistics*, *42*(1), 71–87. doi:10.1111/jbl.12240

Tham, A., & Sigala, M. (2020). Road block(chain): Bit(coin)s for tourism sustainable development goals? *Journal of Hospitality and Tourism Technology*, *11*(2), 203–222. doi:10.1108/JHTT-05-2019-0069

Tsalis, T. A., Malamateniou, K. E., Koulouriotis, D., & Nikolaou, I. E. (2020). New challenges for corporate sustainability reporting: United Nations' 2030 Agenda for sustainable development and the sustainable development goals. *Corporate Social Responsibility and Environmental Management*, *27*(4), 1617–1629. doi:10.1002/csr.1910

Wang, Y., Han, J. H., & Beynon-Davies, P. (2019). Understanding blockchain technology for future supply chains: A systematic literature review and research agenda. *Supply Chain Management*, *24*(1), 62–84. doi:10.1108/SCM-03-2018-0148

Wang, Y., Singgih, M., Wang, J., & Rit, M. (2019). Making sense of blockchain technology: How will it transform supply chains? *International Journal of Production Economics*, *211*, 221–236. doi:10.1016/j.ijpe.2019.02.002

Chapter 12
Blockchain for Academics:
The Key to a More Secure and Efficient Supply Chain in Higher Education

Shiekh Z. H. Ali
K.B. College of Arts and Commerce for Women, India

Mirza A. Haq
Iqra University, Pakistan

Haseeb R. Khan
Solace Sleep, Australia

ABSTRACT

Blockchain technology is revolutionizing countless areas of human life. It has gained significant attention because of its potential to transform supply chain management across various sectors, including education. This chapter explores possible benefits and obstacles associated with adopting a blockchain-enabled supply chain in the educational sector from a management perspective. With blockchain, universities will have more transparency, security, and efficiency in their system. However, implementing a new system includes several challenges in terms of technology, Infrastructure, Finance, Legal, and Human Resources. To overcome these challenges, a comprehensive understanding of the educational sector's unique supply chain requirements, stakeholders' participation, and careful planning are necessary. This chapter provides insights to decision-makers in formulating strategies to leverage blockchain technology effectively and maximize its potential in enhancing supply chain procedures in the educational sector.

INTRODUCTION

Blockchain technology has emerged as a transformative innovation with the potential to revolutionize various industries, including supply chain management. At its core, blockchain is a decentralized and distributed digital ledger that records transactions in a secure and transparent manner (Tapscott & Tapscott 2016; Mihalcea & Ceaușu 2017; Iansiti, & Lakhani 2017; Swan 2015). This technology of-

DOI: 10.4018/979-8-3693-0482-2.ch012

fers a new paradigm for tracking and verifying the movement of goods, information, and assets across complex networks. In traditional supply chain systems, challenges such as opacity, inefficiencies, fraud, and lack of trust among participants have been persistent (Ghouri et al., 2023; Calvera Isabal et al., 2023; Flores-Vivar & García-Peñalvo, 2023; Shaoliu & Tongbai, 2023; Mihalcea, R., & Ceauşu, 2017; Khan et al., 2017; Haq, Khan, Parkash & Jabeen, 2016). However, blockchain's decentralized architecture addresses these challenges by enabling a secure, tamper-proof, and transparent record-keeping system (Zhang, 2019; McKibbin, S. 2017). Transactions, once recorded on the blockchain, cannot be altered or deleted without consensus from the network participants. This ensures data integrity and builds trust among stakeholders. As a result, blockchain has gained significant attention for its potential to enhance transparency, traceability, and overall efficiency within supply chains (McKibbin, 2017; Sheehan, 2017; Iyer, & Kemp, 2019). The previous study provides a comprehensive foundation for understanding how blockchain technology is influencing supply chain management. They emphasize the potential of blockchain to enhance transparency, traceability, and efficiency within supply chains while addressing traditional challenges.

Education revolution has increased the mobility of students as well as teachers across the world. With this educational proliferation, the Universities in developing countries face challenges associated with the issuance of certificates, attestations, and the assessment of academic performance. The problem of forgery and fraud in academic records questions the credibility of university graduates' certificates and reduces their chances of studying or working abroad. Besides, the process of verification and accreditation of documents is time-consuming as well as costly for students and university. The need of the hour is cutting-edge solutions so as to improve the handling of academic records, issuance of certificates, safe and secure exchange and with no scope to tamper and forge the documents.

Fake degrees, credential fraud, delayed verification of credentials and lack of digital credential have been prevalent, leading to credibility issues for educational institutions and employers (David, L., & Courtois, 2018; Demir, I., & Karabatak, 2019), Galvez, 2020). Transferring academic transcripts between institutions can be slow and cumbersome, often requiring manual processes and administrative effort (Kumar, A., & Yadav, (2019). Student data, including personal and academic information, is vulnerable to breaches and misuse (Brown, Chui et al.(2011). Instances of unverified MOOC completion certificates have been in the recent past (Dillahunt et al. (2020). Also, it has been a matter to ponder wherein students have multiple digital identities across different platforms (Liu, Wang, & Zhu, (2019). Besides, issues like plagiarism, data manipulation and lack of transparency is prevalent in academics (Moxham, & Boon, (2019).

Figure 1 depicts the overall flow of the chapter process from beginning to end. The rest of this chapter is structured as follows. Section II introduces the concept of blockchain. Section III explains the preceding research. Section IV discusses the approach, Section V discusses the analysis and results, and Section VI closes with a discussion, limits, future research directions, and conclusion.

Blockchain is a new concept in the field of Education. The significance of blockchain enabled supply chain management is rapidly increasing. It is a distributed network that has specific consensus algorithms used to create a sequence of blocks which includes immutable records of transactions. Blockchain enabled supply chain will solve the problem of transparency, traceability, security, privacy, trust, speed, and tampering documents in Universities. This technology has evolved into a dependable guarantor of transactional integrity and the network of links between economic participants. However, adopting the blockchain enabled supply chain system needs analyses of advantages from management perspective in a developing country. The change would affect all stakeholders in the field of higher education, includ-

Figure 1. Outline of research process

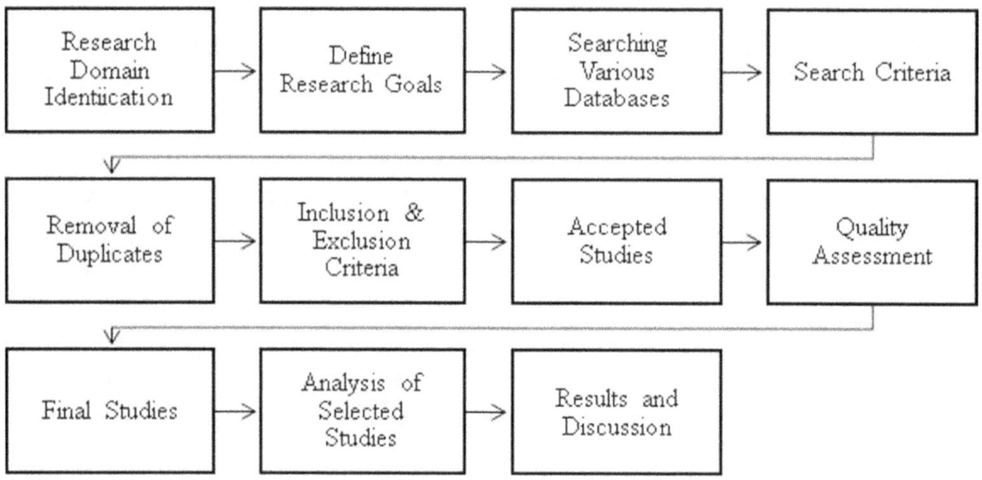

ing students, universities, teaching and non-teaching faculties, government agencies, policymakers, and companies from the business sector. Also, changes have to be integrated in technology, Infrastructure, Finance, Legal and Human Resources which pose questions. To overcome the dilemma, existing scholarly literature synthesis is a way to delve in this subject and investigate into the research question 1. Why should Universities introduce Blockchain enabled supply chains in their system? and 2. What are the potentials and problems in acceptance of a Blockchain enabled supply chain in higher education ?

BLOCKCHAIN TECHNOLOGY

Concept of Blockchain

Paxos protocol was introduced in 1989 by Leslie Lamport. Though it was not directly related to blockchain, its concepts of distributed consensus have influenced the development of consensus mechanisms within blockchain networks, contributing to the broader field of distributed systems and fault-tolerant computing (Lamport, 1998). It clearly started in 2008, with the publication of the Bitcoin whitepaper by an unidentified entity going by the pseudonym Satoshi Nakamoto. This essential document pioneered the concept of a decentralized, peer-to-peer digital currency, which was realized with the 2009 introduction of Bitcoin (Nakamoto, 2008). The blockchain was the innovation that powered Bitcoin. It was a public ledger that recorded all transactions in a safe, transparent, and immutable manner. In the years thereafter, blockchain's potential has expanded beyond digital currencies, leading to the development of platforms such as Ethereum, which introduced smart contracts, programmable self-executing agreements (Buterin, 2013). This paved the way for a variety of applications other than finance, such as supply chain management, healthcare, and identity verification. Blockchain's journey from its Bitcoin origins to a versatile technology disrupting multiple industries reflects its profound conceptual development and its transformative impact on how we store, verify, and exchange information (Mougayar, 2016).

Features of Blockchain

1. **Decentralization:**Blockchain operates on a decentralized network of nodes, eliminating the need for a central authority or intermediary. (Nakamoto, 2008).
2. **Transparency:** All transactions and data recorded on the blockchain are visible to all participants, ensuring transparency and reducing the possibility of fraud (Tapscott, & Tapscott, 2016).
3. **Security:**Blockchain uses cryptographic techniques to secure transactions and data, making it highly resistant to tampering and unauthorized access (Mougayar, 2016).
4. **Immutability:** Once data is added to the blockchain, it cannot be altered or deleted, ensuring the integrity and authenticity of records (Swan, 2015).
5. **Consensus Mechanisms:**Blockchain employs consensus algorithms to achieve agreement among participants about the state of the network, ensuring data consistency (Cachin &Vukolić, 2017).
6. **Provenance and Auditability:**Blockchain provides a transparent record of every transaction's origin and history, enabling easy auditability and traceability (Zheng et al 2017).
7. **Distributed Ledger:** Transactions are recorded on multiple copies of the ledger distributed across the network, enhancing redundancy and fault tolerance (Cocco et al 2018).
8. **Smart Contracts:** Self-executing contracts with predefined conditions are embedded within blockchain transactions, automating processes (Szabo 1997).

Types of Blockchain

There are currently three generally recognized types of blockchain systems which differ in governance and architecture (Zheng, 2017):

1. Public Blockchain: Here all records are accessible to the general public, and anyone can participate in the consensus process without any permission. This type of blockchain has strong immutability but low efficiency. Bitcoin best illustrates using the powers of such permission less blockchain.
2. Private Blockchain: This belongs to a single individual or organization, and only nodes from that organization are permitted to participate in the consensus process. Private blockchains offer weaker immutability but more efficiency than public blockchains. This is also known as permissioned blockchain. Here the consensus mechanism can be similar to a public blockchain or a tool such as Ripple, Corda or Hyperledger.
3. Consortium Blockchain: A hybrid of the two previous types of systems in which a predetermined number of users can participate in the consensus process and not all users are affiliated with the same organization. Immutability and efficiency are similar to private blockchain, while consortium blockchain is a middle ground between decentralized public blockchain and centralized private blockchain in terms of centralization. This is sometimes referred to as a permissioned blockchain. Example: Hyperledger and Quorum

Blockchain Platforms (Use Table)

In recent years, there has been a proliferation of platforms dedicated to the development of blockchain systems. Among the most widely regarded options are as follows:

Ethereum, an open-source and public blockchain technology, was initially conceptualized by VitalikButerin in 2013 (Ethereum, 2019). Ethereum encompasses Ether, a digital asset classified as a cryptocurrency, that serves as a means of payment for "gas." This "gas" refers to a quantifiable unit of computational operations executed by smart contracts, also known as scripts, which operate within the Ethereum Virtual Machine (EVM). Ethereum employs a variant of the Nakamoto consensus, which is the consensus process utilized by Bitcoin. Ethereum is extensively utilized in the creation of Peer to Peer (P2P) Distributed (or Decentralised) Applications (Dapps).

Hyperledger Fabric, developed by IBM and Digital Asset, is a permissioned (private) blockchain infrastructure that exhibits a modular architecture, smart contracts, and configurable consensus and membership services (Hyperledger Fabric, 2019). In addition to its status as a private blockchain, Hyperledger Fabric distinguishes itself from Ethereum by the absence of an inherent token and its higher level of configurability, among other factors. Hyperledger Fabric is a project that falls under the umbrella of the Linux Foundation's "Hyperledger" initiative. It is primarily designed for enterprise use, with a particular focus on facilitating Business to Business (B2B) applications.

Corda, a blockchain technology platform, was developed by the R3 firm (Corda, 2019). Corda is an open-source distributed ledger and smart contract platform known as the KMIS 2019 - 11th International Conference on Knowledge Management and Information Systems. It has been specifically designed to cater to the requirements of businesses. Similar to Hyperledger Fabric, Corda is a permissioned blockchain platform that lacks a native token. However, Corda distinguishes itself by being more specialized, catering exclusively to the unique requirements of the financial services sector.

Openchain, a blockchain technology developed by CoinPrism (Openchain, 2019), is designed to enable organizations to securely issue and manage digital assets in a scalable manner. Smart contracts are implemented and partitioned consensus is employed to enable users to generate distinct instances that possess a singular governing authority. It is possible to establish a fixed exchange rate between tokens on the Openchain platform and Bitcoin. Openchain employs a client-server architecture as opposed to the prevalent peer-to-peer (P2P) architecture utilized by most blockchains. Furthermore, it is important to note that consensus does not necessitate the involvement of a miner. Consequently, transactions can be executed instantaneously and without any associated costs.

BigChainDB is an open-source distributed storage system that seeks to integrate the benefits of NoSQL databases with blockchain technology, including distributed storage, immutability, and the absence of a central authority (BigChainDB, 2019). BigChainDB is constructed utilizing many NoSQL database nodes, such as MongoDB instances, that hold unalterable data pertaining to transactions. These nodes are kept in sync by the utilization of the Tendermint Byzantine Fault Tolerance (BFT) mechanism, which ensures consensus. BigChainDB has the capability to operate in three distinct modes: public, private, or permissioned.

Blockchain Applications in Various Sectors

Literature references provide insights into how blockchain technology has transformed supply chains across diverse sectors, demonstrating the broad-reaching impact of blockchain on enhancing transparency, security, and efficiency.

Table 1. Integration of blockchain technology in various sectors

Industry	Use	Source
Food and Agriculture	Enables traceability of food products from farm to table	Zheng, et al (2017)
Retail and Consumer Goods	Improves the visibility of product provenance	Kim. et al (2019).
Healthcare and Pharmaceuticals	Ensures the authenticity of drugs by tracking their journey through the supply chain	Yue, et al (2016)
Automotive Industry	Enhances transparency in the automotive supply chain, preventing use of counterfeit auto parts	Dorri, et al. (2017).
Fashion and Luxury Goods	Verifies the authenticity of luxury goods, enabling customers to trace the origin	Böhme, et al (2015
Energy and Utilities	Facilitates peer-to-peer energy trading, optimizing energy distribution and enabling renewable energy sharing	Li, et al (2017).
Logistics and Transportation	Enhances transparency in logistics, optimizing freight tracking, and automating customs and documentation processes	Meng, & Lai, K. (2018)
Real Estate	Streamlines property transactions by providing a secure and transparent record of ownership	Xu, et al (2017)
Waste Management	Ensuring proper disposal, recycling, and adherence to regulations	Zheng, et al (2018)
Government	It is s intended to improve egovernment, electronic voting, price archives and virtual identification	Pawlaket al (2018)
Internet of Things	Ensures the integrity and transparency of the gathered data and its interactions, safety, security, device management, identification, and confidentiality	Sullivan et al (2018)

An Overview of Blockchain in Higher Education

In this section we explore the details of blockchain application by few universities as well as educational institutions.

1. **MIT (Massachusetts Institute of Technology), USA:** MIT collaborated with Learning Machine to develop Blockcerts, an open standard for blockchain-based digital certificates. MIT has been actively using Blockcerts to issue and verify digital certificates and diplomas. This allows students to have tamper-proof digital credentials (Allen, J.& Harding, M. 2017).
2. **University of Melbourne, Australia:** The University of Melbourne is known for its work on blockchain technology in academia. They have experimented with using blockchain for issuing digital credentials and academic certificates securely (University of Melbourne).
3. **University of Nicosia, Cyprus:** The University of Nicosia is a pioneer in offering blockchain and cryptocurrency-related courses. They have integrated blockchain technology into their academic programs and have even issued blockchain-based academic certificates (University of Nicosia).
4. **Stanford University, USA:** Stanford University has conducted research into blockchain technology and its applications. They have explored blockchain's potential impact on various industries, including education (Stanford University).
5. **Sony Global Education's Blockchain Platform:** Sony Global Education has implemented blockchain to secure and streamline the sharing of student records. The platform enables students to own and share their academic achievements securely (Sony Global Education).

6. **Holberton School's Blockchain Verification:**Holberton School uses blockchain to allow employers to verify the authenticity of a graduate's diploma quickly and efficiently. This adds trust to their education credentials (Holberton School).
7. **Southern New Hampshire University's Blockchain-Based Credentials:** SNHU has partnered with blockchain startup Learning Machine to issue blockchain-based digital diplomas to its graduates. This enhances the credibility and security of their credentials (Southern New Hampshire University).
8. **Lancaster University, UK:** Lancaster University has used blockchain technology to verify degree certificates. They issued blockchain-based digital certificates to graduates, ensuring the security and authenticity of credentials (Lancaster University).

These implementations demonstrate how blockchain technology is being leveraged to address various challenges and enhance processes in higher education. Research papers and references provided here offer deeper insights into specific use cases and the benefits of blockchain in academia.

PRIOR STUDY/LITERATURE REVIEW

As blockchain is still in its early stages, researchers and practitioners have explored blockchain applications in Higher education in recent years. (Table) presents the existing review studies on blockchain in Universities.

Al-Bayatti et al in 2020 explored the opportunities and challenges of implementing blockchain in higher education, emphasizing how blockchain enhances the authenticity of academic records and credentials.

Many universities around the world have explored and implemented blockchain technology in various ways. Researchers have mentioned that Blockchain can be used to securely store, manage academic records, transcripts, certificates, course completion data timestamp and issue micro-credentials ensuring transparency (Jha, & Abraham 2019; Pardo & Siemens 2014). Blockchain-based identity verification systems are being explored to enhance security during student onboarding and registration, reducing the risk of identity fraud (Liu, Wang, & Zhu, 2019). Blockchain can be applied to manage the supply chain of educational resources, ensuring the authenticity and quality of textbooks, learning materials, and online courses (Khan & Gani 2020). Besides, some universities experiment with blockchain-based voting systems for student elections ensuring transparency and integrity (Bano Sonnino, et al. 2017).

A. MOTIVATION: To the best of our knowledge, higher education has few systematic literature reviews (SLRs), papers, and chapters on blockchain use. We also noticed that few studies have taken other blockchain applications into account. The purpose of this study was to analyze existing blockchain research in higher education and to create an integrated framework for blockchain adoption in higher education. The proposed integrated framework overcomes academic restrictions and encourages academicians, administrators, and practitioners to adopt and efficiently apply it in the educational sector.
B. GOALS: This study systematically reviewed and synthesized prior studies that explored the adoption of BCT in Higher education based on the research questions in (Table)

Table 2. Purpose and type of BCT application in higher education institution

Institution	Purpose/Application	Type of BCT	Blockchain Platform
University of Melbourne	Issuing digital credentials and academic certificates securely	Public and Permissioned	Ethereum, Hyperledger Fabric
University of Nicosia	Offering blockchain and cryptocurrency courses, issuing blockchain-based academic certificates	Public (Bitcoin)	Bitcoin, Ethereum
MIT (Massachusetts Institute of Technology)	Issuing blockchain-based digital diplomas through Blockcerts	Permissioned	Bitcoin, Ethereum, Blockcerts
Southern New Hampshire University	Issuing blockchain-based digital diplomas and certificates to graduates	Permissioned	Bitcoin, Ethereum, Blockcerts
Stanford University	Research into blockchain technology and its applications in various sectors	N/A (Research-focused)	N/A (Research-focused)
Lancaster University, UK	Issuing blockchain-based degree certificates for secure verification	Permissioned	Custom Solution
Open University, UK	Exploring blockchain for academic records management	Permissioned	Custom Solution
Massachusetts Institute of Technology (MIT)	Issuing digital diplomas and integrating blockchain for secure verification	Permissioned	Ethereum, uPort
Central New Mexico Community College	Securely issuing and verifying digital diplomas	Permissioned	Learning Machine, Blockcerts
King Fahd University of Petroleum and Minerals	Exploring blockchain for academic records verification	Permissioned	Custom Solution

Table 3. Research questions and objectives of study

#	Research Question	Objectives
1.	Why should Universities introduce Blockchain enabled supply chains in their system?	To review the existing research on BCT in Higher Education
2.	What are the potentials and problems in acceptance of a Blockchain enabled supply chain in higher education ?	To identify benefits, potentials and challenges of BCT in Higher education

METHODOLOGY

In the current study, using the guidelines of (Kitchenham and Charters and Tranfield et al.) explanatory literature synthesis process was carried out. This study ensures a systematic and rigorous analysis of the existing literature, enabling the identification of key findings and insights related to the adoption of blockchain-enabled supply chain in academic documents within the higher education sector. The in-depth syntheses explains a perspective, reasoning behind it, key findings to shed light on the potential benefits, challenges, and implications of implementing blockchain technology in managing academic documents within educational institutions.

Search Strategies and Data Sources

The pilot search protocol initially was based on trial and error method wherein a few terms like "blockchain", "blockchain" AND "supply chain", "blockchain" AND "higher education" and "blockchain

Table 4. Criteria for inclusion and exclusion

INCLUSION	EXCLUSION
The article must be written in English.	Papers that are not accessible and meta-data
It is imperative that the title, abstract, and complete content of the publication are accessible on the internet.	White papers, Ph.D dissertation, Technical reports, newspapers, magazines
Only scholarly works published in peer-reviewed journals and conference proceedings will be taken into consideration.	Papers that got published before 2017
The primary focus of the article should be around the intersection of block chain technology and its implications for the field of education.	Papers that are duplicated within the search documents

challenges" were used in the chosen scientific databases which included ScienceDirect, IEEE Xplore, SpringerLink, IGI Global and Google Scholar. Following the pilot study, the authors choose to utilize three reputable databases, namely Sciencedirect, Google Scholar, and IGI Global, in order to gather relevant literature for this systematic literature review. The authors replicated the methodological strategy employed in the pilot study.

The search terms used to examine the application of blockchain technology in higher education across the aforementioned three databases encompassed a general query, "blockchain and higher education." Nevertheless, the initial search yielded restricted outcomes, prompting the authors to broaden their investigation by incorporating alternative terms such as "block-chain," "block-chains," "block chain," "blockchains," "blockchain technology," "distributed ledger," "distributed ledger technology," "shared ledger," "decentralized ledger," "smart contracts," "smart contract," "hyper ledger," "Hyperledger," and "Ethereum." Various alternative terms were employed to refer to higher education and education, such as "the educational sector," "academics," "university," "college," "study center," "teaching and learning," "education institutions," "education transparency," "education supply chain," "university supply chain," and "credentials traceability." The search strings were formulated using the logical operators "AND" and "OR".

Inclusion and Exclusion Criteria

The inclusion and exclusion criteria are outlined, following the methodology employed by Taylor et al.

Quality Assessment

In this study, the relevance of the publications was evaluated using a quality assessment checklist, which was based on the approach employed by Taylor et al. and Hosseini et al. The checklist had five distinct steps, as seen in below Table.

Search Results

The initial search was constrained to the examination of titles and abstracts. A total of 357 articles were identified from the three databases based on the specified search parameters. A total of 172 instances of duplicate papers were detected and then eliminated, resulting in a remaining count of 185. The researchers

Table 5. Quality assessment criteria

Stage	Statements
Stage 1	Blockchain – The article must be focused on Blockchain in academics or higher education
Stage 2	Context- The article must have sufficient context to help interpret research results
Stage 3	Blockchain and Higher education- For answering RQ1 the selected literature must include detail adoption of BCT supply chain in education
Stage 4	For answering RQ2 the selected literature must explain the Potentials and Challenges of BCT in higher education
Stage 5	Data- A detail of how data was acquired must be presented

examined the titles and abstracts of various articles to identify those that specifically addressed the topics of "blockchain" in relation to "education" or "higher education". As a consequence, a total of 83 papers were produced. Subsequently, the writers engaged in a comprehensive examination of the whole articles in order to ascertain their relevance or ascertain the availability of full texts. As a consequence, a total of 40 papers were produced. A total of five (5) papers were included in the sample using snowballing procedures, resulting in a final collection of 45 articles and papers for subsequent analysis.

ANALYSIS AND RESULTS

The below figure depicts the publication year distribution of selected works linked to BCT in academia and higher education. Despite the fact that the BCT originally debuted in 2008 (Nakamoto & Bitcoin, 2008), the data show an increase in studies in space from 2018 to 2023. The first piece, according to the writers, was published in 2016. The authors also discovered that the most papers (22) were published in 2022, while the fewest were published in 2019 (02), with only two articles. (Figure) also shows that the majority of studies were conducted between 2021 and 2023, indicating that publications in this field will continue to expand.

Figure 3 exposes the Country Wise distribution of selected literature related to BCT in academics and higher education. The authors discovered that the papers selected were spread across 24 countries, wherein countries included USA, India, China, Indonesia, Singapore, Australia, Portugal etc. It is found that out of 45 papers, most of the (11) papers are from Indian authors on this novel subject. Followed by 5 papers from China and 3 papers each from Germany and Europe.

Figure 4 indicates the Search databases used and the percentage of papers chosen from each database. Three databases explored in this study were Science Direct, Google Scholar and IGI Global. Total 45 papers were selected from three databases out of which 20 papers were from ScienceDirect using the search string and 20 papers were from Google scholar. However, five papers selected from IGI Global were on the basis of search string and snowball sampling.

The subsequent section undertakes an analysis of the papers that have been identified in the literature, with a total of 45 articles being confirmed as the final sample for this study. The table provided presents a comprehensive compilation of the bibliographic details pertaining to each individual article. The papers are arranged according to the journal name in the provided table. The methods utilized in the chosen research papers have been organized and presented, while the ideas employed in these publications have been summarized and presented.

Figure 2. Year-wise publication of selected papers

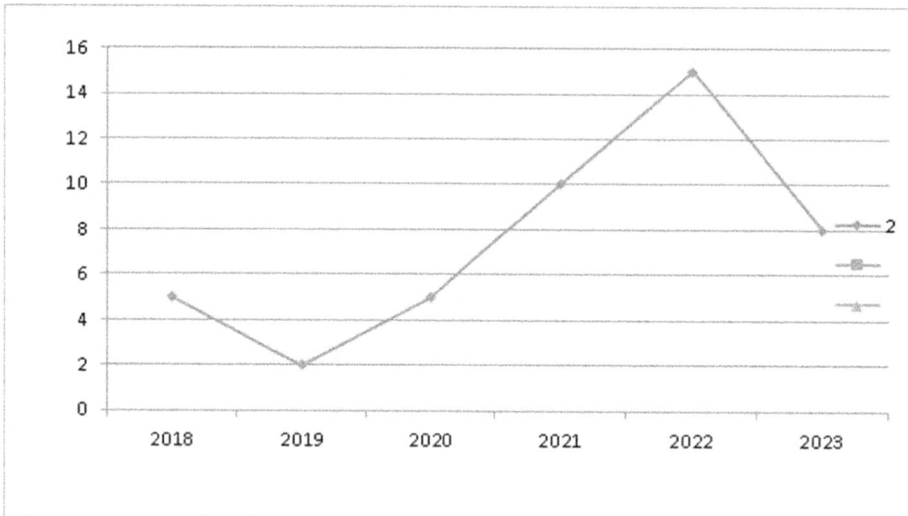

Figure 3. Country-wise distribution of selected papers

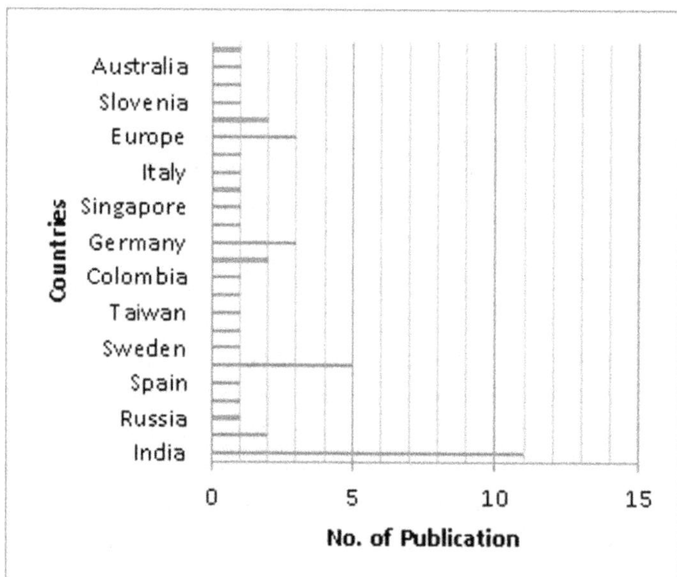

STATE OF RESEARCH ON BCT ADOPTION IN ACADEMICS

The initial step was the identification of existing research pertaining to the application of blockchain technology in the education sector. This identification process was conducted by considering four key characteristics, namely, the summary of studies, the specific topic of each study, the research methodology employed, and the resultant products or outcomes. A comprehensive overview of these aspects can be found in the provided table.

Figure 4. Databases used with percentage

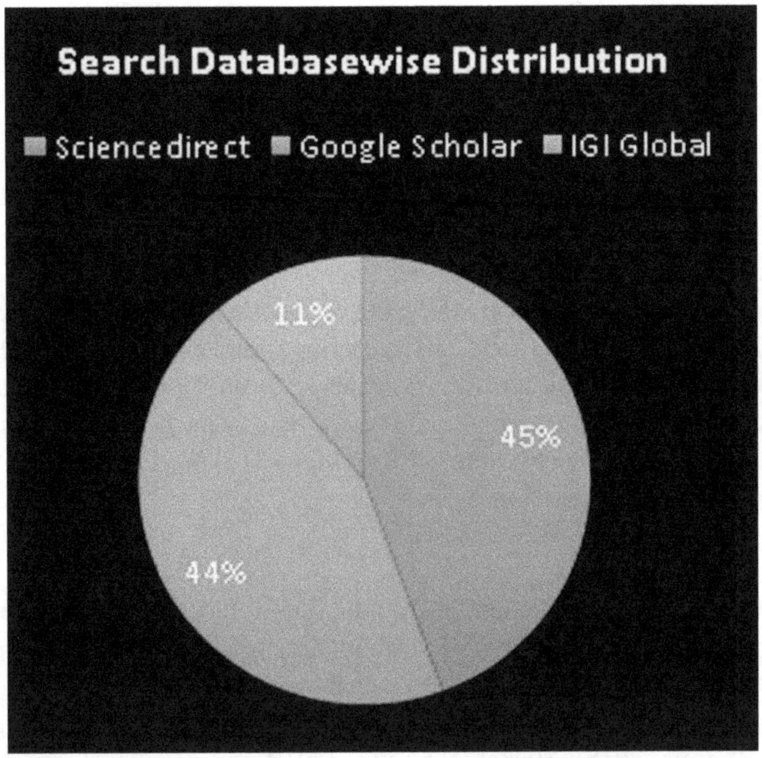

Annexure A.1 throws light on the various journals and proceedings which are the ultimate source of the selected research papers. Papers are selected from one or the other source of the below mentioned list of thirty-three journals and proceedings. Blockchain being a technical concept which is more of an information technology and computer science term, it was found that Journal named "Procedia Computer Science" housed 6 research papers followed by Journal "Applied Sciences" which proved to be a source of 3 research papers.

RESEARCH METHODS USED IN THE LITERATURE

The authors also examined the research methods used in the selected articles, which are summarized (ANNEXURE A.3). Findings showed that qualitative (N = 19) and proof of concept (N = 16) were the most employed methods,

CONCEPTUAL FRAMEWORK

Based on the analysis results, we developed a conceptual framework that brings together the enablers, benefits, and barriers to BTC adoption in Higher education. The following Section discusses the core elements of this framework.

POTENTIAL ENABLERS OF BCT IN HIGHER EDUCATION

The literature identified the enablers of BCT adoption in Higher education. These enablers are discussed in detail below.

Security

Security is a fundamental aspect and primary concern while integrating blockchain technology in educational context in higher education institutions (Ahmed Aziz, et al. 2018). Blockchain technology provides enhanced security features ensuring the protection of sensitive student data, academic records, academic credentials, records are protected from tampering, fraud and unauthorized access (Nir Kshetri2018; Vidalis .et al. 2019). Samson Kwiringira emphasizes on Blockchain's security features, such as encryption and decentralized data storage to enhance data security in education, especially when handling students' sensitive information (Samson Kwiringira et al 2021).

Authenticity

Authenticity is a central and crucial element in the adoption of blockchain technology in education as it ensures the integrity and trustworthiness of academic records, credentials, and certifications. (Ali Al-Bayatti 2020). Blockchain adoption in education enables quick and reliable verification of students' qualifications ensuring the authenticity of academic credentials and creating a lifelong learning passport for students (Bojana Dzinic, 2018). Stiakakis, E. et al (2019).in his paper discusses how Blockchain technology can support learner mobility and support lifelong learning ensuring authenticity of records and credibility of credentials. (Stiakakis et al 2019; Vidalis, 2019).

Immutability

Immutability is a key feature of blockchain technology that ensures that once data is recorded, it cannot be altered. This property is essential in maintaining the integrity and trustworthiness of academic records. Dzinic et al (2018), discusses how blockchain's immutability feature is leveraged to create a lifelong learning passport, ensuring the permanence and integrity of academic records (Dzinic et al (2018). Immutability is a foundational element that prevents unauthorized changes or deletions of academic records, ensuring reliability and authenticity. (Al-Bayatti et al 2020; Kshetri 2018). discusses how blockchain's immutability enhances data integrity in educational contexts (Kshetri 2018).

Transparency

Transparency is a core feature of blockchain technology that ensures all stakeholders have access to the same information, enhancing trust and accountability in educational processes (Stiakakis et al, 2019; Kshetri 2018). It ensures that academic records and credentials are accessible and verifiable by all relevant parties associated with the educational system, highlighting how blockchain's transparency enhances the credibility of academic records (Ali Al-Bayatti 2020). Transparency is a fundamental benefit of blockchain technology in education, as it ensures that data related to academic achievements is readily available for verification ensuring the accessibility, integrity and reliability of academic data (Desteanis et al (2019; Kshetri,2018).

Anonymity

Anonymity is an aspect of blockchain which allows one to maintain privacy. In the educational context blockchain technology can safeguard the privacy of students and educators data while still participating in educational processes.(Al-Bayatti, et al. 2020). Blockchain technology can be leveraged in educational contexts to ensure the confidentiality of sensitive student information with a focus on preserving anonymity (Samson et al 2021;Destefanis 2019), explored the quest of how BCT can enhance anonymity to facilitate secure and private transactions related to educational credentials and records ensuring the confidentiality of academic data (Destefanis,2019; Kshetri 2018) mentions the fact that blockchain's anonymity features enhance data privacy and protect student identity in educational sector (Kshetri, 2018)

Interoperability

Interoperability enables different educational institutions and systems to communicate and share data seamlessly. Lytas M. in his research paper discusses how blockchain-based credentials enhance interoperability in education by allowing for the easy sharing and verification across institutions (Lytras, et al 2019). Interoperability is essential for creating a standardized system for verifying and sharing educational credentials. Blockchain technology enhances interoperability in higher education by providing a standardized framework for credential verification (Destefanis et al. 2019; Dzinic.et al. (2018) explores how interoperability is a fundamental feature of BCT that ensures the compatibility of educational systems and takes care of seamless exchange of academic records supporting global learner mobility (Dzinic et al. 2018; Stiakakis, et al. 2019).

CHALLENGES OF BCT IN HIGHER EDUCATION

The literature identified the challenges of BCT adoption in Higher education. In the below section financial, human resource, technological, infrastructural and regulatory challenges are discussed in detail below.

1. FINANCIAL CHALLENGE: The upfront investment required for developing and integrating blockchain solutions can be substantial. This includes costs for software development, infrastructure setup, and the creation of blockchain applications tailored to educational needs (Lakkala et al 2019). Maintaining the necessary blockchain infrastructure, including nodes, servers, and data storage, can be costly. Also, integrating and customizing blockchain with existing educational systems can be complex and costly. These costs can grow as the number of users and transactions increases (Khan, & Gani,2020;Tarkoma, S. 2018; Gervais,et al. 2016). Continuous maintenance, security updates, and system enhancements to ensure the reliability and security require financial resources (Swan 2015). Meeting regulatory requirements related to data privacy and security can involve additional expenses (Tapscott, Tapscott 2016).
2. HUMAN RESOURCE CHALLENGE: When a new BCT adopted the existing staff does not welcome the change easily (Khedekar 2018). On the other hand when educational institutions integrate BCT, they also face a lack of in-house experts in blockchain technology (Mavridis & Stavropoulos 2019). The process of training and recruitment is costly, time consuming as well as the institution has to compete for a good talent (Huckle, & White2016) Mougayar (2016). Even after

investing in the appointment of blockchain expertise, institutions must work to retain talent. High demand for blockchain professionals can lead to staff turnover (Khan 2020). Besides, implementing blockchain often requires interdisciplinary collaboration between IT experts, administrators, and academic departments. Overcoming silos and fostering interdisciplinary teamwork can be challenging (Halaburda,& Sarvary 2016).

3. REGULATORY CHALLENGE: Blockchain implementation in higher education can encounter regulatory challenges related to data privacy, security, and compliance with existing laws. Determining data ownership and control on a blockchain can be complex (Böhme 2015). Interjurisdictional compliance in case of BCT across borders is challenging (Tapscott & Tapscott 2016). Regulatory frameworks for blockchain are continuously evolving and institutions have to stay abreast of changes and adapt accordingly (Khan & Gani 2020). Implementing BCT involves the storage and sharing of personal student and staff data where the institution has to ensure compliance with data privacy regulations, such as the General Data Protection Regulation (GDPR) in Europe is essential (GDPR (2016). Universities have to ensure the legal recognition and enforcement of smart contracts comply with contract law for their use in educational contexts (De Filippi & Hassan2016). Navigating these regulatory challenges requires collaboration between educational institutions, legal experts, and policymakers. It's essential to strike a balance between the benefits of blockchain technology and compliance with existing laws and regulations
4. INFRASTRUCTURAL CHALLENGE: Implementing BCT in higher education can pose infrastructural challenges that institutions must navigate. There is a need for resource- intensive infrastructure so as to use Proof of Work(PoW) mechanisms. . Ensuring energy-efficient infrastructure is a challenge for sustainable blockchain adoption. (Schorsch & Scheuermann 2016). Another important resource for BCT is the necessity of high-speed internet connectivity to communicate effectively (Zohrevand & Bassett 2017). To ensure the reliability of blockchain networks, educational institutions must establish redundancy and fault-tolerant systems to prevent downtime in the event of node failures (Cachin &Vukolić 2017). Besides, operating blockchain nodes often requires data center facilities with appropriate environmental controls, power supplies, and physical security measures (Swan, 2015). The BCT infrastructure should protect from cyber threats by opting for robust security measures, including firewalls and intrusion detection systems (Zohrevand & Bassett, 2017).
5. TECHNOLOGICAL CHALLENGE: BCT challenges that institutions need to address involve issues related to scalability, interoperability, and the technical complexities of integrating blockchain with existing systems. Blockchain networks may struggle to handle the high volume of transactions and data generated in educational institutions. Scaling the network to accommodate increased load can be technically challenging (Gervais, et al 2016). Besides, many BCT consumes a significant amount of energy leading to higher carbon footprints (Gencer et al 2018). Integrating the existing data systems with BCT and selecting an appropriate consensus mechanism ensuring seamless interoperability between blockchain and legacy systems can be complex (Tarkoma 2018; Bano. et al. 2017). Students and administrators need user-friendly BCT interfaces and applications to overcome usability challenges (Conoscenti, et al. 2016; Zhang, et al 2018). Addressing these technological challenges involves a combination of careful planning, selecting the appropriate blockchain platform, and collaborating with experts in blockchain technology. Solutions must be tailored to the specific needs and goals of the educational institution.

DISCUSSION

This paper provides a comprehensive overview of the current understanding about the possibilities, advantages, and obstacles associated with the implementation of blockchain technology in the context of higher education. The outcomes of the in-depth analysis emphasize the significance of blockchain technology in the realm of academia. The results of the systematic literature review (SLR) study suggest that blockchain technology holds promise in revolutionizing educational supply chains and addressing certain challenges prevalent in the higher education sector. The implementation of blockchain technology has the potential to enhance the traceability of documents and expedite the process of ascertaining their provenance. The eradication of concerns pertaining to forgery, fraud, or other infractions of academic documents is a pressing matter. Blockchain technology offers comprehensive product traceability, enabling the monitoring of educational sector goods throughout the entirety of the education supply chain. The study reveals that several key factors, namely security, trustworthiness, traceability, transparency, decentralized databases, provenance, and ethereum, play a crucial role in facilitating the widespread acceptance and use of blockchain technology. The findings of our study also examine the advantages of blockchain technology (BCT) and its potential to improve the quality of education, provide safety and data security, foster trust and collaboration, enhance performance, and promote sustainability in many activities. The findings also demonstrate the potential of blockchain technology in facilitating collaborative efforts within the realm of higher education. The implementation of blockchain technology facilitates enhanced collaboration and productivity among various stakeholders within the higher education sector. The results of our study indicate that implementing this approach has the potential to enhance the efficiency and long-term viability of educational supply chains. The present study posited a theoretical framework for the implementation of behavior change techniques (BCTs) within the context of higher education. This framework incorporates the various potentials, enablers, and obstacles associated with the adoption of behavior change techniques (BCTs). The framework can also be utilized to conduct further investigation into the adoption of blockchain technology in various industry contexts, with the aim of comprehending the effects and benefits of implementing blockchain.

LIMITATION

While this analysis offers insights into the adoption of Blockchain technology in higher education, it is important to acknowledge several limitations that need to be considered for future research. Primarily, this review is focused on the realm of higher education. Furthermore, the inclusion criteria employed in this study were limited to a select few peer-reviewed publications and conference proceedings. The results of our study indicate a scarcity of scholarly articles in the existing body of literature. Consequently, the authors suggest the inclusion of white papers, reports, journals, and newspapers as a means to prevent the omission of accessible information. Furthermore, our analysis has indicated a dearth of published articles pertaining to the implementation of blockchain technology.

CONCLUSION

This chapter contributes to the existing literature by providing a comprehensive examination of the potential enablers and challenges in adopting blockchain-enabled supply chain management in the educational sector. The management in higher education systems faces problems in integrating a new system due to lack of resources, resistance to change by personnel and other stakeholders, compliance to regulatory matters, governance issues, data privacy concerns and infrastructural bottlenecks. This chapter will provide an invaluable guide for researchers, practitioners, and decision-makers who are interested in gaining a knowledge of the managerial views and implications of blockchain technology within the context of higher education. This chapter provides a comprehensive introduction to the Behaviour Change Technique (BCT) and offers specific insights into its application within the field of education. The utilization of BCT projects in the field of education was explained, with a focus on delineating the key concepts that hold significance for prospective practical implementations.

REFERENCES

Aditya, U. S., Singh, R., Singh, P. K., & Kalla, A. (2021). A survey on blockchain in robotics: Issues, opportunities, challenges and future directions. *Journal of Network and Computer Applications, 196*, 103245. doi:10.1016/j.jnca.2021.103245

Albeanu, G. (2017, October). Blockchain technology and education. In *The 12th International Conference on Virtual Learning ICVL* (pp. 271-275).

Ali, S. I. M., Farouk, H., & Sharaf, H. (2022). A blockchain-based models for student information systems. *Egyptian Informatics Journal, 23*(2), 187–196. doi:10.1016/j.eij.2021.12.002

Alsobhi, H. A., Alakhtar, R. A., Ubaid, A., Hussain, O. K., & Hussain, F. K. (2023). Blockchain-based micro-credentialing system in higher education institutions: Systematic literature review. *Knowledge-Based Systems, 265*, 110238. doi:10.1016/j.knosys.2022.110238

Amaral, V. (2020). Blockchain for the Internet of Things: Current and Future Trends. *In Handbook of Research on Emerging Perspectives in Intelligent Pattern Recognition, Analysis, and Data Mining*. (32-48). IGI Global. https://aws.amazon.com/marketplace/

Arndt, T. (2019). An Overview of Blockchain for Higher Education. *KMIS*, 231-235.

Arndt, T., & Guercio, A. (2020). Blockchain-based transcripts for mobile higher-education. *International Journal of Information and Education Technology (IJIET), 10*(2), 84–89. doi:10.18178/ijiet.2020.10.2.1344

Babu, E. S., Srinivasarao, B. K. N., Kavati, I., & Rao, M. S. (2022). Verifiable authentication and issuance of academic certificates using permissioned blockchain network. [IJISP]. *International Journal of Information Security and Privacy, 16*(1), 1–24. doi:10.4018/ijisp.2022010107

Baden, R., Bender, A., Spring, N., Bhattacharjee, B., & Starin, D. (2009, August). Persona: an online social network with user-defined privacy. In *Proceedings of the ACM SIGCOMM 2009 conference on Data communication* (pp. 135-146). ACM. 10.1145/1592568.1592585

Bano, S., Sonnino, A., Al-Bassam, M., Azouvi, S., McCorry, P., Meiklejohn, S., & Danezis, G. (2017). Consensus in the age of blockchains. *arXiv preprint arXiv:1711.03936.*

Baviskar, D., Ahirrao, S., Potdar, V., & Kotecha, K. (2021). Efficient automated processing of the unstructured documents using artificial intelligence: A systematic literature review and future directions. *IEEE Access : Practical Innovations, Open Solutions*, *9*, 72894–72936. doi:10.1109/ACCESS.2021.3072900

Bhatia, R., & Bhasin, N. K. (2023). A Study of the New Role of Blockchain in the Indian Education System. [IJeC]. *International Journal of e-Collaboration*, *19*(1), 1–19. doi:10.4018/IJeC.315784

Böhme, R., Christin, N., Edelman, B., & Moore, T. (2015). Bitcoin: Economics, technology, and governance. *The Journal of Economic Perspectives*, *29*(2), 213–238. doi:10.1257/jep.29.2.213

Brody, P., Pureswaran, V., Panikkar, S., & Nair, S. (2015). Empowering the edge Practical insights on a decentralized Internet of Things. *IBM Institute for Business Value. Technical Report.* IBM.

Brown, B., Chui, M., & Manyika, J. (2011). Are you ready for the era of 'big data'. *The McKinsey Quarterly*, *4*(1), 24–35.

Buterin, V. (2014). A next-generation smart contract and decentralized application platform. *white paper, 3*(37), 2-1.

Cachin, C., & Vukolic, M. (2017). Blockchain Consensus Protocols in the Wild. preprint. *arXiv preprint arXiv:1707.01873.*

Caldarelli, G., & Ellul, J. (2021). Trusted academic transcripts on the blockchain: A systematic literature review. *Applied Sciences (Basel, Switzerland)*, *11*(4), 1842. doi:10.3390/app11041842

Calvera Isabal, M., Santos, P., Hoppe, H., & Schulten, C. (2023). Cómo automatizar la extracción y análisis de información sobre ciencia ciudadana con propósitos educativos. *Comunicar.*, *31*(74), 13.

Cameron, L. (2020). *The rise of algorithmic work: Implications for organizational control and worker autonomy* [Doctoral dissertation, University of Michigan].

Chen, G., Xu, B., Lu, M., & Chen, N. S. (2018). Exploring blockchain technology and its potential applications for education. *Smart Learning Environments*, *5*(1), 1–10. doi:10.118640561-017-0050-x

Chen, X., Xu, X., & Hsing, P. (2020). Intellectual Property Protection in Blockchain-based Education. In *2020 IEEE International Conference on Blockchain and Cryptocurrency (ICBC)* (pp. 263-268). IEEE.

Chukowry, V., Nanuck, G., & Sungkur, R. K. (2021). The future of continuous learning–Digital badge and microcredential system using blockchain. *Global Transitions Proceedings*, *2*(2), 355–361. doi:10.1016/j.gltp.2021.08.026

Conoscenti, M., Vetro, A., & De Martin, J. C. (2016, November). Blockchain for the Internet of Things: A systematic literature review. In *2016 IEEE/ACS 13th International Conference of Computer Systems and Applications (AICCSA)* (pp. 1-6). IEEE. 10.1109/AICCSA.2016.7945805

David, L., & Courtois, N. T. (2018). Blockchain-based degree fraud detection and prevention in higher education. *IEEE Access : Practical Innovations, Open Solutions*, *6*, 43011–43024.

De Filippi, P., & Hassan, S. (2018). Blockchain technology as a regulatory technology: From code is law to law is code. *arXiv preprint arXiv:1801.02507.*

Delgado-von-Eitzen, C., Anido-Rifón, L., & Fernández-Iglesias, M. J. (2021). Blockchain applications in education: A systematic literature review. *Applied Sciences (Basel, Switzerland)*, *11*(24), 11811. doi:10.3390/app112411811

Demir, I., & Karabatak, M. (2019). Digital diplomas in higher education and blockchain technology. *Contemporary Educational Technology*, *10*(3), 298–312.

Dillahunt, T. R., Park, J. H., & Kim, H. W. (2020). Exploring Asset Management through Blockchain in Higher Education. In *Proceedings of the 2020 CHI Conference on Human Factors in Computing Systems* (pp. 1-14). IEEE.

Dorri, A., Kanhere, S. S., Jurdak, R., & Gauravaram, P. (2017, March). *Blockchain for IoT security and privacy: The case study of a smart home. In 2017 IEEE international conference on pervasive computing and communications workshops (PerCom workshops).* IEEE.

Dudhat, A., Santoso, N. P. L., Santoso, S., & Setiawati, R. (2021). Blockchain in Indonesia University: A Design Viewboard of Digital Technology Education. [ATT]. *Aptisi Transactions on Technopreneurship*, *3*(1), 68–80. doi:10.34306/att.v3i1.146

Dunphy, P., & Petitcolas, F. A. P. (2018). A first look at identity management schemes on the blockchain. *IEEE Security and Privacy*, *16*(4), 20–29. doi:10.1109/MSP.2018.3111247

Duwadi, N. (2021). A Systematic Review on Blockchain in Education: Opportunities and Challenges. *Nepalese Journal of Management Science and Research, 4.*

Edastama, P., Purnama, S., Widayanti, R., Meria, L., & Rivelino, D. (2021). The potential blockchain technology in higher education learning innovations in era 4.0. *Blockchain Frontier Technology*, *1*(01), 104–113. doi:10.34306/bfront.v1i01.18

Fang, B. (2022). Blockchain-Based Educational Management and Secure Software-Defined Networking in Smart Communities. [IJISP]. *International Journal of Information Security and Privacy*, *16*(2), 1–20. doi:10.4018/IJISP.308314

Fedorova, E. P., & Skobleva, E. I. (2020). Application of blockchain technology in higher education. *European Journal of Contemporary Education*, *9*(3), 552–571.

Flores-Vivar, J. M., & García-Peñalvo, F. J. (2023). Reflexiones sobre la ética, potencialidades y retos de la Inteligencia Artificial en el marco de la Educación de Calidad (ODS4). *Comunicar*, *31*(74). doi:10.3916/C74-2023-03

Galvez, J. F. (2020). Towards the enhancement of security and efficiency in academic credentials verification using blockchain technology. *International Journal of Advanced Science and Technology*, *29*(5), 13329–13337.

Gandhi, S., Kiwelekar, A., Netak, L., & Shahare, S. (2023). A blockchain-based data-driven trustworthy approval process system. *International Journal of Information Management Data Insights*, *3*(1), 100162. doi:10.1016/j.jjimei.2023.100162

Gencer, A. E., Basu, S., & Eyal, I. (2018). Decentralization in bitcoin and ethereum networks. In Proceedings of the 2018 IFIP Networking Conference (IFIP Networking) and Workshops. 10.1007/978-3-662-58387-6_24

Gervais, A., Karame, G. O., Wüst, K., Glykantzis, V., Ritzdorf, H., & Capkun, S. (2016, October). On the security and performance of proof of work blockchains. In *Proceedings of the 2016 ACM SIGSAC conference on computer and communications security* (pp. 3-16). ACM. 10.1145/2976749.2978341

Ghouri, A., Akhtar, P., Venkatesh, V. G., Ashraf, A., Arsenyan, G., Tarba, S. Y., & Khan, Z. (2023). Enhancing supply chain innovation and operational agility through knowledge acquisition from the social media: A microfoundational approach. *IEEE Transactions on Engineering Management*, 1–15. doi:10.1109/TEM.2023.3316119

Gräther, W., Kolvenbach, S., Ruland, R., Schütte, J., Torres, C., & Wendland, F. (2018). *Blockchain for education: lifelong learning passport.*

Guerreiro, S., Ferreira, J. F., Fonseca, T., & Correia, M. (2022). Integrating an academic management system with blockchain: A case study. *Blockchain: Research and Applications*, *3*(4), 100099.

Gupta, N. K., Yadav, A. K., & Jain, A. (2021). Using Blockchain for Digital Copyrights Management. In *Blockchain for Information Security and Privacy* (pp. 377–399). Auerbach Publications. doi:10.1201/9781003129486-18

Han, M., Li, Z., He, J., Wu, D., Xie, Y., & Baba, A. (2018, September). A novel blockchain-based education records verification solution. In *Proceedings of the 19th annual SIG conference on information technology education* (pp. 178-183). ACM. 10.1145/3241815.3241870

Härting, R. C., Sprengel, A., Wottle, K., & Rettenmaier, J. (2020). Potentials of blockchain technologies in supply chain management-A conceptual model. *Procedia Computer Science*, *176*, 1950–1959. doi:10.1016/j.procs.2020.09.334

Hofmann, E., & Rüsch, M. (2017). Industry 4.0 and the current status as well as future prospects on logistics. *Computers in Industry*, *89*, 23–34. doi:10.1016/j.compind.2017.04.002

Iansiti, M., & Lakhani, K. R. (2017). The truth about blockchain. *Harvard Business Review*, *95*(1), 118–127.

Inam, R., Hata, A. Y., Prifti, V., & Asadollah, S. A. (2022). A Comprehensive Study on Artificial Intelligence Algorithms to Implement Safety Using Communication Technologies. *arXiv preprint arXiv:2205.08404.*

Iyer, D., & Kemp, J. (2019). Blockchain in global supply chains: Exploring the challenges, opportunities, and future prospects. *Transportation Research Part E, Logistics and Transportation Review*, *125*, 100815.

Iyer, S. S., Seetharaman, A., & Ranjan, B. (2021). Researching Blockchain Technology and its Usefulness in Higher Education. *Machine Learning, IOT and Blockchain Technologies & Trends*, 27-48.

Khan, I. A., & Gani, A. (2020). Blockchain technology: A review on applications and security privacy. *IEEE Access : Practical Innovations, Open Solutions*, *8*, 41106–41124.

Khan, M. A., & Salah, K. (2018). IoT security: Review, blockchain solutions, and open challenges. *Future Generation Computer Systems, 82*, 395–411. doi:10.1016/j.future.2017.11.022

Khan, S., Haleem, A., Husain, Z., Samson, D., & Pathak, R. D. (2023). Barriers to blockchain technology adoption in supply chains: the case of India. *Operations Management Research*, 1-16.

Khedekar, P. (2018). *Blockchain and higher education: From credentials to learning data.* Research Report, Tyton Partners.

Kim, J., & Laskowski, M. (2019). Towards an ontology for blockchain-based supply chain provenance. *Sustainability, 11*(17), 4649.

Kosmarski, A. (2020). Blockchain adoption in academia: Promises and challenges. *Journal of Open Innovation, 6*(4), 117. doi:10.3390/joitmc6040117

Krzysztofek, M. (2018). *GDPR: General Data Protection Regulation (EU) 2016/679: Post-reform Personal Data Protection in the European Union.* Kluwer Law International BV.

Kshetri, N. (2017). Can blockchain strengthen the internet of things? *IT Professional, 19*(4), 68–72. doi:10.1109/MITP.2017.3051335

Kumar, N., Singh, M., Upreti, K., & Mohan, D. (2022). Blockchain adoption intention in higher education: role of trust, perceived security and privacy in technology adoption model. In *Proceedings of International Conference on Emerging Technologies and Intelligent Systems: ICETIS 2021* (Volume 1) (pp. 303-313). Springer International Publishing.

Kumar, R., & Jain, V. (2023). *Convergence of IoT*. Blockchain, and Computational Intelligence in Smart Cities.

Lacity, M., Beck, R., & Böhmann, T. (2019). Blockchain and the future of supply chain transparency in the education sector. *Communications of the Association for Information Systems, 45*, 22–30.

Lakkala, M., Suoranta, J., & Teräs, H. (2019). Blockchain for education: A review. Technology. *Knowledge and Learning, 24*(3), 487–504.

Lamport, L. (1998). The part-time parliament. [TOCS]. *ACM Transactions on Computer Systems, 16*(2), 133–169. doi:10.1145/279227.279229

Li, S., Jiang, P., Wang, X., & Zhang, L. (2018). An Overview of Blockchain Technology: Architecture, Consensus, and Future Trends. In *2018 IEEE International Congress on Big Data (BigData Congress)* (pp. 557-564). IEEE.

Li, Z. (2017). A blockchain based new secure multi-layer network model for internet of things. *IEEE Access : Practical Innovations, Open Solutions, 5*, 5585–5593.

Litoussi, M., Fartitchou, M., El Makkaoui, K., Ezzati, A., & El Allali, Z. (2022). Digital Certifications in Moroccan Universities: Concepts, Challenges, and Solutions. *Procedia Computer Science, 201*, 95–100. doi:10.1016/j.procs.2022.03.015

Liu, Y., Wang, Z., & Zhu, J. (2019). Blockchain-based digital identity management systems in higher education. In *2019 IEEE/RSJ International Conference on Intelligent Robots and Systems (IROS)* (pp. 5677-5684). IEEE.

Loddo, A., Meloni, G., & Pes, B. (2022). Using Artificial Intelligence for COVID-19 Detection in Blood Exams: A Comparative Analysis. *IEEE Access : Practical Innovations, Open Solutions, 10*, 119593–119606. doi:10.1109/ACCESS.2022.3221750

Lu, Y. (2018). Blockchain and the related issues: A review of current research topics. *Journal of Management Analytics, 5*(4), 231–255. doi:10.1080/23270012.2018.1516523

Maestre, R. J., Bermejo Higuera, J., Gámez Gómez, N., Bermejo Higuera, J. R., Sicilia Montalvo, J. A., & Orcos Palma, L. (2023). The application of blockchain algorithms to the management of education certificates. *Evolutionary Intelligence, 16*(6), 1967–1984. doi:10.100712065-022-00812-0 PMID:36597508

Manogaran, G., & Lopez, D. (2017). A survey of big data architectures and machine learning algorithms in healthcare. *International Journal of Biomedical Engineering and Technology, 25*(2-4), 182–211. doi:10.1504/IJBET.2017.087722

Mavridis, N., & Stavropoulos, P. (2019). On the integration of blockchain in education and its impact on the job market: A survey. *Telematics and Informatics, 42*, 1012–1019.

Meiklejohn, S., Pomarole, M., Jordan, G., Levchenko, K., McCoy, D., Voelker, G. M., & Savage, S. (2013, October). A fistful of bitcoins: characterizing payments among men with no names. In *Proceedings of the 2013 conference on Internet measurement conference* (pp. 127-140). ACM. 10.1145/2504730.2504747

Mendling, J. (2010). Foundations of business process modeling. In Business Information Systems: Concepts, Methodologies, Tools and Applications (pp. 6-41). IGI Global. doi:10.4018/978-1-61520-969-9.ch002

Mihalcea, R., & Ceaușu, S. I. (2017). The Impact of Blockchain Technology on the Supply Chain. *Procedia Engineering, 181*, 1218–1223.

Mishra, R. A., Kalla, A., Braeken, A., & Liyanage, M. (2021). Privacy protected blockchain based architecture and implementation for sharing of students' credentials. *Information Processing & Management, 58*(3), 102512. doi:10.1016/j.ipm.2021.102512

Mohammad, A., & Vargas, S. (2022). Challenges of Using Blockchain in the Education Sector: A Literature Review. *Applied Sciences (Basel, Switzerland), 12*(13), 6380. doi:10.3390/app12136380

(2023). Mohammed.A., PotdarV, Mohammed And Wendy Hui (2023). Blockchain Adoption in Food Supply Chains: A Systematic Literature Review on Enablers, Benefits, and Barriers. *IEEE Access : Practical Innovations, Open Solutions, 11*, 14366–14355.

Mokhberi, A. (2023). *Towards understanding trust, privacy, and safety management among Facebook Marketplace users* [Doctoral dissertation, University of British Columbia].

Monostori, L., Kádár, B., Bauernhansl, T., Kondoh, S., Kumara, S., Reinhart, G., Sauer, O., Schuh, G., Sihn, W., & Ueda, K. (2016). Cyber-physical systems in manufacturing. *CIRP Annals, 65*(2), 621–641. doi:10.1016/j.cirp.2016.06.005

Mougayar, W. (2016). *The business blockchain: promise, practice, and application of the next Internet technology*. John Wiley & Sons.

Mourtzis, D., Angelopoulos, J., & Panopoulos, N. (2023). Metaverse and blockchain in education for collaborative product-service system (PSS) design towards University 5.0. *Procedia CIRP*, *119*, 456–461. doi:10.1016/j.procir.2023.01.008

Moxham, N., & Boon, E. (2019). Blockchain in higher education: Possibilities for co-created research and the common good. *Open Review of Educational Research*, *6*(1), 94–112.

Nakamoto, S. (2008). Bitcoin: A peer-to-peer electronic cash system. *Decentralized business review*.

Narváez, M. H., Carrasquilla-Díaz, L., De Luque-Pisciotti, A., Guarin, A. F., Barrios, T. A., & Gallego-Nicholls, J. F. (2022). Legal challenges for Blockchain implementation in Colombia. *Procedia Computer Science*, *210*, 323–327. doi:10.1016/j.procs.2022.10.158

Nousias, N., Tsakalidis, G., Michoulis, G., Petridou, S., & Vergidis, K. (2022). A process-aware approach for blockchain-based verification of academic qualifications. *Simulation Modelling Practice and Theory*, *121*, 102642. doi:10.1016/j.simpat.2022.102642

Ofori-Mensah, J., Yaokumah, W., & Sakyi, E. A. (2022). Design of Authenticated and Trusted Academic Certification Using Blockchain Technology. [IJSI]. *International Journal of Software Innovation*, *10*(1), 1–19. doi:10.4018/IJSI.303580

Oğhan, V. (2022). Environmental policies for green cryptocurrency mining. In *Handbook of research on challenges in public economics in the era of globalization* (pp. 217–227). IGI Global. doi:10.4018/978-1-7998-9083-6.ch013

Pani, S. K., Chatterjee, R., & Mahapatra, N. R. (2019). Towards Trusted, Transparent and Motivational Professional Education System Through Blockchain. [IJISSC]. *International Journal of Information Systems and Social Change*, *10*(2), 62–73. doi:10.4018/IJISSC.2019040105

Pardo, A., & Siemens, G. (2014). Ethical and privacy principles for learning analytics. *British Journal of Educational Technology*, *45*(3), 438–450. doi:10.1111/bjet.12152

Park, J. (2021). Promises and challenges of Blockchain in education. *Smart Learning Environments*, *8*(1), 1–13. doi:10.118640561-021-00179-2

Pawlak, M., Guziur, J., & Poniszewska-Marańda, A. (2019). Voting process with blockchain technology: auditable blockchain voting system. In *Advances in Intelligent Networking and Collaborative Systems: The 10th International Conference on Intelligent Networking and Collaborative Systems (INCoS-2018)* (pp. 233-244). Springer International Publishing. 10.1007/978-3-319-98557-2_21

Pu, S., & Lam, J. S. L. (2023). The benefits of blockchain for digital certificates: A multiple case study analysis. *Technology in Society*, *72*, 102176. doi:10.1016/j.techsoc.2022.102176

Pulmano, C. E., Estuar, M. R. J. E., De Leon, M. M., Tan, H. C. L., Co, N. A. S., & Tamayo, L. P. V. (2023). Towards the Development of a Blockchain-based Decentralized Digital Credential System using Hyperledger Fabric for Participatory Governance. *Procedia Computer Science*, *219*, 99-106.

Ramya, U., Sindhuja, P., Atsaya, R., Dharani, B. B., & Golla, S. M. V. (2018). Reducing forgery in land registry system using blockchain technology. *Proc. Int. Conf. Adv. Informat. Comput. Res.* Berlin, Germany: Springer.

Rizzi, A., Caballini, C., Cagno, E., & Boer, H. (2018). Blockchain for supply chain finance: Benefits and challenges. *Production Planning and Control*, *29*(15), 1265–1276.

Sahoo, S., Kumar, S., Sivarajah, U., Lim, W. M., Westland, J. C., & Kumar, A. (2022). Blockchain for sustainable supply chain management: Trends and ways forward. *Electronic Commerce Research*, 1–56. doi:10.100710660-022-09569-1

Samaniego, M., & Deters, R. (2016, November). Using blockchain to push software-defined IoT components onto edge hosts. In *Proceedings of the international conference on big data and advanced wireless technologies* (pp. 1-9). ACM. 10.1145/3010089.3016027

Shaoliu, D., & Tongbai, L. (2023). Ideological and Physical Education Integration in Higher Education: Strategies for Mental Health Education. *Journal of Sport Psychology*, *32*(4), 203–212.

Sheehan, B. (2017). A blockchain-based approach towards overcoming challenges in supply chain management. *International Journal of Advanced Manufacturing Technology*, *89*(9-12), 3657–3667.

Shen, D. (2021). Research on the sharing mode of educational information resources in colleges and universities based on the Blockchain and new energy. *Energy Reports*, *7*, 458–467. doi:10.1016/j.egyr.2021.10.016

Sicari, S., Rizzardi, A., Grieco, L. A., & Coen-Porisini, A. (2015). Security, privacy and trust in Internet of Things: The road ahead. *Computer Networks*, *76*, 146–164. doi:10.1016/j.comnet.2014.11.008

Sullivan, C., & Burger, E. (2017). E-residency and blockchain. *Computer Law & Security Report*, *33*(4), 470–481. doi:10.1016/j.clsr.2017.03.016

Suyambu, G. T., Anand, M., & Janakirani, M. (2020). Blockchain–A most disruptive technology on the spotlight of world engineering education paradigm. *Procedia Computer Science*, *172*, 152–158. doi:10.1016/j.procs.2020.05.023

Swan, M. (2015). *Blockchain: Blueprint for a new economy*. O'Reilly Media, Inc.

Swan, M., Bullock, J., & Alnuaimi, O. (2020). Blockchain in education: Strategies for decentralized, learner-owned records. *EDUCAUSE Review*, *55*(3), 16–26.

Szabo, N. (1997). Formalizing and securing relationships on public networks. *First Monday*, *2*(9). doi:10.5210/fm.v2i9.548

Tapscott, D., & Tapscott, A. (2016). *Blockchain revolution: how the technology behind bitcoin is changing money, business, and the world*. Penguin.

Tschorsch, F., & Scheuermann, B. (2016). Bitcoin and beyond: A technical survey on decentralized digital currencies. *IEEE Communications Surveys and Tutorials*, *18*(3), 2084–2123. doi:10.1109/COMST.2016.2535718

Turkanović, M., Hölbl, M., Košič, K., Heričko, M., & Kamišalić, A. (2018). EduCTX: A blockchain-based higher education credit platform. *IEEE Access : Practical Innovations, Open Solutions*, *6*, 5112–5127. doi:10.1109/ACCESS.2018.2789929

Vitale, M., & Mavridis, N. (2017). A survey of internet of things technologies for ambient assisted living environments. *Future Generation Computer Systems*, *76*, 855–869.

Vukolić, M. (2017). Rethinking permissioned blockchains. In *Proceedings of the ACM Workshop on Blockchain, Cryptocurrencies and Contracts* (pp. 3-7). ACM. 10.1145/3055518.3055526

Vytelingum, P., Ramchurn, S. D., Voice, T. D., Rogers, A., & Jennings, N. R. (2010). *Trading agents for the smart electricity grid.*

Wang, Y., Cong, X., Zi, L., & Xiang, Q. (2023). Blockchain for Credibility in Educational Development: Key Technology, Application Potential, and Performance Evaluation. *Security and Communication Networks*, *2023*, 2023. doi:10.1155/2023/5614241

Wang, Y., Sun, Q., & Bie, R. (2022). Blockchain-based secure sharing mechanism of online education data. *Procedia Computer Science*, *202*, 283–288. doi:10.1016/j.procs.2022.04.037

Xu, X., Weber, I., Staples, M., Zhu, L., Bosch, J., Bass, L., & Rimba, P. (2017, April). A taxonomy of blockchain-based systems for architecture design. In 2017 IEEE international conference on software architecture (ICSA) (pp. 243-252). IEEE. doi:10.1109/ICSA.2017.33

Yli-Huumo, J., Ko, D., Choi, S., Park, S., & Smolander, K. (2016). Where is current research on blockchain technology?—A systematic review. *PLoS One*, *11*(10), e0163477. doi:10.1371/journal.pone.0163477 PMID:27695049

Yue, X., Wang, H., Jin, D., Li, M., & Jiang, W. (2016). Healthcare data gateways: Found healthcare intelligence on blockchain with novel privacy risk control. *Journal of Medical Systems*, *40*(10), 1–8. doi:10.100710916-016-0574-6 PMID:27565509

Zhang, Y., Wen, Y., & Li, D. (2019). An IoT electric business model based on blockchain technology in the context of the smart grid. *IEEE Access : Practical Innovations, Open Solutions*, *7*, 67623–67633.

Zheng, Z. (2017). An overview of blockchain technology: Architecture, consensus, and future trends. *IEEE Access : Practical Innovations, Open Solutions*, *6*, 9245–9257.

Zheng, Z., Xie, S., Dai, H., Chen, X., & Wang, H. (2017, June). *An overview of blockchain technology: Architecture, consensus, and future trends. In 2017 IEEE international congress on big data (BigData congress)*. IEEE.

Zheng, Z., Xie, S., Dai, H., Chen, X., & Wang, H. (2017, June). *An overview of blockchain technology: Architecture, consensus, and future trends. In 2017 IEEE international congress on big data (BigData congress)*. IEEE.

Zheng, Z., Xie, S., Dai, H., Chen, X., & Wang, H. (2017, June). *An overview of blockchain technology: Architecture, consensus, and future trends. In 2017 IEEE international congress on big data (BigData congress)*. IEEE.

Chapter 13
Use of Blockchain Technologies for Developing Transparent, Efficient, and Resilient Public Sector Supply

Nabeel Mehboob
https://orcid.org/0009-0005-4710-4311
Iqra University, Pakistan

Mirza A. Haq
Iqra University, Pakistan

Muhammad Awais Bhatti
King Faisal University, Saudia Arabia

ABSTRACT

The wide array of functions performed by a state referred to as public sector is increasingly applying the practices of supply chain management. The public sector has special emphasis on the aspects of transparency, efficiency, and resilience as increased awareness among the citizens is forcing the states to provide better value to the taxpayer money. Use of information and communication technologies has been attributed to improve the visibility and efficiency in public sector. Blockchain technology, being an emerging disruptive technology providing immutable distributed ledgers, has strong theoretical application in public sector. Following a systematic literature review the research establishes that Blockchain technology enables transparency, efficiency, and resilience in the supply chain. As these enablers are key determinant of success in public sector supply chain, therefore existing research on application of blockchain technology in the sector are explored to identify the current standing of the research on the subject and propose future course.

DOI: 10.4018/979-8-3693-0482-2.ch013

1. INTRODUCTION

Supply chain management (SCM) has emerged as a discipline that answers to the needs of the competitive modern globalized economy. Private enterprises over the years have shown enhanced productivity with reduction in cost by employing SCM practices (Khan et al., 2017; Skipper et al., 2009). From demand forecasting to successful execution of contracts, SCM principles have transformed the enterprises from operational level methods to the strategic approach to management (Haq, Khan, Parkash & Jabeen, 2016; Chong et al., 2009). One of the key attribute of SCM is that being a transformational paradigm it is open to incorporation of digital technologies in its practices to reach the ultimate goal of improving process efficiency.

However, traditional supply chains struggle to keep pace with modern demands due to opaqueness, inefficiencies, and vulnerabilities to fraud. Recent research (Ghouri et al., 2023; Calvera Isabal et al., 2023; Flores-Vivar & García-Peñalvo, 2023; Shaoliu & Tongbai, 2023) highlights persistent challenges, particularly in building trust and transparency. This lack of trust acts as a major bottleneck, hindering optimal performance and creating opportunities for fraudulent activities (Khan et al., 2017; Haq, Khan, Parkash & Jabeen, 2016). Addressing these systemic issues head-on is not only crucial for improving efficiency, but also for ensuring the long-term viability of traditional supply chains in today's rapidly evolving world.

The current world order created on the premise of nation states holds the governments responsible for the economic and social growth and prosperity of their respective citizens. Therefore, the state has to create a system of providing services that ensures social, political and economic security (Fukuyama, 2012). These services are rendered in a wide array of state functions and the finances for these services are acquired through collection of taxes from the citizens who are in the modern democratic order are also selecting the state representatives. Resultantly, states are held accountable to their own citizen who are the creators of the state wealth and also the beneficiaries of the service. The globalization of trade and with the dawn of digital age, the prospects of creating a services ecosystem by the states that is efficient as well as transparent is very much possible.

The need of the states to create an optimum service ecosystem and SCM principles ability to create an efficient process powered by inclusion of digital technologies implies that public sector can be a major benefactor from adoption of technology driven SCM practices. However, research indicates that public sector has been slow in adopting supply chain framework and have been looking towards private sector for duplication of process innovations (Gianakis & McCue, 2012). Considering its uniqueness in terms of its financial volume, socio-economic impact and compulsion of process transparency, it is imperative for the public sector to be self-innovative in transforming its process and include the new information communication technologies such as Blockchain technologies to improve its efficiency.

This section of the research will elaborate the scope of public sector and will create a rationale about how supply chain management principles are an important contributor to the successful execution of government functions. Later in the section the significance of factors such as transparency, efficiency and resilience in public sector will be touched upon followed by discussion on how ICT helps in improvement of Supply Chain Functions along with brief overview of Blockchain Technologies.

1.1 State Functions and Use of Supply Chain Management in Public Sector

According to the Classification of the Functions of Government (United Nations, 2000) published by United Nation Statistical Division (UNSD) and developed by Organization of Economic Cooperation and Development (OECD), the objectives of the state are classified into ten divisions that include (i) General Public Service, (ii) Defence, (iii) Public Order and Safety, (iv) Economic Affairs, (v) Environmental Protection, (vi) Housing and Community Amenities, (vii) Health, (viii) Recreation, Culture and Religion, (ix) Education and (x) Social Protection (*COFOG*, 2019). An important consideration is that the level and extent of involvement of a state in fulfilling these functions is not universal and depends upon state's economic orientation. As an example, in a free market economy like the USA functions of Health and Higher Education are privatized whereas in many states in European these facilitates are provided through state owned infrastructure. Nevertheless, some state functions are universally owned by the states such as Defence, Public Order and Safety. Irrespective of the position of a particular state on the spectrum of free market economy and socialist economic standpoint, each state is responsible to provide aforementioned services to the citizens of the state to varying extents (Acemoglu & Robinson, 2012; Fukuyama, 2015). These complex and diverse responsibilities of the state require them to maintain workforce, develop infrastructure and procure resources to perform these functions with utmost emphasis on transparency in their conduct as the source of funds is the tax money collected from the public. Literature suggest that the range of services catered for by the public sector create a heterogeneous mix and always have contextual associations posing challenges for the states to adopt an array of management principles for good governance (Hodgkinson et al., 2017). Issues such as state structure, social conflicts, economic crises, armed conflicts that can be internal or external with added layer of geographic and demographic constraints pose challenges to the governments to ensure the uninterrupted and efficient supply of these services by the government (Sienkiewicz-Małyjurek & Szymczak, 2023).

Increased research combining the fields of public sector and supply chain management (SCM) indicates that principles of SCM are applied to address the problems of complexity and efficiency in the public sector. Stentoft Arlbjørn et al. (2011) in the context of municipality services in Denmark have used the principle of Lean SCM to analyze the impact of lean philosophy on the public sector, the study finds that use of these principles results in improvement of effectiveness by cost reduction and enhancement of services. Addressing the supply chain performance management in public sector, Callender (2011) finds that multiple political and administrative challenges are faced by political actors and public sector managers in achieving optimum supply chain performance due to lack of inter-agency alignment of supply chains in public sector. In an empirical study proposing use of SCM principles in Emergency Management, Peterson et al. (2016) have identified different drivers that may influence the implementation of Supply Chain Operations Reference. Similar studies on the subject of humanitarian relief during crises use different principles of SCM to address the challenges and propose improvement in the response by applying principles of lean and agile supply chains (Pillitteri et al., 2021; Scholten et al., 2010; Shafiq & Soratana, 2019, 2020). Application of SCM practices in healthcare sector has also been a major area of research, especially after the supply chain disruptions faced during COVID-19 pandemic, many researches have focused on implementing supply chain resilience principles to formulate resilient healthcare services (Atkinson et al., 2020; Hossain et al., 2022; Phillips et al., 2023).

1.2 Why Transparency, Efficiency, and Resilience in Public Sector?

Tenet of transparency in the conduct of state affairs is central to maintain the balance between a powerful state and its society, who counter each other to maintain the heading of the state in the narrow corridor of progress and prosperity. The idea has been theorized by Acemoglu & Robinson (2019) in their book, where a state and society balances each other to create a "shackled leviathan" which is powerful enough to enforce its writ, yet answerable to the society by ensuring openness and transparency in the state functions. In the context of public sector transparency is defined as "the extent to which a public organization allows external actors to monitor and assess the internal working and performance"(S. G. Grimmelikhuijsen & Meijer, 2014). Transparency is regarded as a key determinant for increasing trust in the government, state legitimacy and to reduce corruption (S. Grimmelikhuijsen et al., 2017). Scholars indicate that transparency is important for democratic accountability, where the power vested in the office holders is kept in check by access to information about political, administrative and financial decision making by the state apparatus (Florini, 2007; Roberts, 2006). In case of developing and underdeveloped countries other important stakeholder who demand transparency in conduct of public functions are the international lenders as they keep particular insight into the areas of spending and methods adopted to ensure transparent functioning of states. In modern world transparency has taken the status of "quasi-religion" (Hood & Heald, 2006) and has been an important part of political vocabulary (Coglianese, 2009). Research has shown that transparency in the conduct of public sector has improved the judicial legitimacy and has given social benefits to public at large (S. Grimmelikhuijsen et al., 2017).

With increase in access to information and transparency in the public spending, the governments are expected to improve their performance by efficient use of public money (Heller, 2003). Hence, efficiency in the use of public resources has emerged as a key agenda in the political spheres (Joumard et al., 2004). Providing more public service with less public spending is an ongoing challenge for many governments across the globe especially in the OECD member countries (Curristine et al., 2007). Considerable volume of public financial resources collected through taxation are spent on the development and upkeep of state functions therefore, increased focus is laid upon the states to be more efficient in terms of financial management and time taken in delivery of services (Afonso et al., 2010). Inefficient public sector results in dissatisfied public at large due to stratified services based on class or poor service quality resulting in public unrest (Acemoglu & Robinson, 2012). Another important drawback of inefficacy is the macroeconomic challenges which emerge in the shape of increased fiscal deficits that gravely affect the economic health of a state (Heller, 2003).

The term resilience is used in different fields of social sciences and its common definition is "the ability of an entity or a system to return to a state of equilibrium after temporary disruptions" (Simmie & Martin, 2010). In the field of Supply Chain the term resilience is referred to as the capability developed in a supply chain to mitigate in timely manner any unforeseen internal or external disruptions and restoring the original position of operations as before the disruption occurred (Ponomarov & Holcomb, 2009). The external disruptions are often unavoidable and exist in the shape of natural calamities as well as man-made disasters such as terrorist attacks, global armed conflicts, cyber-attacks and economic problems (Shekarian & Mellat Parast, 2021). The internal disruptions are related to supply-demand disparities due to bullwhip effect, changes in specification of product, ICT breakdowns, equipment failures and power breakdown (Karl et al., 2018). Since all the sectors are prone to supply chain disruptions in the modern globalized interconnected world therefore, public sector is also not an exception and due to uncontrollable external disruptions, the risk of disruptions can be reduced but cannot be eliminated completely (Barroso et al., 2015). Creating resilient public sector supply chains is critical for the states to continuously provide the important functions of defense, public order, healthcare, disaster management and general public service (Ambe & Badenhorst-Weiss, 2011).

1.3 Use of ICT in Public Sector Supply Chain to Improve Transparency, Efficiency, and Resilience

Ever since the emergence of Internet, the use of it in the improvement of public sector has been widely researched. Since 1990s researchers and practitioners in the developed countries have emphasized the use of internet technologies to revitalize and reinvent the public sector to improve its performance (Osborne, 1993). With improvement in ICT and its access to public at large, use of internet to improve transparency in the public sector has been proposed as early as 2002 by (McIvor et al., 2002). As transparency is relished as a "quasi-religion" (Hood & Heald, 2006) recent researches have provided empirical evidence of improvement in transparency with use of ICT (S. Grimmelikhuijsen et al., 2017). In their research Sienkiewicz-Małyjurek & Szymczak (2023) propose that digital technologies can be used as a tool to help public sector managers to address the problems faced in communication and coordination throughout their supply chains hence improving the efficiency of public sector. In an empirical analysis Wang et al. (2022) has explored the process through which use of internet technologies has positively affected the public sector supply efficiency. Research also suggests that technology advancements must be evaluated for the prospects of their usefulness in enhancing the Supply Chain Resilience against internal and external disruptions (Barroso et al., 2015; Bayramova et al., 2021; Shekarian & Mellat Parast, 2021).

1.4 Blockchain Technology: An Overview

Blockchain technology fundamentally provides an open distributed ledger to all users (technically called nodes) to view or update information depending upon the consensus model for recognition of alteration to any information by any user. One particular set of transaction is stored in a Block and each transaction is preceded with next transaction stored in new Block that is connected with the previous Block hence creating a chain of blocks giving it the name "Blockchain". The aspect of transparency and validity is ensured by "immutability" of the data in the Blockchain. As every block of information is connected to a chain and contains the information of the previous block therefore, any change of information in the previous block will affect the succeeding blocks making the change traceable and visible to all the nodes. In conventional databases the information was stored in the servers and if desired by the system administrators the information was changed at the backend with no intimation to the users however, in case of Blockchains such changes are observable. In every block the information is secured through cryptographic hashing and since each block is linked with its subsequent block in a chain therefore any change (that is highly unlikely due to hashing) will be observable and traceable for all nodes resulting in an immutable distributed ledger. Blockchain Technology creates an ecosystem in which all stakeholders can maintain transparent and efficient record of any set of transaction (Yaga et al., 2018).

Decentralized, transparent, immutability, irreversible, autonomy, open source, anonymity, ownership and uniqueness, source, contract automation are the significant attributes of Blockchain technology, due to which it is finding wide application in different sectors. (Yontar, 2023).

Literature cited above suggest that the functions of the state referred as Public Sector has witnessed an increased use of Supply Chain Management practices and the requirements of maintaining transparency, efficiency and resilience are very significant for the Public Sector to create public trust and value. Furthermore, the use of ICT has been attributed to improve transparency, efficiency and resilience of public sector supply chain and application of new technologies should be explored to further improve the sector. In this context, use of Blockchain technologies that has emerged in recent years as a major breakthrough in the ICT field needs to be explored in the framework of Public Sector Supply Chains.

As both Blockchain Technologies and Public Sector Supply Chains are emerging fields therefore, the research merits to explore the frontiers where Blockchain Technologies can assist Public Sector Supply Chains to improve transparency, efficiency and resilience. The paper will be focused on the research questions that:

Q1. How application of Blockchain Technology in Supply Chain Management can achieve better transparency, efficiency and resilience? And
Q2. How Public Sector Supply Chains can benefit from adoption of Blockchain Technologies to ensure better transparency, efficiency and resilience?

The research will help in finding current trends in the field of Blockchain Technology and its application in Supply Chain Management and to identify potential use in Public Sector by replicating from the experience in different domains of supply chain management. The research will help future researchers and practitioners in both the fields to find new avenues for future collaboration. Public Policy makers can also benefit from the research as it can help them understand the operability of Blockchain Technology in Public Sector and its associated benefits in Public Sector Supply Chain

2. METHODOLOGY

The research carries out a systematic literature review of the existing research in the field of Blockchain combined with Supply Chain Management. Following the steps of Systematic Literature Review formulated by Tsafnat et al. (2014), articles on the subject in the past three years were searched in the SCOPUS database as it is considered as the most reliable and comprehensive database for peer reviewed Journals. With the Title Key of "Blockchain" OR "Blockchain Technology" OR "Distributed Ledger" OR "Smart Contracts" AND "Supply Chain" OR "Supply Chain Management". The Source and Document Type was restricted to "Journals" and "Articles" respectively to attain only scientific enquiries on the subject. Language was restricted to "English" due to comprehension limitations of the author in case of other languages. Subject Area was applied with keywords of "Public Sector" OR "Government" OR "e-Government" OR "Public Procurement" to capture the comprehensive literature in the field to examine the current developments in the field and using it to identify prospects and application in Public Sector.

The selection of articles from year 2020 to 2023 is significant as a total of 43 literature reviews have already been conducted in these three years to capture different aspects of Blockchain Technology in Supply Chain Management. Initial search generated a total of 502 research articles, after initial screening with inclusion criteria of finding articles only relevant to Blockchain Technologies and Supply Chain Management a total of 38 articles were excluded as they were related to the technical aspects of Blockchain Technology. The further screening of articles based on relevance to Supply Chain in general or public sector resulted in rejection of 115 articles exclusively related to private sector. Out of the remaining 349 articles only 32 articles were identified to have direct baring towards public sector and the remaining articles were related to the framework, application and implementation in Supply Chain in general. A total of 50 articles were sorted according to the themes relevant to this research that include transparency, efficiency, resilience, corruption, lean SC, sustainability, traceability and SC disruption. Further 08 articles were sorted based on application of Distributed Ledger Technology and Smart Contracts in SCM. By Adopting snowball technique 04 book chapters and 03 working papers published by The Organization of Economic Coordination and Development (OECD) were also identified and included in the literature review due to their direct relevance to Blockchain Technology and Public Sector.

3. RESULTS

In this section the systematic literature review will be presented to provide an overview of the existing research combining the fields of Blockchain Technology and Supply Chain Management fostering better transparency, efficiency and resilience in supply chain. Findings from the literature pertaining to Public Sector will be presented to provide the state of current application of Blockchain technology along with providing some frameworks for Public Sector based on the analysis presented in different reports of OECD and existing research.

3.1 Use of Blockchain Technology in SCM to Achieve Transparency, Efficiency, and Resilience

The literature review of articles was focused to find the answer to the research question that how Supply Chain can achieve better transparency, efficiency and resilience by adopting Blockchain Technology. In this context, research articles from different fields published in the past three years were reviewed and articles found most appropriate to address the research question are reflected in Table 1.

Supply chain transparency is the extent to which a firm is a sharing the information with the stakeholders (Awaysheh & Klassen, 2010). Better transparency results in improved supply chain efficiency, better image of the firm, better regulatory compliance, attainment of trust of stakeholders and preventing bad publicity (Sodhi & Tang, 2019). Transparency is ensured by sharing of data however, it results in compromise on confidentiality of data. In the research carried out by Xu et al. (2021) proposes that application of Blockchain technology can help to overcome transparency and data security paradox as traceability, immutability and data encoding can ensure that the data is not tempered whilst keeping it

Table 1. Research articles related to transparency, efficiency, and resilience

Supply Chain Objective	Articles
Transparency	Alabaddi et al., 2023; Babu et al., 2022; Bai et al., 2022; Davis et al., 2022; Hellani et al., 2021; M. Liu et al., 2022, 2023; X. Liu et al., 2023; McGrath et al., 2021; Menon & Jain, 2022; Wu & Yu, 2023; Xu et al., 2021
Efficiency	Al-Zaqeba et al., 2022; Aslam et al., 2023; H. Gupta et al., 2021; Jum'a, 2023; Kalbouneh et al., 2023; Kurdi et al., 2022; Markus & Buijs, 2022; Perano et al., 2023; Tian et al., 2022
Resilience	Alabaddi et al., 2023; Babu et al., 2022; Bayramova et al., 2021; Bechtsis et al., 2022; Cheung et al., 2021; S. Gupta et al., 2023; Kazancoglu et al., 2023; Li et al., 2022; Manupati et al., 2022; A. Mishra et al., 2022; Nagariya et al., 2023; Pattanayak et al., 2023; Razak et al., 2023; Roozkhosh et al., 2023; Xiong et al., 2021

accessible to all stakeholders. Recent research in different fields indicates Blockchain technology employment has a significant impact on improving the transparency of supply chain. In a quantitative research based on data from healthcare industry using structural equation modelling Alabaddi et al. (2023) have found that by achieving better data quality, traceability and smart contracts with the help of Blockchain technology, the supply chain transparency improves significantly. Multiple quantitative researches provide framework and proposition for use of Blockchain technology in improving transparency in supply chain (Hellani et al., 2021; McGrath et al., 2021; Wu & Yu, 2023). These findings are based on research in the field of pharmaceutical (Babu et al., 2022), cocoa industry (Bai et al., 2022), manufacturing (M. Liu et al., 2023; Haq, Khan, Parkash & Jabeen, 2016) and agri-food (Menon & Jain, 2022). With the help of Blockchain technology adoption Davis et al. (2022) have proposed that Multinational Enterprises can mitigate corruption by ensuring transparency in the supply chain.

Supply chain efficiency is measured by evaluating the performance of supply chain in three domains: improved customer satisfaction, reduced cost and improved responsiveness (Yadav et al., 2022). Use of digital technologies has significantly improved the supply chain performance by improving the business process (Perano et al., 2023) and Blockchain has been rated high among latest technologies as it provides transparency, security and reduced information asymmetry (H. Gupta et al., 2021). A quantitative study carried out by Jum'a (2023) in Jordanian manufacturing sector reveals that adoption of Blockchain technology has resulted in increase in supply chain efficiency by reduction in transaction cost, improved customer service and increase in speed of supply chain. Research indicates that Blockchain technology when employed with Big Data Analytics results in improved information about inventory, resulting in better demand forecasting and order fulfilment rate thus improving the efficiency of the whole process (Kalbouneh et al., 2023). Similar empirical findings have been reported by Kurdi et al. (2022), where Blockchain technology has been attributed to have significant positive impact on supply chain performance individually as well as when combined with inventory management systems. In the context of international cross-border trade similar empirical findings have been reported by Tian et al. (2022) which show that application of Blockchain technology can exponentially improve the operational efficiency by sharing of immutable, secure and traceable data across the borders. The characteristics of Blockchain technology that include programmability, data sharing, traceability and verifiability have been empirically tested by Al-Zaqeba et al. (2022) to have significant positive affect on supply chain efficiency. On answering the question of how Blockchain technology can enable better supply chain performance Markus & Buijs (2022) has used systematic literature review to propose that distributed ledger technology and smart contracts provide speed, quality, cost and dependability benefits to the supply chain resulting in better efficiency.

Supply chain resilience is a mechanism to counter disruptions that are driven by internal and external factors and in the ICT based supply chain information sharing paradigm these disruptions can be countered by ensuring traceability within the supply chain and protection from external cyber threats. In a systematic literature review carried out by Cheung et al. (2021) on the aspects of cybersecurity in logistics and supply chain management, the researcher summarizes that due to the provision of anonymity, distributed control, immutability and temper-proofness adoption of Blockchain technology is widely advocated in literature. The research also identifies that use of quantitative research in the field of cybersecurity in logistics and supply chain management is very limited. Study carried out by Alabaddi et al. (2023) shows significant positive impact of Blockchain based data traceability and quality on supply chain resilience. In a structured literature review, Bayramova et al. (2021) concludes that out of 28 supply chain resilience metrics identified in literature, Blockchain technology had significant positive impact on visibility, collaboration, integration, risk management and information sharing.

Other than the cybersecurity domain the resilience of the supply chain is also attributed to response of supply chain towards physical disruptions originating from complexities in the globalized supply chain environment (Stranieri et al., 2017) and mitigation of such disruptions is achieved through traceability in supply chain (Razak et al., 2023). In this context Blockchain technology can provide better traceability and can assist in reducing disruptions significantly as demonstrated in the research carried out by Kazancoglu et al. (2023) in the context of food supply chain during COVID-19 pandemic. A similar event study quantifying the financial effects of COVID-19 between a conventional firm and a Blockchain enabled supply chain firm reveals that the effect of pandemic was less in case of firm applying Blockchain Xiong et al. (2021), concluding that Blockchain technology provides better resilience to natural disruptions. Roozkhosh et al., (2023) through simulation study on Blockchain acceptance rate has also concluded that managers can improve the strength of their supply chain structure by adopting Blockchain technology as it increases response speed, backup and inventories during critical disruptions. Pattanayak et al. (2023) have demonstrated through semi-structured interviews and thematic analysis that Blockchain enabled supply chains perform better at different stages of disruptions than contemporary supply chain networks due to their lack of ability to sense, seize and maintain during disruptions. In the context of micro, small and medium-sized enterprises (MSME) different Blockchain enabled supply chain strategies have been identified in a Delphi study and using best-worst method (BWM) by Nagariya et al. (2023) to improve resilience in MSMEs. Employing smart contracts framework of Blockchain technologies Manupati et al. (2022) have modeled a pre and post-disruption models which were more effective in predicting a disruption than conventional supply chain models. Similar findings have been reported by Li et al. (2022), where Blockchain based business models had better supply chain efficiency and resilience.

The aforementioned review of literature indicates that adoption of Blockchain technology can have significant positive effects on improving transparency, efficiency and resilience in the supply chain. These tenets have substantial weightage in the Public Sector and hence application of Blockchain technology in public sector is supported by research in the field of Blockchain and Supply Chain Management.

3.2 OECD on Blockchain Technology in Governance

The research finds out that OECD has published three working papers related to Blockchain Technologies and their application in government functions. These reports present the suitable framework for adoption of Blockchain technology in multitude of different services provided by the government. The first working paper published in 2018 provides the statistical data that 46 different countries have taken over 200 initiatives which are currently at the planning stage. Further the document states that 19 initiatives are pertaining to the field of Supply Chain however, the details of these initiatives is not included. The report explains that Blockchain Technology can be used in every area of Public Sector and a common application in many countries is found in using Blockchain Technology for Land Title Registry. For application in Public Sector Supply Chain the document highlights that Blockchain can be used for better asset tracking and inventorying, contract management, vendor management and streamlining interagency and cross-sector processes (Berryhill et al., 2018). The second paper published in 2020 is aimed to settle different misconceptions about the potential of Blockchain technologies in Public Sector. The paper aims to counter the general perception of different stakeholders who question the application of Blockchain Technology in Public Sector. The report further adds different factors that may positively or negatively affect the success of Blockchain projects in Public Sector (Lindman et al., 2020). The third paper proposes adoption of Blockchain technologies for accomplishment of Sustainable Development Goals 2030 agenda by using it for empowerment, economic development, improving infrastructure and services. The paper clarifies the general misconception of relating Blockchain Technologies only with Cryptocurrencies and provides insight into different types of Blockchain networks such as Open Permissioned, Closed Consortium and Closed Enterprise regulated with "Proof of Authority" can be used in public sector to overcome lack of trust, information and power asymmetry along with inefficiency in general (Boiardi & Stout, 2021). The premise of these working papers demarcate the significant application of Blockchain Technologies in Public Sector and help building the logic to use Blockchain in Public Sector Supply Chain.

3.3 Researches on Blockchain in Public Sector Supply Chain

The existing literature combining Blockchain Technologies and Supply Chain Management with the perspective of Public Sector has been very scarce. The results of the literature review carried out reveals that many researches carried out in the domain have been closely related to the public sector such as Agriculture (21), Energy (03), Environment (09), Food (49), Healthcare (20), Humanitarian Aid and Disaster Management (06), International Arms Trade (01), Logistics and Maritime Trade (18), Procurement (04) and Smart Cities (01). Researches having particular significance to the public sector are discussed subsequently.

3.3.1 E-Procurement in Public Sector

Irrespective of the function, every public sector organization is engaged in the process of procurement. Digitalization of procurement process has been implemented in majority of the developed countries and is acknowledged as an important milestone to ensure transparency and efficiency in the otherwise inefficient and corruption prone process (Baily et al., 2022). Out of the scare literature on application of Blockchain technologies in public sector, adoption in e-procurement system in public sector been one of the most researched topic identified in the literature review. Though the initial research on Scopus did not result in significant number however, after applying "snowball" technique more articles were found on the subject. Most of the research on adoption of Blockchain technologies in public sector procurement is mostly related to frameworks, adoption opportunities and challenges (Akaba et al., 2020; Elalaoui Elabdallaoui et al., 2021). A conference paper presented by Rodríguez-Espíndola et al. (2020) gives some empirical evidence on positive impact of Blockchain enabled e-procurement system on cost and time saving. Application of Blockchain technology in public sector procurement can be very useful due to complexity of workflow and involvement of many different agencies and departments in the process. For example, as mapped by Khan et al. (2020) in their research a public procurement process in the context of a developing country (Pakistan) has minimum fifteen discrete steps with involvement of five different departments starting from demand initiation to issuance of payment instrument, spread over a timeline of 230 days. Such processes can be an ideal candidate for employment of Smart Contracts technology as they will make the process more transparent and efficient. A recent research by Agrawal et al. (2023) has demonstrated a Blockchain framework using Smart Contracts for interaction of different stakeholders in a typical procurement process. Though the research is mapping the framework of private sector, similar frameworks can be formulated for public sector keeping in consideration the peculiar differentiators and drivers in public and private procurement organizations as researched in study by Ambe & Badenhorst-Weiss (2011) and Kuchina-Musina et al. (2020). In the context of public procurement Akaba et al. (2020) has proposed adoption of Blockchain technology by taking a case study from Nigeria and similar proposal has been suggested by Elalaoui Elabdallaoui et al. (2021) for use of Blockchain technology for improving the efficiency, transparency and ease of public procurement system in Morocco. In a systematic literature review Da Silveira et al. (2022) has concluded that Blockchain technology adoption in public procurement can create innovation ecosystem for sustainable purchases. Some valid and insightful critique on the adoption of smart contracts in public procurement has been provided by Sava & Dragoş (2022), as the researchers have concluded that further research is merited on the adoption potential of smart contracts in terms of legal connotations of adopting self-executing smart contracts especially in case of legal disputes. The researchers further questions the motivation of adopting smart contracts for those countries where a transparent and efficient e-procurement system already exists. Though the research does not rule out the useful applicability of Blockchain technology however, as recommended by Sava & Dragoş (2022) further research is merited to substantiate the hype around using smart contracts in public procurement.

3.3.2 Public (Food) Distribution Systems

In India, Targeted Public Distribution System (TPDS) provides food items to its populace to cater to the problem of poverty and hunger among its large population. The system creates a public sector driven food supply chain that is currently facing problem of theft, corruption, misplacement, shrinkage and leakage of food grains. In this context, Kumar (2020) and H. Mishra & Maheshwari (2021) have proposed the use of Blockchain technology to improve the TPDS as it will provide better cost efficiency and control on corruption by mitigating ghost demands and loss of items.

3.3.3 International Arms Trade

Arms and ammunitions trade is one of the biggest market globally albeit it has considerable risk due to its misuse by rogue nations and non-state actors to commit genocide, crime against humanity, organized crime, gun violence and terrorism. To mitigate these critical issues, International arms trade require secure and safe arms transfer under transparent contracts and traceable movement of arms, ammunition and military hardware. In a study carried out by Min & Joo (2022) the researchers propose adoption of Blockchain technologies to meet the requirements of arms trade. The research was first to leverage Blockchain technology in this domain and further researches are merited in the field.

4. CONCLUSION

The systematic literature review establishes that Blockchain technology enables transparency, efficiency and resilience in supply chain and public sector supply chain can benefit from adopting the technology especially in the domain of procurement, logistics, storage and distribution. Blockchain networks can be designed as permissioned with limited users (nodes) and authorization to view, update or change information is regulated by "Proof of Authority" which is identical to a typical information system however, with the distinction that the information cannot be altered without intimation to all nodes, even by the nodes who have complete authority in the Blockchain. This arrangement provided by Permissioned Blockchains has a significant opportunity for the public sector to shift their processes to a more transparent, secure and decentralized information systems which will foster efficiency and resilience in the supply chain. The most researched topic in application of Blockchain technology is use of smart contracts in the public procurement. Taking inspiration from the proposed use of Blockchain technologies for traceability of International Arms Trade (Min & Joo, 2022), a similar use of permissioned Blockchain can be in equipment accounting domain of public sector supply chain where record of assets can be maintained as they are transferred between different users within and outside departments. This system will be able to provide real-time, accurate and transparent record of equipment movement and current ownership.

However, it is pertinent to mention that aforementioned theorization is mostly inspired from the literature available in domain of supply chain management in general and research capturing the unique operations of public sector is scarce. Application of Blockchain technology in Public Sector has been debated in researches (Alketbi et al., 2018; Batubara et al., 2018; Hou, 2017; Navadkar et al., 2018; Ølnes et al., 2017) however, over the years researchers have not been able to capture the empirical evidence supporting the preposition. Recent researches are still limited to providing frameworks (Cagigas et al., 2023) and literature reviews (Alzahrani et al., 2023; Dhingra et al., 2023; Jiang et al., 2023; Kouhizadeh et al., 2023; Van Wassenaer et al., 2023; Vern et al., 2023). Previous research, exemplified by Khan et al. (2017) and Mishra et al. (2022), has highlighted the potential of RFID technology. Notably, Mishra et al.'s (2022) demonstration of a resilient supply chain network using RFID and Blockchain on Ethereum offers valuable insights for the public sector, particularly in simulating information flow and product movement. Similar, researchers can be helpful in providing proof of concept and influence public sector managers to adopt Blockchain technology.

Research indicates that among the different public sector supply chain functions, public procurement has emerged as a significant applicant for adoption on Blockchain technology. Since procurement is part of every government function therefore, its application is exist in every sector and smart contracts in Blockchain technology can transform the procurement process. However, as highlighted by Sava & Dragoş (2022) that the applicability to smart contracts in public sector procurement is a topic "under construction". The researchers argue the application of smart contracts in case of already adopted e-procurement systems that are meeting the efficiency parameters as in EU, the legal implications in case of disputes and lack of frameworks for complex procurements involving sub-contracts. These arguments require further research on the topic. Another important consideration has been highlighted by Al-Rakhami & Al-Mashari, (2022) and Sislian & Jaegler (2022), as the research proposes to look into the prospects of interoperability of Blockchain technology with the existing digital systems and ERPs. If not considered by researchers and practitioners will face problems in designing and implementation phase. Furthermore, the expected benefits from adoption of Blockchain technology cannot be achieved in case of non-integration of data systems.

Due to overemphasis on the aspects of transparency, the supply chain functions of public sector such as procurement, outsourcing, storage and distribution are all constrained by enacted laws followed by peculiar procedures which ensure recording of every transaction in transparent manner with minimum expense and maximum value for money. Such stringent requirements are an ideal ingredient for use of Blockchain technologies where information sharing can be carried out through secure means with access to all stakeholders including public audits (M. Liu et al., 2022). However, reforms in the laws to adopt the digital technologies needs to be carried out to make the digital framework acceptable to all stakeholders. As highlighted by Davis et al. (2022) the implementation of Blockchain technology based supply chains is dependent upon the government will and digital infrastructure of the state therefore, every research must consider the aspects of political environment and digital ecosystem while proposing frameworks and developing prototypes. Similarly the researchers have to consider the aspects of privacy and data security, implementation cost, regulatory lacunas, digital infrastructure, interoperability and complexity with smart contracts (Menon & Jain, 2022).

REFERENCES

Acemoglu, D., & Robinson, J. A. (2012). *Why nations fail: The origins of power, prosperity and poverty* (1st ed.). Crown Publishers.

Acemoglu, D., & Robinson, J. A. (2019). *The narrow corridor: States, societies, and the fate of liberty*. Penguin Press.

Afonso, A., Schuknecht, L., & Tanzi, V. (2010). Public sector efficiency: Evidence for new EU member states and emerging markets. *Applied Economics*, *42*(17), 2147–2164. doi:10.1080/00036840701765460

Agrawal, T. K., Angelis, J., Khilji, W. A., Kalaiarasan, R., & Wiktorsson, M. (2023). Demonstration of a blockchain-based framework using smart contracts for supply chain collaboration. *International Journal of Production Research*, *61*(5), 1497–1516. doi:10.1080/00207543.2022.2039413

Akaba, T. I., Norta, A., Udokwu, C., & Draheim, D. (2020). A Framework for the Adoption of Blockchain-Based e-Procurement Systems in the Public Sector: A Case Study of Nigeria. In M. Hattingh, M. Matthee, H. Smuts, I. Pappas, Y. K. Dwivedi, & M. Mäntymäki (Eds.), *Responsible Design, Implementation and Use of Information and Communication Technology* (Vol. 12066, pp. 3–14). Springer International Publishing. doi:10.1007/978-3-030-44999-5_1

Al-Rakhami, M., & Al-Mashari, M. (2022). Interoperability approaches of blockchain technology for supply chain systems. *Business Process Management Journal*, *28*(5/6), 1251–1276. doi:10.1108/BPMJ-04-2022-0207

Al-Zaqeba, M. A. A., Jarah, B. A. F., Ineizeh, N. I., Almatarneh, Z., & Jarrah, M. A. A. (2022). The effect of management accounting and blockchain technology characteristics on supply chains efficiency. *Uncertain Supply Chain Management*, *10*(3), 973–982. doi:10.5267/j.uscm.2022.2.016

Alabaddi, Z., Obidat, A., & Alziyadat, Z. (2023). Exploring the effect of blockchain technology on supply chain resilience and transparency: Evidence from the healthcare industry. *Uncertain Supply Chain Management*, *11*(2), 787–798. doi:10.5267/j.uscm.2023.1.001

Alketbi, A., Nasir, Q., & Talib, M. A. (2018). Blockchain for government services—Use cases, security benefits and challenges. *2018 15th Learning and Technology Conference (L&T)*, (pp. 112–119). ACM. 10.1109/LT.2018.8368494

Alzahrani, S., Daim, T., & Choo, K.-K. R. (2023). Assessment of the Blockchain Technology Adoption for the Management of the Electronic Health Record Systems. *IEEE Transactions on Engineering Management*, *70*(8), 2846–2863. doi:10.1109/TEM.2022.3158185

Ambe, I. M., & Badenhorst-Weiss, J. A. (2011). Managing and Controlling Public Sector Supply Chains. In Supply Chain Management (Pengzhong Li, pp. 73–92). InTech.

Aslam, J., Saleem, A., & Kim, Y. B. (2023). Blockchain-enabled supply chain management: Integrated impact on firm performance and robustness capabilities. *Business Process Management Journal*, *29*(6), 1680–1705. doi:10.1108/BPMJ-03-2023-0165

Atkinson, C. L., McCue, C., Prier, E., & Atkinson, A. M. (2020). Supply Chain Manipulation, Misrepresentation, and Magical Thinking During the COVID-19 Pandemic. *American Review of Public Administration*, *50*(6–7), 628–634. doi:10.1177/0275074020942055

Awaysheh, A., & Klassen, R. D. (2010). The impact of supply chain structure on the use of supplier socially responsible practices. *International Journal of Operations & Production Management*, *30*(12), 1246–1268. doi:10.1108/01443571011094253

Babu, E. S., Kavati, I., Nayak, S. R., Ghosh, U., & Al Numay, W. (2022). Secure and transparent pharmaceutical supply chain using permissioned blockchain network. *International Journal of Logistics Research and Applications*, 1–28. https://doi.org/ doi:10.1080/13675567.2022.2045578

Bai, C., Quayson, M., & Sarkis, J. (2022). Analysis of Blockchain's enablers for improving sustainable supply chain transparency in Africa cocoa industry. *Journal of Cleaner Production*, *358*, 131896. doi:10.1016/j.jclepro.2022.131896

Baily, P., Farmer, D., Crocker, B., & Jessop, D. (2022). *Procurment Principles and Management in the Digital Age* (12th ed.). Pearson Education Limited.

Barroso, A. P., Machado, V. H., Carvalho, H., & Cruz Machado, V. (2015). Quantifying the Supply Chain Resilience. In H. Tozan & A. Ertürk (Eds.), *Applications of Contemporary Management Approaches in Supply Chains*. InTech., doi:10.5772/59580

Batubara, F. R., Ubacht, J., & Janssen, M. (2018). Challenges of blockchain technology adoption for e-government: A systematic literature review. *Proceedings of the 19th Annual International Conference on Digital Government Research: Governance in the Data Age*, (pp. 1–9). IEEE. https://doi.org/10.1145/3209281.3209317

Bayramova, A., Edwards, D. J., & Roberts, C. (2021). The Role of Blockchain Technology in Augmenting Supply Chain Resilience to Cybercrime. *Buildings*, *11*(7), 283. doi:10.3390/buildings11070283

Bechtsis, D., Tsolakis, N., Iakovou, E., & Vlachos, D. (2022). Data-driven secure, resilient and sustainable supply chains: Gaps, opportunities, and a new generalised data sharing and data monetisation framework. *International Journal of Production Research*, *60*(14), 4397–4417. doi:10.1080/00207543.2021.1957506

Berryhill, J., Bourgery, T., & Hanson, A. (2018). *Blockchains Unchained: Blockchain Technology and its Use in the Public Sector* (OECD Working Papers on Public Governance 28). OECD. https://www.oecd-ilibrary.org/governance/blockchains-unchained_3c32c429-en

Boiardi, P., & Stout, E. (2021). *To what extent can blockchain help development co-operation actors meet the 2030 Agenda?* (OECD Development Co-Operation Working Papers 95). OECD. https://doi.org/ doi:10.1787/22220518

Cagigas, D., Clifton, J., Diaz-Fuentes, D., Fernández-Gutiérrez, M., & Harpes, C. (2023). Blockchain in government: Toward an evaluation framework. *Policy Design and Practice*, *6*(4), 1–18. doi:10.1080/25741292.2023.2230702

Callender, G. (2011). Alignment of inter-agency supply chains to enhance public sector performance management. *International Journal of Productivity and Performance Management*, *60*(1), 9–23. doi:10.1108/17410401111094286

Calvera Isabal, M., Santos, P., Hoppe, H., & Schulten, C. (2023). Cómo automatizar la extracción y análisis de información sobre ciencia ciudadana con propósitos educativos. *Comunicar.*, *31*(74), 13.

Cheung, K.-F., Bell, M. G. H., & Bhattacharjya, J. (2021). Cybersecurity in logistics and supply chain management: An overview and future research directions. *Transportation Research Part E, Logistics and Transportation Review*, *146*, 102217. doi:10.1016/j.tre.2020.102217

Chong, A. Y.-L., Ooi, K.-B., & Sohal, A. (2009). The relationship between supply chain factors and adoption of e-Collaboration tools: An empirical examination. *International Journal of Production Economics*, *122*(1), 150–160. doi:10.1016/j.ijpe.2009.05.012

Classification of the Functions of Government. (2019). European Union. https://ec.europa.eu/eurostat/web/products-manuals-and-guidelines/-/ks-gq-19-010

Coglianese, C. (2009). The Transparency President? The Obama Administration and Open Government. *Governance: An International Journal of Policy, Administration and Institutions*, *22*(4), 529–544. doi:10.1111/j.1468-0491.2009.01451.x

Curristine, T., Lonti, Z., & Joumard, I. (2007). Improving Public Sector Efficiency: Challenges and Opportunities. *OECD Journal on Budgeting*, *7*(1), 1–41. doi:10.1787/budget-v7-art6-en

Da Silveira, V. A., Da Costa, S. R. R., & Resende, D. (2022). Blockchain Technology in Innovation Ecosystems for Sustainable Purchases through the Perception of Public Managers. *WSEAS TRANSACTIONS ON BUSINESS AND ECONOMICS*, *19*, 790–804. doi:10.37394/23207.2022.19.69

Davis, M., Lennerfors, T. T., & Tolstoy, D. (2022). Can blockchain-technology fight corruption in MNEs' operations in emerging markets? *Review of International Business and Strategy*, *32*(1), 39–56. doi:10.1108/RIBS-12-2020-0155

Dhingra, S., Raut, R., Gunasekaran, A., Rao Naik, B. K., & Masuna, V. (2023). Analysis of the challenges for blockchain technology adoption in the Indian health-care sector. *Journal of Modelling in Management*. doi:10.1108/JM2-09-2022-0229

Elalaoui Elabdallaoui, H., Elfazziki, A., & Sadgal, M. (2021). A Blockchain-Based Platform for the e-Procurement Management in the Public Sector. In C. Attiogbé & S. Ben Yahia (Eds.), *Model and Data Engineering* (Vol. 12732, pp. 213–223). Springer International Publishing. doi:10.1007/978-3-030-78428-7_17

Flores-Vivar, J. M., & García-Peñalvo, F. J. (2023). Reflexiones sobre la ética, potencialidades y retos de la Inteligencia Artificial en el marco de la Educación de Calidad (ODS4). *Comunicar*, *31*(74). Advance online publication. doi:10.3916/C74-2023-03

Florini, A. (Ed.). (2007). *The Right to Know: Transparency for an Open World.* Columbia University Press. doi:10.7312/flor14158

Fukuyama, F. (2012). The origins of political order: From prehuman times to the French Revolution (First paperback edition). Farrar, Straus and Giroux.

Fukuyama, F. (2015). Political order and political decay: From the industrial revolution to the globalization of democracy (Paperback ed). Profile Books.

Ghouri, A., Akhtar, P., Venkatesh, V. G., Ashraf, A., Arsenyan, G., Tarba, S. Y., & Khan, Z. (2023). Enhancing supply chain innovation and operational agility through knowledge acquisition from the social media: A microfoundational approach. *IEEE Transactions on Engineering Management*, 1–15. doi:10.1109/TEM.2023.3316119

Gianakis, G., & McCue, C. (2012). Supply management concepts in local government: Four case studies. *Journal of Public Procurement*, *12*(1), 109–141. doi:10.1108/JOPP-12-01-2012-B004

Grimmelikhuijsen, S., Weske, U., Bouwman, R., & Tummers, L. (2017). Public Sector Transparency. In O. James, S. R. Jilke, & G. G. Van Ryzin (Eds.), *Experiments in Public Management Research* (1st ed., pp. 291–312). Cambridge University Press. doi:10.1017/9781316676912.014

Grimmelikhuijsen, S. G., & Meijer, A. J. (2014). Effects of Transparency on the Perceived Trustworthiness of a Government Organization: Evidence from an Online Experiment. *Journal of Public Administration: Research and Theory*, *24*(1), 137–157. doi:10.1093/jopart/mus048

Gupta, H., Kumar, S., Kusi-Sarpong, S., Jabbour, C. J. C., & Agyemang, M. (2021). Enablers to supply chain performance on the basis of digitization technologies. *Industrial Management & Data Systems*, *121*(9), 1915–1938. doi:10.1108/IMDS-07-2020-0421

Gupta, S., Modgil, S., Choi, T.-M., Kumar, A., & Antony, J. (2023). Influences of artificial intelligence and blockchain technology on financial resilience of supply chains. *International Journal of Production Economics*, *261*, 108868. doi:10.1016/j.ijpe.2023.108868

Haq, M. A., Khan, N. R., Parkash, R., & Jabeen, A. (2016). Impact of JIT, waste minimization, and flow management on operational performance of manufacturing companies. *Quality - Access to Success*, *17*(153), 48.

Hellani, H., Sliman, L., Samhat, A. E., & Exposito, E. (2021). On Blockchain Integration with Supply Chain: Overview on Data Transparency. *Logistics*, *5*(3), 46. doi:10.3390/logistics5030046

Heller, P. S. (2003). *Who will pay? Coping with aging societies, climate change, and other long-term fiscal challenges.* International Monetary Fund.

Hodgkinson, I. R., Hannibal, C., Keating, B. W., Chester Buxton, R., & Bateman, N. (2017). Toward a public service management: Past, present, and future directions. *Journal of Service Management*, *28*(5), 998–1023. doi:10.1108/JOSM-01-2017-0020

Hood, C., & Heald, D. (Eds.). (2006). *Transparency: The key to better governance?* Oxford University Press. doi:10.5871/bacad/9780197263839.001.0001

Hossain, M. K., Thakur, V., & Mangla, S. K. (2022). Modeling the emergency health-care supply chains: Responding to the COVID-19 pandemic. *Journal of Business and Industrial Marketing*, *37*(8), 1623–1639. doi:10.1108/JBIM-07-2020-0315

Hou, H. (2017). The Application of Blockchain Technology in E-Government in China. *2017 26th International Conference on Computer Communication and Networks (ICCCN)*, 1–4. 10.1109/ICCCN.2017.8038519

Jiang, F., Jiang, C. X., & Li, J. X. (2023). Deep learning for blockchain in medical supply chain risk management. *International Journal of Grid and Utility Computing*, *14*(2/3), 250. doi:10.1504/IJ-GUC.2023.131014

Joumard, I., Kongsrud, P. M., Nam, Y.-S., & Price, R. (2004). *Enhancing the Effectiveness of Public Spending: Experience in OECD Countries* (OECD Economics Department Working Papers 380; OECD Economics Department Working Papers, Vol. 380). OECD. doi:10.1787/18151973

Jum'a, L. (2023). The role of blockchain-enabled supply chain applications in improving supply chain performance: The case of Jordanian manufacturing sector. *Management Research Review*, *46*(10), 1315–1333. doi:10.1108/MRR-04-2022-0298

Kalbouneh, N. Y., Bataineh, K. A., Al-Hamad, A. A.-S. A., Dwakat, M. K. A., Abualoush, S., Almasarweh, M. S., & Al-Smadi, R. W. (2023). The effects of the blockchain technology and big data analytics on supply chain performance: The mediating effect supply chain risk management. *Uncertain Supply Chain Management*, *11*(3), 903–914. doi:10.5267/j.uscm.2023.5.008

Karl, A. A., Micheluzzi, J., Leite, L. R., & Pereira, C. R. (2018). Supply chain resilience and key performance indicators: A systematic literature review. *Production*, *28*(0). Advance online publication. doi:10.1590/0103-6513.20180020

Kazancoglu, Y., Ozbiltekin-Pala, M., Sezer, M. D., Luthra, S., & Kumar, A. (2023). Resilient reverse logistics with blockchain technology in sustainable food supply chain management during COVID-19. *Business Strategy and the Environment*, *32*(4), 2327–2340. doi:10.1002/bse.3251

Khan, M. S., Ayyaz, M., & Naseem, A. (2020). An Approach for Developing Integrated Decision Support System Model for Optimizing Contracting Process of Public Procurement in Pakistan. *2020 IEEE Technology & Engineering Management Conference (TEMSCON)*, (pp. 1–6). IEEE. doi:10.1109/TEMSCON47658.2020.9140100

Khan, N. R., Haq, M. A., Ghouri, A. M., Raziq, A., & Moiz, S. M. (2017). Adaptation of RFID technology in business supply chain success: Empirical findings from a developing country logistic industry. *Quality - Access to Success*, *18*(160), 93.

Kouhizadeh, M., Zhu, Q., & Sarkis, J. (2023). Circular economy performance measurements and blockchain technology: An examination of relationships. *International Journal of Logistics Management*, *34*(3), 720–743. doi:10.1108/IJLM-04-2022-0145

Kuchina-Musina, D., Morris, J. C., & Steinfeld, J. (2020). Drivers and differentiators: A grounded theory study of procurement in public and private organizations. *Journal of Public Procurement*, *20*(3), 265–285. doi:10.1108/JOPP-10-2019-0068

Kumar, A. (2020). Improvement of public distribution system efficiency applying blockchain technology during pandemic outbreak (COVID-19). *Journal of Humanitarian Logistics and Supply Chain Management, 11*(1), 1–28. doi:10.1108/JHLSCM-06-2020-0050

Kurdi, B. A., Alzoubi, H. M., Akour, I., & Alshurideh, M. T. (2022). The effect of blockchain and smart inventory system on supply chain performance: Empirical evidence from retail industry. *Uncertain Supply Chain Management, 10*(4), 1111–1116. doi:10.5267/j.uscm.2022.9.001

Li, G., Xue, J., Li, N., & Ivanov, D. (2022). Blockchain-supported business model design, supply chain resilience, and firm performance. *Transportation Research Part E, Logistics and Transportation Review, 163*, 102773. doi:10.1016/j.tre.2022.102773

Lindman, J., Berryhill, J., Welby, B., & Barbieri, M. P. (2020). *The uncertain promise of blockchain for government* (OECD Working Papers on Public Governance 43). OECD. doi:10.1787/19934351

Liu, M., Robin, A., Wu, K., & Xu, J. (2022). Blockchain's Impact on Accounting and Auditing: A Use Case on Supply Chain Traceability. *Journal of Emerging Technologies in Accounting, 19*(2), 105–119. doi:10.2308/JETA-2021-002

Liu, M., Zhang, X., & Wu, H. (2023). The impact of platform restriction on manufacturer quality transparency in the blockchain era. *International Journal of Production Research, 61*(11), 3582–3598. doi:10.1080/00207543.2021.1972180

Liu, X., Zhou, Z., Zhong, F., & Shi, J. (2023). Improving supply chain transparency with blockchain technology when considering product returns. *International Transactions in Operational Research.* IEEE. doi:10.1111/itor.13303

Manupati, V. K., Schoenherr, T., Ramkumar, M., Panigrahi, S., Sharma, Y., & Mishra, P. (2022). Recovery strategies for a disrupted supply chain network: Leveraging blockchain technology in pre- and post-disruption scenarios. *International Journal of Production Economics, 245*, 108389. doi:10.1016/j.ijpe.2021.108389

Markus, S., & Buijs, P. (2022). Beyond the hype: How blockchain affects supply chain performance. *Supply Chain Management, 27*(7), 177–193. doi:10.1108/SCM-03-2022-0109

McGrath, P., McCarthy, L., Marshall, D., & Rehme, J. (2021). Tools and Technologies of Transparency in Sustainable Global Supply Chains. *California Management Review, 64*(1), 67–89. doi:10.1177/00081256211045993

McIvor, R., McHugh, M., & Cadden, C. (2002). Internet technologies: Supporting transparency in the public sector. *International Journal of Public Sector Management, 15*(3), 170–187. doi:10.1108/09513550210423352

Menon, S., & Jain, K. (2022). Blockchain Technology for Transparency in Agri-Food Supply Chain: Use Cases, Limitations, and Future Directions. *IEEE Transactions on Engineering Management*, 1–15. doi:10.1109/TEM.2021.3110903

Min, H., & Joo, S. J. (2022). Blockchain technology for international arms trade. *International Journal of Logistics Systems and Management, 42*(2), 223. doi:10.1504/IJLSM.2022.124183

Mishra, A., Karmakar, S., Dutta, A., Bose, A., & Mohapatro, M. (2022). Design and Deployment of IoT enabled Blockchain based resilient Supply-chain Management System using Ethereum. *International Journal of Computing and Digital Systems*, *12*(4), 1029–1050. doi:10.12785/ijcds/120183

Mishra, H., & Maheshwari, P. (2021). Blockchain in Indian Public Distribution System: A conceptual framework to prevent leakage of the supplies and its enablers and disablers. *Journal of Global Operations and Strategic Sourcing*, *14*(2), 312–335. doi:10.1108/JGOSS-07-2020-0044

Nagariya, R., Mukherjee, S., Baral, M. M., & Chittipaka, V. (2023). Analyzing blockchain-based supply chain resilience strategies: Resource-based perspective. *International Journal of Productivity and Performance Management*. doi:10.1108/IJPPM-07-2022-0330

Navadkar, V. H., Nighot, A., & Wantmure, R. (2018). Overview of Blockchain Technology in Government/Public Sectors. *International Research Journal of Engineering and Technology*, *5*(6), 2287–2292.

Ølnes, S., Ubacht, J., & Janssen, M. (2017). Blockchain in government: Benefits and implications of distributed ledger technology for information sharing. *Government Information Quarterly*, *34*(3), 355–364. doi:10.1016/j.giq.2017.09.007

Osborne, D. (1993). Reinventing Government. *Public Productivity & Management Review*, *16*(4), 349. doi:10.2307/3381012

Pattanayak, S., Arputham, R. M., Goswami, M., & Rana, N. P. (2023). Blockchain Technology and Its Relationship With Supply Chain Resilience: A Dynamic Capability Perspective. *IEEE Transactions on Engineering Management*, 1–15. doi:10.1109/TEM.2023.3235771

Perano, M., Cammarano, A., Varriale, V., Del Regno, C., Michelino, F., & Caputo, M. (2023). Embracing supply chain digitalization and unphysicalization to enhance supply chain performance: A conceptual framework. *International Journal of Physical Distribution & Logistics Management*, *53*(5/6), 628–659. doi:10.1108/IJPDLM-06-2022-0201

Peterson, M. R., Young, R. R., & Gordon, G. A. (2016). The application of supply chain management principles to emergency management logistics: An empirical study. *Journal of Emergency Management (Weston, Mass.)*, *14*(4), 245–258. doi:10.5055/jem.2016.0290 PMID:27575640

Phillips, W., Roehrich, J. K., & Kapletia, D. (2023). Responding to information asymmetry in crisis situations: Innovation in the time of the COVID-19 pandemic. *Public Management Review*, *25*(1), 175–198. doi:10.1080/14719037.2021.1960737

Pillitteri, F., Mazzola, E., & Bruccoleri, M. (2021). The four spheres of value co-creation in humanitarian professional services. *Journal of Humanitarian Logistics and Supply Chain Management*, *11*(3), 402–427. doi:10.1108/JHLSCM-06-2020-0049

Ponomarov, S. Y., & Holcomb, M. C. (2009). Understanding the concept of supply chain resilience. *International Journal of Logistics Management*, *20*(1), 124–143. doi:10.1108/09574090910954873

Razak, G. M., Hendry, L. C., & Stevenson, M. (2023). Supply chain traceability: A review of the benefits and its relationship with supply chain resilience. *Production Planning and Control*, *34*(11), 1114–1134. doi:10.1080/09537287.2021.1983661

Roberts, A. (2006). *Blacked out: Government secrecy in the information age*. Cambridge University Press. doi:10.1017/CBO9781139165518

Rodríguez-Espíndola, O., Chowdhury, S., Beltagui, A., & Albores, P. (2020). The potential of emergent disruptive technologies for humanitarian supply chains: The integration of blockchain, Artificial Intelligence and 3D printing. *International Journal of Production Research*, *58*(15), 4610–4630. doi:10.1080/00207543.2020.1761565

Roozkhosh, P., Pooya, A., & Agarwal, R. (2023). Blockchain acceptance rate prediction in the resilient supply chain with hybrid system dynamics and machine learning approach. *Operations Management Research : Advancing Practice Through Research*, *16*(2), 705–725. doi:10.100712063-022-00336-x

Sava, N.-A., & Dragoş, D. (2022). The Legal Regime of Smart Contracts in Public Procurement. *Transylvanian Review of Administrative Sciences*, *66E*(66E), 99–112. doi:10.24193/tras.66E.6

Scholten, K., Sharkey Scott, P., & Fynes, B. (2010). (Le)agility in humanitarian aid (NGO) supply chains. *International Journal of Physical Distribution & Logistics Management*, *40*(8/9), 623–635. doi:10.1108/09600031011079292

Shafiq, M., & Soratana, K. (2019). Humanitarian logistics and supply chain management – a qualitative study. *Logforum*, *15*(1), 19–38. doi:10.17270/J.LOG.2019.325

Shafiq, M., & Soratana, K. (2020). Lean readiness assessment model – a tool for Humanitarian Organizations' social and economic sustainability. *Journal of Humanitarian Logistics and Supply Chain Management*, *10*(2), 77–99. doi:10.1108/JHLSCM-01-2019-0002

Shaoliu, D., & Tongbai, L. (2023). Ideological and Physical Education Integration in Higher Education: Strategies for Mental Health Education. *Journal of Sport Psychology*, *32*(4), 203–212.

Shekarian, M., & Mellat Parast, M. (2021). An Integrative approach to supply chain disruption risk and resilience management: A literature review. *International Journal of Logistics*, *24*(5), 427–455. doi:10.1080/13675567.2020.1763935

Sienkiewicz-Małyjurek, K., & Szymczak, M. (2023). Understanding public service supply chain management: A systematic literature review. *Management Review Quarterly*. doi:10.1007/s11301-023-00350-8

Simmie, J., & Martin, R. (2010). The economic resilience of regions: Towards an evolutionary approach. *Cambridge Journal of Regions, Economy and Society*, *3*(1), 27–43. doi:10.1093/cjres/rsp029

Sislian, L., & Jaegler, A. (2022). Linkage of blockchain to enterprise resource planning systems for improving sustainable performance. *Business Strategy and the Environment*, *31*(3), 737–750. doi:10.1002/bse.2914

Skipper, J. B., Hanna, J. B., & Cegielski, C. G. (2009). Supply Chain Contingency Planning and Firm Adoption: An Initial Look at Differentiating the Innovators. *Transportation Journal*, *48*(2), 40–62. doi:10.2307/25702522

Sodhi, M. S., & Tang, C. S. (2019). Research Opportunities in Supply Chain Transparency. *Production and Operations Management*, *28*(12), 2946–2959. doi:10.1111/poms.13115

Stentoft Arlbjørn, J., Vagn Freytag, P., & De Haas, H. (2011). Service supply chain management: A survey of lean application in the municipal sector. *International Journal of Physical Distribution & Logistics Management*, *41*(3), 277–295. doi:10.1108/09600031111123796

Stranieri, S., Orsi, L., & Banterle, A. (2017). Traceability and risks: An extended transaction cost perspective. *Supply Chain Management*, *22*(2), 145–159. doi:10.1108/SCM-07-2016-0268

Tian, X., Zhu, J., Zhao, X., & Wu, J. (2022). Improving operational efficiency through blockchain: Evidence from a field experiment in cross-border trade. *Production Planning and Control*, 1–16. doi:10.1080/09537287.2022.2058412

Tsafnat, G., Glasziou, P., Choong, M. K., Dunn, A., Galgani, F., & Coiera, E. (2014). Systematic review automation technologies. *Systematic Reviews*, *3*(1), 74. doi:10.1186/2046-4053-3-74 PMID:25005128

United Nations (Ed.). (2000). *Classifications of expenditure according to purpose: Classification of the functions of government (COFOG), classification of individual consumption according to purpose (COICOP), classification of the purposes of non-profit institutions serving households (COPNI), classification of the outlays of producers according to purpose (COPP)*. United Nations.

Van Wassenaer, L., Verdouw, C., Kassahun, A., Van Hilten, M., Van Der Meij, K., & Tekinerdogan, B. (2023). Tokenizing circularity in agri-food systems: A conceptual framework and exploratory study. *Journal of Cleaner Production*, *413*, 137527. doi:10.1016/j.jclepro.2023.137527

Vern, P., Panghal, A., Mor, R. S., Kamble, S. S., Islam, Md. S., & Khan, S. A. R. (2023). Influential barriers to blockchain technology implementation in agri-food supply chain. *Operations Management Research*. doi:10.1007/s12063-023-00388-7

Wang, Y., Liu, Y., & Hu, Y. (2022). An empirical analysis based on a panel threshold model of the effect of Internet development on the efficiency of Chinese government public service supply. *PLoS One*, *17*(7), e0271390. doi:10.1371/journal.pone.0271390 PMID:35830450

Wu, J., & Yu, J. (2023). Blockchain's impact on platform supply chains: Transaction cost and information transparency perspectives. *International Journal of Production Research*, *61*(11), 3703–3716. doi:10.1080/00207543.2022.2027037

Xiong, Y., Lam, H. K. S., Kumar, A., Ngai, E. W. T., Xiu, C., & Wang, X. (2021). The mitigating role of blockchain-enabled supply chains during the COVID-19 pandemic. *International Journal of Operations & Production Management*, *41*(9), 1495–1521. doi:10.1108/IJOPM-12-2020-0901

Xu, P., Lee, J., Barth, J. R., & Richey, R. G. (2021). Blockchain as supply chain technology: Considering transparency and security. *International Journal of Physical Distribution & Logistics Management*, *51*(3), 305–324. doi:10.1108/IJPDLM-08-2019-0234

Yadav, V. S., Singh, A. R., Gunasekaran, A., Raut, R. D., & Narkhede, B. E. (2022). A systematic literature review of the agro-food supply chain: Challenges, network design, and performance measurement perspectives. *Sustainable Production and Consumption*, *29*, 685–704. doi:10.1016/j.spc.2021.11.019

Yaga, D., Mell, P., Roby, N., & Scarfone, K. (2018). Blockchain technology overview (NIST IR 8202; p. NIST IR 8202). National Institute of Standards and Technology. https://doi.org/ doi:10.6028/NIST.IR.8202

Yontar, E. (2023). The role of blockchain technology in the sustainability of supply chain management: Grey based dematel implementation. *Cleaner Logistics and Supply Chain*, *8*, 100113. doi:10.1016/j.clscn.2023.100113

Chapter 14
Blockchain Technology for Smart Contracts:
Enhancing Trust, Transparency, and Efficiency in Supply Chain Management

S M Nazmuz Sakib
https://orcid.org/0000-0001-9310-3014
International MBA Institute, Switzerland & Dhaka International University, Bangladesh, & School of Business and Trade, Switzerland

ABSTRACT

This chapter explores the application of blockchain technology in achieving secure and transparent supply chains. With globalization and increasing complexities in supply chain networks, ensuring the integrity and visibility of products throughout their lifecycle has become a critical challenge for organizations. Blockchain technology offers a promising solution by providing a decentralized and immutable ledger to record and verify transactions, making it an ideal platform for enhancing supply chain transparency and security. The chapter begins by examining the key challenges faced by modern supply chains, including counterfeiting, lack of traceability, inefficient record-keeping, and trust issues among stakeholders. It highlights how these challenges can be addressed through the implementation of blockchain technology, leveraging its key features such as transparency, immutability, and decentralized consensus.

INTRODUCTION TO SMART CONTRACTS AND BLOCKCHAIN TECHNOLOGY

Smart contracts and blockchain technology have emerged as promising tools for revolutionizing the supply chain industry. Blockchain technology is a distributed ledger system that enables secure and transparent transactions without the need for intermediaries. Smart contracts are self-executing contracts that automatically execute the terms of an agreement when the conditions specified in the contract are met. These contracts are stored and executed on a blockchain network, making them immutable, transparent and secure (Khan *et al.*, 2021).

DOI: 10.4018/979-8-3693-0482-2.ch014

Blockchain technology and smart contracts have the potential to significantly improve supply chain management by providing real-time visibility, improving traceability, enhancing security, and reducing costs. With these technologies, supply chain stakeholders can track and trace products throughout the supply chain, from raw materials to finished goods. They can also ensure the authenticity and quality of products, prevent counterfeiting and fraud, and streamline the entire supply chain process (Taherdoost, 2023).

In this chapter, we will provide an overview of blockchain technology and smart contracts and explore their role in supply chain management. We will also discuss the benefits, implementation considerations, and potential limitations of using smart contracts in supply chain management. Finally, we will discuss the future outlook and potential developments in the use of smart contracts and blockchain technology in supply chain management.

OVERVIEW OF THE SUPPLY CHAIN AND ITS CHALLENGES

Supply chain management is the process of managing the flow of goods, services, and information from the point of origin to the point of consumption. The supply chain includes all the activities and processes involved in bringing a product or service to the end consumer. The supply chain industry faces a number of challenges, including:

Lack of transparency: The supply chain industry often lacks transparency, making it difficult to track and trace products from the point of origin to the point of consumption.

Counterfeiting and fraud: Counterfeiting and fraud are common issues in the supply chain industry, which can lead to significant financial losses and damage to brand reputation.

Inefficiency: The supply chain industry is often inefficient, with delays and bottlenecks in the flow of goods and services.

Quality control: Ensuring the quality and authenticity of products throughout the supply chain can be challenging, especially for products that are highly regulated or require strict quality control measures.

Data management: The supply chain industry generates a large amount of data, which can be difficult to manage and analyze effectively.

These challenges can lead to increased costs, reduced efficiency, and damage to brand reputation. In the next section, we will explore how blockchain technology and smart contracts can help solve these challenges in supply chain management (*Benefits of blockchain - IBM Blockchain | IBM*, no date).

HOW BLOCKCHAIN TECHNOLOGY CAN HELP SOLVE SUPPLY CHAIN CHALLENGES

Blockchain technology has gained significant attention for its potential in revolutionizing supply chain management. Blockchain is a distributed ledger system that enables secure and transparent transactions without the need for intermediaries. The technology offers a number of benefits, including real-time visibility, improved traceability, enhanced security, and reduced costs. In this article, we will explore how blockchain technology can help solve supply chain challenges and improve the overall efficiency and transparency of the supply chain (Kouhizadeh, Saberi and Sarkis, 2021).

Transparency and Traceability

One of the biggest challenges in the supply chain industry is the lack of transparency and traceability. This makes it difficult to track and trace products from the point of origin to the point of consumption. Blockchain technology can help solve this challenge by providing a secure and transparent ledger system that allows supply chain stakeholders to track products throughout the supply chain (Sweeney, no date).

Each transaction in the blockchain is recorded and cannot be altered, making it easy to trace the origin and movement of products. This feature is particularly useful for products that require strict quality control measures or those that are highly regulated. With blockchain, supply chain stakeholders can ensure the authenticity and quality of products, prevent counterfeiting and fraud, and streamline the entire supply chain process (Hayes, 2023).

Reduced Costs

Another challenge in the supply chain industry is the inefficiency of the supply chain process. Delays and bottlenecks in the flow of goods and services can lead to increased costs and reduced efficiency. Blockchain technology can help reduce these costs by eliminating intermediaries and automating the supply chain process (Hobbs, 2019).

Smart contracts are self-executing contracts that automatically execute the terms of an agreement when the conditions specified in the contract are met. These contracts are stored and executed on a blockchain network, making them immutable, transparent, and secure. With smart contracts, supply chain stakeholders can automate the supply chain process, reducing the need for intermediaries and minimizing delays and bottlenecks (Frankenfield, 2023).

Enhanced Security

Security is another challenge in the supply chain industry, with counterfeiting and fraud being common issues. Blockchain technology can help enhance security by providing a secure and tamper-proof ledger system. The decentralized nature of blockchain ensures that data is not controlled by any single entity, making it difficult for malicious actors to manipulate the data (Ghadge *et al.*, 2021).

In addition, blockchain uses advanced cryptography to secure the data, making it virtually impossible to hack. With blockchain, supply chain stakeholders can ensure the security and privacy of their data, prevent counterfeiting and fraud, and improve the overall security of the supply chain process (*What is blockchain?*, 2022).

In conclusion, blockchain technology offers a number of benefits that can help solve supply chain challenges and improve the overall efficiency and transparency of the supply chain. By providing real-time visibility, improving traceability, enhancing security, and reducing costs, blockchain can revolutionize the way the supply chain industry operates. While there are implementation considerations and potential limitations that need to be addressed, the potential benefits of blockchain technology in supply chain management are undeniable. The adoption of blockchain technology in the supply chain industry is expected to grow rapidly in the coming years, and it will be interesting to see how this technology will transform the supply chain landscape in the future.

USE CASES OF BLOCKCHAIN TECHNOLOGY IN SUPPLY CHAIN MANAGEMENT

Blockchain technology has the potential to revolutionize the way supply chains operate by providing a transparent, secure, and efficient platform for managing the flow of goods, services, and information. Blockchain is a distributed ledger system that allows secure transactions without the need for intermediaries. With its immutability and transparency, blockchain technology can help address some of the key challenges faced by the supply chain industry, such as lack of transparency, inefficiencies, fraud, and counterfeiting (Saberi et al., 2018b).

In this article, we will explore some of the key use cases of blockchain technology in supply chain management.

Track and Trace

One of the primary use cases of blockchain technology in supply chain management is track and trace. With blockchain, it becomes possible to track and trace products throughout the supply chain, from the point of origin to the point of consumption. This is made possible by the immutability of the blockchain ledger, which ensures that each transaction is recorded and cannot be altered.

This level of traceability can help improve supply chain transparency and provide greater visibility into the movement of goods. For example, blockchain technology can be used to track the origin of raw materials, ensuring that they are ethically sourced and comply with environmental and social standards. It can also be used to track the movement of finished products, providing greater transparency into the supply chain process (An agri-food supply chain traceability system for China based on RFID & blockchain technology, 2016).

Supply Chain Financing

Blockchain technology can also be used to improve supply chain financing. Supply chain financing is a financing method that provides financing to suppliers based on their outstanding invoices. With blockchain technology, it becomes possible to automate the supply chain financing process, reducing the need for intermediaries and improving the speed and efficiency of the process (Gaur, 2020).

Smart contracts, which are self-executing contracts that automatically execute the terms of an agreement when the conditions specified in the contract are met, can be used to automate the supply chain financing process. Suppliers can create invoices on the blockchain, which are then automatically verified and settled once the conditions of the contract are met. This can help improve the cash flow of suppliers and reduce the risk of default (Gluca and Gluca, 2020).

Counterfeiting and Fraud Prevention

Counterfeiting and fraud are common issues in the supply chain industry, which can lead to significant financial losses and damage to brand reputation. Blockchain technology can help prevent counterfeiting and fraud by providing a secure and transparent ledger system that allows stakeholders to verify the authenticity and provenance of products (Using Blockchain Technology to Fight Counterfeiters, no date).

With blockchain technology, it becomes possible to create a digital identity for each product, which is then recorded on the blockchain. This digital identity can include information such as the origin of the product, the materials used in its production, and any certifications or quality control measures. This information can then be verified by supply chain stakeholders, such as suppliers, manufacturers, and retailers, ensuring the authenticity and quality of the product (Blockchain for Digital Identity, no date).

Supply Chain Optimization

Blockchain technology can also be used to optimize the supply chain process. By providing real-time visibility into the movement of goods, blockchain technology can help identify inefficiencies and bottlenecks in the supply chain process (Akroyd and Kober, 2020). This can help supply chain stakeholders to optimize the supply chain process, reducing costs and improving efficiency.

For example, blockchain technology can be used to track the movement of goods from the point of origin to the point of consumption, providing real-time visibility into the supply chain process (Higgins, 2021). This can help supply chain stakeholders to identify bottlenecks and delays in the process, allowing them to take corrective action to improve efficiency (Khan, no date).

Compliance and Regulatory Compliance

Blockchain technology can also be used to ensure compliance and regulatory compliance in the supply chain industry. With blockchain, it becomes possible to create a tamper-proof record of all supply chain transactions, which can be used to ensure compliance with regulations and standards (Saxena et al., 2020).

For example, blockchain technology can be used to ensure compliance with environmental and social standards. By creating a digital identity for each product on the blockchain, supply chain stakeholders can track the origin of raw materials and ensure that they meet environmental and social standards (Park and Li, 2021). This can help reduce the risk of non-compliance and ensure that supply chain stakeholders meet their obligations under local and international regulations.

Supply Chain Visibility

Another use case of blockchain technology in supply chain management is supply chain visibility. Supply chain visibility refers to the ability to track the movement of goods and information throughout the supply chain process. With blockchain technology, it becomes possible to provide real-time visibility into the movement of goods and information, improving supply chain transparency and reducing the risk of fraud and counterfeiting (Min, 2019).

Blockchain technology can be used to create a digital record of all supply chain transactions, which can be accessed by supply chain stakeholders in real-time. This can help improve collaboration and communication between supply chain stakeholders (Rejeb et al., 2021), reducing the risk of miscommunication and delays.

Sustainability and Environmental Impact

Blockchain technology can also be used to promote sustainability and reduce the environmental impact of the supply chain industry (Kouhizadeh and Sarkis, 2018). With blockchain, it becomes possible to create a digital record of the environmental impact of each supply chain transaction, which can be used to monitor and reduce the environmental impact of the supply chain industry.

For example, blockchain technology can be used to track the carbon footprint of each supply chain transaction, providing greater visibility into the environmental impact of the supply chain process (Saberi et al., 2018). This information can then be used to identify opportunities for reducing carbon emissions and improving the sustainability of the supply chain industry.

In conclusion, blockchain technology has the potential to revolutionize the way supply chains operate, providing a transparent, secure, and efficient platform for managing the flow of goods, services, and information. By providing real-time visibility into the movement of goods and information, blockchain technology can help address some of the key challenges faced by the supply chain industry, such as lack of transparency, inefficiencies, fraud, and counterfeiting.

The use cases of blockchain technology in supply chain management are many and varied, ranging from track and trace to supply chain financing, counterfeiting and fraud prevention, supply chain optimization, compliance and regulatory compliance, supply chain visibility, and sustainability and environmental impact. By leveraging the power of blockchain technology, supply chain stakeholders can improve the efficiency, transparency, and sustainability of the supply chain industry, reducing costs and improving customer satisfaction.

BENEFITS OF USING SMART CONTRACTS IN SUPPLY CHAIN MANAGEMENT

Supply chain management involves coordinating the flow of goods, services, and information between multiple stakeholders, which can be time-consuming, inefficient, and prone to errors. Smart contracts, which are self-executing contracts with the terms of the agreement being directly written into lines of code, offer a number of benefits to supply chain management, including increased efficiency, transparency, and security. They automate many manual processes, reduce intermediaries, and streamline the supply chain process, resulting in faster transaction times, lower costs, and increased efficiency (Groschopf, Dobrovnik and Herneth, 2021b). Smart contracts also provide a transparent and tamper-proof record of all supply chain transactions, improving supply chain transparency and helping reduce the risk of fraud and counterfeiting. They are based on blockchain technology, which provides a secure platform for managing supply chain transactions, reducing the risk of fraud and counterfeiting. Real-world examples of smart contracts include tracking food products for food safety issues, tracking the movement of goods in the logistics industry, tracking the origin and movement of diamonds, and automating the process of financing supply chain transactions (Kamble, Gunasekaran and Gawankar, 2018). While there are challenges to implementing smart contract-based systems, such as interoperability and scalability, the benefits are clear and will continue to drive the adoption of this technology in the years to come.

IMPLEMENTATION CONSIDERATIONS FOR USING SMART CONTRACTS IN SUPPLY CHAIN MANAGEMENT

Smart contracts offer numerous benefits to supply chain management, including increased efficiency, transparency, and security. However, implementing smart contracts in supply chain management can be a complex and challenging process. In this article, we will discuss the implementation considerations for using smart contracts in supply chain management.

Interoperability

One of the primary considerations for implementing smart contracts in supply chain management is interoperability. Smart contracts are designed to be self-executing and self-enforcing, but they must also be able to interact with other systems in the supply chain. This requires a standardized protocol for communication and data exchange between different systems (Bottoni *et al.*, 2020).

Interoperability can be a challenge in supply chain management because there are often multiple stakeholders involved, each using different systems and data formats. To overcome this challenge, it is important to establish clear standards for data exchange and communication, such as the use of open APIs and standardized data formats (Musyoka, no date).

Scalability

Another consideration for implementing smart contracts in supply chain management is scalability. Smart contracts are designed to be executed on a decentralized network, which means that the processing power is distributed across multiple nodes (Musyoka, no date; Pan et al., 2021). This can limit the scalability of smart contract-based systems, particularly when processing large volumes of data.

To address scalability issues, it may be necessary to implement a hybrid approach that combines decentralized and centralized processing (Solaiman, Wike and Sfyrakis, 2020). For example, a smart contract-based system could use a centralized processing engine for certain functions, such as data validation and verification, while still leveraging the benefits of decentralized processing for other functions (Gotskind, 2022; What is Decentralization?, no date).

Security

Security is a critical consideration for implementing smart contracts in supply chain management. Smart contracts are designed to be secure and tamper-proof, but they can still be vulnerable to attacks if not implemented correctly (Llp, 2021). This includes attacks such as hacking, data breaches, and other forms of cybercrime (Godfrey-Faussett, 2021; Kshetri, 2017).

To ensure the security of smart contract-based systems, it is important to implement robust security protocols, such as encryption, access controls, and regular security audits (ConsenSys, no date; Wan et al., 2021). It is also important to have a clear incident response plan in place to respond quickly to any security breaches or other incidents (Alharby and Van Moorsel, 2017; Li, 2022; Luu *et al.*, 2016).

Regulatory Compliance

Regulatory compliance is another important consideration for implementing smart contracts in supply chain management. Many industries are subject to strict regulations around data privacy, security, and other issues, and smart contract-based systems must comply with these regulations to ensure legal compliance (Grunert, 2020).

To ensure regulatory compliance, it is important to work closely with regulatory agencies and legal experts to understand the specific requirements for your industry. This may involve implementing additional security measures, such as encryption and access controls, or ensuring that data is stored and transmitted in compliance with local and international regulations.

Integration with Legacy Systems

Finally, integrating smart contract-based systems with legacy systems can be a challenge. Many supply chain management systems are built on legacy technologies that may not be compatible with smart contract-based systems. This can make it difficult to integrate data and processes between these systems.

To overcome this challenge, it may be necessary to develop custom integration solutions that bridge the gap between legacy systems and smart contract-based systems. This may involve using middleware or APIs to facilitate data exchange between different systems, or implementing custom integration solutions to address specific integration challenges.

Implementing smart contracts in supply chain management can be a complex and challenging process, but it offers numerous benefits, including increased efficiency, transparency, and security. By considering the implementation considerations outlined in this article, supply chain stakeholders can successfully implement smart contract-based systems and realize these benefits. This includes establishing clear standards for data exchange and communication, addressing scalability issues, implementing robust security protocols, ensuring regulatory compliance, and developing custom integration solutions to bridge the gap between legacy systems and smart contract-based systems (*Smart Contracts for Innovative Supply chain management | ITeXchange Blog*, 2022).

CHALLENGES AND LIMITATIONS OF USING SMART CONTRACTS IN SUPPLY CHAIN MANAGEMENT

Smart contracts offer numerous benefits to supply chain management, including increased efficiency, transparency, and security. However, like any new technology, there are also challenges and limitations to using smart contracts in supply chain management. In this article, we will discuss the challenges and limitations of using smart contracts in supply chain management.

Complexity of Supply Chain Processes

One of the primary challenges of using smart contracts in supply chain management is the complexity of supply chain processes. Supply chains can involve numerous stakeholders, including suppliers, manufacturers, distributors, retailers, and consumers, each with their own processes and data requirements (Wang *et al.*, 2019). This complexity can make it challenging to design smart contracts that can effectively address all of the different processes and requirements.

To overcome this challenge, it is important to carefully map out supply chain processes and data requirements to identify areas where smart contracts can provide the most value. This may involve developing custom smart contracts for specific processes or stakeholders, rather than trying to create a one-size-fits-all solution.

Limited Data Input Capabilities

Another challenge of using smart contracts in supply chain management is the limited data input capabilities of smart contracts. Smart contracts are designed to be self-executing and self-enforcing based on predetermined rules, but they are limited in their ability to process external data.

This can be a challenge in supply chain management, where data inputs can be highly variable and subject to change. To overcome this challenge, it may be necessary to develop more complex smart contracts that can process a wider range of data inputs, or to integrate smart contracts with other systems that can provide additional data inputs.

Integration with Legacy Systems

Integrating smart contracts with legacy systems can be a challenge. Many supply chain management systems are built on legacy technologies that may not be compatible with smart contract-based systems. This can make it difficult to integrate data and processes between these systems.

To overcome this challenge, it may be necessary to develop custom integration solutions that bridge the gap between legacy systems and smart contract-based systems. This may involve using middleware or APIs to facilitate data exchange between different systems, or implementing custom integration solutions to address specific integration challenges.

Regulatory Compliance

Regulatory compliance is another challenge of using smart contracts in supply chain management. Many industries are subject to strict regulations around data privacy, security, and other issues, and smart contract-based systems must comply with these regulations to ensure legal compliance.

To ensure regulatory compliance, it is important to work closely with regulatory agencies and legal experts to understand the specific requirements for your industry. This may involve implementing additional security measures, such as encryption and access controls, or ensuring that data is stored and transmitted in compliance with local and international regulations.

Lack of Standardization

A lack of standardization can be a challenge when using smart contracts in supply chain management. Smart contracts are still a relatively new technology, and there is not yet a standardized set of best practices or protocols for using them in supply chain management.

To overcome this challenge, it is important to stay up-to-date on the latest developments in smart contract technology and to participate in industry efforts to develop standardized protocols and best practices for using smart contracts in supply chain management.

Limited Scalability

Smart contracts are designed to be executed on a decentralized network, which means that the processing power is distributed across multiple nodes. This can limit the scalability of smart contract-based systems, particularly when processing large volumes of data.

To address scalability issues, it may be necessary to implement a hybrid approach that combines decentralized and centralized processing. For example, a smart contract-based system could use a centralized processing engine for certain functions, such as data validation and verification, while still leveraging the benefits of decentralized processing for other functions.

While smart contracts offer numerous benefits to supply chain management, there are also challenges and limitations that must be addressed to realize these benefits. These challenges include the complexity of supply chain processes, limited data input capabilities, integration with legacy systems, regulatory compliance, lack of standardization, and limited scalability.

To overcome these challenges, it is important to carefully map out supply chain processes and data requirements, develop custom smart contracts for specific processes or stakeholders, and integrate smart contracts with other systems that can provide additional data inputs. It may also be necessary to develop custom integration solutions that bridge the gap between legacy systems and smart contract-based systems, and to work closely with regulatory agencies and legal experts to ensure regulatory compliance (Singh and Kumar, 2022).

In addition, staying up-to-date on the latest developments in smart contract technology and participating in industry efforts to develop standardized protocols and best practices can help address the lack of standardization challenge. Finally, implementing a hybrid approach that combines decentralized and centralized processing can help address scalability issues.

Overall, while there are challenges and limitations to using smart contracts in supply chain management, the potential benefits make it well worth the effort to overcome these challenges. By leveraging smart contract technology, supply chain managers can achieve greater efficiency, transparency, and security, ultimately leading to improved business outcomes.

Some of the challenges and limitations of using smart contracts in supply chain management include:

The need for reliable and trustworthy data sources (oracles) to trigger the execution of smart contracts. Depending on the type and complexity of the oracle, there may be issues with data quality, availability, security, and cost.

The difficulty of integrating smart contracts with existing legacy systems and processes that may not be compatible or interoperable with blockchain technology.

The legal uncertainty and regulatory compliance of smart contracts, especially across different jurisdictions and industries. There may be conflicts or gaps between the code and the law, as well as challenges in enforcing and resolving disputes involving smart contracts.

Some of the benefits of using smart contracts in supply chain management include:

The ability to automate transactions and processes that are otherwise manual, time-consuming, and error-prone. Smart contracts can reduce transaction costs, improve operational efficiency, and enhance customer satisfaction.

The ability to increase transparency and traceability of supply chain activities and events. Smart contracts can provide real-time visibility and accountability of the flow of goods, information, and money throughout the supply chain.

The ability to enhance security and trust among supply chain partners. Smart contracts can prevent fraud, tampering, and unauthorized access by using cryptography and consensus mechanisms to ensure data integrity and authenticity.

To realize these benefits, supply chain managers need to evaluate their supply chain maturity and readiness for adopting smart contract technology. They also need to assess the sustainability impacts of smart contracts on their supply chain performance and stakeholders. A possible framework for doing so is proposed, which maps the relationships between organizational development, sustainability, and technology. According to this framework, smart contracts can contribute to the economic and social development of networked value chains and Society 5.0 by enabling efficient and transparent governance and collaborative self-coordination of human and non-human actors2. However, there are also trade-offs and challenges that need to be addressed, such as ensuring data quality, privacy, ethics, and social inclusion (Groschopf, Dobrovnik and Herneth, 2021).

In conclusion, smart contracts offer a promising opportunity for supply chain management to achieve higher levels of efficiency, transparency, security, and sustainability. However, they also pose significant challenges and limitations that require careful consideration and adaptation. Supply chain managers need to assess their current situation and future goals, as well as the potential impacts of smart contracts on their supply chain operations and stakeholders. By doing so, they can leverage smart contract technology to improve their business outcomes and contribute to social good.

FUTURE OUTLOOK AND POTENTIAL DEVELOPMENTS IN THE USE OF SMART CONTRACTS AND BLOCKCHAIN TECHNOLOGY IN SUPPLY CHAIN MANAGEMENT

The use of smart contracts and blockchain technology in supply chain management has already shown great promise, but the potential for future developments and advancements is even more exciting. In this article, we will explore some of the potential future use cases and developments for smart contracts and blockchain technology in supply chain management.

Interoperability and Standards

One potential area of future development is the establishment of interoperability and standards between different blockchain networks. Currently, different blockchain networks use different protocols and standards, which can make it difficult for businesses to collaborate and share data. However, efforts are underway to develop cross-chain interoperability solutions, which would enable data and assets to be exchanged across different blockchain networks.

Another potential area for standards development is the creation of standardized smart contract templates that can be easily adapted for use in different supply chain processes. This would enable businesses to more easily and efficiently implement smart contracts, and would also promote greater consistency and transparency across different supply chains.

Machine Learning and Artificial Intelligence

Another potential development is the integration of machine learning and artificial intelligence (AI) with blockchain and smart contract technology. By analyzing data from different points in the supply chain, machine learning algorithms can help identify patterns and optimize supply chain processes. For example, AI could be used to predict demand patterns, optimize production schedules, and identify potential supply chain disruptions before they occur [47] [48].

Supply Chain Finance

Smart contracts and blockchain technology could also revolutionize supply chain finance by enabling automated payments and reducing transaction costs. Currently, the financing of supply chains involves multiple parties and complex payment arrangements, which can result in delays and high costs. However, smart contracts could be used to automate payment processes, eliminating the need for intermediaries and reducing transaction costs.

Environmental and Social Sustainability

Blockchain technology could also be used to promote environmental and social sustainability in supply chains. For example, blockchain could be used to track the carbon footprint of products, enabling businesses to make more sustainable sourcing and transportation decisions. It could also be used to promote fair labor practices and ethical sourcing by providing greater transparency into supply chain operations.

Smart contracts and blockchain technology have the potential to transform supply chain management, providing greater efficiency, transparency, and security. However, there are still challenges to be addressed, such as regulatory compliance and scalability issues. Nevertheless, the potential benefits of this technology are too great to ignore, and we can expect to see continued advancements and developments in the coming years. By staying up-to-date on the latest developments and exploring new use cases, businesses can leverage smart contracts and blockchain technology to create more efficient and sustainable supply chains.

CASE STUDIES OF COMPANIES THAT HAVE SUCCESSFULLY IMPLEMENTED SMART CONTRACTS IN THEIR SUPPLY CHAIN MANAGEMENT

Smart contracts and blockchain technology have the potential to revolutionize supply chain management by improving efficiency, transparency, and security. While the technology is still in its early stages, there are already companies that have successfully implemented smart contracts in their supply chain operations. In this article, we will examine some case studies of companies that have successfully implemented smart contracts in their supply chain management (Chang, El-Rayes and Shi, 2022; Chen and Wang, 2019; IEEE Xplore Full-Text PDF:, no date; Liu et al., 2023; Song et al., 2022).

Walmart

Walmart, one of the world's largest retailers, has been a pioneer in the use of blockchain technology and smart contracts in its supply chain operations. In 2016, Walmart began piloting a program to use blockchain technology to track the origin of pork in China. By using blockchain technology, Walmart was able to track the pork from the farm to the processing plant, and then to the store shelves (*Blockchain in the food supply chain - What does the future look like?*, no date; Hyperledger Foundation, 2022).

Following the success of the pilot program, Walmart has expanded its use of blockchain technology to track other products in its supply chain, such as leafy greens, mangoes, and strawberries. By using smart contracts to automate the tracking process, Walmart has been able to improve supply chain transparency and reduce the time it takes to track products in the supply chain (Vitasek, 2022).

Maersk

Maersk, the world's largest container shipping company, has also been experimenting with blockchain technology and smart contracts in its supply chain operations. In collaboration with IBM, Maersk has developed a blockchain-based platform called TradeLens, which aims to improve transparency and efficiency in the global shipping industry (Maersk, 2023; Reuters, 2022).

By using smart contracts to automate the processing of shipping documents, TradeLens has been able to reduce the time it takes to process documents from days to minutes (Scott, 2018). This has enabled Maersk and its customers to more easily track shipments and reduce the risk of lost or delayed shipments.

De Beers

De Beers, the world's largest diamond producer, has also been exploring the use of blockchain technology and smart contracts in its supply chain operations. In collaboration with other members of the diamond industry, De Beers has developed a blockchain-based platform called Tracr, which aims to improve transparency and traceability in the diamond supply chain.

By using smart contracts to automate the tracking and certification process, Tracr has been able to improve supply chain transparency and reduce the risk of fraud and counterfeiting in the diamond industry. The platform has also enabled De Beers and other members of the industry to more easily track the origin of diamonds and ensure that they are ethically sourced.

Provenance

Provenance, a UK-based startup, has developed a blockchain-based platform that enables businesses to track and verify the origin of products in their supply chain. By using smart contracts to automate the tracking and verification process, Provenance has been able to improve supply chain transparency and enable businesses to make more informed decisions about sourcing and sustainability.

One example of a company that has successfully implemented Provenance's platform is Co-op, a UK-based food retailer. By using Provenance's platform to track the origin of its fish products, Co-op has been able to ensure that its products are sustainably sourced and that they meet the company's ethical standards.

These case studies demonstrate the potential of smart contracts and blockchain technology to revolutionize supply chain management by improving transparency, efficiency, and security. While the technology is still in its early stages, these companies have shown that it is possible to successfully implement smart contracts in the supply chain (CoinGeek, no date; Difrancesco, Meena and Kumar, 2022). As more companies explore the use of blockchain technology and smart contracts in their supply chain operations, we can expect to see continued advancements and developments in the coming years. By staying up-to-date on the latest developments and exploring new use cases (Javaid *et al.*, 2022), businesses can leverage smart contracts and blockchain technology to create more efficient and sustainable supply chains (Anser, 2023).

ETHICAL CONSIDERATIONS IN USING BLOCKCHAIN TECHNOLOGY IN SUPPLY CHAIN MANAGEMENT

Blockchain technology has emerged as a promising solution to address supply chain challenges, such as improving traceability, reducing fraud and increasing efficiency. However, as with any technology, there are also ethical considerations that need to be taken into account when using blockchain in supply chain management. In this article, we will explore some of the ethical implications of using blockchain in supply chain management and how companies can navigate them (Tokkozhina, Martins and Ferreira, 2022).

Transparency and Privacy

One of the key benefits of blockchain technology is its ability to provide transparency, allowing all parties in the supply chain to track products and transactions from the point of origin to the point of consumption. However, this also raises concerns about privacy and data protection. For example, if blockchain is used to track sensitive information, such as personal data or trade secrets, there is a risk that this information could be exposed to unauthorized parties (Agi and Jha, 2022).

To address these concerns, companies should implement measures to ensure that only authorized parties have access to sensitive information. This can include using encryption and access control mechanisms to limit access to the blockchain, as well as implementing privacy-enhancing technologies, such as zero-knowledge proofs, which allow parties to prove the validity of data without revealing sensitive information (Sedlmeir *et al.*, 2022).

Environmental Impact

Blockchain technology is based on a distributed ledger, which requires a significant amount of computing power and energy to operate. This has raised concerns about the environmental impact of blockchain, particularly as the technology becomes more widely adopted.

To address these concerns, companies can explore alternative approaches to blockchain, such as using more energy-efficient consensus algorithms or transitioning to more sustainable energy sources. Companies can also consider offsetting their energy usage through carbon credits or other sustainable practices.

Fairness and Inclusivity

Another ethical consideration when using blockchain in supply chain management is the potential impact on fairness and inclusivity. Blockchain technology has the potential to create more transparent and fair supply chains, but it can also reinforce existing power structures and exacerbate inequalities.

To address these concerns, companies can ensure that all parties in the supply chain have equal access to the benefits of blockchain technology. This can include providing training and resources to ensure that all parties have the skills and knowledge to participate in blockchain-based supply chains. Companies can also work to promote diversity and inclusion within their supply chains, and engage with stakeholders to ensure that the benefits of blockchain are distributed fairly.

As with any technology, there are ethical considerations that need to be taken into account when using blockchain in supply chain management. These considerations include privacy and data protection, environmental impact, and fairness and inclusivity. Companies can address these concerns by implementing measures to ensure the privacy and security of sensitive information, exploring more sustainable approaches to blockchain, and promoting fairness and inclusivity within their supply chains. By addressing these ethical considerations, companies can unlock the full potential of blockchain technology to transform supply chain management (Sharif and Ghodoosi, 2022).

THE ROLE OF INTERNET OF THINGS (IOT) DEVICES IN THE IMPLEMENTATION OF SMART CONTRACTS IN SUPPLY CHAIN MANAGEMENT

The Internet of Things (IoT) is the connection of devices and machines to the internet, which can range from simple sensors to complex machinery. The adoption of IoT in various industries has increased due to its potential for enhancing efficiency and productivity. IoT devices play a critical role in the implementation of smart contracts in supply chain management, which are self-executing contracts that operate on a blockchain network. By integrating IoT devices with smart contracts, supply chain processes can be automated, and stakeholders can easily track the movement and condition of products throughout the supply chain, thereby reducing the risk of delays and product spoilage (A. and R., 2011). Additionally, the use of smart contracts and IoT devices in supply chain management enhances security, as all transactions are recorded in a tamper-proof manner. However, challenges such as standardization of IoT devices and data privacy and security need to be addressed. Finally, the use of IoT devices and smart contracts can provide benefits for supply chain management, such as enabling real-time tracking and monitoring of goods and assets, reducing the risk of theft or loss, improving the accuracy of delivery times, and streamlining supply chain operations ("CS Information," 2018; A., 2020; Singh, Shukla and Sajwan, 2021; Khan et al., 2022; OECD, 2019).

THE POTENTIAL IMPACT OF SMART CONTRACTS AND BLOCKCHAIN TECHNOLOGY ON LOGISTICS AND TRANSPORTATION

The food and beverage industry is one of the largest and most complex supply chains in the world, with a variety of stakeholders involved. Blockchain technology and smart contracts can help prevent food contamination and safety issues by increasing transparency and traceability throughout the supply chain. Smart contracts can also be used to automate certain processes in the supply chain, such as payment and quality control, and reduce the need for intermediaries. Another potential use case for smart contracts is in the area of sustainability (Admin, 2023; Chatterjee, Singh and Neha, 2023).

The use of blockchain technology and smart contracts in the food and beverage industry has the potential to revolutionize the way that food products are tracked and traced throughout the supply chain, providing greater transparency, efficiency, and accountability. Companies such as Walmart and Nestle have implemented blockchain-based systems for tracking the origin of certain food products, such as mangoes and pork in China. However, there are several challenges that must be addressed, such as ensuring interoperability between different blockchain systems and data privacy and security (Enwood, 2021). These technologies can help prevent food safety issues and provide consumers with more information about the sustainability and quality of the products (Dellumo, 2023).

In conclusion, the use of smart contracts and blockchain technology in the food and beverage industry has the potential to revolutionize the way that food products are tracked and traced throughout the supply chain. By providing greater transparency, efficiency, and accountability, these technologies can help prevent food safety issues and provide consumers with more information about the sustainability and quality of the products they consume. However, there are also challenges that must be addressed in order to ensure the widespread adoption and success of these technologies in the industry.

REFERENCES

Accenture. (n.d.). *Blockchain for digital identity*. Accenture. https://www.accenture.com/us-en/services/blockchain/digital-identity

Agi, M. A. N., & Jha, A. K. (2022). Blockchain technology in the supply chain: An integrated theoretical perspective of organizational adoption. *International Journal of Production Economics, 108458*, 108458. doi:10.1016/j.ijpe.2022.108458

Alharby, M., & van Moorsel, A. (2017). *Blockchain-based smart contracts: A systematic mapping study*. arXiv preprint arXiv:1710.06372. https://arxiv.org/abs/1710.06372 doi:10.5121/csit.2017.71011

Alharby, N., & Moorsel, A. V. (2013). Blockchain-based IoT security: A survey. *Computers & Security, 88*, 101614. https://www.sciencedirect.com/science/article/abs/pii/S0045790623000198

Alharby, N., & Moorsel, A. V. (2018). *Internet of Things security with blockchain technology: A state-of-the-art review*. Research Gate. https://www.researchgate.net/publication/365584843_Internet_of_Things_IoT_Security_with_Blockchain_Technology_A_State-of-the-Art_Review

Alharby, N., & Moorsel, A. V. (2021). Blockchain-based IoT security: A comprehensive review of architectures and challenges. *Future Generation Computer Systems, 122*, 1–16. doi:10.1016/j.future.2021.07.015

Alraja, S. M. A., & Alraja, M. A. (2021). Smart Contracts and Supply Chain Management Using Blockchain. *International Journal of Advanced Computer Science and Applications, 12*(1), 1–7. https://www.researchgate.net/publication/365027511_Smart_Contracts_and_Supply_Chain_Management_Using_Blockchain

Amazon Web Services. (n.d.). *What is decentralization in blockchain?* AWS. https://aws.amazon.com/blockchain/decentralization-in-blockchain/

A.P. Moller - Maersk. (2022, November 29). *A.P. Moller - Maersk and IBM to discontinue TradeLens, a blockchain-enabled shipping solution*. A.P. Moller-Maersk. https://www.maersk.com/news/articles/2022/11/29/maersk-and-ibm-to-discontinue-tradelens

Asmussen, C. G., & Charles, A. (2020). Blockchain technology in supply chain management: Insights on adoption barriers and enablers. *Management Accounting Research, 47*, 100–113. doi:10.1016/j.mar.2019.07.002

Bergström, A. (2020). *The role of social media in crisis communication and crisis management* [Doctoral dissertation, University of Gothenburg]. https://www.diva-portal.org/smash/get/diva2:1574301/FULLTEXT01.pdf

Blockhead Technologies. (2019, October 16). *How blockchain is revolutionising food supply chains.* Blockhead Technologies. https://blockheadtechnologies.com/how-blockchain-is-revolutionising-food-supply-chains/

Bottoni, P., Gessa, N., Massa, G., Pareschi, R., Selim, H., & Arcuri, E. (2020). Intelligent smart contracts for innovative supply chain management. *Frontiers in Blockchain*, *3*, 535787. doi:10.3389/fbloc.2020.535787

Casper, R. H., Lazaro, J. A., Wang, E., & Wegrzyn, K. E. (2021). *Smart supply chains using smart contracts.* Manufacturing Industry Advisor. https://www.foley.com/en/insights/publications/2021/09/smart-supply-chains-using-smart-contracts

Chen, X., & Wang, Y. (2021). A blockchain-based secure data sharing scheme for cloud storage *Journal of Cybersecurity and Information Intelligence*, *1*(2), 15–22. https://www.mdpi.com/2674-1032/1/2/15

ConsenSys. (n.d.). *Smart contract security best practices.* GitHub. https://github.com/ConsenSys/smart-contract-best-practices

Difrancesco, R. M., Meena, P., & Kumar, G. (2022). How blockchain technology improves sustainable supply chain processes: A practical guide. *Sustainability*, *14*(1), 7894. https://www.ncbi.nlm.nih.gov/pmc/articles/PMC9797894/

Enkronos. (2020). *What is a smart contract? Advantages and disadvantages.* Ekronos. https://content.enkronos.com/what-is-a-smart-contract-advantages-and-disadvantages/

Exchange Web. (2022). *Smart contracts for innovative supply chain management.* Exchange Web. https://www.itexchangeweb.com/blog/smart-contracts-for-innovative-supply-chain-management/

Frankenfield, J. (2023). *Smart contracts and their advantages.* Investopedia. https://www.investopedia.com/terms/s/smart-contracts.asp

Gaiha, A., & Gaur, V. (2020). Building a transparent supply chain. *Harvard Business Review*, *98*(3), 102–109. https://hbr.org/2020/05/building-a-transparent-supply-chain

Gaur, V., & Singh, S. (2020). Blockchain technology for supply chain compliance. In *Blockchain Technology for Industry 4.0* (pp. 1–22). Springer. doi:10.1007/978-981-15-4814-7_1

Ghadge, A., Duck, A., Er, M., & Caldwell, N. (2021). Deceptive counterfeit risk in global supply chains. *Supply Chain Forum: An International Journal, 22*(2), 87-99. https://www.tandfonline.com/doi/full/10.1080/16258312.2021.1908844

Gotskind, A. (2021). *Decentralized finance and the power of smart contracts.* Research Blog. https://researchblog.duke.edu/2021/12/13/decentralized-finance-and-the-power-of-smart-contracts/

Groschopf, W., Dobrovnik, M., & Herneth, C. (2021). Smart contracts for sustainable supply chain management: Conceptual frameworks for supply chain maturity evaluation and smart contract sustainability assessment. *Frontiers in Blockchain*, *4*, 506436. doi:10.3389/fbloc.2021.506436

Grunert, E. W., & Pinsent Masons. (2018). *Regulatory compliance in the global supply chain.* Out-Law. https://www.pinsentmasons.com/out-law/analysis/regulatory-compliance-global-supply-chain

Harvard Business Review. (2022, January). How Walmart Canada uses blockchain to solve supply-chain challenges [Web page]. *Harvard Business Review.* https://hbr.org/2022/01/how-walmart-canada-uses-blockchain-to-solve-supply-chain-challenges

Hayes, A. (2022). Blockchain facts: What is it, how it works, and how it can be used. *Investopedia.* https://www.investopedia.com/terms/b/blockchain.asp

Higgins, M. (2021, November 8). Blockchain In Supply Chain. *Forbes.* https://www.forbes.com/sites/forbestechcouncil/2021/11/08/blockchain-in-supply-chain/

Hobbs, B. (2019). Supply chain inefficiencies can crush customer experience and cost you millions. *Forbes.* https://www.forbes.com/sites/forbesbusinessdevelopmentcouncil/2019/09/30/supply-chain-inefficiencies-can-crush-customer-experience-and-cost-you-millions/

Hyperledger. (n.d.). *Walmart case study [Web page].* Hyperledger. https://www.hyperledger.org/learn/publications/walmart-case-study

IBM. (2018, August 9). *TradeLens, how IBM and Maersk are sharing blockchain to build a global trade platform [Web page].* IBM. https://www.ibm.com/blogs/think/2018/11/tradelens-how-ibm-and-maersk-are-sharing-blockchain-to-build-a-global-trade-platform/

IBM. (n.d.). *Benefits of blockchain.* IBM. https://www.ibm.com/topics/benefits-of-blockchain

Javaid, N., & Khan, I. (2019). Blockchain-based Secure Data Sharing Platform for Research Data Rights Management over the Ethereum Network. In 2019 IEEE 5th International Conference on Engineering Technologies and Applied Sciences (ICETAS). IEEE. https://www.researchgate.net/profile/Nadeem-Javaid/publication/334696593_Blockchain-based_Secure_Data_Sharing_Platform_for_Research_Data_Rights_Management_over_the_Ethereum_Network/links/5d3aa69e92851cd04686d625/Blockchain-based-Secure-Data-Sharing-Platform-for-Research-Data-Rights-Management-over-the-Ethereum-Network.pdf

Kamble, S. S., Gunasekaran, A., & Gawankar, S. A. (2018). Sustainable Industry 4.0 framework: A systematic literature review identifying the current trends and future perspectives. *Process Safety and Environmental Protection, 117,* 408–425. doi:10.1016/j.psep.2018.05.009

Khan, M. (n.d.). *Revolutionizing the Supply Chain: How Blockchain Technology is Enhancing Efficiency and Transparency.* LinkedIn. https://www.linkedin.com/pulse/revolutionizing-supply-chain-how-blockchain-enhancing-maaz-khan-

Khan, S., & Khan, S. (2023). Impact of technological advancements on international trade and finance. *Modern Diplomacy.* https://moderndiplomacy.eu/2023/03/23/impact-of-technological-advancements-on-international-trade-and-finance/

Khan, S. N., Loukil, F., Ghedira-Guegan, C., Benkhelifa, E., & Bani-Hani, A. (2021). Blockchain smart contracts: Applications, challenges, and future trends. *Peer-to-Peer Networking and Applications, 14*(6), 2901–2925. https://link.springer.com/article/10.1007/s12083-021-01127-0. doi:10.100712083-021-01127-0 PMID:33897937

Kouhizadeh, M., Saberi, S., & Sarkis, J. (2020). Blockchain practices, potentials, and perspectives in greening supply chains. *Sustainability*, *12*(21), 8692. doi:10.3390u10103652

Kouhizadeh, M., Saberi, S., & Sarkis, J. (2021). Blockchain technology and the sustainable supply chain: Theoretically exploring adoption barriers. *International Journal of Production Economics*, *231*, 107831. https://www.sciencedirect.com/science/article/pii/S0925527320302012. doi:10.1016/j.ijpe.2020.107831

Kouhizadeh, M., & Sarkis, J. (2021). Smart Contracts for Sustainable Supply Chain Management: Conceptual Frameworks for Supply Chain Maturity Evaluation and Smart Contract Sustainability Assessment. *Frontiers in Blockchain*, *4*, 506436. doi:10.3389/fbloc.2021.506436

Kshetri, N. (2018). Blockchain's roles in strengthening cybersecurity and protecting privacy. *Telecommunications Policy*, *42*(10), 843–852.

Kshetri, N. (2018). Blockchain's roles in strengthening cybersecurity and protecting privacy. *Telecommunications Policy*, *42*(10), 843–852. doi:10.1016/j.telpol.2017.09.003

Kshetri, N., & Voas, J. (2018). On the internet of things, blockchain technology for supply chain management IoT. *IEEE IT Professional*, *20*(4), 15–21. doi:10.1109/MITP.2018.043141660

Lee, J.-H. (2019, May). A Blockchain-Based Smart Contract Design for Supply Chain Management. *Symmetry*, *11*(5), 635. https://www.mdpi.com/2073-8994/11/5/635

Lee, K., & Kim, J. (2019). Blockchain technology for enhancing supply chain resilience. *Business Horizons*, *62*(1), 35–45. doi:10.1016/j.bushor.2017.09.003

Li, J., & Li, J. (2023). A blockchain-based secure data sharing scheme for cloud storage [Journal article]. *Security and Communication Networks*. https://www.hindawi.com/journals/scn/2023/9998433/

Li, J., & Zhang, Y. (2022). *How do smart contracts benefit security protocols?* arXiv preprint arXiv:2202.08699. https://arxiv.org/abs/2202.08699

Liang, X., Liang, Q., & Gao, F. (2022). Blockchain technology in supply chain management: A review of applications and challenges in operations and logistics management contexts [Journal article]. *Sustainability*, *14*(3), 1470. https://www.mdpi.com/2071-1050/14/3/1470

Liu, J., & Zhang, X.-L. (2021). Research on the application of blockchain technology in supply chain finance [Journal article]. *Journal of Industrial Engineering and Engineering Management*, *35*(4), 107–116. https://kns.cnki.net/kcms/detail/detail.aspx?doi=10.14132/j.cnki.1673-5439.2021.04.013

Luu, L., Chu, D.-H., Olickel, H., Saxena, P., & Daian, A. (2016). Making smart contracts smarter. In *Proceedings of the 2016 ACM SIGSAC conference on computer and communications security* (pp. 254-269). ACM. 10.1145/2976749.2978309

McKinsey. (2022). *What is blockchain?* McKinsey. https://www.mckinsey.com/featured-insights/mckinsey-explainers/what-is-blockchain

Musyoka, J. (2022). *Role of smart contracts in supply chain management*. LinkedIn. https://www.linkedin.com/pulse/role-smart-contracts-supply-chain-management-john-musyoka

Naz, S., & Al-Zahrani, A. (2019). A secure data sharing platform using blockchain and smart contracts. In 2019 IEEE 5th International Conference on Engineering Technologies and Applied Sciences (ICETAS). IEEE. https://www.semanticscholar.org/paper/A-Secure-Data-Sharing-Platform-Using-Blockchain-and-Naz-Al-Zahrani/45e5f96cd89f6da12710133b946b85a88d567475

OECD. (2019). *2019 OECD Global Blockchain Policy Forum: Summary report* (Report No. 9789264633230). OECD. https://www.oecd.org/finance/2019-OECD-Global-Blockchain-Policy-Forum-Summary-Report.pdf

Pan, S., Trentesaux, D., McFarlane, D., Montreuil, B., Ballot, E., & Huang, G. Q. (2021). Digital interoperability in logistics and supply chain management: State-of-the-art and research avenues towards Physical Internet. *Computers in Industry*, *128*, 103435. doi:10.1016/j.compind.2021.103435

Pinsent Masons. (2020). *How smart contracts can enable better supply chains*. Out-Law. https://www.pinsentmasons.com/out-law/analysis/smart-contracts-better-supply-chains

QSales. (2020, August 19). *How blockchain is being used today in the food & beverage industries*. qSales. https://qsales.com/how-blockchain-is-being-used-today-in-the-food-beverage-industries/

Queiroz, M. M., Telles, R., & Bonilla, S. H. (2020). Blockchain and supply chain management integration: A systematic review of the literature. *Supply Chain Management*, *25*(2), 241–254. https://www.emerald.com/insight/content/doi/10.1108/SCM-03-2018-0143/full/html. doi:10.1108/SCM-03-2018-0143

Rejeb, A., Keogh, J. G., Simske, S. J., Stafford, T., & Treiblmaier, H. (2021). Potentials of blockchain technologies for supply chain collaboration: A conceptual framework. *International Journal of Logistics Management*, *32*(3), 1005–1026. doi:10.1108/IJLM-02-2020-0098

Reuters. (2022, November 29). *Maersk, IBM discontinue shipping blockchain platform* [Web page]. Reuters. https://www.reuters.com/technology/maersk-ibm-discontinue-shipping-blockchain-platform-2022-11-29/

Saberi, S., Kouhizadeh, M., & Sarkis, J. (2021). Blockchain technology and its relationships to sustainable supply chain management. *International Journal of Production Research*, *59*(3), 621–643. doi:10.1080/00207543.2018.1533261

Saberi, S., Kouhizadeh, M., Sarkis, J., & Shen, L. (2019). Blockchain technology and its relationships to sustainable supply chain management. *International Journal of Production Research*, *57*(7), 2117–2135. https://www.tandfonline.com/doi/full/10.1080/00207543.2018.1533261. doi:10.1080/00207543.2018.1533261

Schoentgen, A., & Wilkinson, R. (2011). The WTO's Trade Policy Review Mechanism: How to create political will for compliance? *World Economy*, *34*(11), 1897–1925. https://www.econstor.eu/bitstream/10419/238052/1/Schoentgen-Wilkinson.pdf

Sedlmeir, J., Lautenschlager, J., Fridgen, G., & Urbach, N. (2022). The transparency challenge of blockchain in organizations. *Electronic Markets*, *32*(3), 1779–1794. doi:10.100712525-022-00536-0 PMID:35602109

Sharif, M., & Ghodoosi, F. (2022). The Ethics of Blockchain in Organizations. *Journal of Business Ethics*, *178*(4), 1009–1025. doi:10.100710551-022-05058-5 PMID:35125568

Solaiman, E., Wike, T., & Sfyrakis, I. (2021). Implementation and evaluation of smart contracts using a hybrid on- and off-blockchain architecture. *Concurrency and Computation*, *33*(1), e5811. doi:10.1002/cpe.5811

Sweeney, E. (2022). The big challenges for supply chains in 2022. *The Conversation*. https://theconversation.com/the-big-challenges-for-supply-chains-in-2022-174420

Taherdoost, H. (2023). Smart contracts in blockchain technology: A critical review. *Information (Basel)*, *14*(2), 117. https://www.mdpi.com/2078-2489/14/2/117. doi:10.3390/info14020117

Tian, F. (2016). An agri-food supply chain traceability system for China based on RFID & blockchain technology. *2016 13th International Conference on Service Systems and Service Management (ICSSSM)*, (pp. 1-6). IEEE. https://ieeexplore.ieee.org/document/7538424

Tokkozhina, U., Martins, A. L., & Ferreira, J. C. (2021). Use of blockchain technology to manage the supply chains: Comparison of perspectives between technology providers and early industry adopters. *Journal of Theoretical and Applied Electronic Commerce Research*, *17*(4), 82–100. doi:10.3390/jtaer17040082

Tracefood.io. (2020). *Benefits of blockchain in food supply chain industry*. Tracefood. https://tracefood.io/benefits-of-blockchain-in-food-supply-chain-industry/

Vandevelde, P. (2018). *Using blockchain technology to fight counterfeiters*. Development Asia. https://development.asia/case-study/using-blockchain-technology-fight-counterfeiters

Walmart Global Tech. (2022, January 12). *Blockchain in the food supply chain [Web page]*. Walmart. https://tech.walmart.com/content/walmart-global-tech/en_us/news/articles/blockchain-in-the-food-supply-chain.html

Wang, S., Li, D., Zhang, Y., & Chen, J. (2019). Smart Contract-Based Product Traceability System in the Supply Chain Scenario. *IEEE Access : Practical Innovations, Open Solutions*, *7*, 115122–115133. doi:10.1109/ACCESS.2019.2935873

Zhang, Y., Li, X., & Wang, Y. (2020). A review on the applications of blockchain technology in international trade and finance. *Frontiers of Engineering Management*, *7*(4), 445–458. doi:10.1016/j.tbench.2022.100073

Zhang, Y., Li, Y., & Liu, J. (2021). Smart contract security: A practitioners' perspective. In *2021 IEEE/ACM 43rd International Conference on Software Engineering (ICSE)* (pp. 127-138). IEEE. 10.1109/ICSE43902.2021.00127

Zhang, Y., & Liu, X. (2021). The Effect of Blockchain Technology on Supply Chain Sustainability: A Review. *Sustainability (Basel)*, *13*(4), 1726. doi:10.3390u13041726

Zhang, Y., & Zhang, Y. (2020). *A blockchain-based secure data sharing scheme for cloud storage. In 2020 IEEE International Conference on Communications Workshops (ICC Workshops)*. IEEE. https://ieeexplore.ieee.org/stamp/stamp.jsp?arnumber=9329051

Chapter 15
Blockchain-Based Supply Chain Management:
A Challenge Yet an Opportunity to Gauge

Fazeelat Masood
https://orcid.org/0000-0003-1487-6882
Bahria University, Pakistan

Naveed R. Khan
UCSI University, Malaysia

Mustafa Rehman Khan
https://orcid.org/0000-0002-0250-9092
UCSI University, Malaysia

ABSTRACT

In the post-COVID business environment, IR 5.0 seems to be one of the causes as well as the cure of immense disruptions in the supply chain and network management. Cause in a sense that IR 5.0 technologies have given a new face to the optimization of supply chain efficiencies with the advent of new technologies. In doing so, IR 5.0 serves as the cure for pandemic-caused scarcity of data exchange, visibility, and traceability. Adding to the notion, blockchain is an IR 5.0 technology that stores and distributes data among all stakeholders. In the supply chain, the use of blockchain technology enables data storage in different databases with ease of data distribution among stakeholders who are a part of the supply chain network. This chapter aims to broaden readers' understanding of blockchain and supply chain management. Complementing academic research with practical examples where possible, this chapter establishes an understanding of the challenges and opportunities in the adoption, promotion, and facilitation of blockchain-based supply chain management.

DOI: 10.4018/979-8-3693-0482-2.ch015

INTRODUCTION

Supply chain (SC) refers to an integrated system of interrelated business processes for acquiring raw materials, transforming these materials into finished products, adding value to finished products, distributing and promoting products to retailers or end consumers, and facilitating the exchange of information among business entities. In short, the supply chain represents a backward flow of information and a forward flow of goods (Min & Zhou, 2002). Over the years, this simple supply chain process has evolved into a discipline named supply chain management (SCM). SCM is accredited to unite the concepts of operations, distribution, and procurement into a network of links and nodes (Carter et al., 2015). SCM addresses the inherently unstable nature of the supply chain by minimizing the associated uncertainties and risks (Stevens & Johnson, 2016). In modern times, however, the scope of the supply chain has broadened due to its inseparable connection with environmental concerns (Zimon et al., 2020).

As of today, 6.66 million tons of toxic chemicals are released into the environment with annual 24.88 billion tons of CO_2 emission and 3.54 million hectares of forest loss (Worldometer, 2023). These statistics paint severe environmental damages owing to the 0.88% annual growth in the world's population that demands more resource consumption with severe environmental impacts (Macrotrends, 2023). Addressing these environmental concerns, back in 2015, the United Nations (UN) initiated a 15-year plan comprising 17 sustainable development goals (SDGs) enlisting 169 SDG targets to be tracked across 232 unique indicators (United Nations, 2020). The 2030 SDG agenda focuses on peace and prosperity for the planet, people, and their properties. The adoption of a sustainability agenda is gradually becoming pervasive within business enterprises that aim to achieve human well-being and higher levels of sustainability (Agrawal et al., 2022). As a result, green supply chain (GSC) and sustainable supply chain (SSC) are emerging as significant concepts for business operations (Cai & Choi, 2020).

The sustainable supply chain is a new domain that simultaneously addresses the modern world's needs for efficiency and natural resource preservation while enabling enterprises to achieve a competitive edge through innovation and waste reduction (Zimon et al., 2020). Sustainable supply chain management (SSCM) bridges the supply chain with performance goals that address the current and future generation needs by implementing socially and environmentally focused solutions. These SDG-enabled SCM practices, however, were put to a halt when the global economies had a pandemic outbreak of coronavirus disease (COVID-19). Global supply chains were challenged to meet large-scale product demands due to poor visibility, resilience, and flexibility (Kayikci et al., 2021). The unavoidable environmental risks such as the pandemic together with internal risks such as delivery delays, data loss, and equipment malfunction made supply chain practices vulnerable to major disruptions with frequent occurrences (Marinagi et al., 2023). In response, academic researchers and practitioners coined terms such as SC 4.0, smart supply chain, and resilient SC 4.0 to emphasize the application of industrial revolution (IR 4.0) technologies to digitalize different functions of supply chain (Groschopf et al., 2021; Marinagi et al., 2023; Nayeri et al., 2023; Xu et al., 2021).

IR 4.0 has endorsed green innovation technologies (GITs) such as Internet of Services (IoS), Artificial Intelligence (AI), Internet of Things (IoT), Big Data Analytics (BDA), Augmented Reality (AR), and Blockchain (BC) aimed to address the resilience element of SC by improving collaboration, information sharing, agility, visibility, and robustness (Marinagi et al., 2023). These GITs, however, are more concerned with the digitalization of SC practices and achieving efficiency goals. Adding to the technology-driven agenda of IR 4.0, IR 5.0 technologies focus on human-centricity, sustainability, and resilience dimensions to improve supply chain responsiveness – SC's ability to meet customer demands during a specified time (Nayeri et al., 2023). Tiptoeing on these developments, blockchain is emerging as a popular technology to promote the use of sustainable practices in SCM (Varriale et al., 2023).

Blockchain technology, known for its security feature, ensures eco-standard compliance and responsible sourcing by creating transparent and traceable supply chains (Marinagi et al., 2023; Varriale et al., 2023). Earlier scholars have explored the integration of blockchain and SCM as an innovative duo with potential implications and challenges for business operations (Cole et al., 2019; Moosavi et al., 2021; Queiroz et al., 2019). This chapter timely answers the call for addressing the research theme on challenges and opportunities for blockchain-based supply chain management. This chapter builds the post-COVID context of supply chain management while highlighting the paradigm shift in how a supply chain works in the current sustainable development goals (SDG) driven economies. In doing so, this chapter brings readers' attention to the role of blockchain technology, an industrial revolution's (IR 5.0) buzzword, in the supply chain domain.

BLOCKCHAIN TECHNOLOGY: AN OVERVIEW

Before the internet boom, people believed in living in an ideal world with physical processes and protocols to perform one-to-one transactions, fulfill obligations, and transfer rights. For them, a physical connection was crucial to building trust between transacting parties, and the level of trust used to determine the need for written/verbal agreements or involvement of a guarantor to avoid fraud and misappropriations. In the late twentieth century, internet technology replaced people's physical ideal type with the virtual world where the global village facilitated interaction over distance. Masses interacting with masses put into question the capability of the existing design mechanisms to manage sheer volumes of large-scale commerce transactions. The answer to this was found in blockchain technology.

David Chaum, in his seminal works on electronic cash (e-cash), set the stepping stone to the emergence of blockchain technology. Building on the theoretical understanding of distributed systems, digital currency or e-cash was accredited to provide a practical implementation of proof of work algorithms. In 1989, the idea was aided by *Leslie Lamport*'s Paxos proposition. As the most famous protocol, Paxos nodes can perform roles as learner, proposer, and acceptor (Bashir, 2017). Later, a group of developers named Satoshi Nakamoto (2008) created a document to combine and apply these concepts to e-cash which served as the base guideline for the establishment of the Bitcoin cryptocurrency blockchain network (Yaga et al., 2018). Cryptocurrency can be described as a medium of exchange where cryptographic protocols not only verify funds transfer but also help control monetary unit creation. Figure 1 demonstrates a typical workflow in blockchain technology-enabled systems. Unlike NetCash and e-cash, blockchain has created a no-single-source-reliance environment to promote Bitcoin implementation in a distributed manner. Addressing the trustworthiness element, blockchain technology eliminated the need for a trusted third party by promoting a direct transaction between users. Blockchain has enabled e-payment systems replacing trust with cryptographic proof to promote willing parties toward direct transactions.

Starting its journey with currency, blockchain technology, as a distributed ledger, has revolutionized traditional trade by using cryptographic techniques to record every transaction in a tamper-free manner (Gad et al., 2022). With a $ 300 million investment in 2016, blockchain emerged as a breakthrough technology to change everyday business processes and activities (Gatteschi et al., 2018). Countries such as El Salvador, Portugal, and Singapore top the list of blockchain-adopting nations that create a conducive environment with heavy government investments in blockchain-related research and development

Figure 1. How blockchain technology works
[Adopted from (Likens, 2023)]

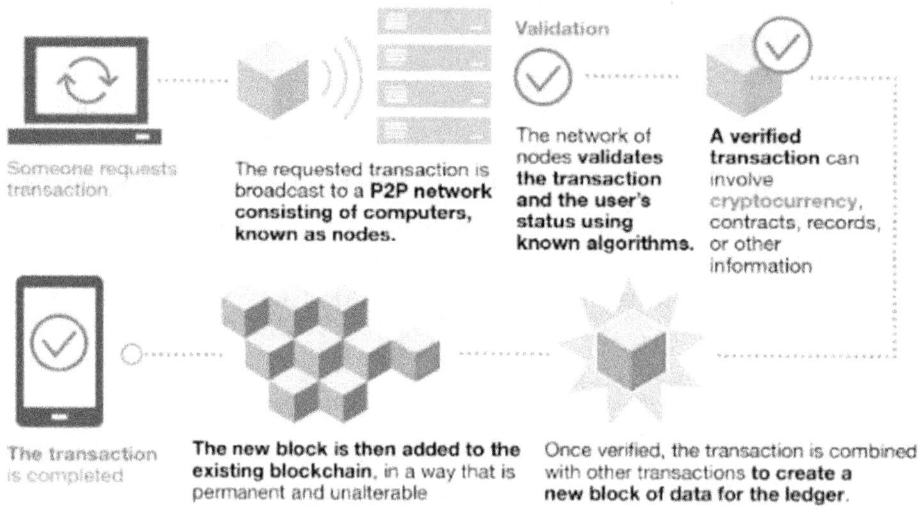

(R&D) and startup projects. Gradually, blockchain has grown into a hotcake desired and endorsed by different nations such as Japan, USA, Russia, South Africa, the UK, China, and India and international institutions such as International Monetary Funds (IMF) and United Nations (UN) (Guo & Liang, 2016). Every passing day created a new avenue for development, thereby witnessing blockchain evolution into versions 1.0, 2.0, and 3.0.

Blockchain 1.0 is money-based and closely attached to cryptocurrencies, in particular Bitcoin (Bashir, 2017). Blockchain 2.0 is centered on *smart contracts* – an algorithm-based contract ensuring fulfillment of obligations between the transacting parties under certain conditions. Blockchain 2.0 is concerned with the registration, confirmation, and transfer of properties or contracts. Blockchain 3.0 has escaped the barriers of restricted application to goods and finance-related transactions; rather it is extending blockchain application to health, education, science, and government (see Figure 2). Government use of blockchain technology can be exemplified with electoral vote records, vehicle registration, health & safety inspection, and business license processing (Gatteschi et al., 2018). These waves of development in blockchain technology can undeniably be accredited to the COVID-19 outbreak that pushed countries and business communities toward investment in digital technology. It also led to the explicitly exclusive implementation of blockchain technology in business operations across the world.

Blockchain Technology – Investment and Application

True to note, the COVID-19 pandemic had global consequences. The pandemic not only caused social immobility and disruption of the economic cycle but also brought a paradigm shift in the business mindset towards the use of business ledger technology. Nearly every economic sector and industry started visualizing digitalization as the only workable solution to continue business operations in a socially handicapped situation of a pandemic. Heavy business investments in reconstructing digital strategies gave rise to the adoption of IR 4.0 technologies such as the Internet of Things (IoT) and cloud but it

Figure 2. Blockchain application scenarios
[Adopted from (Likens, 2023)]

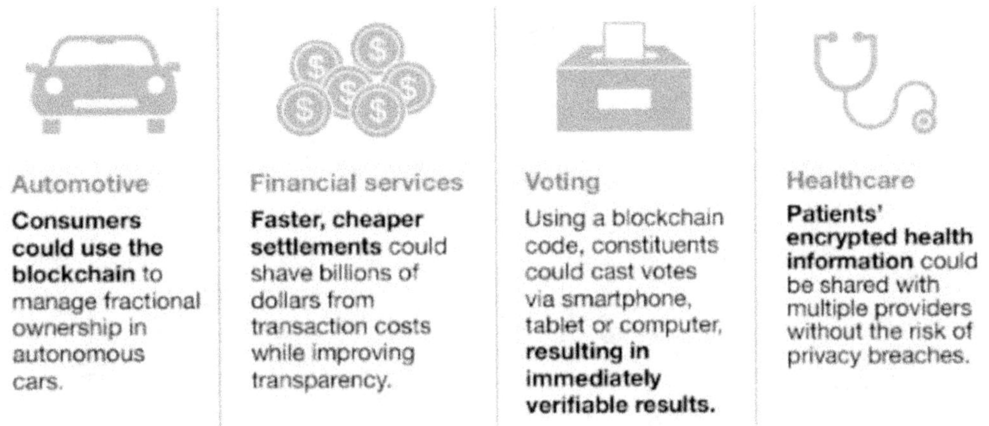

also raised privacy and security concerns. Given the room for the development of IR 5.0 technologies, blockchain surfaced as a digital solution to protect health records, ensure transparency in operations, and provide identity protection. An example of such is MiPasa, a digital ledger-based collaboration project between the World Health Organization (WHO), Oracle, IBM, and Microsoft corporations. In 2020, HACERA designed MiPasa as a distributed data platform for detecting COVID-19 carriers and infection hotspots around the world (FBI, 2023).

Figure 3. Blockchain technology market, region-wise
[Adopted from (FBI, 2023)]

Figure 4. Country-wise venture funding raised by blockchain companies
[Adopted from (Blockdata, 2023)]

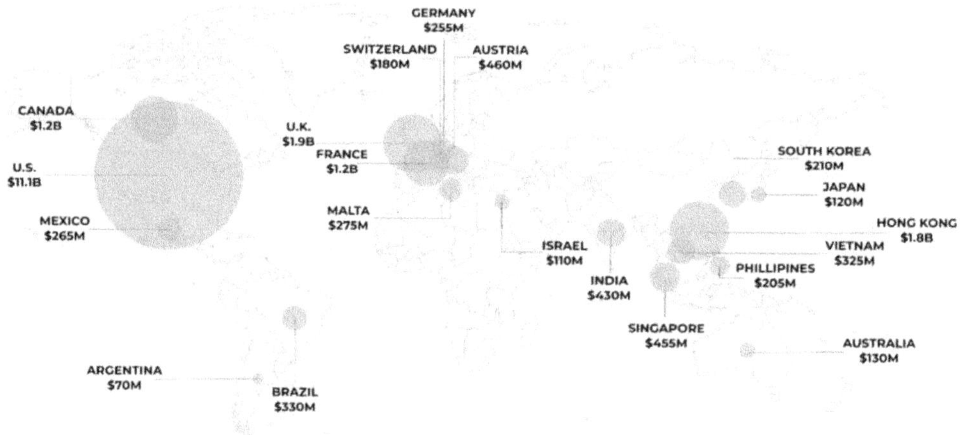

Blockchain technology is recognized as an essential economic contributor with an estimated increase in the global gross domestic product (GDP) of up to $ 2 trillion, by 2030 (Sharma, 2022). Globally, blockchain technology has reached a market value of $ 11.14 billion in 2022 with a forecasted growth of $ 17.57 billion (by 2023) and $ 469.49 billion (by 2030) (FBI, 2023). In blockchain technology, the most active investments during 2021 were made by Coinbase Ventures, Andreessen Horowitz, AU21, Alameda Research, and Pantera Capital (Blockdata, 2023). Geographically, the blockchain technology market is fragmented into European, Middle East & African, North American, Latin American, and Asia Pacific regions (see Figure 3). Among these five geographic regions, North America dominated the market due to the growing presence of Oracle, Microsoft, AWS, Digital Asset Holdings LLC, and IBM. These service providers have been offering client-tailored services across the region. Among these regions, a sizable proportion of vendors for digital ledger services is concentrated in Asia Pacific countries such as China, South Korea, South East Asia, and Japan. According to 2021 Blockchain data, the USA tops the list with $11.1billion blockchain investments followed by the UK ($1.9billion), Hong Kong ($1.7billion), and France ($1.2billion) (see Figure 4). In these economies, blockchain technology investments are not only facilitating business processes but also helping nations meet their sustainable development targets. For example, *Tajikistan* is listed on the World Bank's (WB) unbanked countries where people operate outside the banking systems. Also, 40% of Tajikistani household depends on remittance money. To cater to the money transfer needs of migrant workers, UNDP's AltFinLab collaborated with BitSpark Company to launch a blockchain technology-based mobile application project. This pilot project aims to create means for direct, faster, and cheaper funds transfer through digitally verified identities (UNDP, 2020). In this manner, the application of blockchain technology is enabling SDG-pursuing countries to support financial inclusion.

Industry-level statistics for FY 2022 indicate that 31.5% of the blockchain technology market was captured by the Banking, Financial Services, and Insurance (BFSI) industry, which is followed by telecom, media & entertainment, and manufacturing industries (see Figure 5). Commencing with the digital currency trends, the application of blockchain technology has heavily been condensed to the financial sector where P2P digitalized cryptocurrency networks enable multi-billion dollar anonymous transactions.

Figure 5. Blockchain technology, industry-wise global market share
[Adopted from (FBI, 2023)]

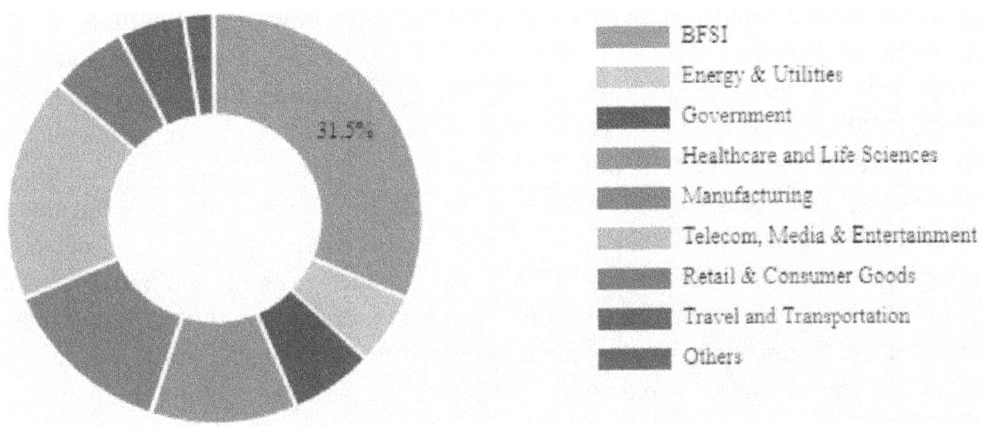

In the financial sector, Blockchain technology is used to combat fraud, track financial transactions, and manage smart contracts and bank guarantees (Cole et al., 2019). Beyond the financial sector, blockchain technology is bringing change to charity, retail, healthcare, media & entertainment, and government sectors. Blockchain technology is making charity donations more transparent by establishing a clear link between charities and the related project outcomes. The application of blockchain technology to healthcare has given rise to e-medical records that not only ensure data authenticity, sharing, and confidentiality but also facilitate tracking of patient progress, especially in post-discharge cases.

Table 1 summarizes the use of blockchain technology across various industries and work contexts

Table 1. BC-based applications and prototypes [Adapted from (Gatteschi et al., 2018)]

S. No.	Industries/ Contexts	Blockchain-based Application Purposes and Prototypes
1.	Software and the Internet	Blockchain technology usage to combat cyber-attacks to alter or delete event histories, promote loaned spacing/cloud storage (such as STorj), and curtail censorship cases (such as Gist).
2.	Finance and trading	Blockchain-based applications such as Chain develop protocols for financial networks; applications such as Augur and Gnosis encourage and collect user predictions about future consequences.
3.	Intellectual property	Blockchain-based e-system of notary services to prove existence and authorship of a document (such as Proof of existence and Superior Notary Services), to license authors' work (such as ascribe), and smart contract triggered automatic payment receipts (such as Monegraph, Mesh).
4.	Healthcare	Akiri, BurstIQ, and MedicalChain are facilitating the use of blockchain to secure health data and promote BC-based healthcare services for recording and managing patient data and location information.
5.	Internet of things	Use of blockchain technology to promote renting and sharing services in a blockchain-based intelligent system such as Slock.it is for room-renting, Blockcharge for electricity sharing, and Lo3Energy for peer-to-peer trading of home-produced energy.
6.	Personal data management	Blockchain wallet recognizes and validates user identity by a certified organization; it is a one-time validation leading to multiple-time usage e.g., bitid, KYC-Chain.
7.	Supply chain & commerce	Blockchain application to handle luxury goods' ownership matters (such as Everledger), identify counterfeit items and exchange of sports tickets, merchandise & subscriptions (such as LuxTag, Reply), trace products through the SC process (such as Provenance, EURGO), and direct exchange of goods without monetary system condition (such as Profeth).
8.	Services	Blockchain technology enabled hail-a-ride or ride-sharing services such as Uber and La'Zooz.

Blockchain Technology in Supply Chain Management

Figure 6 demonstrates the supply chain as a systematic network covering all entities involved in the process of a typical product from its origin till the delivery to the end customer. Blockchain technology revolutionizes this typical supply chain process by facilitating in-part agreements, payments, and deliveries (Al-Farsi et al., 2021). How so? Let's take an example of Company X's SC process under the Supply Chain Operations Reference (SCOR) model. At Company X, a typical SC involves planning, sourcing, making, delivering, and returning stages of managing the supply chain operations. At the planning stage, Company X conducts demand-supply analysis to support operational strategies and decisions related to maintaining resource balance, identifying business rules related to assets and transportation, and determining suppliers. This stage ends with a supply chain plan prepared per the corporate financial plan. At the sourcing stage, Company X handles matters related to raw material procurement and delivery while managing supplier networks, agreements, and payments. Next, the making stage involves records of production activities and networks. Then, the delivery stage concerns with the customer order collection, delivery, and invoicing. The last stage of the process addresses product returns and related rules. Blockchain technology may not apply to the whole SCM system but it ensures implementation of these stages through digital payments and smart contracts.

Typically, a supply chain application has internal (within internal processes) and external interactions (involving external parties or processes). In a BC-based SCM, these interactions are managed in a blockchain-enabled infrastructure that includes smart contracts. Smart contracts serve as agreements between parties for automatic fund transfer when certain conditions are met. In BC-based SCM, smart contracts facilitate secure interaction among parties, and their corresponding interactions are stored in a distributed ledger (Al-Farsi et al., 2021). Figure 7 explains a simple case of smart contracts in the supply chain.

Blockchain technology advances the SCM by adding traceability, transparency, and efficiency to SCM practices. Each of these Blockchain features adds value to the blockchain-based SC system (see Figure 8). Characteristics of a blockchain-based SCM include reliability and security, visibility, traceability, decentralization, cost efficiency, and synchronized transactions. Unlike other SC solutions, blockchain technology is a decentralized system of SC that not only conducts transparent functions but also promotes trust among SC partners. As identified in Table 1, the use of blockchain technology to identify counterfeit items and unlicensed products is gradually growing. Blockchain technology uses its decentralized and traceability properties to identify, blockchain certify, locate, and verify original products on blockchain platforms. In this manner, blockchain technology helps establish a safe, secure, and reliable platform for product, inventory, and logistics management while promoting customer trust and information visibility among participants.

In BC-based SCM, the traceability feature enables suppliers, retailers, customers, and dealers to track products through the whole process i.e., from inception until reception. An example of such is provided with the case of the EMURGO Traceability Solution where the application of blockchain technology supports the supply chain traceability of coffee beans. Further, the application of Blockchain technology improves the efficiency of supply chain operations while reducing operational costs and establishing trust among the SC partners.

Figure 6. Supply chain processes
[Adopted from (Al-Farsi et al., 2021)]

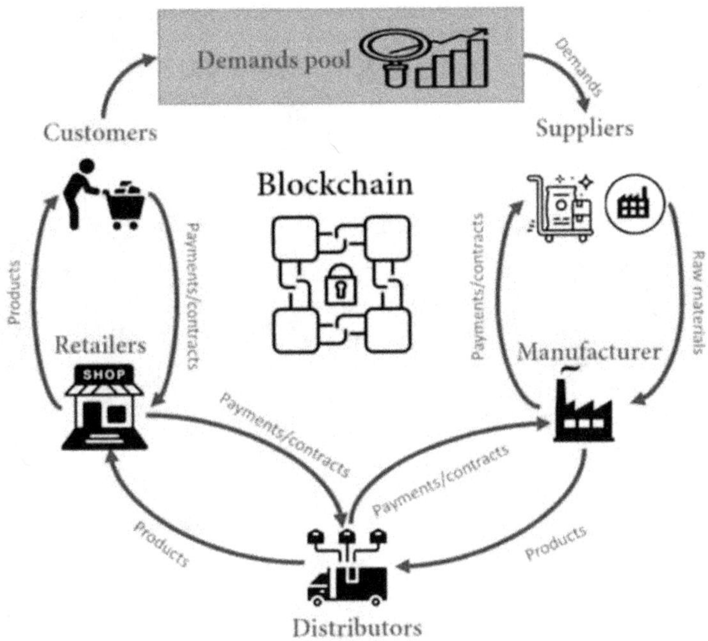

Figure 7. Smart contracts in SCM
[Adopted from (Queiroz et al., 2019)]

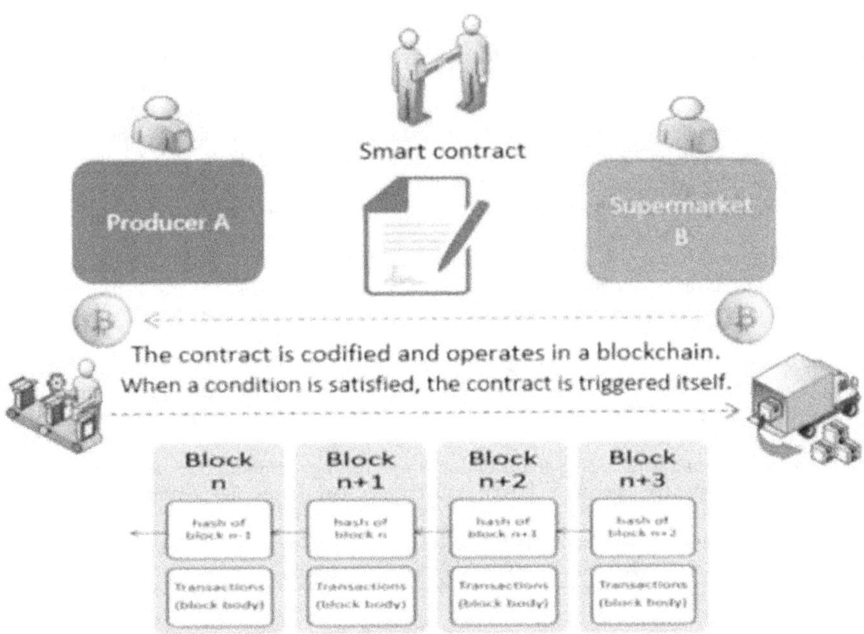

Figure 8. Blockchain-based SCM
[Adopted from (Al-Farsi et al., 2021)]

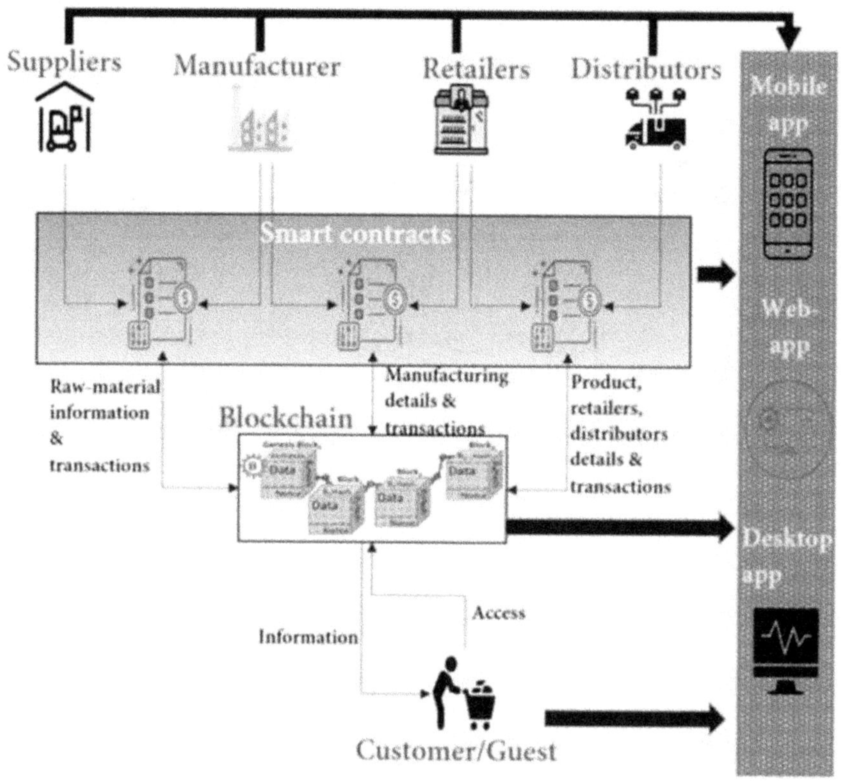

Box 1. Case Study #01

EMURGO Traceability Solution, EMURGO's blockchain technology supporting supply chain traceability of coffee beans

The coffee supply chain is complex for coffee beans pass through many hands before finally reaching the end consumer. This complexity has made those with lesser resources vulnerable to muddy accounting standards and unfair practices that often lead to consumer distrust. This situation becomes grim in Indonesia which is the fourth largest producer and exporter in the global coffee bean supply chain industry. 96% of the Indonesian coffee is produced by smallholders who are unable to maintain adequate count of their bean production. As a result, such small-scale farmers and their consumers remain at the risk of manipulation in the forward stream supply chain by large stakeholders.

Addressing the Indonesian coffee bean industry challenge, *EMURGO* has collaborated with a local coffee brand named *Blue Korintji Coffee*. This partnership project lands the first commercial avenue for EMURGO Traceability Solution to be integrated into Indonesian coffee supply chain to benefit farmers, consumers, and other stakeholders. EMURGO Traceability Solution uses blockchain technology to offer tailored solutions to supply chain inefficiencies and issues related to time, margins, trust, and costs. Also, Blue Korintji Coffee's consumers use mobile QR scan code to access information about the background and origins of coffee they purchase.

"EMURGO is delighted to partner with Blue Korintji Coffee and integrate this solution, bringing a tangible real world application of blockchain technology to farmers, enterprises, and consumers, and shining light on the benefits the technology carries for everyone," said Ken Kodama, EMURGO CEO.

"Blue Korintji Coffee is excited to partner with leading global blockchain technology solutions provider EMURGO, and offer an innovative tech solution that will improve the lives of local Indonesian farmers, businesses, and consumers," said Budi Isman, Blue Korintji Coffee Founder.

EMURGO Traceability Solution powers Cardano's research-drive blockchain technology not only to promote visibility of purchase prices among stakeholders but also to assure immutability of accumulated private information.

IS BLOCKCHAIN MAKING AN OPPORTUNISTIC SPACE IN SCM?

Blockchain technology is a digital logbook of transactions characterized by disintermediation, decentralization, tamper-proof transactions, and transaction sharing. To date, scholars have reported industry-wide application of blockchain technology to healthcare, financial services, manufacturing, energy, construction, logistics, entertainment, and robotics. From the SCM perspective, blockchain technology is likely to disrupt transformations in different industries (Queiroz et al., 2019). In this regard, prior research has identified many drivers and enablers as opportunistic factors for blockchain application to SCM practices (Friedman & Ormiston, 2022; Li & Chen, 2022).

Blockchain technology is an emerging GIT with the potential to address the sustainable transformation concerns of the supply chain. Opportunities for blockchain application to supply chain include technological solutions that (i) enhance product traceability (ii) ensure a transparent and fair supply chain (iii) promote environmental sustainability (iv) combat fraudulent behaviors and human rights violations, and (v) generate shared economic benefits (Friedman & Ormiston, 2022). Concerning opportunities 1 and 4, the case of LuxTag explains how blockchain technology is making its space in the current SCM environment by offering sustainability-oriented innovative solutions. Li & Chen (2022) summarized opportunities arising from blockchain application to SCM as transparency in SC, intelligence in manufacturing, security of logistics, platformisation of sales, and ecology in governance.

Box 2. Case Study #02

LuxTag, Techno-entrepreneurial Success Story

Six years back, bitcoin fever had surged interests in distributed ledger technology (DLT). Around the globe, business enterprises, investors and entrepreneurs discovered new uses for blockchain technology. "We, being the typical tech enthusiasts, would have long discussions and brainstorming sessions on how blockchain could solve the world's problems," said Rene. "One weekend, after one such brainstorming session, we came together with a plan on how we could solve the problem of counterfeiting in the luxury goods sector—hence the name LuxTag."

LuxTag is a startup success story of Rene Bernard, Faeez Noor, and Jeff McDonald. The three techno-entrepreneurs founded LuxTag as a technology driven anti-counterfeit solution for luxury products in Malaysia. Building on NEM blockchain, LuxTag safeguards manufacturers and consumers against the purchase and sale of counterfeit luxury products.

LuxTag utilizes blockchain technology to create LuxTag platform enlisting and connecting every product with manufacturers' luxury goods. Each product enlisted on LuxTag platform is issued a blockchain certificate that holds information about the original manufacturing process of a product. This certificate enables consumers to immediately verify product authenticity. LuxTag uses NEM blockchain to ensure no-certificate-duplication-cases. "The NEM blockchain provides a very intuitive set of APIs (application programming interfaces) that we can quickly build a solid and reliable product on." said Rene.

Using luxury brands as a base case, LuxTag is now replicating the same model across different industries such as fashion products and university diplomas. Currently, LuxTag is offering DLT, BC and IoT based services to clients such as Poesy Liang and DeFeet. In future, LuxTag is planning to offer highly tailored solutions to key customers that includes NFC tags and customizable physical QRs to help customers build their trace solutions.

The emergence of blockchain technology has created numerous opportunities for its application to SCM (Li & Chen, 2022). First, producers and consumers are commonly concerned with the source and safety of a product/good in a typical supply chain. Blockchain technology's traceability features improve product visibility across the supply chain thereby allowing SC participants to trace a particular product/good. BC-based SCM ensures a real-time flow of product-related information among SC participants that includes manufacturers, retailers, suppliers, and customers. By connecting these participants in a digitalized innovative SC platform, blockchain technology improves the transparency of the whole supply chain by ensuring visibility from the start (product origin – raw materials/components) until the end (product sale) point.

Second, blockchain technology is revolutionizing the process of producing goods. Blockchain technology has made an opportunistic move by adding flexibility and integration to the production mechanisms. In literature, this characteristic feature of BC-SCM is recognized as intelligent and organized production (Li & Chen, 2022). In the manufacturing industry, the application of blockchain technology has improved the planning component of supply chain processes by automatically matching demand-supply.

Third, logistics is an important component of the supply chain connecting numerous SC partners including producers, vendors, freight forwarders, and warehouse managers. Among these participants, the paper document is often the only secure means to verify and settle transactions. Paper documentation is not as vulnerable to tampering as e-information; however, it is more prone to damage, dampening, and loss. Consequently, the flow of information in the upstream and downstream SC can be hampered due to slow reconciliation, long delays, and overburdening costs. Blockchain technology addresses these SC concerns by creating a secure and efficient logistics mechanism where the paper document verification need is significantly reduced. In addition, hash functions and block technology not only add to product visibility throughout the supply chain process but also reduce the chances of data tampering.

Fourth, blockchain technology is accredited to not only address the trust issues of SC partners but also to introduce new governing mechanisms for SC collaborations. In BC-SCM ecology of governance concerns the environmental impact of the whole SC process; hence, blockchain technology together with other IR 5.0 technologies helps develop a monitoring system to track ecological environment data. Thus, blockchain technology is likely to make its space in the SCM by enhancing the ecology of governance in the entire supply chain process.

Fifth, blockchain technology brings physical trust-based SC transactions into virtual guarantee to transactions by reducing third-party network dependence. Blockchain technology brings buyers and suppliers together to engage in direct transactions and allows producers access to data. Li & Chen (2022) name it as platformisation of sales where all SC participants can directly join in a transaction with no reliance on the third-party network.

WILL BLOCKCHAIN BE A DREAM TO REALIZE IN SCM?

UN's SDGs have put nations, industries, business enterprises, and other stakeholders in a glob-digit dynamic environment where triple bottom line (TBL) i.e., economic, social, and ecological is at the center stage. With growing concerns for ecological and social sustainability, the external environment is becoming more and more uncertain. On one hand, this uncertainty is serving as a dynamic force to redefine the supply chain operations and business value chains. On the other hand, this uncertainty is itself becoming a challenge to realizing sustainability-oriented SC opportunities. Though blockchain is a buzzword these days, its adoption is not as hassle-free as it may seem. Barriers to the adoption of BC-based SCM have been the focus of the current stream of SCM research (Bag et al., 2020; Kouhizadeh et al., 2021; Moretto & Macchion, 2022; Sahebi et al., 2020). These barriers help answer the question of whether BC-based SCM will be a dream or will transform into a business world reality.

This particular section of the chapter classifies these barriers to BC-based SCM as external and internal barriers. The former pertains to external factors including cultural differences among SC participants, unclear investment outcomes, market barriers, lack of collaboration, external stakeholders' involvement, uncertain regulatory environment, and in-house (organizational cultural resistance) & out-house (industry) acceptability challenges. The latter comprises internal challenges such as workforce obsolescence, financial constraints, poor management vision, privacy concerns, hesitant execution, and lack of in-house blockchain skills (Bag et al., 2020; Kouhizadeh et al., 2021; Sahebi et al., 2020).

External Barriers to BC-Based SCM

The external environment is ever-changing with new technological trends that emerge every day. Factors surfacing in this dynamic external environment are important drivers of organizational endeavors to adapt approaches aiming toward sustainability targets. In this regard, external stakeholders such as regulatory bodies and agencies (government), competitors, social activists, and non-governmental agencies may act as forces pressurizing/hindering the successful adoption of BC-based SCM.

Firstly, SDG-driven economies are endorsing the adoption of GTIs at national and organizational levels; however, adequate policy guidelines and legal frameworks are still missing. A recent surge in the use of cryptocurrencies and digital payment has surely resulted in the development of guidelines for how to use and implement such measures to endorse sustainable practices. For example, US federal and state governments have legalized the use, buying, and selling of cryptocurrencies while the Responsible Financial Innovation Act (RFIA) governs and regulates the digital asset markets. In Germany, BaFin is the regulatory body that oversees cryptocurrency exchanges while the Malaysian Security Commission regulates cryptocurrencies under the Capital Markets and Services Order 2019. True to note, SDG-driven economies have modified or updated their legal and regulatory frameworks to catch up with the developments in IR 4.0 and 5.0 enabled GTIs; yet their upgradation pace is sluggish. In particular, the regulatory environment for blockchain technology and its application to business processes and SCM is unclear. Poor policy framework and unavailability of authentic rules have challenged the adoption of blockchain technology in SCM. Such an uncertain regulatory environment gives birth to another barrier i.e. integrating challenges. The process of adjusting blockchain technology to the existing legal system is complex (Sahebi et al., 2020). It is not only expensive but also time-consuming because the blockchain ecosystem lacks standardization, off-the-shelf interfaces, and no unified legal system.

Secondly, technological standards and SC practices vary from industry to industry. As a result, industry-specific acceptance of technological innovation and its application to SC culture and practices may vary. For instance, the level of a digitalized supply chain in the fashion industry may be different from that of the automobile industry or agriculture. In addition, the absence of a unified technological standard has added to the worries of organizations about having the right supply chain partner and strong collaborations to endorse feasible BC-based SC practices with greater industry acceptance (Moretto & Macchion, 2022). Further, different SC partners adhere to different cultural and economic orientations; hence, technological diffusion may be a challenge.

Thirdly, the customer is a key stakeholder; its changing preferences and environmental awareness an inescapable market barriers. With growing global concerns for environmental protection and national sustainability agendas adhering to SDG#9-industry, innovation & infrastructure, and SDG#12-responsible consumption and production, customers are becoming aware of sustainable products and green business processes. Hence, their growing awareness is altering customer preferences, tastes, and consumption patterns. About blockchain technology, however, customers' lack of tech knowledge and their little awareness of BC application to sustainability agenda may create a hurdle for organizations.

Adding fuel to the fire are firm peers who gauge customer attention with innovative solutions and at times, with market gimmicks. To sum up, changing customer preferences, limited awareness of BC-driven sustainable SC practices, and intensifying market competition are barriers to the implementation of blockchain technology. Fifthly, the constant fear of modern tools and innovative alternatives to GITs has made blockchain-enabled platforms a fruitless attempt for many organizations. Thus, organizations aiming to use blockchain technology often face in-house resistance (organizational culture) making blockchain adoption a hesitant attempt with comparatively low attainability and out-house challenge in terms of low industry acceptance.

Internal Barriers to BC-Based SCM

Where external barriers are exerting systematic effects on BC-endorsing organizations, internal barriers are common yet uniquely varying from business to business. Application of blockchain technology to SCM is beneficial for its added visibility, traceability, and decentralization features but it also has certain organizational constraints that limit its implementation to business operations across organizations in different industries.

First, management vision and commitment to implementing blockchain technology in SCM are crucial. Generally, organizations implementing blockchain technology face issues because the management lacks a clear stance on why the organization is using blockchain technology and how it aligns with the corporate vision & mission. Lack of management vision is one of the key barriers to the adoption of blockchain technology in SCM practices (Bag et al., 2020). When top management is unclear about the purpose and reason for adopting blockchain technology, the subsequent planning for inducting, training, and developing in-house essential skill sets and upgrading the workforce becomes a challenge. Thus, workforce obsolescence and inadequate in-house skills are the second internal barrier to the implementation of blockchain technology. The BC-based supply chain is a strategic move that requires continuous monitoring and dedicated resources with skilled manpower. It is doable when organizations have trained staff with the necessary technical knowledge and sufficient tech skills to use and implement blockchain technology. However, the lack of in-house blockchain skills is hindering the successful adoption of BC-based SCM, as organizations are heavily dependent on external blockchain operators.

Third, blockchain technology does offer innovative solutions to supply chain sustainability issues but its system-related challenges make it a financially constrained investment opportunity. For instance, blockchain technology is in the developmental stage hence it cannot handle simultaneous information sharing and massive transactions. Further, its real-time information-sharing feature is limited while data handling and storage is facing bloat problem. The current immaturity level makes blockchain technology a capital-intensive investment for organizations that pursue BC-based sustainable SC practices. In this regard, low or no subsidy from the government makes blockchain technology a hot cake with a burnt taste. Thereby, hindering organizations from adopting blockchain technology to their SC operations.

Fourth, GITs such as blockchain undoubtedly produce sustainable solutions to everyday business problems but these technologies also receive criticism for privacy concerns. This becomes a challenge when blockchain users are unaware of blockchain technology's privacy protocols. For instance, a distributed digital ledger with smart contracts may enable users to pursue contract errors via an error log but the BC-anonymity feature may backfire in case a malicious user is involved in an illegitimate activity (Sahebi et al., 2020). Thus, data privacy concerns may hinder the implementation of blockchain technology in SC processes.

PRACTICAL IMPLICATIONS OF BC-BASED SCM

The COVID-19 pandemic presented business enterprises with unprecedented challenges of managing operations and supply chain functions in a socially distanced environment. These challenges, in turn, created opportunities for examining the existing supply chain practices from different perspectives. Addressing the trust and transparency issues of the global supply chain, blockchain technology has created a single-control-free virtual environment where supply chain activities are reconciled in a public register. This, however, does not imply disintermediation rather it is a simple replacement of existing intermediaries with the new ones. Hence, stakeholders involved in the blockchain-based SCM need to understand that blockchain does not eliminate intermediaries rather different stakeholders' roles may shift. For instance, an initial service provider may later act as an intermediary in a blockchain-based supply chain network (Tönnissen & Teuteberg, 2020). In a blockchain-based logistics chain, however, the acceptability of a service provider as an intermediary remains unclear. Thus, a key managerial implication here is to devise a clear communication strategy to convince SC participants of the usage and merits of BC-enabled applications. The communication strategy shall emphasize the advantages of adopting blockchain technology-based SC practices for the organizations, SC stakeholders, and the environment. In addition, the strategy shall elicit the process of implementing and using BC-enabled applications in a manner that enhances data transparency. In this way, blockchain-based SC practices will not only receive participant support but also address their concerns about the technology. This initiative leads to the second managerial implication i.e., technology awareness and training.

Despite emerging as a highly efficient solution to SC issues, the acceptability of blockchain technology remains challenged due to its potential as a disruptive technology with uncertain results. In this regard, governments, endorsing blockchain adoption for achieving the sustainability agenda, have a crucial role to play. Government representatives need to shoulder the responsibility to educate stakeholders about the usage, organizational implications, and related merits and demerits of blockchain technology in SC networks. Also, creating developmental opportunities focused on the environmental sustainability agenda through webinars, workshops, and e-tutorials can help promote acceptance of blockchain technology among SC stakeholders. Creating awareness about blockchain technology and its application to the supply chain signifies the third implication i.e. the legal aspect of adopting such GIT.

Starting with the national policy agenda of SDG-endorsing economies, a comprehensive legal framework with relevant laws and regulations shall be designed to address legal requirements of data sharing, privacy, and security. Currently, countries such as the USA, UK, Germany, Malaysia, China, and Japan do have legal frameworks governing digital currencies and blockchain laws in general investing. Similarly, there is a SCOR model of supply chain developed by the Supply Chain Council. This model guides global manufacturing firms in tackling, refining, and disseminating SCM practices revolving around five stages that include plan, source, make, deliver, and return (Al-Farsi et al., 2021). However, guidelines as an amalgamation of the two i.e. blockchain and SCM are still lacking. There is room for developing a mechanism to legally process and guide blockchain technology applications to various supply chain activities. Concerning differences in the legal environment of different countries, there is a need to design a standard user manual/guide for BC application to the global supply chain. This may serve as a general set of guidelines that can further be reformed following the legal requirements of different countries. Within each country's legal framework, organizations shall be encouraged to devise governance mechanisms that ensure legal compliance of data sharing, storage, utilization, and privacy in blockchain-based supply chain networks.

CONCLUSION

The emergence of blockchain technology as a GIT is attributable to the outbreak of COVID-19 which witnessed a surge in the global application of BC to various business processes. True to note, blockchain technology has lessened the worries of business communities by offering a distributed way to establish trust in a sustainable supply chain. Across the globe, from small firms to large corporations, the application of blockchain technology is benefiting business enterprises by offering efficient approaches to managing supply chain disruptions. This chapter has precisely addressed the domain of blockchain-based SCM and sustainable practices. This chapter comprehended the concept of blockchain technology by shedding light on a brief trail from the history of how the concept of 'blockchain technology' has emerged and grown over time along with its recent application across various regions. In addition, this chapter focused on the characteristic features that blockchain has added to supply chain management and how the adoption of such IR 5.0 technology is bringing supply chain management towards sustainability. In particular, this chapter has highlighted the opportunities and challenges in the application of blockchain technology to the supply chain domain.

REFERENCES

Agrawal, R., Majumdar, A., Majumdar, K., Raut, R. D., & Narkhede, B. E. (2022). Attaining sustainable development goals (SDGs) through supply chain practices and business strategies: A systematic review with bibliometric and network analyses. *Business Strategy and the Environment, 31*(7), 3669–3687. doi:10.1002/bse.3057

Al-Farsi, S., Rathore, M. M., & Bakiras, S. (2021). Security of Blockchain-Based Supply Chain Management Systems: Challenges and Opportunities. *Applied Sciences (Basel, Switzerland), 11*(12), 12. doi:10.3390/app11125585

Bag, S., Viktorovich, D. A., Sahu, A. K., & Sahu, A. K. (2020). Barriers to adoption of blockchain technology in green supply chain management. *Journal of Global Operations and Strategic Sourcing, 14*(1), 104–133. doi:10.1108/JGOSS-06-2020-0027

Bashir, I. (2017). Blockchain 101. In *Mastering Blockchain* (1st ed., pp. 7–33). Packt Publishing Ltd. https://books.google.com.pk/books?id=urkrDwAAQBAJ&printsec=frontcover&source=gbs_ge_summary_r&cad=0#v=onepage&q&f=false

Blockdata. (2023). *Blockdata—Accelerating Blockchain Adoption*. Blockdata. https://www.blockdata.tech

Cai, Y.-J., & Choi, T.-M. (2020). A United Nations' Sustainable Development Goals perspective for sustainable textile and apparel supply chain management. *Transportation Research Part E, Logistics and Transportation Review, 141*, 102010. doi:10.1016/j.tre.2020.102010 PMID:32834741

Carter, C. R., Rogers, D. S., & Choi, T. Y. (2015). Toward the Theory of the Supply Chain. *The Journal of Supply Chain Management, 51*(2), 89–97. doi:10.1111/jscm.12073

Cole, R., Stevenson, M., & Aitken, J. (2019). Blockchain technology: Implications for operations and supply chain management. *Supply Chain Management, 24*(4), 469–483. doi:10.1108/SCM-09-2018-0309

FBI. (2023). *Blockchain Technology Market Size, Share & Growth [2030]* (Blockchain Technology Market Size, Share & COVID-19 Impact Analysis FBI100072; pp. 1–160). Fortune Business Insights. https://www.fortunebusinessinsights.com/industry-reports/blockchain-market-100072

Friedman, N., & Ormiston, J. (2022). Blockchain as a sustainability-oriented innovation?: Opportunities for and resistance to Blockchain technology as a driver of sustainability in global food supply chains. *Technological Forecasting and Social Change*, *175*, 121403. doi:10.1016/j.techfore.2021.121403

Gad, A. G., Mosa, D. T., Abualigah, L., & Abohany, A. A. (2022). Emerging Trends in Blockchain Technology and Applications: A Review and Outlook. *Journal of King Saud University. Computer and Information Sciences*, *34*(9), 6719–6742. doi:10.1016/j.jksuci.2022.03.007

Gatteschi, V., Lamberti, F., Demartini, C., Pranteda, C., & Santamaría, V. (2018). To Blockchain or Not to Blockchain: That Is the Question. *IT Professional*, *20*(2), 62–74. doi:10.1109/MITP.2018.021921652

Groschopf, W., Dobrovnik, M., & Herneth, C. (2021). Smart Contracts for Sustainable Supply Chain Management: Conceptual Frameworks for Supply Chain Maturity Evaluation and Smart Contract Sustainability Assessment. *Frontiers in Blockchain, 4*. https://www.frontiersin.org/articles/10.3389/fbloc.2021.506436

Guo, Y., & Liang, C. (2016). Blockchain application and outlook in the banking industry. *Financial Innovation*, *2*(1), 24. doi:10.118640854-016-0034-9

Kayikci, Y., Kazancoglu, Y., Lafci, C., Gozacan-Chase, N., & Mangla, S. K. (2021). Smart circular supply chains to achieving SDGs for post-pandemic preparedness. *Journal of Enterprise Information Management*, *35*(1), 237–265. doi:10.1108/JEIM-06-2021-0271

Kouhizadeh, M., Saberi, S., & Sarkis, J. (2021). Blockchain technology and the sustainable supply chain: Theoretically exploring adoption barriers. *International Journal of Production Economics*, *231*, 107831. doi:10.1016/j.ijpe.2020.107831

Li, Y., & Chen, T. (2022). Blockchain empowers supply chains: Challenges, opportunities and prospects. *Nankai Business Review International*, *14*(2), 230–248. doi:10.1108/NBRI-06-2022-0066

Likens, S. (2023). *Making sense of bitcoin, cryptocurrency and blockchain*. PwC. https://www.pwc.com/us/en/industries/financial-services/fintech/bitcoin-blockchain-cryptocurrency.html

Macrotrends. (2023). *World Population Growth Rate 1950-2023*. Macrotrends. https://www.macrotrends.net/countries/WLD/world/population-growth-rate

Marinagi, C., Reklitis, P., Trivellas, P., & Sakas, D. (2023). The Impact of Industry 4.0 Technologies on Key Performance Indicators for a Resilient Supply Chain 4.0. *Sustainability (Basel)*, *15*(6), 6. doi:10.3390u15065185

Min, H., & Zhou, G. (2002). Supply chain modeling: Past, present and future. *Computers & Industrial Engineering*, *43*(1), 231–249. doi:10.1016/S0360-8352(02)00066-9

Moosavi, J., Naeni, L. M., Fathollahi-Fard, A. M., & Fiore, U. (2021). Blockchain in supply chain management: A review, bibliometric, and network analysis. *Environmental Science and Pollution Research International*. doi:10.100711356-021-13094-3 PMID:33638786

Moretto, A., & Macchion, L. (2022). Drivers, barriers and supply chain variables influencing the adoption of the blockchain to support traceability along fashion supply chains. *Operations Management Research : Advancing Practice Through Research*, *15*(3), 1470–1489. doi:10.100712063-022-00262-y

Nayeri, S., Sazvar, Z., & Heydari, J. (2023). Towards a responsive supply chain based on the industry 5.0 dimensions: A novel decision-making method. *Expert Systems with Applications*, *213*, 119267. doi:10.1016/j.eswa.2022.119267

Queiroz, M. M., Telles, R., & Bonilla, S. H. (2019). Blockchain and supply chain management integration: A systematic review of the literature. *Supply Chain Management*, *25*(2), 241–254. doi:10.1108/SCM-03-2018-0143

Sahebi, I. G., Masoomi, B., & Ghorbani, S. (2020). Expert oriented approach for analyzing the blockchain adoption barriers in humanitarian supply chain. *Technology in Society*, *63*, 101427. doi:10.1016/j.techsoc.2020.101427

Satoshi Nakamoto. (2008). *Bitcoin: A Peer-to-Peer Electronic Cash System*. bitcoin. https://bitcoin.org/bitcoin.pdf

Sharma, T. K. (2022, December 16). *Top 10 Countries Leading Blockchain Technology In The World [Understanding blockchain]*. Blockchain Council. https://www.blockchain-council.org/blockchain/top-10-countries-leading-blockchain-technology-in-the-world/

Stevens, G. C., & Johnson, M. (2016). Integrating the Supply Chain … 25 years on. *International Journal of Physical Distribution & Logistics Management*, *46*(1), 19–42. doi:10.1108/IJPDLM-07-2015-0175

Tönnissen, S., & Teuteberg, F. (2020). Analysing the impact of blockchain-technology for operations and supply chain management: An explanatory model drawn from multiple case studies. *International Journal of Information Management*, *52*, 101953. doi:10.1016/j.ijinfomgt.2019.05.009

UNDP. (2020, March 20). Beyond bitcoin: Using blockchain to advance the SDGs. *Innovation for Development by UNDP Europe and Central Asia*. UN. https://innovation.eurasia.undp.org/beyond-bitcoin-using-blockchain-to-advance-the-sdgs/

United Nations. (2020). *Sustainable Development Goals*. UN. https://sustainabledevelopment.un.org/?menu=1300

Varriale, V., Cammarano, A., Michelino, F., & Caputo, M. (2023). Industry 5.0 and Triple Bottom Line Approach in Supply Chain Management: The State-of-the-Art. *Sustainability (Basel)*, *15*(7), 7. doi:10.3390u15075712

Worldometer. (2023). *Worldometer—Real time world statistics*. Worldometer. https://www.worldometers.info/

Xu, X., Lu, Y., Vogel-Heuser, B., & Wang, L. (2021). Industry 4.0 and Industry 5.0—Inception, conception and perception. *Journal of Manufacturing Systems*, *61*, 530–535. doi:10.1016/j.jmsy.2021.10.006

Yaga, D., Mell, P., Roby, N., & Scarfone, K. (2018). Blockchain Technology Overview (NISTIR 8202; p. NIST IR 8202). National Institute of Standards and Technology (NIST). doi:10.6028/NIST.IR.8202

Zimon, D., Tyan, J., & Sroufe, R. (2020). SCM Drivers of Sustainable Supply Chain Management: Practices to Alignment with UN Sustainable Development Goals. *International Journal of Qualitative Research*, *14*(1), 219–236. doi:10.24874/IJQR14.01-14

Compilation of References

A.P. Moller - Maersk. (2022, November 29). *A.P. Moller - Maersk and IBM to discontinue TradeLens, a blockchain-enabled shipping solution.* A.P. Moller-Maersk. https://www.maersk.com/news/articles/2022/11/29/maersk-and-ibm-to-discontinue-tradelens

Aashima Sharma, S. K. (2021). A comprehensive review on blockchain and Internet of Things in healthcare. *Transactions on Emerging Telecommunications Technologies.*

Ababneh, A. M., Almarashdah, M. A., Jebril, I., Al-Zaqeba, M. A. A., & Assaf, N. (2023). Driving sustainable supply chains: Blockchain-enabled eco-efficiency for resilient customs ports. *Uncertain Supply Chain Management, 11*(4), 1719–1734. doi:10.5267/j.uscm.2023.6.018

Abas, M., Khattak, S. B., Habib, T., & Nadir, U. (2022). Assessment of critical risk and success factors in the construction supply chain: A case of Pakistan. *International Journal of Construction Management., 22*(12), 2258–2266. doi:10.1080/15623599.2020.1783597

Abdelouahid, D., Guerroumi, G., Belaoued, M., & Cheikhrouhou, O. (2021). BMC-SDN: Blockchain-Based Multicontroller Architecture for Secure Software-Defined Networks. *Journal of Wireless Communications and Mobile Computing.* . doi:10.1155/2021/9984666

Abhiroop, T. (2022). A Machine Learning Consensus Based Light-WeightBlockchain Architecture for Internet of Things. *14th International Conference on Communication Systems & Networks.* IEEE. 10.1109/COMSNETS53615.2022.9668487

Abou El Houda, Z., Hafid, A. S., & Khoukhi, L. (2023). MiTFed: A Privacy Preserving Collaborative Network Attack Mitigation Framework Based on Federated Learning Using SDN and Blockchain. *IEEE Transactions on Network Science and Engineering, 10*(4), 1985–2001. doi:10.1109/TNSE.2023.3237367

Accenture. (n.d.). *Blockchain for digital identity.* Accenture. https://www.accenture.com/us-en/services/blockchain/digital-identity

Acemoglu, D., & Robinson, J. A. (2012). *Why nations fail: The origins of power, prosperity and poverty* (1st ed.). Crown Publishers.

Acemoglu, D., & Robinson, J. A. (2019). *The narrow corridor: States, societies, and the fate of liberty.* Penguin Press.

Adams, R., Kewell, B., & Parry, G. (2018). Blockchain for Good? Digital Ledger Technology and Sustainable Development Goals. In *Handbook of Sustainability and Social Science Research* (pp. 127–140). Springer. doi:10.1007/978-3-319-67122-2_7

AdExchanger. (2015). *Defining Viewability: 'The Opportunity To Be Seen Can't Tell You If An Ad Worked Or Not'.* AdExchanger.

Aditya, U. S., Singh, R., Singh, P. K., & Kalla, A. (2021). A survey on blockchain in robotics: Issues, opportunities, challenges and future directions. *Journal of Network and Computer Applications*, *196*, 103245. doi:10.1016/j.jnca.2021.103245

Afonso, A., Schuknecht, L., & Tanzi, V. (2010). Public sector efficiency: Evidence for new EU member states and emerging markets. *Applied Economics*, *42*(17), 2147–2164. doi:10.1080/00036840701765460

Agarwal, S. (2018). *Blockchain technology in supply chain and logistics* [Doctoral dissertation, Massachusetts Institute of Technology].

Agarwal, U., Rishiwal, V., Tanwar, S., Chaudhary, R., Sharma, G., Bokoro, P. N., & Sharma, R. (2022). Blockchain Technology for Secure Supply Chain Management: A Comprehensive Review. *IEEE Access : Practical Innovations, Open Solutions*, *10*, 2022. doi:10.1109/ACCESS.2022.3194319

Agi, M. A. N., & Jha, A. K. (2022). Blockchain technology in the supply chain: An integrated theoretical perspective of organizational adoption. *International Journal of Production Economics*, *108458*, 108458. doi:10.1016/j.ijpe.2022.108458

Agrawal, R., Majumdar, A., Majumdar, K., Raut, R. D., & Narkhede, B. E. (2022). Attaining sustainable development goals (SDGs) through supply chain practices and business strategies: A systematic review with bibliometric and network analyses. *Business Strategy and the Environment*, *31*(7), 3669–3687. doi:10.1002/bse.3057

Agrawal, T. K., Angelis, J., Khilji, W. A., Kalaiarasan, R., & Wiktorsson, M. (2023). Demonstration of a blockchain-based framework using smart contracts for supply chain collaboration. *International Journal of Production Research*, *61*(5), 1497–1516. doi:10.1080/00207543.2022.2039413

Ahad, M. A., Paiva, S., Tripathi, G., & Feroz, N. (2020). Enabling technologies and sustainable smart cities. *Sustainable Cities and Society*, *61*, 102301. doi:10.1016/j.scs.2020.102301

Ahi, P., & Searcy, C. (2015). An analysis of metrics used to measure performance in green and sustainable supply chains. *Journal of Cleaner Production*, *86*, 360–377. doi:10.1016/j.jclepro.2014.08.005

Ahl, A., Yarime, M., Goto, M., Chopra, S. S., Kumar, N. M., Tanakã, K., & Sagawa, D. (2020). Exploring blockchain for the energy transition: Opportunities and challenges based on a case study in Japan. *Renewable & Sustainable Energy Reviews*, *117*, 109488. doi:10.1016/j.rser.2019.109488

Ahmad Musamih, K. S.-H. (2021). A Blockchain-Based Approach for Drug Traceability in Healthcare Supply Chain. *IEEE Access : Practical Innovations, Open Solutions*, *9*, 9728–9743. doi:10.1109/ACCESS.2021.3049920

Ahmad, A., Luo W., & Robles-Kelly, A. (2023). Robust federated learning under statistical heterogeneity via hessian-weighted aggregation. *Journal of Pattern Recognitio n*10.1016/j.patcog.2023.109635

Ahmed Farouk, A. A. (2020). Blockchain Platform for Industrial Healthcare: Vision and Future opportunities. *Computer Communications*, *154*, 223–235. doi:10.1016/j.comcom.2020.02.058

Akaba, T. I., Norta, A., Udokwu, C., & Draheim, D. (2020). A Framework for the Adoption of Blockchain-Based e-Procurement Systems in the Public Sector: A Case Study of Nigeria. In M. Hattingh, M. Matthee, H. Smuts, I. Pappas, Y. K. Dwivedi, & M. Mäntymäki (Eds.), *Responsible Design, Implementation and Use of Information and Communication Technology* (Vol. 12066, pp. 3–14). Springer International Publishing. doi:10.1007/978-3-030-44999-5_1

Al Amin, M., Nabil, D. H., Baldacci, R., & Rahman, M. H. (2023, September 19). Exploring Blockchain Implementation Challenges for Sustainable Supply Chains: An Integrated Fuzzy TOPSIS–ISM Approach. *Sustainability (Basel)*, *15*(18), 13891. doi:10.3390u151813891

Al Asqah M., & Moulahi, T. (2023). Federated Learning and Blockchain Integration for Privacy Protection in the Internet of Things: Challenges and Solutions. *Journal of Future Internet*. . doi:10.3390/fi15060203

Al Sharif, R., & Pokharel, S. (2022). Smart city dimensions and associated risks: Review of literature. *Sustainable Cities and Society*, *77*, 103542. doi:10.1016/j.scs.2021.103542

Alabaddi, Z., Obidat, A., & Alziyadat, Z. (2023). Exploring the effect of blockchain technology on supply chain resilience and transparency: Evidence from the healthcare industry. *Uncertain Supply Chain Management*, *11*(2), 787–798. doi:10.5267/j.uscm.2023.1.001

Alaimo, C., & Kallinikos, J. (2018). *Objects, Metrics and Practices: An Inquiry into the Programmatic Advertising Ecosystem*. Research Gate.

Albeanu, G. (2017, October). Blockchain technology and education. In *The 12th International Conference on Virtual Learning ICVL* (pp. 271-275).

Al-Farsi, S., Rathore, M. M., & Bakiras, S. (2021). Security of blockchain-based supply chain management systems: Challenges and opportunities. *Applied Sciences (Basel, Switzerland)*, *11*(12), 5585. doi:10.3390/app11125585

Algarni, S. (2022) BCNBI: A Blockchain-Based Security Framework forNorthbound Interface in Software-Defined Networking. *Journal of Electronics (China)*. doi:10.3390/electronics11070996

Alharby, M., & van Moorsel, A. (2017). *Blockchain-based smart contracts: A systematic mapping study*. arXiv preprint arXiv:1710.06372. https://arxiv.org/abs/1710.06372 doi:10.5121/csit.2017.71011

Alharby, N., & Moorsel, A. V. (2018). *Internet of Things security with blockchain technology: A state-of-the-art review*. Research Gate. https://www.researchgate.net/publication/365584843_Internet_of_Things_IoT_Security_with_Blockchain_Technology_A_State-of-the-Art_Review

Alharby, N., & Moorsel, A. V. (2013). Blockchain-based IoT security: A survey. *Computers & Security*, *88*, 101614. https://www.sciencedirect.com/science/article/abs/pii/S0045790623000198

Alharby, N., & Moorsel, A. V. (2021). Blockchain-based IoT security: A comprehensive review of architectures and challenges. *Future Generation Computer Systems*, *122*, 1–16. doi:10.1016/j.future.2021.07.015

Alharthi, S., Cerotti, P. R. C., & Maleki Far, S. (2020, October 6). An Exploration of The Role of Blockchain in The Sustainability and Effectiveness of The Pharmaceutical Supply Chain. *Journal of Supply Chain and Customer Relationship Management*, 1–29. doi:10.5171/2020.562376

Ali, S. I. M., Farouk, H., & Sharaf, H. (2022). A blockchain-based models for student information systems. *Egyptian Informatics Journal*, *23*(2), 187–196. doi:10.1016/j.eij.2021.12.002

Alketbi, A., Nasir, Q., & Talib, M. A. (2018). Blockchain for government services—Use cases, security benefits and challenges. *2018 15th Learning and Technology Conference (L&T)*, (pp. 112–119). ACM. 10.1109/LT.2018.8368494

Alraja, S. M. A., & Alraja, M. A. (2021). Smart Contracts and Supply Chain Management Using Blockchain. *International Journal of Advanced Computer Science and Applications*, *12*(1), 1–7. https://www.researchgate.net/publication/365027511_Smart_Contracts_and_Supply_Chain_Management_Using_Blockchain

Al-Rakhami, M., & Al-Mashari, M. (2022). Interoperability approaches of blockchain technology for supply chain systems. *Business Process Management Journal*, *28*(5/6), 1251–1276. doi:10.1108/BPMJ-04-2022-0207

Alsobhi, H. A., Alakhtar, R. A., Ubaid, A., Hussain, O. K., & Hussain, F. K. (2023). Blockchain-based micro-credentialing system in higher education institutions: Systematic literature review. *Knowledge-Based Systems*, *265*, 110238. doi:10.1016/j.knosys.2022.110238

Alzahrani, N., & Bulusu, N. (2018, June). Block-supply chain: A new anti-counterfeiting supply chain using NFC and blockchain. In *Proceedings of the 1st Workshop on Cryptocurrencies and Blockchains for Distributed Systems* (pp. 30-35). ACM. 10.1145/3211933.3211939

Alzahrani, S., Daim, T., & Choo, K.-K. R. (2023). Assessment of the Blockchain Technology Adoption for the Management of the Electronic Health Record Systems. *IEEE Transactions on Engineering Management*, *70*(8), 2846–2863. doi:10.1109/TEM.2022.3158185

Al-Zaqeba, M. A. A., Jarah, B. A. F., Ineizeh, N. I., Almatarneh, Z., & Jarrah, M. A. A. (2022). The effect of management accounting and blockchain technology characteristics on supply chains efficiency. *Uncertain Supply Chain Management*, *10*(3), 973–982. doi:10.5267/j.uscm.2022.2.016

Amaral, V. (2020). Blockchain for the Internet of Things: Current and Future Trends. *In Handbook of Research on Emerging Perspectives in Intelligent Pattern Recognition, Analysis, and Data Mining*. (32-48). IGI Global. https://aws.amazon.com/marketplace/

Amazon Web Services. (n.d.). *What is decentralization in blockchain?* AWS. https://aws.amazon.com/blockchain/decentralization-in-blockchain/

Ambe, I. M., & Badenhorst-Weiss, J. A. (2011). Managing and Controlling Public Sector Supply Chains. In Supply Chain Management (Pengzhong Li, pp. 73–92). InTech.

Amirian, S., Amiri, M., & Taghavifard, M. T. (2022, September 27). The Emergence of a Sustainable and Reliable Supply Chain Paradigm in Supply Chain Network Design. *Complexity*, *2022*, 1–29. doi:10.1155/2022/9415465

Amit Karamchandani, S. K. (2021). Analysing perceived role of blockchain technology in SCM context for the manufacturing industry. *International Journal of Production Research*, *59*(11), 3398–3429. doi:10.1080/00207543.2021.1883761

Amulya Gurtu, J. J. (2019). Potential of blockchain technology in supply chain management: A literature review. *International Journal of Physical Distribution & Logistics Management*, *49*(9), 881–900. doi:10.1108/IJPDLM-11-2018-0371

Andrews, M., Goehring, J., Hui, S., Pancras, J., & Thornswood, L. (2016). Mobile Promotions: A Framework and Research Priorities. *Journal of Interactive Marketing*, *34*, 15–24. doi:10.1016/j.intmar.2016.03.004

Antoniadis, I., & Kontsas, S. (2019). Blockchain Applications in Marketing. *7th International Conference on Contemporary Marketing*. Heraklion: ResearchGate.

Arndt, T. (2019). An Overview of Blockchain for Higher Education. *KMIS*, 231-235.

Arndt, T., & Guercio, A. (2020). Blockchain-based transcripts for mobile higher-education. *International Journal of Information and Education Technology (IJIET)*, *10*(2), 84–89. doi:10.18178/ijiet.2020.10.2.1344

Arun Aryal, Y. L. (2020). The Emerging big Data Analytics and IoT in Supply Chain Management: A Systematic Review. *Supply Chain Management*, 141–156.

Arvind Panwar, V. B. (2022). A Blockchain Framework to Secure Personal Health Record (PHR) in IBM Cloud-Based Data Lake. *Computational Intelligence and Neuroscience*. PMID:35463293

Ashcroft. (2022, October 14). Timeline: Evolution of blockchain tech in supply chain. *Supply Chain Magazine*. https://supplychaindigital.com/digital-supply-chain/timeline-evolution-of-blockchain-tech-in-supply-chain

Ashley, M. J., & Johnson, M. S. (2018). Establishing a secure, transparent, and autonomous blockchain of custody for renewable energy credits and carbon credits. *IEEE Engineering Management Review*, *46*(4), 100–102. doi:10.1109/EMR.2018.2874967

Asif, M., Jajja, M. S. S., & Searcy, C. (2019). Social compliance standards: Re-evaluating the buyer and supplier perspectives. *Journal of Cleaner Production*, *227*, 457–471. doi:10.1016/j.jclepro.2019.04.157

Aslam, J., Saleem, A., & Kim, Y. B. (2023). Blockchain-enabled supply chain management: Integrated impact on firm performance and robustness capabilities. *Business Process Management Journal*, *29*(6), 1680–1705. doi:10.1108/BPMJ-03-2023-0165

Asmussen, C. G., & Charles, A. (2020). Blockchain technology in supply chain management: Insights on adoption barriers and enablers. *Management Accounting Research*, *47*, 100–113. doi:10.1016/j.mar.2019.07.002

Astill, J., Dara, R. A., Campbell, M., Farber, J. M., Fraser, E. D., Sharif, S., & Yada, R. Y. (2019). Transparency in food supply chains: A review of enabling technology solutions. *Trends in Food Science & Technology*, *91*, 240–247. doi:10.1016/j.tifs.2019.07.024

Atkinson, C. L., McCue, C., Prier, E., & Atkinson, A. M. (2020). Supply Chain Manipulation, Misrepresentation, and Magical Thinking During the COVID-19 Pandemic. *American Review of Public Administration*, *50*(6–7), 628–634. doi:10.1177/0275074020942055

Avci, C., Tekinerdogan, B., & Athanasiadis, I. N. (2020). Software architectures for big data: A systematic literature review. *Big Data Analytics*, *5*(1), 1–53. doi:10.118641044-020-00045-1

Awaysheh, A., & Klassen, R. D. (2010). The impact of supply chain structure on the use of supplier socially responsible practices. *International Journal of Operations & Production Management*, *30*(12), 1246–1268. doi:10.1108/01443571011094253

Aysan, A. F., Bergigui, F., & Disli, M. (2021). Blockchain-based solutions in achieving SDGs after COVID-19. *Journal of Open Innovation*, *7*(2), 151. doi:10.3390/joitmc7020151

Azzi, R., Kilany, R., & Sokhn, M. (2019). The power of a blockchain-based supply chain. *Computers & Industrial Engineering*, *135*, 582–592. doi:10.1016/j.cie.2019.06.042

Babu, E. S., Kavati, I., Nayak, S. R., Ghosh, U., & Al Numay, W. (2022). Secure and transparent pharmaceutical supply chain using permissioned blockchain network. *International Journal of Logistics Research and Applications*, 1–28. https://doi.org/ doi:10.1080/13675567.2022.2045578

Babu, E. S., Srinivasarao, B. K. N., Kavati, I., & Rao, M. S. (2022). Verifiable authentication and issuance of academic certificates using permissioned blockchain network. [IJISP]. *International Journal of Information Security and Privacy*, *16*(1), 1–24. doi:10.4018/ijisp.2022010107

Baden, R., Bender, A., Spring, N., Bhattacharjee, B., & Starin, D. (2009, August). Persona: an online social network with user-defined privacy. In *Proceedings of the ACM SIGCOMM 2009 conference on Data communication* (pp. 135-146). ACM. 10.1145/1592568.1592585

Bag, S., Viktorovich, D. A., Sahu, A. K., & Sahu, A. K. (2020). Barriers to adoption of blockchain technology in green supply chain management. *Journal of Global Operations and Strategic Sourcing*, *14*(1), 104–133. doi:10.1108/JGOSS-06-2020-0027

Bai, C., Quayson, M., & Sarkis, J. (2022). Analysis of Blockchain's enablers for improving sustainable supply chain transparency in Africa cocoa industry. *Journal of Cleaner Production*, *358*, 131896. doi:10.1016/j.jclepro.2022.131896

Baily, P., Farmer, D., Crocker, B., & Jessop, D. (2022). *Procurment Principles and Management in the Digital Age* (12th ed.). Pearson Education Limited.

Bannerflow. *The Challenges of Programmatic Advertising.*

Bano, S., Sonnino, A., Al-Bassam, M., Azouvi, S., McCorry, P., Meiklejohn, S., & Danezis, G. (2017). Consensus in the age of blockchains. *arXiv preprint arXiv:1711.03936.*

Barratt, M., & Barratt, R. (2011). Exploring internal and external supply chain linkages: Evidence from the field. *Journal of Operations Management*, *29*(5), 514–528. doi:10.1016/j.jom.2010.11.006

Barroso, A. P., Machado, V. H., Carvalho, H., & Cruz Machado, V. (2015). Quantifying the Supply Chain Resilience. In H. Tozan & A. Ertürk (Eds.), *Applications of Contemporary Management Approaches in Supply Chains*. InTech., doi:10.5772/59580

Bashir, I. (2017). Blockchain 101. In *Mastering Blockchain* (1st ed., pp. 7–33). Packt Publishing Ltd. https://books.google.com.pk/books?id=urkrDwAAQBAJ&printsec=frontcover&source=gbs_ge_summary_r&cad=0#v=onepage&q&f=false

Basu, P., Deb, P., & Singh, A. (2023). Blockchain and the carbon credit ecosystem: sustainable management of the supply chain. *Journal of Business Strategy*.

Batubara, F. R., Ubacht, J., & Janssen, M. (2018). Challenges of blockchain technology adoption for e-government: A systematic literature review. *Proceedings of the 19th Annual International Conference on Digital Government Research: Governance in the Data Age*, (pp. 1–9). IEEE. https://doi.org/10.1145/3209281.3209317

Batwa, A., & Norman, A. (2020). A framework for exploring blockchain technology in supply chain management. *Operations and Supply Chain Management*, *13*(3), 294–306. doi:10.31387/oscm0420271

Baucas, M. J. Petros, S. & Plataniotis, K. (2023). Federated Learning and Blockchain-Enabled Fog-IoT Platform for Wearables in Predictive Healthcare. *IEEE Transactions on Computational Social Systems*. IEEE.

Baviskar, D., Ahirrao, S., Potdar, V., & Kotecha, K. (2021). Efficient automated processing of the unstructured documents using artificial intelligence: A systematic literature review and future directions. *IEEE Access : Practical Innovations, Open Solutions*, *9*, 72894–72936. doi:10.1109/ACCESS.2021.3072900

Bayramova, A., Edwards, D. J., & Roberts, C. (2021). The Role of Blockchain Technology in Augmenting Supply Chain Resilience to Cybercrime. *Buildings*, *11*(7), 283. doi:10.3390/buildings11070283

Bechtsis, D., Tsolakis, N., Iakovou, E., & Vlachos, D. (2022). Data-driven secure, resilient and sustainable supply chains: Gaps, opportunities, and a new generalised data sharing and data monetisation framework. *International Journal of Production Research*, *60*(14), 4397–4417. doi:10.1080/00207543.2021.1957506

Beck, R., Müller-Bloch, C., & King, J. L. (2018). Governance in the blockchain economy: A framework and research agenda. *Journal of the Association for Information Systems*, *19*(10), 1. doi:10.17705/1jais.00518

Behzad Esmaeilian, J. S. (2020). Blockchain for the future of sustainable supply chain management in Industry 4.0. *Resources, Conservation and Recycling*.

Beier, G., Ullrich, A., Niehoff, S., Reißig, M., & Habich, M. (2020). Industry 4.0: How it is defined from a socio-technical perspective and how much sustainability it includes – A literature review. *Journal of Cleaner Production*, *259*, 120856. doi:10.1016/j.jclepro.2020.120856

Benshahar, A. (2021). *Bringing Smart Contracts To The Digital Advertising Industry- SaTT Review*. CryptoPotato.

Benton, M. C., Radziwill, N., Purritano, A., & Gerhart, C. (2018). Blockchain for Supply Chain: Improving Transparency and Efficiency Simultaneously. *Software Quality Professional*, *20*, 28–38.

Bergström, A. (2020). *The role of social media in crisis communication and crisis management* [Doctoral dissertation, University of Gothenburg]. https://www.diva-portal.org/smash/get/diva2:1574301/FULLTEXT01.pdf

Bernards, N., Campbell-Verduyn, M., & Rodima-Taylor, D. (2022, November 25). The veil of transparency: Blockchain and sustainability governance in global supply chains. *Environment and Planning C. Politics and Space, 239965442211427.* doi:10.1177/23996544221142763

Berryhill, J., Bourgery, T., & Hanson, A. (2018). *Blockchains Unchained: Blockchain Technology and its Use in the Public Sector* (OECD Working Papers on Public Governance 28). OECD. https://www.oecd-ilibrary.org/governance/blockchains-unchained_3c32c429-en

Beserra, P. B. (2021). *Blockchain Technology to Improve Supply Chain Management-A Systematic Literature Review* [Doctoral dissertation, Universidade do Algarve (Portugal)].

Bezovski, Z., Apasieva, T. J., & Temjanovski, R. (2021). The Impact and the Potential Disruption of the Blockchain Technology on Marketing. *Journal of Economics*, *6*(1), 13–23. doi:10.46763/JOE216.10013b

Bhatia, R., & Bhasin, N. K. (2023). A Study of the New Role of Blockchain in the Indian Education System. [IJeC]. *International Journal of e-Collaboration*, *19*(1), 1–19. doi:10.4018/IJeC.315784

Bhatti, S. H., Rashid, M., Arsalan, A., Tarba, S., & Liu, Y. (2023). Servitized SMEs performance and the influences of sustainable procurement, packaging, and distribution: The mediating role of eco-innovation. *Technovation*, *127*, 127. doi:10.1016/j.technovation.2023.102831

Biswas, K., Muthukkumarasamy, V., & Tan, W. L. (2017). Blockchain based wine supply chain traceability system. In *Future Technologies Conference (FTC) 2017* (pp. 56-62). The Science and Information Organization.

Blockdata. (2023). *Blockdata—Accelerating Blockchain Adoption*. Blockdata. https://www.blockdata.tech

Blockhead Technologies. (2019, October 16). *How blockchain is revolutionising food supply chains.* Blockhead Technologies. https://blockheadtechnologies.com/how-blockchain-is-revolutionising-food-supply-chains/

Block, S. (2023). Legal Requirements in the Field of Virtual Currencies. In M. Užík, C. Schmitz, & S. Block (Eds.), *Financial Innovation and Value Creation: The Impact of Disruptive Technologies on the Digital World* (pp. 75–86). Springer International Publishing. doi:10.1007/978-3-031-22426-3_5

Böhme, R., Christin, N., Edelman, B., & Moore, T. (2015). Bitcoin: Economics, technology, and governance. *The Journal of Economic Perspectives*, *29*(2), 213–238. doi:10.1257/jep.29.2.213

Boiardi, P., & Stout, E. (2021). *To what extent can blockchain help development co-operation actors meet the 2030 Agenda?* (OECD Development Co-Operation Working Papers 95). OECD. https://doi.org/ doi:10.1787/22220518

Botcha, K. M., & Chakravarthy, V. V. (2019). Enhancing Traceability in Pharmaceutical Supply Chain Using Internet of Things (IoT) and Blockchain. *Proceedings - 2019 IEEE international conference on intelligent systems and green technology*, (pp. 45-48). IEEE.

Bottoni, P., Gessa, N., Massa, G., Pareschi, R., Selim, H., & Arcuri, E. (2020). Intelligent smart contracts for innovative supply chain management. *Frontiers in Blockchain*, *3*, 535787. doi:10.3389/fbloc.2020.535787

Brody, P., Pureswaran, V., Panikkar, S., & Nair, S. (2015). Empowering the edge Practical insights on a decentralized Internet of Things. *IBM Institute for Business Value. Technical Report.* IBM.

Brown, B., Chui, M., & Manyika, J. (2011). Are you ready for the era of 'big data'. *The McKinsey Quarterly*, *4*(1), 24–35.

Bugra, B., Turkmen, H., & Nuriyev, U. (2023),"PPFchain: A novel framework privacy-preserving blockchain-based federated learning method for senor networks", Elseveir: Internet of Things, ISSN: 2542-6605.

Buterin, V. (2014). A next-generation smart contract and decentralized application platform. *white paper, 3*(37), 2-1.

Butterworth, P. (2022). *The Potential of Blockchain in Adtech and Programmatic – for advertisers.* Adwatch.

Bux, C., Varese, E., Amicarelli, V., & Lombardi, M. (2022). Halal Food Sustainability between Certification and Blockchain: A Review. *Sustainability (Basel), 14*(4), 2152. doi:10.3390u14042152

Cachin, C., & Vukolic, M. (2017). Blockchain Consensus Protocols in the Wild. preprint. *arXiv preprint arXiv:1707.01873.*

Cagigas, D., Clifton, J., Diaz-Fuentes, D., Fernández-Gutiérrez, M., & Harpes, C. (2023). Blockchain in government: Toward an evaluation framework. *Policy Design and Practice, 6*(4), 1–18. doi:10.1080/25741292.2023.2230702

Cai, Y.-J., & Choi, T.-M. (2020). A United Nations' Sustainable Development Goals perspective for sustainable textile and apparel supply chain management. *Transportation Research Part E, Logistics and Transportation Review, 141*, 102010. doi:10.1016/j.tre.2020.102010 PMID:32834741

Caldarelli, G., & Ellul, J. (2021). Trusted academic transcripts on the blockchain: A systematic literature review. *Applied Sciences (Basel, Switzerland), 11*(4), 1842. doi:10.3390/app11041842

Callender, G. (2011). Alignment of inter-agency supply chains to enhance public sector performance management. *International Journal of Productivity and Performance Management, 60*(1), 9–23. doi:10.1108/17410401111094286

Callon, M., Yuval, M., & Muniesa, F. (Eds.). (2007). *Market Devices.* Blackwell Publishing.

Calvera Isabal, M., Santos, P., Hoppe, H., & Schulten, C. (2023). Cómo automatizar la extracción y análisis de información sobre ciencia ciudadana con propósitos educativos. *Comunicar., 31*(74), 13.

Cameron, L. (2020). *The rise of algorithmic work: Implications for organizational control and worker autonomy* [Doctoral dissertation, University of Michigan].

Caro, M. P., Ali, M. S., Vecchio, M., & Giaffreda, R. (2018). Blockchain-based traceability in Agri-Food supply chain management: A practical implementation. *2018 IoT Vertical and Topical Summit on Agriculture-Tuscany (IOT Tuscany)*

Carter, C. R., & Rogers, D. S. (2008). A framework of sustainable supply chain management: Moving toward new theory. *International Journal of Physical Distribution & Logistics Management, 38*(5), 360–387. doi:10.1108/09600030810882816

Carter, C. R., Rogers, D. S., & Choi, T. Y. (2015). Toward the Theory of the Supply Chain. *The Journal of Supply Chain Management, 51*(2), 89–97. doi:10.1111/jscm.12073

Casper, R. H., Lazaro, J. A., Wang, E., & Wegrzyn, K. E. (2021). *Smart supply chains using smart contracts.* Manufacturing Industry Advisor. https://www.foley.com/en/insights/publications/2021/09/smart-supply-chains-using-smart-contracts

Catalini, C., & Gans, J. S. (2020). Some simple economics of the blockchain. *Communications of the ACM, 63*(7), 80–90. doi:10.1145/3359552

cerezo, p. (2014). *The media and the challenge of programmatic transformation.* IAB.

Chabani, Z., & Chabani, W. (2022). The role of blockchain technology in enhancing security management in the supply chain. In *Advances in Blockchain Technology for Cyber Physical Systems* (pp. 211–231). Springer International Publishing. doi:10.1007/978-3-030-93646-4_10

Chandan, A., John, M., & Potdar, V. (2023). Achieving UN SDGs in Food Supply Chain Using Blockchain Technology. *Sustainability (Basel), 15*(3), 2109. doi:10.3390u15032109

Chandra, N., Teotia, S., Chaudhary, A., Jain, V., Vashishtha, T., & Dwivedi, N. N. (2022). Noise Reduction Using Cellular Automata. *NeuroQuantology : An Interdisciplinary Journal of Neuroscience and Quantum Physics, 20*(6), 4650–4672.

Chang, S. E., & Chen, Y. (2020). When Blockchain Meets Supply Chain: A systematic literature review on current developments and potential applications. *IEEE Access : Practical Innovations, Open Solutions*, *8*, 2020. doi:10.1109/ACCESS.2020.2983601

Chang, S. E., Chen, Y. C., & Lu, M. F. (2019). Supply chain re-engineering using blockchain technology: A case of smart contract based tracking process. *Technological Forecasting and Social Change*, *144*, 1–11. doi:10.1016/j.techfore.2019.03.015

Chang, Y., Iakovou, E., & Shi, W. (2020). Blockchain in global supply chains and cross border trade: A critical synthesis of the state-of-the-art, challenges and opportunities. *International Journal of Production Research*, *58*(7), 2082–2099. doi:10.1080/00207543.2019.1651946

Chaudhuri, A., Bhatia, M. S., Kayikci, Y., Fernandes, K. J., & Fosso-Wamba, S. (2023). Improving social sustainability and reducing supply chain risks through blockchain implementation: Role of outcome and behavioral mechanism. *Annals of Operations Research*, *327*(1), 401–433. doi:10.100710479-021-04307-6

Chen, W., Shi, Z. X., & Zhao, Y. Z. (2018). A Survey of Blockchain Applications in Different Domains. Association for Computing Machinery, 17-21.

Chen, G., Xu, B., Lu, M., & Chen, N. S. (2018). Exploring blockchain technology and its potential applications for education. *Smart Learning Environments*, *5*(1), 1–10. doi:10.118640561-017-0050-x

Chen, I., & Kitsis, A. (2017). A research framework of sustainable supply chain management: The role of relational capabilities in driving performance. *International Journal of Logistics Management*, *28*(4), 1454–1478. doi:10.1108/IJLM-11-2016-0265

Chen, S., Liu, X., Yan, J., Hu, G., & Shi, Y. (2021). Processes, benefits, and challenges for adoption of blockchain technologies in food supply chains: A thematic analysis. *Information Systems and e-Business Management*, *19*(3), 909–935. doi:10.100710257-020-00467-3

Chen, X., & Wang, Y. (2021). A blockchain-based secure data sharing scheme for cloud storage *Journal of Cybersecurity and Information Intelligence*, *1*(2), 15–22. https://www.mdpi.com/2674-1032/1/2/15

Chen, X., Xu, X., & Hsing, P. (2020). Intellectual Property Protection in Blockchain-based Education. In *2020 IEEE International Conference on Blockchain and Cryptocurrency (ICBC)* (pp. 263-268). IEEE.

Cheung, K.-F., Bell, M. G. H., & Bhattacharjya, J. (2021). Cybersecurity in logistics and supply chain management: An overview and future research directions. *Transportation Research Part E, Logistics and Transportation Review*, *146*, 102217. doi:10.1016/j.tre.2020.102217

Chkanikova, O., & Mont, O. (2015). Corporate supply chain responsibility: Drivers and barriers for sustainable food retailing. *Corporate Social Responsibility and Environmental Management*, *22*(2), 65–82. doi:10.1002/csr.1316

Choi, T. Y., Dooley, K. J., & Rungtusanatham, M. (2001). Supply Networks and Complex Adaptive Systems: Control versus Emergence. *Journal of Operations Management*, *19*(3), 351–366. doi:10.1016/S0272-6963(00)00068-1

Choi, T.-M., & Luo, S. (2019). Data quality challenges for sustainable fashion supply chain operations in emerging markets: Roles of blockchain, government sponsors and environment taxes. *Transportation Research Part E, Logistics and Transportation Review*, *131*, 139–152. doi:10.1016/j.tre.2019.09.019

Chong, A. Y.-L., Ooi, K.-B., & Sohal, A. (2009). The relationship between supply chain factors and adoption of e-Collaboration tools: An empirical examination. *International Journal of Production Economics*, *122*(1), 150–160. doi:10.1016/j.ijpe.2009.05.012

Choo Campbell, R. (2020). The Need for Cyber Resilient Enterprise Distributed Ledger Risk Management Framework. *The Journal of the British Blockchain Association*, *3*(1), 1–9. doi:10.31585/jbba-3-1-(5)2020

Choo, B., & Goh, J. C.-L. (2014) Adapting the ISO31000:2009 Enterprise Risk Management Framework Using the Six-Sigma Approach. *Proceedings of the 2014 IEEE IEEM January 2015* (pp. 39-43). IEEE. 10.1109/IEEM.2014.7058596

Christoph, G., & Schmidt, S. M. (2019). Blockchain and Supply Chain Relations: A Transaction Cost Theory Perspective. *Journal of Purchasing and Supply Management.*

Chua, M. Y., Yee, G. O., Gu, Y. X., & Lung, C. H. (2020). Threats to Online Advertising and Countermeasures: A Technical Survey. *Digital Threats: Research and Practice*, 11.1-11.27.

Chukowry, V., Nanuck, G., & Sungkur, R. K. (2021). The future of continuous learning–Digital badge and microcredential system using blockchain. *Global Transitions Proceedings*, *2*(2), 355–361. doi:10.1016/j.gltp.2021.08.026

CISPL. (2020). *Pros & cons of online food delivery services*. SISPL. https://cispl.com/pros-cons-online-food-delivery-services/

Classification of the Functions of Government. (2019). European Union. https://ec.europa.eu/eurostat/web/products-manuals-and-guidelines/-/ks-gq-19-010

Coglianese, C. (2009). The Transparency President? The Obama Administration and Open Government. *Governance: An International Journal of Policy, Administration and Institutions*, *22*(4), 529–544. doi:10.1111/j.1468-0491.2009.01451.x

Cole, S.A., & Fernando, A.N. (2020). Mobilizing agricultural advice: technology adoption, diffusion, and sustainability. *The Economic Journal, UEAA.*

Cole, R., Stevenson, M., & Aitken, J. (2019). Blockchain technology: Implications for operations and supply chain management. *Supply Chain Management*, *24*(4), 469–483. doi:10.1108/SCM-09-2018-0309

Cong, L. W., & He, Z. (2019). Blockchain disruption and smart contracts. *Review of Financial Studies*, *32*(5), 1754–1797. doi:10.1093/rfs/hhz007

Conoscenti, M., Vetro, A., & De Martin, J. C. (2016, November). Blockchain for the Internet of Things: A systematic literature review. In *2016 IEEE/ACS 13th International Conference of Computer Systems and Applications (AICCSA)* (pp. 1-6). IEEE. 10.1109/AICCSA.2016.7945805

ConsenSys. (n.d.). *Smart contract security best practices*. GitHub. https://github.com/ConsenSys/smart-contract-best-practices

Cording, R., & Lückander, J. (2023). *Blockchain for supply chain transparency and traceability-A contingency framework to implementation challenges.*

Crittenden, C. (2020). Blockchain in California: A Roadmap. *UC Berkeley: Center for Information Technology Research in the Interest of Society (CITRIS)*. https://escholarship.org/uc/item/2j9596dp

Curristine, T., Lonti, Z., & Joumard, I. (2007). Improving Public Sector Efficiency: Challenges and Opportunities. *OECD Journal on Budgeting*, *7*(1), 1–41. doi:10.1787/budget-v7-art6-en

D'Eusanio, M., Zamagni, A., & Petti, L. (2019). Social sustainability and supply chain management: Methods and tools. *Journal of Cleaner Production*, *235*, 178–189. doi:10.1016/j.jclepro.2019.06.323

Da Silveira, V. A., Da Costa, S. R. R., & Resende, D. (2022). Blockchain Technology in Innovation Ecosystems for Sustainable Purchases through the Perception of Public Managers. *WSEAS TRANSACTIONS ON BUSINESS AND ECONOMICS*, *19*, 790–804. doi:10.37394/23207.2022.19.69

Dağ, H., & Erbasi-Gonc, E. (2013). SMIIC and halal food standards. *Journal of Chemical Metrology*, *7*(1).

Danyluk, M. (2019). Fungible space: Competition and volatility in the global logistics network. *International Journal of Urban and Regional Research*, *43*(1), 94–111. doi:10.1111/1468-2427.12675

David, L., & Courtois, N. T. (2018). Blockchain-based degree fraud detection and prevention in higher education. *IEEE Access : Practical Innovations, Open Solutions*, *6*, 43011–43024.

Davis, M., Lennerfors, T. T., & Tolstoy, D. (2022). Can blockchain-technology fight corruption in MNEs' operations in emerging markets? *Review of International Business and Strategy*, *32*(1), 39–56. doi:10.1108/RIBS-12-2020-0155

De Filippi, P., & Hassan, S. (2018). Blockchain technology as a regulatory technology: From code is law to law is code. *arXiv preprint arXiv:1801.02507.*

de Sousa Jabbour, A. B. L., Jabbour, C. J. C., Foropon, C., & Godinho Filho, M. (2018). When titans meet—Can Industry 4.0 revolutionize the environmentally sustainable manufacturing wave? The role of critical success factors. *Technological Forecasting and Social Change*, *132*, 18–25. doi:10.1016/j.techfore.2018.01.017

de Villiers, C., Kuruppu, S., & Dissanayake, D. (2021). A (new) role for business – Promoting the United Nations' Sustainable Development Goals through the internet-of-things and blockchain technology. *Journal of Business Research*, *131*, 598–609. doi:10.1016/j.jbusres.2020.11.066

Dehghani, M., Kennedy, R. W., Mashatan, A., Rese, A., & Karavidas, D. (2022). High interest, low adoption. A mixed-method investigation into the factors influencing organisational adoption of blockchain technology. *Journal of Business Research*, *149*, 393–411. doi:10.1016/j.jbusres.2022.05.015

Delgado-von-Eitzen, C., Anido-Rifón, L., & Fernández-Iglesias, M. J. (2021). Blockchain applications in education: A systematic literature review. *Applied Sciences (Basel, Switzerland)*, *11*(24), 11811. doi:10.3390/app112411811

Deloitte Insights. (2018). *Blockchain – A technical primer*. Deloitte. https://www2. deloitte.com/content/dam/insights/us/articles/4436_Blockchain-primer/DI_ Blockchain_Primer.pdf

Demir, I., & Karabatak, M. (2019). Digital diplomas in higher education and blockchain technology. *Contemporary Educational Technology*, *10*(3), 298–312.

Demirkan, S., Demirkan, I., & McKeec, A. (2020). Blockchain technology in the future of business cyber security and accounting. *Journal of Management Analytics*, 1-20.

Devendra Dhagarra, M. G. (2019). Big Data and blockchain supported conceptual model for enhanced healthcare coverage: The Indian context. *Business Process Management Journal*, BPMJ-06-2018-0164. doi:10.1108/BPMJ-06-2018-0164

Dhingra, S., Raut, R., Gunasekaran, A., Rao Naik, B. K., & Masuna, V. (2023). Analysis of the challenges for blockchain technology adoption in the Indian health-care sector. *Journal of Modelling in Management*. doi:10.1108/JM2-09-2022-0229

Dierksmeier, C., & Seele, P. (2020). Blockchain and business ethics. *Business Ethics (Oxford, England)*, *29*(2), 348–359. doi:10.1111/beer.12259

Difrancesco, R. M., Meena, P., & Kumar, G. (2022). How blockchain technology improves sustainable supply chain processes: A practical guide. *Sustainability*, *14*(1), 7894. https://www.ncbi.nlm.nih.gov/pmc/articles/PMC9797894/

Dillahunt, T. R., Park, J. H., & Kim, H. W. (2020). Exploring Asset Management through Blockchain in Higher Education. In *Proceedings of the 2020 CHI Conference on Human Factors in Computing Systems* (pp. 1-14). IEEE.

Ding, B. (2018). Pharma Industry 4.0: Literature Review and Research Opportunities in Sustainable Pharmaceutical Supply Chains. *Process Safety and Environmental Protection*, *119*, 115–130. doi:10.1016/j.psep.2018.06.031

Dinh, T. T. A., Liu, R., Zhang, M., Chen, G., Ooi, B. C., & Wang, J. (2018). Untangling Blockchain: A data processing view of blockchain systems. *IEEE Transactions on Knowledge and Data Engineering*, *30*(7), 1366–1385. doi:10.1109/TKDE.2017.2781227

Domínguez, J., & Roseiro, P. (2020). *Blockchain: a brief review of agri-food supply chain solutions and opportunities.*

Dong, F., Zhou, P., Liu, Z., Shen, D., Xu, Z., & Luo, J. (2017). Towards a Fast and Secure Design for Enterprise-Oriented Cloud Storage Systems. *Concurrency and Computation*, *29*(19), 77. doi:10.1002/cpe.4177

Dorri, A., Kanhere, S. S., Jurdak, R., & Gauravaram, P. (2017, March). *Blockchain for IoT security and privacy: The case study of a smart home. In 2017 IEEE international conference on pervasive computing and communications workshops (PerCom workshops).* IEEE.

Dou, S., Xu, D., Zhu, Y., & Keenan, R. (2023). Critical mineral sustainable supply: Challenges and governance. *Futures*, *146*, 103101. doi:10.1016/j.futures.2023.103101

Duan, J., Zhang, C., Gong, Y., Brown, S., & Li, Z. (2020). A content-analysis based literature review in blockchain adoption within food supply chain. *International Journal of Environmental Research and Public Health*, *17*(5), 1784. doi:10.3390/ijerph17051784 PMID:32182951

Duan, Y., Dietzenbacher, E., Los, B., & Yang, C. (2021). How much did China's emergence as "the world's factory" contribute to its national income? *China Economic Review*, *69*, 101658. doi:10.1016/j.chieco.2021.101658

Dubey, R. K., Tripathi, V., Dubey, P. K., Singh, H. B., & Abhilash, P. C. (2016). Exploring rhizospheric interactions for agricultural sustainability: The need for integrative research on multi-trophic interactions. *Journal of Cleaner Production*, *115*, 362–365. doi:10.1016/j.jclepro.2015.12.077

Dubey, R., Gunasekaran, A., Papadopoulos, T., Childe, S. J., Shibin, K. T., & Wamba, S. F. (2017). Sustainable supply chain management: Framework and further research directions. *Journal of Cleaner Production*, *142*, 1119–1130. doi:10.1016/j.jclepro.2016.03.117

Dudhat, A., Santoso, N. P. L., Santoso, S., & Setiawati, R. (2021). Blockchain in Indonesia University: A Design Viewboard of Digital Technology Education. [ATT]. *Aptisi Transactions on Technopreneurship*, *3*(1), 68–80. doi:10.34306/att.v3i1.146

Dunphy, P., & Petitcolas, F. A. P. (2018). A first look at identity management schemes on the blockchain. *IEEE Security and Privacy*, *16*(4), 20–29. doi:10.1109/MSP.2018.3111247

Duwadi, N. (2021). A Systematic Review on Blockchain in Education: Opportunities and Challenges. *Nepalese Journal of Management Science and Research, 4.*

Dwivedi, A. D., Srivastava, G., Dhar, S., & Singh, R. (2019). A decentralized privacy-preserving healthcare blockchain for IoT. *Sensors (Basel)*, *19*(2), 326. doi:10.339019020326 PMID:30650612

Dybå, T., & Dingsøyr, T. (2008). Empirical studies of agile software development: A systematic review. *Information and Software Technology*, *50*(9-10), 833–859. doi:10.1016/j.infsof.2008.01.006

Edastama, P., Purnama, S., Widayanti, R., Meria, L., & Rivelino, D. (2021). The potential blockchain technology in higher education learning innovations in era 4.0. *Blockchain Frontier Technology*, *1*(01), 104–113. doi:10.34306/bfront.v1i01.18

El Azzaoui, A., Chen, H., Kim, S. H., Pan, Y., & Park, J. H. (2022). Blockchain-based distributed information hiding framework for data privacy preserving in medical supply chain systems. *Sensors (Basel)*, *22*(4), 1371. doi:10.339022041371 PMID:35214273

El Baz, J., & Ruel, S. (2021). Can supply chain risk management practices mitigate the disruption impacts on supply chains' resilience and robustness? Evidence from an empirical survey in a COVID19 outbreak era. *International Journal of Production Economics, 233*, 107972. doi:10.1016/j.ijpe.2020.107972 PMID:36567758

El Khatib, M., Beshwari, F., Beshwari, M., & Beshwari, A. (2021). The impact of blockchain on project management. *ICIC Express Letters*, *15*(5), 467–474.

Elalaoui Elabdallaoui, H., Elfazziki, A., & Sadgal, M. (2021). A Blockchain-Based Platform for the e-Procurement Management in the Public Sector. In C. Attiogbé & S. Ben Yahia (Eds.), *Model and Data Engineering* (Vol. 12732, pp. 213–223). Springer International Publishing. doi:10.1007/978-3-030-78428-7_17

Elkington, J. (1998). Partnerships from cannibals with forks: The triple bottom line of 21st-century business. *Environmental Quality Management*, *8*(1), 37–51. doi:10.1002/tqem.3310080106

Ellahi, R. M., Wood, L. C., & Bekhit, A. E. D. A. (2023). Blockchain-Based Frameworks for Food Traceability: A Systematic Review. *Foods*, *12*(16), 3026. doi:10.3390/foods12163026 PMID:37628025

Ellen MacArthur Foundation. (2019). Artificial intelligence and the circular economy (pp. 1–39). Ellen MacArthur Foundation Report.

Engbers, N., & Kloppenburg, S. (2020). Bananas Blockchained.

Enkronos. (2020). *What is a smart contract? Advantages and disadvantages*. Ekronos. https://content.enkronos.com/what-is-a-smart-contract-advantages-and-disadvantages/

Erikson Julio De Aguiar, B. S. (2020). A Survey of Blockchain-Based Strategies for Healthcare. ACM Computing Surveys. Association for Computing Machinery (ACM).

Ertemel, A. V. (2018). Implications of Blockchain Technology on Marketing. *Journal of International Trade, Logistics and Law*, 35-44.

Etemadi, N., Borbon-Galvez, Y., Strozzi, F., & Etemade, T. (2021). Supply Chain Disruption Risk Management with Blockchain: A Dynamic Literature Review. *Information (Basel)*, *12*(2), 70. doi:10.3390/info12020070

Exchange Web. (2022). *Smart contracts for innovative supply chain management*. Exchange Web. https://www.itexchangeweb.com/blog/smart-contracts-for-innovative-supply-chain-management/

Facchini Amondarain, F. (2019). *Study of the functional and economic feasibility of the application of Blockchain in a food sector company's supply chain* [Bachelor's thesis, Universitat Politècnica de Catalunya].

Fahimnia, B., Sarkis, J., & Davarzani, D. (2015). Green Supply Chain Management: A Review and Bibliometric Analysis. *International Journal of Production Economics*, *162*, 101–114. doi:10.1016/j.ijpe.2015.01.003

Faisal Jamil, L. H. (2019). A Novel Medical Blockchain Model for Drug Supply Chain Integrity Management in a Smart Hospital. *Electronics (Basel)*.

Fang, B. (2022). Blockchain-Based Educational Management and Secure Software-Defined Networking in Smart Communities. [IJISP]. *International Journal of Information Security and Privacy*, *16*(2), 1–20. doi:10.4018/IJISP.308314

Farahani, B., Firouzi, F., & Luecking, M. (2021). The convergence of IoT and distributed ledger technologies (DLT): Opportunities, challenges, and solutions. *Journal of Network and Computer Applications*, *177*, 102936. doi:10.1016/j.jnca.2020.102936

Farooq, M. S., Riaz, S., Abid, A., Umer, T., & Zikria, Y. B. (2020). Role of IoT technology in agriculture: A systematic literature review. *Electronics (Basel)*, *9*(2), 319. doi:10.3390/electronics9020319

Fátima Leal, A. E.-V.-G.-G. (2021). *Smart Pharmaceutical Manufacturing: Ensuring end-to-end Traceability and Data Integrity in Medicine Production*. Big Data Research.

FBI. (2023). *Blockchain Technology Market Size, Share & Growth [2030]* (Blockchain Technology Market Size, Share & COVID-19 Impact Analysis FBI100072; pp. 1–160). Fortune Business Insights. https://www.fortunebusinessinsights.com/industry-reports/blockchain-market-100072

Fedorova, E. P., & Skobleva, E. I. (2020). Application of blockchain technology in higher education. *European Journal of Contemporary Education*, *9*(3), 552–571.

Fernandez, A., Insfran, E., & Abrahão, S. (2011). Usability evaluation methods for the web: A systematic mapping study. *Information and Software Technology*, *53*(8), 789–817. doi:10.1016/j.infsof.2011.02.007

Fligstein, N. (2001) The Architecture of Markets: An Economic Sociology of Twenty First Century Capitalist Societies). Princeton, Oxford.

Flores-Vivar, J. M., & García-Peñalvo, F. J. (2023). Reflexiones sobre la ética, potencialidades y retos de la Inteligencia Artificial en el marco de la Educación de Calidad (ODS4). *Comunicar*, *31*(74). Advance online publication. doi:10.3916/C74-2023-03

Florini, A. (Ed.). (2007). *The Right to Know: Transparency for an Open World*. Columbia University Press. doi:10.7312/flor14158

Frackiewicz, M. (2023). *The Role of Smart Contracts in Revolutionizing Advertising Transactions*. TS2.

França, A. S. L., Neto, J. A., Gonçalves, R. F., & Almeida, C. (2020). Proposing the use of blockchain to improve the solid waste management in small municipalities. *Journal of Cleaner Production*, *244*, 118529. doi:10.1016/j.jclepro.2019.118529

Francesco Galati, B. B. (2019). Industry 4.0: Emerging Themes and Future Research Avenues Using a Text Mining Approach. *Computers in Industry*, *109*, 100–113. doi:10.1016/j.compind.2019.04.018

Francisco, K., & Swanson, D. (2018). The supply chain has no clothes: Technology adoption of blockchain for supply chain transparency. *Logistics*, *2*(1), 2. doi:10.3390/logistics2010002

Franke, L., Schletz, M., & Salomo, S. (2020). Designing a blockchain model for the paris agreement's carbon market mechanism. *Sustainability (Basel)*, *12*(3), 1068. doi:10.3390u12031068

Frankenfield, J. (2023). *Smart contracts and their advantages*. Investopedia. https://www.investopedia.com/terms/s/smart-contracts.asp

Freeman, F. R. S. A. O. J. (2023, March 22). 10 Companies Using Blockchain Technology for Sustainable Supply Chain. *Medium.* https://medium.com/@OjFRSA/10-companies-using-blockchain-technology-for-sustainable-supply-chain-6d17ca8cca25

Freiberg, D., Park, D., Serafeim, G., & Zochowski, R. (2020). Corporate Environmental Impact: Measurement, Data and Information. In *Harvard Business School Accounting & Management Unit Working Paper.*

Friedman, N., & Ormiston, J. (2022). Blockchain as a sustainability-oriented innovation? Opportunities for and resistance to blockchain technology as a driver of sustainability in global food supply chains. *Technological Forecasting and Social Change*, 175.

Friedman, N., & Ormiston, J. (2022). Blockchain as a sustainability-oriented innovation?: Opportunities for and resistance to Blockchain technology as a driver of sustainability in global food supply chains. *Technological Forecasting and Social Change*, *175*, 121403. doi:10.1016/j.techfore.2021.121403

Fukuyama, F. (2012). The origins of political order: From prehuman times to the French Revolution (First paperback edition). Farrar, Straus and Giroux.

Fukuyama, F. (2015). Political order and political decay: From the industrial revolution to the globalization of democracy (Paperback ed). Profile Books.

Gabriella, M., & Hastig, M. S. (2020). Blockchain for Supply Chain Traceability: Business Requirements and Critical Success Factors. *Production and Operations Management*, 935–954.

Gad, A. G., Mosa, D. T., Abualigah, L., & Abohany, A. A. (2022). Emerging Trends in Blockchain Technology and Applications: A Review and Outlook. *Journal of King Saud University. Computer and Information Sciences*, *34*(9), 6719–6742. doi:10.1016/j.jksuci.2022.03.007

Gaiha, A., & Gaur, V. (2020). Building a transparent supply chain. *Harvard Business Review*, *98*(3), 102–109. https://hbr.org/2020/05/building-a-transparent-supply-chain

Galati, A., Crescimanno, M., Vrontis, D., & Siggia, D. (2020). Contribution to the sustainability challenges of the food-delivery sector: Finding from the deliveroo italy case study. *Sustainability (Basel)*, *12*(17), 7045. doi:10.3390u12177045

Galvez, J. F. (2020). Towards the enhancement of security and efficiency in academic credentials verification using blockchain technology. *International Journal of Advanced Science and Technology*, *29*(5), 13329–13337.

Galvez, J. F., Mejuto, J. C., & Simal-Gandara, J. (2018). Future challenges on the use of blockchain for food traceability analysis. *Trends in Analytical Chemistry*, *107*, 222–232. doi:10.1016/j.trac.2018.08.011

Gandhi, S., Kiwelekar, A., Netak, L., & Shahare, S. (2023). A blockchain-based data-driven trustworthy approval process system. *International Journal of Information Management Data Insights*, *3*(1), 100162. doi:10.1016/j.jjimei.2023.100162

Gao, N., Han, D., Weng, T. H., Xia, B., Li, D., Castiglione, A., & Li, K. C. (2022). Modeling and analysis of port supply chain system based on Fabric blockchain. *Computers & Industrial Engineering*, *172*, 108527. doi:10.1016/j.cie.2022.108527

Gatteschi, V., Lamberti, F., Demartini, C., Pranteda, C., & Santamaría, V. (2018). To Blockchain or Not to Blockchain: That Is the Question. *IT Professional*, *20*(2), 62–74. doi:10.1109/MITP.2018.021921652

Gaur, V., & Singh, S. (2020). Blockchain technology for supply chain compliance. In *Blockchain Technology for Industry 4.0* (pp. 1–22). Springer. doi:10.1007/978-981-15-4814-7_1

Gebremariam, G., Panda, J., & Indu, S. (2023). Blockchain-Based Secure Localization against Malicious Nodes in IoT-Based Wireless Sensor Networks Using Federated Learning. *Hindawi Journal of Wireless Communications and Mobile Computing*. . doi:10.1155/2023/8068038

Gencer, A. E., Basu, S., & Eyal, I. (2018). Decentralization in bitcoin and ethereum networks. In Proceedings of the 2018 IFIP Networking Conference (IFIP Networking) and Workshops. 10.1007/978-3-662-58387-6_24

Gertz, O., & McGlashan, D. (2016). Consumer-Centric Programmatic advertising. In Programmatic Advertising, Management for Professionals, (pp. 55-74). Springer. doi:10.1007/978-3-319-25023-6_5

Gervais, A., Karame, G. O., Wüst, K., Glykantzis, V., Ritzdorf, H., & Capkun, S. (2016, October). On the security and performance of proof of work blockchains. In *Proceedings of the 2016 ACM SIGSAC conference on computer and communications security* (pp. 3-16). ACM. 10.1145/2976749.2978341

Ghadge, A., Duck, A., Er, M., & Caldwell, N. (2021). Deceptive counterfeit risk in global supply chains. *Supply Chain Forum: An International Journal, 22*(2), 87-99. https://www.tandfonline.com/doi/full/10.1080/16258312.2021.1908844

Ghose, A. (2018). What Blockchain Could Mean for Marketing. *Harvard Business Review*.

Ghouri, A., Akhtar, P., Venkatesh, V. G., Ashraf, A., Arsenyan, G., Tarba, S. Y., & Khan, Z. (2023). Enhancing supply chain innovation and operational agility through knowledge acquisition from the social media: A microfoundational approach. *IEEE Transactions on Engineering Management*, 1–15. doi:10.1109/TEM.2023.3316119

Gianakis, G., & McCue, C. (2012). Supply management concepts in local government: Four case studies. *Journal of Public Procurement, 12*(1), 109–141. doi:10.1108/JOPP-12-01-2012-B004

GiannoniC.MeddaF.BartolucciS. (2023). Blockchain Technologies and Art: Opportunities and Open Challenges. *Available at* SSRN 4439318. doi:10.2139/ssrn.4439318

Giuseppe Aceto, V. P. (2020). Industry 4.0 and Health: Internet of Things, Big Data, and Cloud Computing for Healthcare 4.0. *Journal of Industrial Information Integration.*

Glavanits, J. (2020). Sustainable public spending through blockchain. *European Journal of Sustainable Development, 9*(4), 317–327. doi:10.14207/ejsd.2020.v9n4p317

Gold, S., Kunz, N., & Reiner, G. (2017). Sustainable global agrifood supply chains: Exploring the barriers. *Journal of Industrial Ecology*, *21*(2), 249–260. doi:10.1111/jiec.12440

Gómez González, C. (2021). *Blockchain applications in food marketing.*

Gotskind, A. (2021). *Decentralized finance and the power of smart contracts.* Research Blog. https://researchblog.duke.edu/2021/12/13/decentralized-finance-and-the-power-of-smart-contracts/

Gouvea, R., Kapelianis, D., & Kassicieh, S. (2018). Assessing the nexus of sustainability and information & and communications technology. *Technological Forecasting and Social Change*, *130*, 39–44. doi:10.1016/j.techfore.2017.07.023

Govindan, K., Shaw, M., & Majumdar, A. (2020). Social Sustainability Tensions in Multi-Tier Supply Chain: A Systematic Literature Review towards Conceptual Framework Development. *Journal of Cleaner Production*, 123075.

Govindan, K., Soleimani, H., & Kannan, D. (2015). Reverse logistics and closed-loop supply chain: A comprehensive review to explore the suture. *European Journal of Operational Research*, *240*(3), 603–626. doi:10.1016/j.ejor.2014.07.012

Gräther, W., Kolvenbach, S., Ruland, R., Schütte, J., Torres, C., & Wendland, F. (2018). *Blockchain for education: lifelong learning passport.*

Grimmelikhuijsen, S. G., & Meijer, A. J. (2014). Effects of Transparency on the Perceived Trustworthiness of a Government Organization: Evidence from an Online Experiment. *Journal of Public Administration: Research and Theory*, *24*(1), 137–157. doi:10.1093/jopart/mus048

Grimmelikhuijsen, S., Weske, U., Bouwman, R., & Tummers, L. (2017). Public Sector Transparency. In O. James, S. R. Jilke, & G. G. Van Ryzin (Eds.), *Experiments in Public Management Research* (1st ed., pp. 291–312). Cambridge University Press. doi:10.1017/9781316676912.014

Grimm, J. H., Hofstetter, J. S., & Sarkis, J. (2016). Exploring Sub-Suppliers' Compliance with Corporate Sustainability Standards. *Journal of Cleaner Production*, *112*, 1971–1984. doi:10.1016/j.jclepro.2014.11.036

Groschopf, W., Dobrovnik, M., & Herneth, C. (2021). Smart Contracts for Sustainable Supply Chain Management: Conceptual Frameworks for Supply Chain Maturity Evaluation and Smart Contract Sustainability Assessment. *Frontiers in Blockchain, 4.* https://www.frontiersin.org/articles/10.3389/fbloc.2021.506436

Groschopf, W., Dobrovnik, M., & Herneth, C. (2021). Smart contracts for sustainable supply chain management: Conceptual frameworks for supply chain maturity evaluation and smart contract sustainability assessment. *Frontiers in Blockchain*, *4*, 506436. doi:10.3389/fbloc.2021.506436

Grunert, E. W., & Pinsent Masons. (2018). *Regulatory compliance in the global supply chain.* Out-Law. https://www.pinsentmasons.com/out-law/analysis/regulatory-compliance-global-supply-chain

Guerreiro, S., Ferreira, J. F., Fonseca, T., & Correia, M. (2022). Integrating an academic management system with blockchain: A case study. *Blockchain: Research and Applications*, *3*(4), 100099.

Guitton, C., Tamo-Larrieux, A., & Mayer, S. (2022). A typology of automatically processable regulation. *Law, Innovation and Technology*, *14*(2), 267–304. doi:10.1080/17579961.2022.2113668

Gul, I., Khan, N. R., & Ghouri, A. M. (2023). Blockchain- Driven supply chain management and open innovation. In Handbook of Blockchain driven supply chain management: A multi-dimensional perspective. Springer.

Gu, M., Yang, L., & Huo, B. (2021). The Impact of information technology usage on supply chain resilience and performance: An Ambidextrous View. *International Journal of Production Economics*, *232*, 107956. Advance online publication. doi:10.1016/j.ijpe.2020.107956 PMID:33071462

Guo, Y., & Liang, C. (2016). Blockchain application and outlook in the banking industry. *Financial Innovation*, *2*(1), 24. doi:10.118640854-016-0034-9

Gupta, H., Kumar, S., Kusi-Sarpong, S., Jabbour, C. J. C., & Agyemang, M. (2021). Enablers to supply chain performance on the basis of digitization technologies. *Industrial Management & Data Systems*, *121*(9), 1915–1938. doi:10.1108/IMDS-07-2020-0421

Gupta, N. K., Yadav, A. K., & Jain, A. (2021). Using Blockchain for Digital Copyrights Management. In *Blockchain for Information Security and Privacy* (pp. 377–399). Auerbach Publications. doi:10.1201/9781003129486-18

Gupta, S., Modgil, S., Choi, T.-M., Kumar, A., & Antony, J. (2023). Influences of artificial intelligence and blockchain technology on financial resilience of supply chains. *International Journal of Production Economics*, *261*, 108868. doi:10.1016/j.ijpe.2023.108868

Hamir, H; Sum, R M (2021) An Analysis of Risk Management Processes and Comparison with ISO31000:2018. *Asian Journal of Research in Business and Management, 3*, 16-30.

Hammi, M. T., Hammi, B., Bellot, P., & Serhrouchni, A. (2018). Bubbles of Trust: A decentralized Blockchain-based authentication system for IoT. *Computers & Security*, *78*, 126–142. doi:10.1016/j.cose.2018.06.004

Han, M., Li, Z., He, J., Wu, D., Xie, Y., & Baba, A. (2018, September). A novel blockchain-based education records verification solution. In *Proceedings of the 19th annual SIG conference on information technology education* (pp. 178-183). ACM. 10.1145/3241815.3241870

Hannibal, C., & Kauppi, K. (2019). Third-Party Social Sustainability Assessment: Is It a Multi-Tier Supply Chain Solution? *International Journal of Production Economics*, *217*, 78–87. doi:10.1016/j.ijpe.2018.08.030

Hao Sen Andrew Fang, T. H. (2021). Blockchain Personal Health Records: Systematic Review. *Journal of Medical Internet Research*. PMID:33847591

Haq, M. A., Khan, N. R., Parkash, R., & Jabeen, A. (2016). Impact of JIT, waste minimization, and flow management on operational performance of manufacturing companies. *Quality - Access to Success*, *17*(153), 48.

Haq, M. A., Khan, N. R., Parkash, R., & Jabeen, A. (2016). *Impact of JIT*. Waste Minimization, and Flow Management on Operational Performance of Manufacturing Companies in Pakistan.

Harsono, H. (2022). The Blockchain-Based Service Network: The People's Republic of China's Implementation of Digital Authoritarianism in Web3. *SAIS Review (Paul H. Nitze School of Advanced International Studies)*, *42*(2), 45–62. doi:10.1353ais.2022.0010

Härting, R. C., Sprengel, A., Wottle, K., & Rettenmaier, J. (2020). Potentials of blockchain technologies in supply chain management-A conceptual model. *Procedia Computer Science*, *176*, 1950–1959. doi:10.1016/j.procs.2020.09.334

Harvard Business Review. (2022, January). How Walmart Canada uses blockchain to solve supply-chain challenges [Web page]. *Harvard Business Review*. https://hbr.org/2022/01/how-walmart-canada-uses-blockchain-to-solve-supply-chain-challenges

Hashim, Y. Z. H. Y., Ahmad, A. N., Samsudin, N., Abd Lateef, M. H., & Majlan, N. S. (2022). The Evolution Of Halal Research: A Bibliometric For 1996–2020. *Journal of Fatwa Management and Research*, *27*(3), 1–38. doi:10.33102/jfatwa.vol27no3.443

Hassoun, A., Aït-Kaddour, A., Abu-Mahfouz, A. M., Rathod, N. B., Bader, F., Barba, F. J., & Regenstein, J. (2022). The fourth industrial revolution in the food industry—Part I: Industry 4.0 technologies. *Critical Reviews in Food Science and Nutrition*, 1–17. PMID:35114860

Hastig, G. M., & Sodhi, M. S. (2020). Blockchain for supply chain traceability: Business requirements and critical success factors. *Production and Operations Management*, *29*(4), 935–954. doi:10.1111/poms.13147

Hayat, R. F., Aurangzeb, S., & Aleem, M. (2022). ML-DDoS: A Blockchain-Based Multilevel DDoSMitigation Mechanism for IoT Environments. *IEEE Transactions on Engineering Management*. doi:10.1109/TEM.2022.3170519

Hayes, A. (2022). Blockchain facts: What is it, how it works, and how it can be used. *Investopedia*. https://www.investopedia.com/terms/b/blockchain.asp

Helberger, N., Huh, J., Milne, G., Strycharz, J., & Sundaram, H. (2020). Macro and Exogenous Factors in Computational Advertising: Key Issuesand New Research Directions. *Journal of Advertising*, 377-393. iab. (2018). *Blockchain for Video Advertising:A Market Snapshot of Publisher and Buyer Use Cases*. Interactive Advertising Bureau.

Hellani, H., Sliman, L., Samhat, A. E., & Exposito, E. (2021). On blockchain integration with supply chain: Overview on data transparency. *Logistics*, *5*(3), 46. doi:10.3390/logistics5030046

Heller, P. S. (2003). *Who will pay? Coping with aging societies, climate change, and other long-term fiscal challenges*. International Monetary Fund.

Helo, P., & Hao, Y. (2019). Blockchains in operations and supply chains: A model and reference implementation. *Computers & Industrial Engineering*, *136*, 242–251. doi:10.1016/j.cie.2019.07.023

Hemdan, E. E.-D., El-Shafai, W., & Sayed, A. (2023). Integrating Digital Twins with IoT-Based Blockchain: Concept, Architecture, Challenges, and Future Scope. *Wireless Personal Communications*, *131*(3), 2193–2216. doi:10.100711277-023-10538-6 PMID:37360142

Hendayani, R., & Fernando, Y. (2022). Adoption of blockchain technology to improve Halal supply chain performance and competitiveness. *Journal of Islamic Marketing*.

He, Z. (2022). When data protection norms meet digital health technology: China's regulatory approaches to health data protection. *Computer Law & Security Report*, *47*, 105758. doi:10.1016/j.clsr.2022.105758

Higgins, M. (2021, November 8). Blockchain In Supply Chain. *Forbes*. https://www.forbes.com/sites/forbestechcouncil/2021/11/08/blockchain-in-supply-chain/

Higgins, S. (2017). *Walmart: Blockchain food tracking test results are very encouraging*. CoinDesk. https://www.coindesk.com/walmart-blockchain-food-tracking-test-resultsencouraging/

Hobbs, B. (2019). Supply chain inefficiencies can crush customer experience and cost you millions. *Forbes*. https://www.forbes.com/sites/forbesbusinessdevelopmentcouncil/2019/09/30/supply-chain-inefficiencies-can-crush-customer-experience-and-cost-you-millions/

Hodgkinson, I. R., Hannibal, C., Keating, B. W., Chester Buxton, R., & Bateman, N. (2017). Toward a public service management: Past, present, and future directions. *Journal of Service Management*, *28*(5), 998–1023. doi:10.1108/JOSM-01-2017-0020

Hoek, R. v. (2019). Developing a Framework for Considering Blockchain Pilots in the Supply Chain – Lessons from Early Industry adopters. *An International Journal, Emerald Group Publishing Ltd*, 115-121.

Hoekstra, A., & Wiedmann, T. (2014). Humanity's unsustainable environmental footprint. *Science*, *344*(6188), 1114–1117. doi:10.1126cience.1248365 PMID:24904155

Hofmann, E., & Rüsch, M. (2017). Industry 4.0 and the current status as well as future prospects on logistics. *Computers in Industry*, *89*, 23–34. doi:10.1016/j.compind.2017.04.002

Hood, C., & Heald, D. (Eds.). (2006). *Transparency: The key to better governance?* Oxford University Press. doi:10.5871/bacad/9780197263839.001.0001

Hossain, M. K., Thakur, V., & Mangla, S. K. (2022). Modeling the emergency health-care supply chains: Responding to the COVID-19 pandemic. *Journal of Business and Industrial Marketing*, *37*(8), 1623–1639. doi:10.1108/JBIM-07-2020-0315

Hou, H. (2017). The Application of Blockchain Technology in E-Government in China. *2017 26th International Conference on Computer Communication and Networks (ICCCN)*, 1–4. 10.1109/ICCCN.2017.8038519

Howson, P. (2020). Building trust and equity in marine conservation and fisheries supply chain management with blockchain. *Marine Policy*, *115*, 103873. doi:10.1016/j.marpol.2020.103873

Hrouga, M., Sbihi, A., & Chavallard, M. (2022). The potentials of combining Blockchain technology and Internet of Things for digital reverse supply chain: A case study. *Journal of Cleaner Production*, *337*, 130609. doi:10.1016/j.jclepro.2022.130609

Hughes, L., Dwivedi, Y. K., Misra, S. K., Rana, N. P., Raghavan, V., & Akella, V. (2019). Blockchain research, practice and policy: Applications, benefits, limitations, emerging research themes, and research agenda. *International Journal of Information Management*, *49*, 114–129. doi:10.1016/j.ijinfomgt.2019.02.005

Hussien, H. M., Yasin, S. M., Udzir, S. N. I., Zaidan, A. A., & Zaidan, B. B. (2019). A Systematic Review for Enabling of Develop a Blockchain Technology in Healthcare Application: Taxonomy, Substantially Analysis, Motivations, Challenges, Recommendations, and Future Direction. *Journal of Medical Systems*, *43*(10), 320. doi:10.100710916-019-1445-8 PMID:31522262

Hyperledger. (n.d.). *Walmart case study [Web page]*. Hyperledger. https://www.hyperledger.org/learn/publications/walmart-case-study

Iansiti, M., & Lakhani, K. R. (2017). The truth about blockchain. *Harvard Business Review*, 119–127.

IBM. (2018, August 9). *TradeLens, how IBM and Maersk are sharing blockchain to build a global trade platform [Web page]*. IBM. https://www.ibm.com/blogs/think/2018/11/tradelens-how-ibm-and-maersk-are-sharing-blockchain-to-build-a-global-trade-platform/

IBM. (2019, December 16). *Protect Pharmaceutical Product Integrity with the Pharmaceutical Utility Network.* IBM. https://www.ibm.com/blog/protect-pharmaceutical-product-integrity-with-the-pharmaceutical-utility-network/

IBM. (n.d.). *Benefits of blockchain.* IBM. https://www.ibm.com/topics/benefits-of-blockchain

Ijaz, A. Namaly, S., Ylianttilaz M., & Gurtov, S. (2015). Security in Software Defined Networks: A Survey. *IEEE Communications Surveys & Tutorials, 17*(4).

Inam, R., Hata, A. Y., Prifti, V., & Asadollah, S. A. (2022). A Comprehensive Study on Artificial Intelligence Algorithms to Implement Safety Using Communication Technologies. *arXiv preprint arXiv:2205.08404.*

Insights, L. (2020, April 28). *Bahrain to Use Blockchain for Food, pharma traceability, customs amid COVID-19.* Ledger Insights. https://www.ledgerinsights.com/bahrain-to-use-blockchain-for-food-pharma-traceability-customs-amid-covid-19/

ISO. (2009). *ISO Guide 73:2009 Risk Management Vocabulary.* ISO.

ISO. (2018). *ISO31000 Risk Management.* International Organisation for Standardization.

Ivanov, D., Dolgui, A., & Sokolov, B. (2019). The impact of digital technology and Industry 4.0 on the ripple effect and supply chain risk analytics. *International Journal of Production Research, 57*(3), 829–846. doi:10.1080/00207543.2018.1488086

Iyer, S. S. (2022) Application of Digital Technologies: Integrated Blockchain with Emerging Technologies. Handbook of Research on Supply Chain Resiliency, Efficiency and Visibility in the Post-Pandemic Era. IGI Global. doi:10.4018/978-1-7998-9506-0.ch014

Iyer, S. S., Seetharaman, A., & Ranjan, B. (2021). Researching Blockchain Technology and its Usefulness in Higher Education. *Machine Learning, IOT and Blockchain Technologies & Trends*, 27-48.

Iyer, D., & Kemp, J. (2019). Blockchain in global supply chains: Exploring the challenges, opportunities, and future prospects. *Transportation Research Part E, Logistics and Transportation Review, 125*, 100815.

Jabbar, S., Lloyd, H., Hammoudeh, M., Adebisi, B., & Raza, U. (2021). Blockchain-enabled supply chain: Analysis, challenges, and future directions. *Multimedia Systems, 27*(4), 787–806. doi:10.100700530-020-00687-0

Jahid, A., Alsharif, M. H., & Hall, T. J. (2023). The convergence of blockchain, IoT and 6G: Potential, opportunities, challenges and research roadmap. *Journal of Network and Computer Applications, 217*, 103677. doi:10.1016/j.jnca.2023.103677

Javaid, N., & Khan, I. (2019). Blockchain-based Secure Data Sharing Platform for Research Data Rights Management over the Ethereum Network. In 2019 IEEE 5th International Conference on Engineering Technologies and Applied Sciences (ICETAS). IEEE. https://www.researchgate.net/profile/Nadeem-Javaid/publication/334696593_Blockchain-based_Secure_Data_Sharing_Platform_for_Research_Data_Rights_Management_over_the_Ethereum_Network/links/5d3aa69e92851cd04686d625/Blockchain-based-Secure-Data-Sharing-Platform-for-Research-Data-Rights-Management-over-the-Ethereum-Network.pdf

Javed Aslama, A. S. (2021). Factors influencing blockchain adoption in supply chain management practices: A study based on the oil industry. *Journal of Innovation and Knowledge*, 124-134.

Javeed, A., Aljuaid, M., Khan, Z., Mahmood, Z., & Shahid, D. (2022). Role of extrinsic Cues in the formation of quality perceptions. *Frontiers in Psychology, 13*, 913836. doi:10.3389/fpsyg.2022.913836 PMID:35959058

Jen-Hung Tseng, Y.-C. L.-w. (2018). Governance on the Drug Supply Chain via Gcoin Blockchain. *International Journal of Environmental Research and Public Health.* PMID:29882861

Jerath, K. S. (2021). Globalization and the Third and Fourth Industrial Revolution. *Science, Technology and Modernity: An Interdisciplinary Approach*, 119–130.

Jiang, F., Jiang, C. X., & Li, J. X. (2023). Deep learning for blockchain in medical supply chain risk management. *International Journal of Grid and Utility Computing*, *14*(2/3), 250. doi:10.1504/IJGUC.2023.131014

Jiasi, W. J., Liu, J., & Zhang, Y. (2019). Secure Software-Defined Networking Based on Blockchain. *Journal of Cryptography and Security*. doi:/arXiv.1906.04342 doi:10.48550

Jiménez-Carvelo, A. M., Li, P., Erasmus, S. W., Wang, H., & van Ruth, S. M. (2022). Spatial-Temporal Event Analysis as a Prospective Approach for Signalling Emerging Food Fraud-Related Anomalies in Supply Chains. *Foods*, *12*(1), 61. doi:10.3390/foods12010061 PMID:36613277

Ji, S., Zhang, J., Zhang, Y., Han, Z., & Ma, C. (2023). *LAFED: A lightweight authentication mechanism for blockchain-enabled federated learning system*. Elseveir Journal of Future Generation Computer Systems. doi:10.1016/j.future.2023.03.014

John J. Coyle, C. J. (2021). *Supply Chain Management: A Logistics Perspective*. Singapore: Cengage Learning.

Joumard, I., Kongsrud, P. M., Nam, Y.-S., & Price, R. (2004). *Enhancing the Effectiveness of Public Spending: Experience in OECD Countries* (OECD Economics Department Working Papers 380; OECD Economics Department Working Papers, Vol. 380). OECD. doi:10.1787/18151973

Jum'a, L. (2023). The role of blockchain-enabled supply chain applications in improving supply chain performance: The case of Jordanian manufacturing sector. *Management Research Review*, *46*(10), 1315–1333. doi:10.1108/MRR-04-2022-0298

Kagan, A., Draeger, K., & Olive, R. (2020). *Halal and Kosher Minnesota Meat Market Assessment: Analysis*. Implications and Recommendations.

Kalapaaking, A. P., Khalil, I., & Atiquzzaman, M. (2022). *Blockchain-Enabled and Multisignature-Powered Verifiable Model for Securing Federated Learning Systems*. IEEE Transactions on Internets of Things.

Kalbouneh, N. Y., Bataineh, K. A., Al-Hamad, A. A.-S. A., Dwakat, M. K. A., Abualoush, S., Almasarweh, M. S., & Al-Smadi, R. W. (2023). The effects of the blockchain technology and big data analytics on supply chain performance: The mediating effect supply chain risk management. *Uncertain Supply Chain Management*, *11*(3), 903–914. doi:10.5267/j.uscm.2023.5.008

Kamble, S. S., Gunasekaran, A., & Gawankar, S. A. (2018). Sustainable Industry 4.0 framework: A systematic literature review identifying the current trends and future perspectives. *Process Safety and Environmental Protection*, *117*, 408–425. doi:10.1016/j.psep.2018.05.009

Kamble, S. S., Gunasekaran, A., & Gawankar, S. A. (2020). Achieving sustainable performance in a data-driven agriculture supply chain: A review for research and applications. *International Journal of Production Economics*, *219*, 179–194. doi:10.1016/j.ijpe.2019.05.022

Kamilaris, A., Fonts, A., & Prenafeta-Boldύ, F. X. (2019). The rise of blockchain technology in agriculture and food supply chains. *Trends in Food Science & Technology*, *91*, 640–652. doi:10.1016/j.tifs.2019.07.034

Kant, R., Sharma, S., Vikas, V., Chaudhary, S., Jain, A. K., & Sharma, K. K. (2023). Blockchain – A Deployment Mechanism for IoT Based Security. *2023 International Conference on Computational Intelligence, Communication Technology and Networking (CICTN)*, Ghaziabad, India. 10.1109/CICTN57981.2023.10140715

Karl, A. A., Micheluzzi, J., Leite, L. R., & Pereira, C. R. (2018). Supply chain resilience and key performance indicators: A systematic literature review. *Production*, *28*(0). Advance online publication. doi:10.1590/0103-6513.20180020

Karode, T., & Werapun, W. (2022). Robustness against fraudulent activities of a blockchain-based online review system. *Peer-to-Peer Networking and Applications*, *15*(1), 92–106. doi:10.100712083-021-01225-z

Kayikci, Y., Kazancoglu, Y., Lafci, C., Gozacan-Chase, N., & Mangla, S. K. (2021). Smart circular supply chains to achieving SDGs for post-pandemic preparedness. *Journal of Enterprise Information Management*, *35*(1), 237–265. doi:10.1108/JEIM-06-2021-0271

Kazancoglu, Y., Ozbiltekin-Pala, M., Sezer, M. D., Luthra, S., & Kumar, A. (2023). Resilient reverse logistics with blockchain technology in sustainable food supply chain management during COVID-19. *Business Strategy and the Environment*, *32*(4), 2327–2340. doi:10.1002/bse.3251

Keresztes, É. R., Kovács, I., Horváth, A., & Zimányi, K. (2022). Exploratory analysis of blockchain platforms in supply chain management. *Economies*, *10*(9), 206. doi:10.3390/economies10090206

Kewell, B., Adams, R., & Parry, G. (2017). Blockchain for good? *Strategic Change*, *26*(5), 429–437. doi:10.1002/jsc.2143

Khalid, M. S., Upadhyay, A. K., Saxena, S., Yamang, C., & Bansa, S. (2023). BlockChain Technology in Marketing: A Systematic Review of its Potential for Transparency, Trust, and Data Security. *China Petroleum Processing and Petrochemical Technology*, 1882–1893.

Khan, M. (n.d.). *Revolutionizing the Supply Chain: How Blockchain Technology is Enhancing Efficiency and Transparency*. LinkedIn. https://www.linkedin.com/pulse/revolutionizing-supply-chain-how-blockchain-enhancing-maaz-khan-

Khan, M. S., Ayyaz, M., & Naseem, A. (2020). An Approach for Developing Integrated Decision Support System Model for Optimizing Contracting Process of Public Procurement in Pakistan. *2020 IEEE Technology & Engineering Management Conference (TEMSCON)*, (pp. 1–6). IEEE. doi:10.1109/TEMSCON47658.2020.9140100

Khan, N. R., Haq, M. A., Ghouri, A. M., Raziq, A., & Moiz, S. M. (2017). *Adaptation of RFID Technology in Business Supply Chain Success:Empirical Findings from a Developing Country Logistic Industry*. Calitatea.

Khan, S. J., Badghish, S., Kaur, P., Sharma, R., & Dhir, A. (2023). What motivates the purchasing of green apparel products? A systematic review and future research agenda. *Business Strategy and the Environment*. doi:10.1002/bse.3360

Khan, S., & Khan, S. (2023). Impact of technological advancements on international trade and finance. *Modern Diplomacy*. https://moderndiplomacy.eu/2023/03/23/impact-of-technological-advancements-on-international-trade-and-finance/

Khan, S., Haleem, A., Husain, Z., Samson, D., & Pathak, R. D. (2023). Barriers to blockchain technology adoption in supply chains: the case of India. *Operations Management Research*, 1-16.

Khan, I. A., & Gani, A. (2020). Blockchain technology: A review on applications and security privacy. *IEEE Access : Practical Innovations, Open Solutions*, *8*, 41106–41124.

Khan, M. A., & Salah, K. (2018). IoT security: Review, blockchain solutions, and open challenges. *Future Generation Computer Systems*, *82*, 395–411. doi:10.1016/j.future.2017.11.022

Khan, M. R., Khan, M. R., & Nallaluthan, K. (2023). Blockchain Supply Chain Management and Supply Chain Sustainability. In *Blockchain Driven Supply Chain Management: A Multi-dimensional Perspective* (pp. 155–180). Springer. doi:10.1007/978-981-99-0699-4_10

Khan, M. R., & Manzoor, A. (2021). Application and impact of new technologies in the supply chain management during COVID-19 pandemic: A systematic literature review. *International Journal of Economics and Business Administration*, *9*(2), 277–292.

Khan, N. R., Haq, M. A., Ghouri, A. M., Raziq, A., & Moiz, S. M. (2017). Adaptation of RFID technology in business supply chain success: Empirical findings from a developing country logistic industry. *Quality - Access to Success, 18*(160), 93.

Khan, S. N., Loukil, F., Ghedira-Guegan, C., Benkhelifa, E., & Bani-Hani, A. (2021). Blockchain smart contracts: Applications, challenges, and future trends. *Peer-to-Peer Networking and Applications, 14*(6), 2901–2925. https://link.springer.com/article/10.1007/s12083-021-01127-0. doi:10.100712083-021-01127-0 PMID:33897937

Khedekar, P. (2018). *Blockchain and higher education: From credentials to learning data.* Research Report, Tyton Partners.

Khizar Abbas, M. A.-C. (2020). A Blockchain and Machine Learning-Based Drug Supply Chain Management and Recommendation System for Smart Pharmaceutical Industry. *Electronics (Basel).*

KhordadpourP. (2023). Proposed Smart 5G Framework: Incorporating Federated Learning and Transfer Learning. *Tech.* doi:10.36227/techrxiv.22814831.v1

Kim Sundtoft Hald, A. K. (2019). How the Blockchain Enables and Constrains Supply Chain Performance. *International Journal of Physical Distribution & Logistics Management, 49*(4), 376–397. doi:10.1108/IJPDLM-02-2019-0063

Kim, J. S., & Shin, N. (2019). The impact of Blockchain technology application on supply chain partnership and performance. *Sustainability (Basel), 11*(21), 6181. doi:10.3390u11216181

Kim, J., & Laskowski, M. (2019). Towards an ontology for blockchain-based supply chain provenance. *Sustainability, 11*(17), 4649.

Kiran, K. U., & Arumugam, T. (2020). Role of programmatic advertising on effective digital promotion strategy: A conceptual framework. *Journal of Physics: Conference Series*, 1–10.

Kishnani, U., Madabhushi, S., & Das, S. (2023, July). Blockchain in Oil and Gas Supply Chain: A Literature Review from User Security and Privacy Perspective. In *International Symposium on Human Aspects of Information Security and Assurance* (pp. 296-309). Cham: Springer Nature Switzerland. 10.1007/978-3-031-38530-8_24

Klee, C. (2021). AI in Marketing – Curse or Blessing? *Impacts of Programmatic Advertising and Personalized Content on Society.*

Kopyto, M., Lechler, S., von der Gracht, H. A., & Hartmann, E. (2020). Potentials of blockchain technology in supply chain management: Long-term judgments of an international expert panel. *Technological Forecasting and Social Change, 161*, 120330. doi:10.1016/j.techfore.2020.120330

Korpela, K., Hallikas, J., & Dahlberg, T. (2017). *Digital supply chain transformation toward blockchain integration.*

Kosmarski, A. (2020). Blockchain adoption in academia: Promises and challenges. *Journal of Open Innovation, 6*(4), 117. doi:10.3390/joitmc6040117

Kotila, M., Rumin, R. C., & Dhar, S. (2016). *Compendium of ad fraud knowledge for media investors.* World Federation of Advertisers.

Kouhizadeh, M., Saberi, S., & Sarkis, J. (2021). Blockchain technology and the sustainable supply chain: Theoretically exploring adoption barriers. *International Journal of Production Economics, 231*, 107831. doi:10.1016/j.ijpe.2020.107831

Kouhizadeh, M., & Sarkis, J. (2018). Blockchain practices, potentials, and perspectives in greening supply chains. *Sustainability (Basel), 10*(10), 3652. doi:10.3390u10103652

Kouhizadeh, M., Zhu, Q., & Sarkis, J. (2020). Blockchain and the circular economy: Potential tensions and critical reflections from practice. *Production Planning and Control, 31*(11-12), 950–966. doi:10.1080/09537287.2019.1695925

Kouhizadeh, M., Zhu, Q., & Sarkis, J. (2023). Circular economy performance measurements and blockchain technology: An examination of relationships. *International Journal of Logistics Management, 34*(3), 720–743. doi:10.1108/IJLM-04-2022-0145

Kraus, D., Obrist, T., & Hari, O. (2019). *Blockchains, smart contracts, decentralised autonomous organisations and the law*. Edward Elgar Publishing. doi:10.4337/9781788115131

Krzysztofek, M. (2018). *GDPR: General Data Protection Regulation (EU) 2016/679: Post-reform Personal Data Protection in the European Union*. Kluwer Law International BV.

Kshetri, N. (2021). *Blockchain and supply chain management*. Elsevier.

Kshetri, N. (2017). Can blockchain strengthen the internet of things? *IT Professional, 19*(4), 68–72. doi:10.1109/MITP.2017.3051335

Kshetri, N. (2017). Will blockchain emerge as a tool to break the poverty chain in the Global South? *Third World Quarterly, 38*(8), 1710–1732. doi:10.1080/01436597.2017.1298438

Kshetri, N. (2018). Blockchain's roles in meeting key supply chain management objectives. *International Journal of Information Management, 39*, 80–89. doi:10.1016/j.ijinfomgt.2017.12.005

Kshetri, N. (2018). Blockchain's roles in strengthening cybersecurity and protecting privacy. *Telecommunications Policy, 42*(10), 843–852.

Kshetri, N. (2020). Blockchain-based financial technologies and cryptocurrencies for low-income people: Technical potential versus practical reality. *Computer, 53*(1), 18–29. doi:10.1109/MC.2019.2951977

Kshetri, N. (2021). Blockchain and sustainable supply chain management in developing countries. *International Journal of Information Management, 60*, 102376. doi:10.1016/j.ijinfomgt.2021.102376

Kshetri, N., & Voas, J. (2018). On the internet of things, blockchain technology for supply chain management IoT. *IEEE IT Professional, 20*(4), 15–21. doi:10.1109/MITP.2018.043141660

Kuchina-Musina, D., Morris, J. C., & Steinfeld, J. (2020). Drivers and differentiators: A grounded theory study of procurement in public and private organizations. *Journal of Public Procurement, 20*(3), 265–285. doi:10.1108/JOPP-10-2019-0068

Kulkarni, A. (2021). Review of Online Food Delivery Industry of India. *International Journal of Engineering and Advanced Technology, 11*(2), 75–77. doi:10.35940/ijeat.B3317.1211221

Kumar & Dagar. (2021, December 12). Sustainability in Supply Chain with Blockchain: Understanding the Adoption Barriers and Scalability Solution. *International Research Journal of Engineering and Technology, 8*(12), 1135–1144.

Kumar, S. (2002, December 16). *Top 10 Countries Leading Blockchain Technology In The World*. Blockchain Council. https://www.blockchain-council.org/blockchain/top-10-countries-leading-blockchain-technology-in-the-world/

Kumar, A. (2020). Improvement of public distribution system efficiency applying blockchain technology during pandemic outbreak (COVID-19). *Journal of Humanitarian Logistics and Supply Chain Management, 11*(1), 1–28. doi:10.1108/JHLSCM-06-2020-0050

Kumar, A., Liu, R., & Shan, Z. (2020). Is blockchain a silver bullet for supply chain management? Technical challenges and research opportunities. *Decision Sciences, 51*(1), 8–37. doi:10.1111/deci.12396

Kumar, G., Subramanian, N., & Arputham, R. M. (2018). Missing link between sustainability collaborative strategy and supply chain performance: Role of dynamic capability. *International Journal of Production Economics, 203*, 96–109. doi:10.1016/j.ijpe.2018.05.031

Kumar, N., Singh, M., Upreti, K., & Mohan, D. (2022). Blockchain adoption intention in higher education: role of trust, perceived security and privacy in technology adoption model. In *Proceedings of International Conference on Emerging Technologies and Intelligent Systems: ICETIS 2021 (*Volume 1*)* (pp. 303-313). Springer International Publishing.

Kumar, R., & Jain, V. (2023). *Convergence of IoT*. Blockchain, and Computational Intelligence in Smart Cities.

Kurdi, B. A., Alzoubi, H. M., Akour, I., & Alshurideh, M. T. (2022). The effect of blockchain and smart inventory system on supply chain performance: Empirical evidence from retail industry. *Uncertain Supply Chain Management*, *10*(4), 1111–1116. doi:10.5267/j.uscm.2022.9.001

Lacapra, C. (2023, March 9). *5 countries leading blockchain adoption*. Cointelegraph. https://cointelegraph.com/news/5-countries-leading-the-blockchain-adoption

Lacity, M. C. (2018). Addressing key challenges to making enterprise blockchain applications a reality. *MIS Quarterly Executive*, *17*(3), 201–222.

Lacity, M., Beck, R., & Böhmann, T. (2019). Blockchain and the future of supply chain transparency in the education sector. *Communications of the Association for Information Systems*, *45*, 22–30.

Lahkani, M. J., Wang, S., Urbański, M., & Egorova, M. (2020). Sustainable B2B E-commerce and blockchain-based supply chain finance. *Sustainability (Basel)*, *12*(10), 3968. doi:10.3390u12103968

Lai-Wan Wong, G. W.-H.-H.-B. (2020). Unearthing the Determinants of Blockchain Adoption in Supply Chain Management. *International Journal of Production Research*, *58*(7), 2100–2123. doi:10.1080/00207543.2020.1730463

Lakkala, M., Suoranta, J., & Teräs, H. (2019). Blockchain for education: A review. Technology. *Knowledge and Learning*, *24*(3), 487–504.

Lambert, D. M., & Enz, M. G. (2017). Issues in Supply Chain Management: Progress and potential. *Industrial Marketing Management*, *62*(Supplement C), 1–16. doi:10.1016/j.indmarman.2016.12.002

Lamport, L. (1998). The part-time parliament. [TOCS]. *ACM Transactions on Computer Systems*, *16*(2), 133–169. doi:10.1145/279227.279229

Lasi, H., Fettke, P., Kemper, H.-G., Feld, T., & Hoffmann, M. (2014). Industry 4.0. *Business & Information Systems Engineering*, *6*(4), 239–242. doi:10.100712599-014-0334-4

Latino, M. E., Corallo, A., Menegoli, M., & Nuzzo, B. (2022). An integrative conceptual framework of food certifications: Systematic review, research agenda, and macromarketing implications. *Journal of Macromarketing*, *42*(1), 71–99. doi:10.1177/02761467211049071

Laturkar, K., & Laturkar, K. (2023). A Blockchain-Based Approach to Revolutionizing Healthcare. Springer. doi:10.4018/978-1-6684-6509-7.ch003

Laturkar, K., & Laturkar, K. (2022, April). Blockchain and the downstream segment: Increasing efficiency through technology. *Hydrocarbon Processing*.

Laturkar, K., & Laturkar, K. (2023). *Internet of Things: Architectures*. Applications, and Challenges. doi:10.4018/978-1-6684-8145-5.ch023

Leech, T., & Hanlon, L. (2016). Three Lines of Defense versus Five Lines of Assurance: Elevating the Role of the Board and CEO in Risk Governance. The Handbook of Board Governance: A Comprehensive Guide to Public, Private and Not for Profit Board Members. Wiley, London.

Lee, D. K. C., & Low, L. (2018). *Inclusive fintech: blockchain, cryptocurrency and ICO*. World Scientific. doi:10.1142/9789813238640_0007

Lee, J. Y. (2019). A decentralized token economy: How blockchain and cryptocurrency can revolutionize business. *Business Horizons*, *62*(6), 773–784. doi:10.1016/j.bushor.2019.08.003

Lee, J.-H. (2019, May). A Blockchain-Based Smart Contract Design for Supply Chain Management. *Symmetry*, *11*(5), 635. https://www.mdpi.com/2073-8994/11/5/635

Lee, K. L., & Zhang, T. (2023). Revolutionizing Supply Chains: Unveiling the Power of Blockchain Technology for Enhanced Transparency and Performance. *International Journal of Technology* [IJTIM]. *Innovation and Management*, *3*(1), 19–27.

Lee, K., & Kim, J. (2019). Blockchain technology for enhancing supply chain resilience. *Business Horizons*, *62*(1), 35–45. doi:10.1016/j.bushor.2017.09.003

Lemieux, V. L. (2016). Trusting records: Is Blockchain technology the answer? *Records Management Journal*, *26*(2), 110–139. doi:10.1108/RMJ-12-2015-0042

Li, J., & Li, J. (2023). A blockchain-based secure data sharing scheme for cloud storage [Journal article]. *Security and Communication Networks*. https://www.hindawi.com/journals/scn/2023/9998433/

Li, J., & Zhang, Y. (2022). *How do smart contracts benefit security protocols?* arXiv preprint arXiv:2202.08699. https://arxiv.org/abs/2202.08699

Li, S., Jiang, P., Wang, X., & Zhang, L. (2018). An Overview of Blockchain Technology: Architecture, Consensus, and Future Trends. In *2018 IEEE International Congress on Big Data (BigData Congress)* (pp. 557-564). IEEE.

Liang, X., Liang, Q., & Gao, F. (2022). Blockchain technology in supply chain management: A review of applications and challenges in operations and logistics management contexts [Journal article]. *Sustainability*, *14*(3), 1470. https://www.mdpi.com/2071-1050/14/3/1470

Li, G., Hou, Y., & Wu, A. (2017). Fourth Industrial Revolution: Technological drivers, impacts and coping methods. *Chinese Geographical Science*, *27*(4), 626–637. doi:10.100711769-017-0890-x

Li, G., Xue, J., Li, N., & Ivanov, D. (2022). Blockchain-supported business model design, supply chain resilience, and firm performance. *Transportation Research Part E, Logistics and Transportation Review*, *163*, 102773. doi:10.1016/j.tre.2022.102773

Li, J., & Kassem, M. (2021). Applications of distributed ledger technology (DLT) and Blockchain-enabled smart contracts in construction. *Automation in Construction*, *132*, 103955. doi:10.1016/j.autcon.2021.103955

Li, J., Liang, G., & Liu, T. (2017). A Novel Multi-link Integrated Factor Algorithm Considering Node Trust Degree for Blockchain-based Communication. *KSII Transactions on Internet and Information Systems*, 3766–3787.

Likens, S. (2023). *Making sense of bitcoin, cryptocurrency and blockchain*. PwC. https://www.pwc.com/us/en/industries/financial-services/fintech/bitcoin-blockchain-cryptocurrency.html

Lindman, J., Berryhill, J., Welby, B., & Barbieri, M. P. (2020). *The uncertain promise of blockchain for government* (OECD Working Papers on Public Governance 43). OECD. doi:10.1787/19934351

Lindman, J., Tuunainen, V. K., & Rossi, M. (2017). *Opportunities and risks of Blockchain Technologies–a research agenda.*

Liou, R.-S., & Rao-Nicholson, R. (2021). Multinational enterprises and Sustainable Development Goals: A foreign subsidiary perspective on tackling wicked problems. *Journal of International Business Policy*, *4*(1), 136–151. doi:10.105742214-020-00080-8

Litoussi, M., Fartitchou, M., El Makkaoui, K., Ezzati, A., & El Allali, Z. (2022). Digital Certifications in Moroccan Universities: Concepts, Challenges, and Solutions. *Procedia Computer Science*, *201*, 95–100. doi:10.1016/j.procs.2022.03.015

Liu, L., Han, M., Zhou, Y., Parizi, R. M., & Korayem, M. (2020). Blockchain-based certification for education, employment, and skill with incentive mechanism. *Blockchain Cybersecurity, Trust and Privacy*, 269–290.

Liu, M. F. R. (2019). Performance Optimization for Blockchain-Enabled Industrial Internet of Things (IIoT) Systems: A Deep Reinforcement Learning Approach. IEEE Transactions on Industrial Informatics. IEEE Computer Society, 3559-3570. IEEE.

Liu, P., Xu, X., & Wang, W. (2022). *Threats, attacks and defenses to federated learning: issues, taxonomy and perspectives.* Cyber Security, Springer Open Access. . doi:10.1186/s42400-021-00105-6

Liu, X., Zhou, Z., Zhong, F., & Shi, J. (2023). Improving supply chain transparency with blockchain technology when considering product returns. *International Transactions in Operational Research.* IEEE. doi:10.1111/itor.13303

Liu, Y., Wang, Z., & Zhu, J. (2019). Blockchain-based digital identity management systems in higher education. In *2019 IEEE/RSJ International Conference on Intelligent Robots and Systems (IROS)* (pp. 5677-5684). IEEE.

Liu, J., Zhang, H., & Zhen, L. (2023). Blockchain technology in maritime supply chains: Applications, architecture and challenges. *International Journal of Production Research*, *61*(11), 3547–3563. doi:10.1080/00207543.2021.1930239

Liu, J., & Zhang, X.-L. (2021). Research on the application of blockchain technology in supply chain finance [Journal article]. *Journal of Industrial Engineering and Engineering Management*, *35*(4), 107–116. https://kns.cnki.net/kcms/detail/detail.aspx?doi=10.14132/j.cnki.1673-5439.2021.04.013

Liu, L., Zhang, W., & Han, C. (2021). A survey for the application of blockchain technology in the media. *Peer-to-Peer Networking and Applications*, *14*(5), 3143–3165. doi:10.100712083-021-01168-5

Liu, M., Robin, A., Wu, K., & Xu, J. (2022). Blockchain's Impact on Accounting and Auditing: A Use Case on Supply Chain Traceability. *Journal of Emerging Technologies in Accounting*, *19*(2), 105–119. doi:10.2308/JETA-2021-002

Liu, M., Zhang, X., & Wu, H. (2023). The impact of platform restriction on manufacturer quality transparency in the blockchain era. *International Journal of Production Research*, *61*(11), 3582–3598. doi:10.1080/00207543.2021.1972180

Liu, Y., Lee, J. M., & Lee, C. (2020). The challenges and opportunities of a global health crisis: The management and business implications of COVID-19 from an Asian perspective. *Asian Business & Management*, *19*(3), 277–297. doi:10.105741291-020-00119-x

Li, W., Meng, W., & Kwok, L. F. (2016, June). A Survey on OpenFlow-based Software Defined Networks:Security Challenges and Countermeasures. *Journal of Network and Computer Applications*, *68*, 126–139. doi:10.1016/j.jnca.2016.04.011

Li, Y., & Chen, T. (2022). Blockchain empowers supply chains: Challenges, opportunities and prospects. *Nankai Business Review International*, *14*(2), 230–248. doi:10.1108/NBRI-06-2022-0066

Li, Z. (2017). A blockchain based new secure multi-layer network model for internet of things. *IEEE Access : Practical Innovations, Open Solutions*, *5*, 5585–5593.

Loddo, A., Meloni, G., & Pes, B. (2022). Using Artificial Intelligence for COVID-19 Detection in Blood Exams: A Comparative Analysis. *IEEE Access : Practical Innovations, Open Solutions, 10*, 119593–119606. doi:10.1109/ACCESS.2022.3221750

Lund, E. H., Jaccheri, L., Li, J., Cico, O., & Bai, X. (2019). Blockchain and sustainability: A systematic Mapping supply. *1EEE/ ACM 2nd International workshop on emerging trends in software for blockchain (WETSEB).*

Luthra, S., Kumar, A., Zavadskas, E. K., Mangla, S. K., & Garza-Reyes, J. A. (2020). Industry 4.0 as an enabler of sustainability diffusion in the supply chain: An analysis of influential strength of drivers in an emerging economy. *International Journal of Production Research, 58*(5), 1505–1521. doi:10.1080/00207543.2019.1660828

Luu, L., Chu, D.-H., Olickel, H., Saxena, P., & Daian, A. (2016). Making smart contracts smarter. In *Proceedings of the 2016 ACM SIGSAC conference on computer and communications security* (pp. 254-269). ACM. 10.1145/2976749.2978309

Lu, Y. (2017). Industry 4.0: A survey on technologies, applications, and open research issues. *Journal of Industrial Information Integration, 6*, 1–10. doi:10.1016/j.jii.2017.04.005

Lu, Y. (2018). Blockchain and the related issues: A review of current research topics. *Journal of Management Analytics, 5*(4), 231–255. doi:10.1080/23270012.2018.1516523

Luzzani, G., Grandis, E., Frey, M., & Capri, E. (2021). Blockchain technology in wine chain for collecting and addressing sustainable performance: An exploratory study. *Sustainability (Basel), 13*(22), 12898. doi:10.3390u132212898

Macrotrends. (2023). *World Population Growth Rate 1950-2023.* Macrotrends. https://www.macrotrends.net/countries/WLD/world/population-growth-rate

Maestre, R. J., Bermejo Higuera, J., Gámez Gómez, N., Bermejo Higuera, J. R., Sicilia Montalvo, J. A., & Orcos Palma, L. (2023). The application of blockchain algorithms to the management of education certificates. *Evolutionary Intelligence, 16*(6), 1967–1984. doi:10.100712065-022-00812-0 PMID:36597508

Maimoona Bint, E. (2022). Exploiting Machine Learning to Detect Malicious Nodes in Intelligent Sensor-Based Systems Using Blockchain. *Hindawi Journal of Wireless Communications and Mobile Computing.* doi:10.1155/2022/7386049

Majer, A. (2018). *How Blockchain Could Help Regulators.*

Mak, H. Y., & Max Shen, Z. J. (2021). When triple-A supply chains meet digitalization: The case of JD. com's C2M model. *Production and Operations Management, 30*(3), 656–665. doi:10.1111/poms.13307

Malik, A., Gautam, S., Abidin, S., & Bhushan, B. (2019, July). Blockchain technology-future of IoT: including structure, limitations and various possible attacks. In *2019 2nd international conference on intelligent computing, instrumentation and control technologies (ICICICT)* (Vol. 1, pp. 1100-1104). IEEE. 10.1109/ICICICT46008.2019.8993144

Mandolla, C., Petruzzelli, A. M., Percoco, G., & Urbinati, A. (2019). Building a digital twin for additive manufacturing through the exploitation of blockchain: A case analysis of the aircraft industry. *Computers in Industry, 109*, 134–152. doi:10.1016/j.compind.2019.04.011

Manogaran, G., & Lopez, D. (2017). A survey of big data architectures and machine learning algorithms in healthcare. *International Journal of Biomedical Engineering and Technology, 25*(2-4), 182–211. doi:10.1504/IJBET.2017.087722

Manupati, V. K., Schoenherr, T., Ramkumar, M., Panigrahi, S., Sharma, Y., & Mishra, P. (2022). Recovery strategies for a disrupted supply chain network: Leveraging blockchain technology in pre- and post-disruption scenarios. *International Journal of Production Economics, 245*, 108389. doi:10.1016/j.ijpe.2021.108389

Manzoor, U., Iqbal, M. S., & Baig, S. A. (2023). Blockchain Technology in Marketing: Potential Applications and Implications. *Perspective in Management and Society*, 12-23.

Marinagi, C., Reklitis, P., Trivellas, P., & Sakas, D. (2023). The Impact of Industry 4.0 Technologies on Key Performance Indicators for a Resilient Supply Chain 4.0. *Sustainability (Basel), 15*(6), 6. doi:10.3390u15065185

Markus, S., & Buijs, P. (2022). Beyond the hype: How blockchain affects supply chain performance. *Supply Chain Management, 27*(7), 177–193. doi:10.1108/SCM-03-2022-0109

Marotta, A. (2023). Halal as more than a market benchmark: from certification issues to 'Eco-Islam' up to Vegan Muslims. *Amministrativ@ mente-Rivista di ateneo dell'Università degli Studi di Roma "Foro Italico,"* (4).

Marsal-Llacuna, M.-L. (2018). Future living framework: Is blockchain the next enabling network? *Technological Forecasting and Social Change, 128*, 226–234. doi:10.1016/j.techfore.2017.12.005

Masood, A., & Rahim, A. A. (2021). Addressing Halal Industry Sustainability Through Halal Certification Bodies and IR. 4.0 Techonology.

Mavridis, N., & Stavropoulos, P. (2019). On the integration of blockchain in education and its impact on the job market: A survey. *Telematics and Informatics, 42*, 1012–1019.

Mazumder, S., & Bhaumik, A. (2022, June 30). Blockchain: Transforming Supply Chain Management Amidst Covid-19. *International Journal of Engineering Trends and Technology, 70*(6), 100–105. doi:10.14445/22315381/IJETT-V70I6P212

McGrath, P., McCarthy, L., Marshall, D., & Rehme, J. (2021). Tools and Technologies of Transparency in Sustainable Global Supply Chains. *California Management Review, 64*(1), 67–89. doi:10.1177/00081256211045993

McIvor, R., McHugh, M., & Cadden, C. (2002). Internet technologies: Supporting transparency in the public sector. *International Journal of Public Sector Management, 15*(3), 170–187. doi:10.1108/09513550210423352

McKinna, D., & Wall, C. (2020). *Commercial application of supply chain integrity and shelf life systems*. Technical Report. Meat and Livestock Australia Limited.

McKinsey. (2022). *What is blockchain?* McKinsey. https://www.mckinsey.com/featured-insights/mckinsey-explainers/what-is-blockchain

Md. Abdul Moktadir, S. M.-R. (2018). Decision modeling of risks in pharmaceutical supply chains. *Industrial Management & Data Systems.*

Md. Jahir Uddin Palas, R. B. (2021). Exploring Interpretations of Blockchain's Value in Healthcare: A Multi-Stakeholder Approach. *Information Technology & People*, 453–495.

Medaglia, R., & Damsgaard, J. (2020). Blockchain and the United Nations Sustainable Development Goals: Towards an Agenda for IS Research. *PACIS*, 36.

Meemken, E. M., Bellemare, M. F., Reardon, T., & Vargas, C. M. (2022). Research and policy for the food-delivery revolution. *Science, 377*(6608), 810–813. doi:10.1126cience.abo2182 PMID:35981021

Mehrdokht Pournader, Y. S. (2019). Blockchain Applications in Supply Chains, Transport and logistics: A systematic review of the literature. *International Journal of Production Research.*

Meiklejohn, S., Pomarole, M., Jordan, G., Levchenko, K., McCoy, D., Voelker, G. M., & Savage, S. (2013, October). A fistful of bitcoins: characterizing payments among men with no names. In *Proceedings of the 2013 conference on Internet measurement conference* (pp. 127-140). ACM. 10.1145/2504730.2504747

Mejías, A. M., Bellas, R., Pardo, J. E., & Paz, E. (2019). Traceability Management Systems and Capacity Building as New Approaches for Improving Sustainability in the Fashion Multi-Tier Supply Chain. *International Journal of Production Economics*, *217*, 143–158. doi:10.1016/j.ijpe.2019.03.022

Meland, P. H., Bayoumy, Y. F. F., & Sindre, G. (2020). The Ransomware-as-a-Service economy within the darknet. *Computers & Security*, *92*, 101762. doi:10.1016/j.cose.2020.101762

Mendling, J. (2010). Foundations of business process modeling. In Business Information Systems: Concepts, Methodologies, Tools and Applications (pp. 6-41). IGI Global. doi:10.4018/978-1-61520-969-9.ch002

Menon, S., & Jain, K. (2022). Blockchain Technology for Transparency in Agri-Food Supply Chain: Use Cases, Limitations, and Future Directions. *IEEE Transactions on Engineering Management*, 1–15. doi:10.1109/TEM.2021.3110903

Mettler, M. (2016). Blockchain technology in healthcare: The revolution starts here.*2016 IEEE 18th International Conference on e-Health Networking, Applications and Services.* IEEE.

Miguel A. Prada-Delgado, G. D. (2021). A Blockchain-Based Crypto-Anchor Platform for Interoperable Product Authentication. *IEEE international symposium on circuits and systems (ISCAS)*, (pp. 1-5). IEEE.

Miller, D. (2018). Blockchain and the internet of things in the industrial sector. *IT Professional*, *20*(3), 15–18. doi:10.1109/MITP.2018.032501742

Mingyue Wang, Y. G. (2023). MedShare: A Privacy-Preserving Medical Data Sharing System by Using Blockchain. *IEEE Transactions on Services Computing*.

Min, H. (2010). Artificial intelligence in supply chain management: Theory and applications. *International Journal of Logistics*, *13*(1), 13–39. doi:10.1080/13675560902736537

Min, H., & Joo, S. J. (2022). Blockchain technology for international arms trade. *International Journal of Logistics Systems and Management*, *42*(2), 223. doi:10.1504/IJLSM.2022.124183

Min, H., & Zhou, G. (2002). Supply chain modeling: Past, present and future. *Computers & Industrial Engineering*, *43*(1), 231–249. doi:10.1016/S0360-8352(02)00066-9

Mishra, A., Karmakar, S., Dutta, A., Bose, A., & Mohapatro, M. (2022). Design and Deployment of IoT enabled Blockchain based resilient Supply-chain Management System using Ethereum. *International Journal of Computing and Digital Systems*, *12*(4), 1029–1050. doi:10.12785/ijcds/120183

Mishra, H., & Maheshwari, P. (2021). Blockchain in Indian Public Distribution System: A conceptual framework to prevent leakage of the supplies and its enablers and disablers. *Journal of Global Operations and Strategic Sourcing*, *14*(2), 312–335. doi:10.1108/JGOSS-07-2020-0044

Mishra, R. A., Kalla, A., Braeken, A., & Liyanage, M. (2021). Privacy protected blockchain based architecture and implementation for sharing of students' credentials. *Information Processing & Management*, *58*(3), 102512. doi:10.1016/j.ipm.2021.102512

Mitropoulos, P., & Tatum, C. B. (2000). Forces Driving Adoption Of New Information Technologies. *journal of construction engineering and management*, 340-348.

ModusBox. (2017, October 24). Announcing Mojaloop.io – An Open-Source Software Platform for Financial Inclusion to Uplift the World's Poor. *Modusbox.Com.* https://modusboxcom1.wpengine.com/announcing-mojaloop-io-an-open-source-software-platform-for-financial-inclusion-to-uplift-the-worlds-poor/

Mohamad Kassab, J. D. (2019). Exploring Research in Blockchain for Healthcare and a Roadmap for the Future. *IEEE Transactions on Emerging Topics in Computing*, 1835–1852.

Mohamed, S. K., Haddad, S., Barakat, M., & Rosi, B. (2023). Blockchain Technology Adoption for Improved Environmental Supply Chain Performance: The Mediation Effect of Supply Chain Resilience, Customer Integration, and Green Customer Information Sharing. *Sustainability (Basel)*, *15*(10), 7909. doi:10.3390u15107909

Mohammad, A., & Vargas, S. (2022). Challenges of Using Blockchain in the Education Sector: A Literature Review. *Applied Sciences (Basel, Switzerland)*, *12*(13), 6380. doi:10.3390/app12136380

Mohanta, B. K., Jena, D., Panda, S. S., & Sobhanayak, S. (2019). Blockchain technology: A survey on applications and security privacy challenges. *Internet of Things : Engineering Cyber Physical Human Systems*, *8*, 100107. doi:10.1016/j.iot.2019.100107

Mohawesh, R., Xu, S., Tran, S. N., Ollington, R., Springer, M., Jararweh, Y., & Maqsood, S. (2021). Fake reviews detection: A survey. *IEEE Access : Practical Innovations, Open Solutions*, *9*, 65771–65802. doi:10.1109/ACCESS.2021.3075573

Mohit, M., Kaur, S., & Singh, M. (2022). Design and implementation of transaction privacy by virtue of ownership and traceability in blockchain based supply chain. *Cluster Computing*, *25*(3), 1–18. doi:10.100710586-021-03425-x PMID:34744494

Mokhberi, A. (2023). *Towards understanding trust, privacy, and safety management among Facebook Marketplace users* [Doctoral dissertation, University of British Columbia].

Moll, J., & Yigitbasioglu, O. (2019). The role of Internet-related technologies in shaping the work of accountants: New directions for accounting research. *The British Accounting Review*, *51*(6), 100833. doi:10.1016/j.bar.2019.04.002

Monostori, L., Kádár, B., Bauernhansl, T., Kondoh, S., Kumara, S., Reinhart, G., Sauer, O., Schuh, G., Sihn, W., & Ueda, K. (2016). Cyber-physical systems in manufacturing. *CIRP Annals*, *65*(2), 621–641. doi:10.1016/j.cirp.2016.06.005

Montecchi, M., Plangger, K., & Etter, M. (2019). It's real, trust me! Establishing supply chain provenance using blockchain. *Business Horizons*, *62*(3), 283–293. doi:10.1016/j.bushor.2019.01.008

Moosavi, J., Naeni, L. M., Fathollahi-Fard, A. M., & Fiore, U. (2021). Blockchain in supply chain management: A review, bibliometric, and network analysis. *Environmental Science and Pollution Research International*. doi:10.100711356-021-13094-3 PMID:33638786

Mora, H., Mendoza-Tello, J. C., Varela-Guzmán, E. G., & Szymanski, J. (2021). Blockchain technologies to address smart city and society challenges. *Computers in Human Behavior*, *122*, 106854. doi:10.1016/j.chb.2021.106854

Moretto, A., & Macchion, L. (2022). Drivers, barriers and supply chain variables influencing the adoption of the blockchain to support traceability along fashion supply chains. *Operations Management Research : Advancing Practice Through Research*, *15*(3), 1470–1489. doi:10.100712063-022-00262-y

Moro-Visconti, R. (2022). ESG-Driven Valuation: From Father Profit to Mother Nature. In R. Moro-Visconti (Ed.), *Augmented Corporate Valuation: From Digital Networking to ESG Compliance* (pp. 235–314). Springer International Publishing. doi:10.1007/978-3-030-97117-5_8

Morrison, W. M. (2019). China's economic rise: History, trends, challenges, and implications for the United States. *Current Politics and Economics of Northern and Western Asia*, *28*(2/3), 189–242.

Mougayar, W. (2016). *The business blockchain: promise, practice, and application of the next Internet technology*. John Wiley & Sons.

Mourtzis, D., Angelopoulos, J., & Panopoulos, N. (2023). Metaverse and blockchain in education for collaborative product-service system (PSS) design towards University 5.0. *Procedia CIRP*, *119*, 456–461. doi:10.1016/j.procir.2023.01.008

Moxham, N., & Boon, E. (2019). Blockchain in higher education: Possibilities for co-created research and the common good. *Open Review of Educational Research*, *6*(1), 94–112.

Muduli, K., Raut, R., Narkhede, B. E., & Shee, H. (2022, March 11). Blockchain Technology for Enhancing Supply Chain Performance and Reducing the Threats Arising from the COVID-19 Pandemic. *Sustainability (Basel)*, *14*(6), 3290. doi:10.3390u14063290

Muhammad Haseeb, H. I. (2019). Industry 4.0: A Solution Towards Technology Challenges of Sustainable Business Performance. *Social Sciences*.

Mukkamala, R. R., Vatrapu, R., Ray, P. K., Sengupta, G., & Halder, S. (2018). Blockchain for social business: Principles and applications. *IEEE Engineering Management Review*, *46*(4), 94–99. doi:10.1109/EMR.2018.2881149

Murthy, C. V. B., Shri, M. L., Kadry, S., & Lim, S. (2020). Blockchain based cloud computing: Architecture and research challenges. *IEEE Access : Practical Innovations, Open Solutions*, *8*, 205190–205205. doi:10.1109/ACCESS.2020.3036812

Musyoka, J. (2022). *Role of smart contracts in supply chain management.* LinkedIn. https://www.linkedin.com/pulse/role-smart-contracts-supply-chain-management-john-musyoka

Nafik Hadi Ryandono, M., Mawardi, I., Nugraha Rani, L., Widiastuti, T., Tri Ratnasari, R., & Kusuma Wardhana, A. (2023). Trends of research topics related to Halal meat as a commodity between Scopus and Web of Science: A systematic review. *F1000 Research*, *11*, 1562. doi:10.12688/f1000research.123005.2

Nagariya, R., Mukherjee, S., Baral, M. M., & Chittipaka, V. (2023). Analyzing blockchain-based supply chain resilience strategies: Resource-based perspective. *International Journal of Productivity and Performance Management*. doi:10.1108/IJPPM-07-2022-0330

Najjar, M., Small, M. H., & Yasin, M. M. (2019). Adopting and Extending Social Sustainability Practices across the Supply Chain. *Competition Forum*, *17*(1), 105–113.

Najjar, M., Alsurakji, I. H., El-Qanni, A., & Nour, A. I. (2023). The role of blockchain technology in the integration of sustainability practices across multi-tier supply networks: Implications and potential complexities. *Journal of Sustainable Finance & Investment*, *13*(1), 744–762. doi:10.1080/20430795.2022.2030663

Najjar, M., Small, M. H., & Yasin, M. M. (2020). Social Sustainability Strategy across the Supply Chain: A Conceptual Approach from the Organisational Perspective. *Sustainability*, *12*(24), 10438. doi:10.3390u122410438

Nakamoto, S. (2008). Bitcoin: A Peer-To-Peer Electronic *Cash System, 9.*

Nakamoto, S. (2008). Bitcoin: A peer-to-peer electronic cash system. *Decentralized business review.*

Nam Vu, A. G. (2021). Blockchain Adoption in Food Supply Chains: A Review and Implementation Framework. *Production Planning and Control*, 1–18.

Nandi, M. L., Nandi, S., Moya, H., & Kaynak, H. (2020). Blockchain technology-enabled supply chain systems and supply chain performance: A resource-based view. *Supply Chain Management*, *25*(6), 841–862. doi:10.1108/SCM-12-2019-0444

Narváez, M. H., Carrasquilla-Díaz, L., De Luque-Pisciotti, A., Guarin, A. F., Barrios, T. A., & Gallego-Nicholls, J. F. (2022). Legal challenges for Blockchain implementation in Colombia. *Procedia Computer Science*, *210*, 323–327. doi:10.1016/j.procs.2022.10.158

Natanelov, V., Cao, S., Foth, M., & Dulleck, U. (2022). Blockchain smart contracts for supply chain finance: Mapping the innovation potential in Australia-China beef supply chains. *Journal of Industrial Information Integration*, *30*, 100389. doi:10.1016/j.jii.2022.100389

Navadkar, V. H., Nighot, A., & Wantmure, R. (2018). Overview of Blockchain Technology in Government/Public Sectors. *International Research Journal of Engineering and Technology*, *5*(6), 2287–2292.

Nayeri, S., Sazvar, Z., & Heydari, J. (2023). Towards a responsive supply chain based on the industry 5.0 dimensions: A novel decision-making method. *Expert Systems with Applications*, *213*, 119267. doi:10.1016/j.eswa.2022.119267

Naz, S., & Al-Zahrani, A. (2019). A secure data sharing platform using blockchain and smart contracts. In 2019 IEEE 5th International Conference on Engineering Technologies and Applied Sciences (ICETAS). IEEE. https://www.semanticscholar.org/paper/A-Secure-Data-Sharing-Platform-Using-Blockchain-and-Naz-Al-Zahrani/45e5f96cd89f6da127101 33b946b85a88d567475

Nazik Zakari, M. A.-R. (2022). Blockchain technology in the pharmaceutical industry: A systematic review. *PeerJ. Computer Science*. PMID:35634106

Nellemann, C., Stock, J., & Shaw, M. (2018). *World Atlas of Illicit Flows. Sept.* Global Initiatives.

Nguyen, D., Ding, M., Pham, Q., Pathirana, P., & Long, B. (2021). Federated Learning Meets Blockchain in Edge Computing: Opportunities and Challenges. *IEEE Journal of Internet of Things*.

Nikolakis, W., John, L., & Krishnan, H. (2018). How blockchain can shape sustainable global value chains: An evidence, verifiability, and enforceability (EVE) framework. *Sustainability (Basel)*, *10*(11), 3926. doi:10.3390u10113926

Niranjanamurthy, M., Nithya, B. N., & Jagannatha, S. J. C. C. (2019). Analysis of Blockchain technology: Pros, cons and SWOT. *Cluster Computing*, *22*(S6), 14743–14757. doi:10.100710586-018-2387-5

Nordgren, A., & Weckström, E. W. (2019). Blockchain in the Fields of Finance and Accounting: A Distruptive Technology or an Overhyped Phenomenon? *ACRN Journal of Finance and Risk Perspectives*, *8*, 47–58.

Nousias, N., Tsakalidis, G., Michoulis, G., Petridou, S., & Vergidis, K. (2022). A process-aware approach for blockchain-based verification of academic qualifications. *Simulation Modelling Practice and Theory*, *121*, 102642. doi:10.1016/j.simpat.2022.102642

Ntwali, Y. N. C. (2022). *Use of blockchain in the management of land registration system* [Doctoral dissertation, University of Rwanda].

Nzuva, S. (2019). Smart contracts implementation, applications, benefits, and limitations. *Journal of Information Engineering and Applications*, *9*(5), 63–75.

Oates, N. L. (2022). *Blockchain from farm to fork-a new business model for tracing local South African market food supply chains using blockchain technology* [Master's thesis, Faculty of Commerce].

OECD. (2019). *2019 OECD Global Blockchain Policy Forum: Summary report* (Report No. 9789264633230). OECD. https://www.oecd.org/finance/2019-OECD-Global-Blockchain-Policy-Forum-Summary-Report.pdf

Ofori-Mensah, J., Yaokumah, W., & Sakyi, E. A. (2022). Design of Authenticated and Trusted Academic Certification Using Blockchain Technology. [IJSI]. *International Journal of Software Innovation*, *10*(1), 1–19. doi:10.4018/IJSI.303580

Oğhan, V. (2022). Environmental policies for green cryptocurrency mining. In *Handbook of research on challenges in public economics in the era of globalization* (pp. 217–227). IGI Global. doi:10.4018/978-1-7998-9083-6.ch013

Ølnes, S., Ubacht, J., & Janssen, M. (2017). Blockchain in government: Benefits and implications of distributed ledger technology for information sharing. []. Elsevier.]. *Government Information Quarterly*, *34*(3), 355–364. doi:10.1016/j.giq.2017.09.007

Omar, I. A., Jayaraman, R., Salah, K., Debe, M., & Omar, M. (2020). Enhancing vendor managed inventory supply chain operations using blockchain smart contracts. *IEEE Access : Practical Innovations, Open Solutions*, *8*, 182704–182719. doi:10.1109/ACCESS.2020.3028031

Osborne, D. (1993). Reinventing Government. *Public Productivity & Management Review*, *16*(4), 349. doi:10.2307/3381012

Otoum, S., Al Ridhawi, I., & Mouftah, H. (2023). A Federated Learning and Blockchain-Enabled Sustainable Energy Trade at the Edge:A Framework for Industry 4.0. *IEEE Internet of Things Journal*, *10*(4), 3018–3026. doi:10.1109/JIOT.2022.3140430

Paggi, E. (2022). Blockchain in finance: focus on securitization.

Palomares, I., Martínez-Cámara, E., Montes, R., García-Moral, P., Chiachio, M., Chiachio, J., Alonso, S., Melero, F. J., Molina, D., Fernández, B., Moral, C., Marchena, R., de Vargas, J. P., & Herrera, F. (2021). A panoramic view and swot analysis of artificial intelligence for achieving the sustainable development goals by 2030: Progress and prospects. *Applied Intelligence*, *51*(9), 6497–6527. doi:10.100710489-021-02264-y PMID:34764606

Pani, S. K., Chatterjee, R., & Mahapatra, N. R. (2019). Towards Trusted, Transparent and Motivational Professional Education System Through Blockchain. [IJISSC]. *International Journal of Information Systems and Social Change*, *10*(2), 62–73. doi:10.4018/IJISSC.2019040105

Pan, S., Trentesaux, D., McFarlane, D., Montreuil, B., Ballot, E., & Huang, G. Q. (2021). Digital interoperability in logistics and supply chain management: State-of-the-art and research avenues towards Physical Internet. *Computers in Industry*, *128*, 103435. doi:10.1016/j.compind.2021.103435

Pardo, A., & Siemens, G. (2014). Ethical and privacy principles for learning analytics. *British Journal of Educational Technology*, *45*(3), 438–450. doi:10.1111/bjet.12152

Park, A., & Li, H. (2021). The effect of blockchain technology on supply chain sustainability performances. *Sustainability (Basel)*, *13*(4), 176. doi:10.3390u13041726

Park, J. (2021). Promises and challenges of Blockchain in education. *Smart Learning Environments*, *8*(1), 1–13. doi:10.118640561-021-00179-2

Park, L. W., Lee, S., & Chang, H. (2018). A sustainable home energy prosumer-chain methodology with energy tags over the blockchain. *Sustainability (Basel)*, *10*(3), 658. doi:10.3390u10030658

Parmentola, A., Petrillo, A., Tutore, I., & De Felice, F. D. (2021). Is blockchain able to enhance environmental sustainability? A systematic review and research agenda from the perspective of sustainable development goals (SDGs). *Business Strategy and the Environment*, *31*(1), 194–217. doi:10.1002/bse.2882

Patil, P., Sangeetha, M., & Bhaskar, V. (2021). Blockchain for IoT access control, security and privacy: A review. *Wireless Personal Communications*, *117*(3), 1815–1834. doi:10.100711277-020-07947-2

Pattanayak, S., Arputham, R. M., Goswami, M., & Rana, N. P. (2023). Blockchain Technology and Its Relationship With Supply Chain Resilience: A Dynamic Capability Perspective. *IEEE Transactions on Engineering Management*, 1–15. doi:10.1109/TEM.2023.3235771

Paula Fraga-Lamas, T. M.-C. (2020). Fake News, Disinformation, and Deepfakes: Leveraging Distributed Ledger Technologies and Blockchain to Combat Digital Deception and Counterfeit Reality. IT Professional. IEEE.

Pawlak, M., Guziur, J., & Poniszewska-Marańda, A. (2019). Voting process with blockchain technology: auditable blockchain voting system. In *Advances in Intelligent Networking and Collaborative Systems: The 10th International Conference on Intelligent Networking and Collaborative Systems (INCoS-2018)* (pp. 233-244). Springer International Publishing. 10.1007/978-3-319-98557-2_21

Pedro, M., & Reyes, J. K. (2020). Managing the Dynamics of New Technologies in the Global Supply Chain. *IEEE Engineering Management Review*, 156–162.

Peltola, A., Barnat, N., Chernova, E., Cristallo, D., Hoffmeister, O., & MacFeely, S. (2022). The role of international organizations in statistical standards setting and outreach: An overview of the UNCTAD contribution. *Statistical Journal of the IAOS*, *38*(2), 501–509. doi:10.3233/SJI-210894

Perano, M., Cammarano, A., Varriale, V., Del Regno, C., Michelino, F., & Caputo, M. (2023). Embracing supply chain digitalization and unphysicalization to enhance supply chain performance: A conceptual framework. *International Journal of Physical Distribution & Logistics Management*, *53*(5/6), 628–659. doi:10.1108/IJPDLM-06-2022-0201

Perboli, G., Musso, S., & Rosano, M. (2018). Blockchain in logistics and supply chain: A lean approach for designing real-world use cases. *IEEE Access : Practical Innovations, Open Solutions*, *6*, 62018–62028. doi:10.1109/ACCESS.2018.2875782

Perego, A., Sciuto, D., Portale, V., & Bruschi, F. (2019). *Blockchain and distributed ledger*. Osservatori. https://www.osservatori.net/it/ricerche/osservatori-attivi/blockchain-distributed-ledger

Peres, R., Schreier, M., Schweidel, D. A., & Sorescu, A. (2023). Blockchain meets marketing: Opportunities, threats, and avenues for future research. *International Journal of Research in Marketing*, *40*(1), 1–11. doi:10.1016/j.ijresmar.2022.08.001

Permentola, A., Petrillo, A., Tutore, I., & Felice, F.D. (2021). Is blockchain able to enhance environmental sustainability? A systematic review and research agenda from the perspective of sustainable development goals (SDGs). *Business society and the environment*, *31*, 194-217.

Petersen, K., Feldt, R., Mujtaba, S., & Mattsson, M. (2008, June). Systematic mapping studies in software engineering. In *12th International Conference on Evaluation and Assessment in Software Engineering (EASE) 12* (pp. 1-10). IEEE.

Peterson, M. R., Young, R. R., & Gordon, G. A. (2016). The application of supply chain management principles to emergency management logistics: An empirical study. *Journal of Emergency Management (Weston, Mass.)*, *14*(4), 245–258. doi:10.5055/jem.2016.0290 PMID:27575640

Phillips, W., Roehrich, J. K., & Kapletia, D. (2023). Responding to information asymmetry in crisis situations: Innovation in the time of the COVID-19 pandemic. *Public Management Review*, *25*(1), 175–198. doi:10.1080/14719037.2021.1960737

Pillitteri, F., Mazzola, E., & Bruccoleri, M. (2021). The four spheres of value co-creation in humanitarian professional services. *Journal of Humanitarian Logistics and Supply Chain Management*, *11*(3), 402–427. doi:10.1108/JHLSCM-06-2020-0049

Pinsent Masons. (2020). *How smart contracts can enable better supply chains*. Out-Law. https://www.pinsentmasons.com/out-law/analysis/smart-contracts-better-supply-chains

Pixalate. (2021). *Navigating ad fraud and consumer privacy abuse in programmatic advertising*. TechCrunch.

Polvora, A., Nascimento, S., Lourenco, J., & Scapolo, F. (2020). Blockchain for industrial transformations: A forward-looking approach with multi-stakeholder engagement for policy advice. *Technological Forecasting and Social Change*, *157*, 157. doi:10.1016/j.techfore.2020.120091

Ponomarov, S. Y., & Holcomb, M. C. (2009). Understanding the concept of supply chain resilience. *International Journal of Logistics Management, 20*(1), 124–143. doi:10.1108/09574090910954873

Powell, W. (2022). *China, trust and digital supply chains: dynamics of a zero trust world.* Taylor & Francis.

Prakash Agrawal, R. N. (2018). Digital supply chain management: An Overview. *IOP Conference Series. Materials Science and Engineering.*

Priantina, A., & Sapian, S. M. (2021). Halal Food and Compliance: A Bibliometric Analysis.

Publift. (2023). *A Complete Guide to Programmatic Direct.* Publift.

Pulmano, C. E., Estuar, M. R. J. E., De Leon, M. M., Tan, H. C. L., Co, N. A. S., & Tamayo, L. P. V. (2023). Towards the Development of a Blockchain-based Decentralized Digital Credential System using Hyperledger Fabric for Participatory Governance. *Procedia Computer Science, 219*, 99-106.

Puri, V., Mondal, S., Das, S., & Vrana, V. G. (2023, January). Blockchain propels tourism industry—An attempt to explore topics and information in smart tourism management through text mining and machine learning. [). MDPI.]. *Informatics (MDPI), 10*(1), 9. doi:10.3390/informatics10010009

Purvis, B., Mao, Y., & Robinson, D. (2019). Three pillars of sustainability: In search of conceptual origins. *Sustainability Science, 14*(3), 681–695. doi:10.100711625-018-0627-5

Pu, S., & Lam, J. S. L. (2023). The benefits of blockchain for digital certificates: A multiple case study analysis. *Technology in Society, 72*, 102176. doi:10.1016/j.techsoc.2022.102176

Qammar, A., Karim, A., Ning H., & Ding, J. (2022). Securing federated learning with blockchain: a systematic literature review. *Journal of Artificial Intelligence Review.* . doi:10.1007/s10462-022-10271-9

Qi, X., Ye, W., Tao, Z., Wu, J., & Li, Q. (2021). A survey of federated learning for edge computing: Research problems and solutions. *Journal of High-Confidence Computing.* . doi:10.1016/j.hcc.2021.100008

Qian, C., Liu, Y., Barnett-Neefs, C., Salgia, S., Serbetci, O., Adalja, A., & Wiedmann, M. (2022). A perspective on data sharing in digital food safety systems. *Critical Reviews in Food Science and Nutrition*, 1–17. PMID:35880485

QSales. (2020, August 19). *How blockchain is being used today in the food & beverage industries.* qSales. https://qsales.com/how-blockchain-is-being-used-today-in-the-food-beverage-industries/

Queiroz, M. M., Telles, R., & Bonilla, S. H. (2019). Blockchain and supply chain management integration: A systematic review of the literature. *Supply Chain Management, 25*(2), 241–254. doi:10.1108/SCM-03-2018-0143

Rahman, AMontieri, AKundu, DKarim, MIslam, JUmme, SNascita, APescapé, A. (2022). On the Integration ofBlockchain and SDN: Overview, Applications, and Future Perspectives. *Journal of Network and Systems Management.* doi:10.100710922-022-09682-4

Rahmanzadeh, S., Pishvaee, M. S., & Rasouli, M. R. (2020). Integrated innovative product design and supply chain tactical planning within a blockchain platform. *International Journal of Production Research, 58*(7), 2242–2262. doi:10.1080/00207543.2019.1651947

Raja Santhi, A., & Muthuswamy, P. (2022). Influence of blockchain technology in manufacturing supply chain and logistics. *Logistics, 6*(1), 15. doi:10.3390/logistics6010015

Rajani Singh, A. D. (2020). Internet of Things Based Blockchain for Temperature Monitoring and Counterfeit Pharmaceutical Prevention. *Sensors (Basel).* PMID:32708588

Rajasekaran, A. S., Azees, M., & Al-Turjman, F. (2022). A comprehensive survey on blockchain technology. *Sustainable Energy Technologies and Assessments*, *52*, 102039. doi:10.1016/j.seta.2022.102039

Rajeev, A., Pati, R. K., Padhi, S. S., & Govindan, K. (2017). Evolution of sustainability in supply chain management: A literature review. *Journal of Cleaner Production*, *162*, 299–314. doi:10.1016/j.jclepro.2017.05.026

Raj, P. V. R. P., Jauhar, S. K., Ramkumar, M., & Pratap, S. (2022). Procurement, traceability and advance cash credit payment transactions in supply chain using blockchain smart contracts. *Computers & Industrial Engineering*, *167*, 108038. doi:10.1016/j.cie.2022.108038

Ramya, U., Sindhuja, P., Atsaya, R., Dharani, B. B., & Golla, S. M. V. (2018). Reducing forgery in land registry system using blockchain technology. *Proc. Int. Conf. Adv. Informat. Comput. Res.* Berlin, Germany: Springer.

Rauniyar, K., Wu, X., Gupta, S., Modgil, S., & Jabbour, A. B. (2021). *Risk Management of Supply Chains in the Digital Transformation Era: Contribution and Challenges of Blockchain Technology.* Industrial Management and Data System. doi:10.1108/IMDS-04-2021-0235

Raza, A., Asif, M., & Akram, M. (2023). Give your hunger a new option: Understanding consumers' continuous intention to use online food delivery apps using trust transfer theory. *International Journal of Consumer Studies*, *47*(2), 474–495. doi:10.1111/ijcs.12845

Razak, G. M., Hendry, L. C., & Stevenson, M. (2023). Supply chain traceability: A review of the benefits and its relationship with supply chain resilience. *Production Planning and Control*, *34*(11), 1114–1134. doi:10.1080/09537287.2021.1983661

Reiff. (2023, June 5). *How Blockchain Can Help Emerging Economies.* Investopedia. https://www.investopedia.com/tech/how-blockchain-can-help-failing-economies/

Reinsberg, B. (2021). Fully-automated liberalism? Blockchain technology and international cooperation in an anarchic world. *International Theory*, *13*(2), 287–313. doi:10.1017/S1752971920000305

Rejeb, A., & Karim, R. (2019). Blockchain technology in tourism: Applications and possibilities. *World Scientific News*, *137*, 119–144.

Rejeb, A., Keogh, J. G., Simske, S. J., Stafford, T., & Treiblmaier, H. (2021). Potentials of blockchain technologies for supply chain collaboration: A conceptual framework. *International Journal of Logistics Management*, *32*(3), 1005–1026. doi:10.1108/IJLM-02-2020-0098

Reuters. (2022, November 29). *Maersk, IBM discontinue shipping blockchain platform* [Web page]. Reuters. https://www.reuters.com/technology/maersk-ibm-discontinue-shipping-blockchain-platform-2022-11-29/

Riahi, A., Mohamed, A., & Erbad, A. (2023). RL-Based Federated Learning Framework Over Blockchain (RL-FL-BC). *IEEE Transactions on Network and Service Management*, *20*(2), 1587–1599. doi:10.1109/TNSM.2023.3241437

Riley, J. (2021). The current status of cryptocurrency regulation in China and its effect around the world. *China and WTO Review*, *7*(1), 135–152. doi:10.14330/cwr.2021.7.1.06

Rizzi, A., Caballini, C., Cagno, E., & Boer, H. (2018). Blockchain for supply chain finance: Benefits and challenges. *Production Planning and Control*, *29*(15), 1265–1276.

Robbie Morrison, N. C. (2020). The DAO Controversy: The Case for a New Species of Corporate Governance? *Frontiers in Blockchain.*

Robert M. Monczka, R. B. (2020). *Purchasing and Supply Chain Management.* Cengage Learning.

Roberts, A. (2006). *Blacked out: Government secrecy in the information age*. Cambridge University Press. doi:10.1017/CBO9781139165518

Rodgers, M., Raine, G., Thomas, S., Harden, M., & Eastwood, A. (2019). Informing NHS policy in 'digital-first primary care': A rapid evidence synthesis. *Health Services and Delivery Research*, *7*(41), 1–124. doi:10.3310/hsdr07410 PMID:31869020

Rodriguez-Espindola, O., Chowdhury, S., Beltagui, A., & Albores, A. (2020). The potential of emergent disruptive technologies for humanitarian supply chains: The integration of blockchain, artificial intelligence and 3D Printing. *International Journal of Production Research*, *58*(15), 15. doi:10.1080/00207543.2020.1761565

Roozkhosh, P., Pooya, A., & Agarwal, R. (2023). Blockchain acceptance rate prediction in the resilient supply chain with hybrid system dynamics and machine learning approach. *Operations Management Research : Advancing Practice Through Research*, *16*(2), 705–725. doi:10.100712063-022-00336-x

Rossi, M., Mueller-Bloch, C., Thatcher, J. B., & Beck, R. (2019). Blockchain research in information systems: Current trends and an inclusive future research agenda. *Journal of the Association for Information Systems*, *20*(9), 14. doi:10.17705/1jais.00571

Saberi, S., Kouhizadeh, M., & Sarkis, J. (2018). Blockchain technology: A panacea or pariah for resource conservation and recycling? *Resources, Conservation and Recycling*, *130*, 80–81. doi:10.1016/j.resconrec.2017.11.020

Saberi, S., Kouhizadeh, M., & Sarkis, J. (2019). Blockchains and the supply chain: Findings from a broad study of practitioners. *IEEE Engineering Management Review*, *47*(3), 95–103. doi:10.1109/EMR.2019.2928264

Saberi, S., Kouhizadeh, M., Sarkis, J., & Shen, L. (2019). Blockchain technology and its relationships to sustainable supply chain management. *International Journal of Production Research*, *57*(7), 2117–2135. doi:10.1080/00207543.2018.1533261

Sabreen, M. (2021). Legislation on Halal Food in Pakistan: An Analytical Study. *Journal of Islamic and Religious Studies*, *6*(1), 27–40. doi:10.36476/JIRS.6:1.06.2021.14

Sadri, S. (2021). *Enhancing healthcare using blockchain technology: blood donation supply chain* [Doctoral dissertation, École de technologie supérieure].

Sahebi, I. G., Masoomi, B., & Ghorbani, S. (2020). Expert oriented approach for analyzing the blockchain adoption barriers in humanitarian supply chain. *Technology in Society*, *63*, 101427. doi:10.1016/j.techsoc.2020.101427

Sahoo, S., Kumar, S., Sivarajah, U., Lim, W. M., Westland, J. C., & Kumar, A. (2022, May 27). Blockchain for sustainable supply chain management: Trends and ways forward. *Electronic Commerce Research*. doi:10.100710660-022-09569-1

Samaniego, M., & Deters, R. (2016, November). Using blockchain to push software-defined IoT components onto edge hosts. In *Proceedings of the international conference on big data and advanced wireless technologies* (pp. 1-9). ACM. 10.1145/3010089.3016027

Sánchez-Flores, R. B., Cruz-Sotelo, S. E., Ojeda-Benitez, S., & Ramírez-Barreto, M. (2020). Sustainable Supply Chain Management—A Literature Review on Emerging Economies. *Sustainability (Basel)*, *12*(17), 6972. doi:10.3390u12176972

Sandip Jangir, A. M. (2019). A Novel Framework for Pharmaceutical Supply Chain Management using Distributed Ledger and Smart Contracts. *International Conference on Computing, Communication and Networking Technologies (ICCCNT)*. IEEE.

Sannara, E. K. (2021). A Federated Learning Aggregation Algorithm for Pervasive Computing: Evaluation and Comparison. *IEEE International Conference on Pervasive Computing and Communications*. IEEE. 10.1109/PERCOM50583.2021.9439129

Sarwar, A., Zafar, A., & Qadir, A. (2021). Analysis and prioritization of risk factors in the management of Halal supply chain management. *Discover Sustainability*, *2*(1), 1–10. doi:10.100743621-021-00039-6

Satoshi Nakamoto. (2008). *Bitcoin: A Peer-to-Peer Electronic Cash System*. bitcoin. https://bitcoin.org/bitcoin.pdf

Sauer, P. C., & Seuring, S. (2019). Extending the Reach of Multi-Tier Sustainable Supply Chain Management–Insights from Mineral Supply Chains. *International Journal of Production Economics*, *217*, 31–43. doi:10.1016/j.ijpe.2018.05.030

Schinckus, C. (2020). The good, the bad and the ugly: An overview of the blockchain technology. *Energy Research & Social Science*, *69*, 69. doi:10.1016/j.erss.2020.101614

Schmid, D. (2017). *The History of Programmatic Advertising: Everything You Need to Know.*

Schmidt, C. G., & Wagner, S. M. (2019). Blockchain and supply chain relations: A transaction cost theory perspective. *Journal of Purchasing and Supply Management*, *25*(4), 100552. doi:10.1016/j.pursup.2019.100552

Schoentgen, A., & Wilkinson, R. (2011). The WTO's Trade Policy Review Mechanism: How to create political will for compliance? *World Economy*, *34*(11), 1897–1925. https://www.econstor.eu/bitstream/10419/238052/1/Schoentgen-Wilkinson.pdf

Scholten, K., Sharkey Scott, P., & Fynes, B. (2010). (Le)agility in humanitarian aid (NGO) supply chains. *International Journal of Physical Distribution & Logistics Management*, *40*(8/9), 623–635. doi:10.1108/09600031011079292

Securing Industry. (2017, August 24). *BlockRx announces powerhouse partners before the first pharmaceutical ICO offering hits the market*. Securing Industry. https://www.securingindustry.com/press-releases/blockrx-announces-powerhouse-partners-before-the-first-pharmaceutical-ico-offering-hits-the-market/s135/a5484/

Sedlmeir, J., Lautenschlager, J., Fridgen, G., & Urbach, N. (2022). The transparency challenge of blockchain in organizations. *Electronic Markets*, *32*(3), 1779–1794. doi:10.100712525-022-00536-0 PMID:35602109

Setiadi, R., Soetomo, M. A., & Mahawan, B. (2018). Blockchain Governance: An Evaluation from COBIT5 Perspective. *Proceedings of Annual Conference on Management and Information Technology (ACMIT) 2018*. ACM.

Seyed Mojtaba Hosseini Bamakan, S. G. (2021). Blockchain-enabled Pharmaceutical Cold Chain: Applications, key Challenges, and Future Trends. *Journal of Cleaner Production.*

Seyednima Khezr, M. M. (2019). *Blockchain Technology in Healthcare: A Comprehensive Review and Directions for Future Research*. Applied Sciences.

Seyyed-Mahdi Hosseini-Motlagh, M. J. (2020). Recall Management in Pharmaceutical Industry through Supply Chain Coordination. *Annals of Operations Research*, 1–39.

Seyyed-Mahdi Hosseini-Motlagh, M. J. (2020). Recall management in pharmaceutical industry through supply chain coordination. *Annals of Operations Research.*

Seyyed-Mahdi Hosseini-Motlagh, M. N. (2021). Drug Recall Management and Channel Coordination Under Stochastic Product Defect Severity: A Game-Theoretic Analytical Study. *International Journal of Production Research*, *59*(6), 1649–1675. doi:10.1080/00207543.2020.1723813

Shafiq, M., & Soratana, K. (2019). Humanitarian logistics and supply chain management – a qualitative study. *Logforum*, *15*(1), 19–38. doi:10.17270/J.LOG.2019.325

Shafiq, M., & Soratana, K. (2020). Lean readiness assessment model – a tool for Humanitarian Organizations' social and economic sustainability. *Journal of Humanitarian Logistics and Supply Chain Management, 10*(2), 77–99. doi:10.1108/JHLSCM-01-2019-0002

Shanshan Zhao, S. L. (2019). Blockchain Enabled Industrial Internet of Things Technology. *IEEE Transactions on Computational Social Systems, 6*(6), 1442–1453. doi:10.1109/TCSS.2019.2924054

Shaoliu, D., & Tongbai, L. (2023). Ideological and Physical Education Integration in Higher Education: Strategies for Mental Health Education. *Journal of Sport Psychology, 32*(4), 203–212.

Sharif, M., & Ghodoosi, F. (2022). The Ethics of Blockchain in Organizations. *Journal of Business Ethics, 178*(4), 1009–1025. doi:10.100710551-022-05058-5 PMID:35125568

Sharma, S., & Bhadula, S. (2023). Secure Federated Learning for Intelligent Industry 4.0 IoT Enabled Self Skin Care Application System. *IEEE Xplore proceedings of the Second International Conference on Applied Artificial Intelligence and Computing (ICAAIC 2023).* IEEE. 10.1109/ICAAIC56838.2023.10141028

Sharma, T. K. (2022, December 16). *Top 10 Countries Leading Blockchain Technology In The World [Understanding blockchain].* Blockchain Council. https://www.blockchain-council.org/blockchain/top-10-countries-leading-blockchain-technology-in-the-world/

Sharma, V., & Seetharaman, T. (2023). Blockchain and Federated Learning Enabled Smart Traffic Management System for Smart Cities. *4th International Conference on Intelligent Engineering and Management (ICIEM 2023).* IEEE. http:// Doi: 10.1109/ICIEM59379.2023.10167236

Sharma, P. K., Kumar, N., & Park, J. H. (2020). Blockchain technology toward green IoT: Opportunities and challenges. *IEEE Network, 34*(4), 263–269. doi:10.1109/MNET.001.1900526

Sheehan, B. (2017). A blockchain-based approach towards overcoming challenges in supply chain management. *International Journal of Advanced Manufacturing Technology, 89*(9-12), 3657–3667.

Shekarian, M., & Mellat Parast, M. (2021). An Integrative approach to supply chain disruption risk and resilience management: A literature review. *International Journal of Logistics, 24*(5), 427–455. doi:10.1080/13675567.2020.1763935

Shen, D. (2021). Research on the sharing mode of educational information resources in colleges and universities based on the Blockchain and new energy. *Energy Reports, 7,* 458–467. doi:10.1016/j.egyr.2021.10.016

Shin, S., Xu, L., & Hong, S. & Gu, G. (2016). Enhancing Network Security through Software Defined Networking (SDN)",IEEE Explore. *25th International Conference on Computer Communication and Networks (ICCCN).* IEEE. 10.1109/ICCCN.2016.7568520

Shi, X., Yao, S., & Luo, S. (2023). Innovative platform operations with the use of technologies in the blockchain era. *International Journal of Production Research, 61*(11), 3651–3669. doi:10.1080/00207543.2021.1953182

Shi, X., Yao, S., & Ma, Y. (2022). When and how should cross-border platforms manage blockchain technology in the presence of purchasing agents? *Asia-Pacific Journal of Operational Research, 39*(01), 2140020. doi:10.1142/S0217595921400200

Shuchih E. Chang, Y. C. (2020). When Blockchain Meets Supply Chain: A Systematic Literature Review on Current Development and Potential Applications. *IEEE Access, Institute of Electrical and Electronics Engineers Inc.* IEEE.

Sicari, S., Rizzardi, A., Grieco, L. A., & Coen-Porisini, A. (2015). Security, privacy and trust in Internet of Things: The road ahead. *Computer Networks, 76,* 146–164. doi:10.1016/j.comnet.2014.11.008

Sienkiewicz-Małyjurek, K., & Szymczak, M. (2023). Understanding public service supply chain management: A systematic literature review. *Management Review Quarterly*. doi:10.1007/s11301-023-00350-8

Simmie, J., & Martin, R. (2010). The economic resilience of regions: Towards an evolutionary approach. *Cambridge Journal of Regions, Economy and Society*, *3*(1), 27–43. doi:10.1093/cjres/rsp029

Singh, S. K., Jeong, Y.-S., & Park, J. H. (2020). A deep learning-based IoT-oriented infrastructure for a secure smart City. *Sustainable Cities and Society*, *60*, 102252. doi:10.1016/j.scs.2020.102252

Singh, S. K., Yang, L. T., & Park, J. H. (2022). FusionFedBlock: Fusion of blockchain and federated learning to preserve privacy in industry 5.0. *Information Fusion*, *90*, 233–240. doi:10.1016/j.inffus.2022.09.027

Sinistra, P. (2020, November 3). *Future of Blockchain Technology in Supply Chain Management*. Vault Security Systems AG – Blockchain for Supply Chain. https://vaultsecurity.io/blockchain-technology-supply-chain-management

Sislian, L., & Jaegler, A. (2022). Linkage of blockchain to enterprise resource planning systems for improving sustainable performance. *Business Strategy and the Environment*, *31*(3), 737–750. doi:10.1002/bse.2914

Sjahroeddin, F. (2018, October). The role of ES-Qual and food quality on customer satisfaction in online food delivery service. In *Prosiding Industrial Research Workshop and National Seminar* (Vol. 9, pp. 551-558).

Skipper, J. B., Hanna, J. B., & Cegielski, C. G. (2009). Supply Chain Contingency Planning and Firm Adoption: An Initial Look at Differentiating the Innovators. *Transportation Journal*, *48*(2), 40–62. doi:10.2307/25702522

Sluis, S. (2015). *Procter & Gamble CMO Pritchard: Programmatic Delivers Business Lift*. ad Exchanger.

Smits, R. (2002). Innovation studies in the 21st century; Questions from a user's perspective. *Technological Forecasting and Social Change*, *69*(9), 861–883. doi:10.1016/S0040-1625(01)00181-0

Sobia Yaqoob, M. M. (2019). Use of Blockchain in Healthcare: A Systematic Literature Review. *International Journal of Advanced Computer Science and Applications*, 644–653.

Sodhi, M. S., & Tang, C. S. (2019). Research Opportunities in Supply Chain Transparency. *Production and Operations Management*, *28*(12), 2946–2959. doi:10.1111/poms.13115

Sodhi, M. S., & Tang, C. S. (2021). Supply chain management for extreme conditions: Research opportunities. *The Journal of Supply Chain Management*, *57*(1), 7–16. doi:10.1111/jscm.12255

Solaiman, E., Wike, T., & Sfyrakis, I. (2021). Implementation and evaluation of smart contracts using a hybrid on- and off-blockchain architecture. *Concurrency and Computation*, *33*(1), e5811. doi:10.1002/cpe.5811

Son-Turan, S. (2019). The blockchain–sustainability nexus: Can this new technology enhance social, environmental, and economic sustainability? In *Blockchain Economics and Financial Market. Innovation* (pp. 83–89). Springer. doi:10.1007/978-3-030-25275-5_5

Spagnoletti, P., & Terruli, V. (2021). *The application of blockchain technology in the programmatic advertisement ecosystem.*

Stallone, V., Wetzels, M., & Klaas, M. (2021). *Applications of Blockchain Technology in marketing—A systematic review of marketing technology companies. Blockchain: Research and Applications, 1-9. statista. (2023). Estimated cost of digital ad fraud worldwide from 2018 to 2023.* Statista Research Department. doi:10.1016/j.bcra.2021.100023

Statista. (2023, April 27). *Food service industry: global market size 2021-2028*. https://www.statista.com/statistics/1095667/global-food-service-market-size/#statisticContainer

Steenwinckel, B., De Paepe, D., Vanden Hautte, S., Heyvaert, P., Bentefrit, M., Moens, P., Dimou, A., Van Den Bossche, B., De Turck, F., Van Hoecke, S., & Ongenae, F. (2021). FLAGS: A methodology for adaptive anomaly detection and root cause analysis on sensor data streams by fusing expert knowledge with machine learning. *Future Generation Computer Systems*, *116*, 30–48. doi:10.1016/j.future.2020.10.015

Steiner, J., & Baker, J. (2015). *Blockchain: The Solution for Transparency in Product Supply Chains.*

Stentoft Arlbjørn, J., Vagn Freytag, P., & De Haas, H. (2011). Service supply chain management: A survey of lean application in the municipal sector. *International Journal of Physical Distribution & Logistics Management*, *41*(3), 277–295. doi:10.1108/09600031111123796

Sternberg, H. S., Hofmann, E., & Roeck, D. (2021). The struggle is real: Insights from a supply chain blockchain case. *Journal of Business Logistics*, *42*(1), 71–87. doi:10.1111/jbl.12240

Stevens, G. C., & Johnson, M. (2016). Integrating the Supply Chain … 25 years on. *International Journal of Physical Distribution & Logistics Management*, *46*(1), 19–42. doi:10.1108/IJPDLM-07-2015-0175

Stock, T., & Seliger, G. (2016). Opportunities of sustainable manufacturing in Industry 4.0. *Procedia CIRP*, *40*, 536–541. doi:10.1016/j.procir.2016.01.129

Stranieri, S., Orsi, L., & Banterle, A. (2017). Traceability and risks: An extended transaction cost perspective. *Supply Chain Management*, *22*(2), 145–159. doi:10.1108/SCM-07-2016-0268

Sullivan, C., & Burger, E. (2017). E-residency and blockchain. *Computer Law & Security Report*, *33*(4), 470–481. doi:10.1016/j.clsr.2017.03.016

Suyambu, G. T., Anand, M., & Janakirani, M. (2020). Blockchain–A most disruptive technology on the spotlight of world engineering education paradigm. *Procedia Computer Science*, *172*, 152–158. doi:10.1016/j.procs.2020.05.023

Swan, M. (2015). *Blockchain: Blueprint for a new economy*. O'Reilly Media, Inc.

Swan, M., Bullock, J., & Alnuaimi, O. (2020). Blockchain in education: Strategies for decentralized, learner-owned records. *EDUCAUSE Review*, *55*(3), 16–26.

Sweeney, E. (2022). The big challenges for supply chains in 2022. *The Conversation*. https://theconversation.com/the-big-challenges-for-supply-chains-in-2022-174420

Szabo, N. (1997). Formalizing and securing relationships on public networks. *First Monday*, *2*(9). doi:10.5210/fm.v2i9.548

Taherdoost, H. (2023). Smart contracts in blockchain technology: A critical review. *Information (Basel)*, *14*(2), 117. https://www.mdpi.com/2078-2489/14/2/117. doi:10.3390/info14020117

Tanin, T. I., Mobin, M. A., Ng, A., Dewandaru, G., Salim, K., Nkoba, M. A., & Razak, L. A. (2019). How does microfinance prosper? An analysis of environmental, social, and governance context. *Sustainability*, *27*, 1001–1022.

Tan, T. M., & Saraniemi, S. (2022). Trust in blockchain-enabled exchanges: Future directions in blockchain marketing. *Journal of the Academy of Marketing Science*.

Tanwar, S., Parmar, A., Kumari, A., Jadav, N. K., Hong, W. C., & Sharma, R. (2022). Blockchain adoption to secure the food industry: Opportunities and challenges. *Sustainability (Basel)*, *14*(12), 7036. doi:10.3390u14127036

Tapscott, D., & Tapscott, A. (2016). *Blockchain revolution: how the technology behind bitcoin is changing money, business, and the world*. Penguin.

Terruli, V., & Spagnoletti, P. (2021). *The application of blockchain technology in the programmatic advertisement ecosystem.*

Tham, A., & Sigala, M. (2020). Road block(chain): Bit(coin)s for tourism sustainable development goals? *Journal of Hospitality and Tourism Technology*, *11*(2), 203–222. doi:10.1108/JHTT-05-2019-0069

Thanujan, T., Rajapakse, C., & Wickramaarachchi, D. (2021, September). A community-based hybrid blockchain architecture for the organic food supply chain. In *2021 International Research Conference on Smart Computing and Systems Engineering (SCSE)* (Vol. 4, pp. 77-83). IEEE. 10.1109/SCSE53661.2021.9568325

Tharatipyakul, A., & Pongnumkul, S. (2021). User interface of blockchain-based agri-food traceability applications: A review. *IEEE Access : Practical Innovations, Open Solutions*, *9*, 82909–82929. doi:10.1109/ACCESS.2021.3085982

Thess, A., Klein, M., Nienhaus, K., & Pregger, T. (2020). Global carbon surcharge for the reduction of anthropogenic emission of carbon dioxide. *Energy, Sustainability and Society*, *10*(1), 1–9. doi:10.118613705-020-0242-z

Thomas McGhin, K.-K. R. (2019). Blockchain in Healthcare Applications: Research Challenges and opportunities. *Journal of Network and Computer Applications*, *135*, 62–75. doi:10.1016/j.jnca.2019.02.027

Thylin, T., & Duarte, M. F. N. (2019). Leveraging blockchain technology in humanitarian settings–opportunities and risks for women and girls. *Gender and Development*, *27*(2), 317–336. doi:10.1080/13552074.2019.1627778

Tiago, J. (2023). *Why blockchain is the key to sustainable advertising and customer acquisition.* Open Mic.

Tian, F. (2016). An agri-food supply chain traceability system for China based on RFID & blockchain technology. *2016 13th International Conference on Service Systems and Service Management (ICSSSM),* (pp. 1-6). IEEE. https://ieeexplore.ieee.org/document/7538424

Tian, F. (2017). A Supply Chain Traceability System for Food Safety Based on HACCP, Blockchain & Internet of Things. *2017 International Conference on Service Systems and Service Management* (ICSSSM). IEEE. 10.1109/ICSSSM.2017.7996119

Tian, X., Zhu, J., Zhao, X., & Wu, J. (2022). Improving operational efficiency through blockchain: Evidence from a field experiment in cross-border trade. *Production Planning and Control*, 1–16. doi:10.1080/09537287.2022.2058412

Tillemann, T., Price, A., Tillemann-Dick, G., & Knight, A. (2019). *The blueprint for blockchain and social innovation.* New America. https:// d1y8sb8igg2f8e.cloudfront.net/documents/The_Blueprint_for_Blockchain_and_ Social Innovation .pdf

Tokkozhina, U., Martins, A. L., & Ferreira, J. C. (2021). Use of blockchain technology to manage the supply chains: Comparison of perspectives between technology providers and early industry adopters. *Journal of Theoretical and Applied Electronic Commerce Research*, *17*(4), 82–100. doi:10.3390/jtaer17040082

Tönnissen, S., & Teuteberg, F. (2020). Analysing the impact of blockchain-technology for operations and supply chain management: An explanatory model drawn from multiple case studies. *International Journal of Information Management*, *52*, 101953. doi:10.1016/j.ijinfomgt.2019.05.009

Toyoda, K., Mathiopoulos, P. T., Sasase, I., & Ohtsuki, T. (2017). A novel blockchain-based product ownership management system (POMS) for anti-counterfeits in the post supply chain. *IEEE Access : Practical Innovations, Open Solutions*, *5*, 17465–17477. doi:10.1109/ACCESS.2017.2720760

Tracefood.io. (2020). *Benefits of blockchain in food supply chain industry*. Tracefood. https://tracefood.io/benefits-of-blockchain-in-food-supply-chain-industry/

Treiblmaier, H., & Garaus, M. (2023). Using blockchain to signal quality in the food supply chain: The impact on consumer purchase intentions and the moderating effect of brand familiarity. *International Journal of Information Management*, *68*, 102514. doi:10.1016/j.ijinfomgt.2022.102514

Truong, Y., McColl, R., & Kitchen, P. (2010). Practitioners' perceptionsof advertising strategies for digital media. *International Journal of Advertising*, *29*(5), 709–725. doi:10.2501/S0265048710201439

Tsafnat, G., Glasziou, P., Choong, M. K., Dunn, A., Galgani, F., & Coiera, E. (2014). Systematic review automation technologies. *Systematic Reviews*, *3*(1), 74. doi:10.1186/2046-4053-3-74 PMID:25005128

Tsalis, T. A., Malamateniou, K. E., Koulouriotis, D., & Nikolaou, I. E. (2020). New challenges for corporate sustainability reporting: United Nations' 2030 Agenda for sustainable development and the sustainable development goals. *Corporate Social Responsibility and Environmental Management*, *27*(4), 1617–1629. doi:10.1002/csr.1910

Tschorsch, F., & Scheuermann, B. (2016). Bitcoin and beyond: A technical survey on decentralized digital currencies. *IEEE Communications Surveys and Tutorials*, *18*(3), 2084–2123. doi:10.1109/COMST.2016.2535718

Tse, D., Zhang, B., Yang, Y., Cheng, C., & Mu, H. (2017, December). Blockchain application in food supply information security. In *2017 IEEE international conference on industrial engineering and engineering management (IEEM)* (pp. 1357-1361). IEEE. 10.1109/IEEM.2017.8290114

Tsiulin, S., Reinau, K. H., Hilmola, O. P., Goryaev, N., & Karam, A. (2020). Blockchain-based applications in shipping and port management: A literature review towards defining key conceptual frameworks. *Review of International Business and Strategy*, *30*(2), 201–224. doi:10.1108/RIBS-04-2019-0051

Tsoukas, V., Gkogkidis, A., Kampa, A., Spathoulas, G., & Kakarountas, A. (2022). Enhancing food supply chain security through the use of blockchain and TinyML. *Information (Basel)*, *13*(5), 213. doi:10.3390/info13050213

Turkanović, M., Hölbl, M., Košič, K., Heričko, M., & Kamišalić, A. (2018). EduCTX: A blockchain-based higher education credit platform. *IEEE Access : Practical Innovations, Open Solutions*, *6*, 5112–5127. doi:10.1109/ACCESS.2018.2789929

Uddin, M. (2021). Blockchain Medledger: Hyperledger fabric enabled drug traceability system for counterfeit drugs in pharmaceutical industry. *International Journal of Pharmaceutics*, *597*, 120235. doi:10.1016/j.ijpharm.2021.120235 PMID:33549813

Uddin, M. J., Azmat, F., Fujimoto, Y., & Hossain, F. (2023). Exploitation in Bangladeshi ready-made garments supply chain: A case of irresponsible capitalism? *International Journal of Logistics Management*, *34*(1), 164–188. doi:10.1108/IJLM-12-2021-0565

UNDP. (2020, March 20). Beyond bitcoin: Using blockchain to advance the SDGs. *Innovation for Development by UNDP Europe and Central Asia*. UN. https://innovation.eurasia.undp.org/beyond-bitcoin-using-blockchain-to-advance-the-sdgs/

United Nations (Ed.). (2000). *Classifications of expenditure according to purpose: Classification of the functions of government (COFOG), classification of individual consumption according to purpose (COICOP), classification of the purposes of non-profit institutions serving households (COPNI), classification of the outlays of producers according to purpose (COPP)*. United Nations.

United Nations. (2020). *Sustainable Development Goals*. UN. https://sustainabledevelopment.un.org/?menu=1300

Upadhyay, A., Mukhuty, S., Kumar, V., & Kazancoglu, Y. (2021). Blockchain technology and the circular economy: Implications for sustainability and social responsibility. *Journal of Cleaner Production*, *293*, 126130. doi:10.1016/j.jclepro.2021.126130

Upadhyay, N. (2020). Demystifying blockchain: A critical analysis of challenges, applications, and opportunities. *International Journal of Information Management*, *54*, 102120. doi:10.1016/j.ijinfomgt.2020.102120

van Ruth, S. M., Huisman, W., & Luning, P. A. (2017). Food fraud vulnerability and its key factors. *Trends in Food Science & Technology*, *67*, 70–75. doi:10.1016/j.tifs.2017.06.017

Van Wassenaer, L., Verdouw, C., Kassahun, A., Van Hilten, M., Van Der Meij, K., & Tekinerdogan, B. (2023). Tokenizing circularity in agri-food systems: A conceptual framework and exploratory study. *Journal of Cleaner Production*, *413*, 137527. doi:10.1016/j.jclepro.2023.137527

Vandevelde, P. (2018). *Using blockchain technology to fight counterfeiters*. Development Asia. https://development.asia/case-study/using-blockchain-technology-fight-counterfeiters

Varriale, V., Cammarano, A., Michelino, F., & Caputo, M. (2020). The unknown potential of Blockchain for sustainable supply chains. *Sustainability (Basel)*, *12*(22), 1–16. doi:10.3390u12229400

Varriale, V., Cammarano, A., Michelino, F., & Caputo, M. (2023). Industry 5.0 and Triple Bottom Line Approach in Supply Chain Management: The State-of-the-Art. *Sustainability (Basel)*, *15*(7), 7. doi:10.3390u15075712

Vashishth, T. K., Chaudhary, S., Sharma, V., Sharma, S., & Gupat, V. K. (2023). Technological Implementation in Achieving Data Privacy Through Blockchain Technique. *International Journal of Research and Analytical Reviews*, *10*(2), 276–483.

Vashishth, T. K., Chaudhary, S., Sharma, V., Yadav, A., & Panwar, R. (2023). Next Generation Dynamic Distributed Honeypots System Based on Blockchain: A Real Time Network Defense Strategy. *International Journal of Research and Analytical Reviews*, *10*(2), 583–591.

Vashishth, T. K., Sharma, V., Chaudhary, S., Panwar, R., Sharma, S., & Kumar, P. (2023). Advanced Technologies and AI-Enabled IoT Applications in High-Tech Agriculture. In A. Khang (Ed.), *Handbook of Research on AI-Equipped IoT Applications in High-Tech Agriculture* (pp. 155–166). IGI Global., doi:10.4018/978-1-6684-9231-4.ch008

Vatankhah Barenji, A., Li, Z., Wang, W. M., Huang, G. Q., & Guerra-Zubiaga, D. A. (2020). Blockchain-based ubiquitous manufacturing: A secure and reliable cyber-physical system. *International Journal of Production Research*, *58*(7), 2200–2221. doi:10.1080/00207543.2019.1680899

Venkatesh, V., Kang, K., Wang, B., Zhong, R. Y., & Zhang, A. (2020). A System architecture for blockchain-based transparency of supply chain social sustainability. *Robotics and Computer-integrated Manufacturing*, *63*, 101896. doi:10.1016/j.rcim.2019.101896

Verma, P. K., Sharma, V., Kumar, P., Sharma, S., Chaudhary, S., & Preety, P. (2023). IoT Enabled Real Time Appearance System using AI Camera and Deep Learning for Student Tracking. *International Journal on Recent and Innovation Trends in Computing and Communication*, *11*(6s), 249–254. doi:10.17762/ijritcc.v11i6s.6885

Vern, P., Panghal, A., Mor, R. S., Kamble, S. S., Islam, Md. S., & Khan, S. A. R. (2023). Influential barriers to blockchain technology implementation in agri-food supply chain. *Operations Management Research*. doi:10.1007/s12063-023-00388-7

Veuger, J. (2018). Trust in a viable real estate economy with disruption and blockchain. *Facilities*, *36*(1/2), 103–120. doi:10.1108/F-11-2017-0106

Vimaladevi, K., & Dhanabhakaym, M. (2012). A study on the effects of online consumer reviews on purchasing decision. *Prestige In. J. Manag.*, *7*(1), 51–99. doi:10.37922/PIJMIT.2012.V01i01.005

Vincent, N. E., & Barkhi, R. (2021). Evaluating Blockchain Using COSO. *Current Issues in Auditing*, *15*(1), 57–71. doi:10.2308/CIIA-2019-509

Viriyasitavat, W., & Hoonsopon, D. (2019). Blockchain characteristics and consensus in modern. *Journal of Industrial Information Integration*, *13*, 32–39. doi:10.1016/j.jii.2018.07.004

Vitale, M., & Mavridis, N. (2017). A survey of internet of things technologies for ambient assisted living environments. *Future Generation Computer Systems*, *76*, 855–869.

Vukolić, M. (2017). Rethinking permissioned blockchains. In *Proceedings of the ACM Workshop on Blockchain, Cryptocurrencies and Contracts* (pp. 3-7). ACM. 10.1145/3055518.3055526

Vytelingum, P., Ramchurn, S. D., Voice, T. D., Rogers, A., & Jennings, N. R. (2010). *Trading agents for the smart electricity grid.*

Wael, I. (2023), Blockchain-Based Federated Learning for Securing Internet of Things: A Comprehensive Survey. ACM Computing Surveys, 55(9) . doi:10.1145/3560816

Walmart Global Tech. (2022, January 12). *Blockchain in the food supply chain [Web page].* Walmart. https://tech.walmart.com/content/walmart-global-tech/en_us/news/articles/blockchain-in-the-food-supply-chain.html

Walsh, P. P., Murphy, E., & Horan, D. (2020). The role of science, technology and innovation in the UN 2030 agenda. *Technological Forecasting and Social Change*, *154*, 119957. doi:10.1016/j.techfore.2020.119957

Wang, M., Wu, Y., Chen, B., & Evans, M. (2021). Blockchain and supply chain management: A new paradigm for supply chain integration and collaboration. *Operations and Supply Chain Management*, *14*(1), 111–122.

Wang, S., Ding, W., Li, J., Yuan, Y., Ouyang, L., & Wang, F. Y. (2019). Decentralized autonomous organizations: Concept, model, and applications. *IEEE Transactions on Computational Social Systems*, *6*(5), 870–878. doi:10.1109/TCSS.2019.2938190

Wang, S., Li, D., Zhang, Y., & Chen, J. (2019). Smart Contract-Based Product Traceability System in the Supply Chain Scenario. *IEEE Access : Practical Innovations, Open Solutions*, *7*, 115122–115133. doi:10.1109/ACCESS.2019.2935873

Wang, Y., Cong, X., Zi, L., & Xiang, Q. (2023). Blockchain for Credibility in Educational Development: Key Technology, Application Potential, and Performance Evaluation. *Security and Communication Networks*, *2023*, 2023. doi:10.1155/2023/5614241

Wang, Y., Han, J. H., & Beynon-Davies, P. (2019). Understanding blockchain technology for future supply chains: A systematic literature review and research agenda. *Supply Chain Management*, *24*(1), 62–84. doi:10.1108/SCM-03-2018-0148

Wang, Y., Liu, Y., & Hu, Y. (2022). An empirical analysis based on a panel threshold model of the effect of Internet development on the efficiency of Chinese government public service supply. *PLoS One*, *17*(7), e0271390. doi:10.1371/journal.pone.0271390 PMID:35830450

Wang, Y., Singgih, M., Wang, J., & Rit, M. (2019). Making sense of blockchain technology: How will it transform supply chains? *International Journal of Production Economics*, *211*, 221–236. doi:10.1016/j.ijpe.2019.02.002

Wang, Y., Sun, Q., & Bie, R. (2022). Blockchain-based secure sharing mechanism of online education data. *Procedia Computer Science*, *202*, 283–288. doi:10.1016/j.procs.2022.04.037

Wen, B., Wang, Y., Ding, Y., Zheng, H., Qin, B., & Yang, C. (2023). Security and privacy protection technologies in securing blockchain applications. *Information Sciences*, *119322*, 119322. Advance online publication. doi:10.1016/j.ins.2023.119322

World Bank. (2020). Poverty and shared prosperity 2020: Reversals of fortune. The World Bank.

Worldometer. (2023). *Worldometer—Real time world statistics*. Worldometer. https://www.worldometers.info/

Wu, H., Cao, J., Yang, Y., Tung, C. L., Jiang, S., Tang, B., & Deng, Y. (2019, July). Data management in supply chain using blockchain: Challenges and a case study. In *2019 28th international conference on computer communication and networks (ICCCN)* (pp. 1-8). IEEE.

Wu, J., & Yu, J. (2023). Blockchain's impact on platform supply chains: Transaction cost and information transparency perspectives. *International Journal of Production Research*, *61*(11), 3703–3716. doi:10.1080/00207543.2022.2027037

Wünsche, J. F., & Fernqvist, F. (2022). The potential of blockchain technology in the transition towards sustainable food systems. *Sustainability (Basel)*, *14*(13), 7739. doi:10.3390u14137739

Xiong, Y., Lam, H. K., Kumar, A., Ngai, E. W., Xiu, C., & Wang, X. (2021, July 13). The mitigating role of blockchain-enabled supply chains during the COVID-19 pandemic. *International Journal of Operations & Production Management*, *41*(9), 1495–1521. doi:10.1108/IJOPM-12-2020-0901

Xu, X., Weber, I., Staples, M., Zhu, L., Bosch, J., Bass, L., & Rimba, P. (2017, April). A taxonomy of blockchain-based systems for architecture design. In 2017 IEEE international conference on software architecture (ICSA) (pp. 243-252). IEEE. doi:10.1109/ICSA.2017.33

Xuanping Wu, Y. L. (2019). Blockchain Recall Management in Pharmaceutical Industry. *Procedia CIRP*, 590–595.

Xu, M., Chen, X., & Kou, G. (2019). A systematic review of blockchain. *Financial Innovation*, *5*(1), 27. doi:10.118640854-019-0147-z

Xu, P., Lee, J., Barth, J. R., & Richey, R. G. (2021). Blockchain as supply chain technology: Considering transparency and security. *International Journal of Physical Distribution & Logistics Management*, *51*(3), 305–324. doi:10.1108/IJPDLM-08-2019-0234

Xu, X., Lu, Y., Vogel-Heuser, B., & Wang, L. (2021). Industry 4.0 and Industry 5.0—Inception, conception and perception. *Journal of Manufacturing Systems*, *61*, 530–535. doi:10.1016/j.jmsy.2021.10.006

Xu, Y., Li, X., Zeng, X., Cao, J., & Jiang, W. (2022). Application of blockchain technology in food safety control: Current trends and future prospects. *Critical Reviews in Food Science and Nutrition*, *62*(10), 2800–2819. doi:10.1080/10408398.2020.1858752 PMID:33307729

Yadav, S., & Singh, S.P. (2020). Resources, Conservation, and Recycling Blockchain critical success factors for a sustainable supply chain. *Resources, Conservation and Recycling*. Elsevier.

Yadav, S., & Singh, S. P. (2020). Blockchain critical success factors for sustainable supply chain. *Resources, Conservation and Recycling*, *152*, 104505. doi:10.1016/j.resconrec.2019.104505

Yadav, V. S., Singh, A. R., Gunasekaran, A., Raut, R. D., & Narkhede, B. E. (2022). A systematic literature review of the agro-food supply chain: Challenges, network design, and performance measurement perspectives. *Sustainable Production and Consumption*, *29*, 685–704. doi:10.1016/j.spc.2021.11.019

Yaga, D., Roby, N., & Scarfone, K. (2018). *Blockchain Technology Overview*. National Institute of Standards and Technology. doi:10.6028/NIST.IR.8202

Yang, L. (2019). The blockchain: State-of-the-art and research challenges. *Journal of Industrial Information Integration*, 80–90.

Yanling Chang, E. I. (2020). Blockchain in global supply chains and cross border trade: A critical synthesis of the state-of the-art, challenges and opportunities. *International Journal of Production Research*, 1–18.

Yan, Y., & Cao, S. (2021). A Study on Data Monitoring and Effect Optimization of Programmed Advertising Platform: Taking "Ocean Engine" as an Example. *Journal of Physics: Conference Series*, *1883*(1), 1–5. doi:10.1088/1742-6596/1883/1/012170

Yigit (2021). Blockchain technology and the circular economy: implications for sustainability and social responsibility. *Journal of Cleaner Production*, 293.

Yi-Hummo, J., Ko, D., Choi, S., Park, S., & Smolander, K. (2016). Where is current research on blockchain technology? *A systematic Review. PLoS One*, *11*(10). PMID:27695049

Yingjia Wang, J. L.-M. (2020). Gray Market and Counterfeiting in Supply Chains: A Review of the Operations Literature and Implications to Luxury industries. *Transportation Research Part E, Logistics and Transportation Review*.

Yli-Huumo, J., Ko, D., Choi, S., Park, S., & Smolander, K. (2016). Where is current research on blockchain technology?—A systematic review. *PLoS One*, *11*(10), e0163477. doi:10.1371/journal.pone.0163477 PMID:27695049

Yontar, E. (2023, September). The role of blockchain technology in the sustainability of supply chain management: Grey based dematel implementation. *Cleaner Logistics and Supply Chain*, *8*, 100113. doi:10.1016/j.clscn.2023.100113

Yousuf, S., & Svetinovic, D. (2019, October). Blockchain technology in supply chain management: Preliminary study. In *2019 sixth international conference on internet of things: systems, management and security (IOTSMS)* (pp. 537-538). IEEE. DOI: 10.1109/IOTSMS48152.2019.8939222

Yuen, K. F., Wang, X., Ma, F., & Wong, Y. D. (2019). The determinants of customers' intention to use smart lockers for last-mile deliveries. *Journal of Retailing and Consumer Services*, *49*, 316–326. doi:10.1016/j.jretconser.2019.03.022

Yue, X., Wang, H., Jin, D., Li, M., & Jiang, W. (2016). Healthcare data gateways: Found healthcare intelligence on blockchain with novel privacy risk control. *Journal of Medical Systems*, *40*(10), 1–8. doi:10.100710916-016-0574-6 PMID:27565509

Yusoff, F. A. M., Yusof, R. N. R., & Hussin, S. R. (2015). Halal Food Supply Chain Knowledge and Purchase Intention. *International Journal of Economics & Management, 9*.

Zhang, Y., Li, Y., & Liu, J. (2021). Smart contract security: A practitioners' perspective. In *2021 IEEE/ACM 43rd International Conference on Software Engineering (ICSE)* (pp. 127-138). IEEE. 10.1109/ICSE43902.2021.00127

Zhang, Y., Li, X., & Wang, Y. (2020). A review on the applications of blockchain technology in international trade and finance. *Frontiers of Engineering Management*, *7*(4), 445–458. doi:10.1016/j.tbench.2022.100073

Zhang, Y., Wen, Y., & Li, D. (2019). An IoT electric business model based on blockchain technology in the context of the smart grid. *IEEE Access : Practical Innovations, Open Solutions*, *7*, 67623–67633.

Zhang, Y., & Zhang, Y. (2020). *A blockchain-based secure data sharing scheme for cloud storage. In 2020 IEEE International Conference on Communications Workshops (ICC Workshops)*. IEEE. https://ieeexplore.ieee.org/stamp/stamp.jsp?arnumber=9329051

Zhao, G., Olan, F., Liu, S., Hormazabal, J. H., Lopez, C., Zubairu, N., Zhang, J., & Chen, X. (2022). Links between risk source identification and resilience capability building in agri-food supply chains: A comprehensive analysis. *IEEE Transactions on Engineering Management*, 1–18. doi:10.1109/TEM.2022.3221361

Zheng, Y., & Walsham, G. (2008). Inequality of what? Social exclusion in the e-society as capability deprivation. *Information Technology & People*, *21*(3), 222–243. doi:10.1108/09593840810896000

Zheng, Z. (2017). An overview of blockchain technology: Architecture, consensus, and future trends. *IEEE Access : Practical Innovations, Open Solutions*, *6*, 9245–9257.

Zheng, Z., Xie, S., Dai, H., Chen, X., & Wang, H. (2017, June). *An overview of blockchain technology: Architecture, consensus, and future trends. In 2017 IEEE international congress on big data (BigData congress)*. IEEE.

Zheng, Z., Xie, S., Dai, H., Chen, X., & Wang, H. (2018). Blockchain challenges and opportunities: A survey. *International Journal of Web and Grid Services*, *14*(4), 251–274. doi:10.1504/IJWGS.2018.095647

Zhu, C., Zhu, X., Ren, J., & Qin, T. (2022). Blockchain-Enabled Federated Learning for UAV Edge Computing Network: Issues and Solutions. *IEEE Access : Practical Innovations, Open Solutions*, *10*, 56591–56610. Advance online publication. doi:10.1109/ACCESS.2022.3174865

Zibin, Z., Chen, W., Chen, X., Weng, J., & Imran, M. (2019). An Overview on Smart Contracts: Challenges, Advances and Platforms. *Journal of Future Generation of Computer System.* . doi:10.1016/j.future.2019.12.019

Zimon, D., Tyan, J., & Sroufe, R. (2020). SCM Drivers of Sustainable Supply Chain Management: Practices to Alignment with UN Sustainable Development Goals. *International Journal of Qualitative Research*, *14*(1), 219–236. doi:10.24874/IJQR14.01-14

Zreik, M. (2022). The Regional Comprehensive Economic Partnership (RCEP) for the Asia–Pacific region and world. *Journal of Economic and Administrative Sciences*.

Zreik, M. (2023a). Analytical study on Foreign Direct Investment Divestment Inflows and Outflows in Developing Economies: Evidence of China. *Chinese Economy*, *56*(6), 415–430. doi:10.1080/10971475.2023.2193118

Zreik, M. (2023b). Sustainable and Smart Supply Chains in China: A Multidimensional Approach. In B. Bentalha, A. Hmioui, & L. Alla (Eds.), *Integrating Intelligence and Sustainability in Supply Chains* (pp. 179–197). IGI Global. doi:10.4018/979-8-3693-0225-5.ch010

Zreik, M., Iqbal, B. A., & Rahman, M. N. (2022). Outward FDI: determinants and flows in emerging economies: evidence from China. *China and WTO Review*, *8*(2), 385–402. doi:10.14330/cwr.2022.8.2.07

Zyskind, G., & Nathan, O. (2015, May). Decentralizing privacy: Using blockchain to protect personal data. In *2015 IEEE security and privacy workshops* (pp. 180-184). IEEE. 10.1109/SPW.2015.27

About the Contributors

Mustafa Khan has been associated with Graduate Business School, UCSI University, Malaysia. He received PhD in Management Sciences from Universiti Pendidikan Sultan Idris, Malaysia. He has published in several esteemed international journals such as the IEEE Transactions on Engineering Management, Management of Environmental Quality, and the International Journal of Productivity and Performance Management.

Naveed R. Khan received his PhD in Human Resource Management from University Pendidikan Sultan Idris, a public sector university in Malaysia. Later, he was selected for a post-doctoral fellowship. He have been teaching for the last 14 years in higher education institutions. Throughout his career, he has taught graduate and post-graduate levels, both qualification and non-qualification bearing programs. Besides teaching, he is an enthusiastic trainer. He has designed training modules and conducted several pieces of trainings for Corporate employees and University faculty. He won two research grants from USAID and UPSI, and have supervised to completion five PhD scholars. The main themes of his research interest, largely reflected in his research publications, have been Green HRM, Firm Competitiveness, Sustainable Performance, and Gender in Management. One of his latest research papers have been published in European Management Journal. He has been a member of British Academy of Management, UK. Currently, he has been affiliated with the Faculty of Business and Management, UCSI University, Malaysia.

Arsalan Ghouri is Senior Lecturer at London South Bank, UK. He has been involved in teaching and research with Iqra University, Pakistan, and Montpellier Business School (France). He has over 6 years of academic and research experience, in marketing, supply chain management, data science, and innovative research methods/techniques. He has published several articles in peer reviewed journals of repute including Journal of business ethics (FT 50), Technological forecasting and social change and international journal of information management.

***

Pervaiz Akhtar is Director of MBA and Chair (Full Professor) in Business Analytics, Big Data and Supply Chains. Capitalizing on over 20-year of academic and industrial experiences from leading public, private, and non-profit-making organizations, he has published in top-tiered international journals such as International Journal of Operations & Production Management, British Journal of Management, International Journal of Production Economics, Business Ethics, among others.

Mirza Amin-ul-Haq, a distinguished academician and educational leader, is an expert in business research holding a Doctorate in Business Administration. Currently serving as the Registrar at Iqra University, he has consistently demonstrated exemplary leadership and administrative acumen. With over 30 articles published in esteemed journals like the Journal of Business Research, Technological Forecasting and Social Change, and on prestigious platforms such as Web of Science, Social Sciences Citation Index, and Scopus, Dr. Haq boasts an impressive publication record. His work has significantly shaped the trajectory of academia and research in the field, further solidifying his position as a distinguished figure contributing to the advancement of higher education in Pakistan. His book proposal, recognized for its merit, has even been awarded for publication by a leading global publishing house.

Gregory Barnes is a Senior Lecturer in Business Strategy, Operations and Enterprise. Member of the Chartered Institute of Procurement and Supply (CIPS).

Muhammad Awais Bhatti, an accomplished academic and seasoned professional in Human Resource Management, boasts an extensive career spanning over a decade across prominent educational institutions. Currently an Associate Professor at King Faisal University in Hofuf, Kingdom of Saudi Arabia, he specializes in International Human Resource Management, Workforce Diversity Management, and Strategic HRM, among other domains. With a Ph.D. in Management from the University of Malaya, Malaysia, Dr. Bhatti's contributions transcend teaching to impactful research, evident through his numerous publications in esteemed journals. His research interests span Human Resource Management, E-learning, Organizational Behavior, and Supply Chain Management. Recognized for his expertise, he has conducted diverse training programs and holds a repertoire of certifications complementing his academic achievements. Dr. Bhatti continues to make profound strides in academia and industry, influencing the field of HRM with his extensive knowledge and innovative perspectives.

Syed Danish Bukhari is a Ph.D. Scholar (Management Science) Pakistan. His research interest includes Supply Chain Management and COVID-19, Mass Media and Journalism, Project Management, Human Resource, and Marketing. He has more than 13 years of industrial experience in the area of Marketing, Human Resources, Project Management, and Internal Audit and also published research papers in international journals.

Sachin Chaudhary completed his Graduation from MJPRU, and Post Graduation from AKTU, Moradabad, U.P. Currently Pursuing his Ph.D. in Computer Science and Engineering from Govt. Recognized University. Presently, he is working as an Assistant Professor in the Department of Computer Science and Applications, IIMT University, Meerut, U.P, India. He has been awarded as Excellence in teaching award 2019. He is the reviewer member of some reputed journals. He has published several book chapters and research papers of national and international reputed journals.

Omkar Dastane obtained his Ph.D. in Business from Curtin University and is working as an Assistant Professor and Head of Program (MBAs) at the UCSI Graduate Business School, UCSI University, Kuala Lumpur, Malaysia. Dr. Omkar's research mainly emphasizes digital consumer behavior, consumer perception and values, technological impact on businesses, and scale development studies in the marketing domain. His research has been published in several international journals and books including the

Journal of Retailing and Consumer Services, Marketing Intelligence & Planning among others. He is also an active reviewer for Web of Science and Scopus Indexed Journals.

G. Revathy is working as an Assistant Professor in the Department of CSE, SRC-SASTRA Deemed University, Kumbakonam, Tamil Nadu.She did her B.E. CSE in Sudharsan Engineering College, M.E. CSE in Arulmighu Meenakshi Amman College of Engineering and Ph.D under Annamalai University. She has 13 years of teaching experience. Her area of interests are Wireless Mesh Networks and Artificial Intelligence.She has published about 28 International Journals, 9 Books and 4 Book Chapters.

Muhammad Inshal, a recent BBA graduate from Iqra University, excels academically and actively contributes. Notable achievements include leading a winning team in a university entrepreneurship competition and contributing to the UN's Net Zero project. In addition to his academic success, Inshal participated in a postgraduate research competition by Middlesex University Dubai, where his paper reached the final round. Currently a Research Analyst, he specializes in extracting insights from research papers, transforming theoretical concepts into practical solutions, and optimizing processes through data-driven analysis. His versatile skill set spans research, data analysis, and graphic design, positioning him to make a meaningful impact in business and social sciences. Inshal is passionate about merging research and technology for innovative problem-solving, embodying a lifelong learner's mindset with an unwavering pursuit of knowledge.

Haseeb R Khan received his Ph.D. in Information Systems with a specialization in AI from UPSI in Malaysia. He is currently employed as a Data Analyst in Australia's Health and Furniture Industry. Dr. Khan's research focuses on artificial intelligence, recommendation systems, context processing, and user modeling. His research has appeared in several international journals, including the Journal of Business Research and the Annals of Operations.

Bhupendra Kumar completed his Graduation and Post Graduation from Chaudhary Charan Singh University, Meerut, U.P. and Ph.D. in Computer Science and Engineering from Mewar University, Hapur. Presently, he is working as a Professor in the Department of Computer Science and Applications, IIMT University, Meerut, U.P. He has been a huge teaching experience of 19 years. He is the reviewer member of some reputed journals. He has published several book chapters and research papers of national and international reputed journals.

Kasturi Laturkar is currently working as an engineer at the Facility for Rare Isotope Beams, Michigan State University, a US-DOE project in Michigan. He graduated with a M.S in chemical engineering from University of Florida and B.E. in chemical engineering from Panjab University, Chandigarh, India. He has more than 10 years of experience working in the field of process engineering, refinery operations, utility systems design and operation with a special focus on design and commissioning of engineering systems.

Fazeelat Masood is an Assistant Professor at Bahria Business School. Dr. Masood has earned her Ph.D. in Management Sciences from Bahria University, Karachi. Her research interests are quality of life, well-being, social entrepreneurship, and tourism. She has published in HEC-recognized national and international research journals. One of her research papers was accepted for presentation at the

British Academy of Management Conference 2019, and another at the Asian Academy of Management Conference 2021.

Nabeel Mehboob is a research scholar in the field of Supply Chain Management with interest in Public Sector.

P. Brindha is working as an Assistant Professor in the Department of Artificial Intelligence and Data Science in Builders Engineering College, Nathakadaiyur, Kangeyam, Tiruppur District, Tamil Nadu. She did her B.E. CSE and M.E. CSE in Builders Engineering College. She has about 8 years of teaching experience. Her area of Interests are Artificial Intelligence and Wireless Networks.

Rajneesh Panwar Graduated and Post Graduated in Mathematics and Computer Application from Ch. Charan Singh University, Meerut (U.P.) and received his M. Tech. in Computer Science from Shobhit University, Meerut. Presently, he is working as an Assistant Professor in the School of Computer Science and Application IIMT University, Meerut, U.P. He qualifies GATE 2021 and UGC-NET June 2020 and December 2020. He has published several book chapters and research papers of national and international repute.

S. Selvi is working as an Associate Professor & Head in the Department of Artificial Intelligence and Data Science at Builders Engineering College,Nathakadaiyur, Kangeyam, Tamil Nadu. She did her B.E(CSE) in Kongu Engineering College, Perundurai, Tamil Nadu and M.E(CSE) in Velalar College of Engineering and Technology, Thindal, Tamil Nadu. She has completed her Ph.D. under Anna University, Chennai in the year 2019. Her area of interest includes Cloud Computing, Compiler Design and Machine Learning. She has published about 20 papers in various International Journals and 4 Patents. She has provided about 10 Guest Lectures in various renowned Engineering Institutions.

S M Nazmuz Sakib was born in Dinajpur, Bangladesh on the 16th of April in 2001. He achieved his Primary School Certificate (PSC) from Cotton Research Station School, Sreepur, Gazipur and after several months of studying Class 6 in Alhaz Dhanai Bepari Memorial High School, Sreepur, Gazipur, he relocated to Jashore. He accomplished his Junior School Certificate (JSC) from Jagodishpur Mirzapur Ismail Secondary School, Jagodishour, Chaowgacha, Jashore and his Secondary School Certificate (SSC) from A. K. High School And College, Dhania, Dhaka-1236. He obtained his Higher Secondary Certificate (HSC) from Chowgacha Government College, Chowgacha, Jashore. He received a BSc in Business Studies, earning a CGPA of 4 out of 4 (1st class 1st) with 97.06% marks from School of Business and Trade, an online business school situated in Switzerland. He completed an MBA in Human Resources from International MBA Institute, an online business institute in Switzerland. He studied Bachelor of Laws (Hon's) or LLB(Hon's) at Dhaka International University, Dhaka, Bangladesh. He has accomplished CPD verified advanced diploma and diploma programs i.e. Advanced Diploma in Tissue Engineering, Advanced Diploma in Genetic Engineering - Theory and Application, Diploma in Fashion Design, Diploma in Nutrition, Therapeutics and Health, Diploma in Biology, Diploma in Pharmacy Technician, Software Test Engineer Diploma (Advanced), Advanced Diploma in Soil Science and Technology, Diploma in Energy Economics, Energy Systems and Environmental Impact, Advanced Diploma in Political Ideologies, Diploma in Community Psychology, Diploma in Training of Trainers, Advance Diploma in Principles of Industrial Engineering, Advanced Diploma in Production & Operation Management, Advanced Diploma in Modelling and Analytics for Supply Chain Management, Business Administration Diploma (Foundation), Diploma in Effective Human Resource Administration, Diploma in Audio System Engineering, Diploma in ISO Standards - Integrated Management System (IMS), Diploma in Lean Manufacturing - Productive Management with Fundamental Tools, Advanced Diploma in Tourism and Hospitality Management, Diploma in Web Design, Diploma in Human Resources, and Diploma in Basic English Grammar, Diploma in River Engineering and has obtained certifications such as TESOL from Arizona State University, TEFL from Teacher Record, Scrum Master Professional Certificate (SMPC®), EF SET Certificate (C2 Level), Google IT Support Professional Certificate, Google Data Analytics Professional Certificate, Google Project Management Professional Certificate, Google Business Intelligence Professional Certificate, Google Digital Marketing & E-commerce Professional Certificate and IBM New Collar: Customer Engagement Specialist credential etc. As a multidisciplinary researcher, he has published several articles in the Asian Pacific Journal of Environment and Cancer, Simulacra, Journal of Innovation Information Technology and Application (JINITA), Waste Technology, and The IUP Journal of Electrical and Electronics Engineering. Several of his articles are published by Cambridge Open Engage, a publication of Cambridge University Press. Some of the titles of his published research works include “The Impact of Oil and Gas Development on the Landscape and Surface in Nigeria,” “Assessing the Impact of Arctic Melting in the Predominantly Multilateral World System,” “LiDAR Technology - An Overview,” “Exploring the Intersection of Software Engineering and Mobile Technology from 2010 to 2021: A Review of Recent Research” “Comparing the sociology of culture in Bangladesh and India: Similarities and differences in Bangladeshi and Indian cultures” “Electrochemical Waste Water Treatment.”. Published chapters i.e. “Chapter 3: Artificial Intelligence Model for Analyzing the Buying Patterns of Customers” and “Chapter 11: Restaurant Sales Prediction Using Machine Learning” of the book titled “Handbook of Research on AI and Machine Learning Applications in Customer Support and Analytics”, “Chapter 15: The Role of Innovation in Driving the Bioeconomy: The Challenges and Opportunities (pages 288-311)” of the book, “Handbook of Research on Bioeconomy and Economic Ecosystems”. Authored a chapter in the book “Advancement in Business Analytics Tools for Higher Financial Performance” also. The concept of Sakibphobia is invented by him and several researches are ongoing on this topic. In a last research works published by more than 100 scientists were “S M Nazmuz Sakibs Toxic Comparative Theorys Psychiatrys Perspectives on the Sociological Analysis of Sakibphobia using Structural Functionalism, Symbolic Interactionism, and Conflict Perspective” and “S M Nazmuz Sakibs Toxic Comparative Theory, Sakibphobia with Structural Functionalism, Symbolic Interactionism, and Conflict Perspective, A Sociological Analysis”. There are many researches are ongoing in this topic. According to various sources, Sakibphobia is a term coined by S M Nazmuz Sakib, a Bangladeshi researcher and author, to describe the phenomenon of fear, hatred, or discrimination towards those who are perceived as being more successful or accomplished than oneself. Sakibphobia is based on Sakib’s toxic comparative theory (TCT), which suggests that individuals may develop negative emotions and behaviors when they compare themselves unfavorably with others who have achieved higher levels of success in various domains of life, such as education, career, wealth, fame, or social status. According to Sakib, Sakibphobia can manifest in various ways, such as envy, jealousy, resentment, anger, hostility, insecurity, inferiority, anxiety, depression, or isolation. Sakibphobia can also lead to irrational or harmful actions, such as sabotage, slander, violence, discrimination, or self-harm. Sakib argues that Sakibphobia is a widespread and serious problem that affects individuals and society at large. He claims that Sakibphobia can undermine personal well-being, interpersonal relationships, social harmony, and global peace. Sakibphobia is a novel concept that has attracted attention from various fields of study, such as psychology, sociology, economics, politics, education, media, etc. Sakib's toxic comparative theory has been applied to analyze various phenomena and issues related to social comparison and inequality in different contexts. Sakibphobia is a concept that has sparked debate and discussion among various stakeholders and audiences. It has raised awareness and interest about the phenomenon of social comparison and its consequences for individuals and society. It has also challenged and provoked people to rethink their views and values about success and happiness. Whether one agrees or disagrees with Sakibphobia, it is undeniable that it is a concept that deserves attention and exploration. Environmental Scientist, S M Nazmuz Sakib's hypotheses and theories on environmental science and climate studies are highly used and reused in latest papers. S M Nazmuz Sakib's hypothesis of aerosol-sea ice feedback and its implications for climate system dynamics is a a hypothesis that suggests that changes in aerosol emissions significantly impact sea ice concentration and thickness in the Arctic, which, in turn, affect aerosol transport and deposition over the Tibetan Plateau. The paper presents a comprehensive analysis of the hypothesis, including the underlying facts, a proposed formula for the aerosol-sea ice feedback, and the potential variations of this feedback based on regional and temporal patterns of aerosol emission changes. Furthermore, the paper introduces the Sea Ice-Aerosol-Cloud Feedback (SIACF) Index and its application to historical incidents related to aerosol emission changes. The SIACF Index provides a quantitative measure to evaluate the influence of changes in aerosol emissions on sea ice concentration and thickness. The paper concludes by emphasizing the importance of testing this hypothesis through global aerosol models, observations, and historical incidents to gain a deeper understanding of aerosol-climate interactions and develop effective mitigation strategies. Another research presents S M Nazmuz Sakib's Climate Conflict Theory and tests its hypotheses using a quantitative analysis of 36 African countries from 1990-2020. The theory argues that climate change affects armed conflict risk through its impacts on state capacity, ethnic diversity, and regional spillovers. The results of logistic regression analysis provide empirical support for the theory. Lower state capacity, higher ethnic diversity, and greater regional spillovers are found to increase the likelihood of conflict. The effect of ethnic diversity on conflict is also shown to be moderated by exposure to climate change. The findings highlight the importance of strengthening state capacity, promoting ethnic inclusion, and enhancing regional cooperation for preventing climate-induced conflicts in Africa. This research introduces a novel integrated measure of economic growth and development called the Super Advanced SM Nazmuz Sakib's Economic Growth and Development Index (SASEGDI). SASEGDI incorporates 12 key dimensions including GDP per capita, human development, productivity, CO2 emissions, income inequality, economic freedom, corruption, competitiveness, political stability, social welfare, innovation, and environmental sustainability. Quantitative correlation analysis among 180 countries shows SASEGDI has strong positive correlation with human rights protection but negative correlation with civil liberties, political rights, and press freedom. Case studies of Norway, China, Saudi Arabia, and Venezuela using SASEGDI values imply a potential trade-off between economic development and human freedoms. Triangulation with qualitative analysis suggests policies enhancing SASEGDI may also restrict human rights and liberties. The SASEGDI provides a multidimensional tool to evaluate and compare country performance on economic growth and development while highlighting the complex interlinkages with human rights and freedoms. Further research could apply SASEGDI to study impacts of culture, institutions, and regimes on developmental outcomes. Snow cover in the Himalayan region plays a critical role in the regional hydrology, ecosystems, natural hazards, and climate. However, the effects of changes in snow cover on these interconnected systems are complex and uncertain. This article presents an integrated modeling framework developed by SM Nazmuz Sakib to assess and predict the impacts of snow cover changes on water resources (Snow-Cover and Water Resources Optimization Model), biodiversity and ecosystem services (Snow-Cover and Biodiversity Model), geohazards (Snow-Cover and Geohazards Model), regional climate (Snow-Cover and Climate Change Model), and carbon cycle (Snow-Cover and Carbon Cycle Model) in the Himalayan region. The framework couples process-based models with optimization techniques to identify optimal snow cover conditions for minimizing adverse impacts on the environment and society. The models incorporate data on snow cover characteristics, topography, hydrology, vegetation, soil, climate, and socio-economic factors. They can help researchers and policy-makers monitor, diagnose and project the diverse effects of snow cover changes across different sectors under various scenarios. This integrated modeling system provides a novel tool for understanding snow-water-ecosystem-hazard-climate linkages and supporting integrated planning and adaptation in the Himalayan region.

Kewal Krishan Sharma is a professor in computer sc. in IIMT University, Meerut, U.P, India. He did his Ph.D. in computer network with this he has MCA, MBA and Law degree also. He did variously certification courses also. He has an overall experience of around 33 year in academic, business and industry. He wrote a number of research papers and books.

Vikas Sharma completed his Graduation and Post Graduation from Chaudhary Charan Singh University, Meerut, U.P. Currently Pursuing his Ph.D. in Computer Science and Engineering from Govt. Recognized University. Presently, he is working as an Assistant Professor in the Department of Computer Science and Applications, IIMT University, Meerut, U.P. He has been awarded as Excellence in teaching award 2019. He is the reviewer member of some reputed journals. He has published several book chapters and research papers of national and international reputed journals.

Tarun Kumar Vashishth is an active academician and researcher in the field of computer science with 21 years of experience. He earned Ph.D. Mathematics degree specialized in Operations Research; served several academic positions such as HoD, Dy. Director, Academic Coordinator, Member Secretary of Department Research Committee, Assistant Center superintendent and Head Examiner in university examinations. He is involved in academic development and scholarly activities. He is member of International Association of Engineers, The Society of Digital Information and Wireless Communications, Global Professors Welfare Association, International Association of Academic plus Corporate (IAAC), Computer Science Teachers Association and Internet Society. His research interest includes Cloud Computing, Artificial Intelligence, Machine Learning and Operations Research; published more than 20 research articles with 1 book and 10 book chapters in edited books. He is contributing as member of editorial and reviewers boards in conferences and various computer journals published by CRC Press, Taylor and Francis, Springer, IGI global and other universities.

Mohamad Zreik, a Postdoctoral Fellow at Sun Yat-sen University, is a recognized scholar in International Relations, specializing in China's Arab-region foreign policy. His recent work in soft power diplomacy compares China's methods in the Middle East and East Asia. His extensive knowledge spans Middle Eastern Studies, China-Arab relations, East Asian and Asian Affairs, Eurasian geopolitics, and Political Economy, providing him a unique viewpoint in his field. Dr. Zreik is a proud recipient of a PhD from Central China Normal University (Wuhan). He's written numerous acclaimed papers, many focusing on China's Belt and Road Initiative and its Arab-region impact. His groundbreaking research has established him as a leading expert in his field. Presently, he furthers his research on China's soft power diplomacy tactics at Sun Yat-sen University. His significant contributions make him a crucial figure in understanding contemporary international relations.

Index

A

B

C

D

E

F

G

H

I

M

P

Q

R

S

T

U

www.ingramcontent.com/pod-product-compliance
Lightning Source LLC
LaVergne TN
LVHW062136300926
849161LV00010B/2545